GENEALOGICAL
ABSTRACTS
OF

THE LAWS OF PENNSYLVANIA

&

THE STATUTES AT LARGE

Candy Crocker Livengood

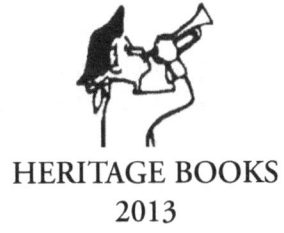

HERITAGE BOOKS
2013

HERITAGE BOOKS
AN IMPRINT OF HERITAGE BOOKS, INC.

Books, CDs, and more—Worldwide

For our listing of thousands of titles see our website at
www.HeritageBooks.com

Published 2013 by
HERITAGE BOOKS, INC.
Publishing Division
5810 Ruatan Street
Berwyn Heights, Md. 20740

Copyright © 1990 Candy Crocker Livengood

All rights reserved. No part of this book may be reproduced or transmitted in any form or by any means, electronic or mechanical, including photocopying, recording or by any information storage and retrieval system without written permission from the author, except for the inclusion of brief quotations in a review.

International Standard Book Numbers
Paperbound: 978-1-58549-176-6
Clothbound: 978-0-7884-6809-4

The Statutes at Large of Pennsylvania and The Laws of Pennsylvania are an untapped genealogical gold mine. Much of the information found in these books may not be duplicated anywhere else. Name changes, children being legitimized for inheritances, divorces and annulments, oaths of allegiance, Revolutionary War pensions, debtors in prison, trustees of early churches, Indian murders, establishment of roads and county boundaries are just a few of the topics these early laws covered. Using these resources, however, has never been easy. Although individual books in these sets have indexes, not all names found in the laws are found in the indexes. This book, then, is a comprehensive abstraction of every name from every book beginning in 1683. Name and place spellings have been left as found in the original law. Therefore, all phonetically applicable names should be checked in this abstract, particularly any names other than English, Irish or Scottish. For example, the name LAVINGAIR is probably an variation of LOWENGIER. All women named Catherine, Kathrine, Katherine had their names spelled Catharine. There were some obvious misspellings and misprints, but, in the interest of accuracy, the names have been left as originally published.

Although some of the quaint spellings and phrasings were kept in order to provide a window to a fascinating historical era, all of the laws have been abstracted and condensed for this book. If further edification is desired, the complete law may be read in the actual books which are available at most law libraries in Pennsylvania and in quite a few public and academic libraries. A bibliography of books covered in this work has been included.

A heartfelt thank you to Joan Appleton Jones of the Pennsylvania Legislative Reference Bureau for her invaluable information on the early Pennsylvania law and statute books.

            Candy Crocker Livengood
            May, 1990

INDIAN PLACE NAMES

Alleghany hills - Apalachian hill
Aughwick
Awandac (Tawandee)
Burnett's hills - Long Mountains
Cantaguy Creek - Maghonioy Creek (Delaware name)
Chadochque
Chesapeak - bay
Conewango Creek
Consohockan - a hill
Cushietunk
Juniata - river
Kayarondinhagh Creek - Penn's Creek (Kaarondinhah)
Kekachtanemin Hills
Kittanning - Place on Ohio River
Kittatinny Mountains - Kittochtinny Hills - Blue Hills
Lechawachsein Creek
Lechay Hills or Mountains
Lycomick - Lycoming
Macopanackhan - Chester River or Creek - Upland
Mahaniay
Makerisk - Kitton - Delaware River
Manaiunk - Schuylkill River
Matiniounsk - island in the Delaware River
Minissinks - 40 miles above Lechay Hills
Neshamina
Neshammony's Creek - Neshemineh
Nittany
Ohio
Oley
Onondago
Opasiskunk
Oreskons - island in Delaware River
Oughcough pockeny
Owegy
Pahkehoma - Perkeomink - Perkioming
Pemmapecka Creek - Dublin Ck. (Pennepack)
Pexton
Playwisky - Delaware Village (Playwickey)
Poquessing
Quing Quingus - Duck Creek
Sapassineks - island in Delaware River
Shamokin
Shingo - town
Sinnemahoning
Soepassineks - a name of some land
Tayamentaschta - hills
Tiadaghton Creek - Pine Creek
Towissinon Creek
Tulpyhockin - Tulpehocken
Tyanuntasachta Mountains (5 Nation name) - Kekac(h)tany Hills
                                                          (Delaware name)
Tyoninhasachta Hills
Wissahickon
Wyomen

CONTENTS

Introduction iii
Indian Place names v
Charter to William Penn 1
The Statutes at Large of Pennsylvania, 1682-1700 1
The Statutes at Large of Pennsylvania, 1700-1712 8
The Statutes at Large of Pennsylvania, 1712-1724 9
The Statutes at Large of Pennsylvania, 1724-1744 ... 11
The Statutes at Large of Pennsylvania, 1744-1759 ... 15
The Statutes at Large of Pennsylvania, 1759-1765 ... 17
The Statutes at Large of Pennsylvania, 1765-1770 ... 22
The Statutes at Large of Pennsylvania, 1770-1776 ... 26
The Statutes at Large of Pennsylvania, 1776-1779 ... 32
The Statutes at Large of Pennsylvania, 1779-1781 ... 41
The Statutes at Large of Pennsylvania, -1782 44
The Laws of Pennsylvania, 1781-1810 52
The Statutes at Large of Pennsylvania, 1785-1787 ... 65
The Statutes at Large of Pennsylvania, 1787-1790 ... 74
The Statutes at Large of Pennsylvania, 1791-1793 ... 81
The Statutes at Large of Pennsylvania, 1794-1797 ... 87
The Statutes at Large of Pennsylvania, 1798-1801 ... 96
The Laws of Pennsylvania, 1801-1803 107
The Laws of Pennsylvania, 1803-1804 116
The Laws of Pennsylvania, 1804-1806 122
The Laws of Pennsylvania, 1806-1808 133
The Laws of Pennsylvania, 1808-1812 152
The Laws of Pennsylvania, 1812-1814 168
The Laws of Pennsylvania, 1814-1816 190
The Laws of Pennsylvania, 1816-1818 207
The Laws of Pennsylvania, 1817-1822 227
The Laws of Pennsylvania, 1818-1820 239
Bibliography 253
Index [of personal names] 255
Index of places 335

THE STATUTES AT LARGE AND THE LAWS OF PENNSYLVANIA

Charter to William Penn, and
Laws of the Province of Pennsylvania
Passed Between The Years 1682 and 1700...

p. 161, 1683: Members of Provinciall Council present at writing of the charter: William MARKHAM, John MOLL, William HAIG, Francis WHITWELL, Christopher TAYLOR, John SIMCOCK, William CLAYTON, John HILLIARD, Thomas HOLME, William CLARK, William INGELO, Ck. Councili.

Members of Assembly: Andrew BANKSON, Bobert BEDWELL, John BEZER, Benoni BISHOP, Henry BOWMAN, James BOYDEN, Robert BRASSIE, Sr., Thomas BRASSIE, Jno. BRINKLOE, Daniel BROWN, William GUEST als BUTLER, John BLUMSTON, William FUTCHER, Robert HALL, John HARDING, John CLOWES, John CURTIS, Jr., John DARBIE, Samuel DARKE, Thomas FITZWATER, Casparus HARMAN, John HART, Thomas HASSOLD, Jno. HASTINGS, John HILL, Valentine HOLLINGSWORTH, Simon IRONS, John KIPSHAVEN, Robert LUCAS, Alexander MOLLISTON, Joseph PHIPPS, Dennis ROCHFORD, William SIMSMORE, John SONGS, John SOUTHWORTHE, Cornelius VERHOOFFE, Robert WADE, Nicholas WALNE, Luke WATSON, Benjamin WILLIAMS, James WILLIAMS, John WOOD, William YARDLIE, Thomas WYNNE.

Some inhabitants of Philadelphia then present: William HOWELL, Edmund WARNER, Henry LEWIS, Samuel MYLES.

p. 417, 1624: Cornelis Jacobsz MEY and Adriaen Jorissz TIENPOIONT build "Fort Nassau" on the "South River" (Delaware River) near Gloucester Point, N.J. Samuel GODYN and Samuel BLOEMMAERT purchased land around Cape Hinlopen on the south side of the Delaware Bay.

p. 418: David Pietersen DE VRIES, GODYN, BLOEMMAERT and others established a colony on this purchase named "Zwanendal" or "Valley of the Swans." Giles HOSSETT handled affairs of the colony after 1631. Wouter VAN TWILLER was Director-General of New Netherlands from 1633 until 1638. William KEIFT was Director-General from 1638 until 1646.

p. 420, 1626: William USSELINCX, a merchant of Brabant, Antwerp, established a Swedish West India Co.

p. 422: Swedish Deputy Governors: Peter MINUET, 1638-1641; Peter HOLLANDARE, 1641-1643 (after his term, he was a major at Skepsholm, Stockholm in 1655); John PRINTZ, 1643-1653 (a Swedish lieutenant of cavalry, he died in 1663); John PAPPEGOYA, 1653-1654 (he was the son-in-law of John PRINTZ, marrying Amigart PRINTZ); John Claude RYSINGE, 1654-1655.

p. 426: Gerrit BIKKER was in command of the Dutch Fort Casimer. Capt. John Admundson BESK received a grant of land in New Sweden and the commission of "captain in the navy."

p. 428: John Paul JACQUET was appointed Vice Director and Chief Magistrate on the South River of New Netherlands on 29 Nov., 1655. Deryck SMIDT was Vice Director as well. Administrators of the Colony of the Company were Gregorius VAN DYKE, 1657-1658 and William BEEKMAN, 1653-1663. Administrators of the Colony of the City were Jacob ALRICKS, 1657-1659 and Alex. D'HINOYOSSA, 1659-1663. Secretary under JACQUET was Andries HUDDE and Elmerhuysen CLEYN was a council member.

p. 432, 25 Dec., 1655: Marriage license is recorded between William MAUNTZ, "a young man from Wallshire, old about 33," and Janitze TOMAS, "old about 16 years."
    19 Jan., 1656: Mathys BUSAIN was appointed by the Director General to be a court messenger at Fort Casimer.
    13 Feb., 1655: Thomas BROEN was charged with striking a servant and placed under arrest.

p. 433: Jacob ALRICHS was commissioned Vice Director or Commissary General of the city's colony on the Delaware, 1656. His wife died in 1659. ALRICHS died on 30 Dec., 1659.

p. 437: Alexander D'HINNOYOSSA named ALRICHS' successor. Abraham VAN RYNEVELT, a council member, died on 28 Oct., 1658. Anthony RADEMAN, a Schepens, died ca Oct., 1658. Other council members were Cor. VAN GEZEL (Secretary). Other Schepens were Herr ELMERHUYSEN, Jam. WILLIAMSON. Gerritt VAN SWERINGEN was Schout. Hendrick KIP took RADEMAN's spot. John CRATO took VAN GEZEL's spot as councillor. Hans BLOCK was a constable. Magistrates in 1658 were: Oloffe STILLE, Matthys HANSON, Pieter RAMBO, Pieter COCK. Swens SCHUTE was Captain, Andries I'ALBO was Lieutenant and Jacob SWENSON was Ensign.

p. 438: Sheriff Gregorius VAN DYCK was removed from office at the beginning of 1661. Duties were taken over by William BEEKMAN.

p. 444: Under the English rule, Deputy Governor was Col. Richard NICOLLS. Sir Robert CARRE, Knight; George CARTWRIGHT and Samuel MAVERICK, Esq. were Commissioners. In May, 1667, Deputy Governor was Col. Francis LOVELACE. Military Commander was Capt. Robert NEEDHAM. On 1 July, 1674, Maj. Edmund ANDROSSE was named Governor of N.Y. The successor, if necessary, was to be Lt. Anthony BROCKHOLLS.

p. 454: Capt. Edmund CANTWELL and William TOM are authorized to take possession of the fort at New Castle. CANTWELL is appointed sheriff and TOM is appointed Secretary. Magistrates at New Castle: Hans BLOCK, John MOLL, Foppo OUTHOUT, Joseph CHEW, Dirck ALBERTS. Magistrates on the River: Peter COCK, Peter RAMBO, Israel HELME, Lars ANDRIESEN, Woolle SWAIN.

p. 455: CANTWELL and TOM were relieved by the appointment of Capt. John COLLIER as Commander on the Delaware River and Ephriam HERMANS as Secretary. Magistrates named in 1676 were: John MOLL, Henry WARD, William TOM, Foppo OUTHOUT, John Paul JACQUETT, Gerritt OTTO. These were for New Castle. Magistrates named for the River: Peter COCK, Peter RAMBO, Israel HELME, Lars ANDRIESEN, Woolle SWAIN, Otto Earnest COCK.

p. 457, 13 Aug., 1677: COLLIER was relieved by Governor ANDROSSE. Capt. Christopher BILLOP was appointed to the command of affairs on the Delaware but he was removed for misconduct in 1679.

p. 458: New Castle Justices of the Peace were: John MOLL, Peter ALRICKS, M. Gerritt OTTO, Mr. Johanes DE HAES, and Mr. William TEMPLE. Justices of the Peace on the Delaware River: Mr. Otto Ernest COCK, Mr. Israel HELME, Mr. Henry JONES, Mr. Lansa COCK, Mr. George BROWNE. Justices for St. Jones County, Delaware Bay: Francis WHITWELL, John HILLYARD, Robert HART, Edward PACK. Justices of Whore Kill: Luke WHATSON, John ROADES, John KIPPSHAVEN, Otto WOOLGAST, William CLARKE. Deputy Gov. of N.Y. was Capt. Anthony BROCKHOLLS.

p. 459, 1669: Marcus JACOBSON, alias Matthew HINKS, alias John BINCKSON (Long Finne or Swede), adventurer, pretended to be the son of CONNIGSMARK, one of the King of Sweden's general officers. His chief follower was Henry COLEMAN, a Finne. Daughter of the former Swedish Governor PRINTZ was Jeffro Armagart PAPPEGOYA.

P. 464, 12 Nov., 1678: Court case of William ORIAN vs. John D'HAES. Jury members were hans MOENS, dunk WILLIAMS, Xtopher BARNES, Edm : DAUFTON, Peter JOCKUM, Isacq SAVOY, Jan HENDRIKS, Jonas KIEN, moens COCK, John BROWNE, Jan BOELSEN, Henry HASTINGS.

P. 470, 11 July, 1681: A document signed by William PENN and witnessed by William BOELHAM, Thomas PRUDYARD, Harbert SPRINGET, Thomas FARRINBORROUGH, John GOODSON, Hugh CHAMBERLEN, R. MURRAY, Harbet SPRINGET, Humphry SOUTH, Thomas BARKER, Samuel JOBSON, John Joseph MOORE, William POWEL, Richard DAVIE, Griffith JONES, Hugh LAMBE. On 10 Apr., 1681, PENN commissioned his cousin, William MARKHAM, to be Deputy Governor of Pa.

p. 471: A Council was called by MARKHAM and included: Robert WADE, Morgan DEWET, William WOODMANSON, William WARNER, Thomas FAIRMAN, James SANDILANDS, William CLAYTON, Otto Ernst COCK, Lacey COCK. They took office on 3 Aug., 1681.

p. 473, 4 Dec., 1682: The Assembly met at Chester. Elections and Privileges Committee: Christopher TAYLOR, Bucks Co.; Nicholas MORE, Philadelphia; Francis WHITEWELL, Kent; John SYMCOCK, Chester; William CLARK, Sussex. "Committee of Foresight," for the preparation of Provincial Bills: John SYMCOCK, Chester; William CLARK, Sussex; Luke WATSON, Sussex; Christopher TAYLOR, Bucks; Griffith JONES, Philadelphia; Nicholas MORE, Philadelphia, Chairman.

p. 474: Committee for Justice and Grievances: Griffith JONES, Philadelphia; Luke WATSON, Sussex; William SAMPLE, New Castle; William YARDLEY, Bucks; Thomas BRASSY, Chester; John BRIGGS, Kent. Those selected to wait on the Governor: Edward SOUTHRIN, Sussex. Two other names mentioned in the minutes: Ralph WITHERS, who asked a leave of absence and John MOLL of New Castle. Governors, Deputy Governors and Presidents of Council prior to 1700: William PENN, William MARKHAM, Thomas LLOYD, John BLACKWELL, Benjamin FLETCHER. Assistants in the Government: John GOODSONN, Samuel CARPENTER. Speakers of Assembly prior to 1700: Thomas WYNNE, Nicholas MORE, Arthur COOKE, Joseph GROWDON, William CLARKE, David LLOYD, Edward SHIPPEN, John SIMCOCKS, John BLUNSTON, Phinehas PEMBERTON.

p. 483, 1682: Sheriffs: John TEST, Philadelphia; Thomas USHER, Chester; Edmund CANTWELL, New Castle; Peter BOWCOMB, Kent; John VINES, Sussex.

p. 484, 1683: Provincial council: William PENN, Proprietary and Governor; Capt. William MARKHAM, New Castle; Christopher TAYLOR, Chester; Thomas HOLMES, Phila.; Lasse COCK, Phila.; William CLARK, Sussex; John HILLIARD, Kent; William HAIGE, Phila.; John MOLL, New Castle; John ROADS, Sussex; Ralph WITHERS, Bucks; John SYMCOCK, Chester; Francis WHITEWELL, Kent; Edmund CANTWELL, New Castle; William CLAYTON, Chester; William BILES, Bucks; James HARRISON, Bucks; John RICHARDSON, Kent; Edward SOUTHRIN, Sussex.

p. 485: Assembly: Kent: John BRIGGS, Simon IRONS, Thomas HAFFOLD, John CURTIS, Robert BEDWELL, William WINSMORE, John BRINCKLOE, Daniel BROWN, Benoni BISHOP. Bucks: William YARDLEY, Samuel DARKE, Robert LUCAS, Nicholas WALNE, John WOOD, John CLOWES, Thomas FITZWATER, Robert HALL, James BOYDEN. Chester: John HASKINS, Dennis ROCHFORD, Joseph PHIPPES, Robert WADE, Thomas BRACY, George WOOD, John BEZER, John BLUNSTON, John HARDING. Philadelphia: John SONGHURST, John HART, Swan SWANSON, Walter KING, Thomas WINN, Andros BINCKSON, Griffith JONES, John MOON, William WARNER. New Castle: John CANN, John DARBY, Valentine HOLLINGSWORTH, Gasparus HERMAN, John DEBOAES, James WILLIAMS, William GUEST, Peter ALDRICH, Heinrich WILLIAM. Sussex: Luke WATSON, Alexander DRAPER, William FRITCHER, Henry BOWMAN, Alexander MOLESTON, John HILL, Bobert BRACY, John KIPSHAVEN, Cornelius VERBOOF.

p. 494: Assembly of 1684: Sussex: John ROADS, Henry BOWMAN, Hercules SHEPPARD, Samuel GRAY, William EMMETT, Henry STRETCHER. Philadelphia: Nicholas MORE, John SONGHURST, Francis FINCHER, Lasse COCK, Joseph GROWDEN, John HART. New Castle: James WILLIAMS, John DARBY, William GRANT, Gasparus HERMAN, Abram MANN, John WHITE. Bucks: William BEAKES, John CLOWES, Richard HOUGH, John OTTER, Edmond BENNET. Chester: Joshua HASTINGS, Robert WADE, John BLUNSTON, George MERIS, Thomas USHER, Henry MADDOCK. Kent: John BRIGGS, John GLOVER, John CURTIS, William SHERWOOD, James WELLS, William BERRY.
    Council of 1684: New Castle: William WELCH, John CANN, Edmund CANTWELL. Kent: Francis WHITEWELL, William SOUTHERSBY, John HILLIARD. Sussex: Luke WATSON, William CLARK, Edward SOUTHRIN. Chester: Christopher TAYLOR, John SYMCOCK, William CLAYTON. Philadelphia: William HAIGE, Thomas LORD, Thomas HOLMES. Bucks: James HARRISON, William WOODS, Thomas JANNEY.

p. 496: 1685 Council: President Thomas LLOYD, Thomas HOLMES, William WOOD, John SYMCOCK, Christopher TAYLOR, Thomas JANNEY, Phineas PEMBERTON, John BARNES, Peter ALRICHS, John CANN, John ROADS, William FRAMPTON, William SOUTHERSBY, William DARVALL, Luke WATSON, Edward GREENE, Nicholas NEWLIN, Richard INGELO, Clerk.

p. 497: 1685 Assembly: Philadelphia: Nicholas MORE, Joseph GROWDEN, Barnaby WILCOX, Lawrence COCK, Gunner RAMBO, Thomas PASCHALL. Chester: John BLUNSTON, George MERIS, John HARDING, Thomas USHER, Francis STANFIELD, Joshua FERNE. Sussex: Henry SMITH, William CARTER, Robert CLIFTON, John HILL, Samuel GRAY, Richard LAW. Bucks: William BEAKES, Gilbert WHEELER, Henry BAKER, William DARK, James DILWORTH, Henry PAXON. New Castle: John WHITE, Gasparus HERMAN, Hendrick WILLIAMS, Abraham MANN, Edward OWEN, Jr., John DARBY. Kent: John BRIDGES, John CURTIS, Daniel JONES, Peter GRONINGDYKE, William BERRY, John BRINCKLOE.

p. 505, 1686: Council: Thomas LLOYD, President. John BARNES, Robert TURNER, Thomas JANNEY, Arthur COOK, Francis HARRISON, Nicholas NEWLIN, John SYMCOCK, William SOUTHERSBY, William FRAMPTON, Luke WATSON, John ROADES, William CLARK, Phineas PEMBERTON, William DARVALL, John CANN, Peter ALRICHS, William MARKHAM, Secretary.
    Assembly: Philadelphia: James CLAYPOOLE, John SONGHURST, Thomas DUCKET, John GOODSON, Griffith OWEN, Andrew BANKSON. New Castle: John WHITE, John DARBY, Cornelius EMPSON, James WILLIAMS, Abraham MANN, William GRANT. Kent: John BRINCKLOE, John BRADSHAW, John WALKER, William BERRY, Robert BEDWELL (died before assembly met), Richard WILSON. Chester: Robert WADE, John

BLUNSTON, George MARIS, Barth. COPPOCK, Samuel LEWIS, Caleb PUSEY. Bucks: William YARDLEY, Joseph GROWDEN, John OTTER, William BILES, Joshua HOOPS, John ROWLAND. Sussex: Henry BOWMAN, Norton CLAYPOOLE, Henry STRETCHER, John VINES, Albertus JACOBS, Samuel GRAY. John CLAYPOOLE was clerk and Richard REYNOLDS was messenger.

p. 509, 1687: President and council: Thomas LLOYD, President. Arthur COOK, William CLARK, William DYER (but council refused to admit him because he had been unfaithful as King's Collector of Customs), John BARNES, Nicholas NEWLIN, James CLAYPOOLE, Phineas PEMBERTON, John SYMCOCK, Robert TURNER, Joseph GROWDEN, John CANN, Peter ALRICHS, John BRISTOW, John CURTIS (was under suspicion of speaking treasonable words, acquitted by Grand Jury, but Council would not have him as a member), Griffith JONES (in place of William FRAMPTON, dec.), William DURVALL, William MARKHAM, Secretary.
    Assembly: Bucks: Thomas LANGHORN, Robert HALL, Nicholas WALNE, Robert LUCAS, Henry BAKER, Edward BENNET. Chester: John BLUNSTON, George MARIS, Barth. COPPOCK, Caleb PUSEY, Edward BEZAR, Randel VERNON. Kent: John BRINKLOE, William BERRY, Richard WILSON, Thomas PEMBERTON, William FREELAND, Benoni BISHOP. Sussex: Luke WATSON, Henry SMITH, Henry MOLESTINE, Henry BOWMAN, Samuel GRAY, Henry STRETCHER. Philadelphia: Humphrey MORREY, William SALWAY, John BEVAN, Lasse COCK, Daniel PASTORIUS, John PAUL. New Castle: Johannes DE HAES, Edward BLAKE, Valentine HOLLINGSWORTH, John WHITE, John DARBY, Richard NOBLE.

p. 515, 1688: Councillors: Thomas LLOYD, Robert TURNER, Arthur COOK, John SYMCOCK, John ECKLEY. Council members: William CLARK, Joseph GROWDEN, John CANN, Griffith JONES, William DARVALL, Luke WATSON, Samuel CARPENTER, Barth. COPPOCK, Johannes D'HAES, William YARDLEY, John BRISTOW, Peter ALRICHS. William MARKHAM, Secretary.
    Assembly: Bucks: Nicholas WALNE, Henry BAKER, Richard HOUGH, Robert LUCAS (dec.), Robert HALL (dec.), Joshua HOOPS. Chester: John BLUNSTON, John BRINKLOE, John BETTS, William RODNEY, John BURTON, Samuel BURBURY, Jno. RICHARDSON, Jr. Philadelphia: Thomas HOOTON, Thomas FITZWATER, Lasse COCK, James FOX, Griffith OWEN, William SOUTHERSBY. New Castle: John WHITE, Edward BLAKE, Peter BAYNTON, Val. HOLLINGSWORTH, John DARBY, Joseph HOLDING. Sussex: Thomas WINNE, Henry BOWMAN, Henry MOLESTINE, Thomas PRICE, John SYMONS, Albertus JACOBS.

p. 523, 1689: John BLACKWELL, Esq., Governor. Council: Griffith JONES, Joseph GROWDON, Luke WATSON, John HILL, William STOCKDALE, John SYMCOCK, Barth. COPPACK, Peter ALRICHS, Jonathan D'HAAS, John ECKLEY, Samuel RICHARDSON, Thomas LLOYD, William MARKHAM, Secretary. John ECKLEY was returned from Philadelphia but not allowed to take his seat because 50 or 60 Welshmen, who were not of the country, had joined the vote. Samuel RICHARDSON, the Governor said, had misdemeaned himself in council and ordered a new writ of election to issue. Thomas LLOYD was objected to by the Governor because he had charges of high crime and misdemeanors, in discharging the government, to prepare against him.
    Assembly: Philadelphia: Joseph FISHER, Abraham UPDEGRAVE, Griffith OWEN, Thomas PASCHALL, Thomas DUCKETT, Henry WADDY. Bucks: Arthur COOK, William BILES, Phineas PEMBERTON, John SWIFT, Nich. WALNE, Edmund BENNET. Kent: Daniel JONES, William BERRY, William MANLOE, John WALKER, Peter GRONINGDYCK, Daniel BROWN. Chester: James SANDILAND, Samuel LEWIS, John BARTRAM, Robert PILE, Michael BLUNSTON, Jonathan HAYES. New Castle: John DARBY, John WHITE (in prison), Val. HOLLINGSWORTH, Edward BLAKE, Isaac WELDON, Rich. MANKIN. Sussex: Baptist NEWCOMB, Samuel GRAY, Robert

CLIFTON, Henry SHEPPARD, Luke WATSON, Jr., Jonathan BAILEY.

p. 531, 1690: Council: Thomas LLOYD, President. John SMYCOCK, Samuel RICHARDSON, John CURTIS, Griffith JONES, Griffith OWEN, John BRINKLOE, William YARDLEY, William STOCKDALE, Luke WATSON, J. D'HAES, John BLUNSTON, William CLARK, Arthur COOKE, Thomas DUCKETT, Barth. COPPICK, Thomas CLIFTON, John CANN, William MARKHAM, Sec.
Assembly: Phila.: William SALWAY, Humphrey MORREY, Thomas FITZWATER, Charles PICKERING, Paul SAUNDERS, Abraham UPDEGROVE. Chester: John BRISTOW, William JENKINS, Robert PILE, Joshua FERN, George MARIS, Caleb PUSEY. Bucks: Joseph GROWDEN, Henry POYNTER, Richard HOUGH, Henry BAKER, Edmund BENNETT, John COOK. Kent: John BARNES, John BETTS, Daniel BROWN, Ez. NEEDHAM, Richard CURTIS, William FREELAND. New Castle: Edward BLAKE, Henry WILLIAMS, Richard HALLWELL, John DARBY, William GRANT, John DONALDSON. Sussex: John HILL, Samuel GRAY, Robert CLIFTON, Henry SMITH, Baptist NEWCOMB, Thomas BRANSCON.

p. 533, 11 Sept., 1684: The death of William WELCH, President, was announced.

p. 534, 17 Aug., 1691: Council met and included: Thomas LLOYD, President. John SYMCOCK, John DELAVALL, William STOCKDALE, Arthur COOK, Joseph GROWDEN, John CURTIS, Thomas DUCKETT, John BRISTOW, Thomas JANNEY, William JENKINS, Griffith OWEN.

p. 537, 1692: Council for the Province: Thomas LLOYD, Deputy Governor. Arthur COOK, Joseph GROWDEN, Griffith OWEN, William JENKINS, John BRISTOW, Samuel LEWIS, William BILES. Council for the Territories: William MARKHAM, Deputy Governor. John CANN, Richard HALLIWELL, George MARTIN, Albertus JACOBS, Samuel GRAY, Richard WILSON, John DELAVALL, Hugh ROBERTS. Assembly: Philadelphia: Samuel RICHARDSON, Philip ROMAN, George MARIS, Bart. COPPOCK, Robert PILES, Caleb PUSEY, Thomas WITHERS. Bucks: John SWIFT, John OTTER, Joshua HOOPS, William PAXON, Nicholas WALNE, John ROLAND. New Castle: John DARBY, John DONALDSON, Joseph ENGLAND, John GRUBB, Robert ASHDON, Edward BLAKE. Kent: William FREELAND, Daniel JONES, Simon IRONS, John BARNES, George MANLOE, William MANLOE. Sussex: William CLARK, Robert CLIFTON, Baptist NEWCOMB, Luke WATSON, Jr., Thomas BRANSCON, William PILES. William CLARK of Sussex is Speaker. William ALLOWAY is clerk. Charles WARE is messenger.

p. 545, 15 May, 1693: Benjamin FLETCHER is Governor. William MARKHAM, Esq., is Lieutenant Governor. Council: Andrew ROBESON, Esq., Robert TURNER, Esq., Patrick ROBINSON, Esq., Lawrence COCK, Esq., William SALWAY, Esq., George FORMAN, Esq., John CANN, Esq., William CLARK, Esq. Assembly: Phila.: Samuel CARPENTER, Samuel RICHARDSON, John WHITE, James FOX. Chester: John SYMCOCK, George MARIS, David LLOYD. New Castle: Edward BLAKE, Cornelius EMPSON, Henry WILLIAMS, Richard HALIWELL. Bucks: Joseph GROWDEN, John SWIFT, Henry POYNTER. Sussex: Albertus JACOBS, Thomas PEMBERTON, Samuel PRESTON. Kent: John BRINKLOE, John WALKER, William MANLOE.

p. 552, 1694: Assembly: Phila.: Samuel RICHARDSON, Samuel CARPENTER, Henry WADDY, James FOX. New Castle: John DONALDSON, Edward BLAKE, Richard HALIWELL, Henry WILLIAMS. Chester: David LLOYD, Caleb PUSEY, Samuel LEVIS. Bucks: William BILES, Phineas PEMBERTON, Jonathan SCAIFE. Kent: John BRINKLOE, William FREEMAN, Richard WILSON. Sussex: Thomas PEMBERTON, Luke WATSON, Roger CORBETT.

p. 559, 1695: William MARKHAM, Governor. John GOODSON, Assistant Governor. Council: Phila.: Samuel CARPENTER, Samuel RICHARDSON, Anthony MORRIS. Bucks: Joseph BROWDEN, Phineas PEMBERTON, William BILES. Sussex: William CLARK, Thomas PEMBERTON, Robert CLIFTON. Kent: John BRINKLOE, Richard WILSON, Griffith JONES. Chester: David LLOYD, Caleb PUSEY, George MARIS. New Castle: John DONALDSON, John WILLIAMS, Richard HALLIWELL. Patrick ROBINSON, Sec.

p. 561, 1695: Assembly: Phila.: Edward SHIPPEN, Alexander BEARDSLEY, James FOX, Robert OWEN, John BEVAN, John PARSONS. Bucks: Joshua HOOPES, Henry PAXTON, Samuel DARK, Nicholas WALNE, John SWIFT, Joseph MILLER. Chester: John BLUNSTON, Barth. COPPOCK, William JENKINS, Robert PILES, Walter FOREST, Philip ROMAN. Kent: John BETTS, William RODNEY, William MORTON, Simon IRONS, Daniel BROWN, John HILLIARD. Sussex: John STOCKLEY, Thomas OLDMAN, Joseph BOOTH, Henry MOLESTON, James PETERKILL, Jonathan BARLEY. New Castle: Joseph ENGLAND, Valentine HOLLINGWORTH, George HARLAND, Edward GIFFS, Henry HOLLINGWORTH, Cornelius EMPSON. Francis COOK is clerk. Meetings will be held in the house of Sarah WHITPAIN.

p. 564, 1696: Council: Edward SHIPPEN, Anthony MORRIS, David LLOYD, Jasper YEATES, John HILL, John BRINKLOE, William CLARKE, John DONALDSON, Patrick ROBINSON.
Assembly: Phila.: Samuel CARPENTER, Samuel RICHARDSON, James FOX, Nicholas WALNE. Chester: John SYMCOCK, John BLUNSTON, Caleb PUSEY. Bucks: William BILES, Joshua HOOPES, William PAXTON. New Castle: John HUSSEY, Cornelius EMPSON, George HOGG, Adam PETERSON. Kent: William RODNEY, William MORTON, Richard WILSON. Sussex: Thomas PEMBERTON, Roger CORBETT, John MIRES.

p. 569, 1697: Council: Edward SHIPPEN and Samuel CARPENTER from Phila. Bucks: Joseph GROWDEN, Phineas PEMBERTON. Chester: John SYMCOCK, Caleb PUSEY. Kent: Griffith JONES, John CURTIS. Sussex: William CLARK, John HILL. New Castle: Peter ALRICHS, Richard HALLIWELL.
Assembly: Phila.: Samuel RICHARDSON, James FOX, Robert OWEN, Nicholas WALNE. Chester: John BLUNSTON, Barth. COPPOCK, Thomas WORTH, Johnathan HAYES. Kent: John WALKER, Thomas BEDWELL, Samuel BURBERRY, John BRADSHAW. Bucks: Joshua HOOPES, Stephen BEAKS, Richard HOUGH, Jere. LANGHORNE. New Castle: Cornelius EMPSON, Benj. GORMLEY, John RICHARDSON, John BUCKLEY. Sussex: Luke WATSON, Thomas OLDMAN, Nehemiah FIELD, Thomas FISHER.

p. 576, 1698: Council: Phila.: Edward SHIPPEN, Samuel CARPENTER. Bucks: Joseph GROWDEN, William BILES. Chester: David LLOYD, John SYMCOCK. New Castle: Richard HALLIWELL, John DONALDSON. Kent: John CURTIS, William RODENEY. Sussex: William CLARKE, John HILL.
Assembly: Phila.: Anthony MORRIS, James FOX, Samuel RICHARDSON, Adnrew BANKSON. Bucks: Phineas PEMBERTON, Joseph HEATON, Joseph KIRKBIRDE, Henry BAKER. Chester: Caleb PUSEY, Samuel LEVIS, Nath. NEWLIN, Robert CARTER. New Castle: Adam PETERSON, Edward GIBBS, John GRUBB, Joseph ENGLAND. Kent: Richard WILSON, Robert EDMOND, Henry MOLESTON, William MORETON. Sussex: Thomas OLDMAN, Jonathan BAILEY, Luke WATSON, Jr., Cornelius WILLBANK. Jonathan DICKINSON is Clerk.

p. 577, 1699: Council: Phila.: Samuel CARPENTER, Edward SHIPPEN. Bucks: William BILES, Phineas PEMBERTON. Chester: David LLOYD, Caleb PUSEY. Kent: William RODNEY, Richard WILSON. Sussex: William CLARK, John HILL. New Castle: none.
Assembly: Phila.: Anthony MORRIS, James FOX, Isaac

NORRIS, John BEVIN. Bucks: John SURKETT, John SWIFT, Richard HOUGH, Enoch YARDLY. Chester: John BLUNSTON, Speaker, Robert PILES, John WORRILAW, Robert Carter. Kent: John FORSTER, Thomas SHARP, Henry MOLESTON, James BROWN. New Castle: No members returned. Sussex: William PILES, William FISHER, Nehemiah FIELD, William DYER.

p. 578: Maj. John DONALDSON was party to a disturbance in New Castle. The Sheriff of New Castle, Joseph WOOD, was dismissed for a joke of sending a blank sheet of paper to the council representing the assemblymen elected from New Castle. DONALDSON was also dismissed without punishment. Elected to fill the vacancies from New Castle for the Assembly: John HENLY, Adam PETERSON, William GUEST, William HOUSTON. For the Council: Richard HALLIWELL, Robert FRENCH.

THE STATUTES AT LARGE OF PENNSYLVANIA FROM 1682 TO 1801
Volume 2 - 1700-1712

p. 278, 1705-06: Joseph GROWDON, Samuel DARK, Tobias DYMOCK, Joseph KIRKBRIDE and William PAXON are to make public sale of the old courthouse and prison in Bristol. The courthouse is to be built on the ground lately occupied by Samuel CARPENTER and given to Joseph GROWDON, Tobias DYMOCK, Joseph KIRKBRIDE and Edward MAYES. The land is north of Peter WEBSTER's property.

p. 280, 1705-06: County justices: Phila.: Samuel FINNEY, Rowland ELLIS, Samuel RICHARDSON, Edward SHIPPEN, William CARTER. Bucks: John SWIFT, Joseph KIRKBRIDE, Tobias DYMOCK, William PAXSON. Chester: Jasper YEATES, Caleb PUSEY, Philip ROMAN (ROMANS), Jonathan HAYES.

p. 291, 1705-06: Chester Co. justices sold the old courthouse to John SIMCOCK, who died and left a will dated 25 July, 1702, bequeathing the land and building to his son-in-law, Ralph FISHBOURN.

p. 299, 1709: The following from Philadephia are to make an oath of allegience: Francis Daniel PASTORIUS, John JAWERT, Caspar HOODT, Dennis KUNDERS and three sons (Cunrad CUNRADS, Mathias CUNRADS and John CUNRADS), Dirk KEYSER and son Peter KEYSER, John LUCKEN, William STREPERS, Abraham [TUNES], Lenartt ARRETS, Reinier TYSON, John LENSON, Isaac DILBECK and son Jacobus DILBECK, John DOEDEN, Cornelius SIORTS, Henry SELLIN, Walter SIMENS, Dirk JANSEN, Jr., Richard VAN DER WERF and son, John Roeloffs VAN DER WERF, John STREEERS, Sr., Peter SHOEMAKER, Jacob SHOEMAKER, George SHOEMAKER, Isaac SHOEMAKER, Matthias VAN BEBBER, Cornelius VAN DER GAEGH, Peter CLEVER, George GOTTSHICK, Paul ENGELL and son, Jacob ENGELL, Hans NEUS, Reinier VAN DER SLUYS and son, Adrian VAN DER SLUYS, Jacob Gaetshalck VAN DER HEGGEN and son, Gaetshalck VAN DER HEGGEN, Caspar KLEINHOOF, Henry BUCHOLTZ, Hermann TUYNEN, Paul KLINUPGES and son, John KLINUGES, John NEUS and sons, Matthias and Cornelius NEUS, Claus RITENHUYSEN, Caspar STALLS, Henry TUBBEN, William HENDRICKS and sons, Hendrick and Lawrence HENDRICKS, Henry KESSLEBERRY, Johannes REBENSTOCK, Peter VERBYNEN, John GORGAES, Senwes BARTELLS and son, Henry BARTELLS, John KREY and son, William KREY, Conrad JANSEN, Claus JANSEN and son, John JANSEN, William JANSEN, Evert IMHOFF and sons, Gerhard, Herman, and Peter IMHOFF, Peter JANSEN, John SMITH, Thomas ECKLESWICH, Johannes SCHOLL, Gabriel SCHULER, William PUTTS, Matthi[a]s TYSEN. Johannes BLEIKERS of Bucks Co.

The oath of allegience must be made within 6 months of 1 Sept., 1709.

p. 374, 1710-11: Commissioners are: Phila.: Edward FARMER, Rowland ELLIS, Thomas MASTERS, Nathan STANBURY. Bucks: Joseph KIRKBRIDE, Thomas STEVENSON, Thomas WATSON, John ROWLAND. Chester: Jasper YEATES, Caleb PUSEY, Nicholas PILE, Henry PEIRCE.

p. 427, 1712: In 1697, the Lower Ferry on the Schuylkill River was commonly called the Benjamin CHAMBERS' ferry.

p. 429, 1712: Ferrys erected: At New Bristol by John SOTCHER of Pennsbury; at the Falls of the Delaware by John CLARK; at William WILLIAMS' landing; at John BALDWIN's on Neshominy Creek.

THE STATUTES AT LARGE OF PENNSYLVANIA FROM 1682 TO 1801
Volume 3 - 1712-1724

p. 6, 1712-13: Commissioners: Phila.: Richard HILL, Thomas MASTERS, Edward FARMAR, Nathan STANBURY, Rowland ELLIS. Chester: Caleb PUSEY, Nicholas PYLE, Henry PIERCE, Isaac TAYLOR, William DAVIS. Bucks: Joseph KIRKBRIDE; Thomas STEVENSON, Thomas WATSON, John ROWLAND, Jeremiah LANGHORNE.

p. 56, 1715: Charles BROCKDEN, Phila., gentleman, shall be Recorder of Deeds for Phila.

p. 84, 1715: Commissioners: Phila.: Richard HILL, Nicholas WALN, John ROBERTS. Bucks: Everard BOLTON, William PAXSON, Robert HARVEY. Chester: David LLOYD, Evan LEWIS, Gaven MILLER.

p. 92, 1715: Samuel PRESTON, Philadelphia, Merchant, is appointed provincial treasurer. Samuel CARPENTER, provincial treasurer during the 11th and 12th years of Queen Anne, died before 16 June, 1713. Executrix of his estate was Hannah CARPENTER.

p. 129, 1717: Commissioners: Phila.: William FISHBOURN, Benjamin VINING, Joseph REDMAN. Chester: David LLOYD, John MARIS, David HARRY. Bucks: Thomas STEVENSON, Jeremiah LANGHORNE, John STOCHER.

p. 163, 1717-18: Owen ROBERTS, gentleman, is appointed collector of duty on Negroes brought into this province.

p. 178, 1717-18: Commissioners: Phila.: Joseph WILLCOX, Abraham BICKLEY, Edward FARMAR, Toby LEECH, Thomas PASCHALL. Chester: David LLOYD, Nathaniel NEWLIN, John WOOD, Henry MILLER. Bucks: Jeremiah LANGHORNE, Thomas STEVENSON, John SOTCHER, Thomas WATSON.

p. 194, 1718: A ferry is established at the Falls on the Delaware River at the place of Joseph KIRKBRIDE.

p. 197, 1718: A ferry continuing from Bristol, Bucks Co. to Burlington, N.J. is kept by John SOTCHER, Pennsbury.

p. 225, 1718: William CLARKE, late of Sussex Co. on the Delaware, gentleman, in 1704, was indebted to sundry persons, among them William HOUSTON, late of New Castle upon Delaware, merchant, dec. William CLARKE and William CLARKE, Jr., on 2 Mar., 1704, bound themselves jointly to William HUSTON for £220. William CLARKE owned a messuage and lot in Philadelphia which he settled on his son,

William CLARKE, Jr. and Rebecca CURTIS (to whom it is said William CLARKE was married). Soon after, William CLARKE died. William CLARKE, Jr., afterwards secretly withdrew himself and his family to the island of Barbados, where he has since died. Anthony HOUSTON is the executor and universal legatee of William HUSTON. The land is now owned by Andrew HAMILTON. Clement PLUMSTED is the attorney for William CLARKE, Jr. On 10 June, 1718, the land is to be vested and settled in Charles READ, William FISHBOURN, Israel PEMBERTON of Philadelphia, merchants.

p. 289, 1722: Samuel CARPENTER, son of Samuel CARPENTER, late of Philadelphia, dec., is appointed to inspect flour.

p. 316, 1722: A ferry is erected at Solebury, Bucks Co., at the place of John WELLS.

p. 318: A ferry is erected in Makefield on the land of Thomas YARDLEY over the Delaware River.

p. 322: Nathaniel GRIFFITTS and Benjamin MORGAN of Phila., are appointed gaugers of wine, rum, molasses and other liquid merchandise.

p. 346, 1722-23: William PENN, on 22 and 23 Mar., 1681, sold land in Pa. to Nicholas MOORE, James CLAYPOOLE, Philip FORD, William SHARLOE, Edward PIERCE, John SIMCOCK, Thomas BRASEY, Thomas BARKER, Edward BROOKES in trust for the Free Society of Traders in Pa. and their successors. Now, Francis RAWLE, John WOOD, Joseph SHIPPEN, Job GOODSON, Stephen JACKSON, Joseph PIDGEON, Joseph COLEMAN, John DURBUROW, William HEARN, and Charles READ want to buy the land. Charles READ, Job GOODSON, Evan OWEN, Georege FITZWATER [and Joseph PIDGEON] are authorized to sell it.

p. 417, 1724: A ferry is established over Neshaminy Ck. on the King's High Road from Phila. to Bristol, Bucks Co. John BALDWIN is the keeper.

p. 419: In 1694, the then justices of the peace and grand jury of Chester Co. bought land from John HOSKINS, for a court house and prison. In a deed of 9 June, 1697, John HOSKINS conveyed to John SIMCOCK, John BLUNSTON, Samuel LEVIS, Jasper YEATES and Jonathan HAYES the piece of ground where the court house stands adj. land of Robert WADE (but now of James LOGAN), Francis LITTLE (now in the tenure of Henry HOLLINGSWORTH). After 28 May, 1724, the land is actually vested in Henry PIERCE, John CROSBY, Robert PYLE, and Isaac TAYLOR.

p. 425, 1724: John CRATHO and Caspar WISTAR were born under allegiance to the Emperor of Germany. Nicholas GATEAU was born under allegiance to the King of France. They are now in amity with the King of Great Britain and being of Protestant or Reformed religion and desirous to come under the power and protection of his British Majesty.

p. 438: Attesting that an act to allow Quakers to be judges, justices, jurymen, and witnesses in criminal and capital matters would be beneficial: Cha. COOKE, P. DOCMINIQUE, J. MOLESWORTH, Dan. PULTENEY, Mart. BLADEN. 1 May, 1719.

p. 455, 17 Jan., 1718-19: Richard DRAFTGATE was injured by an act concerning feme sole traders. He lives at the sign of the Golden

Ball, the same being a haberdasher's shop of small wares in Grace Church.

p. 470, 6 Oct.., 1719: William CLARK, Jr. and wife, Rebecca, had three children, all living and all infants. CLARK, Jr. is dec. Rebecca would not have married CLARK without the settlement mentioned on p. 225. Rebecca married Zachariah RICHARDSON, after being widowed. Anthony HUSTON died and his executor was Jonathan HUSTON. Zachariah RICHARDSON went to London in 1719 and got the act repealed which sold Rebecca's property. He settled on the Island of Jamaica until the latter end of 1724 when he was deprived of the use of his limbs and advised to go to Bath. He left Jamaica and arrived in London in Aug., 1725. He died in London in Jan., 1735. Rebecca came to Phila.

p. 488, 1717-18: An act for erecting a ferry near the land of the late Daniel COOPER.

p. 500, 1725-26: An act to enable Bernard VANLEER, Arent HASSART, Michael SMITHS, William SELLINGER, Arnold BAMBERGER, William HILLGART and Ulrich HAGEMAN, to trade and hold land in this province. All were born in Germany.

THE STATUTES AT LARGE OF PENNSYLVANIA FROM 1682 TO 1801
Volume 4 - 1724-1744

p. 32, 1725: William CHANCELLOR, Phila., sailmaker, is to build a suitable powderhouse on a piece of ground purchased from Daniel PEGG.

p. 73, 1727: Nathaniel GRIFFITTS, Phila., cooper, is appointed officer for brewing, searching, packing or re-packing and branding all beef and pork intended for exportation.

p. 80, 1727: To establish a ferry at the land of the late Daniel COOPER, now William COOPER's, at or near High St., Phila., and near Armstrong SMITH's dwelling place adjoining the town-bounds of Phila. The ferry will go to Gloucester, N.J.

p. 99, 1729: Trustees to provide bills of credit for the province: Thomas TRESS, Edward HORNE, John PARRY, and Abraham CHAPMAN.

p. 147, 1729-30: Granting privileges to Protestants who were subjects of the Emperor of Germany and transported themselves and their estates into Pennsylvania between 1700 and 1718. All from Lancaster Co.: Martyn MYLIN, Hans GRAAF, Christian STONEMAN, Jacob FUNK, Francis NEIFF, Francis NEIFF, Jr., George KINDICK, John BURKHOLDER, John BURKHOLDER, Jr., John BRUBAKER, Jacob GOOT, Christopher SOWERS, Christian PEELMAN, Abraham HARE, John Jacob SNEVELY, Isaac COFFMAN, Henry FUNK, Roody MIRE, John MYLIN, Abraham BURKHOLDER, John HESS, Christopher PRENIMAN, Joseph BUCKWALTER, Adam PRENIMAN, John BOHMAN, Henry NEIFF, Henry BARE, Peter BUMGARNER, Jacob NISLEY, John WOOLSLEGLE, Joseph STONEMAN, John Henry NEIFF, John Henry NEIFF, Jr., Peter LEAMEN, Andrew COFFMAN, Jacob BHEME, Michael DONEDER, John COFFMAN, Michael GOHMAN, John FREDERICK, Martin HARNIST, Felix LANDAS, Jr., John FUNK, John TAYLOR, Michael MIRE, Melcor HUFFORD, Melcor ERISHMAN, John SNEVELY, Jacob MIRE, Daniel ASHLEMAN, John FERIE, Jacob BIERE, Peter YORDEA, Woolrick RODTE, Charles CHRISTOPHER, Andrew SHULTS, John HOWSER, Christian PRENIMAN, Jacob MILLER, black; Christian HERMAN, big John SHANK,

John Woolrick HOUVER, John HAMPHER, John Henry BARE, Jacob WEAVER, Abraham MIRE, Woolrick HOUSER, Michael SHANK, Martin MILLER, Christian STANER, Christopher FRANCISCUS, John LINE, Jonas LEROW, Everard REAM, Henry CARPENTER, Emanuel CARPENTER, Philip FIERE, Jacob CHURTS, John CROYDER, Martyn GRAAF, Jacob BARE, Jr., Henry WEAVER, John MIRE, Jacob MILLER, Peter AYBE, John Jacob LIGHT, Caspar LOUGHMAN, John SHWOPE, Simeon KING, Gabriel CARPENTER, Daniel HERMAN, Mathias SLAREMAKER, Jacob SNEVELY, Jr., John LEIGHTE, Peter SMITH, Peter NEWCOMAT, John WEAVER, David LONGANICKAR, Henry MUSSELMAN, Jacob MILLER, Jr., Hans GOOT, Adam BRAND, Frederick STAY, Bastian ROYER, John AYBE.
From Phila.: John NEGLEY, Bernard RESSOR, Herman YERKHAS, John WISTOR, John Frederick AX, John Philip BOHM, Anthony YERKHAS.

p. 159, 1729-30: Charles READ, Phila., is appointed collector of excise tax on wine, rum, brandy and other spirits. James MITCHELL, Lancaster, is appointed the same, as well as Nathan WATSON, Bucks Co., yeoman, and Caleb COPELAND, Chester Co., gentleman.

p. 190, 1730: Samuel CARPENTER, Jeremiah LANGHORNE, William FISHBOURNE and Nathaniel NEWLIN, all of Pa., gentlemen, were appointed trustees for issuing and letting out upon loan bills of credit for the general loan office of Pa. In 1729, Nathaniel NEWLIN died and Philip TAYLOR, Chester Co., was nominated to fill the spot.

p. 207, 1730: John WRIGHT, Lancaster Co., gentleman, was appointed trustee of the general loan office of Pa.

p. 219, 1730-31: Protestants who were subjects of the Emperor of Germany, to enable them to hold lands and invest them with the privileges of natural born subjects of England. All of Phila. Co.: Peter WENTZ, Martin KOLB, Jacob KOLB, Dielman KOLB, Jacob KOLB, Hubbard GASSELL, Gerhard CLEMENTS, Bastian SMITH, Christian BOWMAN, John JODER, Philip KEILWEIN, John Dieterich KREINER, Isaac LEVAND, Jean BARTOLETT, Jonathan HERBEIN, Johannes LANGENECKER, Isaac VANSINTERN, Blasius Daniel MACKINET, Lorence BELITZ, John Joseph SCHRACK, Jacob SELTZER, Samuel GOULDIN, Hans SIGFRIED, Jacob HETTLESTEIN, Melchor HOCH, John Jacob SCHRACK, Jacob REIF, Antonius HILMAN, John Isaac KLEIN, Michael ZIEGLER, Paul FRIED, Johannes FRIED, Hans DATWEILLER, Johannes LESEBER, Chris. ZIMMERMAN, Mathias GEMELIN, Abraham SCHWAARTZ, John JODER, Jr., Hans HOCH, Peter BALIO, Nicholas LESCHER, Hans Martin GERICH, John BOWMAN, Johannes BUCKWALTER, Johannes Dewalt END, Mathias Adams HOGERMOED, Johann Nicholas KRESSMAN, Philip SCHRACK, George ROWSE, Christian GOULDIN, Peter TREXLER, Daniel LANGENECKER, Jacob HOCH, John George REIF, Conrad REIF, Henry ANTIS, Johannes MAYER, Valantine HUNSUCKER, Jacob SCHEIMER, Johannes KOCKEN, George MARKL, Jacob HERMAN, Jacob METTS, Ulrich MAYER, Hermanus KUSTER, Joest JODER, Peter ENDREAS, Abraham LEVAND, David KOUFFMAN, Martin SCHENKEL, Arnold HUFFNAGLE, Johannes ECKSTEIN, Johannes George BENTZEL, Hans RUP, Christopher FUNK, Johannes SHAFFER, George JAGER, Henry PENNEBECKER, Henry SCHAUT, Hans Jacob BECHTLEY, George HOLLENBAIK, Joh. Geo. REIF, Jr., Peter REIF, Gerhard PETERS, Samuel HOCH, John SNYDER, George BECHTLEY, Joest Hendrick ZAATZMENTZHOUSSEN. All of Phila. City: Marcus HUHL, John KELLER, Jacob KASDROP, Johan BAKER, Abraham KINKING. All of Bucks Co.: Jacob KLEMMER, Jacob SOUDER, Philip KEISINGER, George BACHMAN, John DRIESTLE. All of Chester Co.: Christian MARY, Johannes ROTH, Casper ACKER, Jacob ACKER.

p. 222, 1730-31: Benjamin MAYNE, late of Phila., merchant, traded and lived several years in good credit in Pa. before 1721 and had become a debtor to sundry merchants in the course of business. When he took some merchandise to Salem Co., N.J. to sell, his creditors took attachments against his goods in Phila., sold them for less than ½ the real value and ruined MAYNE.

p. 226, 1730-31: William FISHBOURNE, Phila., gentleman, was appointed a trustee of the general loan office in 1722. In Aug., 1730, he fraudulently concealed and applied to his own use a considerable sum of bills of credit. From publication of this act until five years have passed, William FISHBOURNE cannot be a member of the general assembly or hold and enjoy any office within Pa. FISHBOURNE is indebted to Pa. for £1769 18s 3 farthings.

p. 277, 1735: Joseph CHAPMAN, Bucks Co., yeoman, was elected commissioner of Bucks Co. on 1 Oct., 1733. Sheriff of Bucks Co. failed to return his name. He is declared duly elected. William PAXTON is now dec. William BILES and Simon BUTLER, Bucks Co., gentlemen, are nominated as commissioners and Joseph KIRKBRIDE, Jr. is likewise nominated. William BILES has declined to act as commissioner this year. Benjamin TAYLOR, Richard MITCHELL, Nathan WATSON, John DAWSON, Joseph LUPTON, David WILSON, yeomen, are Bucks Co. assessors.

p. 283, 1735: Protestant subjects of Germany are enabled to hold lands, etc. All from Phila. City: John DIEMER, David SCHOLTZE, Peter HILLEGAS, Wilhelm ZIEGLER, Anthony BENEZET, Paulus KRIPNER, Jacob SEIJL, George SCHOLTZ, Ulrich ALLER, Caspar ULRICH, Henry VAN AKEN, John IDEN, Adam KLAMTER. All of Phila. Co.: Anthony BOHM, Conrad BENSELL, Adam ROMISH, Frederick REYMER, Adam GALAR, Conrad REBLE, Johannes ZIRWER, Jacob HILL, Christian WEBER, Conrad KEER, Anthony ZADOUSKI, Lodwick PITTING, Joseph GRAFF, Henry SLINGLOFF, Michael BERGER, George SOUBER, Nicholas LEISHER, Jr., Hans George WEIGERT, Sebastian Reiff SCHNEIDER, John SOUBER, Nicholas KEYSER, Conrad KUSTOR, Hans PINGEMAN, Alexander DIHL, Jacob BOWMAN, Gottlieb HERGER, Daniel SCHONER, Peter SOUBER, Christopher MINK, Jacob KEMP, Abraham ZIMMERMAN, Martin PITTING, Jacob DUBRE, Andreas KRAVER. All of Bucks Co.: John George KINKNER, William MOREY, Peter SCHNEIDER, John JODER, Ulrich RUBEL, Henry RINKER, Christian KLIMMER, John JODER, Jr., Joseph EBERHART, Michael EBERHART, Jacob KANGWEER, John BRECHT, Henry SCHNEIDER, George ZEIWIZT, Michael WE[I]BER, Diter GAUFF. All of Chester Co.: George DONATT, Garratt BROWNBACK. All of Lancaster Co.: John George BEARD, John Casper STOVER, Jacob BYERLY, Michael WEIDLEY, Frederick ELBERSCHIDT, Jacob LEMAN, Peter ENTZMINGER, Jacob KERSBERGER, Michael BYERLY.

p. 286, 1735: On 25 Oct., 1701, William PENN granted 12000 acres in Phila. Co. to Samuel CARPENTER, Isaac NORRIS, and Edward PENINGTON. 5000 acres of this land is the proper estate of John PENN by the grant of Thomas CALLOWHILL, grandfather of John PENN. William PENN's other children by his wife, Hannah, were Thomas, Richard, Margaret (wife of Thomas FREAME) and William. On 1 and 2 July, 1734, 12,000 acres were sold to John PENN. Samuel CARPENTER and Edward PENINGTON were dec. Isaac NORRIS is dec. His son is Isaac NORRIS. John PENN, on 19 and 20 June, 1735, sold the 12,000 acres, which on resurvey was found to contain 14,060 acres, to George MCCALL for 2000 guineas.

p. 304, 1738: Charles READ, one of the trustees of the general loan office is dec. As of 10 Oct., 1738, Andrew HAMILTON, Jeremiah LANGHORNE and Richard HAYES were discharged from being trustees of the general loan office. John KINSEY, Jonathan ROBESON, Joseph

KIRKBRIDE and Caleb COWPLAND are appointed.

p. 326, 1739: Protestant subjects of Germany are enabled to hold lands, etc. Phila. City and County residents: Joannes DYLANDER, Christian GRASSOLD, Henry SHOCKLIER, Michael Jansen HALLING, Daniel STEINMETZ, Johannes SMITH, David DESHLER, Hans George PASSAGE, David SEESHOLTZ, Stephen GREIFF, Hans George HICKNER, Sebastian MIRRY, Rudolph BONNER, Baltzazar REESER, Jr., Johannes ZACHARIAS, Charles BENSEL, Jr., Daniel MACKNED, Jr., Justis REEB-CAMP, Charles REEB-CAMP, Jacob GALLETE, Anthony HINKEL, Peter RIGHTER, William RERIGH, Henry SHOUB, Christopher ROAB, Caspar SINGER, Ludowick KNAUS, William HAUKE, Leonhart CHRISTLER, Johannes WILHELM, Ludowick CIRKEL, Ludowick HINNIGE, George CREESMAN, Frederick GOTSHALL, Andreas TROMBOUER, Jacob TROMBOUER, Hartman DETTERMER, Philip ENGHERT, Leonhart HARTLINE, Michael KLEIN, Joseph COOB, Henry DEINIG, Johan Ditterig BAUMAN, Johan KLEIM, Frederick MARSTALLER, Matthias KOPLIN, Johannes BENDER, Henry DEERINGER, Adam MOSER, Peter JARGERT, Samuel GOOLDIN, Hans George JARGER, Jacob FREY, Christopher WITMAN, Andreas GEISBERTS, Andreas JAGER, Jacob AISTER, Andreas KEPLER, Benedictus MUNTS, John EIGSTER, Michael HERGER, Philip HAAN, Conrath DOTTERER, Bernhard DOTTERER, Herman FISHER, Frederick HILLENGAS, Philip LABAR, Michael KNAPPENBERGER, Michael DOTTERER, George HUBNER, Conrath KOLB, George Philip DOTTERER, Johan MILLER, Jacob FREEH, Henry SMITH, Leonhart SMITH, Rowland SMITH, Michael KRAUS, Daniel KREESTMAN, Abraham BEYER, Michael GOOD, George GOOD, Henry SNYDER, Adam REED, Christopher OTTINGER, Anthony JAGER, Nicholas JAGER, Johan Hnery WEEBER, Johan Jacob ROTH, Johannes GELDBAGH, Christian GONDY. From Bucks Co.: Henry BERNHART, Mick[a]el NEACE, Adam SHAFFER. From Lancaster Co.: Michael ALBERT, William ALBERT, Leonhart BENDER, Ludowick DETTENBURN, Michael BECKER, John LIBOUGH, Jacob BECKER, Matthew TISE, George Ludowick HORST, Henry Michael IMMEL, George MILLER, John BUSHUNG, Nicholas CANDLE, Jacob BARE, Jr., John Peter COOKER, Bartholomew SHAVER, Tobias PICKLE, Paul REMSBERGER, John LEIBERGER, Christian LOWER, Caspar STUMP, Peter RUTT, George KLINE, Johan Henry BASSELER, Mattheas JUNG, Felix MILLER, Martin WEYBRECHT, Henry NEAFF, Jr., Johan STETLER, Nicholas MILLER, Johan HOCK, Jacob SHAFFER, Valentine KEEFER, Caspar REED, Jacob LOWER, Hans MOOR, Erasmus BUCKENMEYER, Frederick EIGHELBERGER, Sebastian FINK, Anthony BRETTER, Hans GRAFF, Benjamin WITMER, Adam WITMER, Valentine HERGELRAT, Leonhart ROMLER, Johan NOHAKER, Thomas KOPPENHEFFER, Michael KOPPENHEFFER, Jacob ETSHBERGER, Christian MANUSMITH, Christopher LEY, John BLUM, George GROFF, Hans Adam SHREINER, Christian LONG, Leonhart ELLMAKER, Jacob HARTMAN, Joannes PINKLEY, Turst BUCKWALTER, Henry BASSELER, Leonhart HEYER, Peter SHELL, Christian LEEMAN, George UNROOK, Herman WALBURN, Nicholas CUTTS, George WEYRICK, George STEITZ.

p. 382, 1742-43: FISHER's Island, on the southerly side of the mouth of the Schuylkill River in Phila. Co., adjoining the Delaware River, is now called Providence Island. A conveyance taken from Jonathan PASCHAL and his wife, Mary, (late Mary FISHER), John PASCHAL and Henry HODGE, executors of the will of John FISHER, late owner of the island, to Joseph HARVEY, Thomas TATNALL, Joseph TROTTER, James MORRIS and Oswald PEELE, gentlemen. The island will be used as a hospital and pest house for sickly persons imported into this province.

p. 408, 1744: The new trustees of the general loan office: John KINSEY, Thomas LEECH, John WATSON, Thomas CHANDLER, John WRIGHT.

THE STATUTES AT LARGE OF PENNSYLVANIA FROM 1682 TO 1801
VOLUME 5 - 1744-1759

p. 28, 1745-46: Jeremiah LANGHORNE, William BILES, Joseph KIRKBRIDE, Jr., Thomas WATSON, and Abraham CHAPMAN are to build a new courthouse and prison in Bucks Co. in the 11th year of the reign of King George I. Thomas WATSON is a practitioner in physick and is from Newtown. Since this act was made, Jeremiah LANGHORNE, William BILES and Thomas WATSON are dec. Mark WATSON, Mahlon KIRKBRIDE and John WATSON, Jr. of Buckingham are named to replace those three.

p. 54, 1748-49: On 26 May, 1744, John KINSEY, Thomas LEECH, John WATSON, Thomas CHANDLER and John WRIGHT were appointed trustees of the general loan office. Now they are dismissed and on 16 May, 1749, John KINSEY, James MORRIS, Abraham CHAPMAN, Francis YARNAL and James WRIGHT are nominated.

p. 74, 1748-49: David MCCONAUGHY, York Co., is appointed to collect excise taxes. Thomas COX, Michael TANNER, George SWOOPE, Nathan HUSSEY, and John WRIGHT, Jr., all of York Co., yeomen, are to purchase land to erect a courthouse and prison.

p. 78: Joseph PRICHARD, Phila., gentleman, is appointed duty collector.

p. 82: William ALLEN, Esq., sold a piece of ground in Phila. to the government for an almshouse.

p. 90: Robert MCCOY, Benjamin CHAMBERS, David MAGAW, James MCENTIRE and John MCCORMICK, yeomen, are to build a courthouse in Cumberland Co. Benjamin CHAMBERS is appointed excise tax collector.

p. 102: Joseph KING, Phila., is appointed an officer for viewing all flour shipped from Phila. City and County. Joseph ATKINSON, Bucks Co., is appointed an officer for viewing all flour shipped from Bucks Co. Thomas CUMMINGS is appointed the same for Chester Co.

p. 136: Anthony LEE, Francis PARVIN, William MAUGRIDGE, William BIRD, and Joseph MILLARD are to get land in Reading to build a courthouse and prison. John HUGHS of Berks Co. is authorized to collect excise taxes.

p. 138, 1751-52: Edward SCULL, Phila. Co.; Benjamin LIGHTFOOT, Chester Co. and Thomas COOKSON, Lancaster Co., are required to mark out boundary lines between Phila., Chester, Lancaster and Berks Co.

p. 143, 1751-52: Thomas CRAIG, Hugh WILSON, John JONES, Thomas ARMSTRONG, and James MARTIN are to build the courthouse in Northampton Co. Daniel CRAIGE, Northampton Co., is appointed excise tax collector.

p. 189, 1754-55: Bills of credit of 1 shilling or more shall be signed by three of the following: Evan MORGAN, Joseph FOX, James PEMBERTON, Hugh ROBERTS, John REYNELL, Thomas CLIFFORD, Owen JONES, Jonathan EVANS, Joseph WHARTON, John SMITH, Isaac JONES, Isaac GREENLEAF, Thomas CROSBY, Daniel WILLIAMS, William GRANT, Joseph KING, William LOGAN, Charles JONES, Samuel HAZARD, Samuel RHODES, Joseph MORRIS, Samuel SANSOM, Edward PENINGTON, Thomas FAY, Joseph SAUNDERS, Samuel BURGE.

p. 209, 1755-56: Bills of credit of 1 shilling or more shall be signed by three of the following: Evan MORGAN, John BAYNTON, Thomas CROSBY, Thomas WHARTON, Joseph MARRIOTT, Charles MEREDITH, Redmond CONYNGHAM, Daniel BENEZET, William SHIPPEN, William GRIFFITTS, Thomas DAVIS, Daniel ROBERDEAU, Attwood SHUTE, Samuel NEAVE, Charles STEADMAN, Jonathan EVANS, Edmond KEARNEY, William FISHER, George OKILL, Abel JAMES, Enoch FLOWER, Henry HARRISON, Jacob LEWES, John TAYLOR, William GRANT, Amos STRETTELL, Samuel MORRIS, Jacob DUCHE, Thomas GORDON, Joseph KING, William VANDERSPEIGEL, Joseph REDMAN, Charles JONES, Isaac PASCHAL.

p. 212, 1755-56: Petition: David FRANKS for LEVY & Co., Jeremiah WARDER, Samuel NEAVE, William and David MCILVAINE, Buckridge SIMS, Benjamin and Samuel SHOEMAKER, James WALLACE, James BENEZET, Thomas CAMPBELL, William WEST, Adam HOOPS, John POTTER, Joseph MORRIS have petitioned that George CROGHAN and William TRENT, late of Cumberland Co., Indian traders and partners, owe them and others large sums of monies. Losses were occasioned by defection of "our Indian allies" and from their former friendship with this province and conquest by the French on the Ohio and the adjacent country (where for the most part the goods purchased of the aforesaid creditors were sold). Petitioners ask 10 years amnesty for CROGHAN and TRENT. They have to live away from creditors to avoid prosecution and therefore cannot transact business and cannot pay off debts. Ten years is to be computed from 28 Nov., 1755.

p. 216, 1755-56: William GRIFFITTS, Jacob DUCHE and Thomas SAY, Phila., Griffith OWEN, Samuel BROWN, and Abraham DE NORMANDIE, Bucks Co., Nathaniel PENNOCK, Nathaniel GRUBB and John HANNUM, Chester Co., Calvin COOPER, James WEBB, and Samuel LE FEVRE, Lancaster Co., are to appoint the disposition of inhabitants of Nova Scotia, imported into this province, into Phila., Bucks, Chester and Lancaster Co. and help settlement by the purchase of stock or utensils of husbandry as necessary.

p. 243, 1755-56: Bills of credit may be signed by any three: William GRANT, Joseph RICHARDSON, James BENEZET, Samuel WHARTON, Joseph WHARTON, Jr., Daniel RUNDLE, Joseph SAUNDERS, Peter REEVE, Joseph MORRIS, Luke MORRIS, Peter CHEVALIER, William HOPKINS, Stephen WOOLEY, Joshua HOWELL, Joseph GALLOWAY, George BRYAN, Samuel SMITH, John RHEA, Thomas SMITH, Charles THOMSON, Isaac PASCHAL, Charles JONES, John SAYRE, Francis RAWLE, Thomas WHARTON, Jacob COOPER, William FISHER, Joseph REDMAN.

p. 262: Joseph YEATES, Phila., has been long confined to gaol at the suit of Thomas ROBEY for a debt of £100.

p. 298, 1756-57: Signers of bills of credit (any three): Henry HARRISON, Peter REEVE, Joseph MORRIS, William MORRIS, Jr., Buckridge SIMS, James CHILD, Stephen CARMICK, Thomas CLIFFORD, Thomas BOURNE, John SWIFT, John RHEA, James WHARTON, Plunket FLEESON, John ORD, Ed. DUFFIELD, Matthew CLARKSON, John HUGHES, Samuel HOWELL, Thomas SAY, Thomas CARPENTER, Thomas MOORE, John LYNN, George EMLEN, Joseph HILBORN.

p. 305, 1756-57: Signers of bills of credit (any three): Joseph MORRIS, Charles MEREDITH, Ed. PENINGTON, Charles JONES, Richard WISTAR, Samuel BURGE, Evan MORGAN, John LYNN, Plunket FLEESON, Charles THOMSON, John ORD, William FISHER, Thomas WHARTON, Joseph REDMAN, Thomas GORDON, Francis RAWLE, James HUMPHRYS, Henry

HARRISON, Thomas CLIFFORD, Joseph RICHARDSON, Thomas DAVIS, Joseph HILLBORN, William MORRIS, Jr., Thomas SAY, Joseph STRETCH.

p. 315: Samuel Preston MOORE and Richard HILL, dec., were tenants in common of land in Phila. In Richard HILL's will, he named his father, Richard HILL; his brother-in-law, Samuel Preston MOORE and wife, Hannah; his brother, Henry; and his sisters: Mary, Deborah, Harriet, Rachel, Margaret, Sarah and Milcah.

p. 321, 1757-58: Edward PENINGTON, William FISHER, John REYNELL, Joseph RICHARDSON, William WEST, Joseph MORRIS, Amos STRETTLE, Thomas WILLING and James CHILD are appointed commissioners for Indian affairs.

p. 348: Bills of credit may be signed by any three; Peter REEVE, Henry HARRISON, James WHARTON, William FISHER, Evan MORGAN, Daniel WILLIAMS, Stephen WOOLEY, Thomas YORKE, Charles HUMPHREYS, William HOPKINS, George BRYAN, Charles JONES, Joseph WHARTON, Jr., Luke MORRIS, James BENEZET, James HUMPHREYS, John HUGHES, Joseph SAUNDERS, Joseph MORRIS , Samuel MORRIS, Charles THOMPSON, Thomas CLIFFORD, Daniel RUNDLE, Matthew CLARKSON, Samuel WHARTON, Joseph STRETCH, Joseph MARRIOTT, Thomas MOORE, Thomas CARPENTER, Peter CHEVALIER, Thomas GORDON, John ORD, James CHILD.

P. 375: John THOMAS, Phila., is appointed officer for viewing flour shipped from Phila. John PRIESTLY is appointed same for Bucks Co. Edward RUSSEL is appointed same for Chester Co.

p. 392, 1758-59: Bills of credit may be signed by any three: Peter REEVE, Charles THOMSON, Daniel WILLIAMS, Robert BULLY, James WHARTON, Henry HARRISON, Joseph STRETCH, Thomas GORDON, Richard PEARNE, Charles JONES, Joseph SAUNDERS, Evan MORGAN, John ORD, Joseph MARRIOT, Samuel MORRIS, Luke MORRIS, Joseph MORRIS, Thomas CLIFFORD, Thomas TILBURY, Peter CHEVALIER, James CHILD, James HUMPHREYS.

p. 406: Thomas YORKE, James CHILD, Daniel RUNDLE, Peter CHEVALIER, Enoch STORY are to sell the provincial ship-of-war and use the money to purchase or hire one other ship-of-war.

p. 429: Trustees of the general loan office are: Charles NORRIS, Thomas LEECH, John WATSON, Nathaniel GRUBB, Emanuel CARPENTER.

p. 456: An act to lend £50,000 to Col. John HUNTER, agent for John TOMLINSON, John HANBURY, George COLEBROOKE and Arnold NESBIT, contractors.

p. 571, 1756: Isaac NORRIS, James HAMILTON, John MIFFLIN, and Benjamin FRANKLIN, Esqs., Joseph FOX, John HUGHES, Evan MORGAN, gentlemen, are to supply "our friendly Indians," holding treaties, relieving distressed settlers who have been driven from their lands.

THE STATUTES AT LARGE OF PENNSYLVANIA FROM 1682 TO 1801
VOLUME 6 - 1759-1765

p. 19, 1759-60: Lynford LARDNER, Thomas CADWALADER, Joseph FOX, John HUGHES, William MASTERS, Joseph GALLOWAY and John BAYNTON, Esq., are appointed to dispose of money for raising, paying and clothing 2700 men to act in conjunction with His Majesty's British forces until 25 Nov., next.

p. 22, 1759-60: Point No Return Meadows, fronting the River Delaware in the precinct of Richmond, Northern Liberties Twp., Phila. Co., lying between the mouth of Gunner's Creek and the mouth of Frankford Creek, shall be divided into several allotments: The lower and southwest end of the tract claimed by heirs of William BALL, dec., extending up to a creek dividing BALL'S meadow from meadows of heirs of Edward WARNER, dec., extending across the meadow of heirs of WARNER and of Joseph FOX to a line dividing them from a meadow of William CALLENDER is one allotment; across the meadow of William CALLENDER to a line dividing it from PARROCK's meadow is one allotment; across PARROCK's meadow to a line dividing this from a meadow of Michael HILLEGAS is one allotment; across HILLEGAS' meadow to a line dividing it from the meadow late of Joseph LYNN, dec., is one allotment; across the meadow of LYNN to a line dividing it from the meadow of Jeremiah ELFRETH is one allotment; across the meadow of ELFRETH to a line dividing it from Samuel OLDMAN's meadow is one allotment; across the meadow of OLDMAN to a line dividing it from Robert HOPKINS' meadow is one allotment; across the meadow of HOPKINS and Hugh ROBERTS to a line of William MOORE's meadow is one allotment.

p. 34, 1759-60: Joseph FOX, John HUGHES, Hugh ROBERTS, Philip SYNG, Matthew JOHNS, Jacob LEWIS and Jacob COOPER are authorized to divide up Greenwich Island (surrounded by the Delaware River, HOLLANDER's Ck., and HAY Ck. in Moyamensing and Passyunk Twp., Phila. Co.).

p. 54, 1760-61: Meadowland and marsh in Kingsess Twp. on the west side of the Schuylkill River, beginning at David GIBSON' fast land, running to the mouth of INCORN's Kill, now called CHARLES JUSTICE's Ck.. Hugh ROBERTS, Enoch FLOWER, Samuel RHOADS, Andrew BANKSON, Joseph JOHNSON and John SMITH are authorized to divide the banks and repair and maintain them.

p. 72, 1760-61: An act to enable Thomas YORKE, James CHILD, Daniel RUNDLE, Peter CHEVALIER and Enoch STORY to sell the provincial ship of war.

p. 75: Darby Ck. meadows, fronting on the Delaware River in Ridley Twp., Chester Co., is bounded by Crum Ck., Darby and Stone Ck. The meadow is divided into two parts: from the eastern line dividing the meadows of John MORTON from the meadows of John KNOWLES and Israel HENDRICKSON, and extending to Darby and Stone Cks., shall be known as the "Eastern Moiety." The Eastern Moiety is divided into three different district and allotments: from the fast land near the house of Swan CULIN, 56 perches of the said bank shall belong to Daniel CULLIN, Swan CULIN, George CULIN and Samuel CULIN, heirs of George CULIN, dec.; another part will belong to John MORTON; another part will belong to Morton MORTON, Lawrence GARRET and Thomas SMITH. William PARKER, Esq., Isaac PEARSON, John LEWIS are appointed to divide the meadows. Owners of the land are to be called The Ridley Co.

p. 94: Joseph FOX, John HUGHES, Samuel RHOADS, John POTTS, William PALMER, David DAVIS, Mordecai MOORE, Henry PAWLING, James COULTAS, Jonathan COATES, Joseph MILLARD, William BIRD, Francis PARRIN, Benjamin LIGHTFOOT, Isaac LEVAN are appointed commissioners to clear, scour and make the Schuylkill River navigable.

p. 100: Solomon HALL, Phila., tailor, owned land in Oxford Twp. On 15 June, 1724, he sold it to Josiah HARPER and Toby LEECH, the younger, for the use of the minister of the established church at Oxford. The Rev. Robert WEYMAN is the minister. Since then, the church at Whitemarsh has been annexed to the mission of Oxford Church by the Honorable the Society in London for Propagating the Gospel in Foreign Parts. Now, the church wants to sell the land. All rights to the land settled on Rev. Mr. Hugh NEILL, Isaac ASHTON, Esq., Samuel SWIFT, Jacob LEECH (the son of Jacob LEECH) and Jacob DUFFIELD.

p. 111: Thomas COOMBE is appointed to succeed Richard PEARNE as a collector of duty on negroes and mulatto slaves imported into the province.

p. 115: John SARGENT, George AUFRERE, David BARCLAY, Jr., John BARCLAY, merchants in London, are authorized to apply for distributive shares allotted to this Province out of sums of money granted to His Majesty's colonies in America. Thomas LEECH, Charles NORRIS, Mahlon KIRKBRIDE, Francis YARNALL, and James WRIGHT are appointed trustees of the general loan office.

p. 118: William GRIFFITTS, Phila., merchant, 18 months ago found himself incapable of satisfying debts due to losses in trade for several successive years. GRIFFITT's wife was Abigail. Charles NORRIS, John REYNELL, attorney to Elias BLAND; Daniel RUNDLE, Joseph RICHARDSON, William FISHER, Joshua HOWELL, JAMES & DRINKER for themselves, William NEALE, John NIXON, Thomas CARPENTER, Thomas MOORE, Joseph WHARTON, Jr., Charles MONK, Oswald EVE, Robert FIELD, FRANCIS & RELFE, Samuel ORMES, REED & PETIT, Peter WIKOFF for John and Peter WIKOFF, John MEASE, John NELSON attorney for Charles STEUART, William PLUMSTED, Lester FALCONAR, Robert LEWIS & Son, William BROWN, Charles WEST, William RUSH, George ROBOTHAM, Owen JONES, Benjamin KENDALL, Isaac GREENLEAFE, Jacob SHOEMAKER, Jr., James EDDY for PEMBERTON, MOORE & KINSEY, KEARNEY & GILBERT, creditors of the said William GRIFFITTS, ask that he not be imprisoned.

p. 124: Schuylkill Point Meadow Land, Phila. Co., Passyunk Twp., beginning at the fast land of Henry ELVES and John HANNIS, near the mouth of SPIKE's Ck. to the mouth of HOLLANDER Ck., and up the same creek line to the line between Joseph TURNER and Joseph SIMS. Hugh ROBERTS, Enoch FLOWER, Samuel RHOADS, Andrew BANKSON, Joseph JOHNSON and John SMITH are authorized to divide the banks and repair and maintain the meadow.

p. 135, 1761-62: Meadowland in Moyamensing Twp., Phila. Co., is called Wicaco Meadows. Jeremiah ELFRETH, Stephen PASCHALL, Hugh ROBERTS, Andrew BANKSON, William JONES, George GRAY, David GIBSON and Jonathan PASCHALL are empowered to inspect dams around the meadow.

p. 147: Isaac PEARSON, John PAHSCHAL and John SMITH are authorized to divide dams, etc. around a marsh in Kingsessing Twp., Phila. Co., commonly known as BOON's Island and Carcus Hook Marsh and other parcels in Ridley Twp., Chester Co.

p. 162: George GRAY, David GIBSON, Philip PRICE, John SMITH (of Kingsess) and John LEWIS, gentlemen, are authorized to divide banks, etc. around Hay Island and the Little Island, on the west side of Darby Ck., at Calcoon Hook, Darby Twp., Chester Co., excepting the meadow ground of Charles GRANTUM and of the heirs of Adam ARCHER and Jacob ARCHER, both dec.

p. 174: Enoch STORY, Thomas YORKE, James CHILD, Daniel RUNDLE or Peter CHEVALIER, Jr. are authorized to sell the provincial ship-of-war.

p. 175: Enoch STORY, one of the administrators of the estate of Richard PEARNE, is authorized to collect duties.

p. 176: Samuel RHOADS, Esq., Henry HARRISON, Esq., Thomas WILLING, Esq., Thomas WHARTON, George BRYAN, Luke MORRIS, and Peter REEVE, gentlemen, are to buy ground on the Delaware River or Bay to erect piers.

p. 177: Andrew HAMILTON and William ALLEN, Esqs., bought for the use of the province, lots of ground on the south side of Chestnut St. One other lot owned by Andrew MORRIS (bounded by a lot of John BIRD), was bought to erect a State House. John KINSEY, Joseph KIRKBRIDE (the younger), Caleb COWPLAND, and Thomas EDWARDS, Esqs., conveyed assurances. Andrew HAMILTON, John KINSEY, Caleb COWPLAND, and Joseph KIRKBRIDE, Jr., are since dec. The State House is now vested in Isaac NORRIS, Thomas LEECH, Joseph FOX, Samuel RHOADS, Joseph GALLOWAY, John BAYNTON and Edward PENNINGTON, Esqs.

p. 187: The following shall divide their counties into districts to divide responsibilities for public roads: Phila. Co.: Joseph FOX, Esq., Hugh ROBERTS, William CALLENDER, John ROBERTS (miller), Jacob EDGE, John SHRACK, William FOULKE. Bucks Co.: James MELVIN, Esq., Joseph HAMPTON, John WOOLSTON, Alexander BROWN, John BROWN (of Bristol). Lancaster Co.: Emanuel CARPENTER, Esq., Samuel BOUDE, Esq., George LEANORD, John CLEMSON, Peter KUCHER. Cumberland Co.: John BYERS, Esq., James GALBREATH, Esq., Francis CAMPBELL, Esq., Benjamin CHAMBERS, James MCDOWELL. Northampton Co.: Adam JOHE, John MCDOWELL, Christopher WAGONER, John WALKER, George REX. Chester Co.: John MORTON, Esq., John HANNUM, Esq., Jonas PRESTON, Joseph PENNOCK, Jr., John GRIFFITH, John MARSHALL, Thomas PIMM. York Co.: David MCCONAUGHY, Esq., Francis WORLEY, William DUNLAP, Thomas MINSHAL, David GRIFFITH. Berks Co.: Francis PARVIN, Esq., Jonas SEELY, Esq., Isaac LEVAN, Esq., Benjamin SPIKER, Thomas POTTS (of Colebrookdale), Israel ROBESON, Sebastian ZIMMERMAN.

p. 196: Hugh ROBERTS, Philip SYNG, Jacob COOPER, Thomas GORDON, Jacob LEWIS, George BRYAN are commissioners for paving and cleansing streets.

p. 228, 1761-62: Lynford LARDNER, Thomas CADWALADER, Joseph FOX, John HUGHES, Joseph GALLOWAY, John BAYNTON, John MORTON, Esqs., are to appoint the distribution of £15,000 to raise, feed and clothe men to protect and defend Phila.

p. 271, 1762-63: Rev. Charles Magnus WRANGEL, D.D., a subject of Sweden; Andreas Henry GROTH, gentleman of Denmark; Frederich KUHL, gentleman of Denmark; Lewis WEISS, gentleman of Prussia; Nicholas WEAVER, tailor of the Dutchy of Deuxponts, Germany; Johannes LANDAVER, gentleman of the Dutchy of Wirtemberg, Germany; all protestants, are to have the rights and privileges of British subjects.

p. 276, 1762-63: Thomas CRAIG, Hugh WILSON, John JONES, Thomas ARMSTRONG and James MARTIN are to purchase land in Easton, Northampton Co., for a courthouse and prison.

p. 277: John JONES, Thomas ARMSTRONG, James MARTIN, John RINKER, Henry ALLSHOUSE, gentlemen, are authorized to levy money necessary to build a courthouse and prison.

p. 284: John REYNELL, William FISHER, Joseph MORRIS, [Joseph RICHARDSON, merchant], Joseph SIMS, John GIBSON, gentlemen, are appointed commissioners for Indian affairs.

p. 303, 1762-63: Peter REEVE, William RICHARDS, Luke MORRIS, William MORRELL, John KIDD, Joseph STAMPER, John GIBSON are nominated commissioners to build a light-house at the mouth of Delaware Bay at or near Cape Henlopen.

p. 335, 1763-64: Samuel WALLIS has been confined in the gaol of the city and county of Phila. on account of a £586 9s 1p debt to John MOORE. The consideration of the bond was a quantity of goods purchased by WALLIS from MOORE and carried into Quebec. On arrival in Quebec, he found the goods were damaged. Sale was impossible. He transported the goods to the original port.

p. 358: The following are to hear appeals from assessments: Philip SYNG, Phila.; Thomas LIVEZLEY, Phila. Co.; Mahlon KIRKBRIDE, Bucks Co.; James GALBREATH, Cumberland Co.; John MOOR, Northampton Co.; John FAIRLAMB, Chester Co.; Moses IRWIN, Lancaster Co., Michael SWOPE, York Co.; Jonas SEELY, Berks Co.

p. 362: Bills of credit may be signed by three of the following: Henry HARRISON, Joseph SIMS, Joseph STAMPER, William BINGHAM, Samuel NEAVE, Jonathan EVANS, Thomas GORDON, Jacob LEWIS, Isaac GREENLEAFE, Thomas WHARTON, Samuel [Preston MOORE], John GIBSON, Peter REEVE, Joseph SANDERS, Joseph STRETCH, Joseph JACOBS, Isaac STRETCH, John HUGHES, Jr., George ROBERTS, William LLOYD, Samuel RHOADS, Jr., Amos HILBOURN, Cadwalader MORRIS, Thomas MAYBURY, John MEASE, Jr., John BRINGHURST, Thomas CLIFFORD, George CLYMER, Henry DRINKER, Samuel HUDSON, Samuel MORRIS, Jr., Jacob SHOEMAKER, Jr., Enoch STORY, George DILLWYN, Richard WELLS, Charles PETTIT, John MIFFLIN, Abel JAMES, Benjamin MORGAN.

p. 383, 1764-65: Henry HARRISON, Esq., Jacob DUCHEE, Esq., Charles STEDMAN, Thomas GORDON, Joseph SIMS, Edward DUFFIELD, John ORD, John KNOWLES, gentlemen, are managers for a lottery to raise £3003 15s to finish St. Peter's and St. Paul's Episcopal Churches, Phila., and to finish the Episcopal Church at Carlisle and for building an Episcopal Church in York and Reading and for repairing an Episcopal Church at Molattin in Berks Co. and the Episcopal Church in Huntingdon Twp., York Co. and to repair an Episcopal Church at Chichester and Concord and for purchasing a glebe for a church at Chester, Chester Co.

p. 393, 1764-65: Walter DAVIES is now a languishing prisoner in the gaol of Phila., where for 8 months, he has been confined at the suit of Francis HAMITT for a debt of £120 for which he gave his notes of hand to John Charles SAULINER, who is bankrupt.

p. 396: James PEARSON has been confined 17 months in Phila. Co. gaol for a debt at the suit of Messieurs Edmund KEARNEY and Thomas GILBERT, Phila., merchants, for £127 and also at the suits of Messieurs John BAYARD, Buckridge SIMS, and Andrew HODGE.

p. 399: George HITNER, the younger, Phila., saddler; William HARMAN, Phila., baker; Philip BUSH, Blockley Twp., Phila., innholder; are all protestants and Germans. They have been brought into this province during their infancy. They are granted the rights of natural subjects of England.

p. 401: Robert Lettis HOOPER, Jr., meeting with many accidents and losses in trade, was rendered incapable of carrying on his business and paying his just debts, did, on 14 Feb., last past, surrender all estate, real and personal, to Edmund KEARNEY, Gilbert BARCLAY, Thomas WALLACE, and John WIKOFF, for the use of his creditors. Execution issued against him at the suit of Redmond CONYNGHAM and John Maxwell NESBIT for £158 13s 6p. He is now confined to the Phila. gaol.

p. 413: James COULTAS, Esq., George GRAY, and John SMITH, gentlemen, are nominated to divide banks surrounding a marsh in Kinsessing Twp., Phila. Co.

p. 443: Abraham MYER, King's Ward; John CROSS, Queen's Ward; Henry DEHUFF, Prince's Ward, Frederick TOMBAUGH, Duke's Ward, are nominated constables of their wards and John HOPSON, Christopher CRAWFORD and Caleb SHEWART are assessors of Lancaster, Lancaster Co.

p. 469, 1761: A petition of diverse merchants against the bill for duty on the Negroes is signed by: Charles BATHO, Philip KEARNEY, Jr., WILLING, MORRIS & Co., Henry HARRISON, John and Joseph SWIFT, SCOTT & MCMICHAEL, John BELL, William COXE, James CHALMERS, Thomas RICHE, Benjamin LEVY, John NIXON, STOCKER & FULLER, Humphry ROBINSON, REED & PETTIT, Joseph WOOD, David FRANKS, Hugh DONNALDSON, Daniel RUNDLE, FRANCIS & RELFE, John INGLIS, David MCMURTRIE, Samuel and Archibald MCCALL, Joseph MARKS.

THE STATUTES AT LARGE OF PENNSYLVANIA FROM 1682 TO 1801
VOLUME 7 - 1765-1770

p. 19, 1765-66: Abel JAMES, Robert MORRIS, John NIXON, Peter REEVE, Oswell EVE, Michael HULINGS, Thomas PENROSE are appointed wardens of the port of Phila.

p. 47: Frederick MARSHALL, gentleman, was a subject of the Elector of Saxony; Peter Hendrick STRIEPERS, gentleman, was a subject of the King of Prussia; John HERBERGS, gentleman, and Jacob HANSE, mariner, were subjects of the Emperor of Germany. All are Protestants. They are given the privileges of natural born subjects of Great Britain.

p. 53: Robert MILLER, John HOLMES, John MILLER, Robert MCGAW, gentlemen, are nominated to be commissioners to settle accounts of a lottery with the managers. The lottery was to raise money for building a church at Carlisle, Cumberland Co. for the use of the First Presbyterian congregation under the pastoral care of John STEEL, minister.

p. 59, 1766-67: Thomas PRIOR, the younger, Phila., is appointed officer for examining flour sent from Phila. John PRIESTLY, Bucks Co., is flour inspector from that county. Edward RUSSELL, Chester Co., is flour inspector from that county.

p. 69: Thomas REILLY and John WHITPANE are languishing prisoners in the Phila. gaol.

p. 99: Charles MOORE, Samuel MORRIS, Jonathan SHOEMAKER, Richard

HUMPHREYS and Joseph LOWNES are the directors of all affairs related to a road and bridge over HOLLANDER's Ck. leading to the west district of Greenwich Island.

p. 101: Bills of credit are under the care of Joseph GALLOWAY, Joseph FOX, Isaac PEARSON and Michael HILLEGAS.

p. 134: Edward HUGHES, Michael TIEFENDURFER, Philip MARTSTELLER, John SHULTZ, Charles MILLER, George RINE, George STAHLEY, Henry ROCHEY, Lancaster Co., gentlemen, are managers of a lottery to raise £495 19s to pay the debt to build a German Lutheran Church in Earl Twp., Lancaster Co.

p. 172: Godfrey BROWN and wife, Anna Margaret, Wilmington, New Castle Co., yeoman, on 7 May, 1750, mortgaged a plantation in Cheltenham Twp., Phila. Co., near Tacony Ck., John ASHMEAD's land, Samuel BOLTON's land and Edward COLLINS' land. Philip FOX paid £135 11s 6p.

p. 140: Thomas Cotterell GROVE, Frederick PEPLER, Samuel WATTS, Azariah VAUN, Thomas MULLAN, Matthew WARBURTON, James MARTIN and Thomas LEMON are prisoners in the gaols of Phila., Chester and Lancaster.

p. 163, 1767-78: Philip SYNG, Samuel MILES, John CHEVALIER, Thomas SALTER, John GIBSON and Thomas BOND, Jr., Phila., and Peter KNIGHT, Northern Liberties, Phila., gentlemen, are managers of a lottery to raise £5250 to purchase a public landing in Northern Liberties and to pave Phila. streets.

p. 176: Isaac JONES, Luke MORRIS, Jonathan EVANS, Alexander HUSTON, Jacob SHOEMAKER, Jr., Samuel SHOEMAKER, Joseph FOX, Joshua HOWELL, David DESHLOR, Peter REEVE, Gunning BEDFORD and Samuel WEATHERELL, Jr. are the directors of the society "Philadelphia Contributionship for the Insuring of Houses from Loss by Fire."

p. 223, 1768-69: Andrew BANKSON, Moore FURMAN, Francis HOPKINSON, Peter KNIGHT and John ORD, gentlemen, are to sell a church in Phila. to pay debts due for building the same. It is a Calvinist or Reformed Church.

p. 227: William HODGE, William RUSH, James CRAIG, James MEASE, Hugh WILLIAMSON, Robert KNOX, Gunning BEDFORD, John RHEA, John BAYARD, William SHIPPEN, Jr., Jonathan Bayard SMITH, Isaac SNOWDEN, Philip WENTZ, Peter WENTZ, Jacob SNEIDER, Jacob WEAVER, Michael CROAL, Henry CONRAD, Isaac LEFEVER, gentlemen, are managers of a lottery to raise £3099 12s for the First and Third Presbyterian Churches and the Second Presbyterian Church of Phila. and the German Reformed Church, Worcester Twp.

p. 238: Jacob COOPER, William PARR, William BALL, George GRAY, Henry ELWES, David GIBSON, Joseph PENROSE, Phila. Co., gentlemen, are to direct the erection of a dam across the Little Hollander's Ck. below the mouth of Little Hay Ck.

p. 263: Curtis GRUBB married Ann FEW before 1757, sailed from America to Europe and continued absence until the latter end of 1763. In Feb., 1759, Ann had an illegitimate child. On 18 Aug., 1763, Ann married Archibald MCNEAL. Ann had a child to Curtis GRUBB named Peter GRUBB, born 1 Sept., 1758. The marriage is dissolved.

p. 265: James GREEN, Benjamin DAVIS, Paul RIFFET are prisoners in the Phila. gaol.

p. 272: George SANDERSON, James RALFE and Casper SHAFFNER, Jr., Lancaster Borough, are managers to settle accounts of a lottery for £2135 to erect a new school house for the High Dutch Reformed Congregation and to raise £565 to enable wardens of St. James' Church to complete the same.

p. 275: Edward SCULL, Benjamin LIGHTFOOT and Thomas COOKSON are to mark boundary lines between Phila., Chester and Lancaster Co. William MCCLAY, William SCULL and John BIDDLE, Jr. are to survey boundary lines.

p. 278: Thomas SAY, Henry LISLE, Thomas TILBURY, Henry DRINKER, Samuel BRYAN and John MIFFLIN are commissioners to pave streets in Phila.

p. 312: John FELFE was declared a bankrupt in London and confined to King's Bench Prison. Lately, he returned to Phila. and was taken by his special bail in a certain action yet depending and by him, delivered up to the sheriff of Phila. Co. in discharge of the recognizance entered into by his said bail and remains in execution in the gaol of Phila. Co. for a large sum of money. Abraham HOWELL is also in Phila. prison.

p. 317: John GALBREATH is a prisoner in the gaol of Chester Co.

p. 320, 1769-70: Isaac LANE, Joseph JOHNSON, Matthew JOHNS, William JONES, Stephen PASCHALL, Phila. Co., gentlemen, are appointed to survey meadow lands on both sides of Gunner's Ck., Northern Liberties Twp., adj. the precinct of Richmond. William BALL, John CHEVALIER and Charles WEST are to appoint a treasurer for Gunner's Ck. Co.

p. 340: Joseph GALLOWAY, John ROSS, William RODMAN, John MORTON, William LOGAN and William WEST, Esqs., are appointed commissioners to meet with commmissioners of Quebec, N.Y., Md., Va., N.J. and the three lower counties of Delaware to agree on a plan for regulation of Indian trade.

p. 342: Samuel MIFFLIN, Peter REEVE, Andrew CALDWELL, Enoch HOBART, William HEYSHAM, William MORREL, Joseph STOUT, William RICHARDS, Hugh BOWES, Robert WHITE, George MORRISON and Joseph STILES are managers of a society formed for the relief of the poor, aged and infirm masters of ships, their widows and children.

p. 479: Frederick STUMP, a German, murdered some Indians. William BLYTH, Penns Twp., went to the house of George GABRIEL to meet STUMP on 12 Jan., 1768. STUMP said that on Sunday evening before (10 Jan.), six Indians (the White Mingo, an Indian man named CORNELIUS and one other man named John CAMPBELL, one other man named JONES and two women) came to STUMP's house drunk and disorderly. He thought they would do him harm, so he killed them all and dragged them down to a creek near his house, made a hole in the ice and threw them in. Fearing the news might travel to other Indians, he went the next day to two cabins 14 miles away, up Middle Ck., where he found one woman, 2 girls and one child, which he killed. He put them in their cabins and burnt them. His servant was John IRONCUTTER. They were captured and relegated to the Carlisle gaol and later rescued by a party of 70 or 80 men armed with guns and tomahocks on 29 Feb.

p. 505: Mr. James CUNNINGHAM, Lancaster Co., farmer, said that on Friday, 29 Jan. last, about 9:00 or 10:00 A.M., as he was sitting at breakfast with John ARMSTRONG, Esq., in Carlisle, Cumberland Co., he saw men go to the gaol and he and ARMSTRONG ran to the gaol to prevent the escape. ARMSTRONG and Sheriff John HOLMES attempted to go into the gaol but were pushed back. Those endeavoring to disperse the company were ARMSTRONG, Robert MILLER, William LYON, Esq., and Rev. John STEEL. However, the two prisoners were brought forward and carried off. Later, the rescuers desired to meet with ARMSTRONG, LYONS, and HOLMES at the home of John DAVIS. They found that the rescuers had changed their minds and left.

p. 536: In 1763, the massacres of 20 Indians chiefly of the Six Nations were perpetrated at Conestogo and Lancaster. Also, a Delaware Chief was murdered between SHERMAN's Valley and Juniata. In 1765, a Chief of the Six Nations was murdered near Bedford. In 1766, a principal warrior of the Delawares was killed between Red Stone Ck. and Cheat River and three Delaware Chiefs were robbed and murdered near Fort Pitt by two inhabitants of Pa. An Indian was murdered in 1768 in Northampton Co. Along with Frederick STUMP and his servant, who killed 10 Indians, none were brought to punishment.

p. 539: Rev. John STEEL, John ALLISON, Christopher LEMES, Esqs., and Capt. James POTTER, Cumberland Co., are requested to go to Monongahela, Youghiogeny and other places westward of the Allegheny Mountains and set up proclaimations to induce people to give up any land they have settled on that might not have been purchased from the Indians within 30 days.

p. 544: A description of Frederick STUMP and John IRONCUTTER: Frederick STUMP was born in Heidleberg Twp., Lancaster Co. of German parents. He is 33 years old, 5'8", a stout active fellow and well-proportioned with a brown complexion, thin visaged, small black eyes, with a downcast look and wears short black hair. He speaks German well and English indifferently. Wore when rescued: a light brown cloth coat, blue great coat, an old hat, leather breeches, blue leggings and mockasons. John IRONCUTTER, born in Germany about 19 years ago, 5'6", a thick clumsy fellow, round shouldered, dark brown complexiion, a smooth full face, gray eyes, short brown hair and speaks very little English. Wearing a blanket coat, old felt had, buckskin breeches and a pair of long trousers, coarse white yarn stockings and shoes with brass buckles.

p. 546: John ROSS, Joseph FOX, Esqs., Phila.; Charles HUMPHREYS and Isaac PEARSON, Esqs., Chester Co.; William RODMAN, Bucks Co., were to attend the treaty with the Indians but told the Governor that health and concerns and private affairs would not allow them to attend the treaty at Fort Pitt. John ALLEN and Joseph SHIPPEN, Jr., Esqs., were nominated.

p. 580: Philadelphia poor in 1768: Henry GRAY, in Fourth St. with his daughter, is very old; Henry NEWMIRE, near NORRIS' in a house of William MASTERS, is very old and unable to get out; Catherine WILLING, at William PEARSON's in Kensington, can spin; Elizabeth RICKIN, residence unknown; John LOWROW, in Woodrow's Alley, has a stocking loom, is very old and infirm; Luke SUTTON is an idiot; Michael MENDING, with old SCANLIN, on the hill, is very old and debauched; Margaret CURFAS; John COLLINS in Race St., dropsical, is orderly and can do many things and has a wife; Barbara SEELY, in the country with her son-in-law, can spin and knit; Conrad Daniel WALTER lives in German Town, is old, helpless and has a wife industrious; Isaac MILNOR, very near-sighted, is a boy of 15 year old; Margaret KILLWEATHER is old and picks up rags; Michael BRUMECK, with Ewis TREICHEL, near barracks, a tailor, has a hearty old wife and he can do some business.

THE STATUTES AT LARGE OF PENNSYLVANIA FROM 1682 TO 1801
VOLUME 8 - 1770-1776

p. 18, 1770-72: Bills for the defense of Phila. to be signed by: Joseph MORRIS, William FISHER, Joshua HOWELL, Joel EVANS, Luke MORRIS, Daniel ROBERDEAU, Isaac COX, Robert Strettell JONES, Jacob SHOEMAKER, Jr., Francis HOPKINSON, Stephen COLLINS, Thomas MIFFLIN.

p. 32: Commissioners for improving navigation of the Delaware and Lehigh Rivers: Joseph GALLOWAY, Joseph FOX, Michael HILLEGAS, Bael JAMES, Samuel RHODES, James ALLEN, Peter KNIGHT, Daniel WILIAMS, Henry DRINKER, Clement BIDDLE, Jeremiah WARDER, the younger, Jacob BRIGHT, John BALDWIN, Richard WELLS, Thomas YARDLEY, Adam HOOPS, Jacob ORNDT, Peter KECHLINE, Henry KOOKEN, William LEDLEY, Jacob STROUD, Nicholas DEPUI, son of Samuel DEPUI, John ARBO.

p. 37: Commissioners for clearing and making the Susquehanna, Juniata, Bald Eagle, Penn's Ck., Conestogoe, Connedaguinet, Machanoy, Kiskiminetas and Swatara navigable: James WRIGHT, George ROSS, Thomas MINSHALL, John LOUDON, William RICHARDSON, Alexander LOWREY, William MCCLAY, Samuel HUNTER, the younger, William PATTERSON, Robert CALLENDER, Charles STEWART, Reuben HAINES, Thomas HOLT.

p. 49: Arthur ST. CLAIR, Esq., Bernard DAUGHERTY, Esq., Thomas COULTER, William PROCKTER, George WOODS, gentlemen, may purchase land in Bedford for a courthouse and prison. Thomas URIE of Cumberland Co. is appointed tax collector for Bedford Co. Robert MCCREA, William MILLER and Robert MOORE are to mark the boundaries between Bedford and Cumberland Counties.

p. 55, 1770-71: Lazarus STEWART was rescued from the Constable's custody. On 21 Jan., 1771, at Wyoming, Northampton Co., he killed Nathan OGDEN and wounded others. His rescuers were James STEWART, William STEWART, John SIMPSON, William SPEEDY, William YOUNG, John MCDANIEL (alias DONNELL) and Richard COOK.

p. 57: Commissioners for opening and maintaining a road from Reading through Tulpehocken to Susquehanna: John Philip DE HAAS, Frederick WEISER, Benjamin SPYKER, Michael TYCE, Nicholas SWENGLE. Commissioners for opening and maintaining a road from a road near Ellis HUGHES' saw mill and the Schuylkill River to Fort Augusta: Thomas WRIGHT, Joseph PENROSE, Ellis HUGHES, Samuel HUNTER, the younger, Isaac WILLETS, gentlemen.

p. 58: Wardens appointed for the port of Phila.: Peter REEVE, Thomas PENROSE, Robert WHITE, Michael HULINGS, John NIXON, John Maxwell NESBETT, Robert MORRIS, Oswell EVE, Samuel MIFFLIN.

p. 69: George HAWKINS, Conrad KEHNOLE and Jonathan HOBBY are prisoners in the Phila. gaol for debts.

p. 72: Commissioners for building a bridge over Skippack Ck., Phila. Co. are: Benjamin JACOBS, Jacob UMSTAT, John KESTER

(Fuller).

p. 96: Samuel MORTON, Thomas MIFFLIN, Edward DUFFIELD, Jacob WINEY, Moore FURMAN, Joshua HUMPHREYS, gentlemen, are wardens to take care of street lamps.

p. 116: Peter MIERKEN, born at the Imperial and Hanseatic city of Hamburg, in Germany, is a Protestant and would like the privileges of a natural born subject of Britain.

p. 125, 1771-72: Peter REEVE, John GIBSON, William RICHARDS, Luke MORRIS, William MORREL, John KIDD and Joseph STAMPER are nominated to be commissioners to repair a lighthouse at the mouth of Delaware Bay.

p. 139: Richard STEVENS, late of Phila., merchant, now of Perth Amboy, N.J., is in debt to Adam HOOPS, John MEASE, John STARTIN, Nathan HYDE and Robert MORRIS.

p. 146: William MACLAY, Samuel HUNTER, John LOUDON, Joseph WALLIS and Robert MOODY are to buy land for a courthouse and prison for Northumberland Co. Thomas LEMON will be the county tax collector. Joshua ELDER, James POTTER, Jesse LUKENS, and William SCULL are to measure and mark boundaries.

p. 161: William FARIES, John GILLIARD, Charles HICKS and John REYNOLDS are priosners in the Phila. gaol for debt. William BENNETT and Falix MCCOWAN are in the York Co. gaol for debt.

p. 175: Henry WYNKOOP, Esq., John HARRIS, Esq., and Francis MURRAY are commissioners to settle accounts of a lottery.

p. 179: The following persons, late commissioners, assessors and clerks for assessing and levying and keeping the accounts of provincial and county rates for Lancaster Co., have received and illegally detained public money: John HAY, George LEONARD, Samuel STEEL, Joshua ADERSON, George MCCULLOUGH, Isaac SAUNDERS, William JONES, Henry WALTER, John MILLER, Daniel MCPHERSON, James GIBBONS, James WEBB, Jr., Christian HILDEBRAND, John SMITH, Michael GRIMES, James WILSON, Casper CORE. Witnesses against the offenders: Robert ARMOR, Robert WHITEHALL, Michael DIFFEDERFER, Christian WERTZ, Bernard HUBLEY.

p. 199: Names of owners of a tract of meadow land in Chester Borough, Chester Co.: James MATHER, Joseph HOSKINS, Henry Hale GRAHAM, Robert PENNELL, Joseph ASHBRIDGE, Mary NORRIS, James CLAXTON.

p. 206: Signers of bills of credit: John MORTON, Esq., Charles HUMPHREYS, Esq., John SELLER, Esq., Isaac COX, Joseph SIMS, Thomas CLIFFORD, Thomas COOMBE, Thomas FISHER, Samuel PLEASANTS, Joseph DEAN, Joseph SWIFT, Cadwalader MORRIS, Clement BIDDLE, Joel EVANS, Anthony MORRIS, Jr., Samuel HOWELL, Jr., Adam HUBLEY, John MIFFLIN, Joseph PEMBERTON, merchant, Samuel HUDSON, Jams WHARTON, Benjamin WYNKOOP, Jeremiah WARDER, Jr., Samuel COATES.

P. 224: Benjamin KENDALL, Phila., is appointed a searcher and sealer of leather within Phila. Michael HUBLEY in Lancaster.

p. 231: Owen ROBERTS, sheriff of Frederick Twp., phila. Co., seized 450 acres, late the estate of Nathaniel PUCKLE, then deceased, in the hands of Roger EDMONDS and wife, Deborah, executors of Nathaniel PUCKLE, to satisfy Hannah PENN, plaintiff. On Feb., 1723-24, the sheriff sold the 450 acres to Andrew HAMILTON, late of Phila., Esq., for £60. HAMILTON's will, dated 2 Aug., 1741, gave the land to his eldest son, James HAMILTON, Esq. Other partners in the land which contained Perkioming Copper Mine were: John GIBSON, esq., Jacob LEWIS, Jacob SHOEMAKER, the younger, and Henry DRINKER, gentleman.

p. 243: George KEEHMLE, Phila., barber, was, on 23 Aug., 1763, married to Elizabeth MILLER. Elizabeth was convicted of adultery in Apr., 1771, committed by her with John CLARK. The marriage is annulled.

p. 245: A patent dated 13 Oct., 1701, granted 1700 acres to William HARMER. Another patent, dated 22 July, 1713, granted 85 acres of land situated in Perkiomen and Skippack Twp., Phila. Co. to William HARMER. William and Ruth HARMER, on 9 Sept., 1713, sold 1285 acres to Solomon and Philip DUBOIS. On 13 Feb., 1718-19, Solomon released the new part to Philip, recorded at Ulster, N.Y. Philip and Daniel DUBOIS, on 3 Aug., 1724, sold the new property to Abraham DUBOIS. Abraham sold it to John PAWLING and Isaac DUBOIS on 2 Nov., 1724. John PAWLING, Joseph PAWLING, Abraham SAHLER, Peter REIMER, Bernard KEPLER and Andrew HEIZER possess the new part.

p. 249: Hugh HARTSHORNE and Joseph HALL, gentlemen, of Bristol borough, are authorized to view Pigeon Swamp in Bristol Twp., Bucks Co., and map it. Christian MINNICK, Aaron WRIGHT, William BIDGOOD, Jr. are appointed managers.

p. 254: Cadwalader ELLIS, about 57 years ago, owned land in Goshen Twp., Chester Co., containing 295 acres. By deed on 13 May, 1719, he sold it to Joseph PHIPPS. He deeded the same to his son, Samuel PHIPPS. Stephen BEAKS sold an adjoining tract to Samuel PHIPPS, bounded by lands of Rudolph HAINES, Edward HICKS, Thomas GOODWIN, William JONES, George HOOPS, Jonathan GARRET.

p. 256: William HEMBELL, born in Gelnhausen in the dominions of His Serene Highness, the Landgrave of Hesse-Cassel, Germany, a prince in amity with the Crown of Great Britain, is given the privileges of a natural born subject.

p. 257: James HAMILTON, Esq., by deed of 4 Nov., 1736, sold lot #3 in Lancaster near lots of Samuel BETHEL and Mary DUNNING to Henry BOSTLER. BOSTLER, by deed of 4 Dec., 1736, sold the lot to Frederick STRUBLE. STRUBLE sold the lot on 17 Apr., 1738 to Ludowick STONE. By conveyances of Orphan's Court, the premises are vested in Adam Simon KUHN.

p. 274, 1772-73: Jacob WINEY, Charles JERVIS, Benjamin SHOEMAKER, Henry KEPPELE, Jr., Frederick KUHL, John STEINMETZ are appointed signers of bills of credit.

p. 286: Stephen CARMICK, Charles MEREDITH, George EMLEN, Jr., Alexander TODD, Joseph PEMBERTON, Samuel MILES, Owen JONES, Jr., Joseph MIFFLIN, Benjamin MORGAN, Barnaby BARNES, William FISHER, Jr., William WISTAR, Abraham USHER, Reynold KEEN, John FIELD, Jacob HARMAN, Mordecai LEWIS, Isaac WHARTON, William WISHART, Richard WILLING, Benjamin MARSHALL, Samuel FISHER, James HARTLEY, Joseph ALLEN are signers of bills of credit. Samuel Preston MOORE and Amos STRETTELL, Phila.; Abraham CHAPMAN, Bucks Co.; Humphrey MARSHALL, Chester Co.; Moses BRINTON, Lancaster Co., gentlemen, are appointed trustees of the general loan office.

p. 305: A mill dam erected by James PATTON of Shearman's Ck., Cumberland Co., must allow navigation.

p. 309: William RITCHIE is a prisoner in Phila. gaol and John MILLIRON is a prisoner in the Lancaster Co. gaol for debts.

p. 316: Robert HANNA, George WILSON, Samuel SLOAN, Joseph IRWIN and John CAVEAT are to purchase land for a courthouse and prison for the newly erected county of Westmoreland. James KINKEAD is appointed tax collector.

p. 323: A patent dated 1 June, 1749, granted land to Samuel THOMPSON, John MCCLURE, Robert DUNNING, John DAVIES, John MITCHELL and Alexander SAUNDERSON. The tract was in West Penns Borough (now Middleton) Twp., containing 120 acres and was for the use of a society of Presbyterians. A patent dated 16 Apr., 1761, granted to Thomas WILSON, John DAVIES, John BYERS, William SPEER, John MONTGOMERY, and Ezekiel SMITH a lot in Carlisle for the Presbyterian Church. The church is now unfit and a new church will be built in another part of town. Title for the tract is vested in John BYERS, John MONTGOMERY, John AGNEW, Robert MILLER, James WILSON, Robert MCGAW, James POLLOCK, William MILLER, Samuel LAIRD, James YOUNG, John DAVIES, Jonathan HOLMS, William MOOR, James SMITH, George SAUNDERSON and James IRVINE.

p. 327: David RITTENHOUSE, Anthony LEVERING, John ROBERTS, miller, William DEWEES, Jr., David THOMAS, James HOCKLEY, Thomas POTTS, Mark BIRD, James STAR, Jacob KERN and John PAWLING, Jr. are appointed commissioners to clear the Schuylkill River for navigation. They agreed with Charles NORRIS, Esq., lately deceased, that he should be permitted to repair and maintain a mill dam running across the eastern channel of the Schuylkill River from the main eastern shore to Barbadoes Island. Since the agreement, Charles' administrators sold the mill to John BULL, Esq.

p. 335: A patent dated 30 Nov., 1703, granted to John BUDD, Phila., gentleman, 1000 acres in Charlestown Twp., Chester Co. John BUDD and wife Rebecca sold 300 acres to John and William MARTIN on 8 Apr., 1714. John MARTIN and William MARTIN both died intestate, no heirs. Thomas MARTIN and wife, Martha and Llewelyn MARTIN are brothers of John and William MARTIN. A deed of 6 June, 1751 sold land to Lewis MARTIN. He sold 106 acres to his son, William, on 16 Mar., 1767.

p. 337: Francis Caspar HASENCLEVER, Phila., merchant; Frederic PHILE, practitioner in physic; William SHEAFF and Henry SHEAFF, grocers; Jacob MAYER, peruke maker; William REIBLE, trader, all of Phila., Protestants, are all German subjects. All are granted the privileges of natural born subjects of Great Britain.

p. 341: Samuel SWEET is a prisoner in the Phila. gaol and Thomas BANFORD is a prisoner in Lancaster gaol for debt.

p. 393, 1773-74: Levi HOLLINGSWORTH is appointed officer for viewing all flour shipped out of Pa. from Phila. Joseph HALL is appointed same for Bucks Co. Edward RUSSELL is appointed same for Chester Co.

p. 397, 1774-75: James STEPHENS, Thomas LEECH, Benedict DORSEY,

William GRISPIN, John LOWNES, Robert TUCKNISS are appointed signers of bills of credit.

p. 399: Henry William STIEGELL is a prisoner in the Phila. gaol for debt.

p. 407: John BURROWS is a prisoner in the Phila. gaol and William WATERS is a prisoner in the Bucks Co. gaol for debt.

p. 418: Isaac PEARSON, George GRAY, Michael HILLEGAS and Joseph PARKER are to print bills of credit. Lindsay COATES, Job BACON, and Edward ROBERTS are to be signers of bills of credit.

p. 425: James WHARTON, Richard VAUX, Ezekiel EDWARDS, William WISHART, Charles WHARTON and Samuel COATES are signers of bills of credit.

p. 435: William GODDARD and Septimus LEVERING are prisoners for debt in the Phila. gaol.

p. 438: Philip TILLYER of Moorland Manor, Phila. Co., by indenture, sold on 16 May, 1744 to Abraham VANDERGRIFT and Garrett WYNCOOP, elders, and Henry KREWSON and Jacob BENNET, deacons, for the Dutch Presbyterians, Northampton Twp., Bucks Co., a plantation in Byberry Twp., Phila. Co., near land of William HOMER, Nathaniel BRITTAIN, John WORTHINGTON, Samuel COOPER, and William GROOM (dec.). The land is vested in Henry KREWSON, Gilliam CORNELL, John KREWSON and William BENNETT, the younger.

p. 442: On 9 Jan., 1738, a proprietary patent was issued to Clement PLUMSTED, Phila. City, Esq., for land in Bradford Twp., Chester Co., near land of William PIMMS and Jacob ROMAN for 150 acres. The land was granted to Clement PLUMSTED in trust for John TAYLOR, late of Chester Co., a practitioner in physic, dec. TAYLOR died intestate.

p. 444: A patent was made on 28 Oct., 1701, for land in Amity Twp., Berks Co., near land of Peter BOON to Andrew RUDEMAN for 500 acres. On 15 July, 1708, RUDEMAN sold the land to Andrew SANDALL. SANDALL sold the land to Benjamin BURDEN who sold it to Henry BELL. On 6 June, 1723, BELL sold 300 acres to Andrew FOULKE. FOULKE, on 4 Feb., 1729, sold 150 acres to Wendall ANDREW and on 20 Sept., 1730, FOULK sold 150 acres to Charles FOULKE. Charles FOULKE, on 6 Apr., 1742, sold the land to Cornelius DEHART. On 15 Oct., 1746, DEHART sold 22 acres to Wendall ANDREW. Wendall ANDREW willed his 150 acres plus 22 acres to his son, Daniel.

p. 447: Bills of credit can be printed by George GRAY, Michael HILLEGAS, Joseph PARKER and Isaac PEARSON, Esqs. They can be signed by Thomas SHOEMAKER, Charles JERVIS, Philip KINSEY, John KNOWLES, Abel EVANS, John WARDER, Isaac HOWELL, Richard HUMPHREYS, Thomas TILBURY, Henry Hale GRAHAM, Adam GRUBB and Francis JOHNSTON.

p. 456, 1775-76: Richard TAYLOR, Jacob MUCKS, George Jacob HAUSMAN, Richard RAY and Francis OWENS are prisoners in the Phila. gaol for debt. James MACKAY is a prisoner in the Northumberland Co. gaol for debt.

p. 468: William JUDD, John ONIONS, Michael JORDAN and William SANDERS are prisoners in the Phila. gaol for debt.

p. 471: Surveyed unto Peter ALLEN on 5 Nov., 1720, land on

Shickasolungo Ck., then in Chester, now Lancaster Co. near land of James MITCHELL, John STUART, John ROSS, Jane STUART. Peter ALLEN sold the land to Rev. James ANDERSON, now dec. He sold it to William WILKINS. After WILKINS died, Nathaniel LYTEL married Janet WILKINS, widow of William WILKINS. On 6 June, 1737, LYTEL took out a warrant and obtained a patent for the land on 19 Jan., 1738. LYTEL, in his will, left the land to his son, John LYTEL. John LYTEL purchased a release for the land from Janet LYTEL and James WILKINS, son of William WILKINS. John LYTEL sold the land on 12 Aug., 1774 to Andrew HERSHEY for £600. LYTEL is now a prisoner in the Lancaster gaol for debts and needs the £600 to be released.

p. 476: Soffel VANSAND, late of Middletown Twp., Bucks Co., left a will dated 24 June, 1749, in which he gave 50 acres of land to his daughter, Sina, but if she died without issue, the land was to be sold and the money divided between his daughter, Elizabeth's, children and daughters Rachel and Olshe. Sina died without issue. Executors John VANSAND and Lewis RUE are dec. Olshe is dec. leaving two minor children. Elizabeth is also dec., leaving several children. The land is vested in William RODMAN, Esq., John BROWN, Esq., and Gabriel VAN HORN, in trust. Rachel RUE is the widow of Lewis.

p. 480: Alexander STEWART, late of the Kingdom of Ireland, is a prisoner in the gaol of Phila.

p. 487: On 30 June, 1775, a Committee of Safety was named: John DICKINSON, George GRAY, Henry WYNKOOP, Anthony WAYNE, William THOMPSON, Daniel ROBERDEAU, Owen BIDDLE, Thomas WHARTON, Jr., Robert WHITE, Benjamin BARTHOLOMEW, George ROSS, Michael SWOOPE, John MONTGOMERY, Thomas WILLING, John CADWALADER, Francis JOHNSTON, Robert MORRIS, Ed. BIDDLE, William EDMONDS, Bernard DOUGHERTY, Samuel HUNTER, Benjamin FRANKLIN, Andrew ALLEN, Richard REILY, Samuel MORRIS, Jr., gentlemen.

p. 488: Bills of credit may be printed by: George GRAY, Esq., Joseph PARKER, Esq., Isaac PEARSON, William RODMAN, Esqs. Signers of bills of credit are: Adam HUBLEY, John BENEZET, Godfrey TWELLS, William ALLEN, Jr., Sharp DELANY, James MEAS, Samuel Cadwalader MORRIS, John MEAS, Lambert CADWALADER, Isaac HOWELL, Thomas PRIOR, John PURVIANCE. Michael HILLEGAS, Esq., treasurer, is to deliver bond of surety to John MORTON, Esq., and Charles HUMPHREYS, Esq.

p. 494, 18 Nov., 1775: Bills of credit may be signed by: Matthew CLARKSON, William SMITH, Broker, Josiah HEWES, Abel EVANS, Peter THOMSON, Sketchley MORTON, Joseph REDMAN, William CRISPIN, Andrew TYBOUT, Thomas MOORE, Samuel Cadwalader MORRIS, Elisha PRICE, Thomas LEECH, William KENLY, George DOUGLAS, Charles MOORE, Cornelius BARNES, Nicholas FAIRLAMB, gentlemen.

p. 498: Owen BIDDLE, David RITTENHOUSE, Peter DEHAVEN, gentlemen, are a committee to superintend the salt petre works.

p. 559: George ROSS, Esq., of Lancaster Co., is appointed judge of the court of admiralty.

p. 563, 6 Apr., 1776: Signers of bills of credit are: Benjamin BETTERTON, William CLIFFTON, Josiah HEWES, Abel EVANS, Peter THOMPSON, Sketchley MORTON, William SMITH, Broker, William KENLY, Andrew TYBOUT, Thomas MOORE, Samuel Cadwalader MORRIS, Elisha PRICE, Joseph REDMAN, William CRISPIN, George DOUGLASS, Charles MOORE,

Cornelius BARNS, Hugh LLOYD, gentlemen.

THE STATUTES AT LARGE OF PENNSYLVANIA FROM 1682 TO 1801
VOLUME 9 - 1776-1779

p. 7, 1776: The following, all of Phila., are empowered to discharge prisoners in the gaol of Phila.: George BRYAN, John BULL, James YOUNG, Henry HILL, Jacob SCHRYNER, Peter KNIGHT. The following, all of Bucks Co., are empowered to discharge prisoners in the gaol of Bucks Co.: John WILKINSON, Henry WYNKOOP, James WALLACE. The following, all of Chester Co., are empowered to discharge prisoners in the gaol of Chester Co.: David COWPLAND, John CROSBY, John SELLER. The following, all of Lancaster Co., are to do the same for the Lancaster Co. gaol: William HENRY, William BOWSMAN, John HOPSON. The following of York Co. are to do the same for the York Co. gaol: Samuel JOHNSTON, Martin EYCHELBERGER, William LEAS. The following of Cumberland Co. are to do the same for the Cumberland Co. gaol: Robert MILLER, John HOMES, Stephen DUNCAN. The following of Berks Co. are to do the same for the Berks Co. gaol: James READ, William RASER, Daniel HIESTER. The following of Northampton Co. are to do the same for the Northampton Co. gaol: Robert TRAIL, Abraham BERLAIN, Henry BARNET. The following from Bedford Co. are to do the same for the Bedford Co. gaol: William TODD, Charles CISNA, Robert ELLIOT. The following from Northumberland Co. are to do the same for the Northumberland Co. gaol: Samuel HUNTER, Laughlin MCCARTNEY, John BOYD. The following from Westmoreland Co. are to do the same for the Westmoreland Co. gaol: Edward COOK, Robert HANNA, David SEMPLE.

p. 12: Col. James EASTON, a prisoner in the Phila. Co. gaol for debt, is discharged.

p. 13: Justices of the Peace for the Commonwealth: David RITTENHOUSE, Jonathan B. SMITH, Owen BIDDLE, James CANNON, Timothy MATLACK, Samuel MORRIS, the elder, Benjamin BARTHOLOMEW, Peter RHOADS, John MOORE, Esq., Samuel HOWELL, Frederick KUHL, Samuel MORRIS, the younger, Thomas WHARTON, the younger, Henry KEPPLE, the younger, Joseph BLEWER, William LYON, Daniel ESPY, Samuel MIFFLIN, George GRAY, John BULL, Henry WYNKOOP, John HUBLEY, Michael SWOOPE, Daniel HUNTER, John WEITZEL. Justices of the Peace for Phila. city and county: Benjamin FRANKLIN, John DICKINSON, George BRYAN, James YOUNG, James BIDDLE, John MORRIS, the younger, Joseph PARKER, John BAYARD, Sharp DELANEY, John CADWALLADER, Joseph COPPERTHWAITE, Chris. MARSHALL, the elder, Francis GURNEY, Robert KNOX, Matthew CLARKSON, William COATES, William BALL, Philip BOEHM, Thomas CUTHBERT, the elder, Francis Casper HASENCLEVER, Joseph MOULDER, Benjamin HARBESON, Samuel ASHMEAD, Alexander EDWARDS, Rowland EVANS, Moses BARTRAM, Jonathan PASCHAL, Jacob BRIGHT, Frederick ANTIS, Leth QUEE, Charles BENSEL, Jacob SCHREINER, Benjamin PASCHAL, Henry HILL, Samuel ERWIN, Samuel POTTS, Peter EVANS. Justices of the Peace for Bucks Co.: Joseph HART, John WILKINSON, John CLARK, James MCMULLEN, George WICKERT, Richard WALKER, John KIDD, James BENEZET, Theophilus FOULKE, Thomas LONG, Joseph KIRKBRIDE, Robert PATTERSON, Samuel SMITH, Joshua ANDERSON. Justices of the Peace for Chester Co.: Alexander JOHNSTON, William CLINGEN, Evan EVANS, Israel WHALIN, Robert MENDENHALL, Richard BAKER, John SELLARS, Nicholas FAIRLAMBE, William DENEY, John JONES, John WILSON, William HESLET, Samuel BOND. Justices of the Peace for Lancaster Co.: Emanuel CARPENTER, Ludwig LAUMAN, James BIRD, John FERRIE, Zaccheus DAVID, James CLEMSON, Thomas WHITESIDE, Michael BRIGHT, Edward SHIPPEN, William BAUSMAN,

James WORK, Moses IRWIN, David JENKINS, William BROWN, Robert BARBER, Christopher WEGMAN, William HENRY, Michael MUBLY, Timothy GREEN, John THOME, John WHITEHILL, James MURRAY, Robert THOMPSON. Justices of the Peace for York Co.: Robert MCPHERSON, Henry SLAGLE, Matthew DILL, William SMITH, William MCCASKEY, William MCCLEAN, Martin EICHELBERGER, Richard MCCALISTER, William RANKIN, William SCOTT, Josias SCOTT, John MICKLE, the younger, Samuel EDIE, David MCCONAUGHY, William LEES, William BAILEY, Thomas LATTA.
Justices of the Peace for Cumberland Co.: John ARMSTRONG, John BYERS, John REYNOLDS, Jonathan HOGE, Robert MILLER, George ROBINSON, John HOLMES, James OLIVER, John AGNEW, John ALLISON, James MAXWELL, Samuel LYON, William BROWN, James DUNLAP, John MCCLAY, William ELLIOTT, Matthew HENDERSON, Frederick WATT.
Justices of the Peace for Berks Co.: James READ, Peter SPYKER, Jacob MORGAN, Christopher WITMAN, George DOUGLAS, Mark BIRD, Henry CHRIEST, Richard TEA, Balzar GEAR, John PATTON, Thomas DUNDAS, Bastian LEVAN. Justices of the Peace for Northampton Co.: Robert TRAIL, Jacob MOORY, Christopher WAGENER, Robert FORGEMAN, Henry KOOKEN, John WEITZEL, Peter TRAXLER, Sr., Nicholas DUPNI, Evan MORGAN, Henry BARNET. Justices of the Peace for Bedford Co.: Bernard DOUGHERTY, William PROCTOR, George WOOD, William LATTA, Benjamin ELLIOT, David JONES, William MCLEAVY, ed. COOMB, Robert RAMSEY, Samuel THOMPSON, Charles CESSNA, Abraham CABLE, Thomas SMITH, Thomas COULTER, John WILKINS, William PARKER, Henry RHOADS, Gideon RITCHEY, Hugh DAVIS, Benjamin BIRD, William PHILLIPS, John MITCHELL, Henry LLOYD, John PIPER, Samuel DAVIDSON, William TODD, Evan SHELBY, William JOHNSTON, John MELLOTT, Matthew PATTON, John SHAVER, William HOLLIDAY, the younger, Richard BROWN. Justices of the Peace for Westmoreland Co.: Robert HANNA, William LOCKRAY, Alexander MCLEAN, Providence MOUNTS, Joseph CALDWELL, James WILKINS, Samuel BURNS, Andrew MCFARLIN, James POLLOCK, James CAVAL, Samuel SLOANE, Philip ROGERS, William ELLIOT, Thomas SCOTT, Michael HUFNAGLE, James WILSON, David ALLEN, Benjamin DAVIS, George LATIMORE.

p. 24: Assessors for the city of Phila.: Isaac SNOWDEN, James MILLIGAN, Michael SCHUBART, Benjamin HARBESON, William WILL, William HOLLINGSHEAD. Commissioners for the city of Phila.: Jacob MORGAN, Joseph MOULDER, Jacob BRIGHT. Commissioners for the county of Phila.: Thomas POTTS, Samuel ERWIN, John WILLIAMS. Assessors for the county of Phila.: John BROWN, William ROBINSON, Samuel INGLE, Andrew KNOX, Henry DERRINGER, Isaac HUGHES. Commissioners of Bucks Co.: James BENEZET, Capt. William ROBERTS, Abraham MIDDLESWARTS. Assessors of Bucks Co.: Gilliam GORNET, Abraham BRITTON, James WALLACE, Thomas ARMSTRONG, Benjamin SAGAL, George MCILROY. Assessors of Chester Co.: Caleb DAVIS, Richard THOMAS, David CLOYD, Benjamin BRENNON, Thomas EVANS, Joseph GARDNER. Commissioners of Lancaster Co.: Alexander MARTIN, Christian WIRTZ, Casper SNEVELY. Assessors of Lancaster Co.: John BOKENSTOSE, John ROWLAND, Philip GREENWALT, Thomas CLARK of Dromore, Caspar SHAFFNER, John PEMMISON, the younger. Commissioners of York Co.: Peter WOLF, John NESBIT, Archibald MCCLEAN. Assessors for York Co.: Patrick SCOTT, Benjamin PIDON, Frederick WOLF, John AGNEW, Christopher LOWMAN, James DILL. Commissioners for Cumberland Co.: Patrick MAXWELL, Samuel LEARD, James POLLOCK. Assessors for Cumberland Co.: Henry POLLING, John DAVIS, James LYON, Alexander MORROW, John CARSON, William RIPPEY. Commissioners for Northampton Co.: Peter BURKHALTER, Jacob OPP, Henry LAWALD. Assessors for Northampton Co.: Peter KOLER, Abraham ARNDT, Benjamin DUPUI, Peter HAAS, Peter BEISEL, John VAN CAMP. Commissioners of Berks Co.: Henry REITMEYER, Christian LOWER, Mordecai LINCOLN. Assessors of Berks Co.: Conrad HERSHNER, the elder, Nicholas JONES, Frederick MAYERLE, Geoerge KELCHNER, Warner STAM, John ROBINSON. Commissioners of Bedford Co.: Charles CISSNA, Edward COOMB, John CISSNA. Assessors of Bedford Co.: Matthew PATTON, Harman HUSBANDS, William TODD, William PARKER, William PHILLIPS, Benjamin ELLIOTT. Commissioners of Northumberland Co.: Thomas HEWITT, William GRAY, John WEITZEL. Assessors of Northumberland Co.: Jonathan LOUDGE, Walker CLARK, Peter HOLSTERMAN, James HARRISON, Nicholas MILLER, Jacob HEVERLAN. Commissioners of Westmoreland Co.: Robert HANNA, James CAVAT, James POLLOCK. Assessors of Westmoreland Co.: William ELLIOTT, John SHIELDS, Samuel MOORHEAD, James MCCLEAN, James BEARD, Christopher TRUBY.

p. 68, 1776-77: Register of Wills for Phila. is Samuel MORRIS, Esq. For Bucks Co.: Joseph HART, Esq. For Chester Co.: Peter HOOFNAGLE, Esq. For York Co.: Archibald MCCLEAN, Esq. For Cumberland Co.: John CREIGH, Esq. For Berks Co.: Henry CHRIST, Esq. For Northampton Co.: John ORNDT, Esq. For Bedford Co.: Robert GALBRAITH, Esq. For Northumberland Co.: John SIMPSON, Esq. For Westmoreland Co.: James KINKEAD, Esq. Recorder of Deeds for Phila. is John MORRIS, the younger. All of the above men are Recorders of Deeds for their respective counties.

p. 98: Signers of bills of credit: Benjamin BETTERTON, William THORN, William KINLEY, John YOUNG, Jr., [Andrew HODGE], Isaac HOWELL, Caleb DAVID, Joseph GARDNER, James CANNON, Whitehead HUMPHREYS, Benjamin JACOBS, William EVANS, [Levi BUDD], Isaac SNOWDEN, John BROWN, William WILL, Philip ALBERTY, Henry LUITHAUSEN, Samuel SMITH, Frederick ANTIS, Robert LOLLER, James DAVIDSON.

p. 115, 1777: Elections for the city of Phila. will be held at the public house formerly kept by Jacob COLEMAN, Germantown. Elections for the 3rd district of Phila. will be held at Jacob WENTZ's, Worcester Twp. Elections for the 3rd district of Chester Co. will be held at Joseph BENTLEY's house, commonly known as the Red Lion. Elections in the 1st district of Bucks Co. will be held at Andrew KUCHLEIN's, Rockhill. Elections in the 2nd district of Lancaster Co. will be held at James PORTER, Jr.'s, Drumore. Elections in the 2nd district of York Co. will be held at Samuel GATTIS', Cumberland Twp. Elections in the 4th district of York Co. will be held at THOMPSON's Mill near the junction of Fawn, Hopewell and Chanceford Twps. Elections in the 5th district of York Co. will be held at Robert STEVENSON's, Warrington Twp. Elections in the 3rd district of Cumberland Co. will be held at William M. CLURE's. The 4th district of Cumberland Co. will vote at James PURDY's, Farmanagh Twp. The 3rd district of Northampton Co. will vote at Peter ANTHONY's, Lehigh Twp. The 4th district of Northampton Co. will vote at Nicholas DUPUY's, Lower Smithfield Twp. The 2nd district of Bedford Co. will vote at John BURD's, Fort Littleton. The 3rd district of Northumberland Co. will vote at FOUTZ's mill, Buffalo. The 4th election district of Northumberland Co. will vote at Amariah SUTTON's, Muncy Twp. The 1st district of Westmoreland Co. will vote at Capt. Samuel MOORHEAD's mill.

p. 149: John BAYARD, Jonathan SERGEANT, Jonathan B. SMITH, David RITTENHOUSE, Joseph GARDNER, Robert WHITEHILL, Christopher MARSHALL, James SMITH of Yorktown, James ORNDT, Curtis GRUBB, James CANNON, William HENRY of Lancaster, Esqs. are a Council of Safety.

p. 179: Commissioners to certify others to purchase supplies for the army or navy: John MOORE, William ANTIS, Andrew KNOX, Esqs., of

Phila. Co. Gerardus WYNKOOP, Thomas DYER, George WYKART, Esqs., of Bucks Co. George IRWIN, Thomas CHENEY, Philip SCOTT, Esqs., of Chester Co. Morris ERWIN, Christopher MARSHALL, Timothy GREEN, Esqs. of Lancaster Co. Archibald MCLEAN, David WATSON, Benjamin LEDEN, Esqs. of York Co. John CREIGH, John AGNEW, George MATTHEWS, Esqs. of Cumberland Co. Peter SPIKER, Jacob SHOEMAKER, Paul GROFFCOOP, Esqs. of Berks Co. Robert LEVERS, Samuel RAY, William MCNAIR, Esqs. of Northampton Co. William PACKER, Thomas PAXTON and Cornelius MCCAULEY, Esqs. of Bedford Co. Samuel ALLEN, John OURAN, Mordecai MCKINNEY, Esqs. of Northumberland Co. Edward COOK, Charles FOREMAN, John MOORE, Esqs. of Westmoreland Co.

p. 193: Col. Francis JOHNSTON is to be receiver-general of army clothing.

p. 195: Commissioners to form magazines for the army of food and supplies: Phila. Co.--Peter EVANS, Col. John MOORE, Esqs. Bucks Co.--Andrew KICHLIN, Joseph GREER. Chester Co.--Thomas HESLIP, Samuel CULBERTSON. Lancaster Co.--Thomas EDWARDS, David WATSON. York Co.--Maj. James DILL, Maj. William SCOTT. Cumberland Co.--William BLAIR, John ANDREWS. Northampton Co.--John ORNDT, David DESHLER. Bedford Co.--Robert CULBERTSON, Moses REED. Northumberland Co.--William GRAY, John LITTLE, Esqs. Westmoreland Co.--Joseph THORN, John BRANNON.

p. 199: John LESHER, Valentine ECKART, Michael CRAUSE, Christian LAUER, Jr., Berks Co., are commissioners to form magazines for the army of food and supplies.

p. 201: The following men have joined the army of Britain: Joseph GALLOWAY, Andrew ALLEN, Esqs., are late members of Congress of the 13 United Colonies, now the States of America, from Pa. John ALLEN, Esq., is late a member of the committee of inspection for Phila. William ALLEN, the younger, Esq., was at some time a Capt. and afterward, a lieutenant colonel of a regiment or a battalion of foot. James RANKIN, late of York Co., yeoman. Jacob DUCHE, the younger, late Chaplain to the Congress. Gilbert HICKS, late of Bucks Co., yeoman. Samuel SHOEMAKER, late alderman of Phila. City. John POTTS, late of Phila. Co., yeoman. Nathaniel VERNON, late sheriff of Chester Co. Christian FOUTS, late lieutenant-colonel of Lancaster Co. militia. Reynold KEEN, late of Berks Co., yeoman. John BIDDLE, late of Berks Co., yeoman, late excise tax collector of Berks Co. and deputy quartermaster in the U.S. army.

p. 256, 1778: William DEWEES, Esq., was high sheriff of the city and county of Phila. for and during the year ending 14 Oct., 1776, and James CLAYPOOLE, Esq., the present high sheriff of Phila. City and Co., are indemnified for removing the prisoners from the new gaol and imprisoning them in the old gaol.

p. 270: John Abraham DE NORMANDIE, Bucks Co., practitioner in physic, is a citizen of the city of Geneva, the country of his ancestors. He is allowed to sell real estate to move back to Geneva.

p. 293: William HENRY and Ephraim BONHAM, Phila., Esqs., are commissioners for Phila.

p. 300: Albertson WALTON, also called Albinson WALTON, Byberry Twp., Phila. Co., yeoman, said that between 8 May and 25 June, he was in the power of the enemy and could not escape.

35

p. 306: Commissioners of Phila. to administer the oath of allegiance: James YOUNG, Esq., Plunket FLEESON, Esq., John ORD, Esq., Isaac HOWELL, Esq. Commissioners of Phila. Co. to administer the oath of allegiance: John MOORE, Jonathan B. SMITH, David KNOX, Seth QUEE, John RICHARDS, Esqs. Commissioners of Chester Co.: Persifier FRASER, John KINKEAD, John BATON. Commissioners of Bucks Co.: Henry WYNKOOP, Thomas DYER, Thomas LANG. Lancaster Co.: Thomas WHITESIDES, John WHITEHILL, Robert CRAIG, Robert ELDER, John THOM, Christopher MARSHALL, Sr. Commissioners of York Co.; Richard MCALLISTER, David WATSON, William BAILEY, William SMITH, Robert STEVENSON, William MCCLEAN. Commissioners of Cumberland Co.: James OLIVER, John AGNEW, Samuel MCCUNE, Archibald ERWIN, Samuel ROYER, Robert PEEBLES, David ELDER, David MCCLURE, Samuel LYONS, William BROWN. Commissioners of Northampton Co.: John CHAMBERS, John ARNDT, William MCNAIR, Jacob MOREY, Jaocb HORNER, Mathias PROBST. Commissioners of Bedford Co.: David ESPY, Abraham CABLE, Benjamin ELLIOT, Robert SCOTT. Commissioners of Northumberland Co.: Wilton ATKINSON, William SHAW, Andrew CULBERTSON, Samuel ALLEN. Commissioners of Westmoreland Co.: Edward COOK, Charles FOREMAN, James BARR, George READING.

p. 311: William MOORE, Joseph DEAN, David RITTENHOUSE resigned appointments to be auditors of the committee of safety. John NIXON, John Maxwell NESBITT and Benjamin FULLER are appointed in their stead.

p. 315, 1779: A house and lot purchased from James MCCASHLAN in Bedford is to serve as a prison. The land was sold 13 Nov., 1771 to Arthur ST. CLAIR, Barnard DOUGHERTY, George WOODS and William PROCTORS, Esqs., and Thomas COULTER, gentleman.

p. 323: Joseph GALLOWAY is convicted of high treason.

p. 339: George KENNEDY, Peter JANUARY, John PURDON, Robert AITKIN, William RICHARDS, Frazer KINSLEY, John DAVISON, James CONCHY, Rev. William MARSHALL are the minister, elders and deacons of the Scots Presbyterian Church, Spruce St. near 3rd St., Phila.

p. 358: Joseph BLEWER, Philip BOEHM, Thomas CUTHBERT, Jacob GRAFF, John MEASE, John NIXON, William RUSH, Daniel ROBERDEAU, William HENRY, John SHEE, Christopher LUDWICK, James WHARTON are managers of the almshouse of Phila. Francis HOPKINSON is treasurer.

p. 407: Reynold KEEN, on 28 Nov., last, rendered himself to the chief justice of the supreme court on charges of treason.

p. 407: Thomas VERNON, a captain in the 5th Pa. regiment of continental troops and John VERNON (under 18), are children of Nathaniel VERNON, late of Chester Co. Nathaniel was convicted of high treason and his estate was forfeited.

p. 417: Thomas BEANS of Abington Twp., Phila. Co., yeoman, owns 145 acres in Abington Twp. which he purchased from Henry SHISLER and his wife. It was bounded by lands of Richard WILTON, William ROBERTS, Thomas KING and Moses VANCOURT. He also owned 112 1/2 acres in Southampton Twp., Bucks Co., which he purchased from Elizabeth FLETCHER, bounded by the lands of the Baptist meeting house of Daniel HOOGLAND and Wilhelmus CORNELL, lands of Stephen WATTS and Charles GARRISON. He owned 200 acres and 52 perches of land in Warminster Twp., Bucks Co., purchased from Thomas DUNGAN and his wife and bounded by lands of Thomas CRAVEN, John BROOKS, Giles CRAVEN, Joseph HART, Jonathan WALTON and Thomas DUNGAN.

p. 419: John SOMMERS of Moreland Manor, Phila. Co., yeoman, owned 92 acres adjoining Samuel SWIFT, William WALTON, Jonathan WILSON, Henry WALTON; he owned 7 acres at Smithfield adjoining John BRITAIN, Isaac COMELY; he owned 1 acre and 22 perches adjoining the road to Crooked Billet by Newton Rd.; and 82 perches adjoining Henry WALTON and John DORLEY.

p. 427: Commissioners for the city and liberties of Phila.: William HENRY, George ORD, Paul COX, Ephraim BONHAM, Emanuel EYRES, William SHARP, Frederick HAGNER, William JACKSON. Commissioners for the Co. of Phila.: James HAZLET, (Capt.) David SCHNEIDER, John RICHARDS, Israel JONES, Andrew CRAWFORD, Josiah HART, Michael CROLL. Commissioners for Chester Co.: David DENNY, Andrew BOYD, Jr., Peter BELL, John KINKEAD, John BEATON, Persifer FRAZIER, Adam GRUBB. Commissioners for Bucks Co.: John GILL, Abraham DUBOIS, Nathaniel ELLIOTT, Joseph THOMAS, Theophilus FOULKE. Commissioners for Lancaster Co.: Thomas WHITESIDES, John WHITEHILL, Robert CRAIG, William HENRY, John HARRIS (at HARRIS' ferry), John THOMB. Commissioners for Berks Co.: Adam WHITMAN, Henry HILLER, Valentine ECKART, Christian LOWER, Jr., Daniel UTREE. Commissioners for Northampton Co.: Robert LEVERS, John ARNDT, William MCNAIR. Commissioners for York Co.: Henry SLAGLE, William MCLEAN, Benjamin PEDAN, John HAY, Philip GARNDER, Peter SCHULTZ, Andrew SHRIVER, Jr., James DILL. Commissioners for Cumberland Co.: William BROWN of Carlisle, James TAYLOR, James YOUNG, William MCCLURE. Commissioners for Bedford Co.: David ESPY, Samuel DAVIDSON, Jacob HALL, Benjamin BURD. Commissioners for Northumberland Co.: Frederick ANTIS, David MCKENNY. Commissioners for Westmoreland Co.: John PROCTOR, Hugh MITCHELL, Philip JENKINS, John KYLE.

p. 432: William DEWEES, Esq. is late sheriff and James CLAYPOOL, Esq. is present sheriff of the city and county of Phila.

p. 433: During the absence of James MARTIN, Phila., from the city when the British army was in possession, his wife, Elizabeth, took one Sgt. HAVELL of the British army to bed. After the British left Phila., she went off with HAVELL. MARTIN is granted a divorce.

p. 438: Commissioners of Phila. are to meet at Abraham WENTZ's. Commissioners of Bucks Co. are to meet at William BENNETT's, tavern-keeper. Commissioners of Chester Co. are to meet at Elijah WEED's. Commissioners of Northampton Co. are to meet at Jonas HERTZEL's, Esq. Commissioners for Phila. Co. are: Jacob REED, Nathan LEVERING, Thomas DUNGAN, Jenkin EVANS, Robert MCDOWELL, Andrew REED, Peter HOLSTON. Commissioners for Bucks Co. are: John THOMPSON, Joshua ANDERSON, Andrew LONG, Sr., Robert ROBINSON, Robert STEWART, Nathaniel VANSANT. Commissioners for Chester Co. are: Andrew BOYD, Sr., Thomas CHENEY, John BEATON, Edward PARKER, Thomas HESLIP. Commissioners for Lancaster Co. are: Richard FOREE, David WATTSON, Thomas EDWARDS, James ANDERSON, Jr., Hugh PEDON, William SWAN, Jacob FOUTS, Martin HOLMAN, James JACK, Esq., William CLARK. Commissioners for Berks Co.: Joseph HEESTER, Michael LINDEMUTH, Jacob WEAVER, Henry SPYCHER, Jacob BOYER, Jacob BISHOP, Jacob MORGAN, Sr. Commissioners for Northampton Co.: Anthony LEARCH, David DESHLER, Thomas MOORE, Thomas WILSON.

p. 468, 1776: Men deputised to join the provincial conference (*=did not attend): For Phila. City: Dr. Benjamin FRANKLIN (*),

Col. Thomas MCKEAN, Christopher MARSHALL, Sr., Maj. John BAYARD, Col. TimontY MATLACK, Col. Joseph DEAN, Capt. Francis GURNEY, Maj. William COATES, Mr. George SCHLOSSER, Capt. Jonathan B. SMITH, Capt. George GOODWIN, Jacob BARGE, Samuel C. MORRIS, Capt. Samuel BREWSTER, Capt. Joseph BLEWER, William ROBINSON, Capt. Benjamin LOXLEY, Maj. John COX, Capt. Sharp DELANEY, Jacob SCHRINER, James MILLIGAN, Christopher LUDWIG, Dr. Benjamin RUSH, William LOWMAN, Capt. Joseph MOULDER. For Phila. Co.: Col. Henry HILL, Col. Robert LEWIS, Dr. Enoch EDWARDS, Col. William HAMILTON (*), Col. John BULL, Col. Frederick ANTIS, Maj. James POTTS (*), Maj. Robert LOLLER, Joseph MATHER, Matthew BROOKS, Edward BARTHOLOMEW (*). For Bucks Co.: John KIDD, Esq., Maj. Henry WYNKOOP, Benjamin SEGLE, James WALLACE, Col. Joseph HART. For Chester Co.: Col. Richard THOMAS, Maj. William EVANS, Col. Thomas HOCKLEY, Maj. Caleb DAVIS, Elisha PRICE, Esq., Samuel FAIRLAMB, Capt. Thomas LEVIS, Col. William MONTGOMERY, Col. Hugh LLOYD, Richard REILEY, Esq., Col. Evan EVANS, Col. Lewis GRONO, Maj. Sketchley MORTON. For Lancaster Co.: William ATLEE, Esq., Lodowick LOWMAN, Col. Bartram GALBRAITH, Col. Alexander LOWREY, Maj. David JENKINS, Capt. Andrew GRAAF, William BROWN, John SMILEY, Maj. James CUNNINGHAM. For Berks Co.: Col. Jacob MORGAN, Col. Henry HALLER, Col. Mark BIRD, Bodo OTTO, Col. Daniel HUNTER, Col. Valentine EAKERD, Col. Nicholas LUTZ, Capt. Joseph HIESTER, Charles SHOEMAKER. For Northampton Co.: Robert LEVERS, Esq., Col. Neigal GRAY, John WEITZEL, Esq., Nicholas DEPUE, Esq., David DESHLER, Benjamin DEPUE, Col. William RANKIN, Col. Henry SLAGLE, James EDGAR, John HAY (*). For Cumberland Co.: James MCLANE, Col. John ALLISON (*), John MCCLAY, Esq., William ELLIOT, Esq., Col. William CLARK, Dr. John COLHOON, John CREIGH, Hugh MCCORMICK, John HARRIS, Hugh ALEXANDER. For Bedford Co.: Col. David ESPY, Samuel DAVIDSON, Esq., Col. John PIPER. For Westmoreland Co.: Edward COOK, James PERRY.

p. 483: Judges of the elections: For Phila. City: Samuel MASSEY, Frederick KUHL, Thomas CUTHBERT. For Phila. Co.: William COATES, Frederick ANTIS, Robert LOLLAR. For Bucks Co. at Newtown: Henry WYNCOOP, James WALLACE, Joseph HART. For Chester Co.: first division at Chester: Hugh LLOYD, Thomas LEVIS, Mark WILCOX. Second division at Chatham: John M'KAY, Joseph GARDINER, Thomas WELSH. Third division at White Horse: Richard THOMAS, Lewis GRONO, Thomas BULL. For Berks Co. at Reading: Valentine EAKERD, Jacob MORGAN, Daniel HUNTER. For Lancaster Co.: First division at Lancaster borough: William BOWSMAN, H. DEHUFF, Jacob ERB. Second division at James PORTER, Jr.'s: Richard FERREE, John M'MULLEN, Robert TWEED. Third division at Elizabeth town: Daniel ELLIOT, Robert CLARK, Jacob HALDEMAN. Fourth division at Lebanon: Casper KUHN, Jacob ECKART, Philip GREENAWALT. Eighth division at New Holland: J's MCCAMANT, Gab. DAVIS, Michael WHITMAN. Sixth division at GARBER's mill: John ROGERS, John HARRIS, James MORROW. For Cumberland Co.: First division at Carlisle: Robert MILLER, Benjamin BLYTH, James GREGORY. Second division at Chambersburg: John ALLISON, James MAXWELL, John BEARD. Third divison at Robert CAMPBELL's. William BROWN, Alexander MORROW, James TAYLOR. For York Co.: First division at York-town: Charles LUKENS, John HAY, Michael HAYN. Second division at Samuel GADDIS': William M'CLELLAN, John AGNEW, James DICKSON. Third division at Hanover: Joseph JEFFERIES, Thomas LILLY, Frederick WOLFE. Fourth division at NICHOLSON's mill: James LEIPER, Patrick SCOTT, James SAVAGE. Fifth division at Robert STEVENSON's: John NESBIT, James NAYLOR, William MITCHELL. For Bedford Co.: Samuel DAVIDSON, James ANDERSON, William TODD. For Northumberland Co. at George MCCANDLISH's: Thomas HEWIT, William SHAW, Joseph GREEN. For Westmoreland Co.: First division at

SPARK's fort: George WILSON, John KILE, Robert MCCONNELL. Second division at Hannah's town: James BARR, John MOORE, Clement M'GEARY. For Northampton Co.: First divison at Easton: Abraham BERLIN, Jesse JONES, Jonas HARTZELL. Second division at ALLEN's town: John GERHART, David DESHLER, George BREINIG. Third division at Peter ANTHONY's: Simon DREISBACH, Neigel GRAY, Peter ANTHONY. Fourth division at Nicholas DUPUE's: Robert LEVERS, Nicholas DEPUE, Jacobus VANGARDER.

p. 500: Returns of election, 15 July, 1776: Phila. City: Timothy MATLACK, Benjamin FRANKLIN, Frederick KUHL, Owen BIDDLE, James CANNON, George CLYMER, George SCHLOSSER, David RITTENHOUSE. Lancaster Co.: George ROSS, Philip MARSTELLER, Thomas PORTER, Bartram GALBREATH, Joseph SHERRER, John HUBLEY, Henry SLAYMAKER, Alexander LOWREY. Northampton Co.: Siman DRESHBACH, Jacob ARNDT, Peter BUCKHOLDER, Peter RHOADS, Jacob STROUD, Neigal GRAY, Abraham MILLER, John RALSTON. Phila. Co.: Frederick ANTIS, Henry HILL, Robert LOLLER, Joseph BLEWER, John BULL, Thomas POTTS, Edward BARTHOLOMEW, William COATES. York Co.: John HAY, James EDGAR, William RANKIN, Henry SLAGLE, Francis CROZART, James SMITH, Robert MCPHERSON, Joseph DONALDSON. Bedford Co.: Thomas SMITH, John WILKINS, Benjamin ELLIOTT, Thomas COULTER, Joseph POWELL, Henry RHOADS, John BURD, John CESSNA. Bucks Co.: Joseph HART, John WILKINSON, Samuel SMITH, John KELLER, William VANHORN, John GRIER, Abraham VAN MIDLESWARTS, Joseph KIRKBRIDE. Cumberland Co.: John HARRIS, Jonathan HOGE, William CLARKE, Robert WHITEHILL, William DUFFIELD, James BROWN, Hugh ALEXANDER, James MCCLEAN. Northumberland Co.: William COOKE, James POTTER, Robert MARTIN, Matthew BROWN, Walter CLARK, John KELLY, James CRAWFORD, John WEITZELL. Chester Co.: Benjamin BARTHOLOMEW, John JACOB, Thomas STRAWBRIDGE, Robert SMITH, Samuel CUNNINGHAM, John HART, John MACKEY, John FLEMMING. Berks Co.: Jacob MORGAN, Gabriel HEISTER, John LESHER, Benjamin SPYKER, Daniel HUNTER, Valentine ECKART, Charles SHOEMAKER, Thomas JONES. Westmoreland Co.: James BARR, Edward COOK, James SMITH, John MOORE, John CARMICHAEL, James PERRY, John M'CLELLAN, Christopher LAVINGAIR.

p. 502: The Constitutional Convention met 16 July, 1776: Dr. Benjamin FRANKLIN, Pres.; Col. George ROSS, Vice-Pres.; John MORRIS, Esq., Sec.; Jacob GARRIGUES, Assistant Clerk to Sec.; William SHEED, appointed door keeper. Council of Safety elected: David RITTENHOUSE, Jonathan B. SMITH, Owen BIDDLE, James CANNON, Timothy MATLACK, Nathaniel FALCONER, Samuel MORRIS, Jr., Samuel HOWELL, Frederick KUHL, Samuel MORRIS, Sr., Thomas WHARTON, Jr., Henry KEPPELE, Jr., Joseph BLEWER, Samuel MIFFLIN, George GRAY, John BULL for Phila. Co. Henry WYNKOP for Bucks Co. John HUBLEY for Lancaster Co. Benjamin BARTHOLOMEW for Chester Co. William LYON for Cumberland Co. Peter RHOADS for Northampton Co. John WEITZEL for Northumberland Co. Daniel HUNTER for Berks Co. Michael SWOOPE for York Co. David ESPY for Bedford Co. John MOOR for Westmoreland Co.

p. 505, 1776: Rev. William WHITE is to perform divine service on 18 July, 1776 before the convention. Col. MILES is appointed Brigadier-General and Commander in Chief of the forces of Pa.

p. 514: Col. James EASTON is a prisoner in the Phila. gaol.

p. 521: John WILLIAMS, James FORBES and William PATTON are prisoners in the Lancaster Co. gaol.

p. 523: William NICHOLS' petition was referred to the overseers of the poor to take care of the petitioner.

p. 524: Mathew KNOX and William CALDWELL petition to be released from gaol.

p. 528: Joshua FISHER and sons are salt importers.

p. 528: Thomas WIGTON, a prisoner in the gaol of Northampton Co., is complaining of arbitrary imprisonment by Mr. GORDON and Mr. BERLIN.

p. 536: Andrew HAGENBUCK and William STUMPFF, Albany Twp., Berks Co., have asked to be excused from marching into Jersy due to living in a frontier county and being apprehensive of an Indian war.

p. 546: John SMITH and Benjamin LEWIS are prisoners in the Phila. gaol.

p. 552: £834 is to be paid to Neigle GRAY and Maj. Jacob ARNDT to be sent to Northampton Co. to pay the bounty for the second quota for the Flying Camp.

p. 554: Peter WITHINGTON petitions to be appointed a captain in one of the companies to be raised in Northampton and Northumberland. Stephen and Joseph SHEWELL justify their conduct with respect to their salt. Col. KIRKBRIDE requested a leave of absence to join his battalion at Amboy.

p. 555: John TIMMONS is a prisoner in Carlisle jail on suspicion of murder. Col. ROSS and Col. Thomas SMITH are on a committee.

p. 556: Col. M'PHERSON received an account of the loss of a son in the battle on Long Island.

p. 557: Messrs. CARAHAN and PROCTOR are two colonels of the Westmoreland Co. Militia. Andrew LEDLIE, Easton, Northampton Co., complains of ill treatment due to his attachment to the cause of liberty. William HARDY petitions to be appointed officer for Pa. to register those who shall be disabled in the service of the U.S.

p. 561: Col. Thomas SMITH, Col. POTTER, Maj. James SMITH are to be on a committee to confer with the Committee of Congress for Indian Affairs.

p. 563: William WILD sends a memorial to Congress. Lawrence FEAGAN petitions relating to damage he sustained during a riot among the soldiers at the barracks.

p. 566: The following men are empowered to order such part of the associators as they think necessary in case of an actual invasion, to march to the protection of said counties as may be exposed to the depredations of the Indians: Bernard DOUGHERTY, William M'COMB, James ANDERSON and Robert ELLIOTT, Bedford Co. Nicholas DUPUI, David DESHLER, Herman SCHNEYDER and Arthur LATTIMORE, Northampton Co. William M'CLAY, Michael TROY, Walter CLARK, Laughlin M'CARTNEY, Northumberland Co. Samuel SLOANE, William LOCKRAY, John GIFFEN, Christopher TRUBEY, Westmoreland Co.

p. 573: Mr. JACOBS, Col. LOWREY, and Maj. James SMITH are a committee to prepare a speech and wampum for a conference with the

Shawanese Indians.

p. 576: Col. KACHLEAN sent a letter from Amboy ON 11 Sept., 1776, informing of some deserters from his battalion of Bucks Co. Militia.

p. 579: Paul FOOKS wants an appointment as a sworn interpreter for foreign languages and a notary public.

p. 584: Maj. LOLLAR, Maj. COATES and John MORRIS, Jr. are elected commissioners.

THE STATUTES AT LARGE OF PENNSYLVANIA FROM 1682 TO 1801
VOLUME 10 - 1779-1781

p. 49, 1780: The land of the estate of Joseph GALLOWAY, Esq., is appropriated for the use of the President of the Supreme Executive Council. The land is held in trust by Joseph HARVEY, Thomas TATNEL, Joseph TROTTER, James MORRIS and Oswald PEEL and afterwards, was conveyed by Joseph TROTTER, the survivor of said trustees to Joseph FOX, Samuel RHOADS, Joseph GALLOWAY, John BAYNTON, Edward PENNINGTON, Charles HUMPHREYS and Michael HILLEGAS. The land was purchased from Anthony WILKINSON and John JENNINGS and wife to erect a barracks. The land is now vested in the heirs of Joseph FOX, now dec. The land is now held by James WEBB in trust for the public.

p. 51: Joshua CARPENTER held land in trust for Phila. Co. and City.

p. 52: Jeremiah LANGHORNE, William BILES, Joseph KIRKBRIDE, Jr., Thomas WATSON, practitioner in physic and Abraham CHAPMAN are to build a new courthouse and prison for Bucks Co.

p. 89: Trustees of the 2nd Presbyterian Church, Phila.: Joseph REED, Thomas BOURNE, Andrew HODGE, Gunning BEDFORD, John BAIRD, Hugh HODGE, William FAULKNER, William SMITH, Isaac SNOWDEN, Daniel GOODMAN, Benjamin HARBESON, Nathan COOK, William GEDDIS, Jared INGERSOLL, William HOLLINSHEAD, James HUNTER, Samuel MCCLEAN, James ROBESON, Abraham DUBOIS, Hugh LENOX, Jonathan B. SMITH, Thomas NEVILL, William M'ILHENNEY, Joseph EASTBURNE.

p. 93: Samuel MIFFLIN, William HYSHAM, James CRAIG, George ORD, Nathaniel FALCONER, Joseph BLEWER, John WOODS, William BROWN, Henry DOUGHERTY, William ALIBONE, John HAZELWOOD and Leeson SIMMONS are managers of the society for the relief of the poor, aged and infirm masters of ships, their widows and children.

p. 117: On 4 Oct., 1779, sundry persons were unhappily killed in and near the house of James WILSON, Esq., in Walnut St., Phila.

p. 131: Henry GUEST, now of New Brunswick, N.J., has petitioned to be allowed to make an oil called "Currier's Oil and Blubber" exclusively.

p. 142: William CLINGAN, Thomas BULL, John KINKEAD, Roger KIRK, John SELLERS, John WILSON, Joseph DAVIS are to sell the old courthouse, prison and workhouse in Chester Co.

p. 173: Petition of John REDMAN, Phila., practitioner in physic, and Nathaniel FALCONER, Phila., mariner, says that in 1723-24, a road was laid out from Germantown marketplace to Robert ROBERT's ferry on the Schuylkill River. It entered the lands of William

PALMER (now owned by John REDMAN and Nathaniel FALCONER). In 1760, another road was laid out. The first road is now abolished.

p. 185: Daniel WISTER, Levi BUDD, Philip BOEHM, Robert CATHER, Jedediah SNOWDEN, William Lawrence BLAIR, Elias Lewis TREACHEL, John MILLER, Joseph WATKINS, John KNOX, Nathan JONES, William THORNE are signers of bills of credit.

p. 219: It was found inconvenient for freemen of the fourth district of Cumberland Co. to attend the annual election at the house of James PURDY, Farmanaugh Twp. Now the election will be held at the house of Thomas WILSON, Millford Twp. It was found inconvenient for freemen in Air and Bethel Twps., Bedford Co. to attend the annual election. They will now vote at William HART's, Bethel Twp.

p. 267: Giles HICKS, Esq., Captain in the 10th regiment, petitions that in Nov., 1776, when he was a minor of the age of 15 years, he was seduced by artifices of Hester MCDANIEL and her relations to contract marriage with her against the consent of his guardians. Hester, at the time, was a common prostitute and has become so diseased of the lues venerea as to be declared incurable after seven months in the Pa. Hospital. Giles is given a bill of divorcement on 21 Nov., 1780.

p. 270: David RITTENHOUSE, Owen BIDDLE, Mark BIRD, Balser GHEER, Thomas POTTS, David THOMAS, Patrick ANDERSON, John MEAR, Isaac HEWES, Nathan LEVERING, George DOUGLASS, John HEISTER, Christian STEER are appointed commissioners for clearing the Schuylkill River.

p. 273: Washington Co. is erected. Elections are to be held at Catfishes Camp, the house of David HOGE. James EDGAR, Hugh SCOTT, Van SWEARINGHAM, Daniel LITE, John ARMSTRONG are to buy land for a courthouse and prison. Henry TAYLOR is appointed excise tax collector.

p. 279: Daniel RUNDLE and Matthias ASPDEN, merchants, late of Phila., are required to render themselves to a justice of the peace for high treason. They are now probably in Europe.

p. 281: Henry Hugh FERGUSON, late of Horsham Twp., Phila. Co., is attainted of high treason. His estate is forfeited. When he married Elizabeth GRAEME, he became seized of an estate called Graeme Park, Horsham Twp., Phila. Co.

p. 295: Flour inspectors: Phila. City and Co.-- Jacob BRIGHT. Chester Co.--Adam GRUBB. Bucks Co.--Joseph MCELVAINE.

p. 302: Bills of credit are to be printed by: George GRAY, John STEINMETZ, Henry HILL, Samuel PENROSE, Henry HAYES, William HARRIS. They may be signed by: Cadwalader MORRIS, Samuel MEREDITH, James BUDDEN, Joseph WHARTON, Joseph BULLOCK, Samuel CALDWELL, Michael SHUBART, David H. CUNNINGHAM, Jacob BARGE, Philip BOEHM, John PURVIANCE, Joseph DEAN, John MILLER, Jonathan MIFFLIN, Isaac HOWELL, Richard BACHE, John BAYNTON, Tench FRANCIS, David SHAFFER, Sr., Thomas PRYOR, Robert KNOX, John MEASE, Jacob S. HOWELL, John PATTON.

p. 322: Care and custody of lots appurtenant to Reading is vested in Samuel MIFFLIN, Henry CHRIST, Henry HALLER. Care and custody of lots appurtenant to York is vested in Archibald MCCLEAN, Michael SWOOPE, William SCOTT. Care and custody of lots appurtenant to

Carlisle is vested in John MONTGOMERY, Samuel LAIRD, James POLLOCK. Care and custody of lots appurtenant to several towns of Easton, Bedford, Sunbury, and Hannah's town is vested in the Justices of the Peace.

p. 355: Officers of the German Society Contributing for the Relief of Distressed Germans in the State of Pa. are: Pres. Henry KEPPELE; Vice-Pres. Lewis WEISS; Secretaries Lewis FARMER and Henry LEIGHTHOUSER; overseers Christopher LUDWICK, Peter OZEAS, Andrew BURCKHART, John FRITZ, Peter KRAFT, Melchior STEINER; Treasurer Michael SHUBART; Solicitor Henry KAMMERER; Deacon William LEHMAN.

p. 366: John RANKIN, Esq., York Co., petitions that a house and lot in Lisburn, Cumberland Co., was taken in execution as the estate of Richard CARSON and eventually sold to James RANKIN. Afterward, James RANKIN joined the enemy in Phila. The land was vested in John RANKIN.

p. 368: Jacob BILLMEYER, York, petitions that his wife, Mary, about eight years ago, eloped from his bed and board. In Feb., 1778, Mary became acquainted with William COLE with whom she intermarried and cohabitated and left the state. She has born a child to COLE. BILLMEYER's marriage is dissolved.

p. 381: William BINGHAM, Elijah WEED, Charles MILLER, William TURNBULL and John TAYLOR are managers of State Island (late Province Island). John WILCOCKS is treasurer.

p. 407: Officers of the Bank of North America: Thomas WILLING, Pres. and Director. Thomas FITZSIMMONS, John Maxwell NESBITT, James WILSON, Henry HILL, Samuel OSGOOD, Cadwallader MORRIS, Samuel INGLIS, Samuel MEREDITH, William BINGHAM, Timothy MATLACK, Andrew CALDWELL, directors.

p. 412: John PATTON, Francis GURNEY and William ALLIBONE are appointed commissioners to furnish and arm vessels to guard the Delaware River and Bay.

p. 421: John AMIEL is a prisoner in the Phila. gaol for debt.

p. 424: Some early land owners of Carlisle when it was named a borough in 1781: Thomas WILSON's heirs; Widow MCDONALD, Jonathan HOLME, James DAVIS, Charles MCCLURE, Ephraim BLAINE, Hugh PARKER, John SMITH & Co., James YOUNG, Ross MITCHELL. Burgesses were Robert MILLER, Samuel POSTLETHWAITE. Assistants: William IRWIN, William HOLMES, James POLLOCK and Casper CROPT. Robert SMITH was high constable. John HEAP was town clerk. Samuel LAIRD was clerk of the market.

p. 457: John NICHOLSON is comptroller-general of the Dept. of Accounts.

p. 471: William CRAWFORD is to erect a ferry over the Youghiogheny at STUART's crossing and John DEVOIR, executor of the estate of Jacobus DEVOIR, late of Westmoreland Co., on behalf of the orphan children to whom the said estate belongs and Joseph PARKINSON, be also allowed the privilege of having a ferry erected over the Monongahela River 30 perches below the mouth of Pigeon Ck.

p. 476: Hough ROBERTS, Enoch FLOWER, Samuel RHOADS, Andrew BANKSON, Joseph JOHNSON, John SMITH are appointed to maintain dams, etc. in

Schuylkill Point Meadow.

p. 480: Luke MORRIS, Thomas PENROSE, James PENROSE, in 1768, purchased from John JEKYL lots of ground in Southwark to build a public landing. Robert KNOX, Joseph BLEWER, Joseph TURNER, John BROWN, William CLIFTON, Isaac PENROSE are a committee to transact business concerning the lot. Able JAMES is the guardian of Clement PENROSE, only child of James PENROSE, since dec. James PEMBERTON, Joseph SWIFT, Peter KNIGHT, Henry DRINKER, Richard WELLS are the auditors to settle the accounts.

p. 495: James ALLEN is the late owner of the town of Northampton. By will, he devised the town to his son, James, an infant about 4 years old and income from the town to his wife, Elizabeth, until James is 16 years old.

p. 519: Trustees of the Presbyterian Church of Warwick, Bucks Co.: Richard WALKER, Benjamin SNODGRASS, William SCOTT, William LONG, Nathan MCKINSTRY, Gills CRAVEN, William WALKER, John CARR, Joseph HARB.

p. 526: Dutch Protestant Reformed Church, Northampton and Southampton Twps., Bucks Co.: Rev. Mathhew LIGHT, minister; Henry KROESEN, Gilliam CORNELL and Henry WYNCOOP, elders; William BENNET, Aart LEFFERTS and Daniel HOGELAND, deacons.

THE STATUTES AT LARGE OF PENNSYLVANIA FROM 1682 TO 1801
VOLUME 11 - 1782

p. 5: John SENSINIGH is a prisoner in the Lancaster Co. gaol for debt.

p. 6: John SPERING, late of Easton, Northampton Co., in Mar., 1778, left his family, passed through enemy lines and supposedly went to England where he had been born. His eldest son, Henry, and his younger son, John, are soldiers in the U.S. army in the Pa. line. He had daughters Jane and Elizabeth.

p. 17: John NICHOLAS, late of Phila., house-carpenter, dec. His will was dated 7 May, 1755 and named heirs Jane (wife); sister Martha ROBERTS; Martha's daughter, Sarah LLOYD; Sarah's three children: Samuel, Robert, and Martha; his sister, Mary EVANS; Mary's daughter, Margaret; Jane ROBERTS (daughter of Aubrey); Samuel, Mary and Sarah NICHOLAS (children of his dec. brother, Anthony). Samuel LLOYD died without issue. Robert LLOYD leaving four minor children: Thomas, Samuel, Rees and Robert. Martha LLOYD married Samuel HUDSON and died, leaving five minor children: Robert, Sarah, Mary, William and Harry HUDSON. Mary EVANS married Marmaduke COOPER. Jane ROBERTS married Benjamin MORGAN and died, leaving one minor child, Benjamin. Mary NICHOLAS married Jonathan COWPLAND and died, leaving five children: Caleb, Mary and Ann (all minors), Grace COWPLAND and Sarah PARKINSON (of full age). Sarah married --- SHUTE. NICHOLAS had land near Joseph CRUKSHANK, Jonathan MIFFLIN, dec., Casper WISTAR's heirs, Elizabeth PASCHALL's heirs, Johy REYNELL, Samuel MICKLE's heirs and Edward WARNER, dec.

p. 26: Harry GORDON, now or late a military officer in the British service, now or late of Chester Co., on 20 Mar., 1781, bought two tracts of land in Bedford Co.

p. 30: John MORRIS, Eastown Twp., Chester Co., petitions that he owns 150 acres in West Whiteland Twp., bounded by land of the late John JACOBS, Esq., John CUTHBERT, Richard THOMAS and Morris ZOOTZS. It was once owned by David HOWELL, dec., and taken in execution by Jesse MARIS, Esq., high sheriff of Chester Co. The land was sold 26 Aug., 1771, to John MORRIS and a deed from John CUTHBERT for part of the land which was sold to David HOWELL was lost in a fire at John CUTHBERT's house. Papers belonging to Samuel PHIPPS were stolen.

p. 38: Henry DORRACH, New Britain Twp., Bucks Co., yeoman, petitions that a public road was laid out through David REES' land which is now Henry DORRACH's land.

p. 40: Trustees of the Presbyterian Church, Newtown, Bucks Co.: James MCNAIR, Joseph SACKET, Esq., John THOMPSON, Esq., Joshua ANDERSON, Esq., Rev. James BOYD, John BURLEY.

p. 46: John GOSLINE, Bristol, Bucks Co., cordwainer and tanner, was summoned by the name of John GOSLING, shoemaker, to surrender for high treason.

p. 51: Joseph JUDSON, James ROBINSON, James LEES are prisoners in the Phila. gaol for debt.

p. 64: William EMERSON is flour inspector for Westmoreland Co. Hugh GARDNER is flour inspector for Washington Co.

p. 102: John WILT, Bedford Co., wants to erect a fulling mill two miles below Bedford on the Raystown Branch of the Juniata River. It was approved 23 Nov., 1781.

p. 104: Isaac COATES, David ROSE, George FOREPAUGH, George LEIB, Peter BROWN, John BRITTON are superintendents of markets on both sides of Callowhill St. and New Market St., Northern Liberties, Phila.

p. 109: Caleb PAUL, John PAUL, Robert STEEL, Aaron DOANE, Mahlon DOANE, Edward CONNARD, Henry CONNARD, Jeremiah COOPER, Amos WHITE, Joseph DOANE, Abraham DOANE, Levi DOANE are attainted by outlawry in the Pa. Supreme Court. Gideon VERNON, Thomas BULLA, Amos WILLIAMS, Edward RICHARDSON and George BURNS are suspected and charged with being accomplices in robberies.

p. 115: Trustees of the College at Carlisle, Cumberland Co. (Dickinson College): John DICKINSON, Esq., Pres.; Henry HILL, Esq., James WILSON, Esq., William BINGHAM, Esq., Dr. Benjamin RUSH, all of Phila.; Rev. James BOYD, Bucks Co.; Dr. John MCDOWELL, Chester Co.; Rev. Henry MUHLENBERG, Rev. A.M. and William HANDELL, Esqs. and Rev. James JACKS, Esq., all of Lancaster; Rev. John BLACK, Rev. Alexander DOBBINS, Rev. John MCKNIGHT, Hon. James EWING, Esq., Robert MCPHERSON, Henry SCHLEGLE, Thomas HARTLEY and Michael HAHN, all of York Co.; Rev. John KING, Rev. Robert COOPER, Rev. James LAND, Rev. Samuel WAUGH, Rev. William LINN, Rev. John LINN, John ARMSTRONG, Esq., John MONTGOMERY, Esq., Stephen DUNCAN, Thomas SMITH, Robert MAGAU, Esqs., Dr. Samuel MCCLOSKEY, all of Cumberland Co.; Rev. Christopher Emanuel SHULTZ and Peter SPYKER, Esq., of Berks Co.; John ARDNT, Esq., Northampton Co.; William MONTGOMERY, William MCCLAY, Northumberland Co.; Bernard DOUGHERTY, Esq., David ESPY, Esq., Bedford Co.; Rev. James SUTTON, Alexander MCCLEAN, Esq., Northumberland Co., William MCCLEARY, Esq., Washington Co.

p. 123: David MEAD, Robert MARTIN, John CHAMBERS, Nathan DENNISON are elected Justices of the Peace for the North West District. Alexander PATTERSON, John SEELY, Luke BROADHEAD and Henry SHOEMAKER are elected for the South East District, Wyoming Twp., Northumberland Co.

p. 124: Early landowners in Reading, Berks Co.: Adam WITMAN, Esq., dec., Philip SAYLOR, Jonathan POTTS, Esq., dec., Michael BRIGHT, Isaac LEVAN, Michael CROWSER. Daniel LEVAN and William SCULL, Esqs., are burgesses of Reading. Peter NAGLE, John SPOON, Benjamin SPYKER, Jr., and James MAY are assistants.

p. 147: Charles RUBEY, Bedford town, Bedford Co., cordwainer, petitions that his wife, Jane, late Jane SMITH, has been unfaithful, committing adultry with divers persons and wants the marriage annulled.

p. 152: Commissioners appointed to settle jurisdiction of the Delaware River: George GRAY, William BINGHAM, George BRYAN, Pa. Abraham CLARK, Joseph COOPER, Thomas HENDERSON, N.J.

p. 157: William BROWN, late of Phila., baker, is in the Phila. gaol for debt.

p. 168: St. Paul's Episcopal Church, Phila.: John WOOD and Lambert WILMER, present wardens. Vestrymen: Plunket FLEESON, John YOUNG, Andrew DOZ, George GOODWIN, John CAMPBELL, George ORD, Blair MCCLENACHAN, William GRAHAM, George GLENTWORTH, Joseph BULLOCK, Samuel PENROSE, George NELSON, Richard RENSHAW, Joseph TURNER, John KEBLE, John BATES, James DOUGHTY, Benjamin TOWNE, grocer.

p. 173: Francis MURRAY, John DUGUID, Robert PATTON, William CRAWFORD, Andrew DOVER, Thomas JENNEY, Andrew ROBINSON, late officers of the Pa. line, were captives of the enemy. They are awarded higher ranks: Francis MURRAY is a lieutenant-colonel; John DUGUID, Robert PATTON, William CRAWFORD are captains; DOVER, JENNEY and ROBINSON are lieutenants.

p. 174: Catharine SUMMERS, Phila., wife of Peter SUMMERS, victualler, says her husband has left her, frequently beat her, and committed adultry. The marriage is dissolved.

p. 175: Archibald MORRISON, York Co., Cumberland Twp., owned land near John MCFARLAND (now Robert LAIRD's), Hugh MURPHY, James RIDDLE. MORRISON, dec., authorized Archibald MORRISON, Jr. to sell the land to Joshua RUSSELL.

p. 177: Brigadier Gen. William IRVINE, during his separate command at Pittsburg, rendered essential service. An island in the Ohio River below Pittsburg, known as MONTOUR's Island is granted to IRVINE.

p. 178: Thomas HUTCHINS, Esq., former captain and engineer in the British service, is now a geographer to the U.S. He worked for the British at the British port of Pensacola.

p. 180: Joseph JUDSON, Shem THOMPSON, Lawrence POWELL are prisoners in the Phila. gaol for debt.

p. 181: George ROTH, Marlborough Twp., Phila. Co., yeoman, on 17 Feb., 1773, mortgaged land near Peter HEIST, Philip MOOD, George

ROTH, Philip REED, George Michael RIDER, Adam HILLEGASS, Andrew OHL, Leonard THOMAS, Jacob SCHAFFER, Daniel ROBERDEAU. The title deed is missing which transferred the property from Hugh ROBERTS to Daniel LABAR, from Daniel LABAR to Philip LABAR, a patent to Philip LABAR, a deed from Philip LABAR to John YEACKLE, a deed from Adam HILLEGAS to John YEACKLE, a deed from Philip REED to John YECKLE, two deeds from John YECKLE to John ROTH.

p. 185: Persifor FRAZER, Thornbury Twp., Chester Co., owns land in E. Whiteland Twp., Chester Co., near land of Thomas EVANS, Thomas BOWEN, John HAMBRIGHT.

p. 186: John KLEIN is a prisoner in the Lancaster Co. gaol for debt.

p. 193: William BUTLER, Esq., lieutenant colonel in the Pa. line, asks to erect a ferry over the Allegheny River at Pittsburg.

p. 194: May MCKAY, Pittsburg, widow of Col. Aeneas MCKAY, asks to erect a ferry on the Monongahela River at a new store on the land of Col. MCKAY. Their children are Samuel and Elizabeth.

p. 195: Andrew TRUMBOWER is a prisoner in the Newtown gaol, Bucks Co. for debt.

p. 197: The erection of Fayette Co.: Edward COOK, Robert ADAMS, Theophilus PHILLIPS, James DOUGHERTY, Thomas RODGERS, yeomen, are to buy land for the courthouse and prison at Uniontown. Samuel ADAMS is the tax collector.

p. 203: Baptist Church, Montgomery Twp., Phila. Co.: Minister is David LOOFBOURROW. Trustees are Isaac JAMES, Peter EVANS, Jenkin EVANS, George SMITH.

p. 211: Joseph STILES is to superintend the power magazine in Phila.

p. 214: Abraham COMRON, Phila., sail maker, petitions that his grandfather, Nicholas CASSELL, dec., gave to Mary COMRON, mother of Abraham, a lot in Phila. near land of Henry DUNN, dec., James COOPER, John COMRON (father of Abraham). John and Mary died intestate leaving Abraham and Rebecca. When the enemy was in Phila., Abraham's family removed to Gloucester, N.J., a place called Clonmell, where the enemy burned all their possessions. Rebecca is now Rebecca ENGLISH.

p. 227: Public auctioneers are John BAYARD, William BROWN and Alexander BOYD.

p. 228: William MCILHENNY, Phila., tailor, purchased land from the estate of John NICHOLAS, dec., bounded by land of John REYNELL, heirs of Edward WARNER, heirs of Samuel MICKLE. The land was vested in Samuel HUDSON, Marmaduke COOPER, Benjamin MORGAN. James STEEL, Phila., gentleman, and his wife, Martha, by indenture of 22 Jan., 1719, sold the land to John EVANS. EVANS sold the land to Thomas REDMAN, Phila., bricklayer. REDMAN sold the land to Samuel NICHOLAS, brother of John NICHOLAS.

p. 230: Joseph HART, Esq., and David LONGSTRETH, yeoman, say a public road in Warminster Twp., Bucks Co., divided Jacob CHAMBERLAIN's plantation Nov., 1731. In Mar., 1748, another road was laid out by Bartholomew LONGSTRETH's (now Daniel LONGSTRETH's) and Gideon DECAMP's (now Silas HART's) land, James VANSANT's and William SPENCER and Joseph HART's land.

p. 232: John MCKEE petitions that he had a ferry over the Monongahela and Youghiogheny Rivers.

p. 235: Richard GARDINER, Phila., yeoman, petitions his title to a lot near William FISHER, dec., and Joshua TITTERY, dec., Mr. WHITE and Mr. TAYLOR is lost. Phoebe HAWKINS, widow and administrator of William HAWKINS' estate, sold the land to Sarah GARDINER, grandmother of the petitioner.

p. 236: Henry GURNEY, Northern Liberties, buried a trunk in the ground containing deeds when the British were approaching Phila. A deed from Thomas ENGLAND and Matthew BELLIS dated 10 July, 1700, selling ground to Thomas TAYLOR (land bounded by land of Henry GURNEY, Matthew DRASON, dec.). A deed from Thomas TAYLOR dated 4 July, 1702, selling the land to Thomas WHARTON. A deed from Thomas WHARTON dated 5 Jan., 1703, selling the land to John HART. A deed from William PARR, Esq., sheriff of Phila. on 15 Dec., 1766, selling at the suit of George MOORE against Albertus SHOCHELEAR, administrator of John MILLS, unto John ROSS, Esq., a lot now in the tenure of James WILSON, Esq. A deed of lease and release from Benjamin Morgan DATED 27 and 28 Apr., 1744, selling land to Evan MORGAN. A deed from Evan MORGAN, John ROSS, and Catharine MORGAN, executors of the will of Benjamin MORGAN, dated 9 Feb., 1749, granting to Nathaniel ALLEN some land. A deed from Nathaniel ALLEN, 10 Feb., 1749, granting to Evan MORGAN some land. A deed from Evan MORGAN, 12 Jan., 1763, selling to John ROSS land now in the tenure of James WILSON, Esq. A deed dated 3 Dec., 1751, from Richard SEWELL, Esq., sheriff of Phila. Co., granting to Thomas LAWRENCE land on the south side of Apple Tree Alley, Phila., adj. land of John KNOWLES, dec., and John Nicholas CRESMAN and Henry GURNEY, now in the possession of the Widow PYLES. A deed, uncertain date, from Thomas LAWRENCE selling land to John ROSS, Esq. A deed, 27 Mar., 1719, from Anthony MORRIS to George COATS, a lot between High and Mulberry Sts., adj. Widow ELFRITH, Henry GURNEY, now owned by Martha SCOTT. A deed, date uncertain, from George COATS to Thomas MASTERS. A deed, date uncertain, from Joseph PIDGEON to Thomas MASTERS, land on the west side of TURNER's Lane, now Chancery Lane, adj. William CRAIG and Anthony MORRIS. A deed, 25 Nov., 1752, from Samuel APPOWEN and wife, Hannah (late Hannah COX) selling land to John ROSS, Esq., with buildings, in the tenure of James THOMSON. Deeds of lease and release, 28 and 29 Sept., 1722, from Francis RAWLE and wife, Martha, selling to John HEAP land adj. William CRAIG and Henry GURNEY. Buildings in the tenure of Martha SCOTT. A deed from Owen OWEN, Esq., sheriff of Phila. Co., 6 Sept., 1727, selling ground to Richard HILL, Esq., the same taken in execution and sold as the estate of John HEAP. A deed, 5 Apr., 1757, from Samuel Preston MOORE, Esq., and wife, Hannah, selling to John ROSS, Esq. A deed, 4 Sept., 1746, from Nicholas SCULL, sheriff of Phila. Co., to James BOYDEN, land in Oxford Twp., adj. James BINGHAM, Jacob HALL, Thomas KENT, late the estate of Arthur JONES, dec., and sold at the suit of William ALLEN, Esq., against John EVANS and Griffith JONES, exr. of JONES' will. A deed, 10 Mar., 1749, from Richard SEWELL, Esq., sheriff of Phila. Co., selling to Jacob HALL, land taken in execution at the suit of William JACKSON against Robert GREENWAY, exr. of the will of James BOYDEN. A deed, 11 Mar., 1749, from Jacob HALL, selling to John ROSS, Esq., premises now in the tenure of James GLEN. A deed, uncertain date, from William HAYES to John

ROSS, Esq., for a lot in Kensington, Phila. Co., adj. Jacob MILLER and William BALL.

p. 241: John SUMRALL has kept a ferry over the Youghiogheny River.

p. 242: John ORMSBY has kept a ferry from Pittsburg over the Monongahela River.

p. 243: Daniel ELLIOT, Washington Co., wants to establish a ferry over the Ohio River at the mouth of Saw-Mill Run, 1 mile below Fort Pitt.

p. 245: Trustees of the Presbyterian Church, Hanover Twp., Lancaster Co.: John COOPER, James JOHNSTON, James MCCREIGHT, Daniel BROADLEY, George CRAIN, John MCEWEN, John ROBINSON, Richard DERMOND, Ambrose CREAIN, Rev. Matthew WOODS.

P. 252: Michael HILLEGAS, Benjamin FULLER, and Mathew CLARKSON are managers for a lottery.

p. 265: John ALEXANDER and wife, Margaret, Phila., were married. Margaret has left bed and board and committed adultery. The marriage is dissolved.

p. 267: David RITTENHOUSE, Lindsey COATS, Anthony LEVERING, John JONES, Gulph Mill; Robert CURRY, Isaac POTTS, Joseph PAUL, David THOMAS, Providence; Matthias PENNEBAKER, James HOCKLEY, John BROOKS, Jacob LIGHT, Abraham LINCOLN, Mordecai MILLER, John BISHIP, George GARDINER, John MEARS, Charles SHOEMAKER, George MILLER, Henry HALLER, Samuel BAIRD, Frederick CLECKNER are commissioners to clear navigation on the Schuylkill River.

p. 273: Robert HANNA, George WILSON, Samuel SLOAN, Joseph IRWIN, John CAVET are empowered to purchase land for a courthouse and prison for Westmoreland Co. John IRWIN, Benjamin DAVIS, Charles CAMPBELL, James POLLOCK and James WILKINS are county trustees.

p. 276: William CLINGAN, Thomas BULL, John KINKEAD, Roger KIRK, John SELLERS, John WILSON, Joseph DAVIS were to build a new courthouse and prison for Chester Co. but their duty has not been executed. John HANNUM, Esq., John TAYLOR, Esq., and John JACOBS are appointed commissioners for this purpose.

p. 278: Edith KIDD, late of Phila., wife of Alexander KIDD, late of Phila., merchant, says that Alexander has left her bed and board, frequently beat her and has committed adultry. The marriage is dissolved.

p. 279: Leonard ECKSTINE, Westmoreland Co., farmer, says his wife, Mary, (late Mary SHIPLER) has been unfaithful and has lived in prostitution for several years. The marriage is dissolved.

p. 280: Robert STEWARD, Phila., mariner, says wife, Catharine, late Catharine KINCHLEY, has been unfaithful. The marriage is dissolved.

p. 285: 2nd district, Bedford Co. election district will now vote at George CLUGGAGE's, Shirley Twp., instead of at John BURD's, Dublin Twp. Third district, Westmoreland Co., will vote at William MOORE's, Rostraver Twp. Pitt Twp., Westmoreland Co., will vote at Deveraux SMITH's, Fort Pitt, instead of at Robert HANNA's.

p. 320: Francis GURNEY, John DONALDSON, Samuel CALDWELL, Thomas PRYER, George ORD, Nathaniel FALCONER and John HAZELWOOD are appointed wardens of Phila. Jacob S. HOWELL is appointed collector of duties.

p. 330: John LONG, John MCFADDEN, Daniel DRAIS, Mary CURRIE, and Elizabeth CARNAGHAN are prisoners in the Phila. gaol for debt.

p. 334: Henry EBERLE is a prisoner in the Lancaster Co. gaol for debt.

p. 336: George BRYAN, John EWING, David RITTENHOUSE are commissioners to meet with Virginia commissioners. The meeting will be held 31 Aug., 1779. The Virginia commissioners are James MADDISON and Robert ANDREWS.

p. 345: Trustees of the United Presbyterian Church, Lower Paxton Twp., Lancaster Co.: Jacob AWL, John CAVET, Samuel COCHRAN, Joshua ELDER, John FOSTER, John GILCRIST, John HARRIS, William KERR, Thomas MCARTHUR, Jr., Alexander MCCLURE, John WIGGINS, John WILSON, and Rev. John ELDER.

p. 352: Isaac AUSTIN, Phila., gentleman, petitions that his brother, William AUSTIN, late of Phila., was attainted of high treason.

p. 356: A public road in York Co. is near lands of Robert JONES, Manchester Twp., James WRIGHT and heirs of John WRIGHT, dec., and John HAY.

p. 362: James MAXWELL, James MCCALMONT, Josiah CRAWFORD, David STONER, and John JOHNSON are trustees of Franklin Co.

p. 367: Henry PAWLING, Jr., Jonathan ROBERTS, George SMITH, Robert SHANNON, Henry CUNNARD, Whitpain Twp., Montgomery Co., are to purchase land for a courthouse and prison. Edward DUFFIELD, Enoch EDWARDS, Nathan GIBSON, Joseph FERREE, John HOLMES are to survey county boundaries.

p. 372: Trustees of the public school in Germantown, Phila. Co.: Henry HILL, Esq., Samuel ASHMEAD, Esq., Jacob RUST, Esq., Rev. Albert HELFENSTEIN, Frederick SMITH, John VANDEREN, John BRINGHURST, Joseph FERREE, Christian SNIDER, James HASLET, Samuel MECHLIN, Noah TOWNSEND, Samuel BRINGHURST, George BRINGHURST, Justus FOX, William ASHMEAD, David DESHLER, Dr. Jacob FRELICH, Paul ENGLE, John FRY, Abraham RITTENHOUSE.

p. 376: Marcus HULINGS, Cumberland Co., will build a mill dam near the mouth of SHEERMAN's Ck., Cumberland Co.

p. 381: John SHEARER, Whitpain Twp., Phila. Co., tile maker, lost a deed for property from Charles KRESS. John SHEARER, on 1 Apr., 1763, bought land from Charles KRESS, Whitpain Twp., Phila. Co., adj. land of Bernard SHEARER and George KASNER.

p. 393: Isaac PEARSON, William PARKER, Andrew BANKSON are appointed to divide banks around a meadow in Kingsessing Twp., Phila. Co.

p. 405: Trustees of the Presbyterian congregation of Pequea, Salisbury Twp., Lancaster Co.: Isaac MCCALMONT, Amos SLAYMAKER, James ARMOR, Thomas SLEMONS, Andrew CALDWELL, Robert BYERS, David

JENKINS, Thomas PATTON, Rev. Robert SMITH.

p. 411: Arthur DONALDSON, Phila., shipwright, in 1774, invented a machine called a hippopotamos for cleaning docks.

p. 426: Nathaniel IRWIN, Warrington Twp., Bucks Co., minister of the gospel, says that his wife, Martha, is guilty of adultery. A divorce is granted.

p. 441: William AUSTIN, attainted of high treason, had property on the north side of Mulberry St., Phila. The land is vested in Isaac AUSTIN. An ejectment is instituted by George Adam BAKER against Isaac AUSTIN.

p. 445: Trustees of the Presbyterian Church, Abington Twp., Montgomery Co.: William M. TENNENT, Samuel MCNEAR, William WILSON, Joseph MCCLEAN, Garret WYNKOOP, John MANN, Samuel LEECH, Samuel ERWIN, John COLLOM.

p. 451: Dauphin Co. is erected. Elections for Upper Paxton Twp. will be at Peter HOFFMAN's. John HARRIS' house will hold the elections of Lower Paxton Twp. and West Hanover. Land for a courthouse and prison is to be bought by Jacob AWL, Joshua ELDER, Andrew STEWART, James COWDAN and William BROWN, Paxton.

p. 483: John BIDDLE, George SOLOSSER, Joseph DEAN, John WHARTON are to print bills of credit. John CHALONER, Willliam TURNBULL, George LATTIMER, Reynold KEEN, Andrew TYBOUT, Edward FOX, James COLLINS, Peter BAYNTOR, William SMITH, druggist; Samuel MURDOCH, James BAYARD, Joseph REDMAN, Robert SMITH, merchant; John RHEA, William GRAY, brewer; William TILTON, Francis WADE, Thomas IRVIN, Charles RISK, Andrew PETTIT, James MCCREA, John TAYLOR, Samuel CALDWELL, Stacy HEPBURN and John DUFFIELD are signers of the bills.

p. 496: Baron STEUBEN is entitled to a grant of land equal to a major-general. Lt. Col. TILGHMAN is entitled to a grant of land equal to a Lt. Col.

p. 508: Trustees of the Presbyterian Church, Falling Springs, Franklin Co.: Patrick VANCE, Esq., Benjamin CHAMBERS, Sr., Matthew WILSON, Esq., Josiah CRAWFORD, John BOGGS, Esq., Edward CRAWFORD, Jr., Rev. James LAND, James MOOR.

p. 517: James RUMSEY has discovered a way to navigate large heavy boats up rapid rivers.

p. 535: William CLINGAN, Thomas BULL, John KINKEAD, Roger KIRK, John SELLERS, John WILSON, Joseph DAVIS are to build a new courthouse and prison in Chester Co.

p. 539: Henry WILLIS, Virginia, says his wife, Mary ROSS (they were married in Pa. and are living in Va.), has committed adultery. The marriage is dissolved.

p. 558: Francis GURNEY, John DONALDSON, Samuel CALDWELL, Thomas PRIOR, George ORD, Nathaniel FALCONER and John HAZELWOOD are wardens of the port of Phila. Jacob S. HOWELL is tax collector.

p. 581: Thomas PAINE, Esq., is given £500 for services.

p. 591: Gen. James POTTER is granted 1000 acres in the forks of

LAWS OF PENNSYLVANIA FROM 14 OCT., 1790 TO 20 MAR, 1810
VOLUME 2 - 1781-1790

p. 108: Seven who drew lots of Schuylkill frontage to the center of Phila.: William PENN, Jr., William LOWTHER, Lawrence GROWDON, Philip FORD, Nicholas MOORE, The Society, John MARSH.

p. 109: Early Indian deeds contained the following names: 1682--IDQUAHON, IANNOTTOWE, IDQUOQUEYWON, SAHOPPE, OKONICHON, MERKENKOWON, OREEKTON, NANNAMSY, SHAURWASIGHON, SWANPISSE, NAHOOSEY, TOMACKHICKON, WESKEKITT, TALAWSIS, all Indian Shackamakers. The land began at John WOODS' (called Gray-stones), over against the fall of the Delaware River. On 1 Aug., 1682, Indian owners of land and an island called Socpassineks were: IDQUOQUEYWAN, SWANPISSE, FILERAPPOMOND, ESSEXAMARTHAKE, NANNESHESSHAD, PYSERHAY. On 23 June, 1683, ESSEPENAIKE, swanpees, OKETTARICKON, WESSAPOAK sold land between the Pemmapecka and Neshemineh Creeks. Other sellers were TAMANEN and METAMEQUAN. On 25 June, 1683, WINGEBONE sold land. On 14 July, 1683, ICQUOQUSHAN and SECANE, Indian Shackamakers, sold land. Others selling land on the same date are NENESHICKAN, MALEBORE alias PENDANOUGHHAH, NESHANOCKE, and OSEREREON. 10 Sept., 1683: KEKETAPPAN of OPASISKUNK. 18 Oct., 1683: MACHALOHA (this deed is signed in the presence of many Indians whose names are partly eaten off by mice). 3 June, 1684: MANGHOUGSIN for land upon Pahkehoma (Perkeomink now Perkioming). 7 June, 1684: Richard METTAMICONT. 30 July, 1685: SHAKHOPPOH, SECANE, MALIBORE, TANGORAS. 2 Oct., 1685: PARE, PACKENAH, TAREEKHAN, SICHAIS, PITQUASSIT, TOWIS, ESSEPENAICK, PESKOY, KEKELAPPAN, EOMUS, MACHALOHA, MESHECONGA, WISSAPOWEY, all Indian Kings and Shackamakers. 15 June, 1692: King TAMINENT, King TANGORUS, King SWAMPES, King HICKOQUEON. 13 Jan., 1696: Thomas TONGAN (DUNGAN), afterward Earl of Limerick, Ireland, late Governor of N.Y. DONGAN purchased land from the Susquehanna Indians with a warranty from the Sasquehanna Indians. 5 July, 1697: A deed from Sachem TAMINY, his brother and sons--"TAMINY SATHIMACK, WEHEELAND, my brother, and WEHEQUEEKHON, alias ANDREW, who is to be king after my death, YAQUEEKHON, alias NICHOLAS, and QUENAMOCKQUID, alias CHARLES, my sons. 13 Sept., 1700: WIDAGH and ANDAGGY-JUNKQUAGH, Kings of the Susquehanna Indians. 17 Sept., 1718: SASSOONAH, MEETASHECHAY, GHETTYPENEEMAN, POKEHAIS, AYAMACKAN, OPEKASSET and PEPAWMAMAM. The aged SASSOONAN complained that settlers were encroaching on Indian land in in 1728. 7 Sept., 1732: SASSOONAH, alias ALLUMMAPIS, sachem of the Schuylkill Indians, ELALAPIS, OHOPAMEN, PESQUETOMEN, MAYEMOE, PARTRIDGE, TEPAKOASET, alias JOE. The deed was ratified by LINGAHONA, a Schuylkill Indian. James LOGAN wrote to Thomas WATSON on 20 Nov., 1727. Joseph WHEELER proposes to lay out a warrant on Minissink lands. Joe TAYLOR mentioned Conrad WEISER, an important agent. 25 Aug., 1737: TESHAKOMEN alias TISHEKUNK, and NOOTAMIS alias NUTIMUS, two chiefs of the Delaware Indians. Another Delaware Indian is LAPPAWINZOE. MAYKEERICKKISHO, SAYHOPPY, TAUGHHAUGHSEY are Kings of the Northern Indians on the Delaware. Chief Sachema is MONOCKYKICHAN. A release of 1737 was signed by MANOCKYKICHON, LAPPAWINZOE, TESHACOMIN, NOOTAMIS. CANASSATEGO said that "they saw the Delawares had been an unruly people and were altogether in the wrong; that they had concluded to remove them and oblige them to go over the river Delaware and quit all claim to any lands on this side for the future.

p. 119: Thomas MAGEE is an Indian trader. CANASATAGO, SATAGANACHLY, KANALSHYIACAYON, CANECHWADEERON are Sachems of the

Onotagers. CAYANOCKEA, KANATSANY-AGASHTASS, CARUCHIANACHAQUI are Sachems of the Sinickers. Peter ONTACHSAX and Christian DIARYHOGON are Sachems of the Mohocks. SARISTAGNOAH, WATSHATUHON and ANUCHNAXQUA are Saches of Oneyders. TAWIS TAWIS, KACHNOARAASEHA and TAKACHQUONTAS are Sachems of the Cayiukers. TYLEROX, BALICHWANONACH-SHY are Sachems of the Tuscorrorow. IACHNECHDORUS, SAGOGUCHIATHON, CACHNAORA-KATACK-KE are Sachems of the Shomokens. NUTIMUS and QUALPAGHACH are Sachems of the Delawares. BACHSINOSA is a Sachem of the Shawanes. Richard PETERS is the secretary of the land office in 1750. In 1753, CANASSATEGO was dead.

p. 120: Henry PETERS, Abraham PETERS, BLANDT, Johannes SATFYHOWANO, Johannes KANADAKAYON, Abraham SASTAGHREDOHY are Sachems of the Mohock nation. ANEEGHNAXQUA TARAGHORUS, TOHAGHDAGHGUYSERRY, alias KACHNEGHDACKON are Sachems of the Oneyda nation. OTSINUGHYADA alias BUNT signs deed in behalf of himself and all Sachems of the ONONDAGO nation. SCANURATY, TANNAGHDORUS, TOKAAIYON, KAGHRADODON are Sachems of the Cayuga nation. KAHICHDODON alias GROOTE YOUNGE, TAKEGHSATI, TIYONENKOKARAW are Sachems of the Seneca nation. SUNTRUGHWACKON, SAGOCHSIDODAGON, TOHASHOWANGARUS, ORONTAKAYON alias John NIXON, TISTOAGHTON are Sachems of the Tuscarora nation.

p. 121: Nichai KARAGHIAGDATIE is a Sachem of the Mohock nation. ASSARODUNQUA is a Sachem of the Onondago nation. SAGEHSADON or TAGESHATA is a Sachem of the Seneca nation. Thomas KING alias SAQUHSONYONT is a Sachem of the Oneyda nation. TOKAHOYON is a Sachem of the Cayuga nation. WISHAQUONTAGUSH is a Sachem of the Tuscarora nation.

p. 122: TYANHASARE alias ABRAHAM is a Sachem of the Mohock nation. SENUGHSIS is a Sachem of the Oneydas. CHENUGHIATA is a Sachem of the Onondagos. GAUSTARAX is a Sachem of the Senecas. SEQUARISERA is a Sachem of the Tuscaroras. TAGAAIA is a Sachem of the CAYUGAS.

p. 124: George CROGHAN is the department supervisor of Indian affairs under Sir William JOHNSON on the Ohio. CANASSATEGO spoke at the Treaty of 1749.

p. 126: On the Big Juniata, 25 miles from the mouth, William WHITE owned 1 of 5 log cabins. Others were owned by George CAHOON, HIDDLESTON, GALLOWAY and LYCON. All but LYCON were convicted by magistrates of settling on Indian land. The cabins were burnt. Cabins were also burnt at SHEARMAN's Ck. Also burnt was a cabin of CHARLTON. Andrew MONTOUR is to preserve the lands from being settled on by others.

p. 127: Christopher RUDEBAGH, Westmoreland Co., settled on land in 1761 due to a military permit from Col. BOUQUET. A land dispute case: David SHERER v. Thomas M'FARLAND, Westmoreland Co., 1797. There is a deed from John LOYDICK to William MOUNT dated 11 Jan., 1775. Abraham LEASURE improved lands in 1768-69.

p. 128: A land dispute case: Peter WEISER v. Samuel MOODY: WEISER claimed a patent issued 7 July, 1755 to his grandfather, Conrad WEISER, in consideration for his services as an interpreter to the Six Indian Nations. Nicholas SCULL was the surveyor-general to Samuel WEISER.

p. 129: Land dispute case: Bernard GRATZ v. Patrick CAMPBELL, Westmoreland Co., 1800. The plaintiff claimed a moiety of the land under a special order to David FRANKS of the 1st of April, 1769.

FRANKS' agent was Christopher HAYES. £300 is granted to Reading HOWELL for delineating lines of the state on his map.

p. 131: Land dispute case: Bazil BROWN, Fayette Co., 1795 v. SMITH's Lessee. Samuel HYDE v. William TORRENCE, Washington Co., 1799. An early improvement was made by Thomas PROVENCE in 1767. He sold the land to Aaron JENKINS on 8 May, 1782. He leased it to Joseph ROSS for 150 bu. of corn per year. The tenant improperly permitted Martin HARDEN, son of the defendant's landlord, to come into possession. John HARDEN was lessor. John HUSK applied for 300 acres on the west side of the Monongahela River at the mouth of Big White Lick Ck., 13 June, 1769. Edward ARSKEN is entitled to 400 acres on the Monongahela River at the mouth of Whitely Ck., 9 Feb., 1780. Land dispute case: Thomas JONES v. James PARK and Benjamin KINSOLE, Allegheny Co., May, 1799. Zadock WRIGHT, on 18 Feb., 1783, said he was entitled to 400 acres at the mouth of Montour Run in Youghogheny Co. In 1772, WRIGHT settled a tract at the mouth of Montour's Run which was different from the land in question. John WESTFALL settled another tract 3/4 of a mile above the mouth and Abel WESTFALL, a tract below it's mouth. The title of WRIGHT's land is since vested in Jeremiah WRIGHT. Land dispute case: Thomas LILLY v. George KITZMILLER, York, May, 1791. Warrant was made to Martin KITZMILLER for 150 acres on 5 Feb., 1747.

p. 143: Edward PENNINGTON, 2nd surveyor-general of Pa., died 10 Jan., 1701.

p. 144: On 6 & 7 Oct., 1708, the proprietor mortgaged the province to Henry GOULDNEY, Joshua GEE, Sylvanus GROVE, John WOODS, Thomas CALLOWHILL, Thomas OADE and Jeffery PINNEL. Surveyors-general for Pa.: Jacob TAYLOR (Mar, 1706-07), Benjamin EASTBURNE (29 Oct., 1733), William PARSONS (22 Aug., 1741), Nicholas SCULL (1748), John LUKENS (Dec., 1761--he died in 1789), Daniel BRODHEAD (3 Nov., 1789), Samuel COCHRAN (23 Apr., 1800), Andrew PORTER (4 Apr., 1809).

p. 146: Samuel BLUNSTON was issued a commission 11 Jan., 1733, to grant licenses to settle on the west side of the Susquehanna River. William WILLIS was to have 500 acres at Conestogoe on 3 Feb., 1719.

p. 158: Thomas CROYLE had an ancient settlement near the head of Snake Spring Ck., begun in 1754 and held until Dec., 1788. In June, 1762, he sent his son with money to get a warrant for 300 acres. He was only allowed to take 100 acres on 10 June, 1762, adj. to George CROGHAN. On 3 Aug., 1767, Thomas CROYLE applied for 200 acres adj. his warranteed land in CROYLE's Valley, on the east side of Rays-town branch of the Juniata. On 14 Apr., 1774, CROYLE executed a deed to Robert ELLIOTT. CROYLE had an actual personal residence settlement at the head of the Spring though he had a shed and some cleared land at the mouth.

p. 165: Jacob MILLISON, father of John MILLISON, on 4 Dec., 1784, obtained two warrants for 300 acres each in Westmoreland Co., one in his name and one in the name of his son, Philip.

p. 174: Matthew KARR made a small improvement on a plantation in Washington Co. in 1768. Next year, Joseph PROCTOR settled near him. KARR sold his improvement to Charles BURKHAM.

p. 176: Names in land cases: James CALDWELL, Richard TEA, Robert OWINGS, Robert ADAMS, Jr., Thomas STURGEON, Alexander WAUGH, Hugh NEILLY, Benjamin M'CORMICK, Richard CARROL, Robert ANDREWS, Samuel

PARKHURST, Stephen CARTER, Thaddeus DODD, David REDDICK, Daniel M'FARLAND, Lawrence CRAFT, John HOGE, John NICHOLLS, William LAFFERTY, William HARVEY, William M'MURRAY, Gotliep REIGART, Conrad HAVERSTOCK, Christiana SAMUEL, william M'MANIMY, William HARVEY, John HOLMES, Thomas KAY, Frederick PIGOU, Nicholas NEVILL, James GRAHAM, Ludwig KARCHER, Conrad SHARPE, Bartram GALBREATH, Philip MAUS, Thomas GRANT, Daniel EDDY, Ephraim BLAINE, George CRAWFORD, Henry FORE, James BYERS, Jr., Alexander ROSS, James MCKEE, Capt. Charles EDMONSTONE, Henry DRINKER, William HOLLIDAY, John EWING, Daniel BARTON, Nathaniel BREDEN, William ROSS, John GALLOWAY, William SCULL, William MCCORD, Daniel GRIPE, Rev. David BAIRD, John IRWIN, Andrew MOORE, James IRWIN, Casper GEYER, Jesse FUNSTON, John M'MAHON, William BELL, Robert LEVERS, Abraham M'KINNEY, Jacob HOUSER, Reuben HAINES.

p. 196: John HUGHES, Henry DOUGHERTY, James HUGHES (brother of John), Northumberland Co. In 1773, James HUGHES settled on the land in question. The next year, he built a house of logs. The following winter, he went to his father's in Donegal, Lancaster Co. and died there. His eldest brother, Thomas, was settled on Indian land. In 1778, Henry DOUGHERTY joined the army.

p. 201: Alexander WRIGHT, Benjamin WELLS, Pressly NEVIL, Matthew RITCHIE were involved in a land dispute. This case concerned land called "Danger" situated on Raccoon Ck.

p. 206: Lewis BOND, Robert FITZRANDOLPH, Cornelius VANHORNE, and a man called LICQUERS who married an Indian woman were involved in a land dispute. The land in question was on French Ck. In 1789, Cornelius VANHORNE erected a cabin of logs on the land. The lessor of the plaintiff, in 1792, was an officer of the army under Gen. WAYNE.

p. 207: A case was called the Lessee of Benoni DAWSON v. William LAUGHLIN, Allegheny.

p. 208: Cases: Lessee of Alexander WRIGHT v. Benjamin WELLS, Washington, May, 1793. Lessee of James HEPBURN v. William HUTCHINSON, Northumberland, Oct., 1798. Lessee of Samuel EWALT v. Martha HIGHLANDS. EWALT claimed 400 acres of land across the Allegheny at GIRTY's run. Jonathan LEET surveyed the land on 9 Apr., 1794. On 10 Feb., 1796, EWALT leased it to Peter SMITH, who came over the river, kindled a fire in the cabin, staid there an hour, and then removed.

p. 209: Case: Neal M'GLAUGHLIN v. Nicholas DAWSON. The plaintiff, on 4 Apr., 1792, crossed the Ohio, grubbed a small piece of ground near a cabin which had been erected by LINK, in 1790. Only M'GLAUGHLIN and Charles PHILIPS were known to have resided on the NW side of the Ohio, with the intention of making settlements, in 1792. During the year, Nicholas DAWSON lived with his brother, Benoni DAWSON, at the mouth of Mill Ck., about 4 miles from the land in dispute. Nicholas and George CLARK were seen together in the blockhouse and Daniel SWERINGEN demanded a survey be made.

p. 211: Cases: The Lessee of James SCOTT v. William ANDERSON. The Lessee of Robert MORRIS v. William NEIGHMAN, Allegheny, May, 1799. Lessee of Robert MORRIS v. Adam SHEINER. Jacob RUDOLPH was a tenant who had accepted a lease under MORRIS.

p. 213:   Lessee of GAZARD v. LOWREY. Warrant of 13 Apr., 1792 for 400 acres adj. land of Walter STEWART.

p. 224:   Cases: Lessee of Thomas BUCHANAN v. Adam MEYER, Westmoreland Co., Nov., 1803. This was an ejectment for land in Buffalo Twp., Armstrong Co.

p. 230:   In 1793, George BALFOUR was a surgeon in the army, in garrison at Fort Franklin. In Apr., 1795, he had five tracts of land surveyed in the name of himself, Elizabeth BALFOUR & three others. One WILSON was directed to make the surveys. He couldn't & one STEEL was employed to do it. The deputy-surveyor was STOKELY.

p. 233:   Case: Alexander WRIGHT vs. Brice M'GEHAN, Allegheny, Nov., 1801. There was a warrant dated 14 Apr., 1792 to Michael SHUBERT for 400 acres north & west of Ohio, adj. land granted to Marshal SPRING, & a survey of 400 acres made 13 Mar., 1795 to John POWER. The leading warrant was issued in the name of Matthew M'CONNELL for 400 acres extending along big Beaver Ck., near the falls. James CAROTHERS was deputy-surveyor of the district on 10 June, 1793.

p. 234:   Case: Lessee of William CLEMMINS v. Philip GOTTSHALL & Robert JOHNSTON, Venango, Oct., 1806. David MEADE, William JOHNSTON, Philip GOTTSHALL, William CLEMMINS & Robert JOHNSTON entered into a written agreement with CUSSEWAGO on 26 Dec., 1794. They erected their cabins in the Spring of 1795 but deserted the land on hearing of the murder of two of the inhabitants by the Indians in June, 1795 at the mouth of little Coneaut Ck. CLEMMINS, at the close of the same summer, came out & did some work but returned to Westmoreland Co. in the Fall. In 1795, he sold his interest in 3 tracts to one PATTERSON. CLEMMINS married in Apr., 1796. He improperly obtained possession of a tract of land above Meadville claimed by one MAGOFFIN but quitted the same & sold to John DAVIS. He later stopped at the claim of Richard VANSICKEL, known as WENTWORTH's tract, & seized possession of it. In late 1796 or early 1797, his wife was pregnant. In Mar. or Apr., 1797, the cabin he claimed was consumed by fire. The following June, CLEMMINS, his wife, their two month old infant & his wife's father went back to the land where the cabin had been. Robert JOHNSTON sold his land to Thomas RUSSEL who afterwards sold to GOTTSHALL. Samuel DALE was the deputy-surveyor.

p. 240:   Case: George MOORE v. John MUNDORFF. Ejectment was for a small island in the Susquehanna River. On 8 June, 1797, MOORE made a second application for the island & on 24 Aug., 1802, John MUNDORFF, in behalf of himself & other heirs of George MUNDORFF, claimed an improvement was made ten years before.

p. 243:   Case: Lessee of David MEADE v. Frederick HAYMAKER & Luke STEPHENS, Allegheny, Oct., 1800. Land was surveyed on a warrant for Henry MEADE, 17 Mar., 1796, for 400 acres between the outlet of little Coneaut Lake & Sandy Ck. STEVENS, the other defendant, had a family on the west branch of the Susquehanna under the care of Jesse GLANCEY, his step-son.

p. 246:   Lessee of John WILKINS, Jr. vs. John ALLENTON, Allegheny, Nov., 1801. Plaintiff claimed 400 acres north & west on French Ck., adj. a survey for one BAUM & including the claim formerly of John WENTWORTH. A survey of 373 acres was made by J. POWERS.

p. 249:   William GREGG & John GREGG, two brothers, seated themselves down on French Ck. in the summer of 1789. William was killed by Indians on his land in the Spring of 1791. One HAYMAKER married GREGG's widow. William M'ADAMS is the guardian of her minor children.

p. 249: An act was passed for the relief of Peter WIKOFF, Jonathan Bayard SMITH & others.

p. 255: Lessee of Henry DRINKER v. William HOLLIDAY, Jr., Huntingdon, May, 1796. Lessee of Robert PORTER v. James FERGUSON & Abraham FEAGLY in ejectment for 139 acres on Mingo Ck. Under an entry made by Francis HULL of 400 acres on the Monongahela River, with the Va. commissioners on 13 Nov., 1779, on which a survey was made by NEVIL & RITCHIE. Another survey was made by Thomas STOKELY.

p. 256: Cases: Lessee of Henry DRINKER v. Samuel HUNTER, Northumberland, Oct., 1796. Lessee of DAVIS v. BUTTERBACK, Franklin, Apr., 1797. Lessee of SHIELDS v. BUCHANNAN, Westmoreland, May, 1797. Lessee of FUNSTON v. M'MAHON, Northumberland, Oct., 1797. Lessee of John YODER v. William FLEMMING, Mifflin, May, 1798. Lessee of John WALKER vs. Jacob FURRY & Michael KREHL, Carlisle, 26 Nov., 1790. DAWSON' Lessee v. LAUGHLIN, Allegheny, May, 1799. Lessee of NICHOLAS & others v. HOLLIDAY, Huntingdon, May, 1802. Plaintiff claimed a warrant to Edward NICHOLAS made 25 May, 1765. Samuel FINLAY, who acted under Richard TEA, the surveyor, was the surveyor for this warrant.

p. 257: Cases: BIDDLE'S Lessee v. DOUGAL. EVANS v. NARGONG. ADDLEMAN v. WAY, Huntingdon, May, 1805. M'KINZIE v. CROW. NESBIT's Lessee v. TITUS, Huntingdon, May, 1793. John HUBLEY & others v. Benjamin CHEW, Northumberland, Oct., 1796. Plaintiff claimed under 18 different warrants, dated 16 Aug., 1773 to Bernard HUBLEY & others. Jessee LUKENS began a survey on 7 Sept., 1773. Surveys completed in Apr., 1777 by Joseph WALLIS, under Charles LUKENS, deputy-surveyor.

p. 265: Trustees for Franklin Co.: James MAXWELL, James M'CALMONT, Josiah CRAWFORD, David STONER, John JOHNSTON.

p. 267: Elections for Montgomery Co. will be at Hannah THOMSON's, innkeeper, Norriton Twp. Commissioners to purchase land for county buildings: Henry PAWLING, Jr., Jonathan ROBERTS, George SMITH, Robert SHANNON, Henry CUNNARD, Whitpain Twp.

p. 270: Marcus HULINGS is to erect a dam near SHEARMAN's Ck., Cumberland Co.

p. 285, 1785: Elections for Dauphin Co. for Upper Paxton Twp., on the North side of Peter's Mountain, will be held at Peter HOFFMAN's. For Lower Paxton Twp., on the South side of Peter's Mountain, they will be held at John HARRIS' till the courthouse is built. Jacob AWL, Joshua ELDER, Andrew STEWART, James COWDEN & William BROWN, Paxton, are trustees to take assurance of a lot for county buildings.

p. 291: Baron STEUBEN, late Inspector General of the American Army, is to receive donation lands equal to a Maj. Gen. Lt. Col. TILGHMAN is entitled to lands equal to a Lt. Col.

p. 299: Thomas GRANT's brother, an officer, was killed in the service of the U.S. during the war & died unmarried.

p. 301: Land record names: Samuel SIMPSON, Christian MILLER, Samuel MILES, Henry FUNK, Hugh NEILLY, Benjamin M'CORMICK, Ephraim WALLACE, Thomas DICKEY, William DICKEY, Joseph IRWIN, David DICKEY, John MOORE, George HENRY, Robert WHITE, James & John CAROTHERS, William CAROTHERS, William LYON, William HARKNESS, Samuel LYON, John DAVISON, John COCHRAN, Samuel MOBLEY, Denton MOBLEY, William MOBLEY, Robert CUNNINGHAM & wife, Margaret; Susanna MOBLEY, Christian OCKER, Clover Ck., Woodburry Twp., Huntingdon. Samuel, Denton, William MOBLEY, Margaret CUNNINGHAM & Susanna MOBLEY were children of Ezekiel MOBLEY. Ezekiel settled on his land in 1774 or 1775. Michael CRYDER was a neighbor. Settlers were driven off by Indians in 1777. MOBLEY went to Md. & died. His widow returned in 1785 with her five children (the eldest was 15, the youngest was 2) & was assisted by her brother, William PHILIPS. PHILIPS took out warrants in the name of Susanna MOBLEY.
Joshua CLARK v. George HACKETHORN. James BRICE v. Richard CURRAN, Mifflin, May, 1802. Plaintiff claimed under a warrant to John BROWN, 5 Apr., 1788, 50 acres.

p. 332: Charles BESSONET, Bristol borough, Bucks Co., & Gershom JOHNSON, Phila., were proprietors of stages from Phila. to Trenton. They are to make a public road from Phila. to Bristol & then to Joshua VANDEGRIFT's land through William ALLEN's land, John EDGAR's land & Joseph TOMLINSON's.

p. 334: Election districts: Part of Bucks Co. will vote at Abraham KEICHLEIN's, inn-keeper. Part of Chester Co. will vote at the sign of the Pa. Arms at John CULBERTSON's, Esq., E. Caln Twp. Part of Lancaster Co. at Col. James PORTER's, Dromore Twp. Donegal, Mountjoy, Rapho, Hempfield, Elizabeth, & Warwick Twps., Lancaster Co., will vote at Capt. Hugh PEDEN's, Rapho Twp. Salisbury, Earl, Caernarvon, Brecknock, Cocolico & Leacock Twp., Lancaster Co., will vote at Thomas HENDERSON's, Newholland, Earl Twp. Part of York Co. will vote at Samuel GETTIS'. Fawn, Hopewell, Chanceford Twp., York Co., will vote at TURNER's mill, Chanceford Twp. Newberry, Warrington, Monahan, Huntingdon, Reading Twps., York Co., will vote at Robert STEVENSON's. Rye, Tyrone, Teboyn Twps., Cumberland Co., will vote at William M'CLURE's, Tyrone Twp. Greenwood, Fermanagh, Leek, Milford Twp., Cumberland Co., will vote at Thomas WILSON's, Milford Twp. Derry, Armagh, Wayne Twps., Cumberland Co., will vote at Arthur BUCHANAN'S., Derry Twp. Allen, Moore, Chesnut-Hill, Towamensing, Penn & Lehigh Twps., Northampton Co., will vote at Peter ANTHONY's Lehigh. Hamilton, Lower Smithfield, Delaware, Upper Smithfield Twps., Northampton Co., will vote at Nicholas DEPUI's, Lower Smithfield Twp. Bethel & Air Twps., Bedford Co., will vote at Ephraim WALLACE's, Bethel Twp. Brothers Valley, Quesmahoning, Turkey Foot, Wilford Twps., Bedford Co., will vote at James BLACK's, Quesmahoning. Dublin, Shirely Twps., Bedford Co., will vote at George CLUGGAGE's, Shirley Twp. Buffaloe, White Deer, Potter Twps., Northumberland Co., will vote at GREEN's mill (formerly FOUTZ's), Buffaloe. Munsey, Bald Eagle Twps., Northumberland Co., will vote at Amariah SUTTON's, Munsey. Kiskiminitas Twp. & Connemach River (those living on the north side), Westmoreland Co., are to vote at Samuel DICKSON's. Those bounded by Laurel Hill, Connemach, Chesnut Ridge & the Fayette Co. line will vote at William JAMESON's. Huntingdon & Rastrover Twp., Westmoreland Co., will vote at William MOORE's, Rastrover Twp. Fort Pitt Twp., Westmoreland Co., will vote at Devereux SMITH's, Fort Pitt. Fannet Twp., Franklin Co. will vote at Widow ELLIOT's. Part of Montgomery Co. will vote at George ECKART's tavern, Whitemarsh. Limerick, New Hanover, Douglass, Upper

Hanover, Marlborough, Upper Salford Twp., Montgomery Co., will vote at Michael KREPSE's tavern, New Hanover. Heidelberg, Lebanon, Bethel & E. Hanover Twps., Dauphin Co., will vote at Anthony KECHLER's, Lebanon-town. Derry, Londonderry, W. Hanover Twps., Dauphin Co., will vote at Peter FRIEDLEY's, Hummel's town, Derry Twp. Upper Pextang, the north side of Peter's Mountain, will vote at Peter HOFFMAN's, Upper Pextang.

p. 239: Benjamin DAVIS, Michael ROUGH, John SHIELDS, John POMROY & Hugh MARTIN, Westmoreland Co., are to be trustees to purchase land for a courthouse & prison.

p. 343: Jacob BAUSMAN is to erect a ferry from the southwest side of the Monongahela River opposite Pittsburg.

p. 353: A rent of 30 bushels of wheat is payable to trustees of the University of Pa. on land situated in Northern Liberties Twp., Phila. Co., bounded by Henry NAGLE, & TURNER's Lane. It was granted to John DUNLAP, Thomas LAWRENCE, James BUDDEN by deed on 1 Aug., 1780, late the estate of Joseph GRISWOLD.
 Rent of 12 11/12 bu. payable to trustees on land situated in the Manor of Moreland, Phila. Co., bounded by John BUTCHER, Jonathan COMLEY, Joseph MICHEL, Casper FETTER, granted to Charles WALKER 31 July, 1780, late the estate of Joseph CROMLEY.
 Rent of 20 bu. on a lot divided from a lot late of John PARROCK (now granted to Peter PARRIS) granted to Christian WERTZ, John SCHAFFER, Jacob GEIGER on 19 Aug., 1780, late the estate of John PARROCK.
 Rent of 22 bu. on a building bounded by Edward BROOKS, Jonathan RICHARDS, granted to Francis LEE 26 Nov., 1780, late the estate of George KNAPPER.
 Rent of 135 4/5 bu. on land in Lower Merion Twp.: Two tracts, one bounded by Margaret JONES, William LEWIS, Owen JONES, Benjamin HUMPHREYS, Conrad SCHITZ, John ROBINSON, John RIGHTER. The other bounded by Owen JONES, William LEWIS. Granted to Edward MILNER 16 Dec., 1780, late the estate of John ROBERTS.
 Rent of 2 9/20 bu. on land bounded by John PETERS, granted to William COATS, Esq., 31 Jan., 1781, late the estate of Samuel SHOEMAKER.
 Rent of 13 ½ bu. on land in Northern Liberties bounded by Henry CISS, late the land of Isaac NORRIS, Thomas BOND. Granted to James BUDDEN, John DUNLAP, Thomas LAWRENCE, late the estate of Joseph GRISWOLD.
 Rent of 7 ½ bu. for land in Blockley Twp., bounded by Daniel HIBBARD, Thomas PASCHALL. Granted to James BUDDEN, John DUNLAP, Thomas LAWRENCE 4 Feb., 1780, late the estate of Joel EVANS.
 Rent of 24 ½ bu. for land bounded by Selwood GRIFFIN, granted to Joseph DEANE 31 Jan., 1781, late the estate of John HENDERSON.
 Rent of 10 1/5 bu. in the Manor of Moreland, bounded by Richard MAPLE, Derrick KREWSON, William TILLIER, William ROBERTS, granted to George BENNER 4 Feb., 1781, late the estate of John LOUGHBOROUGH.
 Rent of 5 7/10 bu. for land in Hatfield Twp. bounded by land of ---- BUCHAMER, Martin WIREMAN, Thomas DAVIS, Abijah WRIGHT, Thomas STILTFORD, granted to Joseph DEANE 31 Jan., 1781, late the estate of Jonathan WRIGHT.
 Rent of 7 4/10 bu. for land in Blockley Twp., bounded by Widow PETERS, ---- GEORGE, John PENN, Esq., granted to Joseph DEANE, 31 Jan., 1781, late the estate of John BUTCHER.
 Rent of 5 11/20 bu. for land in Germantown, bounded by

Peter BOCHIUS & Melchoir MENG, granted to Joseph DEANE 31 Jan., 1781, late the estate of Holton JONES.

Rent of 8 3/40 bu. granted to Jonas PHILIPS 15 Mar., 1781, late the estate of John PARROCK.

Rent of 54 bu. for two lots in Oxford Twp. One bounded by Robert HARPER & William ASHBRIDGE. The other bounded by Thomas PEARL, granted to John EVE 21 Mar., 1781, late the estate of Oswell EVE.

Rent of 2 11/20 bu. for land in Hatfield Twp. bounded by Melchior YEDER, Thomas STILTFORD, Abijah WRIGHT, John YEGLESS, granted to Owen FARIES 21 Mar., 1781, late the estate of John WRIGHT.

Rent of 3 1/20 bu. for land in the Manor of Moreland, bounded by Albertson WALTON, John BLACKFORD, Detrick KREWSON, William TYLLIER, granted to James VANSANT 21 Mar., 1781, late the estate of John BURKE.

Rent of 10 bu. for land bounded by Edward STILES, William RUSH, granted to Robert BETHELL 20 Dec., 1780, late the estate of Abraham CARLISLE.

Rent of 3 bu. for land in Roxborough Twp., bounded by Samuel POWELL, Daniel CLYMER, Christian VANLASHETS, granted to Benjamin HARBESON 4 Feb., 1781, late the estate of Christopher SOUR.

Rent of 2 1/20 bu. for land bounded by Alexander ADAMS, John SMITH, Anthony DUCHE, granted to Charles ALEXANDER 28 Feb., 1781, late the estate of William RHODDEN.

Rent of 55 ½ bu. for land bounded by land late of John PARROCK, now of Jacob BUNNER, granted to James PARR, 7 June, 1781, late the estate of John PARROCK.

Rent of 16 8/10 bu. for land bounded by Jacob BUNNER, Joseph WARNER, granted to Michael SIMPSON 14 June, 1781, late the estate of John PARROCK.

Rent of 22 8/10 bu. for land bounded by James SKINNER, James ROWAN, granted to Alexander POWERS 30 June, 1781, late the estate of John FOX.

Rent of 6 bu. for land bounded by Isaiah BELL, John GIBSON, granted to Benjamin HARBESON 3 Feb., 1781, late the estate of Isaac ALLEN.

Rent of 39 3/20 bu. for land granted to John WEIDMAN 10 July, 1781, late the estate of John PARROCK.

Rent of 11 9/11 bu. for land in Heidelberg Twp., Berks Co., for land bounded by Adam WEGERLY, Jacob STALEY, George LOUSH, granted to John PLEIN 21 July, 1781, late the estate of Andrew ALLEN.

Rent of 18 ½ bu. for land in Abingdon Twp., Phila. Co., one lot bounded by Thomas TYSON, the other bounded by William HASKINS, granted to Henry DOTTS in the right of Philip MOORE 27 June last, late the estate of Joshua KNIGHT.

Rent of 6 6/10 bu. for land bounded by ground late of John PARROCK & since granted to Christian WIRTZ. Granted to Peter PARIS 12 May, 1780, late the estate of John PARROCK.

Rent of 12 2/10 bu. for land adj. land late of Samuel SHOEMAKER, granted to James HUTCHINSON 23 July, 1781, late the estate of Joseph GALLOWAY.

Rent of 32 7/10 bu. for land granted to Jacob BUNNER 1 Aug., 1781, late the estate of John PARROCK.

Rent of 232 ½ bu. for land granted to Hon. Thomas M'KEAN, Esq., 9 Aug., 1781, late the estate of Jacob DUCHE, the younger.

Rent of 82 19/20 bu. for land granted to William POWERS 15 Aug., 1781, late the estate of David JONES.

Rent of 3 bu. for land in Moyamensing Twp., Phila. Co., bounded by Plunket FLEESON & John HALL, granted to Joseph CARSON 1

Sept., 1781, late the estate of Peter CAMPBELL.
Rent of 9 bu. for land in New Garden Twp., Chester Co., bounded by ---- SCARLET, Isaac RICHARDS, ----- KNIGHT, granted to James PARR 31 Aug., 1781, late the estate of Stephen ANDERSON.
Rent of 2 2/15 bu. for land in E. Marlborough Twp., bounded by John JACKSON, Sr., & William BAILEY, granted to James PARR 31 Aug., 1781, late the estate of John JACKSON.
Rent of 2 103/240 bu. for land in E. Marlborough Twp., bounded by Jonathan JACKSON, Samuel HAYES, George JACKSON, granted to James PARR 31 Aug., 1781, late the estate of Stephen ANDERSON.
Rent of 13 15/40 bu. for land in E. Caln Twp., Chester Co., bounded by John PIERCE, Joseph PARKE, Thomas BABLE, William DAWSON, granted to James HUTCHINSON 31 Aug., 1781, late the estate of Philip MARCHINTON.
Rent of 163 19/120 bu. for land in Heidelberg Twp., Berks Co., bounded by -----HAINES, Matthias WENRICK, Baltzer WENRICK. Granted to John CHRISTIE, 1 Sept., 1781, late the estate of Andrew ALLEN.
Rent of 117 79/240 bu. for land in Heidelberg Twp., Berks Co. bounded by land late of Andrew ALLEN, John HAINES, Isaac COPELAND, Adam SHOWERS, granted to John CRAIG 1 Sept., 1781, late the estate of Andrew ALLEN.
Rent of 18 bu. for land in W. Caln Twp., Chester Co., bounded by Thomas ROGERS, Samuel LOVE, William DUNN, Francis FINCHER, granted to Francis JOHNSON, 31 Aug., 1781, late the estate of Richard SWANWICK.
Rent of 2 1/4 bu. in West. Bradford, Chester Co., bounded by James CHALFANT, ---- EASTBURN, Thomas BUFFINGTON, granted to James PARR, 6 Oct., 1781, late the estate of Philip MARCHINTON.
Rent of 4 ½ bu. for land granted to Benjamin EVANS 26 Oct., 1781, late the estate of William EVANS.
Rent of 1 7/10 bu. for land bounded by Edward STILES, Andrew DUCHE, in Southwark, granted to Patrick ROBINSON, 15 Dec., 1781, late the estate of John TOLLY.
Rent of 45 9/20 bu. for land adj. John WEIDMAN, granted to David ZEIGLER 10 Jan., 1782, late the estate of John PARROCK.
Rent of 1 1/5 bu. for land in Lebanon, Lancaster Co., adj. Philip MARSTELLER, granted to William BAILEY, 19 Feb., 1782, late the estate of Nicholas HOUSECKER.
Rent of 9 4/5 bu. for land in Hilltown Twp., Bucks Co., bounded by Henry RICE, Amos VASTINE, William THOMAS, Charles LEIDIG, Levy THOMAS, granted to George BENNER 23 Feb., 1782, late the estate of Evan THOMAS.
Rent of 36 bu. for land in Tinicum Twp., Bucks Co., bounded by John PATTERSON, Edward PENNINGTON, William SHOEMAKER, Michael WALTER, John REED, granted to Jacob BENNER 23 Feb., 1782, late the estate of Jacob OVERHOLTZ.
Rent of 5 8/10 bu. for land in Abington Twp., bounded by Abraham TYSON, granted to William DEANE 30 Oct., 1781, late the estate of Joshua KNIGHT.
Rent of 87 ½ bu. for land on Hog Island in the Delaware River granted to Samuel CALDWELL, 9 May, 1782, late the estate of Joseph GALLOWAY.
Rent of 23 4/30 bu. for land in Heidelberg Twp., Berks Co., granted to Jacob STEHELY, 15 June, 1782, late the estate of Andrew ALLEN.
Rent of 5 19/20 bu. for land in Northern Liberties Twp., Phila. Co., granted to James CALDWELL 15 June, 1782, late the estate of John PARROCK.

Rent of 21 9/20 bu. for land in Whitpaine Twp., Phila. Co.,

granted to Edmund MILNE, 15 June, 1782, late the estate of John ROBINSON.
Rent of 20 76/120 bu. for land in Heidelberg Twp., Berks Co., granted to Peter FILBERT 15 Aug., 1782, late the estate of Andrew ALLEN.
Rent of 17 1/5 bu. for land in Heidelberg Twp., Berks Co., granted to Peter NAGLE, 15 Aug., 1782, late the estate of Andrew ALLEN.
Rent of 11 11/12 bu. for land in Brunswick Twp., Berks Co., bounded by Jacob HOFFMAN, Matthias KRAEMER, Jacob KENGETH, granted to Charles GOBLIN 25 July, 1782, late the estate of John KOSTER.
A lot, messuage & ferry wharf, late the estate of William AUSTIN.
A lot, messuage, adj. to Rudolph BUNNER, John ELLICK, rent of £4 18s 6p, late the estate of Jonathan ADAMS & wife.
A lot, house & wharf, subject to rent of £9 10s, late the estate of Matthias ASPDEN.
A tract in Middletown Twp., Bucks Co., bounded by the land late of William PAXTON, Joshua RICHARDSON, Garret VANSANT, Joseph KNIGHT, late the estate of Joseph PAXTON.
A lot & messuage, late the estate of Hudson BURR.
A lot & messuage, late the estate of Robert LOOSLEY, £2 rent.
A lot & smith's shop, late the estate of Alexander SMITH, £8, 12s, 6p rent.
A lot late in the tenure of William WESTON, bounded by John COXE & land late of Charles NORRIS, late the estate of Andrew ALLEN.
A lot & messuage, late the estate of Joel EVANS.
A lot & messuage, late the estate of William ROSS, 30s rent.
A lot & messuage late in the tenure of John JACKSON, dec., bounded by land late of Thomas MONTGOMERY, land late of Joseph FOX, late the estate of Andrew ELLIOT, £4 rent.
A lot & messuage in Northern Liberties, late the estate of Lawrence FAGAN.
A lot & messuage in Northern Liberties, bounded by Samuel GARRIGUES, Thomas RICHE, John MORGAN, late the estate of Oswell EVE.
A tract in Abington Twp., bounded by Joshua KNIGHT, Ryner TYSON, Isaac KNIGHT, Sr., Jacob LIPPENCOTT, late the estate of John KNIGHT.
Land in Whitpaine Twp., adj. James MORRIS & John ROBERTS, late the estate of Isaac TAYLOR.
Land in Germantown, adj. John BRINGHURST, Dr. WARNER, late the estate of Abraham PASTORIUS.
30s payable by Joseph JOHNSON for a lot & messuage, late the estate of Samuel SHOEMAKER.
£2 per year payable to John DRINKER for a lot & messuage late the estate of Samuel SHOEMAKER.
30s payable by Philip SYNG for a lot & messuage late the estate of Samuel SHOEMAKER.
£7 10s payable by Frederick SHINKLE for a lot & messuage late the estate of Samuel SHOEMAKER.
£2 payable by Elizabeth HARMAN for a lot & messuage late the estate of Samuel SHOEMAKER.
£2 payable by Richard PARKER for a lot & messuage late the estate of Samuel SHOEMAKER.
£17 for a lot & messuage late the estate of John PARROCK.
£10 for land late in the tenure of William NILES, late the estate of John PARROCK.
£2 14s for land late in the tenure of Edward BROOKS, late the estate of John PARROCK.

62

£7 10s for land late in the tenure of William SALSBURY, late the estate of John PARROCK.
£4 for land late in the tenure of Michael DAWSON, late the estate of John PARROCK.
£3 6s for land late in the tenure of George HERGER, late the estate of John PARROCK.
£3 10s for land late in the tenure of Adolph GILMAN, late the estate of John PARROCK.
£3 10s for land late in the tenure of Frederick MAUSE, late the estate of John PARROCK.
£3 2s for land late in the tenure of Charles MEREDITH, late the estate of John PARROCK.
£6 for land late in the tenure of Jacob BROWN, late the estate of John PARROCK.

p. 383, 1786: Election districts: Some twps. of Phila. Co. will vote at John BARNESLY's, Bustletown, Lower Dublin Twp. Part of Chester Co. will vote at Mary WITHY's, Chester Twp. Part of Lancaster Co. will vote at Col. James PORTER's, Drumore Twp. Another part of Lancaster Co. will vote at Michael NICHOLAS', Cross Road, Donegal Twp. Carnarvon, Brecknock, Earl, Leacock, Salsbury Twps., Lancaster Co. will vote at Thomas HENDERSON's, New Holland. The 2nd district, Bedford Co. will vote at William KERNEY's. Frankstown, Morrison's Cove Twp., will vote at Lazarus LOWREY's, Frankstown. Potter's Twp., Northumberland Co., will vote at George M'CORMICK's, Penns Valley, Potter's Twp. The 4th district of Dauphin Co. will vote at KLEINE's mill. East Hanover & Bethel Twps., Dauphin Co. will vote at Matthias HENING's, Williamsburg, Bethel Twp.

p. 387: Zebulon BUTLER, Nathaniel LANDEN, Jonah ROGERS, John PHILIPS & Simon SPAWLDING are trustees to purchase land for a courthouse & prison for Luzerne Co.

p. 389: George WALL, John OKELY, Jonas HARTZEL are commissioners for Pa. Moore FURMAN, Esq., is a commissioner for N.J. They are appointed to distinguish several islands: BIRD's Island, SLACK's three islands, DUN's Island, HARVEY's lower island, HARVEY's upper island, LOWNES's Island, SMITH's Island & bar, PAXTON's Island & bar, PRALL's two islands, WALL's Island, Resolution Island, MARSHALL's Island, LAUGHLY's Island, Pohatcung Island, SHOEMAKER's Island, LOOR's Island, Easton Island, MASON's Island, Foul Rift Island, M'ILHENNEY's Island, ATTIN's tow islands, HANDIE's Island, GOODWIN's two islands, SHAWANAUGH's Island, VANCAMPEN's Island, Nicholas DEPUI's Island, CHAMBERS' Island, VANOKEN's Island, SWARTSWOOD's Island, Isaac VANCAMPEN's Island, PUNKEY's Island.

p. 412: 1787: Election districts--Fannet Twp., Franklin Co. will vote at Widow ELLIOT's. Antrim & Washington Twps., Franklin Co., will vote at George CLARK's, Greencastle. Peters & Montgomery Twps., Franklin Co. will vote at James CRAWFORD's, Mercersburgh. Tyrone Twp., Bedford Co., will vote at David LOWREY's. Greenwood & Rye Twps., Cumberland Co. will vote at David ENGLISH's, ENGLISH's Mill, Rye Twp.

p. 416: From 10 mile Creek to the head of David GRAY's branch at Jacob CLINE's on Muddy Ck. will be an election district for Washington Co. From near Martin DAGGER's to David ENOCH's Mill will vote at Shasbazer BENLEY's Mill, Pidgeon Ck. Near PETER's Ck. will vote at Daniel SHAUGHAN's. Near William CAMPBEL's will vote at the courthouse. Near MILLER's Run will vote at Joshua MEEK's. The rest of the county is to vote at George BLAZER's on the waters of Kings Ck.

p. 419: Election district for Huntingdon Co.: Huntingdon town will vote at George CLUGGAGE's. Shirley Twp. will vote at David LOWREY's, Tyrone Twp. Benjamin ELLIOT, Thomas Duncan SMITH, Ludwig SELL, George ASHMAN, William M'ELVEY are trustees for Huntingdon Co.

p. 421: Abraham WITMER is to build a bridge across Conestogoe Ck., Lancaster Co.

p. 435: Francis GURNEY, Richard WELLS, Presley BLACKISTON, Thomas SHIELDS, Gunning BEDFORD are commissioners to regulate streets in Southwark.

p. 440, 1788: West Chester Borough, Chester Co., is erected & bounded by land of Charles RYAN, John DARLINGTON, land late of Thomas WILLIAMSON, Gideon WILLIAMSON, Thomas DARLINGTON, Jr., land of George MATLOCK, William SHARPLESS, Jonathan MATLOCK, John PATTON, Isaiah MATLOCK, Dr. Joseph MOORE, Thomas HOOPS, Benaniel OGDEN.

p. 451: Election districts: Washington Co. near Joseph SCOTT, Esq.'s, on Montour's Run, to ARMSTRONG's mill on MILLER's Run, will vote at Elizabeth M'CANLESS'. Northumberland Co., Penn & Beaver Twp. will vote at Albright SWINEFORD's, Penn Twp. The 3rd district of Northumberland Co. will vote at Andrew BILLMEYER's, Buffaloe Twp. Derry, Lower Paxtang Twps., Dauphin Co., near Jacob BRANT's & Christopher EARNEST's to a line between the companies of Capt. James CLUNI & Capt. Robert M'KEE will vote at Conrad NOLFLY's, Middletown, Lower Paxtang Twp. Lurgan & Southampton Twps., Franklin Co., will vote at Joseph FINLEY's, Southampton Twp.

p. 488, 1789: Manahan, Warrington, Huntingdon, Reading, Newberry Twps., York Co., will vote at William BUTTS', Warrington.

p. 489: Tioga district, Luzerne Co., will vote at Simon SPALDING's. Tunkhannock district will vote at Gideon OSTERHOUT's. Wilkesbarre district will vote at the courthouse. Kingstown district will vote at Lawrence MYERS'. Salem district will vote at Nathan BEACH's.

p. 490: George FREY, Middletown, Dauphin Co., is authorized to build a mill dam across Sweetara Ck.

p. 492: A part of Washington Co. is annexed to Allegheny Co.--the part near WHITE's mill on Raccoon Ck., ARMSTRONG's mill on MILLER's Run. Peter KIDD & John BEAVER are authorized to mark the boundaries.

p. 493: Mifflin Co. is erected. George M'CORMICK's land is to remain in Northumberland Co. Courts will sit at Arthur BUCHANAN's until the courthouse is built. Elections will be at Enoch HESTING's. Trustees are John OLIVER, William BROWN, David BEALE, John STEWART, David BOLE, Andrew GREGG.

p. 496: Berks Co. elections districts: Reading Borough, Alsace, Cumru, Exeter, Heidleberg, Brecknock, Maiden Ck., Carnarvon, Oley, Robinson, Ruscomb Manor & the lower part of Bern Twp. (near Anthony SHOMO & Abraham STOUT's land & John NOECKER's mill) will vote at the courthouse. Maxatawny, Long-Swamp, Hereford district, Richmond, Rockland & Greenwich Twps., will vote at Philip GEHR's, Kutz-town, Maxatawney Twp. Windsor, Brunswick, Albany, the upper part of Bern

Twp., will vote at John MOYER's, Hamburg, Windsor Twp. Tulpehoccon, Bethel, Pine Grove Twps. will vote at Godfrey ROEHRER's, Tulpehoccon. Earl, Amity, Union, Colebrookdale, Douglass Twps., will vote at William WITMAN's, Amity Twp.

p. 499: Delaware Co. is erected near the land of Elizabeth CHADS & Caleb BRINTON. Henry Hale GRAHAM, Richard REILLY, Josiah LEWIS, Edward JONES, Benjamin BRANNAN are trustees.

p. 507: The part of Allegheny Co. within the forks of the Monongahela & Youghiogheny Rivers will vote at David ROBISON's. Plumb & Versailles Twps., Allegheny Co., will vote at Matthew SIMPSON's. Restraver Twp., Westmoreland Co., will vote at Samuel WILSON's. Derry Twp., Westmoreland Co., will vote at Moses DONALD's.

p. 508: Londonderry Twp., Bedford Co., will vote at John BRIGHT's. Air & Dublin Twps., Bedford Co., will vote at Daniel M'CONNEL's, Air Twp. Greenwood Twp., Mifflin Co., will vote at Henry M'CONNEL's. Lack Twp., Mifflin Co., will no longer vote at Thomas WILSON's, but at the house lately occupied by James STACKPOLE.

p. 510: Samuel HOLLAND, Esq., & David RITTENHOUSE were to fix the boundary of New York & Pa. in 1774. Andrew ELLICOT, Esq., is the commissioner to run the Northern boundary of Pa. & N.Y. In 1786, James CLINTON & Simeon DEWITT are commissioners from N.Y. to mark the boundary.

p. 525: Andrew HENDERSON & Richard SMITH, Huntingdon Co., are named trustees for the county.

p. 530: John OLIVER, William BROWN, David BEAL, John STEWART, David BOWEL & Andrew GREGG are appointed trustees for Mifflin Co. David BOWEL doesn't reside with the limits of Mifflin Co. Dr. James ARMSTRONG is appointed in his stead.

THE STATUTES AT LARGE OF PENNSYLVANIA FROM 1682 TO 1801
VOLUME 12 - 1785-1787

p. 6, 1785: Trustees of the German Lutheran Church, Germantown Twp., Phila. Co.: Rev. John Frederick SCHMIDT, Wichard MILLER, Christian SCHNEIDER, Charles HAY, Samuel MACHLIN, John FREY, George HACKER. Present elders are: John George GRAEFLY, Henry BECK, Bernard BISBING, John ALTEMUS, Jacob NEES, Sebastian RIEBER. Present deacons: William SOMMERLAT, John EGERSDORF, Philip KIESY, John DOWMAN.

p. 17: Charles BESSONET, Bristol, Bucks Co., & Gershom JOHNSON, Phila., are proprietors of the Phila. to Trenton stage. They purchased land for a public highway adj. land of Joshua VANDERGRIFT, William ALLEN, John EDGAR, & Joseph TOMLINSON.

p. 20: On 1 Apr., 1754, the Free Masons purchased from Thomas & Mary GORDON, a lot. The land is vested in William PLUMSTEAD, Thomas BOND, Hugh DAVEY, Edward SHIPPEN, Samuel MIFFLIN, John SWIFT, Daniel ROBERDEAU, John WALLACE & William FRANKLIN, Esqs.

p. 25: Levy BUDD, James LAUGHEAD, George LEIB, John BAKER, William WERTZ, Francis MENTGES, Joseph KERR, John MILLER, James GLENTWORTH, John STEEL, George GOODWIN, Joseph MARSH, Henry KAMMERER, Michael

SHUBART & Robert BRIDGES are signers for bills of credit.

p. 27: Half of Bucks Co. will vote at Abraham KECHLEIN, inn-keeper. Voters in Lancaster Co. will vote at: Col. James PORTER's, Dromore Twp.; Capt. Hugh PEDEN's, Rapho Twp.; Thomas HENDERSON's, New Holland, Earl Twp. Voters in York Co. will vote at: Samuel GETTIS' & Robert STEVENSON's. Voters in Cumberland Co. will vote at: William MCCLURE's, Tyrone Twp.; Thomas WILSON's, Milford Twp.; Arthur BUCHANAN's, Derry Twp. Voters in Northampton Co. will vote at: Peter ANTHONY's, Lehigh Twp, & Nicholas DEPUI's, Lower Smithfield Twp. Voters in Bedford Co. will vote at Ephraim WALLACE's, Bethel Twp.; James BLACK's, Quesmahoning Twp.; George CLUGGAGE's, Shirley Twp. Some voters in Northampton Co. will vote at Amariah SUTTON's, Muncy Twp. Voters in Westmoreland Co. will vote at Samuel DICKSON's; William JAMESON's; William MOORE's, Rastrover Twp.; Debereux SMITH's, Ft. Pitt. Some voters of Franklin Co. will vote at Widow ELLIOTT's, Fannet Twp. Some voters in Montgomery Co. will vote at George ECKART's tavern, Whitemarsh; Michael KREPS' tavern, New Hanover. Some voters in Dauphin Co. will vote at Peter FRIEDLEY's, Hummelstown, Derry Twp; Peter HOFFMAN's, Upper Paxton Twp.

p. 52: Benjamin DAVIS, Michael ROUGH, John SHIELDS, John POMEROY, Hugh MARTIN, all of Westmoreland Co., are to purchase land to erect a courthouse.

p. 67: Jacob BAUSMAN has kept a ferry from the southwest side of the Monongahela River opposite Pittsburg.

p. 91: Robert PORTER, Robert CARRY, William ARMSTRONG are appointed managers of a lottery to build Newark Academy & a German Lutheran Church in Whitpain Twp., Phila. Co., & to repair Norriton Meeting-House. The lottery will finance the building. Michael CROLL, Esq. & Michael MCGLATHARTY, Montgomery Co., & William OLIPHANT, Phila., are commissioners of the lottery.

p. 107: David MEADE, Esq., is appointed justice of the peace for Wyoming, Northumberland Co.

p. 108: Capt. James IRVINE is late an officer in the Army. His wife, Deborah, has received a certificate for interest on depreciation certificates while her husband is a prisoner with the Algerines.

p. 119: Land is granted to John DUNLAP, Thomas LAWRENCE & James BUDDEN on 4 Aug., 1780, late the estate of Joseph GRIESWOLD. A tract of land in the Manor of Moreland, then in Phila. Co., bounded by land of John BUTCHER, Jonathan COMLEY, Joseph MITCHEL, Casper FETTER, is sold by the commonwealth to Charles WALKER on 31 July, 1780, late the estate of Joseph COMLEY. A lot on the northeast corner of 2nd St. from Delaware & Sassafras St. in Phila., adj. John PARROCK (now granted to Peter PARIS), is granted to Christian WERTZ, John SHAFFER & Jacob GEIGER 19 Aug., 1780, late the estate of John PARROCK. A house & lot bounded by ground of Edward BROOKS & Jonathan RICHARDS is granted to Francis LEE on 25 Nov., 1780, late the estate of George KNAPPER. Land in Lower Merion Twp., Phila., bounded by Margaret JONES, William LEWIS, Owen JONES, Benjamin HUMPHREYS, Conrad SCHITZ, John ROBINSON, John RIGHTER, granted to Edward MILNER on 16 Dec., 1780, late the estate of John ROBERTS. Land in Northern Liberties, bounded by John PETERS, is granted to William COATES, Esq. on 31 Jan., 1781, late the estate of Samuel

SHOEMAKER. Land in Northern Liberties, bounded by Henry CISS & land late of Isaac NORRIS & Thomas BOND, granted to James BUDDEN, John DUNLAP & Thomas LAWRENCE, late the estate of Joseph GRIESWOLD. Land in Blockley Twp., Phila. Co., bounded by Daniel HIBBARD & Thomas PASCHALL, granted to James BUDDEN, John DUNLAP, & Thomas LAWRENCE, late the estate of Joel EVANS. Land in Phila., bounded by land late of Selwood GRIFFIN, granted to Joseph DEANE on 31 Jan., 1781, late the estate of John HENDERSON. Land in the Manor of Moreland, Phila. Co., bounded by Richard MAPLE, Derrick KREWSON, William TILLER & William ROBERTS, granted to George BENNER 4 Feb., 1781, late the estate of John LONGBOROUGH. Land in Hatfield Twp., bounded by ---- BUCHAMER, Martin WIREMAN, Thomas DAVIS, Abijah WRIGHT & Thomas STILTFORD, granted to Joseph DEANE 31 Jan., 1781, late the estate of Jonathan WRIGHT. Land in Blockley Twp. Co., bounded by the Widow PETERS, George & John PENN, Esqs., granted to Joseph DEANE 31 Jan., 1781, late the estate of John BUTCHER. Land in Germantown, bounded by Peter BOCHIUS & Melchior MENG, granted to Joseph DEANE 31 Jan., 1781, late the estate of Holton JONES. Land in Phila. granted to Jonas PHILIPS 15 Mar., 1781, late the estate of John PARROCK. Land in Oxford Twp., Phila. Co., bounded by Robert HARPER, William ASHBRIDGE, Thomas PEARL, granted to John EVE 21 Mar., 1781, late the estate of Oswell EVE. Land in Hatfield Twp., bounded by Melchior YEDER, Thomas STILTFORD, Abijah WRIGHT & John YEGLESS, granted to Owen FARIES 21 Mar., 1781, late the estate of John WRIGHT. Land in the Manor of Moreland, bounded by Albertson WALTON, John BLACKFORD, Detrick KREWSON & William TILLER, granted to James VANSANT 21 Mar., 1781, late the estate of John BURKE. Land in Phila., bounded by Edward STILES, William RUSH, granted to Robert BETHELL 20 Dec., 1780, late the estate of Abraham CARLISLE. Land in Roxborough Twp., bounded by Samuel POWELL, Daniel CLYMER, Christian VANLASKETS, granted to Benjamin HARBESON 4 Feb., 1781, late the estate of Christopher SOUR. Land in Phila. bounded by Alexander ADAMS, John SMITH, Anthony DUCHE, granted to Charles ALEXANDER 28 Feb., 1781, late the estate of William RHODDEN. Land in Phila., bounded by John PARROCK (now John BUNNER), granted to James PARR 7 June, 1781, late the estate of John PARROCK. Land in Phila. bounded by Jacob BUNNER & Joseph WARNER, granted to Michael SIMPSON 14 June, 1781, late the estate of John PARROCK. Land in Phila. bounded by James SKINNER & James ROWAN, granted to Alexander POWERS 30 June, 1781, late the estate of John FOX. Land in Phila. bounded by Isaiah BELL & John GIBSON, granted to Benjamin HARBESON 3 Feb., 1781, late the estate of Isaac ALLEN. Land in Phila. granted to John WEIDMAN 10 July, 1781, late the estate of John PARROCK. Land in Heidelberg, Berks Co., bounded by Adam WEGERLY, Jacob STALEY & George LOUSH granted to John PLEIN 21 July, 1781, late the estate of Andrew ALLEN. Land in Abington Twp., Phila. Co., bounded by Thomas TYSON & William HASKINS, granted to Henry DOTTS in the right of Philip MOORE 27 June, 1785, late the estate of Joshua KNIGHT. Land in Phila. bounded by John PARROCK & Christian WIRTZ, granted to Peter PARIS 12 May, 1780, late the estate of John PARROCK. Land in Northern Liberties, bounded by Samuel SHOEMAKER, granted to James HUTCHINSON 23 July, 1781, late the estate of Joseph GALLOWAY. Land in Phila. granted to Jacob BUNNER 1 Aug., 1781, late the estate of John PARROCK. Land in Phila. granted to Thomas MCKEAN 9 Aug., 1781, late the estate of Jacob DUCHE. Land in Phila. granted to William POWERS 15 Aug., 1781, late the estate of David JONES. Land in Moyamensing Twp., Phila. Co., bounded by Plunkett FLEESON & John HALL, granted to
Joseph CARSON 1 Sept., 1781, late the estate of Peter CAMPBELL. Land in New Garden Twp., Chester Co., bounded by Mr. ---- SCARLET, Isaac RICHARDS, ----KNIGHT, granted to James PARR 31 Aug., 1781,

late the estate of Stephen ANDERSON. Land in E. Malborough Twp., Chester Co., bounded by John JACKSON, Sr., & William BAILEY, granted to James PARR 31 Aug., 1781, late the estate of John JACKSON. Land in E. Malborough Twp., Chester Co., bounded by Jonathan JACKSON, Samuel HAYS, George JACKSON, granted to James PARR 31 Aug., 1781, late the estate of Samuel ANDERSON. Land in E. Caln Twp., Chester Co., bounded by John PIERCE, Joseph PARKE, Thomas BABLE, William DAWSON, granted to James HUTCHINSON 31 Aug., 1781, late the estate of George SINCLAIR. Land in W. Bradford Twp., Chester Co., bounded by William BUFFINGTON, Samuel WORTH, Widow PEOPLES, William MCLAUGHLIN, granted to James HUTCHINSON 31 Aug., 1781, late the estate of Philip MARCHINTON. Land in Heidelberg Twp., Berks Co., bounded by ---- HAINES, Matthias WENRICK, Baltzer WENRICK, granted to John CHRISTIE 1 Sept., 1781, late the estate of Andrew ALLEN. Land in Heidelberg Twp., Berks Co., bounded by Andrew ALLEN, John HAINES, Isaac COPELAND, Adam SHOWERS, granted to John CRAIG 1 Sept., 1781, late the estate of Andrew ALLEN. Land in W. Caln Twp., Chester Co., bounded by land of Thomas ROGERS, Samuel LOVE, William DUNN, Francis FINCHER, granted to Francis JOHNSTON 31 Aug., 1781, late the estate of Richard SWANWICK. Land in W. Bradford Twp., Chester Co., bounded by James CHALFANT, ---- EASTBURN, Thomas BUFFINGTON, granted to James PARR 6 Oct., 1781, late the estate of Philip MARCHINTON. Land in Phila. granted to Benjamin EVANS 26 Oct., 1781, late the estate of William EVANS. Land in the Southwark district of Phila., bounded by Edward STILES & Andrew DUCHE, granted to Patrick ROBINSON 15 Dec., 1781, late the estate of John TOLLY. Land in Phila., bounded by John WEIDMAN, granted to David ZEIGLER 10 Jan., 1782, late the estate of John PARROCK. Land in Lebanon, Lancaster Co., bounded by Philip MARSTELLER, granted to William BAILEY, 19 Feb., 1782, late the estate of Nicholas HOUSECKER. Land in Hilltown Twp., Bucks Co., bounded by Henry RICE, Amos VASTINE, William THOMAS, Charles LEIDIG, Levy THOMAS, granted to George BENNER 23 Feb., 1782, late the estate of Evan THOMAS. Land in Tinicum Twp., Bucks Co., bounded by John PATTERSON, Edward PENNINGTON, William SHOEMAKER, Michael WALTER, John REED, granted to Jacob BENNER 23 Feb., 1782, late the estate of John OVERHOLTZ. Land in Abington Twp., Phila. Co., bounded by land of Abraham TYSON, granted to William DEANE 30 Oct., 1781, late the estate of Joshua KNIGHT. Land on Hog Island, granted to Samuel CALDWELL 9 May, 1782, late the estate of Joseph GALLOWAY. Land in Heidelberg Twp., Berks Co., granted to Jacob STEHELY 15 June, 1782, late the estate of Andrew ALLEN. Land in Northern Liberties Twp., granted to James CALDWELL 15 June, 1782, late the estate of John PARROCK. Land in Whitpain Twp., Phila. Co., granted to Edmund MILNE 15 June, 1782, late the estate of John ROBINSON. Land in Heidelberg Twp., Berks Co., granted to Peter FILBERT 15 Aug., 1782, late the estate of Andrew ALLEN. Land in Heidelberg Twp., Berks Co., granted to Peter NAGLE 15 Aug., 1782, late the estate of Andrew ALLEN. Land in Brunswick Twp., Berks Co., bounded by Jacob JOFFMAN, Matthias KREAMER, Jacob KENGETH, granted to Charles GOBLIN 25 July, 1782, late the estate of John KOSTER. Land in Phila., bounded by Rudolph BUNNER & John ELLICK, late the estate of Jonathan ADAMS & wife. Land in Phila., late the estate of Matthias ASPDEN. Land in Middletown Twp., Bucks Co., bounded by William PAXTON, Joshua RICHARDSON, Garret VANSANT & Joseph KNIGHT, late the estate of Joseph PAXTON. Other land owners mentioned: John PARROCK, Hudson BURR, Robert LOOSLEY, Alexander SMITH, Joel EVANS, William ROSS, John JACKSON, dec., William WESTON, John COXE, Charles NORRIS, Andrew ALLEN, Thomas MONTGOMERY, Joseph FOX, Andrew ELLIOT, Lawrence FAGAN, Samuel GARRIGUES, Thomas RICHE, John MORGAN, Oswell EVE, Joshua KNIGHT, Rynear TYSON, Isaac KNIGHT, Sr., Jacob LIPPENCOTT,

John KNIGHT, James MORRIS, John ROBERTS, Isaac TAYLOR, John BRINGHURST, Dr. WARNER, Abraham PASTORIUS, John DRINKER, Samuel SHOEMAKER, Joseph JOHNSON, Philip SYNG, Elizabeth HARMAN, Richard PARKER, William NILES, Edward BROOKS, Robert BLACK, William SALSBURY, Michael DAWSON, George HERGER, Adolph GILMAN, Frederick MAUSE, Charles MEREDITH, Jacob BROWN.

p. 142: Thomas EDWARDS, Edward BERWICK, John COWAN, Thomas DAWSON, all owned land in Salisbury Twp., Lancaster Co. William DARLINGTON & John COWAN owned land in Salisbury Twp. Samuel ATLEE, Esq., James CLEMSON, Thomas DOUGLASS & John ANDERSON are authorized to sell land for the Protestant Episcopal Church of St. John on Pequea.

p. 144: John DOUGLASS, Warwick Twp., Lancaster Co., miller, by indenture of 29 Sept., 1775, sold land to William ATLEE & Jasper YEATES, Esq. The land was in Salisbury Twp. The will of Edward SMOUT, Esq., dated 14 June, 1751, authorized William ATLEE, Jasper YEATES, Stephen CHAMBERS, Joseph SHIPPEN, Jr., & Edward HAND, Esq. to sell the property for the church.

p. 153, 1786: Trustees of the Mutual Assurance Co.: Matthew CLARKSON, William CRAIG, Benjamin WYNKOOP, John PHILLIPS, John Clement STOCKER, Thomas FRANKLIN, Isaac JONES, John HARRISON, Joseph SIMS, Philip WAGER, James COOPER, Presley BLACKISTON & John WHARTON.

p. 164: Protestant Episcopal Church (Bangor Church), Churchtown, Carnarvan Twp., Lancaster Co., wardens: Amos EVANS, Aaron RATTEN. Jacob MORGAN, Esq., John EVANS, farmer, James OLD, Gabriel DAVIES, William SMITH, James EVANS, Samuel ELLIOTT, John REES, John HUSTON, Nathan EVANS (son of John), Francis WILMER, Richard LINDSEY are vestrymen.

p. 181: Episcopal cong. of St. Peter's Church, Great Valley, Tredyfferim Twp., Chester Co.: Trustees: Thomas BULL, Esq., Benjamin THOMAS, Richard RICHISON, John RALSTON, Esq., John ROWLAND, John FRANCIS, Cromel PIERCE, Thomas WILSON, Joseph ROWLAND, Richard ROBINSON, John EVANS, Roger LUTLE.

p. 183: Thomas MORGAN, Carnarvon Twp., Berks Co., in his will of 6 Dec., 1740, devised to his four sons: John MORGAN, Francis MORGAN, William MORGAN, & Jacob MORGAN. Now John, Francis & William are dec. Jacob is still alive. They were devised 1 acre of land in Carnarvan Twp. (then in Lancaster Co., now in Berks Co.) so they could erect a church. The church was St. Thomas' Chapel, MORGAN'S town. Trustees were Jacob MORGAN, Esq., & David MORGAN, wardens. Mordecai PIERSOL, Thomas BULL, Esq., Daniel CLYMER, Esq., Samuel VANLEAR, John JONES, John JONES, Jr., Aaron RATTEU, Richard PIERSOL, Nathan EVANS, John HUDSON, Joseph JENKINS are vestrymen.

p. 214: Nathaniel TAYLOR, late of Allen Twp., Northampton Co., yeoman, dec., owned land adj. Robert CLENDANIN, John RIDDLE, John BOYD, John WALKER. An application was made by Neigal GRAY to remedy the loss of the title of land.

p. 226: A house & lot on Market St. is forfeited by Joseph GALLOWAY.

p. 242: Land adj. to John TAYLOR is vested in Christopher MARSHALL, Joseph STILES, Nathaniel BROWN, Isaac HOWELL, Peter THOMPSON, Benjamin SAY, Joseph WARNER, all Quakers, for the Quaker burial ground in Phila.

p. 244: Rev. Dr. Robert DAVIDSON is minister of the Presby. Church, Carlisle Borough, Cumberland Co. Trustees are Robert MILLER, John ARMSTRONG, William MOORE, Thomas CRAIGHEAD, William LYONS, George DAVIDSON, James IRVINE, John AGNEW, John MONTGOMERY, Samuel A. MCCLOSKEY, Samuel LAIRD.

p. 250: Trustees of the Brandywine Presby. Church, Westnantmel Twp., Chester Co.: Samuel CUNNINGHAM, John CULBERTSON, Nathaniel PORTER, Robert SMITH, David DENNY, Robert LOCKHART, James DUNWOODY, James MCCLURE, William ANDERSON.

p. 252: Trustees of the Baptist Church, New Britain Twp., Bucks Co.: Edward MATTHEW, Thomas JONES, Morris MORRIS, Benjamin MATTHEW. Minister is Joshua JONES.

p. 258: Trustees of the Scots Presby. Church, Phila.: William MARSHALL, John PURDON, Frazer KINSLEY, Robert AITKIN, James FULTON, James COCHRAN, Samuel MCCLURE, John DAVIDSON, Robert HUNTER, Peter STEEL. Rev. William MONCRIEFF is the Minister of the Gospel in Alloa. James ALLICE is the Minister of the Gospel in Paisley. John WILSON is the Minister of the Gospel in Methben.

p. 266: Trustees of the Presby. Church, Donegal Twp., Lancaster Co.: Rev. Collin MCFARQUHAR, John BAILIE, James BAILIE, James ANDERSON, Robert SPEARS, Bryce CLARK, Samuel WOODS, James MUIRHEAD, Joseph LITTLE.

p. 272: Minister of the German Reformed Church, Lancaster Co.: Rev. William HENDEL. Present trustees: Peter HOOFNAGLE, Nicholas JOB, Christopher CRAWFORD. Elders: Jacob WEAVER, Peter BEIER, Conrad HAAS, John HATZ, Barnard WOLFF, Andrew BAUSMAN. Deacons: Andrew BACHENSTOFE, Caspar FORDNEY, John GETZ, Jacob KOELER, Andrew TEYER, Michael GRUBB.

p. 279: Trustees of the Presby. Congregation of Bensalem, Bucks Co.: John CLARK, John PROUL, John VANDERGRIFT, Esqs.; Jacob VANDERGRIFT, Daniel LAREW, Jr., Herman VANSAVT.

p. 293: Election districts: All townships excepting the city of Phila., Phila. Co. will vote at John BARNESLY's, Bustletown, Lower Dublin Twp. Part of Chester Co. will vote at Mary WITHY's, Chester. Part of Lancaster Co. will vote at Col. James PORTER's, Drumore Twp. Raphoe, Donegal & Mountjoy Twps., Lancaster Co. will vote at Michael NICHOLAS' at the crossroads in Donegal Twp.

p. 297: In 1741, James MCGINLEY, Archibald BAIRD, John WITHROW, Jeremiah LOCKRY contracted with Charles CAROL, Esq., to buy CAROL's Delight, then supposed to be in Frederick Co., Md. but now in Hamilton's Bann & Cumberland Twps., York Co. Money is owed by David BLYTHE, Moses MCCLEAN, William WAUGH, James BRICE, John MAGINLEY & James STEPHENSON. On 20 Dec., 1770, Charles CAROL sold land to Amos MCGINLEY. MCGINLEY died intestate & left a widow, Ann, who later married Samuel MCFARREN. His goods were committed to Ann, John AGNEW & William MCCLEAN. Amos MCGINLEY's lawful issue were: James MCGINLEY, eldest son; Hance MCGINLEY, Temperance MCGINLEY, Samuel MCGINLEY, Amos MCGINLEY, Sarah MCGINLEY (all but James are under age).

p. 302: Elections for Luzerne Co. will be held at Zebulon BUTLER's, Wilkesbarre.

p. 311: William CLINGAN, Thomas BULL, John KINKEAD, Roger KIRK, John SELLERS, John WILSON, Joseph DAVIS are to build a new courthouse & prison in Chester Co. John HANNUM, Esq., Isaac TAYLOR, Esq., & John JACOBS are commissioners for Chester Co.

p. 322: George SCHLOSSER, Phila., in 1778, paid £1000 to purchase supplies for the federal army. The same was paid to David DESHLER & Jacob ARNDT, Esq., commissioners for Northampton Co. The money was delivered to Hugh MONTGOMERY, Esq.

p. 325: Andrew GALBRAITH, Samuel WALLACE, David BOYD, John WALKER, Hugh LAIRD, Samuel VAUGH, William MCTEER, Francis SILVER, & David HOGE are trustees of the Presby. Church, Silver Spring, Cumberland Co.

p. 331: William THARPE, Phila., merchant, sued Robert STEWART & John CARR, commissioners of clothing in Bucks Co.

p. 332: Margaret SMITH, before her espousals, owned property in Phila., bounded by Benjamin & Elizabeth CHEW. Margaret married Frederick SMITH & granted the property to John PENN, Edward SHIPPEN & Thomas PARKE. Margaret has debts from her late uncle, Joseph TURNER's, estate.

p. 340: Timothy PICKERING, Esq., is prothonotary of Luzerne Co. Zebulon BUTLER & John FRANKLIN are inhabitants of said county.

p. 346: Benjamin DAVIS, Michael ROUGH, John SHIELDS, John POMEROY & Hugh MARTIN are to give accounts of the money spent to purchase land for the Westmoreland Co. courthouse to William MOORE, Charles CAMPBELL & James BRYSON.

p. 347: Isaac WYNN, Philip BUCKIUS, John HARMAR, Adam ALBERGER, Edward DICKINSON, George KNOX, Charles BROWN, Elias ROSA, Harnam COURTER, Dennison HUME, Thomas HARRISON, William RITCHIE & Cato HILL are prisoners in the Phila. gaol for debt.

p. 352: Thomas MIFFLIN, Robert MORRIS, George CLYMER, Jaret INGERSOLL, Thomas FITZSIMMONS, James WILSON, & Gov. MORRIS, Esq., are deputies to the Federal Constitution Convention in Phila.

p. 357: Trustees of the Pittsburg Academy: Rev. Samuel BARR, Rev. James FINLEY, Rev. James POWERS, Rev. John MCMILLAN, Rev. Joseph SMITH, Rev. Matthew HENDERSON, Gen. John GIBSON, Col. Priestly NEVIL, Col. William BUTLER, Col. Stephen BAYARD, James ROSS, David BRADFORD, Robert GALBRAITH, George THOMPSON, George WALLACE, Edward COOK, John MORE, William TODD, Alexander FOWLER, Dr. Nathaniel BEDFORD, Dr. Thomas PARKER.

p. 361: Minister of the German Lutheran Church, Lancaster Borough: Rev. Henry MUHLENBERG. Trustees: Bernard HUBLEY, Ludwig LAUMAN, Michael HUBLEY. Elders: Matthias SLOUGH, George MUSSER, Jacob KRUG, George Adam LINDENBERGER, Michael MUSSER, Christian APP, John HUBLEY, Paul ZANTZINGER, Melchior RUIDSILL. Wardens: Ludwig HECK, John BLOTTENBERGER, Michael APP, Charles HEINITSH, Stophel HEGER, John BURG.

p. 368: David CLOYD, former treasurer of state taxes in Chester Co., was robbed of £270 9s.

p. 369: Seventh Day Baptists Church, Chester Co., E. Nantmel Twp., board: David THOMAS, Daniel GRIFFITH, Esq., William GRIFFITH, Sr., Levi GRIFFITH, John MCCRACKING, James ROBERTS, Samuel THOMAS, Hazael THOMAS, Jeremiah JARMAN.

p. 375: John VANDEREN is non compos mentis for 3 months past. Robert TOWERS, John DONALDSON, Owen JONES, the younger, & Caleb CARMALE, all of Phila., are a committee of the estate of John VANDEREN, who owns land in Phila., Bedford, Westmoreland, Washington, Fayette, Northampton, & Northumberland Counties. VANDEREN has a wife & minor children.

p. 379: Daniel SHARP, Luke DAY, Adam WHEELER & Eli PARSONS are principals in a rebellion against the state of Massachusetts Bay.

p. 383: Trustees of the Presby. Church, Leacock Twp., Lancaster Co.: James MERCER, John CRAIG, John SLAYMAKER, George MCELWAINE, William PORTER, Henry SLAYMAKER, Jr., William CRAYTON & James COOPER. Minister is Rev. Nathaniel SEMPLE.

p. 386: Rev. Joseph PILMORE is the Rector of the United Episcopal Churches of Trinity Church, Oxford Twp. & All Saint's Church, Lower Dublin Twp., Phila. Co. & St. Thomas' Church, Whitemarsh Twp., Montgomery Co. Benjamin COTTMAN, Jacob ASHTON are wardens of Trinity Church. Benjamin JOHNSTON & Jacob DUFFIELD are wardens of All Saint's Church & Joseph THORNHILL, Matthew INGRAM, Nathan WHITMAN & Demos WORRELL are vestrymen for Trinity Church. Joseph COTTMAN, Josiah JACKSON, Thomas ASHTON & Joseph ASHTON are vestrymen for All Saint's Church. Andrew REDHEFFER & John Bernard GILPIN are wardens for St. Thomas' & Edward BURK, Lewis STANGERT, Frederick HITNER & William HICKS are vestrymen for St. Thomas'.

p. 391: Trustees of Franklin College, Lancaster, Lancaster Co.: Hon. Thomas MIFFLIN, Esq.; Hon. Thomas MCKEAN, Esq., Dr. of Laws; Rev. Dr. John Henry Christian HELMUTH; Rev. Caspar WEIBURG; Rev. Henry MUHLENBERG; Rev. William HANDELL; Rev. Nicholas KURTZ; Rev. George TROLDENIER; Rev. John HERBST; Rev. Joseph HUTCHINS; Rev. Frederick WEYLAND; Rev. Albertus HELFENSTEIN, Rev. William INGOLD; Rev. Jacob VANBUSKIRK, Rev. Abraham BLUMER, Rev. Frederick Valentine MILTZEIMER; Rev. Frederick DALECKER, Rev. Christopher Emanuel SHULTZ; Rev. John B. COUSIE; Peter MUHLENBERG, Esq.; John HUBLEY, Esq.; Joseph HEISTER, Esq.; Casper SCHAFFNER; Peter HOOFNAGLE, Esq.; Christopher CRAWFORD; Paul ZANTZINGER; Adam HUBLEY, Esq.; Adam REIGART; Jasper YEATES, Esq.; Stephen CHAMBERS, Esq.; Hon. Robert MORRIS, Esq.; George CLYMER, Esq.; Philip WAGNER; Hon. William BINGHAM, Esq.; William HAMILTON; William SHEAF; Dr. Benjamin RUSH; Daniel HEISTER, Esq.; William RAWLE, Esq.; Lewis FARMER, Esq.; Christopher KUCHER; John MUSSER; Philip GROENWALDT; Michael HAHN; George STAKE, Sr., Esq.

p. 441: John FITCH, Bucks Co., is given the right to make & use a steamboat.

p. 442: Trustees of the Presby. Church, Londonderry, Dauphin Co.: John RODGERS, James WILSON, Sr., James RODGERS, William SNODGRASS, Robert CLARK, Robert ROBERTSON, Thomas MCCALLEM, William LAIRD, David HAY, Robert MOODY, Joseph PARKS, James WILSON, Rev. John ELDER.

p. 448: Trustees of the Presby. Church, Tinicum Twp., Bucks Co.: Thomas LONG, Esq., John BARCLAY, Esq., John THOMPSON, Robert

STEWART, Jr., John BAILEY.

p. 455: Trustees of the Presby. Church, New London, Chester Co.: Robert FINNEY, Sr., Elijah MCGLENACHEN, Andrew BOYD, David MACKEY, Esq., William SHERER, Alexander FULTON, Alexander MORRISON, Joseph STRAWBRIDGE, John MCDOWELL.

p. 465: Jonathan SHOEMAKER, Seneca LUKENS & John HOUGH are directors & Mordecai THOMAS, treasurer, of the Union Library Co., Hatboro, Moreland Manor, Montgomery Co.

p. 466: Minister of the Baptist Church, Lower Dublin Twp., Phila. Co: Rev. Dr. Samuel JONES. Thomas WEBSTER, Benjamin DUNGAN, Joseph MILES, John HOLMES, Enoch EDWARDS, Esq., Richard WHITTON, Joshua JONES, Stephen WATT are all members.

p. 477: Conrad MINICK has a saw-mill on the Northumberland-Berks Co. line.

p. 480: Trustees of the Academy of Protestant Episcopal Church, Phila.: Rev. William WHITE, Rev. Samuel MAGAU, Rev. Robert BLACKWELL, Robert MORRIS, Thomas WILLING, Edward SHIPPEN, Richard PETERS, Andrew DOZ, Abraham MARKOE, Peter BAYNTON, Gerardus CLARKSON, Francis HOPKINSON, Joseph SWIFT, William POLLARD, John WILCOCKS, Andrew WILCOCKS.

p. 483: Oliver EVANS, New Castle Co., Delaware, miller, invented two machines for the use in merchant's mills.

p. 485: Peter LE GAUX owns property on the Schuylkill River near Spring Mill. He will run a public ferry.

p. 491: Trustees of the German Lutheran Congregation, Reading, Berks Co.: Henry HAHN, the elder, Michael KRAUSE, Christian MERKEL. Deacons: Matthias BABB, Henry SPENGLER, Christopher RIGHTMEYER, Jacob LEITHEUSER, John SHOEMAKER, Henry HAHN, the younger. Elders: Jacob ZOLL, John STROHECKER, Michael BUSH.

p. 495: George WALL, Jr., Bucks Co., designed a mathematical instrument.

p. 497: United Swedish Lutheran Church of Wicacoa, Kingessing & Upper Merion, called Gloria Dei, St. James' & Christ Church rector is Rev. Nicholas COLLEEN. Wardens are Reynold KEEN, John STILLE, Matthew JONES, Samuel HOLSTEIN. Vestrymen are Samuel WHEELER, Hugh DEHAVEN, Joseph BLEWER, William JONES, George ORD, Paul BECK, Jr., Charles JUSTICE, Sr., Lawrence JUSTICE, Andrew BOON, Jr., John ROBINSON, Andrew COXE, Andrew LONGACRE, Ezekiel RAMBO, Peter RAMBO, Lindsay COATES.

p. 502: Upper Presby. Church, Marsh Ck., York Co.: Trustees are John ROSS, David MCCLELLAN, John HOSAC, James JOHNSTON, Quintain ARMSTRONG, Michael KINCAID, William MCPHERSON, Joshua RUSSELL, William MCCLELLAN.

p. 509: Paul HAUSMAN, late collector of taxes in Manor Twp., Lancaster Co., is now in gaol for nonpayment of £294 2s 2 1/2p.

p. 518: Protestant Episcopal Church of St. John, Yorktown, York Co. The lot on which the church stands was granted to Joseph ADLUM. Present Rector is Rev. John CAMPBELL. Wardens: Thomas HARTLEY,

John CLARK. Vestrymen: William BAILEY, Henry MILLER, Robert JONES,
William JOHNSTON, Garrett CAVODE, Joseph ADLUM, Robert HAMMERSLEY &
George WELSH.

p. 528: Trustees of the Academy of Washington, Washington Co.:
Rev. John MCMILLAN, Rev. Joseph SMITH, Rev. Thaddeus DODD, Rev. John
CLARK, Rev. Matthew HENDERSON, Rev. John CORBLY, James MARSHALL,
Esq., James EDGAR, Esq., John MCDOWELL, Esq., Alexander WRIGHT,
Esq., James ALLISON, Thomas SCOTT, Esq., David BRADFORD, James ROSS,
David REDICK, John HOGE, Alexander ADDISON, Thomas CROOKS, James
FLANAGAN, Dr. Alexander BAIRD, James BRICE.

p. 532: York Borough is erected. It is bounded by land of John
HAY, William BAILEY, Esq., WRIGHT's ferry, James SMITH, Esq.,
KAUSMAN's lands. Henry MILLER, Esq., David CANTLER are burgesses.
Advisors are Baltzer SPANGLER, Michael DOWDLE, Christopher LAUMAN,
Peter MUNDORF, David GREER, Esq., James SMITH, Esq. High Constable
is Christian STAYER. Town Clerk is George Lewis LEFFLER.

p. 566: German Reformed Church, Frankford, Oxford Twp., Phila. Co.:
Minister is Philip PAULE. Trustees: Rudolph NEFF, Jacob NEFF,
George CASTOR, Sr., Frederick CASTOR. Elders: Jacob MEYERS,
Rudolph MOWER, Jacob SIBLEY, Joseph DEARMAN. Deacons: John ROHRER,
Adam BAKER, George ROHRER, Jacob CASTOR.

p. 588: Timothy PICKERING, William MONTGOMERY & Stephen BALLIOT,
Esq., are to hire a surveyor for lands claimed by settlers of
Wyoming.

p. 589: John KEARSLEY, Phila., practitioner in physic, willed land
he purchased from Levi BUDD & Thomas HART in Northern Liberties to
be sold & the money given to the rector, wardens & vestrymen of the
United Episcopal Church of Christ Church & St. Peter's Church,
Phila., for an infirmary or almshouse. Robert TROWERS, John
SAWNWICH & George BICKHAM are to sell the ground.

p. 591: The Presby. Church of Pittsburg & Westmoreland Co. Rev.
Samuel BARR is pastor. John WITHERS, Robert GALBREATH, Stephen
BAYARD, Alexander FOWLER, George WALLACE, David DUNCAN, Adamson
TANNYHILL, John GIBSON, Richard BUTLER, Isaac CRAIG are trustees.

THE STATUTES AT LARGE OF PENNSYLVANIA FROM 1682 TO 1801
VOLUME 13 - 1787-1790

p. 10: Alexander M'DOWELL is appointed surveyor of a district. He
is owed £79 10s.

p. 12: Rev. John ETTWEIN is one of the bishops of the church called
Unitas Fratrum or United Brethern. Rev. John MEDER is a pastor in
ordinary of said church in Phila. In 1740, the church began to make
settlements in America to carry the gospel to the Indians.
Directors: Frederick William VON MARSHALL, gentleman; Rev. Andrew
HUBNER; Paul MUNSTER; Hans Christian VON SCHWEINITZ, gentleman; Rev.
David ZEISBERGER, Jr.; John August KLINGSOHR; Jeremiah DENCKE;
Charles Gotthold REICHEL; Daniel KOEHLER; Christian BENZEIN; Godfrey
PRAEZEL. Associate directors: Rev. Bernhard Adam GRUBE; Frederick
PETER, Sr.; Jacob VAN VLECK. Ministers of different Brethern
congregations: Rev. John HERBST, John MEDAR, Francis BOAHLER, James
BIRKBY, Lewis BOEHLER, Abraham REINECKE.

p. 16: Trustees of the First Presby. Church, Newtown Twp., Cumberland Co.: David STERRET, Robert PATTERSON, Charles LEIPER, Randle BLAIR, John M'KEEHAN, Samuel FINLEY, John CARSON.

p. 23: West Chester, Chester Co., is erected into a borough near the land of Charles RYAN, John DARLINGTON, land late of Thomas WILLIAMSON, Gideon WILLIAMSON, Thomas DARLINGTON, Jr., George MATLACK, William SHARPLESS, Jonothan MATLOCK, John PATTON, Dr. Joseph MOORE, Isaiah MATLACK, Thomas HOOPS, Benaniel OGDEN.

p. 24: Land in East Caln Twp., Chester Co., was purchased from Rosanna SHEWARD for use of Chester Co. by William CLINGAN, Thomas BULL, John KINKEAD, Roger KIRK, John SELLERS, John WILSON & Joseph DAVIS.

p. 25: Marsh & meadowland in Kingsessing Twp., Phila. Co., known as BOONE's Island & Carcus-Hook marsh & a drained marsh in Tinicum Twp., Chester Co., is near the land of Christopher ELLIOTT & the Widow COCKS.

p. 38: Trustees of the Academy of the Borough of Reading, Berks Co.: Hon. Thomas MIFFLIN, Esq., Rev. William INGOLD, Rev. Frederick WILDBOHN, Rev. William BOOS, Daniel BROADHEAD, Daniel HEISTER, Jr., James BIDDLE, Joseph HEISTER, Collinson READ, Daniel CLYMER, Dr. James DIEMER, Cadwalader MORRIS, George EGE, Joseph SANDS, Christopher LOWER, Charles SHOEMAKER, Nicholas LUTZ, John BISHOP, Thomas DUNDASS, Paul GROSSCUP, John ECKERT, John OTTON, Daniel LEVAM, Esqs., Jacob WINEY, John HARTMAN, Henry HAHN, Sr., Peter NAGLE, John STROHECKER, Daniel UDRE. They are to meet 14 May, 1788 in Reading at the house of John HARTMAN.

p. 50: James MCMANAS petitions that while employed in the service of Pa. as a laborer running the northern boundary line, he received a wound & bruises by the falling of a tree in a storm on him. He is rendered totally incapable of ever supporting himself by labor. £100 is given to him for his immediate support.

p. 51: Joseph FRY, door-keeper, says an account has been exhibited against him by the comptroller-general for rent for occupying the part of the western wing of the State House in which he & his family dwell & for herbage of the State House yard consumed by cattle.

p. 66: James PARKER is a prisoner in the Phila. gaol for debt.

p. 67: Thomas GORDON, Oxford Twp., Phila. Co., was commanded by proclamation of the Supreme Executive Council on 22 June, 1779, to surrender himself for trial for high treason. He was a minor & absent from this continent at the time of his attainder, having been placed upon a British vessel in Phila. in 1778 by his mother, against his own inclination. His estates are restored.

p. 71: Rev. Robert MOLYNEAUAUX, Rev. Francis BEESTON, Rev. Lawrence GRAESAL are the present pastors & George MEADE, Thomas FITZSIMMONS, James BYRNE, Paul ESLING, John COTTRINGER, Joseph ECK, Mark WILCOX, John CARROL are members of St. Mary's Roman Catholic Church, Phila.

p. 75: Robert BAILY, John PAXTON, John JOHNSTON, Andrew WORK, John ANDERSON, Thomas WHITESIDE, Samuel MCCLELLAND, Alexander MORRISON & Rev. Nathaniel W. SEMPLE (present pastor) are the trustees of the Presby. Church, Middle Octarara, Bart Twp., Lancaster Co.

p. 82: Lt. Col. Francis MENTGES has inspected the militia & receives £100 compensation for his duties.

p. 89: Eli COULTER, Peter KIDD, Benjamin LODGE are to mark the boundary lines between Westmoreland, Washington, & Allegheny Co.

p. 90: Washington Co. election district #5 will vote at Joshua MEEKS' instead of Elizabeth MCCANLESS'.

p. 91: Penn & Beaver Twps., Northumberland Co., will vote at Albright SWINEFORD's, Penn Twp. The 3rd district, Northumberland Co., will vote at Andrew BILLMEYER's, Buffaloe Twp.

p. 92: Derry & Lower Paxtang Twps., Dauphin Co., near Jacob BRANDT's, Christopher EARNEST's, between the companies of Capt. James CLUNI & Capt. Robert MCKEE, will vote at Conrad NOLFLY's.

p. 126, 1765: William DEWEES, Michael HILLEGAS & Benjamin DAVIS were appointed commissioners to erect a bridge over Skippack Ck. In 1771, Benjamin JACOBS, Jacob UMSTAT & John KESTAR were also appointed commissioners to build a bridge over Skippack Ck. UMSTAT & KESTAR are now deceased. Anthony CRUTHERS, Thomas DAVIS & William ARMSTRONG are now nominated commissioners for this purpose.

p. 131: Episcopal Congregation of St. James' Church, Perkiomen, New Providence Twp., Montgomery Co.: Rev. Slaitor CLAY, minister. James SHANNON, Nathan PAWLING, wardens. Henry PAWLING, Sr., Edward LANE, John BEAN, Henry NEWBERRY, Joseph PAWLING, Robert SHANNON, Benjamin RITTENHOUSE, Henry PAWLING, Jr., John PAWLING, Jr. are vestrymen.

p. 133: Thomas & Richard PENN patented on 3 Mar., 1733 to John MONTGOMERY, Robert MILLER, John ARMSTRONG, James WILSON, George STEVENSON, Robert MAGAW, Stephen DUNCAN, William LYON, & William IRWIN for land in Carlisle, Cumberland Co.

p. 135: James GIBBONS, John SHALLCROSS, Thomas MAY, Vincent BONSALL, Isaac HENDRICKSON, gentlemen of Wilmington Borough, are to settle the matters of the Wilmington Lottery.

p. 138: John HAGUE is being recompensed for introducing a cotton carding machine into Pa.

p. 162: Capt. William ROSS, Luzerne Co., has been employed in suppressing insurrections & checking the violent & lawless proceedings of certain insurgents & rioters who have disturbed the peace of Luzerne Co. In an attempt to take certain persons who had captivated Col. Timothy PICKERING, Esq., ROSS received several dangerous wounds, losing the use of his right hand. He is awarded £187 10s.

p. 163: David LINTON, in March last, apprehended in Manheim, Lancaster Co., & safely lodged in the gaol, George SINCLAIRE, who was attainted by outlawry in the Supreme Court from several robberies, burglaries & felonies. LINTON is to receive £50.

p. 166: Trustees of the religious society of German Roman Catholics of Holy Trinity Church, Phia.: George Ernest LECHLER, Sr., James OELLERS, Christopher SHORTY, Sr., Henry HORNE, Adam PREMIR, Anthony HOOKY, Jacob THREIN, Charles BAUMAN.

p. 169: Sarah CALDWELL, on 18 Jan., 1788, held certificates made out to her & to Andrew CALDWELL for money. She lost them the same day. The total amount was £2513 12s.

p. 175: Henry Cleland BAKER, Joseph Richard ROBESON, Benjamin BURTON, Robert HUNTER are prisoners in the Phila. gaol for debt.

p. 177: John DAVIS, John CHRISTIE, John GRIFFITH, John TEMPLETON, David WILSON, David CLOYD, John MAXWELL, Robert TODD, Thomas HARRIS, Matthew NEARLY, James DAVIS, Thomas R. KENNEDY are trustees of the Presby. Congregation of Tredyffrin Twp., Chester Co.

p. 227, 1789: Robert BEATTY, late a tax collector for Shippensburg Twp., Cumberland Co., & Benjamin MOORE, late a tax collector for Lebanon Twp. (then Lancaster Co.), now in Dauphin Co., are confined to gaol for nonpayment of money received as public taxes.

p. 233: In 1767, Lewis KNOWS, Henry RADER, Peter METZ & John SHARP owned a house an lot in Easton, Northampton Co., near the lot late of William NYCE, for the use of the Protestant Evangelic Reformed German Congregation of Easton, Bethlehem, Plainfield Twps., Northampton Co., & Greenwich Twp., Sussex, N.J. Philip ODEWELDER, the younger, Peter SHARP, Jonas HARTZELL & Joseph KELLER are to sell the property.

p. 241: The governing body of the College of Physicians of Phila: John REDMAN, Pres.; John JONES, V. Pres.; William SHIPPEN, Jr., Adam KUHN, John MORGAN, Benjamin RUSH, Samuel DUFFIELD, Gerardus CLARKSON, George GLENTWORTH, Thomas PARKE, James HUTCHINSON, Robert HARRIS, John CARSON, Benjamin DUFFIELD, William W. SMITH, John FOULKE, Samuel Powel GRIFFITS, William CLARKSON, William CURRIE, Benjamin SAY, Andrew ROSS, John MORRIS, Nathan DORSEY, James CUNNINGHAM, Caspar WISTAR, Jr., Michael LEIB, John H. GIBBONS.

p. 283: James BUDDEN, late of Phila., merchant, is now dec. He wrote his will on 20 Oct., 1783. He was indebted to different persons in Europe. He thought the debts had been paid by his late partner, William STRICKER. Francis BUDDEN is the administrator of the estate.

p. 287: Henry WYNKOOP, Thomas JENKS, Francis MURRAY, Samuel BENEZET, [Abraham] DU BOIS are the present directors of the Newtown Library Co., Bucks Co. Present treasurer is William LINTON.

p. 288: John HEWSON, Northern Liberties, Phila., is a calico printer & bleacher.

p. 294: The Darby Ck. Co.: Philip PRICE, John PEARSON, Hugh LLOYD, John HUNT, Jr., Isaac SERRILL, gentlemen, are to divide meadow land in Tinicum Twp., Chester Co., for repair.

p. 307: Luzerne Co. election districts: Tioga District will vote at Simon SPALDING's. Tunkhannock District will vote at Gideon OSTERHOUT's. Kingston District will vote at Lawrence MEYER's. Salem District will vote at Nathan BEACH's.

p. 309: Robert LESLIE, Phila., a clock & watchmaker, is to have exclusive rights to construct improvements he has invented for clocks in Pa.

p. 312: James PETTIGREW, late excise tax collector in Northampton

Co., is in gaol for arrearages in his collected taxes.

p. 313: George FREY, Middletown, Dauphin Co., has erected a mill near the mouth of Swatara Ck.

p. 320: Peter KIDD & John BEAVER are authorized to mark the boundary when part of Washington Co. is annexed to Allegheny Co.

p. 327: Elections for Mifflin Co. will be at Arthur BUCHANAN's. Trustees for Mifflin Co. are John OLIVER, William BROWN, David BEALE, John STEWART, David BOLE & Andrew GREGG.

p. 328: Some early Easton Borough residents: Andrew KROUP, George MESSINGER, Barnett WALTER. Burgesses: Peter KACHLEIN, Henry BARNET, Jacob WEYGAND, William RAUP, John PROTSMAN. Frederick BARTHOLD is High Constable. Samuel SITGREAVES is town-clerk.

p. 338: John SELLARS, Thomas TUCKER, Charles DILWORTH are commissioners to mark the boundary line of Delaware Co.

p. 343: Meadowland in Northern Liberties, Phila., is near land of Frederick PIGOU (late Abel JAMES), Thomas Lloyd MOORE (late William MOORE, Esq.).

p. 358: John HOUSTON is appointed surveyor of one of the districts. He is owed £88 10s.

p. 358: Robert Edge PINE, dec., in 1784, removed with his family from London to Phila., & brought with him a large & valuable collection of original historical paintings, drawings, & designs & he purchased a lot in 8th St., between Market & Arch St., & erected a building thereon to exhibit the collection & carry on his business as a painter. Mary PINE is the widow & executrix. John JONES, Francis HOPKINSON, George MEADE, Walter STEWART, Charles HEATLY, John VAUGHN, Temple FRANKLIN are managers for a lottery to dispose of the lot & buildings & collections.

p. 361: James RUMSEY, Berkley Co., Va., has invented & improved boilers, mills & engines.

p. 373: Sharp DELANY, Esq., is appointed collector of imports & duties. Frederick PHILE, Esq., is the naval officer of Pa.

p. 379: John PENN, Esq., Governor of the province of Pa., in 1774, nominated David RITTENHOUSE, Esq., to fix the boundary line between Pa. & N.Y. Cadwallader COLDEN, Esq., Governor of N.Y., nominated Samuel HOLLAND, Esq., to fix the boundary line between Pa. & N.Y. Pennsylvania, under a commission headed by Charles BIDDLE, Esq., in 1786, appointed Andrew ELLICOT, Esq., to mark the northern boundary of Pa. James CLINTON & Simeon DEWITT, Esq., were appointed commissioners to mark the boundary by N.Y.

p. 382: Joseph PERKINS, Abram MORROW, John NICHOLSON repaired public arms for the militia.

p. 383: Francis WHITE, Robert ROSS are prisoners in the Phila. Co. gaol & were adjudged bankrupt.

p. 387: The Society for the Relief of Distressed & Decayed Pilots, Their Widows & Children was incorporated on 10 Nov., 1788. Henry FISHER, Aaron BENNET, Richard HOWARD, William ROSS, Andrew HIGGINS,

Samuel THOMPSON, James ART, Henry STEPHENS, William WEST, John BARNES, Aaron EDMONDS, John SNYDER were managers. Isaac ROACH is treasurer. Nathaniel GALT is clerk.

p. 393: German Lutheran Congregation, St. Peter's, Pikeland Twp., Chester Co.: Rev. Ludwig VOIGT, minister. Jacob DANNEFELSER, George DERIE, Zachariah REIS, Trustees. Elders: Valentine ORNER, John KING, Valentine FUSS, Charles STELL, Jacob LUDWIG, Conrad HENRY. Deacons: Michael HALLMAN, Frederick STRAUCK, Lawrence KING.

p. 403: German Lutheran Congregation, Zion Church, Pikeland Twp., Chester Co.: Rev. Ludwig VOIGT, minister. Trustees: John HASS, John WALTER, Henry CHRISTMEN. Elders: Nicholas SCHNEIDER, Conrad HERLEMAN, Stephen HEILMAN, George CHRISTMAN, Philip MILLER, Henry KNERR. Deacons: John FERTICH, Nicholas LAHR, George EMRICH.

p. 425: Members of the Pennsylvania Society for Promoting the Abolition of Slavery & the Relief of Free Negroes Unlawfully Held in Bondage & for Improving the Condition of the African Race: Dr. Benjamin FRANKLIN, James PEMBERTON, Jonathan PENROSE, Thomas HARRISON, James STARR, William LIPPINCOTT, John THOMAS, Benjamin HORNER, Samuel RICHARDS, John EVANS, John TODD, James WHITEALL, Edward BROOKS, Thomas ARMAT, John WARNER, Samuel DAVIS, Thomas BARTOW, Robert EVANS, Robert WOOD, Seymour HART, Richard HUMPHREYS, Robert TOWERS, Joseph MOORE, Joseph RUSSELL, William ZANE, Israel WHELEN, Samuel BAKER, Richard PRICE, Charles JERVIS, Israel HALLOWELL, Clement BIDDLE, Amos WICKERSHAM, Pattison HARSHORN, Nathan SELLERS, David SELLERS, Isaac PARRISH, Zacariah JESS, Dr. Benjamin RUSH, John FIELD, Richard JONES, William POYNTELL, Andrew CARSON, Philip PRICE, John HUNT, Jr., Norris JONES, John NORTON, Thomas PENROSE, Thomas POULTNEY, Thomas EDDY, Isaac WEAVER, Jr., Caleb ALTMORE, Joseph BUDD, Abraham SHARPLESS, Isaac MASSEY, James LEWIS, Thomas SHOEMAKER, Robert MORRIS, Jeremiah PAUL, Thomas SAVERY, Francis BAILEY, Thomas SHIELDS, George EDDY, John MORRISON, John MORRIS, Joseph CLARK, Zachariah POULSON, Jr., Thomas PARKER, William GRAHAM, Thomas RODGERS, John POULTNEY, Isaac BONSALL, Joseph CRUCKSHANK, John JACOBS, Nathan BOYS, William ASHBY, Jacob TRASEL, William JACKSON, Charles CRAWFORD, Ellis YARNALL, John OLDEN, Tench COXE, Jonathan PUGH, Reece JOHN, Jacob SHOEMAKER, Jr., William MCILHENNY, Caleb LOWNES, John LETCHWORTH, William WEST, Isaac PEASON, Burton WALLACE, Francis JOHNSTON, Joseph SHARPLESS, Thomas WISTAR, Joseph LOWNES, Dr. Benjamin SAY, Joseph ANTHONY, Caspar W. HAINES, Joseph BACON, George RUTTER, David LOWNES, Bartholomew WISTAR, George FOX, William T. FRANKLIN, William RAWLE, James TRENCHARD, Conrad HANSE, Samuel COATES, Richard WELLS, Sharp DELANEY, Johnathan WILLIS, Jr., Joseph GIBBONS, Samuel PANCOAST, Jr., Kearney WHARTON, Dr. James HUTCHINSON, Charles WILLIAMS, John CLAYPOLE, John DOWERS, Hilary BAKER, George LATIMER, Andrew GEYER, James READ, Peter WOGLOM, John HAGHN, John TODD, Jr., Philip BENEZET, Joseph JAMES, Dr. Caspar WISTAR, Jr., Dr. Samuel P. GRIFFITHS, Thomas FITZGERALD, Stephen MAXFIELD, Philip PRICE, Jr., Israel PLEASANTS, Mordicai CHURCHMAN, Thomas ANNESLY, Benjamin W. MORRIS, John MCCREE, George RICHIE, James OLDEN, John HUNTCHINSON, George WILSON, Jacob PARKE, Thomas LAWRENCE, Dr. John FOULKE, Jesse WATERMAN, James TRIMBLE, Dr. William ROGERS, Dr. Nicholas COLLIN, Samuel M. FOX, Benjamin SHOEMAKER, Joseph Parker NORRIS, George ROBERTS, Jeremiah PARKER, Abraham LIDDON, John BLEAKLEY, John INSKEEP, Robert WALN, Richard PARKER, John STARR, Nathan Allen SMITH, Thomas NORTON, Robert TAGGART, Samuel KINGSLEY, Nathan FIELD, Daniel TROTTER, Benjamin TAYLOR, James SMITH, Jr., Caleb CARMALT, Robert ROBERTS, William CHANCELLOR, Thomas FORREST, Jonathan JONES,

Ebenezer BREED, George ASHTON, Thomas PROCTOR, George DAVIS, John SMILIE, Thomas PALMER, Anthony Felix WUIBERT, Matthew HALE, Richard PETERS, Joseph THOMAS, Thomas ROSS, Isaac BUCKBEE, Joshua GILPIN, Dr. Amos GREGG, Gerard VOGELS, Richard RILEY, Samuel CLAPHAMSON, Zaccheus COLLINS, Henry Hale GRAHAM, John ELY, Richard H. MORRIS, John STAPLER, Jr., Daniel MAY, Andrew JOHNSTON, S. BARNETT, William WELSH, Isaiah HAM, Charles LUKINS, James SMITH, S. MORRIS, Ambrose UPDEGRAFF, Peter MONDERF, Thomas FISHER, Robert KAMMERSLY, John SMITH, William WEBB, John ROBERTS, John KITTERE, William BRISBAND, William GIBBONS, Samuel UPDEGRAFF, Caleb JOHNSTON, Robert VEREE, Dr. John CHAPMAN, Alexander ANDERSON, Samuel REDWOOD, Rees CADWALLADER, Samuel JACKSON, Dr. John LUTHER, Dr. John STORY, Benjamin WRIGHT, Eli LEWIS, all of Pa. Joseph SHOTWELL, Jr., David COOPER, Samuel ALLISON, Thomas REDMAN, Thomas STOKES, John WISTAR, Thomas CLEMENS, Joseph SLOAN, Ebenezer HOWELL, Clement HALL, James JESS, Benjamin WRIGHT, Richard WALN, Stacy BIDDLE, Hezekiah HUGHES, Thomas GITHEN, all of N.J. Hon. John JAY, Matthew CLARKSON, both of N.Y. John BOGGS, Caleb KIRK, Warner MIFFLIN of Delaware. Zebulon HOLLINGSWORTH, John RICHARDSON, Woolman HICKSON, John FEIGLE, Joseph WILKINSON, John NEEDLES of Maryland. Samuel HOPKINS, Benjamin FOSTER, Enos HITCHCOCK, Benjamin WEST, Moses BROWN, William PATTON, Samuel VINSON, Thomas ROBINSON, Jonathan EASTON, of Rhode Island. John SAUNDERS, George TEGAL, George CORBYN, of Virginia. Noah WEBSTER, Thomas GAIN, Benjamin WEST of Mass. Capel LOFT, David BARCLAY, Granville SHARPE, Dr. Richard PRICE, James PHILIPS, Thomas DAY, Dr. Thomas CLARSON, The Right Honorable William PITT, Dr. John Okely LETTSOM, William DILWYN, Robert ROBESON, William HOLLICK, Great Britain. LeAbbe RAYNAL, Le Marquis de LA FAYETTE, I.P. Brissot de WARVILLE, Charton de LA TERRIERRE, Francis Clery DUPONT, France. Benjamin FRANKLIN is President. Jonathan PENROSE & James PEMBERTON are Vice Presidents. Benjamin RUSH & Caspar WISTAR are Secretaries. James STARR is treasurer. William LEWIS, Miers FISHER, William RAWLE & John D. COXE are councillors.

p. 432: Minister of the Methodist Episcopal Church, Phila., is Rev. John DICKINS. Directors are Robert FITZGERRALD, Jacob BAKER, Thomas ARMAT, James DOUGHTY, Josiah LUSBY, John HOOD, Burton WALLACE, John BOND, Henry MANLY.

p. 444, 1790: Trustees of the public school in Huntingdon Twp., Huntingdon Co.: Benjamin ELLIOT, Andrew HENDERSON, Esqs., Hon. John CANNON, Esq., George FOLKNER, Alexander DEAN, John DEAN, John WILLIAMS, gentlemen.

p. 452: Fayette Co. election districts: Springhill, German & George's Twps. will vote at Nicholas RIFFLE's, German Twp. Tyronea & Bullskin Twps. will vote at Samuel HICKS', Bullskin Twp.

p. 452: William LYON, Esq., Prothonotary of Cumberland Co., lost his house by fire on the night of 1 Apr., 1789. He lost all his possessions but saved the public papers. He is exempted from paying tax.

p. 453: In 1780, Gabriel COX, George VALENDIGHAM & Andrew SWERINGEN hired Capt. Thomas BAY to raise a company of rangers for the defense of the Washington Co. frontier.

p. 458: James ROWAN was appointed tax collector of Phila. He is now in the Phila. gaol. Robert KNOX, Joseph BLEUER, Isaac PENROSE are commissioners to purchase a public landing in Southwark, Phila. Co. They are all now dec. The three surviving commissioners are

Joseph TURNER, William CLIFTON & John BROWN.

p. 462: Election district for Washington Co., Bentley's District, will vote at Thomas HILL's.

p. 476: John LYTLE, John WEBB & William MURRAY borrowed money from the loan office to improve farms in 1774. In the late Indian war, they were driven from their habitations & lost all personal property.

p. 476: Laughlin MCCARTNEY, John SIMPSON, Thomas GASKINS, William SAYERS, William MCKIM, Frederick STONE, Aaron LEVY, Robert MARTIN, William MACKEY, in 1775, furnished sundry supplies to the civil officers of Northumberland Co.

p. 477: Reading HOWELL, Phila., has procured material for compiling an accurate map of Pa. He is to receive £200 until the completion of the map.

p. 495: Two additional trustees are appointed for Huntingdon Co.: Andrew HENDERSON & Richard SMITH.

p. 501: Carpenters Company of Phila. is incorporated: Isaac ZANE, John MIFFLIN, Joseph THORNHILL, Benjamin LOXLEY, James WORREL, Gunning BRADFORD, Thomas NEVELL, James ARMTIAGE, Samuel ***, James POTTER, George WOOD, Joseph RAKESTRAW, Silas ENGLIS, William LOWNES, Samuel POWEL, William ROBINSON, James BRINGHURST, James GRAYSBURY, Thomas SHOEMAKER, David EVANS, William COLLIDAY, William ASHTON, Samuel JERVIS, Samuel WALLIS, Matthew M'GLATHERY, Thomas PROCTOR, Adam ZANTZINGER, John KEEN, John LORT, Joseph GOVETT, Joseph OGILBY, William WILLIAMS, Robert ALLISON, George FOREPAUGH, John SMITH, Matthias SADLER, James GIBSON, George INGELS, Frazer KINGSLEY, James CORKRIN, Joseph RAKESTRAW, Jr., Joseph THORNHILL, Jr., John KING, Andrew BOYD, Conrad BARTLING, William GARRIGUES, John RUGAN, Mark ROODES, Robert EVANS, Joseph WETHEREL, Hugh ROBERTS, Isaac JONES, Samuel PANCOAST, Matthias VALKEEN, William STEVENSON, Robert MORREL, Richard MOSLEY, John REINHARD, Samuel PASTORIUS, Josiah MATLACK, John PILES, Joseph CLARK, William ZANE, Benjamin MITCHELL, Thomas SAVERY, Nathan Allen SMITH, Samuel JONES, John HALL, Joseph HOWELL, Jr., Israel HALLOWELL, John HARRISON, Ebenezer FERGUSON, John COOPER, William LINNARD, Jonathan EVANS, Joseph WORREL, James BOYER.

***line is missing from the volume

p. 509: John OLIVER, William BROWN, Daniel BEAL, John STEWART, David BOWEL, Andrew GREGG, all of Mifflin Co., are trustees. Also Dr. James ARMSTRONG.

p. 529: Robert THORN, Bucks Co., has spent money over & above subscriptions given him to remove obstructions in the Delaware River at Wells' Falls & Howell's Falls. He is repaid £40 12s.

p. 532: Manuel JOSEPHSON, Solomon LYON, William WISTAR, John DUFFIELD, Samuel HAYES, Solomon ETTING are managers of a lottery to raise money for the Hebrew Congregation of Phila.

THE STATUTES OF PENNSYLVANIA FROM 1682 TO 1801
VOLUME 14 - 1791-1793

p. 8: Patent granted to BIG-TREE, one of the Seneca nation chiefs, for an island in the Allegheny River, 3 miles below Conewango River, called Conewango Island.

p. 9:   A warrant for $800 is to be paid to CORN-PLANTER, HALF-TOWN & BIG-TREE, Seneca chiefs, now in Phila. The town of Jenuch Shadega, two islands opposite the town, a Delaware town called Conenugayya & 300 acres on Oil Ck. are patented to CORN-PLANTER for a total of 1500 acres.

p. 12:   Dr. Francis ALISON, the surviving executor of the will of his brother, Benjamin ALISON. On orders of John PENN, Esq., on 25 Nov., 1775, the deceased furnished supplies & medicines.

p. 15:   Northampton Co. election district: Hamilton, Lower Smithfield Twps. will vote at Col. Jacob STROUT's. Upper Smithfield, Delaware Twps. will vote at Johannes VAN ETTEN's.

p. 22:   Election judges for Phila. & Bucks Co. will meet at George BENNER's, Bustleton, Phila. Co. Chester & Montgomery Co. judges will meet at Casper FAWNSTOCK's, East Whiteland Twp., Chester Co. Berks, Northampton, Luzerne Co. judges will meet at Jeremiah TREXLER's, Maccungy Twp., Northampton Co. Lancaster, Dauphin Co. judges will meet at Alexander BOGGS', near Elizabethtown, Lancaster Co. York & Cumberland Co. judges will meet at Daniel CARPENTER's, Warrington Twp., York Co. Westmoreland, Fayette, Washington, Allegheny Co. judges will meet at Stephen BAYARD's, Elizabethtown, Elizabeth Twp., Allegheny Co.

p. 25:   Robert KING carried public dispatches to the Seneca nation, respecting the murder of two Indians on Pine Ck. He exerted himself to bring the offenders to justice. He was given £139 10s 10p compensation & a patent for land in the 9th donation district.

p. 28:   Christian SELTZER has maintained a ferry over Swartara Ck. for several years.

p. 31:   Freeholders & taxables of Northern Liberties Twp. are to meet at John STRICKER's.

p. 47:   James CUNNINGHAM, David STEWART & John OLIVER, Esqs., are to run the boundary line between Huntingdon & Mifflin Cos.

p. 53:   Blackall William BALL, late a lieutenant in the Pa. Line, has lost certificate #2 for £220 12s 7p given to him for depreciation due on his pay.

p. 55:   Shauchan's election district & Bently's (2nd district of Washington Co.) find it inconvenient to vote at John HILL's. They will now vote at David HAMILTON's.

p. 56:   Jane JONES, Blaithwait JONES, Mary JONES, & Gibbs JONES, all of Phila., minors under 21, are entitled to 1/6 part of a messuage & lot near Leonard SHALLCROSS', James FISHER's. John WOOD is the guardian for the minors. Eleazer OSWALL has the authority to sell the property for the maintenance of the minors.

p. 57:   John SONGHURST, Samuel RICHARDSON, Anthony MORRIS owned a lot on which was erected the Bank meeting house, Phila., on 20 Feb., 1702. They sold it to Samuel CARPENTER, John KINSEY, John PARSONS, William HUDSON, Pentecost TEAGUE & Isaac NORRIS in trust for the Quakers. They are all long-since deceased. Samuel CARPENTER died beyone the sea. His heirs reside beyond the sea & are non-members of the society. William PENN granted, on 18 Oct., 1701, two lots on the southeast corner of Mulberry & 4th St. to Edward SHIPPEN &

Samuel CARPENTER for the use of the Quakers as a burying place. The two above properties are vested in Samuel SANSOM, John FIELD, Joshua CRESSON, John DRINKER, trustees appointed by the monthly meeting of Phila. Henry DRINKER, Samuel HOPKINS, Isaac CATHRALL & Thomas SCATTERGOOD are trustees appointed by the monthly meeting of Phila. for the northern district; Nicholas WALN, James BRINGHURST, Thomas FISHER, Samuel COATES are trustees appointed by the monthly meeting of Phila. for the southern district.

p. 60: John FOX, late of Phila., cutler, is attainted of high treason. His estate is forfeited. At the time of being attainted, he was indebted by bond to Elizabeth JONES, then a minor. Elizabeth JONES has since intermarried with Robert LUKENS. Bond was assigned to Abraham LUKENS, Horsham Twp., Montgomery Co.

p. 61: James OFFICER says two certificates (#5084 & #6490), issued on account of his services in the Cumberland Co. militia, were destroyed by fire. Two new ones were issued.

p. 69: Thomas BRADFORD is to receive £192 5s 6p for printing bills & laws. Eleazer OSWALD is to receive £14 7s 6p for printing bills. Andrew BROWN is to receive £15 6s 6p for newspapers furnished for the general assembly. Daniel HUMPHREYS is to receive £6 10s for newspapers furnished for the general assembly. Michael BILLMEYER is to receive £287 8s 2p for printing the minutes of the general assembly in German. Melchior STEINER is to receive £36 15s 9p for printing bills in German. Peter Zachary LLOYD is to receive £131 19s 9p as clerk of the general assembly. Jacob SHALLUS is to receive £119 13s 4p for extra services to the general assembly. James MARTIN is to receive £15 for extra services as Sergeant-at-arms. Joseph FRY is to receive £15 for extra services as doorkeeper.

p. 79: Union Twp., Mifflin Co., will vote at Capt. Hugh MCLELEN's. Wayne Twp., Mifflin Co., will vote at Edward JOHNSTON's. Potters Twp., Northumberland Co., will vote at George MCCORMICK's. The 5th election district of Northumberland Co. will vote at Aaron LEVY's.

p. 81: £130,000 is granted to the devisees of Thomas & Richard PENN & the widow of Thomas PENN on 27 Nov., 1779. On 28 Mar., 1787, a warrant was issued to John PENN, the younger, & John PENN, Esq.

p. 86: Evan OWEN is to receive £26 10s 9p for completing a road between the Susquehanna River & the Lehigh River (Nescopeck Rd.). Robert GALBRAITH is to receive £70 12s 6p for opening a road from Frankstown to Conemaugh.

p. 88: Philip PETER, by his attorney, John AURANT, applied by law for settlement of account of the officers & soldiers of the Pa. Line.

p. 89: Robert CUNNINGHAM, late master of the Brigantine "Conyngham," was convicted of bringing into the port of Phila., a number of passengers from Londonderry, Ireland, without having provided them with sufficient provisions & water & is fined £500. For want of payment, he was, in Dec. last, committed to gaol.

p. 124: John VANNOST, Phila., drafted a fee bill. He was paid £15 for services.

p. 140: Thomas GORDON was attainted of high treason. On 29 Mar.,

p. 140: Thomas GORDON was attainted of high treason. On 29 Mar., 1788, his estate was restored to him.

p. 147: Mary HARRISON's claim against the state is suspended, respecting a certain bond due from Joseph GALLOWAY.

p. 148: Robert SMITH, William RICHARDS are sureties of Alexander BOYD. BOYD owed the commonwealth £370 4s 2p for duties received by him as an auctioneer for the northern district of Phila.

p. 150: Henry DRINKER, Robert HARE, Joseph HIESTER, George LATIMER, George FRY, William MONTGOMERY, Samuel MILES are commissioners of the county to open a canal & lock-navigation between the Schuylkill River & the Susquehanna River.

p. 165: Election districts of Northumberland Co.: Turbutt, Derry, Washington & part of Muncy Twp. will vote at David SHANNON's, Turbutt Twp; the 9th election district will vote at Hugh ANDREW's, Pine Creek Twp. Teboyne & Tyrone Twps., Cumberland Co., will vote at George ROBINSON's, Tyrone Twp. Washington & Franklin Twps., Westmoreland Co. will vote at David FINLEY's. Tubmill Ck. to Chestnut Ridge will vote at Robert RODGERS', Wheatfield Twp. Moon Twp., Allegheny Co., from FLAUGHERTY's Run, BROADHEAD's Road, to the house of John SHORT to MONTGOMERY's mill, will vote at Col. Samuel WILSON's. Union, Caernarvon, Robeson Twps., Berks Co., will vote at Isaac BONSALL's, Robeson Twp.

p. 168: Sarah CALDWELL had certificates for £2513 12s 6p & they are now lost. Mary BEERE, Phila., widow, lost a new loan certificate #865 for £32 16s 3p. James STEEN, Chester Co., had a new loan certificate #14283, dated 23 Mar., 1787, for £29 16s 3p. It was lost 18 Dec., 1788. John THOMPSON, Bucks Co., on 20 Oct., 1789, was robbed of new loan certificates numbered from 3593 through 3600, #3610, #280, #8654, #8655, #8651.

p. 187: Richard RICHARDSON & some heirs of Joseph RICHARDSON, formerly of Providence Twp., Phila. Co., yeoman, dec., say that Joseph & Elizabeth & their son, Samuel RICHARDSON, by indenture dated 27 July, 1722, granted to Mary COOK, Phila., widow, a messuage & lot bounded by a lot formerly of Griffith JONES, dec., & a lot formerly of Abraham BICKLEY, dec., a messuage & lot bounded by James PORTEUS, dec. Elizabeth died first. Joseph's will of 6 Dec., 1745, devised yearly rent to his four sons: Samuel, Awbray, Edward & Richard. Awbray & Edward died before their father. Samuel also died many years ago. Richard is very ancient & infirm. Samuel, Awbray & Edward left behind a great number of children. Several children are dec. & they left behind numerous offspring scattered over the U.S.

p. 199: Small portions of the estates of John ROBERTS & Abraham CARLILE were forfeited by their attainder but were never sold. Jane ROBERTS, widow of John ROBERTS, & Abraham CARLILE, the only son of Abraham CARLILE, were the heirs.

p. 218: Part of the Luzerne Co. election district will vote at Isaac HANCOCK, Esq.'s. The 2nd election district, Lancaster Co., will vote at William WHITE's, known by the name of Unicorn, Drumore Twp.

p. 219: The first district of Westmoreland Co. will vote at William NEAL's, Armstrong Twp.

p. 223: James LOGAN, formerly of Stenton, Phila. Co., squire, by deed of 8 Mar., 1745, conveyed to trustees a lot as a library for the inhabitants of Phila. In his will of 25 Nov., 1749, he named his sons William, James & John, & Hannah SMITH (a daughter of James LOGAN, the elder) as the executors of the estate. On 28 Aug., 1754, they vested the building in Israel PEMBERTON, Jr., William ALLEN, Richard PETERS & Benjamin FRANKLIN. A tract of land in Solebury Twp., Bucks Co., was granted to Jonathan INGHAM by James LOGAN on 1 May, 1750. On 26 May, 1750, a tract was granted by James LOGAN, the elder, to Jacob DEAN. William LOGAN was the first librarian. The whole library now consists of 3500 volumes. James LOGAN is the only surviving trustee.

p. 227: John WETZEL, on 14 July, 1778, was directed to call forth the 1st, 2nd, 3rd, & 4th classes of militia in Northampton to procure 300 men to act in conjunction with Col. HARTLEY's regiment against the Indians on the frontier of the county. He could only raise 280 so he enlisted the remaining 20 men for £750 continental currency.

p. 229: Bedford Co. election districts: Quemahoning, Brothers Valley, Elklick Twps. will vote at Robert PHILSON's, Berlin, Brothers Valley Twp. Turkeyfoot, Milford Twps. will vote at Jesse BRAKIN's, Turkeyfoot Twp.

p. 231: The Little Lehigh, Northampton Co., will be a public highway from it's mouth to Adam DESHLER's mill dam. Passage can be made in Jacob WEISS' mill dam across Pocopoco or Big Ck., Northampton Co.

p. 240: John SHROPP desires to build a bridge over the Lehigh River at or near the present ferry at Bethlehem.

p. 243: Christopher SOWER, dec., forfeited real & personal estate to the commonwealth by his attainder. What wasn't forfeited is vested in Christopher ZIMMERMAN & David SOWER.

p. 251: Lancaster: Casper EHRMAN is warden for the n.e. ward. Henry LECHLER is warden for the n.w. ward. Daniel EHLER is warden for the s.e. ward. John REITZALL is warden for the s.w. ward. Christopher PETERY, Jacob WEAVER, Matthias YOUNG & Caleb COPE are assessors.

p. 260: Charles Wilson PEALE, Phila., on 25 Aug., 1779, purchased an estate in the Southwark district of Phila. Co.

p. 263: The 5th & 6th election districts in Washington Co. will vote at George BURGET's, miller.

p. 279: Elliston PEROT, Henry DRINKER, Jr., Owen JONES, Jr., Israel WHELEN, Cadwallader EVANS, Phila., gentlemen; Edward HAND, John HUBLEY, Paul ZANTZINGER, Matthias SLOUGH, Abraham WITMER, Lancaster Co., gentlemen, are commissioners to make a road from Phila. to Lancaster.

p. 294: The 2nd election district, Bedford Co., will vote at Michael STALL's, Belfast Twp.

p. 296: Jane COLLINS, a widow, lost a certificate prior to 23 Apr., 1788. Certificate #5490 was issued in favor of Ralph COLLINS, her late husband, for £78 13s 6p.

p. 332: Elections of the 5th district, Bedford Co., will vote at John SHOFF's, Milford Twp.

p. 337: John ALEXANDER, on 20 July, 1792, surrendered by his bail & is confined to gaol in Phila. for debt.

p. 338: Daniel LEET, deputy-surveyor, is to lay out a town at the Mouth of Beaver Ck.

p. 342: John MILLER, Adam WEAVER, John SWENK, John MILEY are to erect a bridge over the Conostogoe Ck. where Martick Forge Rd. crosses in Lancaster Co.

p. 353: John HERSH, a soldier in the Pa. Line, dec., lost a certificate for depreciation of pay, #259, for £60 17s 7p.

p. 356: Peter LAGAUX has experimented with cultivating the vine in Pa. Samuel MILES, Fench FRANCIS, John SWANWICK, Timothy PICKERING & Israel WHELEN are commissioners of the county to promote cultivation of vines.

p. 361: Mifflin & St. Clair Twps., Allegheny Co., near James PERRY's ferry, BECK's Run, John BELL's, Nicholas BAUSMAN's are to vote at John REED's, stone mason, Mifflin Twp.

p. 366: Superintendents of the Bank of Pa.: Samuel HOWELL, John BARCLAY, Clement BIDDLE, John ROSS, Edward FOX, John SWANWICK, George MEADE, at Phila. Edward HAND, Robert COLEMAN, George ROSS, Adam REIGART & Casper SHAFFNER, at Lancaster. James DEIMER, Joseph HEISTER, James MAY, Jacob BOWER, Thomas DUNDAS, at Reading.

p. 384: John KEAN, Henry BAYLOR, Valentine HUMMEL are commissioners for Dauphin Co. & are intrusted with HARRIS' ferry, late of John HARRIS, dec., & conveyed to Jacob AWL, Andrew STEWART, James COWDEN, Joshua ELDER & William BROWN. John KEAN, Robert HARRIS, Michael KOPP are to procure materials to build a courthouse on a lot in Harrisburg.

p. 388: John WALKER is authorized to erect a wing-dam on Conedogwinet Ck., Cumberland Co.

p. 390: Richard KEYS, Thomas BAILEY, John GRIER, James HOPKINS are proprietors of land adj. Connewago Falls on the eastern side of Susquehanna River, Lancaster Co.

p. 397: Adam HAMAKER is authorized to maintain a dam across Swatara Ck., Dauphin Co.

p. 400: The Conewago Canal Co. trustees: Robert MORRIS, William SMITH, Walter STEWART, Samuel MEREDITH, John STEINMETZ, Tench FRANCIS, John NICHOLSON, John DONALDSON, Samuel MILES, Timothy MATLACK, David RITTENHOUSE, Samuel POWEL, Alexander James DALLAS, William BINGHAM, Henry MILLER, Abraham WITMER, Robert HARRIS.

p. 404: Simon SNYDER & the heirs of Anthony SELIN, dec., may erect a dam across Penn's Ck., Northumberland Co.

p. 406: Lots vested in Christopher MARSHALL, Joseph STILES, Nathaniel BROWN, Isaac HOWELL, Peter THOMSON, Benjamin SAY & Joseph

p. 412: Commissioners to open a canal & lock navigation system on the Brandywine Ck.: Abijah DAWES, Joseph Parker NORRIS, Samuel Mickle FOX, Jonathan HARVEY, Andrew PETTIT, Hugh ROBERTS, John FLEMING, Charles DILWORTH, Nathan SCOFIELD, Robert HAMILTON, John HAYES, William POOLE. Josiah MATLACK, Moses COATES, Rumford DAWES, Job HENRY, Samuel HOLLINGSWORTH are commissioners to lay courses & distances of canals.

p. 426: Andrew PIERCE, Allegheny Co., erected a mill-dam across the Monongahela River.

p. 428: Elections for Woodbury Twp., Bedford Co., will be held at William HART's. Elections for Cumberland Valley Twp., Bedford Co., will be held at Peter BUGH's.

p. 428: The estate of James RANKIN was forfeited by his attainder. Portions were never sold on behalf of the Commonwealth. George NEBINGER has asked that those portions be vested in Abraham RANKIN & Ann NEBINGER, wife of George, two children of James RANKIN.

p. 432: Fleming WILSON, Northumberland Co., says a tract of land which is now his property, was mortgaged by John STEVENS, the original grantee, to a trustee of the loan office. He transferred the tract to Cornelius VINCENT & Samuel GOULD who sold it to Fleming WILSON.

p. 445: James SHORT, George DUFFIN, Jacob TREAT, Jacob CARPENTER, Samuel Mickle FOX & John HANNUM are commissioners to build a bridge over the Susquehanna River near the Blue Rock, 4 miles below WRIGHT's ferry, Lancaster Co.

p. 511: Elections for Letterkenny Twp., Franklin Co., will be at Andrew RALSTON's, Strasburg, Letterkenny Twp.

THE STATUTES AT LARGE OF PENNSYLVANIA FROM 1682 TO 1801
VOLUME 15 - 1794-1797

p. 5: Samuel MILES, John SWANWICK, Walter STEWART, John FRY, Israel WHELEN & Benjamin BARTON are commissioners to promote the cultivation of vines.

p. 8: Elections in Macungie, Upper Milford Twps., Northampton Co., will be at Leonard SLOUGH's, Millerstown, Macungie Twp. Elections in Heidelburg, Lowhill, Weissenburg, Lynn, Penn Twps., Northampton Co. will be held at Henry OHL's, Heidelburg.

p. 9: Standing Stone Ck., near the house of William MCALEVY, is declared a public highway.

p. 10: In 1790, Peter DEHAVEN was appointed a trustee of the State Island & Hospital. He was paid $80.83 for his services.

p. 11: Elections for Tinicum, Nockamixon, Durham Twps., Bucks Co., will be at Jacob YOUNG's, Nockamixon Twp.

p. 11: Elections for Quemahoning & Stony Ck. Twps., Bedford Co., will be at Joseph BUCK's, Quemahoning Twp.

p. 12: Cocolamus Ck., near David CARGIL's, is a public highway.

p. 16: Blackall William BALL, a lieutenant in the late Pa. Line, lost a certificate #94 for £220 12s 7p which was given to him for depreciation of pay.

p. 17: Thomas BUTLER lost a new loan certificate #2350 for £87 15s for personal services performed during the war. Henry BROWN lost a certificate #3645 for $50 for like services.

p. 20: Colebrookdale, Earle District, Hereford Twp., Berks Co., will vote at Joseph MUTHARD's, Colebrookdale Twp.

p. 21: Edward SHYMER, Bethlehem Twp., Northampton Co., is authorized to erect a dam on the Lehigh River in order to erect a grist mill.

p. 28: Adam MELCHER, at a sale of confiscated estates held by George SMITH, agent for the Commonwealth, in 1787, purchased 1/4 part of a tract in Lower Merion Twp., Montgomery Co., which was forfeited to the state by John MEREDITH, attainted of high treason.

p. 30: James WALLACE, W. Hanover Twp., Dauphin Co., & Rudolph PICKEL, Lebanon Twp., are authorized to build mill dams two miles above Hummelstown & 2 ½ miles below Jonestown, opposite the land of George TITTLE.

p. 31: Christian MARY, a tax collector in Charleston Twp., Chester Co., was obliged to employ Lawrence KING as an assistant. On 23 Feb., 1788, KING was robbed of £45 2s 6p of public money.

p. 32: Springfield, Haycock, Rockhill, Richland, Milford Twps., Bucks Co. will vote at Jacob FREES, Richland Twp.

p. 33: New Britain, Plumstead, Buckingham, Warwick, Warrington, Bedminster, Hilltown Twps., Bucks Co., will vote at William CHAPMAN's, Esq., Buckingham Twp.

p. 34: The 6th district, Washington Co., near John MARSHALL's saw mill, SMITH's meeting house, WALLER's Fort, will vote at Samuel URIES.

p. 35: Charles CAMPBELL was a lieutenant of the Westmoreland Co. militia. Absalom BAIRD was a lieutenant in the Washington Co. militia.

p. 38: Patrick ROBERTS, a soldier in the late Pa. Line, lost certificate #77 for £56 6s 4p for depreciation pay. Charles WEST, Jr., lost a new loan certificate #11874 for £294 5s.

p. 40: Archibald MCGREW said that Thomas BRACKEN, late of York Co., dec., owned land in Manallen Twp., bounded by Joseph ELGAR, Thomas MCCOUSLAND & James MCGREW. On 6 Apr., 1779, a will was made that directed Archibald MCGREW & William BRACKEN, executors, to sell the land. William BRACKEN died before the sale.

p. 44: John Maxwell NESBIT is the president of the Insurance Co. of America. Directors are Joseph BALL, John CRAIG, John LEAMY, John SWANWICK, Walter STEWART, Samuel BLODGET, the younger, Magnus MILLER, Thomas FITZSIMONS, William MCMURTRIE, John VAUGHN, Charles PETTIT, John ROSS, Robert RALSTON, Francis WEST, Standish FORD, Peter BLIGHT, Thomas Lloyd MOORE, Robert SMITH, John FRY, the younger, Jehu HOLLINGSWORTH, John WILCOX, Thomas TINGEY, Archibald

MCCALL, Philip NICKLIN.

p. 65: Payment for incidental expenses: Michael BILLMEYER for printing the House of Representatives journals in German. Francis SHALLUS for transcribing the constitution. Joseph FRY, door-keeper. Thomas DOBSON for stationery. Anthony WRIGHT for powder. James MARTIN. William SCHEAFF for vinegar to purify rooms after the late epidemic. Andrew BROWN, newspapers. Benjamin Franklin BACHE. John DUNLAP. Francis KIRKPATRICK. William O'HARRA. William BARRET.

p. 70: Stockholders of the Insurance Co. of Pa.: Archibald MCCALL, Jesse & Robert WALN, Thomas WILLING, WHEELEN & MILLER, Thomas FITZSIMONS, George LATIMER, Francis GURNEY, John SWANWICK, Levi HOLLINGSWORTH, Joshua GILPIN, Mordecai LEWIS, James YARD, Joseph MAGOFFIN, Ambrose VASSE, John STEINMETZ, Ferguson MCILVAINE, Jacob DOWNING, Joseph & Richard WALN, Josiah HEWES, Thomas MORGAN, Miers FISHER, SMITH & RIDGEWAY, Benjamin FULLER, Thomas ELLISTON & John PEROT, JACKSON & EVANS, RUNDLE & MURGATROYD, William ROBESON, Daniel TYSON, John WALN, Philip NICKLIN & Co., George PLUMSTEAD, Robert WHARTON, SNOWDEN & NORTH, Thomas CANBY, Joseph ANTHONY, PLUMSTEAD & MCCALL, John & William MONTGOMERY, Alexander FOSTER, John NIXON, George EDDY; PHILIPS, CRAMOND & CO.; Jehu HOLLINGSWORTH & Co., Isaac WHARTON, Thomas M. WILLING, Isaac HAZLEHURST, Mathew LAWLER, James C. & Samuel FISHER, George MEADE; HARTSHORNE, LARGE & Co.; Edward DUNANT, Robert SMITH, WHARTON & GREEVES, Alexander WILCOCKS, George EMLIN, John SITGREAVES, John Clement STOCKER, George MCCALL, John DONALDSON, Anthony BUTLER, Charles WHARTON, Jesse WALN, John FIELD & Son, James CRAIG, John WILCOCKS, Peter KUHN, Samuel HOWELL, WELLS & MORRIS, Jeremiah WARDER, Blair MCCLENACHAN, Patrick MOORE, Jeremiah PARKER, Joseph SWIFT, Benjamin MORGAN, David H. CONYNGHAM, Rumford & Abijah DAWES, William SMITH, William RAWLE, John FRY, Samuel M. FOX, William SANSOM, Joseph Parker NORRIS, Joseph SIMS, James COX, Stephen GIRARD, Daniel SMITH, John HUNN, Edward RUSSEL, Nalbro & John FRAZIER, Samuel COATES, MORGAN & PRICE, James ASH, John WHARTON, John MILLER, Jr., John ANGUS, BRITTON & MASSEY, Edward CARRELL, William FORREST, Mathias KEELY, Philemon DICKENSON, John STILLE, Peter KEMBLE; NOTTNAGLE, MONTMOLIN & Co.; Adam KUHN, James MAZURIE, Henry PRATT, Lambert CADWALLADER, Archibald MCCALL, Jr., Nathan FIELD, Bohl BOHLEN, Josiah W. & W. GIBBS, DUTHILL & WACHSMUTH, Alexander MURRAY, James VANUXEM, David PINKERTON, Thomas EWING, Peter BLIGHT, PRAGERS & Co., Samuel JACKSON, Benjamin HOLLAND, Stephen DECATUR, Curtis CLAY, Joseph RUSSEL, George WESCOTT, Thomas BELL, HOLMES & RAINEY, Nathaniel LEWIS, William PLUMSTEAD, STEWART & BARR, Wilson HUNT, George HARRISON, Woolman SUTTON, Thomas TINGEY, William ALLIBONE, Thomas PENROSE, Paul BECK, George CLAY, Samuel PENROSE, Philip CARE, Lowis CROUSILLET.

p. 77: Election district--part of Luzerne Co. will vote at Horatio STRONG's.

p. 104: John BLAKE is a tax collector in Phila. Co.

p. 107: George WALL, late a sub-lieutenant in Bucks Co., obtained a judgment against Robert ROBINSON, late of Bedminister Twp., Bucks Co., dec. for money for militia fines. Grizel ROBINSON, widow of Robert ROBINSON, is subject to occasional lunacy. Thomas PRICE bought the messuage & lot of Grizel ROBINSON.

p. 146: John LAIRD, in Aug., 1778, pursuant of orders given by John TRAVERS, then sub-lieutenant of York Co., spent £280 to hire seven men to march to the Standing Stone for defence of the Western frontiers.

p. 147: Samuel HARVEY, late of Falls Twp., Bucks Co., owned a plantation & in his will written 29 July, 1770, he authorized William YARDLEY & HARVEY's widow, Catharine, to sell it & divide the money between his brothers, Thomas, William & John, & sister, Elizabeth GILLINGHAM (wife of Joseph GILLINGHAM); his widow, Catharine; William, Mary, Jane, John, Peter, Vanransiller & Samuel TENBROOK. William YARDLEY & Catharine HARVEY have since died. Joseph GREER is the administrator of Jane GREER, late Jane TENBROOK, dec. William HARVEY is the executor of the estate of John HARVEY, dec. Isaac & Sarah PENNINGTON are the administrators of Thomas HARVEY, dec. Elijah PHILLIPS is the administrator of Catherine PHILLIPS, late Catherine HARVEY, dec.

p. 154: Delaware Co. election district: Concord, Birmingham, Thornbury, Ashton, Bethel & Upper Chichester Twps. will vote at Joshua VERNON's, Concord Twp.

p. 155: Delaware Co. election district: Newton, Edgemont, Upper Providence, Marple & Radnor Twps. will vote at William BEAUMONT's, Newton Twp. Darby, Upper Darby, Haverford, Springfield, Tinicum Twps. will vote at Samuel SMITH's, Darby Twp.

p. 155: Matthew CLARKSON, Elliston PEROT, Israel ISRAEL, Caleb LOWNES, James KERR, John LETCHWORTH, James SHARSWOOD are guardians of orphan children of Phila. city & suburbs who have been left parentless by a "malignant disorder" recently afflicted on Phila.

p. 157: William LINDSEY, late of Uwchlan Twp., Chester co., dec., nominated Richard THOMAS & George THOMAS, both of West Whiteland Twp. as executors of his estate. George is now dec.

p. 159: Judges of Berks & Dauphin Co. will meet at Jacob SELTZER's, Middletown, Berks Co. Judges of Westmoreland & Fayette Co. will meet at William LATTA's, South Huntingdon Twp., Westmoreland Co.

p. 173: Judges of Bucks, Northampton & Montgomery Co. will meet at Jacob FRIE's, innkeeper, Richland Twp., Bucks Co. Judges of Berks & Luzerne Co. will meet at Samuel WEBB's, Manheim Twp., Berks Co. Judges of Dauphin & Northumberland Co. will meet at Matthias DEIBLER's, Dauphin Co. Judges of Cumberland & Mifflin Co. will meet at John STERRETT's, Greenwood Twp., Cumberland Co. Judges of Bedford, Franklin, & Huntingdon Co. will meet at John JAVISON's, Burnt Cabins, Bedford Co.

p. 182: Israel WHELEN, James MILLER, George BICKHAM, Francis JOHNSTON, Jonathan JONES, Phila.; Edward HAND, John HUBLEY, Adam REIGART, Jr., Thomas BOUDE, Paul ZANTZINGER, Lancaster Co., are commissioners to make a road from Lancaster to the Susquehanna River, near WRIGHT's ferry.

p. 198: William WALLACE petitions to erect a bridge across Raystown branch of the Juniata River.

p. 200: Peter SHAFFNER, late tax collector in Lancaster borough, is now confined to the gaol of Lancaster Co. for non-payment of money which he received from taxes.

p. 206: Election districts: Huntingdon Co.--Woodbury, Frankstown, part of Allegheny Twp. west of Widow EDINGTON's will vote at

Alexander MCDOWELL's, Frankstown Twp. Franklin, Tyrone, Morris & part of Allegheny Twp. east of Widow EDINGTON's will vote at Alexander RAMSEY, Jr's., Franklin Twp.

p. 207: John WALKER, E. Pennsboro Twp., Cumberland Co., petitions to extend the wing-dam across Conedogwinit Ck.

p. 210: Nathaniel FALCONER is the late health officer of the port of Phila.

p. 215, 1795: Westmoreland Co. election district: South Huntingdon district near Jacob PAINTER, Esq's. mill on Sewickley Ck. will vote at Jacob HOUGH, Jr's.

p. 217: Middle Paxton, Dauphin Co. election district will vote at John AYRES'.

p. 218: Zachariah POULSON, Jr., printer of the state journal, is paid $130. Thomas DOBSON is paid $40.14 for stationery. Michael BILLMEYER is paid $182 for printing the journal in German.

p. 220: Luzerne Co. election district: Lackawanna, Exeter, Providence Twps., will vote at William Hooker SMITH's, Lackawanna Twp.

p. 221: Benjamin ELLIOT is authorized to erect a wing-dam on the east side of the Juniata River, Huntingdon Co.

p. 225: James MILLER owned land in New Garden Twp., Chester Co. On 26 Oct., 1717, he sold 6 acres to Simon HADLEY, James STARR, Thomas JACKSON, Michael LIGHTFOOT on which they erected a brick meetinghouse & a stone schoolhouse. On 12 Dec., 1723, they declared the land was conveyed to them as trustees of the Quakers. Simon HADLEY is the only survivor. His heirs have removed to Carolina. The land is now vested in John PHILLIPS, Isaac RICHARDS, Jr., William THOMPSON, Thomas HOOPS, Holliday JACKSON, Joseph SHARP.

p. 226: Jeremiah REES & Samuel FISHER are authorized to maintain a dam across Connedogwinit Ck., Cumberland Co.

p. 229: Warrants are drawn for Godfrey HAGA, Edward PENNINGTON, Robert RALSTON, Samuel P. GRIFFITS, Joseph LOWNES, Samuel MECKLIN, Joseph SANSOM, commissioners, to give relief to distressed French emigrants from Hispaniola.

p. 230: Philip ODENWELDER (the younger), Jonas HARTZELL, Henry ENGLE, Peter SHARP all owned land in Easton, Northampton Co., near Jacob GROTZ, Jr's. They are authorized to sell land to purchase a parsonage for the minister of four protestant Evangelic Reformed German congregations--Easton, Nazareth, Plainfield Twps., Northampton Co. & Greenwich Twp., Sussex Co., N.J.

p. 233: Some residents of Chester, Delaware Co., were David COWPLAND & John SALKELD.

p. 236: Levi HOLLINGSWORTH, Jesse WALN, John NICHOLSON, Phila., John ARNDT, William HENRY, John HERSTER, Northampton Co., James HYNDSHAW, Thomas PAUL, Thomas BULLMAN, N.J., are commissioners to build a bridge over the Delaware River at Easton, Northampton Co.

p. 246: Bedford Co. election district: Hopewell Twp. will vote at

Mordecai WILLIAMS'.

p. 246: William BEATTY is authorized to erect a dam from Sheep Island to the west side of the Juniata River, Cumberland Co.

p. 247: Bald Eagle Twp. & part of Potter Twp. near Nathaniel ADAMS, Mifflin Co. will vote at Richard MILES', Milesborough. The rest of Potter Twp. will vote at William KING's.

p. 253: William COATES, Esq., Jacob WEAVER, Esq., Dr. John WEAVER, Dr. Peter PERES, Jacob WHITMAN, William Peter SPRAGUE, Daniel MILLER, John BROWN, Michael GROVES, John Nicholas WAGNER are superintendents of a town house & market place between Coates St. & Poplar Lane, Northern Liberties, Phila.

p. 257: Heidelberg Twp., Dauphin Co. will vote at Samuel RIX's, Shafferstown.

p. 258: William GARDNER, Jr. is authorized to erect a bridge from a certain Rocky Island in the Youghiogheny River, Westmoreland Co., to his own land.

p. 259: Ann RUSSEL said that in 1792, she lost a new loan certificate #13769 dated 1 Jan., 1787, issued in the name of John Chew THOMAS for £129 2s 9p.

p. 262: There is a tract of marsh & meadow land in Kingsessing Twp., Phila. Co., near fast land of John HUNT, Matthew JONES, Samuel BUNTING, Benjamin SAY & James B. BONSALL.

p. 274: Green Twp., Washington Co., will vote at JARRET's Fort at the house of George COX.

p. 283: John HAWGER is authorized to erect a dam on Penn's Ck., Northumberland Co.

p. 284: Those voting near Miller's Run, Montour's Run & James BAGG's fork will vote at Henry NOBLE's, Noblesburg.

p. 292: Mahanoy Twp., Northumberland Co., will vote at William DOBSON's.

p. 293: Cocalico & Elizabeth Twp., Lancaster Co., will vote at Henry MILLER's, near Ephrata.

p. 294: East Pennsborough & Allen Twp., Cumberland Co., near John CLENDENEN's & Archibald LOWDEN's, will vote at the Silver Spring meeting house, East Pennsborough.

p. 295: John METOXEN, on the Stockbridge tribe of Oneida Indians, will be provided with suitable lodging, clothing & entertainment for two years & will be placed in a school for education.

p. 300: Commissioners for ascertaining arrearages of taxes in various counties: For Phila. & Montgomery Co.--Henry DRINKER, Jr., son of John DRINKER; John BROWN, Northern Liberties; John MANN, Montgomery Co. For Chester & Delaware Co.--William GIBBONS, William TREMBLE, Jr., Chester Co.; Hugh LLOYD. For Lancaster & Dauphin Co.--Andrew CALDWELL, Mathias YOUNG, Alexander BERRYHILL. For Northumberland & Luzerne Co.--John SIMPSON, John KIDD, Lawrence MYERS. For Cumberland, Franklin & Mifflin Co.--John ARTHURS,

William ELLIOT, Fanet Twp.; Joseph MCCLELLAND. For Bedford & Huntingdon Co.--David STEWART, Thomas VICORY & Jacob NAGLE. For Westmoreland, Washington, Fayette & Allegheny Co.--William JACK, Daniel LEET, Samuel KING, George WALLACE. For Bucks Co.--Isaac WATSON, Isaac VANHORN, Thomas LONG. For Berks Co.--John WITMAN, son of Christopher WITMAN; John SPIKER & Peter FEATHER, Jr. For York Co.--Alexander RUSSELL, George Lewis LEFFLER, John CAMPBELL, Sr. For Northampton Co.--Jacob EYERLY, Jr., Robert TRAIL, George RHOADS.

p. 308: William DUNTON served as sailing master & Bernard MERKLE served as seaman on board the ship Hyder Ally, commanded by Capt. Joshua BARNEY. On 8 Apr., 1782, in an engagement between the Hyder Ally & a British ship, the General Monk, both men were wounded & are disabled. John KLINE, late a private in the Berks Co. militia was disabled by a wound received in his arm while in the service. None are entitled to relief from the U.S. having only been in the service of Pa. DUNTON will receive $7/month, MERKLE will receive $4/month, KLINE will receive $3.33/month.

p. 317: John GORDON, Phila., while acting in the service of Pa. as a sergeant in the artillery at Fort Mifflin, in the Delaware River, Sept., 1793, received an injury in one of his feet by the fall of a piece of cannon. He is probably crippled for life. He is granted $400.

p. 347: David RITTENHOUSE, Francis GURNEY, Thomas PROCTOR are commissioners to inspect gunpowder.

p. 376: John NICHOLAS is the late comptroller-general.

p. 378, 1796: Hannah SOWER has vested in herself & her children certain parts of the forfeited estate of Christopher SOWER, the younger.

p. 385: Oliver POLLOCK & Henry NEAFF are authorized to erect a wing-dam on Conedogwinit Ck., Cumberland Co.

p. 391: Brintnel ROBBINS is authorized to erect a mill-dam over part of the Youghiogheny River, Westmoreland Co.

p. 392: Agents for confiscated estates in Northumberland Co. sold to Valentine ECKHART, a tract of land on Fishing Ck., part of the confiscated estate of Alexander BARTRAM for £826.

p. 393: William HARRIS & Joseph MCCLELLAND established a ferry over the Juniata River on the main road leading from Sunbury & Northumberland to Path Valley.

p. 398: Evan OWEN is authorized to erect a wing dam on the north side of the Susquehanna River, Northumberland & Luzerne Co.

p. 399: Christopher ERNST & Samuel SHERER maintained a ferry over Swatara Ck. on the main road leading from Reading through Hummelstown to Harrisburg.

p. 403: Thomas WHITAKER is to establish a ferry over the Juniata River opposite the town of Huntingdon, Huntingdon Co.

p. 404: William Ennis CORTWRIGHT, late a private in the Northampton Co. militia, was disabled by a wound in the thigh while in Pa. service.

p. 405: The commissioners of the Lancaster, Elizabethtown, Middletown, Harrisburg Turnpike Road Co.: Alexander BERRYHILL, William BROWN, William CRABB, Jasper EWING, George FISHER, John A. HANNA, Christian KUNCKLE, Robert MCKEE, Mordecai MCKINNEY, William MONTGOMERY, John NORRIS, Adam RIEGART, Jr., James RUSSELL, Daniel SMITH, Thomas STUBBS, John SWAR, Abraham WITMER, William NELSON, Paul ZANTZINGER.

p. 420: Owen MCLAUGHLIN, late a soldier in Col. HAZEN's regiment of the quota of this commonwealth in the U.S. Army, lost a certificate #76 for £90 19s 7p for depreciation pay. John SKILLING, Lycoming Co., lost certificate #106 for £64 6s 8p for personal services rendered during the late war.

p. 423: Joseph HEISTER, James DIEMER, Thomas DUNDAS, James MAY, John OTTO, John KEIM, Daniel GRAFF, Sebastian MILLER are commissioners to raise by lottery $60,000 to erect a stone bridge over the Schuylkill River at Reading.

p. 432: George LATIMER, Robert WALN, Nathaniel LEWIS, Abijah DAWES, Phila.; Joshua PUSEY, Jacob LINDLEY, John M'DOWELL, James BOYD, Chester Co.; Abraham CARPENTER, John FUNK, Michael WITHER, John BARR, Paul ZANTZINGER, Adam REIGART, Jr., John FRY, Lancaster Co.; Henry LATIMER, Joseph TATNAL, William ROBESON, Nehemiah DELAPLAINE, Cyrus NEWLIN, New Castle Co., Delaware, are commissioners to make a road from Gap Tavern on the Phila. & Lancaster Turnpike to Newport & Wilmington Delaware.

p. 451: A warrant is drawn in favor of Joseph HORSEFIELD for removing fallen timber & obstructions in the road from Jacob HELLER's tavern, Northampton Co. to Wilkesbarre, Luzerne Co.

p. 464: Martin NISSLY is authorized to erect a wing-dam on the west side of the Conestoga River, Lancaster Co.

p. 474, 1797: Henry PENFINGER, a disabled soldier of the 4th Pa. regiment in the late Revolutionary War is paid #600.

p. 476: John MILLER, East Hanover Twp., Dauphin Co., is authorized to erect a mill dam across Swatara Ck., 4 miles below Jonestown, Dauphin Co.

p. 478: Paul Frazer is authorized to erect a dam across Shearman's Ck., Cumberland Co.

p. 479: Robert SAMPLE, a captain in the late continental army in the Pa. line, received a patent for 500 acres of donation land which fell in N.Y. The patent is mislaid or lost. A new patent is granted for land in Pa.

p. 482: Peter MUHLENBERG, John RICHARDS, Benjamin MARKLEY, Samuel BAIRD, Pottsgrove; Francis SWAINE, Moses HOBSON, Frederick CONRAD, Samuel MAULSBY, Francis NICHOLS, William SMITH, Philip BOYER, Elisha EVANS, James BEAN, John MARKLEY, tanner, Robert KENNEDY, John ELIOT are commissioners to raise funds to erect a stone arch bridge over Perkiomen Ck., Montgomery Co., on the road from Phila. to Reading.

p. 485: Marsh land in Derby Twp., Delaware Co., is near land late of John GRANTHAM, John FREDERICK & Daniel HUMPHRIES, dec. Hugh LLOYD, Jacob GIBBONS, John HUNT are to determine the deficiency of

p. 497: Robert DEAN & Joseph SMITH are authorized to erect a wing-dam on the south side of the Frankstown branch of the Juniata, Huntingdon Co.

p. 498: Edward HAND, Paul ZANTZINGER, Abraham WITMER, Matthias SLOUGH, Adam REIGART, Jr., Jacob GRAFF, Philip DIFFENDERFER, Jacob KRUGH, George MUSSER, John MILLER, Joseph CRAWFORD, Caspar SHAFFNER, John HUBER, Adam WEAVER, John HUBLEY are commissioners to raise money to pave streets in Lancaster Borough.

p. 503: James PATTERSON owned land in Hamilton Twp., Franklin Co. adj. Christian MILLER, Isaac PEARSON, William RAMSEY, Thomas RAMSEY & William MCCUNE. In Apr., 1795, he sold it to George CRIDER. PATTERSON died intestate leaving a numerous family, some still minors, & a widow.

p. 505: Election districts: Elizabeth Twp., Allegheny Co. will vote at Samuel BAYARD's. Bethel & East Hanover Twps., Dauphin Co. will vote at Christopher CAPP, Jr's, Williamsburg, Bethel Twp. Turkey Foot Twp., Somerset Co., will vote at John NICHLOW's. Milford & Somerset Twp., Somerset Co., will vote at Henry & Jacob SCHNEYDER's, Somerset. The north end of Belfast Twp., Bedford Co. will vote at Daniel MCCONNEL's, Air Twp. Muncy Twp., & part of Washington Twp., Lycoming Co., will vote at Henry SHOEMAKER, Jr's., Muncy Twp. Part of Lycoming Twp. & Nippenose Twp., Lycoming Co., will vote at Thomas RAMSEY's, Pine Ck. Pine Ck. Twp., Lycoming Co., will vote at Hugh ANDREWS', Dunnsburg. Bald Eagle Twp., Lycoming Co., will vote at Frederick RICHARDS'. West Caln, Sadsbury, East & West Fallowfield Twps., Chester Co., will vote at James HOLLIS', East Fallowfield. East & West Nottingham Twps., Upper & Lower Oxford Twps., Chester Co., will vote at Samuel HOOD's. Charlestown, Tredyffrin, Easttown, Willistown, East Whiteland Twps., Chester Co., will vote at Richard ROBINSON's, Tredyffrin Twp. Woodbury, Morris Twps., Huntingdon Co., will vote at Robert SMITH's, Williamsbug (sic). Hopewell & Union Twps. near John FRETE's will vote at Isaac CRUM's on the Raystown branch of the Juniata River. Franklin Twp., Greene Co., will vote at Thomas SLATER's near Waynesburg. Cumberland Twp., Greene Co., will vote at Philip KITCHAM's. Part of Northampton Co. will vote at Elijah DIX's. Washington Twp. & part of White Deer Twp., Northumberland Co., near Matthew LAIRD's plantation to where Peter AWARTZ formerly lived, near James STEDMAN's, near William REED's on Childeisquaque Ck., will vote at William GALLAGHER's, Milton.

p. 513: John KONAPOT, Jr., a youth of the Stockbridge tribe of Oneida Indians, is given lodging, clothing & entertainment money & will be educated at public expense. John KONAPOT, Sr. is to be paid $60 to defray expenses until he returns to his own nation.

p. 527: William TILGHMAN & George EDDY, Phila.; Peter ROADS, Peter EALER, Henry HAUGHENBAUGH, Thomas MAWHORTER, Northampton Co., are commissioners to erect a bridge over the Lehigh River near Northampton.

p. 535: The election district of Bethlehem & part of Bethlehem Twp. & Allen Twp. will vote at Adam SHENER's, Allen Twp.

p. 535: The election district of Strasburg, Sadsbury, Bart & part of Martic Twp. near Henry ECKMAN's & LONG's tavern will vote at George RINE's, Strasburg.

p. p. 537: Montgomery Co. election districts: Whitemarsh, Springfield, Upper Dublin, Horsham Twps. will vote at Philip RIFFERT's, Whitemarsh Twp. Abington, Cheltenham & Moreland Twps. will vote at William MCCALLA's, Abington Twp. Gwynedd, Montgomery, Towamensing, Hatfield, Franconia, Lower Salford, Skippack & Perkiomen Twps. will vote at Christian WEABER's, Twoamensing Twp. Limerick, New Hanover, Upper Hanover, Douglas, Marlborough & Frederick Twps. will vote at Catharine SCHNIDER's, New Hanover Twp.

p. 542: Berks Co. election districts: Bethel, Tulpehocken, part of Heidelberg Twp. will vote at Conrad STAUCH's, Middletown, Heidelberg Twp. Pine Grove Twp. will vote at Jacob GUNCKEL's.

p. 550: Commissioners, in the commission of bankrupt issued against Joseph DEAN, Thomas BARCLAY, Jonathan WILLIAMS, Jr., & Robert MCCLENACHAN, shall have the power to demand & receive all moneys recovered by them for debts due to the co-partnership of DEAN & PURVIANCE, BARCLAY & MITCHELL, WILLIAMS, MOORE & Co., & THOMPSON & MCLENACHAN.

p. 556: Thomas PROCTOR is authorized to commence suit against the Commonwealth.

p. 560: In Montgomery Co., Margaret GILBERT was found to be of unsound mind. She owns land in Warminster Twp., Bucks Co. Jonathan JARRET, Montgomery Co., is appointed to take care of her estate. William GILBERT is brother & heir to Margaret.

p. 562: On 5 Apr., 1790, Dr. James ARMSTRONG was appointed trustee for Mifflin Co. He has since moved out of the country. William HARRIS is appointed in his stead.

p. 563: Nicholas KERN, Jonas HARTZELL, John CRAIG, Samuel STEWART, John KIDD, & Richard MARTIN are to be paid for services performed in obtaining information respecting intrustions made within Pa. by persons claiming under Connecticut.

THE STATUTES AT LARGE OF PENNSYLVANIA FROM 1682 TO 1801
VOLUME 16 - 1798-1801

p. 6: Lewis DERR, late of Buffalo Twp., Northumberland Co., dec., made an indenture on 26 Mar., 1785, granting three lots in Lewisburg, Buffalo Twp., to Walter CLARK, William GRAY & William WILSON. They can sell the land for the use of the Presbyterian Church of Buffalo Twp.

p. 7: Alexander MCDOWELL surveyed land granted to CORNPLANTER, a chief of the Seneca nation.

p. 8: Berks Co. election district near John DAVIS' improvement, Robert A. FARMER, John HARRISON will vote at Philip MARQUART's, Robeson Twp.

p. 9: Dauphin Co. election district of Upper Paxton Twp. will vote at Adam BENDER's.

p. 9: David JONES is the late collector of taxes in Blockley Twp., Phila. Co.

p. 14: John STEWART was appointed trustee for Mifflin Co. on 19 Sept., 1789. He has since died. David BOAL is appointed in his place.

p. 18: Joshua ASHBRIDGE, Edward DARLINGTON, Moses MARSHALL, Esq., Robert MILLER, John DAVIS, John RINCHART, James M. GIBBONS, Esq., Samuel CARTER, James JOHNSTON, Chester Co.; Edward HAND, Thomas BOUDE, George MOSSER, James MORRISON, John FUNK, Peter ELLMAKER, Frederick SEGER, George ELICK, Zachariah MOORE, Lancaster Co. are to hear applications for building a house of poor in Chester & Lancaster Co.

p. 23: William TILGHMAN, Godfrey HAGA, John M. TAYLOR, Phila., & John BARNET, Joseph HORSEFIELD, Nicholas KERN, Northampton Co.; Matthias HOLLENBACK, Rosewell WELLES, Lord BUTLER, Luzerne Co. are commissioners to improve the navigation of the Lehigh River.

p. 36: Richard PETER, John PEROT, Godfrey HAGA, Matthew M'CONNEL, William SHEAFF are commissioners to erect a bridge over the Schuylkill River near Phila.

p. 48: Thomas BROOK, Israel ORLEIP, John YOST, Isaac SHANTZ, Henry MESSIMER, Cassimer MESSIMER, John LIGHTNER, Jacob MESSIMER, Adam BRANDT, Francis BIGONY are commissioners to raise money through a lottery for a school house in New Hanover Twp., Montgomery Co. Robert HARRIS, George WHITEHILL, Christian KUNKLE, William GRAYDON, George BRINZER, Adam BOYD, Jacob BUCHER, Archibald MCALLISTER, Samuel ELDER are commissioners to raise money for the Presbyterian Cong., Harrisburg.

p. 49: John HOLME, John B. GILPIN, Edward DUFFIELD, Jr., William LARDNER, John KEEN, Humphrey WATERMAN, Thomas HOLME, Strickland FOSTER are commissioners to raise money for the Lower Dublin Academy. Frederick BOYER, Jr., Dr. Robert JOHNSON, John MCCLENACHAN, John GERHART, John NEIGH, Jr., John BEZORE are commissioners to raise money to construct the German Episcopal Church, Green Castle, Franklin Co. Prestly NEVILL, George STEVENSON, John SCULL, Isaac CRAIG, Nathaniel BEDFORD, James BRISON, George SHIRAS, Jeremiah BARKER, Nathaniel IRISH are commissioners to raise money to construct piers, wharves, etc. within Pittsburgh, Allegheny Co.

p. 52: William CAMPBELL, Valentine SHOUSLER, Robert BOAL, Peter BEASORE, Michael LEIDIGH, William STEWART, Isaac HERRISON, Michael STROW, Sr., Henry STEIN, Peter SPYKER are commissioners to raise money for a bridge over Big Swatara Ck., Jonestown, Dauphin Co.

p. 53: Bristol Island meadows are the property of John MASSEY, James STERLING, Israel TONKIN, John HUSTON, William HEWSON, Bristol Twp., Bucks Co. Managers are to be chosen at the house of Charles BESSONET, Bristol Borough.

p. 60: Election districts for North Quemahoning Twp., Somerset Co., will vote at Miles PHILIPS'.

p. 61: Edmund MILNE bought land in Whitpain Twp., Phila. Co., that had been forfeited by John ROBINSON. At the time of the sale, it was subject to annual payments to the widows of John & William ROBINSON by their will instructions.

p. 64:   George MICHAEL is an owner of land near the boundary of the new county of Wayne. George BUCHANAN, Milford, Wayne Co., will have court & elections in his house.

p. 72:   Joseph HEISTER, Jacob BOWER, Daniel ROSE, Samuel LAFFERTY, George DOUGLASS, Abraham LINCOLN, Berks Co.; Benjamin CHEW, Jr., Casper W. HAINES, Samuel BETTON, John FROMBERGER, George LOGAN, Isaac FRANKS, Phila., are commissioners of the Germantown & Reading Turnpike Road Co.

p. 91:   Daniel UDREE, Daniel LUDWIG, John WHITMAN, Jr., are to liquidate the accounts of the commissioners who were to build a stone bridge over the Schuylkill River at Reading.

p. 93:   John GLEN is a disabled soldier who served in the militia during the Revolution.

p. 96:   David C. & Septimus CLAYPOOLE furnished newspapers to the legislature. Alexander James DALLAS drafted bills for the committees of the House of Representatives.

p. 114:   Morris Twp., Huntingdon Co. will vote at Capt. Alexander RAMSEY, Jr.'s. Brunswick & Manheim Twp., Berks Co., will vote at John HAMMER's, Orwigsburgh. Erie Twp., Allegheny Co., will vote at James BAIRD's, Erie. Irwin Twp., Allegheny Co., will vote at John ANDREWS', Franklin. Allegheny Co. near the donation & depreciation lands will vote at Samuel JOHNSTON's, Beaver. Allegheny Co. area within Elder's district & part of Deer Twp. will vote at James MCCORMICK's, Freeport. Northumberland Co., West Buffalo Twp., will vote at James FOSTER's, Mifflinsburg. Mohontongo & Penns Twps., Northumberland Co., near Michael WARLIN's ferry on the Susquehanna River, near HESLER's old mill on Penns Ck., near SOUTHERLAND's mill, near Peter GOLTSHALK's on Middle Ck., will vote at Jacob ANDERSON's, Selins Grove. Torbut Twp., Northumberland Co. near James HARRISON's, James COCHRAN's, John WILSON's, John BUCKALEW's will vote at Daniel BERRY's, Washington, Derry Twp. Catawissa Twp., 7th district (now 12th district), Northumberland Co., will vote at Isaiah WILLETT's, Catawissa town. Mifflin Twp., Northumberland Co., will vote at David GITLING's, Mifflinsburg. Derry & Armagh Twps., Mifflin Co., will vote at Arthur BUCHANAN's. Washington Co. near John MCDONALD's, Hickory Tavern, TOMPSON's Mill, PESS' Mill, Andrew ARMSTRONG's, will vote at the Academy, Cannonsburg. Luzerne Co. will vote at William CORBIT's.

p. 135:   Abraham WITMER, Lancaster Co., is authorized to erect a bridge over Conestoga Ck., Lancaster Co.

p. 138:   Philip WAGER, James C. FISHER, Charles BIDDLE, Phila., John BEATTY, Peter GORDON, Asron HOWELL, New Jersey, are commissioners to erect a bridge over the Delaware River at Trenton.

p. 148:   Shirley Twp. & part of Springfield Twp., Huntingdon Co., will vote at John PALMER's, Shirleysburg. Dublin Twp., & part of Springfield Twp., Huntingdon Co., will vote at George HUDSON's, Dublin Twp.

p. 148:   Frankford Ck., near Joseph I. MILLER's, is declared a public highway.

p. 151:   John CANAN is authorized to erect a toll bridge over the Frankstown branch of the Juniata River.

p. 154: Greensburg, Westmoreland Co., is made a borough & is bounded by lands of William JACK, William BEST, George ODERMAN, WILLIAM BARNES, James WATERSON, James GUTHRIE, Robert WILLIAMS & Christopher TRUBY.

p. 161: Samuel BRYSON, James KNOX, John WATSON, William HARRIS, James RODMAN are commissioners to raise money by lottery for a Presbyterian Meeting House in Mifflintown, Mifflin Co.

p. 183: John CAMPBELL, Jacob GORING, Daniel WAGGONER, John BLACK, Robert KITHCART, William PAXTON, Thomas HARTLEY, James SMITH, John EDIE, John CLARK, Jacob HAY, Jacob RUDICIL, Elihu UNDERWOOD, William ROSS of Chanceford; Jacob BARNITZ, Michael SNYDER, Conrad LAUBE, William M'LEAN, William SCOTT, Philip GOSLAR, George BARD are trustees of the York Co. Academy.

p. 194: Benjamin HERR is authorized to erect a mill-dam & wing-dam in the Allegheny River from WILSON's Island to his own land.

p. 195: Matthias FLAM & David WATTS are to establish a ferry over the Susquehanna River near the mouth of the Juniata.

p. 208: Jesse RANKIN performed a tour of duty under Col. CRAWFORD on the Sandusky expedition.

p. 209: William RANKIN, dec., had part of his estate forfeited by attainder. William WEBB asks that it be vested in the heirs of RANKIN.

p. 210: Brigadier General William IRWINE is granted the right of pre-emption to Montour's Island on the Ohio River, since claimed by Col. Charles SYMS, under a warrant issued by Virginia. In lieu of the island, IRWINE is granted 2000 acres at the mouth of Harbor Ck., Allegheny Co.

p. 213: Martin GARTNER & Jacob WELTZHOOVER, Sr. are granted, in trust for the German Lutheran & Reformed congregations of Creutz Ck., Hellam Twp., York Co., a warrant on 29 Jan., 1799, for land adjoining Henry SCHULTZBACH, John KAUFMAN, & Henry KENDING.

p. 220: John ROGERS, Alexander M'WHORTER, Samuel Stanhope SMITH, Ashbel GREEN, William M. TENANT, Patrick ALLISON, Nathan IRWIN, Joseph CLARK, Andrew HUNTER, Jaret INGERSOLL, Robert RALSTON, Jonathan B. SMITH, Andrew BAYARD, Elias BOUDINOT, John NELSON, Ebenezer HAZARD, David JACKSON, Robert SMITH, merchant, are trustees of the General Assembly of the Presbyterian Church of the U.S.

p. 224: A Baptist Church was established on 19 Aug., 1738 in Cumru Twp., now Berks Co. (then Lancaster Co.). Thomas JONES is the only remaining member. He & Peter FILBERT are authorized to sell the church's land.

p. 225: West Chester is erected into a borough. It is bounded by land of Richard JACOBS, John DARLINGTON, Amos DARLINGTON, Joseph M'CLELLAN, George MATLACK, Jonathan MATLACK, John PATTON, dec., Dr. Joseph MOORE, Jesse MATLACK, John BIDDLE, Abner HOOPS, Benaniel OGDEN.

p. 230: Lebanon is erected into a borough. It is bounded by lands of Christopher LAIB, dec., John LIGHT, Christopher UHLER, Jacob

WIRICH, Henry GILBERT, Peter SHINDLE.

p. 235: Jonathan WILLIAMS, now of Phila., & his wife, Mariamne (late Mariamne ALEXANDER), made an agreement before their marriage for a tract of land called Mt. Pleasant, Northern Liberties Twp., Phila. Co. It was bought with money furnished by Alexander John ALEXANDER & now is vested in William ALEXANDER & Robert ALEXANDER in trust for Jonathan & Mariamne WILLIAMS.

p. 238: John BRINK, Ebenezer JEANS, John HILBORN, John B. RODGERS, John BUNTING are trustees for Wayne Co.

p. 240: Matthias BARTON, Jacob STRICLER, Thomas BOUDE are commissioners to move the seat of government for Pa. to Lancaster.

p. 242: Thomas FITZGERALD, John LEAMY, Edward CARROLL are commissioners to raise money to build the Roman Catholic Church of St. Augustin, Phila.

p. 245: Isaac WHELEN, Chester Co., Thomas BOUDE, Lancaster Co., Gen. William IRWINE, Cumberland Co., are commissioners to examine land within Seventeen Twps., Luzerne Co.

p. 252: Lawrence ALLMAN was a lieutenant in the service attached to the Pa. Line during the Revolution. Hannah ALLMAN is executrix for the estate of ALLMAN, dec.

p. 256: Rev. Joseph CLARKSON, Minister; Archibald HENDERSON, Jr., James DUNLAP, present wardens; Jerman DAVIS, John ANDERSON, James LYTLE, Matthew HENDERSON, Archibald HENDERSON, John HOPKINS, Daniel BUCKLEY, John WILSON, Leonard ELMAKER, James CLEMSON, Christopher GRIFFITH, James HENDERSON, present vestrymen, are to incorporate the Protestant Episcopal Church of St. John in West Caln, Chester Co.

p. 261: Salt Lick Twp., Fayette Co., will have elections at Andrew TRAPP's, Esq.

p. 261: Part of Allegheny Co. will vote at Andrew M'CLURE's.

p. 262: Limerick Twp., part of Douglass & New Hanover Twps., Berks Co., near the house of Rev. Frederick WYERELAND, the 5th district of Montgomery Co., will vote at George PFLEIGER's, Pottstown, Douglass Twp. Upper Hanover, Marlborough, Frederick & part of Douglass & New Hanover Twps., Berks Co., will vote at Henry CREPS, New Hanover Twp. Greene District, Greene Co., will vote at John BURLEY's. Warwick & Rapho Twps., Lancaster Co., will vote at John HEINTZELMAN's, Manheim, Rapho Twp. Donegal & Mt. Joy Twps., Lancaster Co., will vote at Alexander BOGGS' house, formerly occupied by John WOLFEY near Elizabethtown, Donegal Twp. Upper & Lower Mt. Bethel Twps., Northampton Co., will vote at Samuel GULICK's. Beaver Twp. near Francis LONG's & George THOMAS', Northumberland Co., will vote at Henry GROCE, Sr.'s, Beaver Twp. Wharton Twp., Fayette Co., will vote at Samuel BELL's. Jefferson Twp. & part of Morgan Twp., Greene Co., will vote at Samuel SALMON's, Jefferson town. Erie Twp., Allegheny Co. will vote at Timothy TUTLE's. POWER's district, Allegheny Co., will vote at John M'GUNNIGLE's. Near Lexington, Allegheny Co., will vote at Thomas HAMILTON's. Near Waterford, Allegheny Co., will vote at Daniel HENDERSON's. Near Erie, MCDOWELL's, NICHOLSON's, & POWER's districts, Allegheny Co., will vote at William MILES'. Near ALEXANDER's district, Allegheny Co., will vote at James BUCHANAN's. Near the donation lands, Allegheny

Co., will vote at David SAMPLE's. The 3rd election district, Phila. Co., will vote at John SAGAR, Jr.'s, Bristleton. The 4th election district, Huntingdon Co., will vote at Frederick CHRISTMAN's, Hollidaysburg. Heidleburg Twp. near Jacob MEASES', ZIMMERMAN's mill, Dauphin Co., will vote at Godfrey KEINER's, Moyerstown. Greenwich & Albany Twp., Berks Co., will vote at Michael CROLL's, Greenwich.

p. 275: Gen. William JACK, Greensburg, Westmoreland Co., in 1794, called a small corps of militia to support the laws of the town of Greensburg.

p. 288: Militia regiments, commanders & numbers:
Philadelphia: #24--Lt. Col. GURNEY; #25--Lt. Col. GUYER; #28--Lt. Col. NICHOLS; #50--Lt. Col. MCLANE; #84--Lt. Col. SCOTT.
Philadelphia Co.: #42--Lt. Col. SHRUPP; #67--Lt. Col. PATTERSON; #75--Lt. Col. FRANKS; #80--Lt. Col. WORRELL; #88--Lt. col. COATS.
Bucks Co.: #13--Lt. Col. SMITH; #31--Lt. Col. ERWIN; #32--Lt. Col. HANNA; #48--Lt. Col. HART.
Chester Co.: #27--Lt. Col. WHELEN; #44--Lt. Col. HARRIS; #47--Lt. Col. CORRYS; #85--Lt. Col. CRAIG; #92--Lt. Col. HEISTER; #97--Lt. Col. BOYD.
Lancaster Co.: #5--Lt. Col. HAMBRIGHT; #7--Lt. Col. ENSMINGER; #34--Lt. Col. STRICKLER; #60--Lt. Col. MILLS; #98--Lt. Col. FOUTZ; #104--Lt. Col. STEEL; #120--Lt. Col. REAM; #121--Lt. Col. MOSHER.
York Co.: #9--Lt. Col. SHEARMAN; #20--Lt. Col. READ; #40--Lt. Col. CAMPBELL; #41--Lt. Col. KELLY; #61--Lt. Col. MAY; #93--Lt. Col. KING; #111--Lt. Col. DIEHL; #113--Lt. Col. EDIE.
Cumberland Co.: #12--Lt. Col. ALEXANDER; #21--Lt. Col. MITCHELL; #49--Lt. Col. ANDERSON; #59--Lt. Col. LUSH; #87--Lt. Col. MCFARLAND; #116--Lt. Col. MCDONALD.
Berks Co.: #43--Lt. Col. FRAILEY; #69--Lt. Col. SPANG; #79--Lt. Col. MOYERS; #95--Lt. Col. LOWER; #110--Lt. Col. BAUNA; #114--Lt. Col. GEHR.
Northampton Co.: #8--Lt. Col. MCFARREN; #13--Lt. Col. GRIM; #38--Lt. Col. BACHMAN; #71--Lt. Col. MULHALLON; #101--Lt. Col. BAUCHMAN; #94--Lt. Col. RINKER; #115--Lt. Col. STARBIRD; #118--Lt. Col. KERN.
Westmoreland Co.:#2--Lt. [Col.] BONNET; #19--Lt. Col. KUHN; #30--Lt. [Col.] CRAIG; #54--Lt. Col. POWERS; #63--Lt. Col. HALFERTY; #70--Lt. Col. HUNTER.
Northumberland Co.: #18--Lt. Col. MCKENNY; #39--Lt. Col. KELLEY; #77--Lt. Col. PRICE; #81--Lt. Col. MONTGOMERY; #106--Lt. Col. LAZARUS; #112--Lt. Col. SALMON; #123--Lt. Col. TIETSWORTH.
Franklin Co.: #1--Lt. Col. PARKER; #73--Lt. Col. RHEA; #64--Lt. Col. ELLIOTT; #68--Lt. Col. JOHNSTON; #96--Lt. Col. MILLER.
Montgomery Co.: #36--Lt. Col. PUGH; #51--Lt. Col. WENTZ; #56--Lt. Col. HINES; #86--Lt. Col. MARKLEY.
Dauphin Co.: #3--Lt. Col. WOODS; #66--Lt. Col. FORSTER; #78--Lt. Col. MCKEE; #117--Lt. Col. SHAUFLER.
Luzerne Co.: #35--Lt. Col. RANSOM; #45--Lt. Col. FAULKNER; #57--Lt. Col. FRANKLIN.
Mifflin Co.: #11--Lt. Col. MCFARLANE; #52--Lt. Col. STERRETT; #74--Lt. Col. WILLIAMSON; #83--Lt. Col. NELSON; #89--Lt. Col. HOLT.
Delaware Co.: #65--Lt. Col. LEVIS; #110--Lt. Col. WILCOCKS.
Huntingdon Co.: #14--Lt. Col. MOORE; #33--Lt. Col. FEE; #46--Lt. Col. CROMELL; #58--Lt. Col. HOLLIDAY; #119--Lt. Col. SPENCER.
Allegheny Co.: #16--Lt. Col. PATTERSON; #17--Lt. Col. FORSTER; #26--Lt. Col. SPROUT; #29--Lt. Col. GILLAND; #62--Lt. Col. MCNAIR; #76--Lt. Col. WILSON; #107--Lt. Col. MCDOWELL.
Washington Co.: #22--Lt. Col. STOCKELY; #23--Lt. Col. MARSHALL;

#53--Lt. Col. HAMILTON; #82--Lt. Col. WILLIAMSON; #99--Lt. Col. JENKINS.
Greene Co.: #6--Lt. Col. WOOLVERTON; #122--Lt. Col. SWAN.
Fayette Co.: #72--Lt. Col. PAUL; #90--Lt. Col. SPRINGER; #91--Lt. Col. LYNN; #108--Lt. Col. WHALEY.
Bedford Co.: #55--Lt. Col. PATTERSON; #105--Lt. Col. WARD.
Somerset Co.: #10--Lt. Col. STALL; #109--Lt. Col. KIMMEL.
Wayne Co.: #73--Lt. Col. SCHRUNK; #103--Lt. Col. COOLBAUGH.
Lycoming Co.: #4--Lt. Col. CUMMINGS; #102--Lt. Col. CRANE.

p. 309: Little Schuylkill River, near George ROUSH's saw-mill & Jacob SHELLEY's saw-mill is declared a public highway.

p. 309: John JONES purchased land in Earl Twp., Lancaster Co. (the confisgated property of Isaac GRAFTS). The land had been sold on 7 Apr., 1794, by the sheriff of Lancaster Co. as the estate of Isaac GRAFTS at the suit of the administrators of David MORGAN, dec. The sale to JONES was an error. JONES is deceased.

p. 312: Arnold RICHARDSON, late of Phila., dec., owned land in Northern Liberties & sold it to George WALTON. RICHARDSON died before executing the deed.

p. 315: Election districts: Hamilton & Chestnut Hill Twps., Northampton Co., will vote at Simon HELLER's, Hamilton Twp. Luzerne Co. near Breakneck Mt. & Rummerfield Ck., will vote at William MEENES', Wyorocks Twp. Washington Co. near Thomas PARKINSON's old mill, BENTLEY's, mill, Nathan HEALD's saw-mill, will vote at Edward WEST's.

p. 317: Francis JOHNSTON is receiver-general.

p. 319: Andrew ALLEN, as guardian for his daughter, Elizabeth ALLEN; William ALLEN; Ann PENN ALLEN; William TILGHMAN; Henry Walter LEVINGSTON & his wife, & others are residuary devisees of William ALLEN, formerly of Phila., dec. Elizabeth ALLEN is an infant. Elizabeth Margaret TILGHMAN is the only child of William TILGHMAN & his late wife, Margaret Elizabeth, one of the daughters of James ALLEN, dec. Edward SHIPPEN is authorized to sell Elizabeth ALLEN's part of the estate.

p. 329: Fishing Ck., Northumberland Co., near John EVE's mill is declared a public highway.

p. 330: Indenture dated 7 May, 1790 was executed by Robert RICHART & his wife, Elizabeth, John SCOTT, David AYRES, William RICHART for land in Upper & Lower Bethel Twps., Northampton Co., near Samuel MILLER, William PLUMMER & Isaac HILLIARD. David AYRES, with the consent of Joseph BOWMAN, Esq., Peter MIDDAGH, John HUTCHESON, Jephta ARRISON, William CONNELLY, are to sell the land for the Presby. Church of Lower Mt. Bethel Twp.

p. 336: On 24 Mar., 1797, the legislature granted $200 for the education of John KONKAPOT, Jr.'s education. He is an Oneida Indian.

p. 390: French emigrant, Alexander DE TILLY (commonly called Count DE TILLY), bribed & corrupted servants of William BINGHAM, Phila., & began a correspondence with Maria M. DE TILLY (then Maria M. BINGHAM), daughter of William BINGHAM, then 15 years old, & caused her to elope at midnight & marry him. DE TILLY exhorted money from William BINGHAM. He has since deserted Maria.

p. 401: Jacob WEIRICH, Philip GREENAWALT, Jr., Jacob PFEIFFER, Henry SHEFFER, John GRUM & Valentine MILLER are commissioners to raise money to build the German Reformed Church, Lebanon, Dauphin Co., & one in Heidelberg. David KRAUSE, Frederick HUBLEY, John WEIDMAN, Henry GILBERT, Peter SHINDLE, Christopher UHLER are commissioners to raise money for the German Lutheran Congregation in Lebanon.

p. 403: Court for Centre Co. will be at James DUNLOP's house, Bellefont. Andrew GREGG, William SWANZEY, Robert BOGGS, Bald Eagle, are trustees for Centre Co.

p. 407: John RANKIN, late of York Co., dec., bought in Dec., 1779, land in Newbury Twp., which had been forfeited by James RANKIN. Elizabeth RANKIN is his widow. A writ of ejectment was brought against Samuel BRADY.

p. 408: The remains of the late Maj. Gen. Thomas MIFFLIN are to be interred at the expense of the commonwealth. William PENROSE is the chairman of the committee of accounts.

p. 409: Shaver's Ck., Huntingdon Co., near John & James CRAWFORD's, is a public highway.

p. 414: There is marsh meadow on the west side of Darby Ck., adj. the Delaware River, Ridley Twp., near Swan CULIN, dec., Caleb DAVIS, Esq., William PAUL, William HOSKIN, Jacob PAINTER, Thomas SMITH, dec., John CROZER, Aaron MORTON & Peter HILL.

p. 420: John B. PALMER & Frederick HEISZ are a committee to take care of the estate of Jacob PALMER, lunatic.

p. 433: James BOGGS, John BOGGS, William ATKINS are refunded their militia pay.

p. 440: Frankford Borough is erected. It is bounded by land of Rudolph NEFF, Henry ROVER, Jacob SMITH & Robert SMITH.

p. 446: John STEIN, late of Phila., dec., owned land in Upper Merion Twp., Montgomery Co. He sold it to William HENDERSON but died before execution of the deed. Catharine STEIN, Abraham STEIN & Charles MARQUEDANT are executors. The land is adj. to John PHILIPS, Henry GRIFFITHS & Thomas REES.

p. 447: Christiana M'CAMMON is the adminstrix of the estate of Samuel MCCAMMON, her late husband, who died intestate. He laid out ten lots in Shirelysburg, Huntingdon Co.

p. 448: William ROGERS, Evan EVANS, John MENOUGH, Jr. are commissioners of Chester Co.

p. 449: Christian BEAR is to erect a mill dam on Swatara Ck., Dauphin Co., ½ mile from Hummelstown, having obtained the consent of Peter EVERSOLL. Adam HAMAKER's privileges to open a canal from Susquehanna River to Schuylkill River will not be impaired.

p. 451: William ADCOCK & Christian RITIZ had a patent for land in Phila. A house & lots on High St., Phila., late the estate of Joseph GALLOWAY, is forfeited to the Commonwealth.

p. 460: Armstrong Co. elections will be at John SMITH's house.

p. 463: David MEADE, Frederick HAMAKER, James GIBSON are trustees for Crawford Co. Jonathan COULTER, Joseph HEMPHILL, Denny M'LURE are trustees for Beaver Co. Judah COLT, Thomas REES, John D. HAY are trustees for Erie Co. William MILES, Thomas MILES & John ANDREWS are trustees for Warren Co. George FOWLER, Alexander M'DOWELL & James M'CLARION are trustees for Venango Co. Adiel M'LURE, James AMBERSON, William ELLIOTT are trustees for Butler Co. Benjamin STOKELY, William M'MILLAN, John WILLIAMSON are trustees for Mercer Co. John CRAIG, James SLOAN, James BARR are trustees for Armstrong Co.

p. 472: Edward CARRELL, John TAGGARD, Thomas SHORTALL are commissioners for a lottery for St. Augustin Catholic Church, Phila.

p. 475: Isaac MEASON & Zachariah CONNELL are permitted to build a toll bridge across the Youghiogheny River, Connellsville.

p. 478: Rev. Alexander DOBBIN & David MOORE are trustees for Adams Co. William M'CLELLAN, Henry HOKE & William HAMILTON are to buy ground in Gettysburg for a courthouse & prison.

p. 480: The Fourth Presby. Church, Phila., is to buy land near Amos WICKERSHAM & Richard PRICE.

p. 487: A road from David BEALE's, Mifflin Co., over the end of the Tuscarora & over the W. Conecocheague Mts. to George M'MULLIN's, Shearman's Valley, Cumberland Co., will be improved under Commissioners David BEALE & Joseph M'COY, Mifflin Co.

p. 491: Thomas PARKER paid $532.43 for repairs to the state house clock by the legislature. The heirs of William JANUARY, dec., are to be paid $26.75 for his services as a transcribing clerk to the House of Representatives in 1797.

p. 495: Elections in Huntingdon Twp., Luzerne Co., will be at Charles E. GAYLORD's. Brantum Twp., Luzerne Co., will vote at James WHEELER's. Luzerne Co. districts of Wyalusing, Wysock, Tioga & Willingborough will vote at Ezekiel HYDE's.

p. 496: Frederick SEGAR, Adam MILLER, Jr., George ECARD, Jr., Jacob COLFRODE, Jacob RENGEWALT, Philip DIFFENDEFFER, Henry REAM are commissioners to raise money for the German Calvinist congregation, New Holland, Lancaster Co.

p. 498: Washington Co. near John GRAHAM's, Alexander GRAY's, Joseph LAURAMORE's will vote at James KERR's. Washington Co. near Alexander GRAY's & John GRAHAM's will vote at Robert STEVENSON's. Washington Co. near Rev. Joseph SMITH's, dec., WELL's Mill, John MARSHALL's, Rev. Thomas MARQUAS' old place & Harmonis COLE's, will vote at the place formerly designated.

p. 499: Huntingdon Co. near Philip CURFMAN's saw-mill, Joshua CHILCOT, Jr's., Alexander MCCORMICK's mill, will vote at the courthouse.

p. 502: Northumberland Co. near William WEYRICK's, Frederick STONE's, John DIBLER's, Jacob BISHOP's, George MARKLEY's, Peter BURNS', Abraham IRELEY's, Toran O'QUIN's, SEABOLD's mill, will vote at Christopher SEABOLD's, New Berlin. Shamokin District, Northumberland Co. will vote at Jacob REED's. Fishing Ck. Twp. & Greenwood Twp. will vote at Samuel SMITH's, Fishing Ck. Twp. Bloom

& Brier Ck. Twp. will vote at David FOWLER's, Brier Ck. Twp., not at Samuel BOONE's.

p. 506: Isaac VAN HORNE was a captain in the late continental army in the Pa. Line. He is given lot #51 in the 3rd donation land dist.

p. 506: Abraham MORROW, Phila., is appointed to repair some public arms of Pa.

p. 507: James HURLING is authorized to erect a wing dam on French Ck., Venango Co.

p. 509: Roger ALDEN is authorized to erect a wing dam on French Ck., 6 miles above Meadville.

p. 510: Adams Co. near SHRIVER's mill will vote at George LASHEL's. Adams Co. twps. of Mt. Joy, Germany, Heidelberg & Manheim will vote at Jacob WINROTT's, Petersburg, Germany Twp. Adams Co. twps. of Berwick, Mt. Pleasant, part of Strabane near SCHRIVER's mill & George LASHEL's, will vote at William STURGEON's, Oxford. Adams Co. twps. of Tyrone, part of Huntingdon, Monaghan, Reading & Warrington will vote at John FICKES'. The twps. of Hamilton's ban & Liberty will vote at John M'GINLEY's, Millerstown.

p. 512: Blockley & Kingsessing Twps., Phila. Co., will vote at John LEECH's, Blockley Twp.

p. 513: Anvil Twp. & part of Londonderry Twp., Dauphin Co., near the land of Robert & Thomas M'CALLEN, Henry GATE, Martin THOMAS, Thomas M'ELWRATH, John BOAL, Jacob LONGNECKER, David BRAND, Jacob LIHMAN, William LOGAN will vote at Christian CASSEL's, Millers town.

p. 514: Thomas JONES is dec. Samuel JONES, Phila. Co., will continue to be a commissioner with Peter FILBERT.

p. 518: Part of Allegheny Co. will vote at Adam PATTERSON's, Middletown.

p. 520: Michael RUGH & Anthony ALTMAN, trustees of the Lutheran congregation, Hempfield Twp., Westmoreland Co., on 22 Aug., 1785, got a warrant for land for the church. On 23 May, 1789, they received a patent. They sold the land to Rev. Anthony Ulrich LUTGE.

p. 525: York Co. twps. of Heidelberg & part of Manheim near George BEACK's, Nicholas ANDREW's, George MAYER's, Michael FISSELL & part of Codorus Twp. near Jost RUNK's, Henry STRIKEHOUSER's, Christian ROHRBACH's, Peter KREPS', Ludwig FRASHER's, will vote at Daniel CLAPSADLE's, Hanover. Newbury Twp. will vote at Eli LEWIS', Lewisbury. Warrington, Reading, Monahan & Huntingdon Twps. will vote at John M'CLELLAN's on the York-Carlisle Rd.

p. 526: Benjamin CHEW, Jr., Casper W. HAINS, Matthew HUSTON, Samuel BETTON, John FROMBERGER, Joseph P. NORRIS are commissioners to make a road from Phila. to Ten Mile Stone on Chestnut Hill & then to New Stone Bridge over Perkiomen Ck., Montgomery Co.

p. 548: Peter WICKOFF, Jonathan Bayard SMITH received land patents that have fallen in N.Y. since the northern border was determined.

p. 550: Levi HOLLINGSWORTH, John HUNN, James C. FISHER, Benjamin R. MORGAN, Jonathan Bayard SMITH, Phila.; William MONTGOMERY, John

HALDIMAN, Lancaster Borough; Robert HARRIS, Harrisburg Borough; Jesse MOORE, Sunbury, Northumberland Co.; Andrew HENDERSON, Huntingdon Borough; are commissioners to make a canal between the Delaware River & the Chesapeake Bay.

p. 555: Part of Crawford & Venango Cos. near Andrew CRESS' & Adam FELT's will vote at Joel GREENE's.

p. 555: Alexander M'DOWELL & Thomas REES are to be paid for surveying islands in the Ohio & Allegheny Rivers.

p. 556: A bridge is to be erected over the Little Juniata River, Huntingdon Co., above George EVY's mill.

p. 557: Christian BINKLEY erected a stone bridge over the River Conestoga.

p. 558: Bristol borough is bounded by lands of Joseph BOND & Phineas BUCKLEY.

p. 562: Bedford Co., Londonderry Twp., elections will be at Andrew SHEARER's.

p. 563: James BLACK, now of Adams Co., is adjudged a lunatic. William GILLILAND, Alexander RUSSELL & Samuel COBEAN are a committee to take care of his estate.

p. 564: A German Lutheran Church was built in 1759 at Barren Hill, White Marsh Twp., Phila. Co. (now Montgomery) on land bought from Philip SHARP. Count SOLMS, of Germany, loaned the congregation money to pay off debts which was from his legacy. Rev. Henry MUHLENBERG repaid the debts. Philip SHARP, White Marsh, yeoman, & his wife, Eva, on 11 Oct., 1766, sold land to the church. Henry KATZ, Leonard KOLB & John HEINS are trustees.

p. 567: Mifflin Co., Lack Twp., will vote at the merchant mill of Dr. Thomas LAUGHLIN, Waterford. Union Twp. will vote at John REED's, Bellville. Potter & Ferguson Twps., Centre Co., will vote at John BENNER's, Potter Twp.

p. 569: In 1796, 1797, & 1798, James PEARSON made reference books of city & barrack lots.

p. 570: Andrew BOYD, late treasurer of Chester Co., owes the state £2386 14s 4p. BOYD sold real estate in Chester Co. to John M'DOWELL.

p. 571: John RENISON, formerly an ensign in the 7th Pa. regiment of the late Rev. War, has since become blind & disabled.

p. 572: William TURNBULL & Co. are agents for the royal marine of France.

p. 573: Lycoming Co., Muncy Twp., will vote at Jacob MIRRIL's, Pennsburg, Muncy Ck. Twp. Baldeagle Twp. will vote at Hugh ANDREWS', Dunsburg.

p. 578: George ROSS, formerly a judge of the court of vice-admiralty, paid the late David RITTENHOUSE, then treasurer of the commonwealth, certain continental certificates worth $24,700.

p. 579: Lancaster Co., Sal] ? at John YOUNG's house on the turnpike road, Salisb

p. 581: George HAY, Martin WISER, Baltzer KUNKLE are supervisors of the River Codorus. John SHARP, William ROSS & James M'MILLEN are supervisors of the River Conewago.

p. 587: Salem Twp., Mercer Co., will vote at John WILLIAMSON's mill. Mercer Co. west of the donation land will vote at Benjamin MENTLY's. Those citizens who voted at John ELLIOT's will now vote at Benjamin STOKELY's.

THE LAWS OF PENNSYLVANIA
1801-02, 1802-03

p. 6: Edmund MILNE says he paid John NICHOLSON, then comptroller-general, the balance of a judgment against him. Satisfaction entered on the record in a suit for John HAZLEWOOD, in behalf of the commonwealth against Edmund MILNE & John VANDEEREN.

p. 9: Rev. John M'MILLAN, Joseph PATTERSON, Thomas MARQUIS, Samuel RALSTON, John BLACK, James POWERS, James DUNLAP, John M'PHARRIN, James EDGAR, John M'DOWELL, James ALLISON, William FINDLEY, Craig RITCHIE, John HAMILTON, Joseph VANCE, Robert MAHON, James KERR, Aaron LYLE, Esq., Alexander COOKE, John MERCER, William HUGHES are trustees of a college in Canonsburg, Washington Co.

p. 15: Penn Twp., Northampton Co., will vote at George Simon WEHR's. Southampton Twp., Somerset Co., will vote at Andrew EMRICK's. Half-Moon & Patton Twps., Centre Co., will vote at Abraham ELDER's, Half-Moon Twp. Limerick, Skippack & Perkiomen & part of Providence Twps. will vote at David DEWEES', Providence Twp. Upper Hanover, Marlborough, Upper Salford, Franconia Twps., will vote at John SCHEID's, Summeny town, Marlborough Twp.

p. 28: Peter WILLIAMS, formerly a drummer in the third Pa. Regiment, lost a certificate numbered 471 for £88 1s 9p for depreciation of pay.

p. 30: Catharine ERRINGER is a lunatic. She was a sister of Frederick ERRINGER. She owns a three-story brick house on the east side of Delaware Third-St., Phila., late the estate of her father, Jacob ERRINGER. Peter BROWNE, Northern Liberties Twp., Phila. Co., Esq., is auth. to sell the estate.

p. 45: William HILL, now a resident of Massachusetts, & his wife, Esther, say that at the time of their marriage, Esther was under the will of her late father, Rev. Jacob DUCHE, seized of a messuage un Phila. on Chestnut St. A mortgage was executed by John Bernard GILPIN to her father for £461 1s 4p. An indenture on 7 Aug., 1798, between Esther & Rev. William WHITE, a doctor of divinity & bishop of the Protestant Episcopal Church of Pa. & Miers FISHER, Phila., gentleman, & William HILL. Esther's only sister is Sophia DUCHE HENRY, wife of John HENRY, now in Mass. Burton WALLACE, Phila., bought the messuage.

p. 54: Berks Co., Mahantango Twp., will vote at Michael ARTZ's.

p. 55: John TYSON, late of Abington Twp., Montgomery Co., dec., owned land in Abington Twp. & agree to sell it to John BERRELL.

107

TYSON died before executing the deed. Isaac TYSON & Thomas TYSON are executors of the will. The land is adj. to David KRIERS, Samuel SHOEMAKER, John THAW & John HOBENSACK.

p. 58: The 5th district, Bedford Co., will vote at Jacob FOUR's, McConnelsburgh. Connemaugh Twp., Somerset Co., will vote at John HORNER, Jr's.

p. 61: Warrington, Reading, Huntingdon Twps., York Co., will vote at James M'MILLEN's, Rosstown. Manahan Twp. will vote at Leonard EICHELBERGER's. Shrewsbury Twp. will vote at Thomas EHRHART's. Codorus Twp. will vote at Adam ZIGLER's. Dover Twp. will vote at Patrick M'FARLIN's Dovertown.

p. 62: Joseph TERRANCE purchased 156 acres in German Twp., Fayette Co., which was confisgated from the estate of Anthony YELDALL, which by deed poll dated 23 Feb., 1793, the land was under the hand of Thomas MIFFLIN, Gov. Joseph TERRANCE & his wife sold the land to William OLIPHANT who then sold with his wife to Michael COX who on 13 Dec., 1800, was evicted by a title paramount to Edward GREEN.

p. 64: James WICKERSHAM, Samuel GARRETSON, Ezekiel KIRK are trustees of the Quaker meeting at Warrington Twp., York Co. They say land in Newbury Twp. was granted to John GARRETSON & Joseph HUTTON, now dec. by patent of 20 May, 1796, in trust for the society. They sold 13 acres to Cornelius GARRETSON.

p. 79: The 4th district, Northampton Co., will vote at Ulrich HOUSER's, Lower Smithfield Twp. Juniata, Greenwood, Buffalo Twps., (the part above Falls-hill), Cumberland Co., will vote at William WOODS', Millar's town, Greenwood Twp.

p. 80: John SHERER is authorized to erect a wing dam on the Monongahela River, 1 mile below MCKEE's port, known as BRADDOCK's upper fording.

p. 82: Deer Twp., Allegheny Co., will vote at Thomas MCCONNELL's. Washington & Franklin Twps., Westmoreland Co., will vote at John KING's, Washington Twp. Wheatfield & part of Fairfield Twps., Westmoreland Co., will vote at Richard DIMSEY's, Armagh.

p. 86: Wolf-Ck., Twp., Mercer Co., will vote at Charles BLAIR's. Coolspring Twp. will vote at Peter WILSON's. Sandy Ck. Twp. will vote at David CONDIT's. Salen Twp. will vote at John WILLIAMSON's. Pymatuning & part of Neshanock Twps. will vote at Vincent ROBBINS'. Part of Neshanock Twp. will vote at James HUSTON's.

p. 90: Wyalusing Twp., Luzerne Co., will vote at Justus GAYLORD's. Bald-Eagle Twp., Centre Co., will vote at Casper RICHARDS'.

p. 91: Lewis GARANGER, on 1 Apr., 1786, was issued two new loan certificates for services in the Rev. War, numbered 7455 & 7466 for £737 12s 6p.

p. 92: Henry MEYER, Mountjoy Twp., Lancaster Co., owned land adj. to land of the Moravians or the United Brethern. Jacob RIXECKER & John RIXECKER are the present trustees of the Moravians.

p. 94: A patent was issued to Thomas SMITH & John SMITH (sons of Thomas SMITH of Solebury Twp., Bucks Co., yeoman, dec.) for an island & bar in the Delaware River.

p. 97: Samuel & Sarah WILSON, on 2 Mar., 1761, sold to Thomas ARMSTRONG, late of Allen Twp., Northampton Co., Esq., & James RALSTON, yeoman, land near Jacob HORNER & Hugh WILSON. Trustees of the English Presbyterian Church, Allen Twp., sold the land to Jacob BEAR. James RALSTON is dec.

p. 103: Jacob JENNINGS, clerk, & wife, Hannah, late Hannah CARNAHAN, & John MILLEGAN, are administrators of the estate of James CARNAHAN, dec. Charles FOREMAN & David VANCE are the surviving obligors in a bond with William PERRY, dec. Joseph THOMPSON & John PROBST are the surviving obligors in a bond with William PERRY.

p. 105: Gen. John STEELE & William CALHOUN are authorized to sell land in Drumore Twp., Lancaster Co., which was sold by Bryan QUIN on 26 Dec., 1767 to Robert LONG & Samuel M'CONNEL, overseers of the poor.

p. 106: The Magdalen Society of Phila., whose purpose is to meliorate the distressed condition of unhappy females who have been seduced from paths of virtue & are desirous of returning to a life of rectitude. Directors: William WHITE, Robert COE, Arthur HOWELL, Joseph CLARK, Joseph BUDD, Jacob SHOEMAKER, Samuel Powell GRIFFITHS, Benjamin KITE, Jeremiah PAUL, George WILLIAMS, John LITCHWORTH, Benjamin PRICE, Edward GARRIGUES, Samuel GARRIGUES, Jr., Abraham M. GARRIGUES, Emmor KIMBER, Richard FREEMAN, William SAVERY, Thomas ATTMORE, Samuel SMITH, John EVANS, Robert RALSTON, John INSKEEP, Christopher MARSHALL, Charles MARSHALL, Benjamin RUSH, Joseph COWPERTHWAIT, James ROWLAND, William T. DONNALDSON, Peter KEYSER, Jesse CLEVER, Thomas SAVERY, William GARRIGUES, James MILNOR, James SMITH, John Clement STOCKER, Robert WHARTON, Philip S. PHYSICK, Thomas ALLIBONE, Benjamin SAY, Ashbel GREEN, John COOKE, Malcolm M'DONALD, Thomas WILLING, Isaac T. HOPPER, William YOUNG, Joseph LOWNS, Levi HOLLINGSWORTH, Samuel F, BRADFORD, Thomas DOBSON, Isaac PEARSON, Philip S. BUNTING, Newberry SMITH, Jacob BAKER, Samuel WHELER, Ellis YARNALL, Gilbert GAW, John WISTAR, Jr., Lawrence HERBERT, John DAVIS, Joseph SIMMONS, Samuel HARVEY, John PEROT, William CHANCELLER, John HART, Casper WISTAR, Jr., George KREBBS, William RAWLE, Elias BOUDENOT, David LEWIS, Thomas HODGSON, Joseph PRICE, John M. PRICE, Josiah BALDWIN, William CURREE, William PENROSE, Alexander STEEL, Thomas CUMPSTON, John M'MULLIN, Joseph TOWNSEND, John TOWNSEND, William LINNARD, Richard PRICE, Daniel DAWSON, Even GRIFFITH, Robert COE, Jr., Joseph Parker NORRIS, Robert HARE, Thomas BILLINGTON, Aaron MUSSGRAVE, Jr., Godfrey HAGA, William POYNTELL, Joseph HUDDELL, Robert WALN, James BRINGHURST, James TAYLOR, Peter BROWNE, James TRAQUAIR, John WAGNER, James POUPARD, Thomas SMITH, David JACKSON, Charles SWIFT, Ebenezer FERGUSON, James STOKES, John T. MIFFLIN, Isaac PARISH, John HARRIS, Enoch WHEELER, Thomas ANSLY.

p. 111: Allegheny Twp., Armstrong Co., will vote at George PAINTER's, Miller, near the mouth of Cherry-run.

p. 112: David JACKSON & Barnabas BINNEY are deceased.

p. 113: Sarah CALDWELL held certificates & lost them. She is now deceased. Thomas LEIPER is the administrator of her estate.

p. 123: Peter ARNOLT shall maintain a dam across Raystown branch of the Juniata abutting his land in Colerain Twp., Bedford Co.

p. 125: Isaac WILEY, Cumberland Co., was wounded 2 May, 1782, while serving as a militia man under the command of Capt. Samuel LEAMAN in Col. Samuel HUNTER's battaliion, defending the frontier inhabitants of Northumberland Co. against the Indians. James CALHOUN, now a resident of Westmoreland Co., was in May, 1778, wounded & taken prisoner by the British at Crooked Billet, while serving as a militia man under Capt. Robert M'COY, in Col. WATT's regiment. They are given $40/year.

p. 129: David M'KISSICK was convicted of a rape in Westmoreland Co. & sentenced to gaol in Phila. for 15 years. Margaret M'KISSICK has asked for a divorce from David who escaped & has not yet been retaken.

p. 131: Lower Saucon Twp., Northampton Co., will vote at Frederick KING's. Providence & Colerain Twp., Bedford Co., near Robert CULBERTSON's, will vote at Daniel DAVIS', Providence Twp.

p. 132: Nathan EVANS left a legacy of £100 to the Protestant Episcopal Church of Bangor, Carnarvon Twp.

p. 136: Brecknock Twp., Cocalico Twp., near Michael HOAG's mill, Jacob HAGEY's tavern, MILLER's tavern, WRIGHT's tavern, will vote at Jacob STAHLEY's, Reamstown, Cocalico Twp.

p. 137: Trustees for Mifflin Co.: John BRATTON, Dr. Ezra DOTY, George M'CLELLAND, Robert STERRET, Thomas TORBUTT, James BANKS.

p. 138: John KUNIUS, Germantown, Phila. Co., says he was married on 25 July, 1800 to Bathsheba TROTH. She was pregnant at the time of the marriage. She had the child on 22 Sept., 1800. On that day, she is accused of killing the infant. On 27 Sept., she deserted the house of KUNIUS. He believes her to be secreted somewhere in her native state of New Jersey. The marriage is annulled.

p. 141: Peter Bonaventure D'ARTOIS, late of Northern Liberties, Phila. Co., owned a messuage & lot. A nuncupative will was made in the presence of James VALLIANT & Peter BELSTERLING. D'ARTOIS devised land to St. Mary's Roman Catholic Church, Phila., for the use of the poor. The property has escheated to the commonwealth. The property is assigned in trust to John ROSSETER, Patrick LINEHAN, Nicholas ESLING, John RUDOLPH, John O'HARA, Michael LACY, Joseph SNYDER, John CARRELL, Thomas SHORTALL, James RYAN, all trustees of St. Mary's Church.

p. 147: Judges for elections will meet:
Wayne, Bucks, Montgomery, Northampton, Luzerne Cos. at John LEONARD's, innkeeper, Bethleham. Chester, Berks, Lancaster Cos. at Everet M'CLEES', innkeeper, Morgan's town, Berks Co. Dauphin, Cumberland, Mifflin, Huntingdon Cos. at William STERRET's, Mifflin Town. Northumberland, Lycoming, Centre Cos. at Andrew ALBRIGHT's, Lewisburg. York & Adams Cos. at Peter ESKES', Abbot's Town, Adams Co. Franklin & Bedford Cos. at Jacob FOUR's, M'Connelsburg, Bedford Co. Westmoreland, Somerset & Armstrong Cos. at George KELTZ's, Ligonia Valley, Westmoreland Co. Fayette, Greene Cos. at Thomas CLARE's, Fayette Co. Allegheny, Beaver, Butler, Crawford, Mercer, Venango, Warren & Erie Cos. at Adam FUNK's, Butler Co.

p. 161: David MEADE, James GIBSON, Roger ALDEN, Joseph STOCKTON, Thomas R. KENNEDY, Samuel DALE, Jr., Patrick M'GILL are trustees for a public seminary of learning in Meadville, Crawford Co.

p. 165: John BIDDIS, John BRINK, et al, are to provide suitable buildings for a temporary courthouse in Milford, Wayne Co.

p. 167: Marcus HULINGS is auth. to build a toll-bridge over French Ck., opposite Turkey St., Franklin Co.

p. 170: West Hanover, Dauphin co., will vote at Thomas SMITH's, near GREEN's mill.

p. 171: Commissioners to fix on places for seats of justice in Armstrong, Butler & Mercer Cos. are to meet at the house of Thomas FERREE, Pittsburg.

p. 227: Militia commanders:
Phila.: #24--Lt. Col. PANCAKE; #25--Lt. Col. WILLIS; #28--Lt. Col. BRIGHT; #50--Lt. Col. M'LANE; #84--Lt. Col. BARKER.
Phila. Co.: #42--Lt. Col. FOREPAUCH; #67--Lt. Col. M'MULLEN; #75--Lt. Col. BECK; #80--Lt. Col. WORREL; #88--Lt. Col. COATS.
Montgomery Co.: #36--Lt. Col. HENDERSON; #51--Lt. Col. WENTZ; #56--Lt. Col. HART; #86--Lt. Col. DAVIS.
Bucks Co.: #15--Lt. Col. SMITH; #31--Lt. Col. PIPER; #32--Lt. Col. GLUNN; #48--Lt. Col. VANSANT.
Chester Co.: #27--Lt. Col. GRIER; #47--Lt. Col. ARMSTRONG; #85--Lt. Col. TAYLOR; #97--Lt. Col. COCHRAN; #44--Lt. Col. HARRIS; #92--Lt. Col. RALSTON.
Delaware Co.: #65--Lt. Col. SMITH; #100--Lt. Col. RICHARDS.
Lancaster Co.: #5--Lt. Col. WRIGHT; #7--Lt. Col. ENSMINGER; #120--Lt. Col. KLINE; #121--Lt. Col. THOMAS; #34--Lt. Col. BOYD; #60--Lt. Col. BOAL; #98--Lt. Col. WHITEHILL; #104--Lt. Col. LONG.
York Co.: #40--Lt. Col. BLACK; #41--Lt. Col. KELLY; #61--Lt. Col. REISINGER; #111--Lt. Col. HENDRICKS; #113--Lt. Col. SPANGLER; #124--Lt. Col. HINCKEL.
Adams Co.: #9--Lt. Col. KUHN; #20--Lt. Col. GETTY; #93--Lt. Col. KING.
Berks & Dauphin Co.: #37--Lt. Col. BAUM; #43--Lt. Col. FRAILEY; #69--Lt. Col. SCHREADER; #79--Lt. Col. EPLER; #114--Lt. Col. KLINE.
Dauphin Co.: #3--Lt. Col. WEIRICH; #66--Lt. Col. ELDER; #78--Lt. Col. TOOT; #95--Lt. Col. ANSPACH; #117--Lt. Col. SEBOLD.
Cumberland Co.: #12--Lt. Col. BOVARD; #21--Lt. Col. EWALT; #49--Lt. Col. URIE; #59--Lt. Col. ROAN; #87--Lt. Col. MARTIN; #116--Lt. Col. RUPLY.
Franklin Co.: #1--Lt. Col. FINDLAY; #64--Lt. Col. ALEXANDER; #68--Lt. Col. STATLER; #73--Lt. Col. RHEA; #96--Lt. Col. SCOTT.
Northampton & Wayne Co.: #13--Lt. Col. WETZEL; #38--Lt. Col. OHL; #94--Lt. Col. RINKER; #101--Lt. Col. KESTLER; #118--Lt. Col. M'KEEN; #8--Lt. Col. M'FERREN; #71--Lt. Col. HORN; #103--Lt. Col. DINGMAN; #110--Lt. Col. STANTON; #115--Lt. Col. SHOUP.
Northumberland, Lycoming, Luzerne Co.: #35--Lt. Col. RANSOM; #45--Lt. Col. FAULKNER; #57--Lt. Col. SPALDING; #81--Lt. Col. MONTGOMERY; #112--Lt. Col. RUPERT; #123--Lt. Col. GIFFIN; #129--Lt. Col. HYDE; #4--Lt. Col. CUMINGS; #18--Lt. Col. Abraham M'KENNY; #39--Lt. Col. BALDY; #77--Lt. Col. DRUM; #102--Lt. Col. John M'KENNY; #106--Lt. Col. ROBERTS.
Mifflin, part of Centre Co.: #11--Lt. Col. M'DOWELL; #52--Lt. Col. BEALE; #74--Lt. Col. BRATTON; #83--Lt. Col. BANKS; #89--Lt. Col. CRAIG; #131--Lt. Col. MYERS.
Huntingdon & part of Centre Co.: #14--Lt. Col. MOORE; #33--Lt. Col. FEE; #46--Lt. Col. CROMWELL; #58--Lt. Col. HOLLIDAY; #119--Lt. Col. ENTRICKEN.
Fayette Co.: #72--Lt. Col. COLLINS; #90--Lt. Col. OLIPHANT; #91--Lt. Col. BRASHIERS; #108--Lt. Col. WHALEY.

#91--Lt. Col. BRASHIERS; #108--Lt. Col. WHALEY.
Bedford & Somerset Co.:   #10--Lt. Col. CLARKE; #55--Lt. Col. AGNEW;
#105--Lt. Col. BONNET; #109--Lt. Col. KIMMEL; #127--Lt. Col. MOORE;
#128--Lt. Col. BOYLS.
Washington & Greene Co.:   #22--Lt. Col. ATCHISON; #23--Lt. Col.
MARSHALL; #53--Lt. Col. HARE; #82--Lt. Col. STEVENSON; #6--Lt. Col.
HEATON; #99--Lt. Col. JENKINS; #122--Lt. Col. M'CLELAND; #130--Lt.
Col. CATHER.
Allegheny, part of Butler & part of Beaver Co.:   #16--Lt. Col.
MARTIN; #29--Lt. Col. GILLILAND; #62--Lt. Col. CUNNINGHAM; #76--Lt.
Col. NOBLE; #125--Lt. Col. M'FARLAND.
Westmoreland Co.:   #2--Lt. Col. BONNET; #19--Lt. Col. WAGLE;
#30--Lt. Col. M'COMBS; #54--Lt. Col. CAMPBELL; #63--Lt. Col.
M'DOWELL; #70--Lt. Col. HUNTER.
Armstrong, Erie, Butler, Crawford, Warren, Mercer, Venango, & part
of Beaver Co.:   #17--Lt. Col. FORSTER; #26--Lt. Col. SPROAT;
#107--Lt. Col. REED; #126--Lt. Col. SLOAN.

p. 264:   Mathew CAREY & John BIOREN are to print copies of the laws
of Pa.

p. 274:   Solomon MEYER printed German journals of the last session.
William & Robert DICKSON printed the bills of the last House of
Representatives.   Francis BAILEY printed the English journals for
the House of Representatives.   George BRYAN drafted bills for the
House of Reps.   Charles CULNAN took care of the State House & yard.
Benjamin H. LATROBE improved navigation of the Susquehanna River.

p. 276:   Peter MUHLENBURGH resigned his Senate seat.

p. 280:   Christian J. HUTTER printed a statement of finances of Pa.

p. 282:   William TURNBULL, representative for the Royal Marine of
France as a member of William TURNBULL & Co., agents, sued the
Commonwealth.   David RITTENHOUSE is the late state treasurer.

p. 283:   Charles Wilson PEALE is auth. to use the east end of the
State House for a museum.

p. 285:   Andrew ELLICOT, Esq., is to have use of the telescope
purchased in 1769 which is now property of the state.

p. 290, 1802-03:   Plumb Twp., part of Versailles Twp., Allegheny
Co., will vote at John LITTLE's, Frankstown St. road, Plumb Twp.

p. 291:   E. Pennsborough & Allen Twps., Cumberland Co., will vote at
Nicholas KRITZER's, E. Pennsborough.   Beaver Co. near William
ANDERSON's, will vote at Robert JOHNSTON's on Beaver Run.   Beaver
Co., near Henry LAWRENCE's on Big Beaver Ck., will vote at Ananias
ALLEN's,   The Beavertown election district will vote at Samuel
JOHNSTON's (near Michael BAKER's & Jacob MYERS').   The Georgetown
election district will vote at Samuel LYONS'.   Milford Twp.,
Somerset Co., will vote at John GEPHART's.   Greenfield Twp., Erie
Co. near Robert SMITH's, will vote at Andrew LOWRY's.   The
Noblesburgh district, Allegheny Co., will vote at George WILLIAMS'.

p. 299:   Abraham LANDIS is auth. to erect a mill dam in Swatara Ck.,
Dauphin Co.

p. 300:   Hugh BEATY is acting administrator of James BEATY, late of
Northumberland Co., decd.   James & Alexander BEATY, in 1792, sold

lots adj. the town of New Berlin, Buffaloe Twp., Northumberland Co.

p. 302: James MOORE made an actual settlement at an early period on a fractional part of the reserved tract of land at the mouth of Big Beaver Ck. He had 220 acres granted to him for $1.50/acre.

p. 303: Catharine DICK, late Catharine WOLF, Lancaster Borough, says that in Apr., 1801, she was married to Alexander DICK. He had been guilty of larceny before the marriage & convicted & held at Lancaster on the second Monday in May, 1801. He was fined $3467.67 & caused to serve 18 months in Lancaster Co. gaol. He probably will be in gaol for life. The marriage is annulled.

p. 307: Buffaloe Twp., Armstrong Co., will vote at John M'DOWELL's.

p. 308: John CALHOUN, Benjamin CHAMBERS, Dr. Robert JOHNSTON, John BROWN, Jacob ZANCK, George CLARK, David KENNEDY, Col. William ALEXANDER, James M'CALMONT, Jacob CASSEL, Esq., James RAMSEY, Archibald IRVIN, William M. BROWN, Samuel COLHOON, Josiah CRAWFORD, Archibald BAIRD, Esq., are commissioners of a company to open the navigation of Conecocheague Ck. from the mouth of Falling Spring, Chambersburgh to the Maryland line.

p. 314: Godfrey LENHART, Andrew ROBINSON, John ERNST, Peter SMALL, Daniel SPANGLER, John ROTHROCK, George BARNITZ, Christopher LOWMAN are commissioners to raise money to rebuild a German Presby. Church, York Borough & Co., which was destroyed by fire.

p. 316: Charles SMITH, Lancaster Borough, is auth. to erect a wing dam in the Juniata River, Frankstown Branch.

p. 319: Rockdale Twp., Crawford Co., will vote at William GRENLEE's.

p. 320: Henry DRINKER, Benjamin R. MORGAN, Thomas ALLIBONE, Phila.; Samuel SITGREAVES, John HERSTER, Daniel WAGENER, Easton Borough; Lord BUTLER, Lawrence MYERS, Thomas WRIGHT, Luzerne Co., are commissioners to incorporate a company to make a road from Easton, Northampton Co. to Wilkesbarre, Luzerne Co.

p. 343: William WRIGHT, proprietor of land adj. Chiquis Falls on the west side of the Susquehanna River, Hellain Twp., York Co., requests permission to lead off part of the waters of said river.

p. 348: John BIDDLE forfeited his estate by his attainder. Sophia BIDDLE is his widow.

p. 350: John LAWRENCE, Esq., Guion GRIER, James ALEXANDER & Samuel JOHNSTON are trustees for Beaver Co.

p. 352: Jacob CARPENTER, Esq., late state treasurer, is decd.

p. 355: Buckingham, Demascus & part of Lackawaxen Twp., Wayne Co., will vote at Reuben SKINNER's.

p. 361: Isaac WEAVER, John HAMILTON, Thomas MORTON, James BRADY, Presly Carr LANE, Esq., are commissioners to establish a place for courts of justice in Butler Co. John M'BRIDE, Esq., William ELLIOTT, Esq., & John DAVID are trustees for Butler Co. 300 acres of land on the north side of Conequinessing Ck., near Samuel

CUNNINGHAM's mill, are granted by Samuel & John CUNNINGHAM & Robert GRAHAM for the use of Butler Co.

p. 365: Samuel SWIFT, Strickland FOSTER, Jacob SHEARER, John HOLMES, Jr., John THOMPSON, Elisha GORDON, Edward SWIFT, Jacob HALL, Bernard J. MALFESON, William DUNCAN are commissioners to raise funds for completing the building of Bustleton Academy, Phila. Co.

p. 369: Dauphin Co. election district will vote at John EVIG's, Halifax. Middle Paxton Twp. will vote at John FILSON's. Upper Paxton Twp. will vote at George BUFFINGTON's.

p. 371: Mahoning, Hemlock Twp., Northumberland Co., will vote at William SHERRIFF's, Danville, Mahoning Twp. The 6th district will vote at John SWINEFORD', Middleburgh, Penns Twp., instead of at Albright SWINEFORD's. The New Berlin district, beginning at Toran O'QUIN's, near Hugh WILSON's, near Joshua DAVIS' to John STEELE's & to Christopher SEABOLD's mill, is changed from what it was.

p. 372: Samuel & Rebecca MILES say that William WISTER, late of Phila., died intestate with respect to certain real estate in Northumberland Co. It was purchased after his will was written. Catharine, Samuel, William & James MILES are minors & grandchildren of Samuel MILES & children of James MILES, decd. & his wife, Rebecca. John WISTAR, Phila., bought the children's 1/18 shares of William WISTER's real estate. Samuel MILES has a son, Charles.

p. 377: Bethel Twp., Berks Co., will vote at Michael MILLER's.

p. 379: Some landowners of land surrounding Chambersburg, Franklin Co.: James WELSH, John KERR, Frederick REAMER, D. MADERIA, Edward CRAWFORD, Benjamin CHAMBERS, Joseph CHAMBERS, Nicholas CLOPPER, John SHRYOCK, Mr. STOCK.

p. 387: Teboyne Twp., Cumberland Co., will vote at Henry SIMMERMAN's.

p. 388: Pennsbury, Kennett, East Marlborough, Newlin Twps., Chester Co., will vote at Joseph PIERCE's, E. Marlborough Twp., at the Red Lion Tavern.

p. 393: William M'MULLEN, John FINDLEY, William MORTIMORE are trustees for Mercer Co. They are to survey 200 acres on the west side of Otter Ck. on which John GARVER & John PUE (PUGH) settled by John HOGE.

p. 397: Robert LOLLAR, Joshua TYSON, John SHOEMAKER, Jr., John BARCLAY, John INSKEEP, John HART (druggist), George REX, Daniel DE BENEVILLE, Richard T. LEECH are commissioners to make a road from the Rising Sun Tavern through Shoemakerstown to the Red Lion on the old York Rd.

p. 418: Joseph CLUNN, John M'ELROY, Derick PETERSON, Isaac WORRELL, Nathan HARPER, James C. FISHER, Richard GERNON are commissioners to make a road from Front St. & Germantown Rd., Northern Liberties, Phila., through Frankford & Bristol to a ferry at Morrisville on the Delaware River.

p. 441: Richard THOMAS, Matthew STANLY, James M'CONNEL, Chester Co.; Cyrus JACOBS, Jacob KELLER, John ERB, Lancaster Co.; Moses GILMORE, John ELDER, Gotlieb ORTH, Dauphin Co., are commissioners to make a road near Downingstown, Chester Co., to Cornwall Furnace, Dauphin Co., & then to Harrisburgh.

p. 469: Robert JOHNSTON alleges that he was a regimental surgeon to the 6th Regiment of the Pa. Line from the commencement of the war until 1781, where in obedience to the orders of Gen. GREENE, he was obliged to leave the regimental service to assist the wounded officers & soldiers of the American Army, then prisoners in the British hospital in Charleston. He is granted a patent for land.

p. 471: Ann M'FARREN, John AGNEW & William M'CLEAN are auth. to convey by deeds in fee to David BLYTH, Moses M'CLEAN, William WAUGH, James BRICE, John M'GINLEY & James STEPHENSON, certain lots.

p. 506: Martin HOCKER bought from his brother, John HOCKER, a lot in Paxton Twp., Dauphin Co. John is now decd.

p. 569: Sarah CALDWELL is decd. Administrator of her estate is Thomas LEIPER.

p. 571: David HAYES, Chester Co., is a lunatic. Caleb SWAYNE, Samuel SWAYNE, Jr., & Thomas CHALFANT are trustees of estate.

p. 575: William JACK, James PARR, John POMROY, Westmoreland Co., are trustees for Indiana Co.

p. 577: Nicholas UNGERMAN, late a sergeant in Capt. John MEARSE's Co., belonging to the 4th Pa. Regiment, commanded by Col. William BUTLER, on or about Sept., 1779, was killed by Indians in an expedition commanded by Gen. SULLIVAN. UNGERMAN had no relatives in this country other than his now aged mother, Elizabeth UNGERMAN SMITH, who during the infancy of the decd., married Peter SMITH, now of Northumberland Co. Donation land is granted to Peter & Elizabeth SMITH.

p. 579: Flavel ROAN, Solomon MARKLEY & David TAGGART are commissioners of Northumberland Co.

p. 581: Benjamin ALEXANDER, Thomas M'MILLAN are to ascertain the center of Mercer Co.

p. 587: Part of the 5th election district of Lancaster Co. will vote at Nathaniel LIGHTNER's, Cocalico Twp. Part of Warwick Twp., Lancaster Co., near Christian STAUFFER's mill, John PFAUT's mill, will also vote at LIGHTNER's. Part of the 5th election district, Lancaster Co. near MILLER's Tavern will vote at Jacob STAHLEY's, Reamstown.

p. 620: John PARROCK's estate is forfeited by attainder. He is decd. The part not sold on behalf of the commonwealth is vested in Richard SMALLWOOD & others, devisees of James PARROCK, father of John.

p. 626: The British sloop, Active, was captured as a prize on the high seas in Sept., 1778 & brought into Phila. port & there libeled in a Court of Admiralty held before George ROSS, Esq., judge of the said court. Libellants were Gideon URMSTEAD or OLMSTEAD, Artimus WHITE, Aquila RUMSDALE, David CLARKE, who claimed the whole vessel & cargo; Thomas HUSTON, master of the brig, Convention, a vessel of war belonging to Pa.; James JOSIAH, master of the sloop, Girard or Gerard, a private vessel of war. George ROSS directed Matthew

CLARKSON, marshal of Admiralty Court, to pay proceeds of the prize. David RITTENHOUSE was then treasurer of Pa.
ROSS is now decd. Richard PETERS was a judge of the district court. William LEWIS, Esq., was an attorney. Elizabeth SERGEANT & Esther WATERS are surviving executrixes of David RITTENHOUSE, decd.

p. 641: Courts for Beaver County will be held at Abner LAYCOCK's. Courts for Erie Co. will be held at George BEELER's, Erie.

p. 643: S. Irwin Twp., Venango Co. near Daniel FRY's, will vote at Patrick DAVIDSON's. Beaver & Cussewago Twp., Crawford Co., will vote at Robert NELSON's. Conneaut & Sadsbury Twp., Crawford Co., will vote at Joseph GARWOOD's. Shenango & Followfield Twp., & part of Conneaut Twp., Crawford Co., will vote at Thomas MCMICHAEL's. Fairfield Twp., Crawford Co., will vote at James HERRINGTON's.

p. 646: James SLOAN, James MATTHEWS, Alexander WALKER are appointed trustees for Armstrong Co. The courthouse is to be built in Kittanning, on the property of James & John ARMSTRONG.

P. 676: The trial of Alexander ADDISON is printed by George HELMBOLD.

THE LAWS OF PENNSYLVANIA
1803-04

p. 10: All that part of Stoney Ck. Twp., Somerset Co., lying north of a line near SCHRIOCK's cabin is annexed to Quimahoning District & elections will be held at John POWL's, Stoystown. The rest of Stoney Ck. Twp, will vote at John FLACHER's, Berlin. Elk-lick, Somerset Co., will vote at John WELCH's. Addison Twp., Somerset Co., will vote at John MITCHELL's, Esq., Addison Twp.

p. 12: Gen. James GUNN, late a Senator of the U.S. from Georgia, died without issue. He owned land in Pa. Supposedly, he left a will but it has since been lost or destroyed. It appeared to have been the intention of GUNN that his nephew, James GUNN, of Va., should inherit the estate.

p. 14: Elizabeth SHINER, Christian SHINER & John MEYMAN are administrators of the estate of Christophel SHINER, late of Colebrookdale Twp., Berks Co. Melchior SHINER, late of New Hanover Twp., Montgomery Co. (then Phila. Co.), decd., owned land in New Hanover Twp. (140 acres). His will of 19 June, 1778, proved in Phila. Co., said that after the decease of his widow, his son, Christophel, should sell the premises. He did on 2 Jan., 1802, to Amos JONES for £3 16s per acre. Christophel died intestate.

p. 19: John LONEY, in June, 1797, settled on a tract of land on the headwaters of Oil Ck., Union Twp., Erie Co. He lived there with his family until March, 1799, when he was crushed & wounded by a fall of a tree. He can't continue his improvement & will be crippled for life. The title is completed for the land.

p. 20: Henry MECKLEY, York Co., is a lunatic. George MECKLEY, Anthony WILLET, Jacob KELLER are trustees of his estate.

p. 23: Hannah SWAN, Northumberland Co., petitioned that in 1781, she married Samuel SWAN. They lived together till 1791. In May, 1791, Samuel relinquished her & never returned. In 1795, Samuel was married to another woman & lives in Kentucky. The marriage is annulled.

p. 24: Dr. Joseph PRIESTLY gives a library of scarce literature & scientific books to Northumberland Co.

p. 26: Rockhill, Bedminster & Hilltown Twps., Bucks Co., will vote at Henry TRUMBOUR's, Rockhill Twp.

p. 27: Alexander BOATICAR & wife, Lucy, natives of Great Britain, arrived in Pa. in July, 1802. They purchased land from William READ & wife, Ann, & Matthew PEARCE & wife, Mary, at Creesham (Chestnut-hill), Germantown Twp., Phila. Co. One tract was bounded by land late in the tenure of Wiggard MILLER, land late of Samuel MUMMY near the Phila. & Plymouth road, by land of Michael MILBERGER & Abraham TUNIS, & by land late of Julius KARPER. Since then, Alexander BOATICAR sold the land to Lewis BOLLMAN.

p. 37: Elizabeth BURK, Washington Co., represented to the legislature that her husband, Cornelius BURK, has deserted her. He has been gone 5 years, 6 months. It is believed he was married to another woman who is still living before he was married to Elizabeth. She is too poor to travel to Phila. to get a divorce. The marriage is annulled.

p. 54: Present directors of the Phoenix Insurance Co. of Phila.: Isaac WHARTON, David LEWIS, Rumford DAWES, Robert E. GRIFFITH, Joshua GILPIN, Joseph SNOWDEN, Paul BECK, Jr., Paschal HOLLINGSWORTH, Joseph CURVEN.

p. 61: John INSKEEP, William POYNTELL, Samuel WHEELER, John C. STOCKER, Thomas CUMPSTON, Robert MCMULLEN, William RICHARDS are commissioners to raise money (up to $8000) to discharge debts of the minister, wardens & vestrymen of the African Episcopal Church of St. Thomas, Phila.

p. 63: Andrew GREGG was appointed trustee in Centre Co., 13 Feb., 1800. James POTTER is appointed trustee in his stead 6 Feb, 1804.

p. 64: Wysox Ck., Claverack, Luzerne Co., from it's mouth to Jacob MYER's mill dam, is declared a public stream.

p. 87: Alexander PATTERSON, Easton, Northampton Co., was a captain in the Rev. He is granted $400 & $100 per year.

p. 88: Commissioners of the Erie & Waterford Turnpike Rd.: George BUHLER, Callender IRVINE, Judah COLT, Thomas FORSTER, Abraham SMITH, Martin STRONG, James NAYLOR, Wilson SMITH, Charles MARTEN, John COUCHRIN, Roger ALDEN, David MEAD, Thomas R. KENNEDY, Joseph HACKNEY, Jabiz COLT, John WILKINS, Jr., Henry BAULDIN, John MCMASTERS, Samuel EWALT, William GAZZAM, James GIBSON, Paul BUSTIE, William CRAMMOND, Andrew PETIT, Michael KEPPELE.

p. 120: George STEVENSON, now an inhabitant of Washington Co., entered into the service of the U.S. & was appointed a lieutenant in the army. After several year's service, he was made a prisoner in 1779 at West Liberty by Indians & severely wounded in the head with a tomahawk, taken to Detroit & given to the British, carried by them to Quebec where he was imprisoned until Oct., 1782. He was then discharged on parol & made his way to Phila. He is old & has a large family of children to support. He is placed on a list of soldiers entitled to donation lands.

p. 124: Southampton Twp., Somerset Co., will vote at Michael KORN's.

p. 125: John GILCHRIST, Harrisburg, in Rev. War service, received a wound & can't do manual labour. He is allowed an annuity of $64 for life.

p. 126: Heirs of John HIRST, Sr., decd., petition on 14 Dec., 1802, that their title to a lot in Phila. is rendered defective by the loss of a certain deed dated 1 Jan., 1762, from William ALLEN, Esq., late Chief Justice of Pa., to William FOX, joiner, rendering an annual rent, on the South side of Sassafras St., bounded by Edward EVANS, Philip FAIL, Jacob PAINTER, Peter MILLER. Regina FOX, relict, & Henry Justus FOX are executors of the will of William FOX.

p. 129: John EVANS has lost a certificate #162 for £70 10p 3s issued to Thomas MCFARLANE for depreciation of his pay as a matross in the 4th Regiment of artillery. John EVANS is the lawful administrator of Thomas MCFARLANE, decd.

p. 132: George FRY, William CRABB, James HAMILTON, Elijah GREEN, Daniel MONTGOMERY, Jr., George REDFEKER, John CAROLUS, John PEDEN, Adam REIGART, Jr., Samuel HUMES, William KIRKPATRICK, Christopher MYER, John SWAR, Peter GONTER, Adam WEBER, Jacob DICKERT, Abraham WITMER, William MONTGOMERY, John GUNDAKER, William G. LATIMER are commissioners of the Lancaster, Elizabethtown & Middletown Turnpike Rd.

p. 152: George EICHOLTZ, Lancaster Borough, in the Rev. War, served as a private in the Pa. Line, in Capt. DEHUFF's company & Col. ATLEE's Regiment. In the battle of Flatbush, Long Island, he received a severe wound in his groin with a musket ball. He is wholly unable to maintain himself or his family. He is given an annuity of $60.

p. 154: Commissioners of the Bustleton & Smithfield Turnpike Rd.: Henry WYNKOOP, Richard LEEDOM, Augustine WILLOT, Bucks Co.; Jacob SOMMERS, Moreland; Thomas PAUL, William DUNCAN, Isaac WORRELL, Joshua COMLY, Frederick WOLBERT, Phila. Co.; Clement BIDDLE, John BARKER, N. Second St. & Stephen GIRARD, Phila.

p. 175: Huntingdon Co. will vote at Samuel HENRY's, Barree Twp.

p. 176: Commissioners of the Union & Cumberland Turnpike Rd.: Ephraim DOUGLASS, Alexander MCCLEAN, Nathaniel BREADING, Isaac MEASON, Jacob BEESON, Jacob BOWMAN, Samuel JACKSON, James W. NICHOLSON, Joseph TORRENCE, Charles PORTER, John CUNNINGHAM, Samuel TREVOR & John GIBSON, Fayette Co.; John HEATON, John MINOR, Hugh BARCLAY, John BADOLET, Greene Co.; Neal GILLESPIE, Zephania BELL, Thomas ACHESON, James KERR, Joseph PENTICOST, Washington Co.; Thomas SPENCE, Abraham MORRISON, James MITCHELL, John M'CLEAN, Somerset Co.

p. 207: Conrad WEISER, late of Penn's Twp., Northumberland Co., decd., laid out a piece of ground adj. Selinsgrove, which he called Weiserburg. Barbara WEISER & Benjamin WEISER are administrators of the estate.

p. 215: John HUSTON, Cadwallader EVANS, George WEAVER, John BURK, John ROBERTS, Nicholas KLINE, Christian DULL, Jacob DAGER, John

STEELE are commissioners of the Chestnut Hill & Springhouse Turnpike Rd.

p. 251: Robert HARRIS, a native of Scotland, arrived with the intention of residing here in June, 1802. In Aug., he purchased from James M'CAHRIN, 217 acres of a plantation in Westnantmill Twp., Chester Co., bounded by lands of Charles REED, David DENNY & Samuel BYERS for £1200.

p. 252: Zebulon POTTS, late of Montgomery Co., decd., owned real estate in Plymouth Twp., Montgomery Co. He willed it to his wife, Martha POTTS. She has since died intestate. Joseph POTTS & Joseph THOMAS are administrators of her estate. The land adj. David LUKINS, William SHEPHERD.

p. 254: Commissioners of a bridge to be built over the Delaware River near Milford, Wayne Co.: Samuel JOHNSTON, John BIDDIS, John BRODHEAD, John BRINK, Hugh ROSS, Wayne Co.; Thomas ANDERSON, Daniel STEWARD, John GUSTON, Jedediah SAYR, Sussex Co., N.J.

p. 267: Chillisquaque Twp., Northumberland Co., will vote at William DALE's. The 7th election district will vote at Abraham MILLER's, Bloom Twp., instead of at David FOWLER's. The 14th election district will vote at Peter APPLE's, Beaver Twp., instead of at Henry GROSS'.

p. 268: Weisenberg & Lynn Twp., Northampton Co., will vote at George GRIM's, Weisenberg.

p. 268: Alexander MCPHERSON purchased from his brother-in-law, David COWAN & wife, Catharine, a lot of 26 ½ acres in Sadsbury Twp., Chester Co.

p. 278: Directors of the Delaware Insurance Co. of Phila.: Thomas FITZSIMONS, John CRAIG, Griffith EVANS, Tournier ROSTAIN, Jacob SHOEMAKER, Richard GERNON, James LATTIMER, Joseph D. DRINKER, Augustine BOUSQUET, Samuel MEEKER, Bohl BOHLEN, William BUCKLEY, Jacob SPERRY, William MCFADEN, John WELSH, George CUREVEN, Stephen DUTILH.

p. 284: Names of land owners near the marsh meadow in the twps. of Lower Chichester & Chester, Delaware Co.: Marthan SMITH, John PRICE, Jacob DEREBACHER, David & Sarah TRAINER, heirs of Samuel PRICE, Benjamin JOHNSTON, heirs of David JOHNSTON, Jonathan DUTTON, Jacob RICHARDS, Erasmus MORTON, Thomas COBOURN.

p. 293: Alexander MOORE, Robert GORDON, David MILLER, Edward HANNA, Archibald LITTLE, Robert ERWIN, Robert MCCULLOUGH are commissioners to superintend the lottery of up to $10,000 to discharge debts of the 4th Presby. Church, Phila.

p. 295: Fannet Twp., Franklin Co., will vote at the school house on the land of John HOLLIDAY & James WALLACE.

p. 297: Alexander SIMONTON, an inhabitant of Mercer Co., late a sergeant in the Pa. Line in Col. CHAMBERS' Regiment, was wounded at the battle of Brandywine, & discharged previous to the conclusion of the war. The wound renders him incapable of earning subsistence by labor. He is put on the list of soldiers entitled to donation land.

p. 300: Peter KOON, Philip REEMER, Michael TICE, John FINDLEY, John

MCMURDIE, John SCOTT are commissioners to raise up to $2060 to complete the German Presby. Church in Greencastle & the Presby. Church in Mercersburg.

p. 302: Jacob WALTER is administrator of the estate of his late brother, Michael WALTER, decd., who had been a soldier of the 3rd Pa. Regiment during the Rev. War. Michael did not receive depreciation due on his pay. It appears by a certificate from the comptroller-general that the amount of depreciation certificate in the name of Michael WALTER was charged to the U.S. in the accounts of this commonwealth with the U.S. The certificate was never redeemed by this state.

p. 305: John BRADY, late of Northumberland Co., decd., was appointed Capt. in the 12th Pa. Regiment, commanded by Col. William COOKE. He served until 1778. He obtained a leave of absence for the purpose of assisting & defending his family against the Indians. He was returning from a scout to a small fort in which he had placed his family for safety & "fell a victim to savage cruelty." The family is granted a guaranty of donation land.

p. 307: Commissioners for the Susquehanna & York Borough Turnpike Rd.: John STEWART, George HAY, George SPANGLER, Jonathan MIFFLIN, George BARD, Conrad LAUB, John STROMAN, Samuel SPANGLER, Christian STONER, John GRIER, Jacob UPP.

p. 328: Margaret KEITH petitions that Charles MCHAFFEY owned land in Cumberland Co., 190 ½ acres warranteed 29 Jan., 1753. The land was surveyed by William LYON, Esq. on 18 Aug., 1761. Charles MCHAFFEY died intestate in Middletown, Cumberland Co. Margaret KEITH, alias Margaret M'HAFFEY, is the only daughter & heir to the estate. About 30 years ago, Margaret married Timothy KEITH, a foreigner from Ireland. KEITH absconded from Cumberland Co. about 20 years ago & never returned.

p. 331: $150 is granted to Peter KEPLINGER & an annuity of $50.

p. 334: Commissioners to receive subscriptions to the Susquehanna & Lehigh Turnpike Rd.: William TILGHMAN, Benjamin SAY, William TURNBULL, Samuel HODGDON, Thomas C. JAMES, Levi HOLLINGSWORTH, Phila.; Gen. Thomas CRAIG, George SEVITZ, Peter RHODES, Jr., Northampton Co.; Nathan BEECH, Luzerne Co.; Jacob BITTENBENDER & John BROWN, Berwick, Northampton Co.

p. 373: John MURRAY, Jr., Jacob SHIEFFELIN, Thomas BUCKLEY, Effingham EMBREE, minor children of Effingham LAWRENCE, decd., & minor children of Samuel BOWNE, decd., all of the city or state of N.Y.; Samuel W. FISHER in his own right & in trust for Isaac WHARTON, Jesse WALN, Robert WALN, & James C. FISHER, all of Phila.; Samuel PARKER of London....all are owners of 112,300 acres of land on the waters of Pine Ck., & the south branch of Tioga, formerly in the county of Northumberland, now in Lycoming. William ELLIS is a surveyor in Muncy Twp., Lycoming Co.

p. 380: On 11 Apr., 1793, £10,000 was granted to the Pa. Hospital. Philip REILEY is employed to collect the monies. His bond is assured by Christian FEBIGER. After REILEY collected the money, he absconded. Managers of the Pa. Hospital obtained a judgment against Elizabeth FEBIGER, exr. of Christian FEBIGER, for $5331.35.

p. 403: Henry DRINKER, Edward TILGHMAN, Thomas HARRISON, William

POYNTELL, Phila.; John CONKLIN, Jason TORRY, Samuel STANTON, Wayne Co.; Asuhel GREGORY, John TYLER & Menna DUBOIS, Luzerne Co., are commissioners to receive subscriptions for the Coshecton & Great Bend Turnpike Rd.

p. 424: Michael IRICK, late of York Co., decd., enlisted as a soldier in 1777, in Col. HARTLEY's regiment for three years or until the end of the Rev. War. Being on command at Wyoming in the winter of 1780, he had his feet nearly frozen off. Thus he was disabled from continuing in the service of his country or providing for himself or his family. A share of donation lands is granted.

p. 426: William TENNENT, Slator CLAY, John GEMMIL, ministers; Andrew PORTER, Francis SWAINE, Cadwallader EVANS, John JONES, Seth CHAPMAN, Levi PAWLING, Isaac HUDDLESON, John MARKLEY, Alexander CRAWFORD, Robert HAMILL are trustees for the Norristown Academy, Montgomery Co.

p. 434: Morrisville, Bucks Co., is erected into a borough. It is located near property of William JENKS, Lewis LE GUEN, Henry CLYMER, Mahlon MILNOR, Mahlon LONGSTRETH, John CARLILE.

p. 442: Richard KENEHAN had a noncupative will which was certified by William LYON, Esq., register of probates & wills for Cumberland Co. He gave Sarah WILSON a tract of donation land in the 6th district & numbered 1292. Afterward, she became the wife of Samuel HOGGE. They sold the tract to Alexander POWER who sold it to Marcus HULINGS, Jr.

p. 449: Jacob EICHELBERGER & Frederick SHULTZ are authorized to sell a piece of land in York Co. near Heidleburgh for the German Lutheran Congregation near Hanover. The land was sold by John & Elizabeth CREAT on 5 Oct., 1779 to Frederick GILVEX, Henry SLAGLE, et al, for the congregation.

p. 451: Chambers GAW says his infant daughter, Mary, in the right of her mother & uncle, John GALLOWAY, decd., is entitled to a small interest in two tracts of land in Buffaloe Twp., Cumberland Co. Mary is the only child of Chambers & his late wife, Catharine GAW.

p. 464: David JACKSON, during the Rev. War, was called out on a tour of duty in Chester Co. militia in Capt. David HAY's Co., Col. Evan EVAN's Regiment. In the cannonade at Trenton on 2 Jan., 1777, he had his left hand shot off by a cannonball. He was allowed $4/month. He is now aged & infirm & is granted $12/year plus the $48/year he now receives.

p. 465: Nicholas REEM (alias Nicholas RHEAM), Northumberland Co., as early as 1776, enlisted in the Rev. army for three years. He continued as a sergeant until 1781. He was discharged because of wounds. He is granted a share of donation lands.

p. 485: Sarah CALDWELL, John THOMPSON, Mary BEERE, James STEENE, Charles WEST, Thomas BUTLER, Henry BROWN all lost loan certificates which were exchanged for continental certificates. Thomas LEIPER is executor of the estate of Sarah CALDWELL.

p. 486: James WALLIS bought a lot from Llewellin DAVIS in Charlestown, Chester Co. DAVIS is since decd.

p. 493: Mary DEWEES, late Mary KID, Montgomery Co., was lawfully married to Thomas DEWEES, June, 1801. Within a few months after the marriage, he was convicted of forgery in Berks Co. & sentenced to hard labour & imprisonment. After 18 months imprisonment, he was pardoned by the Governor. After remaining with Mary for two weeks after his liberation, he abandoned her. The Allegheny County court on 28 Dec., 1803, convicted Thomas of aiding & abetting the passing of counterfeit money. He was sentenced to 5 years hard labour & imprisonment. The marriage is annulled.

p. 495: Alexander MCINTIRE is auth. to erect a toll bridge over French Ck., Crawford Co.

p. 503: Fermanagh & Milford Twps., Mifflin Co., will vote in the school-house now occupied by David STEELE, Mifflin-town. Cumberland Valley Twp., Bedford Co., will vote at John MCCOY's. Armstrong Twp., Indiana Co., near James M'CLANAHAN's farm on Crooked Ck., including Adam PILSON's house, will vote at Jacob HAAS'. Part of Venango Co. near Andrew CRESS' or CARSON's on Oil Ck., will vote at Thomas GOTT's. Londonderry Twp., Dauphin Co., will vote at Abraham STANDFORD's. Tioga Twp., Lycoming Co., will vote at Thomas BERRY's. Moon Twp., Allegheny Co., will vote at William MARKS' house. The 5th district, Butler Co., will vote at Alexander RAMSAY's. Middlesex & Buffalo Twps., Butler Co., will vote at John NEIGHLY's, Butler. The 6th district, Butler Co., will vote at Washington PORTER's.

THE LAWS OF PENNSYLVANIA
1804-06

p. 6: Miles Twp., including the part of Sugar Valley which falls into Centre Co., will vote at Nicholas GAST's.

p. 10: John INSKEEP, William POYNTELL, John C. STOCKER, Robert M'MULLEN, & William RICHARDS have declined to raise $8000 by lottery for St. Thomas' Church, Phila. William MURDOCK, Joseph Benet EVES, Ephraim CLARK, Peter BROWN, Daniel SMITH are appointed in their stead.

p. 11: Donegal Twp., Lancaster Co., will vote at Frederick GELBAUGH's, in May-town.

p. 13: Trustees of Bellfont Academy, Centre Co.: Henry R. WILSON, Minister; James DENLOP, Roland CURTIN, William PETRIKIN, Robert M'CLANAHAN & John HALL, Bellefont; William STEWART, Minister; Andrew GREGG, James POTTAR, Pottar's Twp.; James DUNCAN, John HALL, Jacob HOSTERMAN, Haines Twp.; John KRIDER, Miles Twp.; Thomas FERGUSON, Ferguson Twp.; Jacob TAYLOR, Half-moon Twp.; David WHITEHILL, Patton Twp.; Richard MILES, Robert BOGGS, Joseph MILES, John DUNLOP, Spring Twp.; William MCEWEN, Thomas MCCALMON, Centre Twp.; John FEARON, Matthew ALLISON, James BOYD, Bald Eagle Twp.

p. 17: Elizabeth SPROGEL, widow, Phila., has children Elizabeth & Ann, both minors. She is destitute & owns a 3 acre lot in Northern Liberties Twp. (which had been devised to Elizabeth for life & the remainder to John SPROGEL, Ludwick SPROGEL & Elizabeth & Ann, in fee) which is unproductive. Isaac JOHNSON & Elizabeth SPROGEL are guardians of Elizabeth & Ann.

p. 20: Franklin Twp., Fayette Co., will vote at John FREEMAN's.

p. 22: Nicholas ECKART, Henry HIRSH, George EGE, Jr., Conrad STOUCH, John KAISS, John WEIFFER, Daniel GREAFF are commissioners to raise $1500 to erect Zion Church & two schools in Wolmesdorf, Berks Co.

p. 24: Andrew DUNLAP, Christian CLAMENS, John HOUGH, Thomas STEWART, Hugh MEREDITH, Nathaniel SHEWELL & Josiah Y. SHAW are commissioners to raise $3000 for debts of Union Academy, Doylestown, Bucks Co.

p. 28: Peter KIMMEL, James CLARK, John TANTLINGER, Ottho SHARDER, Abraham MORRISON, George TUTROW, Abraham MILLER, Jacob SCHNIDER are commissioners to raise $3000 to build a house of worship in Somerset for Lutheran & Calvinist societies.

p. 30: Buffalo twp., Cumberland Co., will vote at William THOMSON's.

p. 31: John MEREDITH is decd. One of his heirs is Charles MEREDITH.

p. 34: Henry SPIKER, late paymaster of Berks Co. militia, said £20 was due to Maj. Martin KERCHER for services rendered by him during the Rev. War. He directed Daniel LEVAN, late treasurer of Berks Co., to pay the money. Martin KERCHER transferred the certificate to Frederick STOEVER.

p. 38: John MAXWELL, late of Caernarvon Twp., Lancaster Co., yeoman, died intestate in 1786. He had land adj. land of Edward DAVIS, Christian HARTZLER & David JENKINS. He left no widow, lawful issue, brothers or sisters. He had married a woman named Isabella with whom he intermarried under the disability of a prior marriage & by whom he had six children: John, Margaret, Martha, Mary, Sarah, & Isabella. All except Margaret were born after the death of his first wife. They were living with him at the time of his death. The estate is vested in the children.

p. 39: Thomas BOUDE, Christian BRENNEMAN, Joseph POOLE, John EVANS, William P. BEATTY, Jacob STRICKLER, Samuel BETHEL, Adam REIGART, Jr., William FERREE, Philip DIFFENDERFER, Michael GUNDAKER, Leonard EICHHOLTZ are managers to raise $20,000 to improve the Susquehanna River. The following men are to superintend divisions: John HALDEMAN, Samuel MILLER from Columbia to the mouth of Swatara; Thomas STUBBS, William MURRAY from Swatara to the mouth of the Juniata; Simon HEROLD, Abraham M'KENNY from the mouth of the Juniata to the forks of the Susquehanna at Northumberland town; John CLARK, Robert ERWIN of Catawissa-town & Daniel MONTGOMERY, Jr. for the Northeast branch of said river from Northumberland to the head of the rapids at Nanticoke Ck., Luzerne Co.; Hugh WHITE, George CRANE & Bethuel VINCENT for the west branch of said river from Northumberland-town to Anderson's Ck., Clearfield Co.; John GILLESPIE, John BRATTON, Robert PROVINCE, William THOMPSON of Thompsontown for the Juniata River from the mouth to Frankstown, Huntingdon Co.; Henry SHOUB, James ENTRICKEN, Peter MORGARET for the Raystown branch of the Juniata from the mouth to Bedford; Robert BOGGS, Isaac M'KINNEY for Bald Eagle Ck. from the mouth to the forks at Milesburgh.

p. 45: John TRAVIS, late of Phila., merchant, on a deed of 30 Oct., 1801, he said he was one of the partners of the firm of Nathaniel & Falkner PHILLIPS & Co. of Manchester, merchants. He was also agent to the house of John & Jeremiah NAYLOR, Wakefield, on the island of Great Britain, merchants. He died & his widow, Elizabeth, was administratrix. He died intestate, not having settled the partnership transactions. The estate is vested in his infant son.

p. 57: Jacob ENGLE & Engle BENFELL were, on 10 Jan., 1793, empowered by devisees of the estate of Paul ENGLE, decd. (except Levi ENGLE, who was absent) to convey real estate they were entitled to by Paul ENGLE's will. The land sold was called "Engina" & was located near the south side of Crooked Ck., formerly in Westmoreland Co., now in Armstrong Co., bounded by lands surveyed in the name of Thomas YORK & Thomas BURD, containing 357 3/4 acres with allowance to Leonard STONEBURNER. £50 was paid by STONEBURNER for the land. He has since died intestate leaving four children: Sarah PARIS, Hester WOODROW, Mary RUSH, & Ann STONEBURNER. Sarah PARIS is since decd. She left a will & left her real estate to George S. BENFELL. Jacob ENGLE is now decd. Engle BENFELL has an indisposition of mind.

p. 66: John HUGHES received patents from Pa. for two tracts, each containing 400 acres. The lands have fallen into the state of Virginia when the western boundary was fixed between PA & VA.

p. 69: Robina DUNLAP, late of Dauphin Co. (now Mifflin Co.), widow of John DUNLAP, decd., who was killed in the Rev. at the battle of Chestnut Hill in 1777 while serving under Capt. James CROUCH, Dauphin Co., has been granted 25s per month as a pension. It is payable from 21 Sept., 1785.

p. 71: John LAURENCE, Beaver; Samuel WILSON, David POTTER, Beaver Co., are auth. to sell 1/4 of the town lots of Beaver.

p. 73: Rebecca ADKINSON, late Rebecca RITTENHOUSE, Fayette Co., says that she married Thomas ADKINSON on 12 Nov., 1801. In May, 1803, Thomas was arrested & committed to the Fayette Co. jail & indicted of larceny. He escaped & was returned Mar., 1804. He was convicted at Allegheny Co. court of divers felonies & sentenced to 5 years in the Phila. penitentiary. The marriage is dissolved.

p. 75: Joseph HEISTER, Peter FRAILEY, John HUY, John KEIM, Sr., George EGE, Conrad STAUGH, Christian LOWER, Berks Co.; John MAYER, Philip GREENAWALT, Peter SHINDLE, David KRAUSE, Henry GILPIN, Henry MEYER, Abram RAGUEL, Henry BERRY, Andrew KELLINGER, John KEAN, Jacob GREENAWALT, George HOYER, Robert HARRIS, Dauphin Co., are commissioners for Berks & Dauphin Turnpike Rd.

p. 95: John R. COATS, Esq., is agent for the inhabitants of York.

p. 104: John M'ELNAY, a soldier in Capt. Philip ALBRIGHT's Co. of the 1st Regiment of Riflemen, commanded by Col. Samuel MILES, in the service of the U.S. during the Rev. War. In the spring of 1776, he enlisted to serve till 1 Jan., 1778. He continued to serve until the battle of Long Island. In the following August, he was taken prisoner by the British. He was in a bad state of health on release & spent a considerable time in the hospital in Phila. He continued sick & incapable of doing duty until his enlistment expired. He was never paid.

p. 105: Theophilais HARRIS, Joshua JONES, Jonathan SCHOLFIELD, Jacob DUFFIELD, Richard WHITTON, John NORTHROP, Enoch WRIGHT are commissioners to raise $5000 to defray expenses of building

Pennepack School House, Phila.

p. 107: Andrew BOYD, late treasurer of Chester Co., owes the commonwealth £2386 14s 4p.

p. 108: James BELL, John R. GRIFFITHS, Adam TRAQUAIR own land in Northampton Co. with a slate quarry. They go together with Thomas DOBSON, James TRAQUAIR, Paul BECK, John BENNET & John MILLER, stone cutter, as commissioners to open the Pa. Slate Co.

p. 116: Frederick FULTZ, now an inhabitant of Chester Co., entered the service of the U.S. for 3 years during the Rev. War on 12 Feb., 1777 under the command of Capt. John DENNIS, in Col. John PATTON's Regiment of foot. He was taken prisoner on 25 Apr., 1777, held captive in a N.Y. sugar house near 3 years. He was wounded in the service & lost one eye in captivity. He is now aged & infirm. He receives $3.33 per month.

p. 118: Marcis HULINGS is allowed two years more to build a bridge over French Ck.

p. 121: William JACK, James PARR, John POMROY are commissioners to erect public buildings for Indiana Co. Charles CAMPBEL, Randel LOUGHLIN, John WILLSON are trustees for Indiana Co. Alexander CRAIG sells ground for George CLYMER.

p. 125: Esther VANSCIVER, late of Northern Liberties, Phila., decd., had 1/5 part of a messuage & lot in Phila. adj. William MALTBY, William HUDSON. She died intestate leaving sons George & Jacob VANSCIVER, daughter Susanna LANE, granddaughter Esther THOMAS. John KEEN, Northern Liberties, house carpenter, is guardian of Esther THOMAS.

p. 127: David RANKIN was an early resident of Greencastle, Franklin Co.

p. 134, 1805: George HOLLINGER, John HOLDEMAN, Jacob LONG, Philip GORNER, James EAGEN, Frederick GALBUCK are commissioners for a lottery to build the German Presby. Church, Maytown, Lancaster Co.

p. 137: Joseph PRIESTLY, John COWDEN, Northumberland; Charles HALL, Sunbury; Dr. James DOOGALL, Milton; Daniel MONTGOMERY, Jr., Danville; Jacob TOPPELL, Hamburgh alias Kercherstown; Joseph HEISTER, James MAY, Reading; Samuel MORRIS, Thomas LEIPER, William TILGHMAN, James GIBSON, Phila.; William HEPBURN, Lycoming Co. are commissioners for the Centre Turnpike Co.

p. 158: John CHANDLER, a native of Great Britain, in Mar., 1803, arrived in Pa. with the intention of residing here. In the following July, he purchased from Joseph WILKINSON & Abraham TRIMBLE, a plantation in Nether Providence Twp., Delaware Co., adj. Edward TILGHMAN & Mahlon PERSONS.

p. 168: Benjamin CLARK, now an inhabitant of Greene Co., entered the service for 3 years in the Rev. He was in the command of Capt. KILGORE, 8th Pa. Regiment. In 1777, he received a wound in the forehead near Boundbrook, N.J. In 1778, he was wounded with two balls in one thigh & another in his hand in a march to Fort M'Intosh, under the command of Col. John CLARK, against the Indians. Shortly after receiving the wounds, he became much affected in his hearing & eyesight & is now nearly deaf & blind, due to the effects of his wounds. He receives $3.33 per month.

p. 169: John HORNER, John J. EVANS, Alexander OGLE are trustees for Cambria Co. Land in Ebensburg is stipulated for by Rees LLOYD, John LLOYD & Stephen LLOYD.

p. 200: Wyconisco Ck., Dauphin Co., near Isaac FERREE's mill dam is declared a public highway.

p. 202: Asa BAILEY & John LYTLE, Sr., are supervisors for Waterford Twp., Erie Co.

p. 210: David MEADE, Peter WIKOFF & Jonathan Bayard SMITH are credited for certificates called "Wyoming Credits" issued 9 Mar., 1796.

p. 215: Jacob CLEMMENS, John ROBERTS, Esq., Christian DULL, Montgomery Co.; David THOMAS, Thomas MATTHIAS, John STOKES, Bucks Co.; Abraham LEVERING, Thomas M'KEEN, Abraham MINCH, Northampton Co., are commissioners for the Springhouse & Bethlehem Tpk.

p. 252: Thomas PRICE, early in the Rev. War, was a sergeant in Col. MILE's Regiment. In the battle of Long-Island, he was wounded & taken prisoner & to preserve his life, he was forced to enlist with the enemy. He was transported to Nova Scotia, escaped by traveling by land round the head of the Bay of Fundy to New England & thence to the army where he served out the remainder of his enlistment. He is to receive donation land.

p. 254: Commissioners are to meet a Benjamin PATTON's, Bellefont, Clearfield Co.

p. 255: Mahantango Twp., Northumberland Co., will vote at Frederick STEES'. Pitt Twp., Allegheny Co., will vote at Thomas WILSON's. St. Clair Twp., Allegheny Co., will vote at Thomas M'CULLEY's. Ohio Twp., Allegheny Co., will vote at John MOORE's. Moon Twp., Allegheny Co., will vote at John BYERS'. Greene Co. near the land of Thomas CARTER, Michael TURNER, Benjamin CLARK will vote at Daniel GRAY's. Caernarvon Twp., part of Earl & Salsbury Twp., Lancaster Co., near James M'CALMONT's mill, William GAULT, Henry GABLE, Matthew HENDERSON, Henry ORLEDY, Christian WEAVER's mill, George KINSER, Martin OVERHOLSER will vote at the house formerly occupied by Thomas PERKINS & now by Jesse LAVERTY, Churchtown. Mount-Joy Twp., Lancaster Co., will vote at Henry MAYER's. Bald Eagle Twp., Centre Co., will vote at John FREDERICKS'. Greenfield Twp., Bedford Co., will vote at Ulrich ZETH's. M'Kean Twp., Erie Co., will vote at Alexander HAMILTON's. Venango Twp., Crawford Co., will vote at Philip STRAW's. Sadsbury & West Caln Twp., Chester Co., will vote at John SLOAN's house which is now occupied by John JONES, innkeeper, Sadsbury Twp. Pittstown election district, Luzerne Co., will vote at John HARDING's. Burlington election district, Lycoming Co., will vote at Nathaniel ALTER's. Georgetown election district, Beaver Co., will vote at William KERNEGHEY's. Antrim Twp., Franklin Co., will vote at John BESHORE's, Greencastle. Fairfield Twp., Westmoreland Co., will vote at William RAMSAY's, Palmer's Fort. Donegal Twp., Westmoreland Co., will vote at Maj. John AMBROSE's. Conemaugh Twp., Somerset Co., will vote at John FORREY's. Sandy Lake Twp., Mercer Co., will vote at Adam HILL's. Wolf Ck. Twp., Mercer Co., will vote at David M'KINLEY's. Slipperyrock Twp., Mercer Co., will vote at Joseph CAMPBELL's.

p. 265: John RITTER & Charles KESSLER published the laws of Pa. in German.

p. 272: Samuel NICHOLSON & Samuel BLYTHE are to pay the government all liens on the estate of the late John NICHOLSON.

p. 276: James BIRCHFIELD, James HERRINGTON, John BROOKS, Henry REICHARD, William MOORE, John PATTERSON, John LIMBER, Henry HURST are trustees of Crawford Co. to erect a building for a seminary of learning in Meadville.

p. 295: Samuel BOWER, Isaac WHITE, Jacob KEEN, Isaac JOHNSON, Thomas TIMINGS, Cornelius TRIMNUL, John COLLARD are commissioners for a lottery to erect the 2nd Baptist Church, Northern Liberties, Phila.

p. 297: Frederick SMITH, Matthias RICHARDS, Nicholas DICK, George D.B. KEIM, William WITMAN, Jr., John R. MESSERSMITH are commissioners to raise money by lottery to erect an English school house & house of English worship in Reading, Berks Co.

p. 299: Anthony CARMONY, Henry BERRY, David MARSHALL, Daniel HENNING, Abraham RAIGUEL, John SHERTZER are commissioners for a lottery to raise money for a church for Lutheran & Presbyterian congregations in Anville, Dauphin Co.

p. 301, 1806: Arthur ST. CLAIR was an auctioneer for Phila. An erroneous statement of his account by John NICHOLSON, comptroller general, 4 years later, made him a debtor of the commonwealth instead of a creditor. $2719.74 is to be paid to ST. CLAIR.

p. 302: The title of land is vested in Sebastian ROYER & Michael MYER in Centre Twp., Northumberland Co. for the Lutheran & Presbyterian congregations. The land is adj. ROYER, MYER & Abraham HASSINGER.

p. 306: John BIDDIS discovered improvements in manufacturing potatoe-starch, sago & hair powder & a machine for opening or reducing again to wool offcast woolen clothing.

p. 307: Return judges for Fayette & Greene Co. will meet at Henry JENNINGS', German Twp., Fayette Co., not at the house of Thomas CLARE, Fayette Co.

p. 312: Jacob JOHN, Bedford Co., farmer, left a will dated 14 July, 1786, in which he devised lands to his seven children: Eldest son David, Margaret, Jacob, Daniel, Samuel, Joseph, & Benjamin. The lands were then in Bedford Co. & now in Franklin Co. Margaret married Owen DAVID & afterwards died leaving four children still minors. Samuel died without issue. Benjamin is still a minor. David JOHN, Daniel JOHN, Joseph JOHN & Jacob ZIMMERMAN are assignees of Jacob JOHN & they pray that David JOHN, David BOWEN, Jr., & David BOWEN of Samuel are appointed to partition land. James M'FARLANE, David BOWEN, Jr., & David BOWEN of Samuel of Montgomery Twp., Franklin Co., are trustees for Benjamin JOHN, a minor, son of Jacob JOHN, Bedford Co., dec., & four minor children of Margaret DAVID, decd.

p. 315: Enoch GRIFFETH, Chester Co., is adjudged a lunatic. John HAMBLETON & Joseph SHARP are appointed trustees.

p. 317: John DEAN & Mary DEAN are administrators of the estate of Joseph DEAN, decd., & James M'COMB is guardian of William DEAN, minor child of Joseph DEAN. They are all of Armstrong Twp., Indiana Co. Joseph DEAN died intestate.

p. 320: Henry PRATT, Stephen GERARD, Moore WHARTON, Isaac WORRELL, Francis MURRAY, Jacob SOMMER, Joseph HART, Augustine WILLETT, Richard LEEDOM, Jonathan WYNKOOP, Joshua JONES, Thomas BIDDLE are commissioners to raise money by a lottery to discharge debts of the Bustleton & Smithfield Turnpike Co.

p. 322: Simon TOEY, formerly an inhabitant of that part of Lancaster Co. which now composes Dauphin Co., served a tour in the militia in 1776 & afterwards, was drafted into the Flying Camp & served as a non-commissioned officer. He was taken prisoner by the British at Fort Washington & forced on board a prison ship. He soon died, leaving a widow & 9 helpless children. Catharine TOEY is awarded $40/year.

p. 326: Jacob SELL, Adams Co., when a young man in 1777, married Eva HELMAN. Five months later, she had a female child. The child was not SELL's. They agreed to separate. In 1780, SELL married again & they had six children. SELL is now old & in declining health. The SELL-HELMAN marriage is annulled.

p. 328: Samuel MEEKER, Jacob SPERRY, Samuel HAYS, Moses NATHANS, Benjamin NONES are a commission to raise money in a lottery in behalf of the president adjuntas & members of the Hebrew Congregation of Phila.

p. 330: William PENNELL is guardian of Matthias Richards SAYRES & Edward Smith SAYRES, minors. Real estate belonging to them is in Lower Chichester Twp., Delaware Co. near land of Benjamin MOULDER & William CRABB.

p. 332: John VANDERIN, Jr. is lately decd. Edmund MILNE, through his agent, John HAZLEWOOD (city purchaser for the army during the late Rev. War), became flour contractor for Pa. On 25 Nov., 1780, he delivered 185 barrels of flour.

p. 349: Samuel MEEKER, Godfrey HAGA, George CLYMER, William GUYER, George BICKHAM, Thomas ALLIBONE, Phila.; Adam REIGART, Jr., Abraham WITMER, Samuel HUMES, William MONTGOMERY, Lancaster; Robert COLEMAN, Robert JENKINS, Lancaster Co.; Moses GILMORE, Christian KUNCKLE, Robert HARRIS, Henry BADER, Adam BOYD, George WEINMAN, Harrisburg; John BAUMAN, John CAROTHERS, Christopher QUIGLEY, James DUNCAN, Joseph PIERCE, Alexander SHARP, John M'KEE, Jacob RAUM, John SIMPSON, Cumberland Co.; Andrew DUNLAP, Jacob HEISER, John GILMORE, Christian KEEVER, Franklin Co.; George BAIRD, John GRIER, Jacob HAY, York Co.; John DAVIS, Jacob BONNETT, John ANDERSON, Henry WERTZ, Jr., Bedford Co.; George KIMMEL, Michael REAM, Abraham MORRISON, Peter KIMMEL, John FLETCHER, John SCHULL, Alexander OGLE, Somerset Co.; William JACK, James GUTHRIE, John IRVIN, Hugh MARTIN, Joseph BALDRIGE, John BONNETT, Robert DICKEY, Thomas JONES, Westmoreland Co.; Nathaniel IRISH, Thomas BEARD, James O'HARRA, Samuel EWALT, Adamson TANNEHILL, Allegheny Co.; Roger ALDAN, David MEADE, Thomas R. KENNEDY, William CLARK, Crawford Co., are commissioners to direct the Harrisburgh to Pittsburg Tpk. Co.

p. 371: David BRADFORD has a mill on the main branch of Chartiers Ck.

p. 371: Trustees of the Griersburgh, Beaver Co. academy: Rev. John M'FARREN, Rev. George M. SCOTT, Rev. Thomas E. HUGHES, Rev. William WICK, Rev. James SUTTERFIELD, Rev. Nicholas PITTINGER, Alexander WRIGHT, Esq., David POTTER, Esq., Dr. Samuel ADAMS, John BEER, George DILWORTH, William SCOTT, Joseph POLLOCK, Hugh HAGGERTY, Caldwell SEMPLE.

p. 375: John Jacob HIRLEMAN died in Phila. in 1793, intestate. The property, for want of known heirs, escheated to the commonwealth. He had 5 brothers & 2 sisters: John Michael, John Henry, Eve Dorthea GREISS, Catharine Salome BICKLER, John, John Philip, John Stephen. All are still living & residing in Alsace, Lower Rhine, France. The attorney is Peter ULRICH.

p. 379: John NICHOLSON, then comptroller-general of Pa., on 15 Sept., 1791, delivered to James ASH, Esq., then sheriff of Phila., a writ at the suit of the commonwealth against Daniel BRODHEAD who owed £893 16s 9p to the commonwealth.

p. 381: John LEWIS, late a sergeant in the 11th Pa. regiment, commanded by Col. Richard HUMPTON, was enlisted on 7 June, 1777. He has not received pay since 1 June, 1778 to the 1st Nov., next following.

p. 383: John GREGG is to keep a ferry over Swatara Ck., near it's junction with the Susquehanna River, Dauphin Co.

p. 398: Williamsport, Lycoming Co., is bounded by land of Michael ROSS & James HEPBURN.

p. 419: Gettysburg, Adams Co., is bounded by land of Thomas BRADON, Alexander DOBBIN, William BUCHANAN, NEWCOMER's out-lot, HUTCHINSON's out-lot, Alexander COBEAN's out-lot, James SCOTT, Alexander BOYD, Henry WEAVER.

p. 428: Joseph Robert Eustache BUNEL, a native of Ponteaudemer, in the late province of Normandy, France, arrived in Pa. in 1792 to reside here. In May, 1804, he purchased Jacob VOGDES' plantation in Bristol Twp., Bucks Co., bounded by land of Samuel ALLEN, land late of Richard NOBELL, Thomas CLIFFORD. Jacob VOGDES' wife is Elizabeth.

p. 444: Thomas LEIPER, Phila.; James KNOWLES, farmer, Delaware Co.; Evan W. THOMAS, farmer, Phila. Co.; George MORTON, farmer; Dell PENNELL, farmer, are commissioners of a company to erect a bridge over the Schuylkill R. near GRAY's ferry. George GRAY, decd., owned the ferry. His heirs are: Ann GRAY, Curtis GRUBB, George G. GRUBB, Martha G. GRUBB, children of Mary GRUBB; George W. GRAY, Mary B. GRAY, children of George GRAY, Jr.; Martha GRAY & William GRAY, children of William GRAY.

p. 461: Andrew MOORE, Lancaster Co., was declared a lunatic Feb., 1799. Henry SLAYMAKER, Jeremiah MOSHER, Christopher NEISLEY, Donegal Twp., were auth. to sell his real estate.

p. 463: George MOORE, Jacob KRUG, Casper SHAFFNER, Jr., William BAUSMAN, Henry DEHUFF, Lancaster Co., & John FUNK, Strasburgh village, are commissioners to make the Conestogo R. navigable from it's confluence with the Susquehanna R. to Abraham HOSTETTER's mill.

p. 479: John WELCH, now an inhabitant of Butler Co., entered the service as a private soldier for 3 years or during the war in Capt. John M'DOWELL's Co., 7th Pa. Regiment, commanded by Lt. Col. John GREER. At the battle of Germantown, he received a severe wound in his left shoulder. A patent is issued for donation land.

p. 486:   Lewis REESE & Thomas MILLS are auth. to erect a wing dam on the Schuylkill R., Berks Co.

p. 526:   Daniel WELKER, now an inhabitant of Franklin Co., enlisted in Col. John PATTON's regiment in 1777 & was wounded at Ash Swamp, N.J. & discharged in 1781 because of the wound. He is now incapable of labour. He is entitled to donation land.

p. 529:   Wilkesbarre, Luzerne Co., is bounded by land of Jacob JOHNSON.

p. 539:   An indenture of 24 Sept., 1787 in which John PENN, Jr., & John PENN, Esq., granted two lots in Pittsburg to John GIBSON, Esq., John ORMSBY, Merchant, Deveraux SMITH, gentleman, & Dr. Nathaniel BEDFORD was for a Protestant Episcopal Church (Trinity Church).

p. 541:   Barbara CONOWAY, Phila., died in 1802 & left property which has escheated to the state for want of heirs. The property & £22 5s 7p was intended for Daniel SHARP but Barbara was seized by a fit of apoplexy & died before her will could be executed. He is to receive the property.

p. 542:   Adam KOCH, now an inhabitant of Berks Co., entered the late Rev. War at it's commencement under the command of Capt. M'CLELLAN, 9th Pa. Regiment, commanded by Col. NAGLE. He was dangerously wounded in the head at the battle of Brandywine by a musquet ball which entered below his right eye & passed out below his right ear. He was afterwards hurt at the building of West Point Fort & the former injury periodically affects his intellects together with the latter increases the infirmities of age. He can no longer support himself. He is to receive $40/year.

p. 550:   John FLEMING, William Hill WELLS, William ELLIS are trustees of Tioga Co. Benjamin W. MORRIS has proposed the seat of justice. They have surveyed land near Samuel W. FISHER's near Wellsborough.

p. 553:   Isaac WHARTON, David LEWIS, Jesse WALN, Robert WALN, William WALN & Alexander FULLERTON, Phila.; Thomas FIZIMMONS, John MILLER, Jr., Robert BIRD, assignees of John VAUGHN, Jane HUMPHREYS, 6 year old daughter of John HUMPHREYS, late of Northumberland Co., are tenants in common of 197 lots (195,063) acres in Lycoming Co. John Philip DE GRUCHY & John BOYD are guardians of Jane.

p. 556:   John FLINTHAM, a minor, is entitled to 1/3 part of real estate in Phila. William FLINTHAM is his father.

p. 581:   John HALDEMAN, Jacob BRENEMAN, Frederick GILBAUGH, James HEGAN, Alexander BOGGS, Henry SHARE, Brice CLARK, Lancaster, are commissioners to make a road from Maytown, Lancaster co. to NICHOLAS' tavern, at the x roads intersecting the Lancaster & Middletown Tpk.

p. 585:   William TILGHMAN & James GREENLEAF, Phila.; George WEAVER, Montgomery Co.; Samuel SELLERS, William GREEN, James CHAPMAN, Andreas TRIEWIG, Bucks Co.; Stephen BALLIOT, Daniel COOPER, Peter

KNIPLEY, John KEEPER, George SAVITZ, Northampton Co., are commissioners to make a road from TRIEWIG's tavern, Bucks Co., by way of Samuel SELLER's tavern, Quakertown meetinghouse & COOPER's tavern, Northampton-town, Northampton Co.

p. 607: Benjamin BROWN, late of Boston, Mass., decd., owned a messuage & lot on the northerly side of Lancaster Tpk., Blockley Twp., Phila. Co. In his will, he left it to his widow, Mary Frances BROWN & daughter, Hannah Fisher BROWN (who is a minor under 14 & is absent in Europe). Her guardian is James LLOYD, Jr., Boston.

p. 610: Officers of the Pa. Academy of Fine Arts: George CLYMER, Pres.; William TILGHMAN, William RAWLE, Moses LEVY, Joseph HOPKINSON, Joseph B. M'KEAN, William MEREDITH, William RUSH, John R. COXE, John DORSEY, William POYNTELL, Thomas C. JAMES, Charles Wilson PEALE, Directors.

p. 611: Levi HOLLINGSWORTH, William TURNBULL, Anthony MORRIS, Benjamin R. MORGAN, Samuel M. FOX, Samuel MIFFLIN, Phila.; Nathan BEACH, Abel FELLOWS, Luzerne Co.; Thomas BOWMAN, Northumberland Co.; John FRANKLIN, Stephen TUTTLE, Reuben HALE, Lycoming Co., are commissioners to make a road from Berwick on the NE branch of the Susquehanna R. from the mouth of Lower Wopehawney to a point on the north line of the state nearest Newtown, on the Tioga R. in N.Y. state.

p. 615: Bellefonte, Centre Co., is bounded by land of John DUNLOP, Nathaniel SIMPSON, James DUNLOP & James HARRIS.

p. 617: John GILL & William COOPER obtained patents from Pa. for two tracts of donation land, #1255 granted to GILL for Rev. services, #57 granted to COOPER fro Rev. services. John CUMMINS owns the tract granted to GILL. The tracts are in the 5th donation district. CUMMINS & COOPER are enabled to take other lands in lieu of lands held by a defective title.

p. 619: James GREENLEAF, Jacob CLAYDER, George ROADS, John KEIPER, George BUTTS, Jeremiah TREXLER are commissioners to erect a bridge over the Lehigh River near Northampton-town.

p. 620: John RYAN, Phila. Co., served in the Rev. War in the 1st Pa. Regiment commanded by Col. HAND & afterwards, by Col. CHAMBERS & was wounded at Miles Square in N.Y. He is to receive $40/yr.

p. 622: John JOURDAN, Greenwood Twp., Cumberland Co., on 26 Nov., 1804, sold verbally to Michael M'GARRY, a house & lot in Miller's town. JOURDAN unexpectedly died. Amos JOURDAN & Sophia are executors of John JOURDAN, decd.

p. 624: Christian KUNCKLE, Isaac FERREE, Jr., Thomas STUBBS, George LOWER, Valentine SHOUFFLER, Martin MEILY, Abraham DOEBLER, Rudolph KINTZEL, Henry MAYER, Dauphin Co., are to erect a house for employment & support of the poor.

p. 633: George VANCE, Mifflin Co., served a tour & also was a volunteer scout in the militia against the Indians in 1781 in the company of Capt. Walter M'KINNEY, under the command of Col. Alexander BROWN. He received a certificate #7179 for £9 for his first tour & a certificate #7162 for £1 4s 6p for his second tour. Both certificates were destroyed by fire.

p. 635: At the time Franklin, Venango Co. was laid out, an in-lot & a house occupied by officers of the U.S. Army was not numbered with the other lots in town & when they evacuated the old garrison, the house was sold by the quarter-master general to John ANDREWS. The right is now vested in Samuel PLUMMER. Commissioners for the sale of lots in Franklin are George FOWLER, George POWER & James G. HERON.

p. 637: A road from Bald Eagle's Nest, Centre Co., to the Allegheny River, Venango Co. as lies between David EUAN's mill, Centre Co. & Joseph BARNETT's mill on Sandy Lick Ck. & a road between BARNETT's mill & the dwelling place of Elias HOLMAN on the Allegheny River will be improved. A Greene Co. road will be improved from David GRAY's to the western boundary of the state toward the flats of Grave Ck.

p. 640: Henry DOUGHERTY, Jr., now an inhabitant of Lycoming Co., when on a tour of duty as a private soldier in Col. POTTER's regiment of Northumberland Co. militia, in an action with the enemy at Piscatawy, N.J., in Feb., 1777, received a wound through the right shoulder, which dislocated the joint & otherwise fractured the bones. He now receives $16/year which is not enough to support him & a large family. He is to have donation land.

p. 643: Thomas RYERSON is to pay the commonwealth $500 within 9 months for a lien against land in Fayette Co. that was part of John NICHOLSON's estate. Included is a grist & saw mill at Haydensburg, lately occupied by Jesse EVANS, 86½ acres on the waters of George's Ck., in George's Twp., surveyed on a warrant 26 Jan., 1791, known as Magnus TATE's place adjoining Thomas HEADY, 196 acres on the waters of George's Ck., surveyed for Thomas HEADY, Jr. & Jesse EVAN's log-house where he resided several years ago.

p. 646: Thomas BOUDE, Samuel BETHEL, Jacob STRICKLER, William P. BEATTY, John EVANS, Christian BRENNEMAN are the 6 managers named 18 Feb., 1805 to raise money to remove obstructions to improve navigation in the Susquehanna River. Adam REIGART, Jr., Philip DIFFENDERFER & Michael GUNDACKER are three managers who have declined the duty. Emanuel REIGART, Hugh WILSON, Michael RINE are appointed managers. Abraham WITMER, Christian STONER, Andrew KAUFFMAN, George PRETZLER, Nathaniel BARBER, Philip GOSLER, George SNYDER, Lancaster Co.; Thomas GRANT, Northumberland-town; James DUNCAN, Aaronsburg, Centre Co.; John BLAIR, Robert ALLISON, Huntingdon, Huntingdon Co.; George M'CLELLAND, Lewistown, Mifflin Co.; are appointed add'l managers with BOUDE, BETHEL, STRICKLER, BEATTY, EVANS, BRENNEMAN, Joseph POOLE, William FERREE & Leonard EICHOLTZ are auth. to execute the act.

p. 648: Simon FORD, a servant of Rudolph SPANGLER, York Co., in 1777, enlisted in Col. Thomas HARTLY's regiment in the Pa. line & at the time of the enlistment, had 1 year 11 months to serve, agreeable to the terms of his indenture which his master never received any satisfaction for. SPANGLER is allowed $53.33 with interest.

p. 650: Thomas JONES, Westmoreland Co.; William BACKHOUSE, Somerset Co., have begun at their own expense to repair a road from Somerset to Washington on Laurel Hill.

p. 654: Tinicum, Nockamixon & Derham Twps., Bucks Co., will vote at Michael OTT's, Nockamixon Twp. Hopewell Twp., York Co., will vote at John BORDNER's. Fan Twp., York Co., will vote at Widow

CUNNINGHAM's. Chansford Twp., York Co., will vote at Charles William POTTER's. The 3rd election district, Berks Co., will vote at Abraham BAILEY's, Hamburgh. The 2nd election district, Northampton Co., will vote at George SEVITZ's, inn-keeper. Moore Twp., & part of Allen Twp., north of Easton Rd., Northampton Co., will vote at Michael MYERS'. Northampton Co. near Frederick NAGLE's & then to Henry BEIL's mill will vote at Abraham MENSH's, Allen Twp. Morris, Amwell, West Bethlehem Twp., Washington Co., near GANTZ's mill, Demas LINDSLEY's mill, Caleb LINDSLEY's, & Jacob BOBBITT's will vote at Ziba COOK's, Esq., Amity, Washington Co. Jefferson Co. will vote at Joseph BARNET's, Sandy Lick. Southampton Twp., Bedford Co., will vote at Jacob ADAM's. Lower Merion Twp., Montgomery Co., will vote at Titus YERKES'. Franconia Twp., Montgomery Co., will vote at John HUGHES', Towamensing Twp. Nicholson's District, Luzerne Co., will vote at Ebenezer STEVENS'. Tunkhannock district, Luzerne Co., will vote at John M'CORD's. The 9th district, Huntingdon Co., will vote at Thomas RICKET's, near GLASSGOWE's farm. Grape Island in the Ohio River to James INGLES' & George BRUCE's will vote at Samuel JOHNSTON, Jr.'s, Beaver-town, Beaver Co. The 1st district, Butler Co., will vote at Adam FUNK's. Buffaloe Twp., Butler Co., will vote at Benjamin SERVER's. Middlesex Twp., Butler Co., will vote at Alexander M'BRIDE's mill. Conequenessing & Muddy Ck. Twp., will vote at Matthew WHITE's, Conequenessing Twp. Armagh Twp., Mifflin Co., will vote at George M'CANDLESS'. Elklick Twp., Somerset Co., will vote at Martin WEYMER, Jr's., Salsbury. The district of Burlington, Lycoming Co., will vote at Nathaniel ALLEN's. Greene Co. near John MEREDITH's will vote at John M'KEE's. Whitely district, Greene Co., near VERNON's mill & LANTZ's mill will vote at the courthouse. Potters Twp., Forguson Twp., Centre Co., will vote at John IRWIN's. Part of Crawford Co. will vote at Shadlock NEGUS'. Sadsbury Twp. near Baner EVANS', Randolph FREEMEN's, will vote at the courthouse, Meadville, Crawford Co. Mead Twp., HENNINGTON's district, Crawford Co., will vote at James HENNINGTON's, Fairfield Twp.

p. 671: Richard SMITH, Maj. Anthony SIMMONS, John GOODWIN, Peter CHRISTIAN, Robert BETHEL, Benjamin S. BARTON, M.D., James VANNUXEM are commissioners to raise money by lottery to promote the cultivation of vines to pay their debts. Philip GABLE, Jr., George HERTZIL, Lawrence JACOBY, Philip ZEFF, Daniel SMITH & Philip HAHN, Jr. are commissioners to raise money to erect a school house near Summony-town, Montgomery co. on a lot of ground given by Daniel HEISTER, decd.

p. 674: Cadwalader EVANS, Montgomery Co.; John STEELE, Lancaster Co.; John LYON, Uniontown, Fayette Co. are commissioners to procure copies of deeds, etc., relating to the estate of John NICHOLSON, decd. Samuel BRYAN is late comptroller-general.

p. 682: James ROSS, Pittsburg, & James HOPKINS are appointed counsel to appear for the inhabitants within the supposed manor of Springetsbury.

p. 684: William HAMILTON is to report on the trial of three judges of the Supreme Court.

THE LAWS OF PENNSYLVANIA
1806-07 & 1807-08

p. 3: William WILLIAMS, Montgomery Co., in a deed of 26 July, 1804, sold land to Michael BARRON, Montgomery Co., in Plymouth Twp., Montgomery Co. On 26 Apr., 1805, BARRON sold the lot to John HART, Plymouth Twp., Montgomery Co.

p. 5: Joseph & John DEVOSS owned land in E. Huntingdon Twp., Westmoreland Co. Joseph DEVOSS died intestate. John DEVOSS sold his interest to Jacob HOUGH. Nicholas SWOPE is administrator of Joseph DEVOSS. Benjamin LODGE is the late deputy surveyor of Westmoreland Co.

p. 6: Pelatiah WEBSTER, late of Phila., decd., owned a messuage & lot on the Schuylkill River, Passyunk Twp., Phila. Co. By his will, he devised land to his two granddaughters, Maria PERIT & Rebecca Hunt PERIT. Rebecca is under 16 & resides in Connecticut. Her guardian is Peter W. GALLAUDET of Connecticut.

p. 10: John LAWRENCE, Beaver-town; Samuel WILSON & David POTTER, Beaver Co., are commissioners to sell town lots in Beaver.

p. 10: James OGLIVIA, Montgomery Co., at the commencement of the Rev. War, served several tours of duty in the militia. On 5 Oct., 1778, he enlisted in Capt. CHRISTIE's Company of the 5th Pa. Regiment commanded by Col. Francis JOHNSTON & continued therein until 1780. Then he was put in the 2nd battalion of Pa. troops commanded by Col. Richard BUTLER. His term of enlistment expired on 5 Oct., 1781, but he did not ask for his discharge until after he saw the capture of CORNWALLIS at York-town in Va. On 5 Nov., he received his discharge & now has become infirm by age & by accident & destitute of support. He is to receive $60 & $50/year is to be paid to Nathaniel B. BOILEAU to be spent providing clothing & diet for OGLIVIA.

p. 11: Daniel HILL, Beaver Co., decd., conveyed 50 acres to Thomas WILLIAMS.

p. 12: James CARMICHAEL, late of Greene Co., decd., had a warrant for land in Washington (now Greene) Co. The warrant was issued in the name of his brother-in-law, Francis SEATON. The land was in Lisburn or Carmichaelstown. CARMICHAEL died intestate. His children were William S. CARMICHAEL & Margaret Eskridge CARMICHAEL.

p. 14: Joseph TYSON, Andrew TODD, Andrew MORGAN, Joseph PRICE, Matthew BROOKE, Christian SHEIDE, Philip GAUBLE are to find a site for a poor house in Montgomery Co.

p. 15: John SHEE, Abraham BICKLEY, William PHILLIPS, & Tench COXE, Phila.; John BRINK, John BRODHEAD, James BARTON, John BIDDIS, Lewis COLLINS, Asa STANTON, John H. SCHANK, Wayne Co.; Isaac BROWNSON & Thomas PARKE, Luzerne Co., are commissioners of the Milford & Owego Tpk. Rd.

p. 18: Dennis M'KNIGHT, a soldier of the 8th battalion of Chester Co. militia, was sorely wounded in battle, taken prisoner & suffered a long & grievous captivity. He is now far advanced in years. He gets $80 & $40 per year will be paid to Alexander OGLE to provide clothing, diet & lodging for M'KNIGHT.

p. 19: Mary CLARK may establish a ferry over the Susquehanna R.

p. 24: Daniel EVANS, late of W. Whitefield Twp., Chester Co., named in his will of 27 Aug., 1775 the Anna-Baptist Church, Vincent Twp.,

Chester Co. & the Episcopal Church of St. Peter, Tredyffrin Twp. They were to receive land in W. Whitefield where he lived after his wife, Sarah's, decease. Sarah is now decd.

p. 26: James MITCHEL entered the U.S. army in 1776, was wounded in the ancle (sic) at the battle of Long Island in 1776. It rendered him unfit for duty for some time. He did not receive full pay. On recovery, he resumed service & was appointed sergeant-major in the regiment commanded by Col. Richard BUTLER. He served till the surrender of CORNWALLIS. He is entitled to donation land.

p. 27: Henry GORDON was accused of high treason on 20 Mar., 1781. He did not turn himself in & his land was deeded to James WOODS on 2 Oct., 1783. WOODS sold the land to Daniel MARTIN & the devisees of Adam HOLLIDAY, Huntingdon Co.; David Hayfield CONYNGHAM, Phila. Co. David STEWART, Andrew HENDERSON & John CANAN are to view tracts of land.

p. 32: Isaac ELY, Reading, Berks Co., on 8 Aug., 1776, enlisted in the company of Capt. Andrew REDHEFFER in Col. John MOORE's battalion of Pa. Flying Camp. On 18 Nov., following, he was taken prisoner at Fort Lee & continued in confinement until mid-February (the greater part in a prison ship, where he suffered considerably). He was then permitted to go home on parole for a considerable time & was exchanged some time in May, 1780, being 3 years, 9 months & some days from the time of enlistment to the time of exchange. $103 is paid for pay missed.

p. 33: Jacob EYERLY, Jr., late of Nazareth, Northampton co., decd., & George HUBER, Bethlehem, Northampton Co., blacksmith, owned a tract of land on the west branch of the Delaware River, Bethlehem Twp., adj. Patrick GRAEME, Thomas GRAEME, Caspar WISTAR & an island in the west branch of the Delaware called "Number Nine" opposite land of Richard FREEMAN. Jacob EYERLY, Jr., on 3 July, 1796, sold his half to George HUBER. It was witnessed by Daniel ELIENST, Esq., now decd., & John WAGENER, Bethlehem. Jacob EYERLY, Jr. died 11 May, 1800. Anna Maria HANKE, wife of Matthew HANKE, later Anna Maria EVERLY, widow of Jacob, is administratrix.

p. 35: Abraham GRIFFITHS enlisted as a soldier during the Rev. War & served 3 years in the Pa. Line. He receives $100.

p. 36: Dr. Samuel EDMISTON entered the service in 1777 as a surgeon, attended the sick & wounded on board armed vessels of war. Then he was ordered to accompany a flying camp & then to attend at the general hospital until the termination of the war. He is given a patent for donation land.

p. 37: John KEATING, Richard GERNON & John S. ROULET are to deed land to McKean Co. in Smeth's port.

p. 38: John G. LOWRY is appted. trustee for Centre Co. in the room of Robert BOGGS, Esq., decd.

p. 39: Andrew PATTERSON, York Co., enlisted soldier during the war, served as an artificer in a company of artificers commanded by Capt. Thomas WILEY. He received a wound in his wrist after serving 3 years & was discharged. He is given donation land.

p. 39: Jonathan MIFFLIN married Frances (Fanny) MIFFLIN. She owned land on the east side of French Ck., adj. Peter LEVY, Emily MIFFLIN,

Paul LEVY, Crawford Co. Jonathan MIFFLIN covenanted with James DIXON to settle & improve land. Frances MIFFLIN is since decd., leaving issue not yet capable to sell land due to minority.

p. 41: James RALSTON is granted $373.67 for services as an agent under an act to prevent intrusions on land in Northampton, Northumberland & Luzerne Cos.

p. 41: William SHERRARD, father of William SHERRARD, Washington Co., decd., said the commonwealth issued a warrant to Philip WHITEBY on 25 Oct., 1784, for land on the waters of Fish-Ck., Washington Co. On 29 July, 1785, WHITEBY sold to John HUGHES & Timothy RYAN. On 4 Aug., 1785, a patent was issued to HUGHES & RYAN. RYAN sold the land to HUGHES who sold the land to William SHERRARD, Jr. He died between 21-22 years old, intestate, no issue or widow. The land, on running the western boundary, was found to be in VA not PA.

p. 44: John HORN, John ROTH, George KECK, George WENNER, George RHOADS & George YOUNDT, Northampton Co., are commissioners to raise money with a lottery for the German Lutheran congregation to erect a school house in Northampton-town. John CLARK, Christian BROBST, Isaiah WILLIS, Gabriel LAUNT, Hezekiah BOON, Northumberland Co., are commissioners to raise money to repair a road from Catawissa to Reading.

p. 49: Robert RALSTON, Thomas STEWARDSON, Simon GRATZ, Michael KEPPELE, Manuel EYRE, John WISTAR, Samuel MEEKER, Phila.; Charles SMITH, Samuel HUMES, John HUBLEY, Alexander PATTERSON, John HALDEMAN, Lancaster Co.; John IRWIN, George HOYER, John SHOCH, George ZIEGLER, Obed FAHNESTOCK, Jacob WAIN, Dauphin Co.; Isaac CRAVEN, William NORTH, John SHEWMAN, David MILLER, George MITCHEL, Thomas COCHRAN, Cumberland Co.; Jacob ZEGLER, Peter FILBERT, John SPAYD, George D.B. KIME, Valentine BOYER, George DOUGLASS, Berks Co.; David DAVIDSON, William THOMPSON, Dr. Ezra DOTY, James KNOX, John BROWN, George M'CLELLAND, John NORRIS, John BRATTON, Mifflin Co.; Andrew HENDERSON, Patrick GUIN, William STEEL, John CANNON, William MOORE, Alexandria; Thomas PROVINCE, Lazarus LOWRY, Huntingdon Co.; Joseph LILLY, Thomas PHILIPS, Thomas W. JONES, John J. EVANS, Michael REIGART, Samuel WHITE, Cambria Co.; James MARTIN, George ROBISON, Alexander HILL, John IRWIN, John DARRAH, Alexander M'LAUGHLIN, Anthony BEELER, Allegheny Co.; Henry HURST, Moses SCOTT, James GIBSON, Edward WORK, John W. HUNTER, Meadville; William CLARK, Charles CAMPBELL, William M'FARLAND, Thomas N. SLOANE, James MARSHALL, Indiana Co.; Nicholas DAY, James KELLY, William FINDLEY, John POMROY, Peter WALLACE, John KUHNS, Nicholas CHAPMAN, Jeremiah MURRAY, William JOHNSTON, Westmoreland Co.; Absalom WOODWARD, Joseph CLARK, Robert BROWN, Col. James SLOAN, Armstrong Co., are commissioners to make a road from Harrisburg to Pittsburg.

p. 51: Jeremiah LOUGHREY, Westmoreland Co., served during the war with Great Britain & afterwards in defence of frontiers of the western part of Pa. against Indians. He was wounded in his shoulder, by which he is much disabled. $40 per year will be paid to Hugh MARTIN, Esq., Westmoreland Co., for his use.

p. 54: Joseph SALMON, Capt. in Col. James MURRAY's Regiment of Northumberland Co. militia during the Rev. War, was taken prisoner by Indians & detained upwards of 2 years. His infant family was left destitute & himself treated with all the rigour incident to savage warfare. He is given a tract of donation land.

p. 55: Gaspar DRIVER, a soldier in Col. WAYNE's Regiment, at the battle of Three Rivers, Canada, he received two wounds, one from a ball passing through his arm & the other from a bayonet passing through his thigh. At the same time, he was made a prisoner & remained so for a considerable length of time. After his exchange, though disabled from wounds, he enlisted again into the Regiment commanded by Col. HUMPTON in the Pa. Line & continued until termination of the war. He receives $40 & $40 per year will be paid to Francis M'CLURE for his use.

p. 56: John METZLER, late of Manheim, Lancaster Co., died intestate & owned a lot in Manheim bounded by Samuel ENSMINGER. A small brick barn was erected on it. He left a widow, Elizabetha & four children: Jacob, John, Elizabeth, & Ann, all minors.

p. 58: Sampson CRAWFORD, Hugh WHITE, Robert M'CLURE are trustees for Potter Co. John KEATING, Richard GERNON & John S. ROULET are to lay out Coudersport.

p. 66: John ALLESON, late of Washington Co., decd., owned land. He willed 1/3 to his wife, Jane; 100 acres to his son, James. His other children were Archibald, Thomas, Hugh, Gawin. Samuel AGNEW is the guardian of the minor children of John ALLESON, Jr., decd. James ALLESON is deaf & dumb.

p. 67: Thomas WEST, late of Ridley Twp., Delaware Co., died intestate. He left a mother, a widow & 6 minor children. James MARIS & Samuel DAVIS are administrators. WEST owned land bounded by William BROWN, Curtis LOWNS, George DAVIS, Cyrus NEWLIN, George WARNER, Esther & John THOMPSON.

p. 70: Paul COX, John DORSEY, Robert M'MULLIN, William MITCHELL, William LINNARD, Henry ORTH, Samuel HARVEY, Samuel WILLIAMSON, William Y. BURCH, Ebenezer FERGUSON, Samuel SMITH, Hugh HENRY are directors of the Phila. Society to Encourage Domestic Manufactures.

p. 73: James SMITH, Lycoming Co., a private soldier in Capt. James MURRY's Company of Flying Camp, was taken prisoner at Fort Washington on 16 Nov., 1776. He stayed a prisoner till the March following. Owing to sickness & debility, he did not reach home until one month after. He is given $100.

p. 83: William KIRKPATRICK, Adam REIGART, Jr., Samuel HUMES, John HUBLEY, Jacob KRUG, James HOPKINS, Samuel BETHEL, Thomas BOUDE, Dr. John WATSON, Michael GUNDACKER, James WHITEHILL, George GRAEFF, George DUFFIELD, James HOUSTON, Edward BRIEN, Samuel WHITE, Abraham WITMER are directors of the Lancaster & Susquehanna Insurance Co.

p. 88: Trustees of the Wilkesbarre Academy: Rev. Andrew HOYT, Lord BUTLER, Jesse FELL, Matthias HOLLERBACK, William ROSS, Rosewell WELLES, Ebenezer BOWMAN, Samuel BOWMAN, John P. ARNDT, Arnold COLT, Peleg TRACY, Matthew COVELL, Joseph SLOCUM, Benjamin PERRY, Thomas GRAHAM, Charles MINER, Thomas DYER.

p. 90: Samuel CUSTER purchased of Isaac MORGAN, a tract in Charlestown Twp., Chester Co. Isaac MORGAN is now decd. Sarah MORGAN & Jonathan MORGAN are administrators.

p. 92: Mahlon MILNOR, Daniel LOVETT, John CARLISLE, Charles BROWN, William WARNER, John MOTT, are trustees of Falls Twp. Free School, Bucks Co.

p. 93: Bernard HUBLEY, late an officer in the U.S. Army, vested his certificates of pay in the purchase of part of a confiscated estate of William RANKIN, late of York Co., an attainted traitor. A title paramount for the land was in Thomas CAMPBELL's name.

p. 94: Trustees of the Meadville Academy, Crawford Co.: Roger ALDEN, Jesse MOORE, John BROOKS, Robert STOCKDON, Joseph HACKNEY, James HERRINGTON, James BURCHFIELD, John DAVIS, Aaron WRIGHT, John LIMBER, Joseph ANDREWS, James GIBSON, Henry RICHARD, Robert COCHRAN, John PATTERSON, Henry HURST, David MEADE, Dr. Thomas R. KENNEDY, Moses SCOTT.

p. 99: George HUBER & Michael ZELLER, Dauphin Co., enlisted as privates into a company commanded by Capt. DECKERT, 5th Pa. Regiment. They were made prisoners at the surrender of Fort Washington & suffered from cold & hunger. 200 acres of donation land are given them as tenants in common.

p. 104: John WORMLEY, James DUNCAN, John BOWMAN, John CAROTHERS, Samuel WEEKLEY, Alexander SHARP, John M'KEE, Jacob RAUM, John SIMPSON, Cumberland Co.; Andrew DUNLAP, Jacob HEISER, Thomas GREER, Jacob SNYDER, John R. CAMPBELL, Patrick M'DOWELL, Franklin Co.; John DAVIS, Benjamin MARTIN, John ANDERSON, Henry WERTZ, Jr., Bedford Co.; Adam MILLER, Ludwick BAKER, Michael RHEEM, John KIMMEL, John SHULL, Peter KIMMEL, Frederick NEFF, Alexander OGLE, John CAMPBELL, Somerset Co.; Thomas JONES, William JACK, John IRWIN, Hugh MARTIN, John M. SNOWDEN, John EDGAR, Joshua BUDD, John DALEY, John LOBENGIER, Westmoreland Co.; Nathaniel IRISH, Thomas BEARD, James O'HARA, Adamson TANNEHILL, John WOODS, George ROBESON, Allegheny Co., are commissioners to make a road from the Susquehanna River opposite Harrisburg to Pittsburg.

p. 117: Adam HENDRIX, George LOTMAN, George BARD, Caleb KIRK, Philip FREDERICK, Robert HAMERSLY, Jacob LOUKS, Isaac KIRK, John BRILLINGER, York Co., are commissioners to receive subscriptions to the York & Md. line turnpike.

p. 119: Samuel TEMPLETON, George LONG, Robert BARBER, Peter FISHER, James DUNCAN, Adam WILT, Christopher SEEBOLD, Jr.; George WEYRICK, are commissioners to raise money to improve navigation of Penn's Ck., Northumberland Co.

p. 120: Archibald M'FALL, Chester Co., enlisted in the service at an early period of the American Revolution & fought in the Pa. Line, 2nd Brigade, 5th Regiment. After experiencing the severities of 7 glorious campaigns, a rigid captivity & two wounds, he was permitted to retire from the field. $40 per year is paid to John G. BULL, Chester Co., for his use.

p. 122: Conrad SWARTZ, Michael GUNDACKER, George MESSERSMITH, John GUNDACKER, Benjamin SHAUM, Peter SHINDLE, Leonard EICHHOLTZ, Jacob STAHL, Jonas METZGAR, John BURG, Christopher KURTZ, John HOFF, Henry SWENTZEL are commissioners to raise money for expenses of trustees of the German Lutheran Congregation, Lancaster borough.

p. 126: Henry DONNEL, George HAINES, John FOSTER are commissioners to mark out a road from the point where Coshecton & Great Bend Turnpike Rd. passes through Moosic Mountain to Coudersport, Potter Co. Samuel DALE, John BOYD, Francis KING are commissioners to mark out a road from Coudersport to Warren, Warren Co.

p. 128: Prudence SLATER, decd., willed to her children Thomas, John, James, Ann, Elizabeth, Mary & Sibby two messuages & a lot in Lancaster. Elizabeth has since died leaving one minor daughter. Henry HAWKINS is a guardian of Maria BICKER, Phila. The lot is adj. Jacob METOR, decd.

p. 129: Samuel JACKSON, Allegheny Co., married Susanna RENO. Susanna's father died intestate. She became entitled to land in St. Clair Twp. All other heirs sold their interest to Pressly NEVILL.

p. 131: John Philip DE GRUCHY & John BOYD are guardians of Jane HUMPHRYS, a minor. The following are tenants in common of land, Lycoming Co.: Isaac WHARTON, David LEWIS, Jesse WALN, Robert WALN, William WALN, Alexander FULLERTON, Thomas FITZSIMONS, John MILLER, Jr., Robert BIRD, John HUMPHRYS. Jesse WALN died intestate leaving issue; Sarah (married to Thomas BULKELEY); Jesse WALN; Rebecca (married to Edward TILGHMAN, Jr.); Ann WALN; Rebecca WHARTON, Susan WHARTON, daughters of Mary, the former wife of Moore WHARTON & daughter of said Jesse WALN, decd. Mary WHARTON died in the life time of her father. Rebecca TILGHMAN, Ann WALN, Rebecca WHARTON & Susan WHARTON are minors.

p. 132: John DUNLAP, Thomas LEIPER, Mathew SHAW, Stephen DECATUR, John SINGER are appointed to sell the Phila. Powder Magazine.

p. 136: Robert E. GRIFFITH is surviving partner of Philip NICKLIN, decd. Juliana NICKLIN, widow of Philip & natural guardian of his minor children, & Benjamin CHEW, Jr., are administrators of his estate. NICKLIN & GRIFFITH were merchants & co-partners in Phila. NICKLIN died intestate leaving 7 minor children.

p. 138: Martha MARSHALL, late Martha MILES, petitions that James Isaac Thomas MARSHALL & Martha were married 15 May, 1804. On 3 Nov., 1806, MARSHALL was convicted in Mayor's court, Phila., for forging a bank note of the Trenton Banking Co. He was sentenced to hard labor & two years in the Phila. gaol. MARSHALL is also called KENSETT. The marriage is annulled.

p. 139: Michael SPIEGLE, Springfield Twp., Phila. Co., willed to his wife, Mary, & Philip DRESHER, a 16 acre lot. Mary afterward married John KENNER. Mary died intestate, leaving no children or known kin. On 31 Mar., 1795, KENNER sold the land to Nicholas KLINE. KENNER is since decd. He willed portions of his estate to persons who have become lunatic & are now in the hospital. KLINE sold land to George BILGER.

p. 140: James BOYD, Ellis PUSEY, William WEST, Robert COCHRAN, Joseph JOHNSON, Chester Co.; Henry SLAYMAKER, Michael GUNDACKER, Francis BAILEY, James MOORE, Jr., Lancaster Co. are commissioners to make a road from the Phila. & Lancaster turnpike rd. at the Gap tavern to the Delaware State line.

p. 153: Jacob BOTTIMORE, a soldier in the 2nd Regiment of Pa. for upwards of 4 years, on 2 Jan., 1777, in a skirmish which ensued after the battle of Trenton, he was wounded by a musket ball which passed through his body & broke two ribs. Now, he is honorably discharged, old & infirm. He is to receive 200 acres of donation land.

p. 154: Edward CHISSELDEN, a soldier in the 8th Pa. Regiment during the Rev., received a certificate for depreciation of pay for £75 1s.

It was redeemed through the land office after being presented by Peter BENSON on 8 June, 1785. Letters of administration were fraudulently obtained by John MALONE. CHISSELDEN sued MALONE in Dec., 1789. MALONE disappeared. CHISSELDEN is now old & blind. A warrant drawn for James KERR for $512 was made for the benefit of CHISSELDEN.

p. 159: Abraham DAWSON willed to the inhabitants of West-Caln Twp., Chester Co., land (32 ½ acres) for the use of the poor of the twp. James M'CLELLAN & Hugh THOMPSON, Esq., are authorized to sell the land.

p. 162: John ALLEN, late of Morris Co., N.J., served as a soldier in the 1st Regiment of Pa. for upwards of 3 years. At the battle of Yorktown, he received a wound & subsequently was discharged on 22 Jan., 1782. His discharge was signed by Lt. Col. F. MENTGES. He never received donation land. Now he is given 200 acres.

p. 164: Alexander M'GREADY, late of Mt. Pleasant Twp., Westmoreland Co., decd., laid out Mt. Pleasant. He sold land by verbal contract to: Patrick CUNNINGHAM, Clements BURLEIGH, John EDGAR, Sr., Michael SMITH, Patrick M'GREADY. Alexander M'GREADY died intestate. John EDGAR & John GALLOWAY are guardians of the minor children of M'GREADY.

p. 168: James M'SHERRY, John SHORP, Jacob WINTEROTT, James GETTYS, Alexander COBEAN, Henry HOKE are commissioners to make a road from the courthouse in Gettysburg through Petersburgh to the Md. line near BIDDLE's mill.

p. 174: A warrant was issued for 60 acres in Mahonoy Twp., Northumberland co. & adj. land of Adam CAMPBELL, Nicholas BOB, Anthony DOCKEY, Jacob YEAGLEY, to Adam LENKER, Esq. & John BINGMAN for the use of Mahony Twp. congregation of Presbyterians & Lutherans.

p. 175: David MAHON, John SIMPSON, George M'CANDLESS, Robert PORTER, John DUNCAN, inhabitants of Shippensburgh, say they need water in their wells. An ancient stream sunk into the ground on the plantation of Adam MYER, Southampton Twp., adj. land of John M'LEAN's heirs, land of Thomas NICHOLS' heirs, land late of the heirs of John M'KNIGHT & now of John WALLACE & land of the heirs of Robert COFFY.

p. 182: Michael WITHERS, George WITHERS, William DUFFIELD, Esq., John KERR, Esq., James WHITEHILL, Jacob BAER, Nathaniel SAMPLE, Jr., John BAER, Isaac BURROWS, Abraham HUBER, Moses HEMOR are commissioners to raise money to defray expenses incurred by trustees of the Lutheran congregation near Strasburgh, Lancaster Co.

p. 186: William BARBER, George HAY, John STEWART, Jacob HAHN, William NESS, Samuel SPANGLER, Jacob EICHELBERGER & John FISHER are commissioners to raise money to enable inhabitants of York borough to bring in a stream of water to supply their fire-engines.

p. 189: Robert KENNEDY, Northern Liberties Twp., Phila. Co., innkeeper, is auth. to dig a mill race near the falls of the Schuylkill River.

p. 191: George GRAHAM, Henry FISHER, Joseph BOISLE, Henry BEANER, Michael ZIMMERMAN, Michael MOUREY, John FORRY, Charles BOYLE, John LEHMER are commissioners to raise money to defray expenses of building a church in Stoys-town, Somerset Co., & to build a bridge over Quemahoning Ck.

p. 192: Lord BUTLER, Lawrence MEYER, Luzerne Co.; Samuel SITGREAVES, Daniel WAGGONER, Easton; John B. WALLACE & Thomas ALLIBONE, Phila., are commissioners to erect a bridge over the Susquehanna River at Wilkesbarre, Luzerne Co.

p. 196: A tract of land in Wilkesbarre extends from the land of Jabez FISH.

p. 197: Anthony MORRIS, Samuel MIFFLIN, Dr. Benjamin SAY, Phila.; Daniel WAGGONER, William HENRY, George SAVITZ, Northampton Co.; George K. HANISON, John BROWN, Abraham MILLER, Northumberland Co., are commissioners to erect a bridge over the Susquehanna River at the falls of Nescopeck, Luzerne Co.

p. 218: Pa. Militia Regiments & Commanders:
Phila.: #24--Lt. Col. PANCAKE; #25--Lt. Col. DUANE; #28--Lt. Col. BRIGHT; #50--Lt. Col. SIMONDS; #84--Lt. Col. FERGUSON.
Phila. Co.: #42--Lt. Col. KRIPS; #67--Lt. Col. M'MULLEN; #75--Lt. Col. BECK; #80--Lt. Col. SULLIVAN; #88--Lt. Col. KESSLER; #140--Lt. Col. MORTON.
Montgomery Co.: #36--Lt. Col. HENDERSON; #51--Lt. Col. WENTZ; #56--Lt. Col. SNYDER; #86--Lt. Col. DAVIS.
Bucks Co.: #15--Lt. Col. SMITH; #31--Lt. Col. PIPER; #32--Lt. Col. CLUNN; #48--Lt. Col. VANSANT.
Chester & Delaware Co.: #27--Lt. Col. GREER; #47--Lt. Col. ARMSTRONG; #85--Lt. Col. PIERCE; #97--Lt. Col. COCHRAN; #44--Lt. Col. DAVIS; #65--Lt. Col. PEARSON; #92--Lt. Col. RALSTON; #100--Lt. Col. RICHARDS.
Lancaster Co.: #5--Lt. Col. WRIGHT; #7--Lt. Col. ENSMINGER; #120--Lt. Col. REAM; #121--Lt. Col. THOMAS; #34--Lt. Col. STRICKLER; #98--Lt. Col. BOYD; #60--Lt. Col. BOAL; #104--Lt. Col. LONG.
York & Adams Co.: #41--Lt. Col. KELLY; #61--Lt. Col. REISINGER; #111--Lt. Col. LAWSON; #113--Lt. Col. PENNINGTON; #124--Lt. Col. HIMES.
Adams Co.: #9--Lt. Col. HORNER; #20--Lt. Col. KERR; #40--Lt. Col. BLACK; #93--Lt. Col. BROWN.
Berks Co.: #37--Lt. Col. BAUM; #43--Lt. Col. SHOEMAKER; #69--Lt. Col. SCHRADER; #79--Lt. Col. EPLER; #114--Lt. Col. KLINE.
Dauphin Co.: #3--Lt. Col. BOWMAN; #66--Lt. Col. WAYNE; #78--Lt. Col. WOLFERSBERGER; #95--Lt. Col. LAVENGUTH; #117--Lt. Col. SEEBOLT.
Cumberland Co.: #12--Lt. Col. BOVARD; #21--Lt. Col. EWALT; #49--Lt. Col. URIE; #59--Lt. Col. M'BEATH; #87--Lt. Col. MARTIN; #116--Lt. Col. RUPLEY.
Franklin Co.: #1--Lt. Col. FINDLEY; #64--Lt. Col. ALEXANDER; #68--Lt. Col. BEATTY; #73--Lt. Col. SNIDER; #96--Lt. Col. SCOTT.
Northampton & Wayne Co.: #13--Lt. Col. WETZEL; #38--Lt. Col. MILLER; #94--Lt. Col. KEIPER; #101--Lt. Col. DESTLER; #118--Lt. Col. M'KEEN; #8--Lt. Col. JACOBY; #71--Lt. Col. HORN; #110--Lt. Col. TANNER; #103--Lt. Col. DINGMAN; #115--Lt. Col. SCHNYDER.
Northumberland & Luzerne Co.: #35--Lt. Col. INMAN; #81--Lt. Col. MONTGOMERY; #112--Lt. Col. RUPERT; #123--Lt. Col. GIFFIN; #18--Lt. Col. M'KENNY; #39--Lt. Col. BALDY; #77--Lt. Col. DRUM; #106--Lt. Col. MOORE; #45--Lt. Col. DENNISTON.
Lycoming, Tioga, Potter, Jefferson, M'Kean, Clearfield Co.: #4--Lt. Col. CUMINGS; #102--Lt. Col. QUIGLE; #57--Lt. Col. SPALDING.
Huntingdon, Mifflin & Centre Co.: #11--Lt. Col. M'DOWEL; #52--Lt. Col. BEALE; #74--Lt. Col. BRATTON; #83--Lt. Col. BANKS; #89--Lt. Col. BENNER; #131--Lt. Col. MYERS; #14--Lt. Col. MOORE; #33--Lt.

Col. HENDERSON; #46--Lt. Col. CROMWELL; #58--Lt. Col. KELLUP; #119--Lt. Col. ENTRICKEN.
Somerset, Bedford & Cambria Co.: #10--Lt. Col. JONES; #109--Lt. Col. KIMMEL; #128--Lt. Col. BOYLS; #127--Lt. Col. MOORE; #105--Lt. Col. REYNOLDS; #55--Lt. Col. AGNEW.
Fayette Co.: #72--Lt. Col. COLLINS; #90--Lt. Col. OLIPHANT; #91--Lt. Col. BRASHEAR; #108--Lt. Col. WHALEY.
Washington & Greene Co.: #22--Lt. Col. ACHISON; #23--Lt. Col. DONALDSON; #53--Lt. Col. MITCHELL; #82--Lt. Col. STEPHENSON; #6--Lt. Col. CLARK; #99--Lt. Col. JENKINS; #122--Lt. Col. HUSTON; #130--Lt. Col. CATHER.
Westmoreland Co.: #2--Lt. Col. BONNET; #19--Lt. Col. WAGLE; #54--Lt. Col. CAMPBELL; #63--Lt. Col. M'DOWELL; #70--Lt. Col. HUNTER.
Allegheny, Armstrong, & Indiana Co.: #141--Lt. Col. BAIRD; #76--Lt. Col. BALDWIN; #16--Lt. Col. FREE; #62--Lt. Col. CUNNINGHAM; #30--Lt. Col. M'COMB; #126--Lt. Col. MOUNTS; #125--Lt. Col. ELROD.
Beaver, Butler, Mercer, Crawford, Erie, Warren, Venango Co.: #26--Lt. Col. SPROAT; #139--Lt. Col. LAURENS; #107--Lt. Col. REED; #137--Lt. Col. HACKNEY; #136--Lt. Col. MARVIN; #135--Lt. Col. HUSTON; #134--Lt. Col. STOKELY; #133--Lt. Col. STOCKTON; #17--Lt. Col. FORSTER; #132--Lt. Col. DALE; #29--Lt. Col. GILLILAND; #138--Lt. Col. CAROTHERS.

p. 239: Lt. Col. John CONNELLY is a commander of a regiment of artillery.

p. 241: William POYNTELL, Matthew CAREY, John INSKEEP, Phila; Roger ALDEN, Meadville, are appointed to raise money to defray expenses of making an aqueduct to conduct water into Meadville. John BROOKS, Henry HURST, Thomas R. KENNEDY are commissioners to build the aqueduct & improve streets.

p. 250: Thomas LAURENCE, James BUDDEN & John DUNLAP, Phila., purchased land in Northern Liberties Twp., which was the confiscated estate of Joseph GRISWOLD & was devised to John FROMBERGER, Phila. On 4 Feb., 1802, he was evicted by reason of a title paramount to Joseph GRISWOLD, New York City. FROMBERGER is now decd. A warrant is drawn on the treasury in favor of John GRYMER & Jacob CHRYSTLER, adminis. of the FROMBERGER estate.

p. 251: David R. BARTON, George SLOUGH, Edward BRIEN, William HAMILTON, Richard GRAY & William P. ATTLEE are commissioners to raise money to repair the Protestant Episcopal Church, Lancaster.

p. 258: Charles THOMPSON, Montgomery Co., in 1783, bought land as the Secretary of Congress for 30 bu. of wheat per year to be paid to the trustees of the U. of Pennsylvania. Charles THOMPSON was evicted 14 Apr., 1806 by a title paramount in Joseph GRISWOLD, New York City.

p. 268: Elections in Armstrong Co.: Buffalo Twp. will vote at Jacob YOUNG's. Sugar Ck. Twp. will vote at Josh WEILE's. Toby Twp. will vote at Thomas MCKIBBIN's. Allegheny Twp. will vote at Solomon SHOEMAKER's. Red Bank Twp. will vote at Samuel C. ORR's. Slippery Rock Twp., Beaver Co., previously voted at Ananias ALLEN's & will now vote at Jonas KELLY's. Elections in Bedford Co.: Providence Twp. will vote at Michael BARNDOLLAR's. Dublin Twp. will vote at George DANSDELL's. Bethel Twp. will vote at James PARSON's, Warfordsburg. Cambria Co. near GALBREATH's road to Henry REUGLE's house will vote at John BRANNIFF's. West Hanover Twp., Dauphin Co., near William ALLEN's to EARLY's mill to DIXON's fording on Swatara Ck., will vote at Jacob GREENAWALT's, Hummelstown. East Hanover Twp., Dauphin Co., will vote at John HARPER's. Elections in Erie Co.: Coniatue & M'Kean Twp. will vote at James M'GINNIS'. Fairview Twp. will vote at William STURGEON's. Springfield Twp. will vote at William PORTER's. Conniat & Elk Ck. Twp. will vote at Joshua RANDEL's, Lexington. LeBoeuff & Waterford Twp. will vote at Jonas CLARK's, Waterford-town. Beaver Dam & Harbour Ck. Twp. will vote at Thomas MORTON's. Northeast Twp. will vote at Andrew LOWRY's. Greenfield & Venango Twp. will vote at Philo PARKER's. Broken Straw & Union Twp. will vote at John TAYLOR's. Saltlick Twp., Fayette Co., will vote at Benjamin DAVIS', near Indian Ck. Southampton Twp., Franklin Co., will vote at William SCOTT's, Esq. Morris Twp., Huntingdon Co., will vote at Lazarus Brown M'CLEAN's, Alexandria. Indiana Co. elections: Armstrong, Washington & Centre Twp. will vote at Peter SUTTEN's. Black-lick Twp. will vote at Patrick M'GEE's. Connemaugh Twp. will vote at John MARSHALL's. Mahoning Twp. will vote at James BREADY, Sr.'s. Martock Twp., Lancaster Co., will vote at George HESS' house, now occupied by Tempest WILSON. Mountjoy Twp., Lancaster Co., will vote at Alexander BOGGS', Elizabethtown. Donegal Twp., adj. the Dauphin Co. line near the landing place late of Bartram GALBRAITH, decd., to the houses of John HURST, Frederick GRAM, Michael GROSS & Abraham HEARNLY, will vote at Alexander BOGGS'. 11th district, Lancaster Co. will vote at John HUSTON's, Churchtown, now occupied by John ROBERTS. Orwell Twp., Luzerne Co., will vote at Josiah GRANT's. Clifford Twp., Luzerne Co., will vote at Asahel GREGORY's. 3rd district, Lycoming Co., will vote at James SHEARER's, innkeeper, Jersey Shore village. Delmar Twp., Lycoming Co., will vote at Joshua EMLEN's, Wellsborough. 5th district, Mifflin Co., will vote at George GALBRAITH's, inn-keeper, Waynesburg. 6th district, Montgomery Co., will vote at William LESHER's, Pottstown. The rest of Douglass & New Hanover Twp., will vote at Henry KREPS', New Hanover. The rest of Allen Twp., Northampton Co., voted previously at Adam SHOENER's, Hanover Twp. & now will vote at Abraham MENSH's, Allen Twp. Upper Mahonoy Twp., Northumberland co., will vote at Leonard REITZ's. Mahoney Twp., Northumberland Co., will now vote at Michael EMRICK's, decd., instead of at William DOBSON's. 18th district, Northumberland Co., will vote at William DALE's. Irwin Twp., Venango Co., will vote at John ANDREWS', Franklin Town. Fawn Twp., York Co., will vote at Robert RAMSEY's, innkeeper. Mahoning Twp., Mercer Co., will vote at George ALLISON's. Sadsbury Twp., Crawford Co., will vote at James MOUNT's. Neshanock Twp., Mercer Co., will vote at William JEWELL's. Centre Twp., Centre Co., will vote at Thomas SPENCER's.

p. 276: $9000 has been appropriated from the estate of John NICHOLSON, decd., for improving the navigation of the Schuylkill River, from the falls to the mouth of the Little Schuylkill. Peter RICHARDS, Joseph HEISTER, Robert KENNEDY are commissioners to superintend the improvements.

p. 278: A warrant is drawn on the state treasury for $1500 in favor of John HALDIMAN, Thomas BOUDE, Alexander BOGGS to improve navigation of the Susquehanna River from Columbia to Middletown. Another warrant in favor of James HAMILTON, Thomas STUBBS, Reuben LOCKART for improving the road from Middletown to the mouth of the Juniata. A warrant for $500 in favor of George M'CELLAND, John GALLESPIE, John BROWN for improving navigation of the Juniata River from it's mouth to the mouth of the Kishecoquillis. A warrant for $1000 in favor of James SMITH, John DUNLOP & Rowland CURTIN for improving the navigation of Bald-Eagle Ck. from it's mouth to

Milesburg, Centre Co.

p. 281: Frederick D. SHAFFER, Henry KATZ, Leonard KOLB, John HART, George BISBING, William HALLMAN, are commissioners to raise money to finish the German Lutheran Church at Barrenhill, Montgomery Co.

p. 283: A balance is due to the estate of John ALBRIGHT, decd., for printing the journal of the House of Representatives in German. $117.92 is appropriated to reimburse Joseph REED, Prothonotary of the Supreme Court, Eastern District, for the price of a seal & press for court.

p. 285: George ROSS is one of the commissioners to run the boundary lines of M'Kean, Potter & Tioga Co. He is accountable to the legal representatives of William ELLIS, decd.

p. 290: Donation land is allotted to John STEEL, late a Captain in the Rev. army.

p. 290: Westmoreland Co. is vacating part of the state road between JONES' mill & the Somerset Co. line. They are also to view a road opened by Thomas JONES & William BACKHOUSE.

p. 292: Samuel GLASKOW, Fayette Co., in his will of 9 Mar., 1805, willed to daughter, Margaret, £50; to daughter, Jennet, £300; to daughter, Mary, £200; to daughter, Ann, £250; to daughter, Rachel, £400. Executors are Mathew GAUT & William ESPY.

p. 293: John WOELFLEY, Frederick HIPPLE, Abraham FISH, John SHARDLE are commissioners to raise money to pay the expenses incurred by trustees of the German Lutheran Congregation near Elizabethtown, Lancaster Co.

p. 294: Robert SCOTT, George MILLER, Philip KLINE, Philip SEIDLE, John MEYER, Abraham BAILEY, Berks Co., are commissioners to raise money to build a church for the Lutheran & Calvinist Congregation, Hamburg, Berks Co. & for finishing the Presbyterian Church in Pittsburg. John WILKINS, Sr., John JOHNSTON, William BOGGS & William PORTER are commissioners for the second mentioned item.

1807-1808

p. 7: Abraham RAMBO sold land in Upper Merion Twp., Montgomery Co. to William BAILEY. Ann RAMBO is executrix of the estate. Jacob SHAINLINE is executor.

p. 8: Samuel BOWER, Isaac WHITE, Jacob KEEN, Isaac JOHNSON, Thomas TIMINGS, John COLLARD, Cornelius TRIMNUL are trustees of the 2nd Baptist Church, Phila.

p. 10: Sixty acres of land in Somerset Twp., Somerset Co., adj. John NEEL, Frederick MORSTOLLER, Nicholas SCHNIDER was warranteed to Andrew WEY, Jacob SWANK, Henry SHARER for the Presby. & Lutheran Congregations in Somerset Twp.

p. 11: Jacob ROHRER & wife, Mary, are administ. of the estate of Henry KEYSER, Cheltenham Twp., Montgomery Co., powder-maker, who sold a tenement & lot adj. Michael KEYSER & John CROUT, to the German Reformed Congregation, Germantown, Phila. Co. They also purchased a tenement & lot from the adminis. of John FROMBERGER, decd.

p. 12: Alexander MOORE, William KASE, John KELLY, Silvanus BIRD, Samuel MOORE are commissioners to raise money to complete the Presby. meeting house in Shamoken Twp., Northumberland Co.

p. 14: John Hare POWEL, son of Robert HARE, Phila., had agreed, at the request of a near relation, to change his name to John Powel HARE.

p. 15: James DIXON, Delmar Twp., Samuel W. MORRIS, Wellsborough, Tioga Co., are trustees for Tioga Co. in the room of William ELLIS, decd., & William H. WELLS, who has resigned. John FLEMING is the other trustee.

p. 19: Biles Island, Falls Twp., Bucks Co., in the Delaware River, was purchased from the Indians in 1680 by William BILES.

p. 19: Samuel KOOCKOOYAEI served as a musician in the Pa. Regiment of Artillery, commanded by Col. Thomas FORREST, honorably discharged because of an epileptic disease. A patent for a tract of donation land is given to him.

p. 27: Martin HARTLEY, Adam ECKFELT, John LESHER, John GRAFF, Christieb BARTLING, Daniel BREUTIGAM, Isaac WAMPOLE, John SINGER, John GOODMAN, Jr., Conrad HAAS, John RUGAN, George REES, Charles SCHAFFER, Jacob BENNINGHOVE, Samuel LEHMAN, Baltes EMRICH, George BANTLEON, Michael FOX, John HAY, Daniel BICKLEY, John GREINER are trustees of the Evangelical Lutheran Congregation of St. John's Church, Phila.

p. 33: James MORRIS (now an inhabitant of Phila.) entered very early into the late Rev. Army. In consequence of merit, he was advanced to a lieutenantcy under Capt. VAN HEER. He continued to render essential services until Nov., 1780, when, owning to extreme hardship, a severe fit of illness reduced him to the necessity of resigning his commission, his life being in imminent danger. He never recovered his health. He is given a share of donation land.

p. 35: Rev. Henry Melchior MUHLENBERG, on 10 July, 1770, conveyed a church & tract of 50 acres to Philip STAMBACH, Jacob GORTNER, Valentine BROBST, George KESTLER, trustees of the German Lutheran Congregation, Albany Twp., Linn Twp., Berks & Northampton Co.

p. 37: Thomas COX, Bucks Co., enlisted in the service in the beginning of 1777. He received a wound in the thigh at the battle of Germantown. He continued in the service until 1781. He is to receive $40 & $40/yr. will be paid to Samuel JOHNSON, Esq., Buckingham Twp., Bucks Co., for Thomas COX's use.

p. 38: Israel ISRAEL, Elisha GORDON, Thomas AMIES, Jacob THOMAS, John MURRAY, Thomas KINGSTON, Thomas TOMKINS, Thomas F. GORDON are commissioners to raise money for purchasing a burial ground for the Society of Universalists, Phila.

p. 39: Trustees of Union Academy: James GUTHRIE, Thomas HADDEN, Presley Car LANE, James W. NICHOLSON, Christian TARR, Charles PORTE, Thomas MEASON, John KENNEDY, Zadoc WALKER, James ALLEN, Maurice FREEMAN, Jesse PENNEL, James FINDLAY.

p. 42: Nathaniel COULTER, Washington Co., is granted $60 for military service. In 1781, 1782, 1783, he performed several tours of militia duty in defence of the Western frontier of Pa. against hostile attacks of Indians.

p. 44: Owen EVANS, James B. HARRIS, Matthew BROOKE, James EVANS, Jr., Isaac MARCKLEY, John BARLOW, Jacob KEELEY, John BROOKE are commissioners to raise money to build a church in Limerick Twp., Montgomery Co.

p. 45: Dillaplain RIDGWAY, Phila., bricklayer, on 17 Oct., last, became bound in a bond for $60,000 along with William T. DONALDSON & 16 others as sureties for William T. DONALDSON's faithful execution of the office of sheriff of Phila.

p. 46: Ebenezer BOWMAN, Lord BUTLER, William ROSS, Rosewell WELLES, Mathias HOLLENBACK, Matthew COVELL, Ebenezer LOCUM, Thomas WRIGHT, Arnold COLT, Cornelius COURTRIGHT, Nathan PALMER, Nathan WALLER, John ROBINSON are commissioners to raise money to finish a meeting house in Wilkesbarre.

p. 47: Andrew MARSHALL, Hamilton Twp., Franklin Co., decd., willed all his land to his 5 sons: Joseph, William, Samuel, John, Andrew. Samuel is since decd. intestate with no issue. John, decd., left issue of three sons & 1 daughter, all minors.

p. 50: Daniel SNYDER, Frederick HOUSMAN, Peter KERN, Michael DEIBER, Stephen BALLIOT, Sr., Peter BUTZ are commissioners to raise money to erect a school house for use of the Lutheran & Reformed Congregation of Union Church, White-hall Twp., Northampton Co.

p. 51: Joseph GWYNE, now residing in Greene Co., enlisted in the 8th Pa. Regiment for 3 years. He receives $156 in depreciation pay.

p. 52: Terence CAMPBELL, William PROCTOR, Jr., John ANDERSON, George HENRY, William GRIFFITH, Samuel TATE, Martin REILY, Samuel DAVIDSON, Henry WERTZ, Jr., are commissioners to raise money for a school & church in Bedford.

p. 53: John LYON, Jacob FLETCHER, Charles M'DOWELL, William REYNOLDS & Anthony NAWGEL are trustees for Bedford Co.

p. 53: Conrad SHERMAN, Henry WELSH, Peter STORM, Frederick WENTZ, Francis LAWMOT, Jacob METZGER & Peter ECKARD are commissioners of a company to make a road from Hanover, York Co., to the Md. line.

p. 56: John ELDER, Matthew IRWIN, Daniel WONDERLICH, John ERNST, John DOWNY, Levi G. HOLLINGSWORTH are commissioners to raise money for the inhabitants of Palmyra, LondonDerry Twp., Dauphin Co. Levi G. HOLLINGSWORTH, Daniel WONDERLICH, Henry LONGENECKER, John KEAN, Joseph CARMONY are commissioners to raise money to supply water.

p. 59: Thomas DILL, late of Monahan Twp., York Co., died intestate. He left a widow, Priscilla, & issue: Caleb, John, Priscilla, James & Elizabeth, all minor except Caleb. William WIREMAN, Sr., is guardian of the minor children. Caleb DILL has since died.

p. 61: William M'CORMICK, now residing in Mercer Co., served 4 years in the 1st Pa. Regiment in the late Rev. War & also in the militia of Lancaster Co. He was taken prisoner at Paole & detained for 8 months in captivity. He is granted donation land.

p. 62: Jacob HENDEL, Joseph SHROM, Jacob WEAVER, Jacob MATTER, Philip REISINGER, Peter FISHBURN, Cumberland Co., are commissioners to raise money to pay the debts of the German Presby. & German Lutheran Churches, Carlisle, Cumberland Co.

p. 63: Christian Carson FEBIGER, Phila., was adopted by an uncle, Col. Christian FEBIGER. The Col. is now decd. In compliance with his will, he has changed his name to Christian Febiger CARSON.

p. 64: William WITMAN, Christian TREAT, Jacob GEIGER, Christian DANNEHOWER, John WESTLEY, John ZEIMER are commissioners to raise money to build a meeting house & school house for the Presby. & Lutheran congregations in Robinson Twp., Berks Co.

p. 65: John MORRIS, now residing in Lancaster Co., enlisted as a soldier in Capt. MARE's Co., 4th Pa. Regiment, commanded by Col. William BUTLER. He served until 1780. He then enlisted in Capt. VAN HEER's troop of horse until the close of the war.

p. 66: Henry SLAGLE, Ludwig OVERDUR, Frederick SHULTZ, Jacob EICHELBERGER, Jr., Jacob METZGER, Henry MARTER are commissioners to raise money to finish a church in Hanover, York Co.

p. 67: David M'KNIGHT, John SIMPSON, Jacob RAHM, Samuel M'CLURE, Alexander STEWART, James LOWREY, Cumberland Co., are commissioners to raise money to build a school in Shippensburg, Cumberland Co.

p. 69: On 19 Sept, 1804, Samuel ASHTON, Phila. Co., purchased from William PLAYFORD, an alien, a plantation in Ridley Twp., Delaware Co.

p. 69: William M'ENTIRE, Metal Twp., Franklin Co., decd., laid out the town of Fanetsburg. Archibald S. M'CUNE, Fanetsburg, James M'CURDY, John WALKER, Metal Twp., are commissioners to procure patents for the sons of William MCENTIRE.

p. 72: Robert KENNEDY, Conrad CARPENTER, owners of ground on both sides of the Schuylkill River, want to erect a bridge.

p. 77: Thomas LEIPER, John DUNLAP, Matthew SHAW, Stephen DECATUR, John SINGER are commissioners to complete a powder magazine in Phila.

p. 77: Christian WOLFF, Edward CRAWFORD, Daniel SMITH, John HOLLADY, Jacob SNIDER, John CALHOUN, Frederick RHEMOR, Andrew DUNLOP are commissioners to raise money toward building a German Reformed Calvinist Church in Chambersburg, Franklin Co.

p. 78: Seth PANCOAST, late of Marple Twp., Delaware Co., died intestate & left a widow & 4 minor children. Israel ROBERTS, John OGDEN, William LEVIS, Jr., are guardians of the children. They are to sell PANCOAST land bounded by Samuel PANCOAST, Elisha WORREL, Elizabeth MARIS, Joseph RHOADS.

p. 81: John KEBLE, decd., willed to the minister of St. Paul's Church, Phila., a messuage & lot for the use of aged widows. Richard NORTH, Levi HOLLINGSWORTH, Plunket F. GLENTWORTH, John MATTHEWS, John VALANCE are members of St. Paul's.

p. 82: Peter ANKENY, late of Somerset Co., decd., owned part of the town of Somerset. Rosina ANKENY, Michael HUGUS, Abraham MILLER are adminis. of his estate.

p. 83: Philip SNYDER, Adam FANDERALL, Jacob KLINE, Jacob COMFORT, George SCHNEIDER, John HOUTZ, John BARBER, John MATHIOTT, Adam OTSTOT, Caspar SCHNEIDER, John EBERLIEN are commissioners to raise money to finish the Lutheran & Calvinist Church, Columbia, Lancaster Co.

p. 87: Election judges for Northampton & Wayne Co. will meet at Peter HOLLINGSHEAD's, late Jacob STROUD's, Stroudsburg, Northampton Co. Those for Luzerne & Northumberland Co. will meet at John KENNEDY's, Bloom Twp., Northumberland Co. Judges for Lycoming, Centre, Clearfield, M'Kean, Tioga & Potter Co. will meet at Jesse HUNT's, Bald Eagle Twp., Lycoming Co. Judges for Mifflin & Huntingdon Co. will meet at John CULBERTSON's, Wayne Twp., Mifflin Co. Judges for Bedford, Somerset, & Cambria Co. will meet at George GRAHAM's, Stoystown, Somerset Co. Judges of Westmoreland, Armstrong, Indiana & Jefferson Co. will meet at the widow ELDER's, Blacklick Twp., Indiana Co. Judges of Greene & Washington Co. will meet at Zeba COOKS', Amity, Washington Co. Judges of Allegheny, Beaver, Butler co. will meet at William DICKSON's, Pine Twp., Allegheny Co. These judges are all election judges for the Senate. Election judges for the House of Representatives: Judges of Northumberland, Washington, Westmoreland, Armstrong, Jefferson, Indiana Co. will meet at Absalom WOODWARD's, Armstrong Co. Judges of Fayette, Bedford, Franklin, Montgomery, Dauphin, Luzerne, Huntingdon, Beaver, Allegheny, Butler Co. will meet at William DICKSON's, Pine Twp., Allegheny Co.

p. 89: George KERL, late of Manheim Twp., York Co., decd., sold a lot before his death to William YOUNG. Jacob RUDISELL & George KERL are adminis. of the estate.

p. 90: Thomas SNOWDEN, citizen of Montgomery Co., late a sergeant in the 9th Pa. Regiment, enlisted in 1776 in the U.S. Army for 1 year in Capt. Samuel BENNEZETT's Co., 5th Battalion of Pa. troops commanded by Col. M'GAW. At the expiration of his term, he enlisted in Capt. Thomas B. BOWEN's Co., 9th Pa. Regiment, commanded by Col. Richard BUTLER & served until the war's conclusion. On 28 July, 1778, at the Battle of Monmouth, N.J., he was wounded by a musket ball in the ancle (sic). He is to receive $40 & $40/year will be paid to Hiram M'NEILL, Montgomery Co., for his use.

p. 91: James WATERS, a soldier in the Pa. Line, received 3 wounds. William BOYD, Esq., Lancaster Co., will receive $40 & $40/year for the use of James WATERS.

p. 93: Godlieb KINTZLY, John BATDORF, Henry HOEKLY, Peter SHULZE, Peter SPANGLER, Philip BREIDENBACH, Henry HILGER, Henry KOPPENHAFER are commissioners to raise money to erect a school house in Mayerstown, Dauphin Co.

p. 94: Jonathan PENROSE, decd., is late sheriff of Phila. Widow is Ann PENROSE.

p. 102: Ann HENRY is treasurer of Lancaster Co. An action was brought against Joseph GEHR, a delinquent collector of Cocalico Twp. He was arrested & Adam NEIS became his bail. NEIS is now decd.

p. 104: John HANNUM, late of West Chester Borough, Chester Co., & his wife, Alice, on 28 Mar., 1793, sold land in West Chester, late of Goshen Twp., Chester Co. to Stephen MOYLAN, Anthony HEARN, Mark WILCOX, Daniel FITZPATRICK, Peter M'GURK, Edward M'CLOSKEY, Lewis JENKINS, Jacob WISINBURG, for the use of the Roman Catholic

Congregation of Christ Church, West Chester, Chester Co. Rev. Patrick KENNY, clergyman of said church, Anthony HEARN, Mark WILCOX, Charles KENNY & John M'LAUGHLIN are trustees of the church.

p. 107: Christian SHOCKEY, now an inhabitant of Southampton Twp., Somerset Co., enlisted as a soldier during the war in Capt. Samuel HEARLY's Co. & was drafted into Capt. George CLAYPOOLE's Co., in the 11th Pa. Regiment commanded by Lt. Col. HUBLEY & then transferred to the 3rd Pa. Regiment, commanded by Col. Thomas CRAIG, then to Capt. William HENDERSON's Co. & then to Capt. John DOYLE's Co. He received a wound in his left arm at the siege of Yorktown, Va. He is to receive $40 & $40/yr. will be paid to Alexander OGLE for his use.

p. 107: In 1798, commissioners of Northampton Co. contracted with John STROUD to build a stone bridge over Jones Ck., Lower Smithfield Twp. STROUD is since decd. His executors are John STARBIRD, James HOLLINGSHEAD & Peter HOLLINGSHEAD.

p. 109: Edward TILGHMAN, William LEVIS, Joseph LOWNES, Phila.; Mark WILLCOX, William TRIMBLE, Caleb LOWNES, Delaware Co.; Amos HARVEY, James KELTON, John MENOUGH, Chester Co., are commissioners to make a road from Phila. to the state line.

p. 118: Philip PELTZ, John KESSLER, John MAITLAND are commissioners to survey the streets in Moyamensing Twp.

p. 126: Martin UPDEGRAFF is to make a landing on the north side of the west branch of the Susquehanna River on his estate situated on the great road leading from the town of Dunnsburg (laid out on UPDEGRAFF's land) to John MYER's, Lycoming Co.

p. 128: John BUCH, otherwise PUGH, late of Lancaster Co., decd., served his country for several years in the Rev. War. For 5 months, he served in Capt. Jacob LIVENGUTH's Rifle Co., in the winter of 1781 & 1782. His widow, Elizabeth BUCH, otherwise PUGH, is to receive $40.

p. 139: Elizabeth HEVERSTRITE & Thomas SHOEMAKER are adminis. of the estate of Jonas HEVERSTRITE, decd. HEVERSTRITE had sold to George WUNDER, a lot in Abington Twp., Montgomery Co.

p. 140: Samuel HAMM, York Co., was induced to marry Mary BEERBROWER with whom Samuel utterly refused to live after the marriage. It is annulled.

p. 143: Paul WILT, late of Dover Twp., York Co., willed part of his estate to his daughter, Maria, who is married to Philip WELDY. John WILT & George SHETTLE are executors of Paul WILT.

p. 146: Ruth KERR, Washington Co., in 1795, married Alexander KERR with whom she lived in a miserable situation (often being beaten & her life was frequently threatened). Until 1803, the situation continued & then KERR deserted her with four small children. The marriage is annulled.

p. 149: James ROBESON, Washington Co., a native of Ireland, arrived here on 14 Aug., 1791. In Sept., 1798, he purchased land of David BRADFORD, Esq., on the headwaters of Wheeling Ck., Finly Twp., Washington Co., bounded by land of James STEVENSON, other lands of David BRADFORD, Esq., now of Lewis MORRIS, lands of one SHAW, Robert ROBESON. On 22 Nov., 1805, he purchased land from James STEVENSON adj. James COOPER, Manning MARTIN, David GIBSON. ROBESON has since become a citizen.

p. 151: Belfast Twp., Bedford Co., will vote at Aaron CLEVINGER's. Rush Twp., Lausanne Twp., Northampton Co., will vote at Elias BERLITS', Lausanne Twp. Harford Twp., Luzerne Co., will vote at Hosea TIFFENY's, Esq. Dublin Twp., Bedford Co. near Christian WAGONER's & Mathias AMBROSURE's farm will vote at Jacob FORE's, M'Connelstown. Abington Twp., Luzerne Co., will vote at Robert STONE's., Abington. Mt. Pleasant Twp., Washington Co., will vote at Samuel MILLER's, innkeeper. Bridgwater Twp., Luzerne Co., will vote at Edward FULLER's. Bloom & Brier Ck. Twp., Northumberland Co., will vote at David WHITMIRE's, Brier Ck. Canaan Twp., Wayne Co., will vote at John SHAFFER's. Brokenstraw Twp., & Union Twp., Erie Co., will vote at William CARSON's. Fairview Twp., Erie Co., will vote at Jonathan BARKER's. Willingsborough district, Luzerne Co., will vote at Josiah STUART's, Great Bend Ferry. St. Clair Twp., Bedford Co., will vote at Thomas VICKROY's. Bart Twp., Lancaster Co., will vote at Nathan THOMPSON's, innkeeper. Elk Lands Twp., Shrewsbury Twp., (north of the summit of the Allegheny Mountains), Lycoming Co., will vote at William MOLYNEUX's, at the Forks of Loyalsock Ck. Burlington Twp., Lycoming Co., to Tioga Co., called the Cliftsburgh District, will vote at John CUMMINGS'. Venango Twp., Erie Co., will vote at John YOST's. Washington Twp., Fayette Co., will vote at John SHREVE's land at the stone school house. Solebury Twp., Bucks Co., will vote at John RUCKMAN's. Indiana Twp., Allegheny Co., will vote at Henry STROMES'. Armstrong Twp., Indiana Co. will vote at David M'COLLOUGH's. Allegheny Twp., Somerset Co., will vote at Henry IMHOFF's, at the foot of Allegheny Mt. The Conemough district, Cambria Co., has changed voting from John HORNER, Jr.'s to John GROSENICKEL's. Beccaria, Bradford & Half-moon Twp., Clearfield Co., will vote at John GYERHART's. Upper Paxton Twp., Dauphin Co., from the summit of Berry's Mountain to the Lutheran St. John's Church to John HAPPLE's house on Mahantango Mountain, will vote at Henry MACK's. The other half will vote at Jacob SNYDER's. Bethel Twp., Dauphin Co., will vote at Jacob RUTY's, Stumpstown. Versailles Twp., Allegheny Co., will vote at William SHAW, Sr.'s. Potter Twp., Centre Co., will vote at John BENNER's. Ferguson Twp., Centre Co., will vote at David NICHOLSON's. Conewango Twp., Warren Co., will vote at Daniel JACKSON's, Warren. Richland Twp., Venango Co., will vote at Alexander M'DONALD's. New-London Twp., London-Britain Twp., Chester Co., will vote at John MENOUGH's. Wysox Twp., Luzerne Co., will vote at Amos MIX's. Buckingham Twp., Wayne Co., will vote at Samuel PRESTON, Esq's. Bensalem Twp., Bucks co., will vote at John JOHNSTON's. The part of Northumberland Co. annexed to Luzerne Co., will vote at James CAMPBELL's. Pymatuning Twp., Mercer Co., will vote at Godfrey KAERNS'.

p. 157: Robert HUNTER, Huntingdon Twp., Westmoreland Co., served as a private soldier in Capt. John FINDLEY's Co., in Col. M'COY's Regiment & at a skirmish of Boundbrook, he received a slight wound in one of his legs which is become incurable. It further appears that he met with a severe accident at the Paole, in crossing a fence in a retreat from the enemy, which occasioned a rupture, which has so much increased that he cannot enjoy the benefit of a truss in this situation. He receives $40 & $40/yr. which will be paid to David HUNTER, Sr., Huntingdon Twp., for his use.

p. 158: James COSTILLOE, late of Phila., decd., willed real estate on Boon's Island, Phila. Co., in trust to his executors, Redmond BYRNE & John CARRELL. They were directed to lease the land to persons approved by the church of St. Mary's, Phila.

p. 160: Redman CUNNINGHAM, Henry DONNEL & George HAINES are appointed commissioners to mark the boundary line of part of Northumberland Co. annexed to Luzerne Co.

p. 161: John M'CONAHEY is allowed $64 from the commonwealth.

p. 161: Richard BACKHOUSE, late of Bucks Co., purchased in 1779 & 1780, several tracts of land from George WALL, commissioners of confiscated estates, for the natural life of Joseph GALLOWAY. Mary BACKHOUSE, widow of Richard, was evicted from tracts by a judgment of the Supreme Court.

p. 162: Albright WEAVER, soldier of the Pa. line, received a wound in the right hand at the Battle of Brunswick. A warrant is drawn in favor of John DORSEY, Phila., for $40 & $40/yr. for his use.

p. 164: Michael DRURY, now an inhabitant of Turkey Foot Twp., Somerset Co., enlisted as a soldier in Capt. John CHRISTY's Co. He was rendered unfit for service by a hurt in his head, which occasioned a deafness that still continues. He receives $40 & $40/yr. is paid to Thomas WILSON for his use.

p. 168: Immediately after the remarriage of Jacob MAYER, Leacock Twp., Lancaster Co., & Catharine, & before consummation, an unaccountable antipathy & dislike on her part took place to her said husband, which led to her separating from him & although all reasonable pains have been taken by him & her father to overcome her aversion & to reconcile her to her said husband, there remains no prospect of reconciliation. The marriage is annulled.

p. 170: The commissioners of any county may not sell for taxes any land late the property of John NICHOLSON or Peter BAYNTON.

p. 170: Edward CAVANOUGH enlisted in Capt. Mathew SMITH's Co. of Riflemen for one year, marched to Boston in 1775 & from there to Quebec & after that severe tour of duty, he continued in the 1st Regiment commanded by Col. Edward HAND for 2 years, at the expiration of which time, he was discharged on account of his ill state of health & being much afflicted with rheumatic pains owing to old age & hard service, he is not able to obtain subsistence by manual labor. He receives $40 & $40/yr. is paid to Thomas CAMPBELL for his use.

p. 173: Henry DONNEL, George HAINES, John FOSTER, Samuel DALE, John BOYD & Francis KING are commissioners in 1807 to mark out a road from a point where Coshecton & Great Bend Turnpike passes through Moosic Mountain to the west line of the state.

p. 177: Jonathan GUY, a sergeant in Capt. VAN ZANT's Co., 5th Pa. Battalion, commanded by Col. M'GAW, received a wound in the service of the U.S. on the night preceding the capture of Ft. Washington, Nov., 1776. After being cured, he enlisted in Col. Walter STEWART's Regiment on 29 Apr., 1778 & continued in the service until 16 Jan., 1781. He is now old & affected by the palsy. He receives $40 & $40/yr. is granted to John WEBER for his use.

p. 180: John MALONEY, Lancaster, served as a soldier in the American Army during the Rev. from June, 1775 until Jan., 1781 & at the battle of Brandywine, was wounded. With other injuries &

hardships incident to military service, he is incapable of bodily labour. He receives $40 & $40/yr. is given to Samuel WHITE for his use.

p. 181: John BRANDON, Dolly WALTHOUR, Martin ASHBAUGH are adminis. of the estate of Christopher WALTHOUR, Jr., decd. John BRANDON, Casper WALTHOUR, James IRWIN are a committee appointed to care for Catharine WALTHOUR, a lunatic. Christopher WALTHOUR, Sr., Westmoreland Co., died intestate, leaving 6 children: Michael, Joseph, Catharine, Casper, Barbara (intermarried with John FRITCHMAN), & Christopher.

p. 185: John CAVENOUGH enlisted early as a soldier in the Rev. He was honorably discharged. At the Battle of Brandywine, he received a wound in his left shoulder by a musket ball. He will receive $40 & $40/yr. is paid to Thomas CAMPBELL, York Co., for his use.

THE LAWS OF PENNSYLVANIA
1808-1812

p. iii: Laws repealed, obsolete & expired: The adminis. of Henry Lennox SHEPPARD, late of Westmoreland co., decd., are to sell land--obsolete. Thomas M'Kean THOMPSON is auth. to sell donation land--obsolete. Casper SHAFFNER is given relief--obsolete. Marriage annulment for John & Margaret M'CLELLEN--a private act. The auth. for Jonathan Bayard SMITH, Gavin HAMILTON & Peter Le Barbier DUPLESSIS to sell land in Phila.--obsolete. Relief for the heirs of Frederick VERNON, decd.--obsolete. Jacob KIMMEL & Abraham KONIGMACHER, Lancaster Co., are auth. to sell land--obsolete. Manning MARTAIN has title to certain lands--obsolete. The adminis. of Basil BROWN, late of Fayette Co., decd., are auth. to sell ground near Brownsville.

p. iv: Guardians of Dr. John HUSTON, Lancaster Co., are auth. to sell land--obsolete. John SHARP, acting adminis. of John SUTTON, decd., is auth. to sell land--obsolete. Money granted to Catharine SHIBE for her husband's Rev. services--obsolete. The title of Samuel WORK's land is confirmed--obsolete. Heirs of Frederick VERNON are given relief--obsolete. John KNAUSS & John LERCH, adminis. of Paul KNAUSS, decd., are auth. to sell land in Northampton Co. Patent issued to George BAKER for a lot of ground--obsolete. The adminis. of James CARNAHAN, late of Westmoreland Co., decd., are auth. to sell land. William M'KIBBEN & George LONG are given relief--obsolete. John VANLEAR is given relief--obsolete. James SEALS & Samuel ISRAEL are given relief--obsolete. The marriage of Peter & Ann RICKENBACH is dissolved. The title of Matthias GREENAWALT to land is confirmed--obsolete.

p. v, 1810: The adminis. of Emmor JEFFERIES, late of Lancaster Co., are auth. to sell ground. John JORDAN is given relief--obsolete. The adminis. of Mark DEARY, of Pittsburg, decd., are auth. to sell land. An act to perfect the title of Thomas HARRISON, Philip JONES & Robert C. MARTIN to a lot in Phila. Co. The adminis. of William RODGERS, decd., are auth. to sell land. John COREY, adminis. of the estate of Levy COREY, is auth. to sell land. Patrick M'GEE is given relief--obsolete.

p. vi: Catharine SHAEFFER, adminis. of John SHAEFFER, late of Berks Co., is auth. to sell land to Philip WEAVER. An act for the benefit of John RITTER & Charles KESSLER--obsolete. John HOPKINS, Robert A. BYERS are auth. to sell land. Michael WANN, old soldier, is given relief--obsolete. Michael NOWLIN is given relief--obsolete. John BAIRD, Hugh BAIRD, Samuel ADAMS, executors of John BAIRD, decd, are auth. to sell land. William LIGGINS is auth. to receive a patent for donation land in trust for his wife, Mary--obsolete. Richard BACHE receives relief--obsolete. James PARRY's title to land in Chester Co. is confirmed. John CONNOR receives relief. The marriage of Lewis & Zilla ALBERTUS is dissolved. Titles of James HICKMAN, John KING in land are confirmed. The title of Pa. to land lately held by Adam SMITH is relinquished. An act to remedy a defect in the title of Isaac WISENER to land in New London Twp., Chester Co. John LONGENECKER is given relief.

p. vii, 1811: William BLAKENEY, a soldier of the Rev. War, is granted money--obsolete. William MEARS & John RITTER, executor of the will of George EASTERLY, decd., is auth. to sell land. Jacob WINNOTT is auth., as executor of the estate of Adam KNOUFF, decd., to sell land to George BURGESSER. The adminis. of James SCOTT, late of Gettysburgh, are to sell land to George LASHELLS. James FRENCH, an alien & man of colour, is granted title to land in Chester Co. An act to remedy a defect in the title of Jacob C. WELPER to lots in Berwick, Luzerne Co., & in Easton, Northampton Co. Relief is granted to Frederick HAKE--obsolete. An act to remunerate the heirs of John MURRAY, Middle Paxton Twp., Dauphin Co.--obsolete. Relief is granted to James HORNER, Robert HORNER, William HORNER, Hugh HORNER, heirs of Hugh HORNER, decd.--obsolete. Relief is granted to Thomas M'KEEN--obsolete. The marriage of William MOLAND & Hannah is dissolved. Relief is granted to Clement BIDDLE--obsolete. Relief is granted to Robert LYON--obsolete. An act remunerating William CECIL for a lot--obsolete. William Henry KILBUCK, chief of the Delaware Indians, is compensated--obsolete.

p. viii: Relief is granted to the widow & children of David SHARPLESS, decd., late a soldier in the Pa. line--obsolete. Trustees of Meadville seminary are empowered to remit a debt due from Patrick DAVIS--obsolete. John WIERMAN & John WRIGHT, executors of the estate of Henry WIERMAN, are auth. to sell land. Relief is granted to the heirs of Samuel CUNNINGHAM, decd. James WALTON, Samuel BLACK are empowered to sell real estate of John SUTOR, a lunatic. Relief is granted to George YOUNDT, the younger, a prisoner in gaol, of Lancaster--obsolete. John CARSON is granted land. The right of Pa. in land lately held by Charles MORRIS & Henry MORRIS is vested in Mary M'CURDY & Jane HENRY. Tracts are granted to Michael SECHLER, Archibald M'NAIR & the widow & children of George CLARK, Rev. soldiers.

1812: The adminis. of James WHEELER are to sell land. Relief is granted to Miles CROWLEY, an old soldier of the Rev.--obsolete. Guardians of Phebe WADHAMS & Lydia WADHAMS, minors & heirs of Moses WADHAMS, late of Luzerne Co., decd., are auth. to sell land. The marriage of John & Mary SMITH is dissolved. Relief is granted to James MELOY--obsolete. Relief is granted to Robert COLEMAN & Cyrus JACOBS--obsolete. John BROWN is granted in trust for the children of Nathaniel SIMPSON, a tract of donation land in the right of Simpson HARRIS--obsolete. Relinquishment of a state loan in favour of the estate of the late Thomas GALLAHER--obsolete. Relief is granted to John WILSON & David HESS--obsolete. A tract of land is granted to Jacob SPEIDER, an old soldier. Relief is granted to Richard HARDING--obsolete. Relief is granted to Robert LOVE--obsolete. Thomas CAMPBELL is granted two tracts of donation land--obsolete. A donation tract is granted to the heirs of Joseph

POTTS, Capt. in the Pa. Line during the Rev. Joseph SHOCK is compensated for services in the Am. Rev.--obsolete. Relief is granted to John SCHRIBER & Sebilla SCHRIBER--obsolete. Relief is granted to Stoffel WEIGELL, a wounded soldier--obsolete. A final settlement & full discharge of the claim of Edmund MILNE-- obsolete. Charles MARTIN is granted donation land. Relief of Emanuel BOLLINGER & valentine WEIRICK--obsolete. Donation land is granted to Susanna STOKELY, widow of Capt. Nehemiah STOKELY, decd. Donation land is granted to Elizabeth WILLIAMS, formerly wife of Richard FLEMING. Relief is granted to John BROWN, a wounded soldier--obsolete. Relief is granted to William BROWN & Jacob SHEIFLEY, old soldiers--obsolete. The marriage of James & Rachael HUSTON is dissolved. Relief is granted to Jacob KUHN & Samuel PULLIN, old soldiers--obsolete. The marriage of Jacob ZINN, Jr., & wife, Eve, is dissolved. Relief is granted to Susanna BURRAS--obsolete. The marriage of Samuel & Sarah ROSE, Jr., is annulled. Robert ALLISON is auth. to sell land. Relief is granted to William TENANT, an old soldier, wounded at the storming of Stony Point--obsolete.

p. x, 1809: Certificate, notes & extracts: Charles ASHCOM, William PENN, Edward SHIPPEN, Griffith OWEN, Thomas STOREY, James LOGAN, Isaac TAYLOR, Richard HILL, Samuel CARPENTER, Isaac NORRIS, Thomas PENN, Richard PENN.

p. xii: Benjamin EASTBURN.

p. xiii: Thomas FREAME, John KINSEY, James HAMILTON, George THOMAS, Robert Hunter MORRIS.

p. xv: Warrants granted to David HASTINGS in 1751; to Thomas GEORGE in Fallowfield Twp. in 1714; to William COX, Esq., assignee of Joseph HIGBY, on the north side of the Juniata in 1762; Thomas SMITH; Dominick BRADLEY; John BACKHOUSE; Robert RAMSEY in 1775; Daniel WILLIAMS; Edward WILLIAMS; Stephen PASCHALL; William GRAY; William WATSON.

p. xvii: Philip HARDING, land on Chilisquaque Ck.; James FOULKS, Mary REESE & Col. FRANCIS on Chilisquaque Ck. Land on the Ck. was adjudged to Seth M'CORMICK, Richard IRWIN & John SMITH. Others on the Ck.: William SCULL, George IRWIN, Francis IRWIN, James MORROW, William JOHNSTON, Robert FOWLER.

p. xviii: Robert CON & George LEADLY were applying for the same land. William MOORE applied for land in Drumore Twp., Lancaster Co., 1768, adj. James ROBISON, John M'DOWEL & William MITCHEL. Joseph SCULL was deputy surveyor. On 12 June, 1767, John KING had surveyed to him land between Fishing Ck. & the east branch of the Susquehanna, Northampton Co. A patent was issued to Dr. William PLUNKET, in whom the right of John MAGRATH is vested, for land surveyed in 1769 called Black Hole, on the south side of the west branch of the Susquehanna, formerly in Berks Co., now in Northumberland Co.

p. xix: George CHURCHMAN's survey is made on a warrant prior to James & Henry WESLEY. George SHRADER has an application, #1727, for 100 acres, purchased by Andrew GRAFT which is older than George SMITH's. Leonard KERSTITLER claims under an application of Valentine WOLF, which is prior to Jacob SEAGRIST's, but according to Mr. M'CLAY's information, WOLF's is located in a different place than SEAGRIST's. Jasper SCULL has the prior location & John HERSHEY has the prior survey. Benjamin DEAN is the assignee of FRAZIER. Jacob & John CARPENTER had applications prior to FRAZIER's, however CARPENTER's survey is rejected. Thomas LEMMON claims under the CARPENTERS. In the case of Thomas JOHNSTON for Martha JOHNSTON, his wife, vs. Paul DEWIT, it appears that Paul DEWIT's location was for another place.

p. xx: In the case of Mary WILLIAMS, executrix of David WILLIAMS, vs. Daniel POALK, the land was surveyed to WILLIAMS in 1749. POALK's resurvey is confirmed. In the lottery application book, some were allowed in the case of losing the land first applied for, to enter another. One of these was to John EWING, one to Patrick CONOR & one to John JENNINGS. In the case of Dr. SMITH vs. Charles COX, the warrant to Barnaby BARNES, under whom Dr. SMITH claimed, was irregular, & yet had a preference given to it, against one regularly issued to Samuel PURVIANCE. The warrant of BARNES is dated 8 Mar., 1755 & that of PURVIANCE is dated 25 Oct., 1765.

p. xxi: Philip FOUST, father of Henry FOUST, had surveyed to him a warrant in 1748, as appears by the field notes of Edward SCULL.

p. xxii: Two early judges were Judge M'KEAN & Judge YEATES.

p. xxii: 200 acres were surveyed to John LOUGHRY.

p. xxiii: Signatures on a bond of 20 Sept., 1752: Peter LABAR, Hans HOUSER, Christian JOCKIE, Jacob STRING, Peter COCKER, Bernard WALTER, Henry WOLF, Jonathan PARKER, Christopher FUCKESS, Adam FRIEDMAN, Thomas SYLLIMAN & Henry WEEDMAN. Samuel BLUNSTON, Lanc. Co., was auth. to grant licenses to settlers over the Susquehanna, 1733.

p. xxiv: Col. ARMSTRONG represented that the settlers about the Big Springs, Cumberland Co., are greatly dissatisfied concerning a number of applications located amongst their settlements. James WILKINS bought an improvement right that was in conflict with M'KNIGHT's survey. James CALHOON had a case against John HARDY. 12 years ago, the place in dispute was settled by one M'CLEAN, who sold his improvement to Arthur M'CONNELL for £8. HARDY later gave M'CONNELL £50 for it & lived on it until driven off by Indians. In ELDER vs. ISH, Joshua ELDER had the first application & survey but Peter ISH alleges that he has made some improvement on the land. It is left to the judgment of William PATTERSON, Esq., & James GALLAHER, what value those improvements are to the place. ELDER is to pay ISH the value. W. ABERNATHY is only able to prove he has grubbed a few acres, plowed a little of it & enclosed it only with a fence two rails high. The survey is granted to Thomas BARTON.

p. xxv: Samuel RICHARDS had 300 acres of land situated on a stream of water running into a lake on the north side thereof, adj. Judah FOULKS & in Northumberland co., 9 May, 1774.

p. xxvi: In FLEMING vs. PLUNKET, Dr. PLUNKET had Dr. WILLIAMSON acting for him. James FLEMING affirms that the application was offered by Dr. PLUNKET to him. In LUKENS vs. COX, it is urged by Dr. COX & the report of William M'CLAY upon the case, it is ordered that Dr. COX have the liberty of laying the application of William NORCROSS, #1437, on the place surveyed for Jesse LUKENS, upon application of Robert IREDEL, Jr., #1733, provided he make title to the application of NORCROSS, & the survey made on the application of Charles IREDEL, #594, be confirmed to Jesse LUKENS. John JENNINGS was allowed to take up 1000 acres. George CROHAN took up 1500 acres in one tract & 7 other tracts amounting to 3200 acres more. In an old day book, the same person is allowed to take up to 14,000 acres, which was transferred to John BAYNTON & Samuel WHARTON & warrants issued to them for the same.

p. xxvii: A letter from James LOGAN to the proprietor, dated 1705, is in the land office. In the warrant book of 1772-5, a new warrant was granted to John GRAY, which had been forfeited by John SCOTT.

p. 1: Hugh FERGUSON is appointed commissioners in the room of others.

p. 2: An annuity is granted to Thomas SNOWDEN.

p. 2: Christian ARRETT is to receive land in Hempfield Twp., Westmoreland Co., in trust for the use of the schools.

p. 3: William NICHOLS, decd., was a clerk of the Mayor's Court, Phila. He owed the U.S. $29,271. To pay, he mortgaged his real estate to Henry MILLER.

p. 4: George BRYAN is auth. to sell unimproved lot in Pittsburg & apply the proceeds of the sale for the benefit of Sarah BRYAN.

p. 5: An annuity is granted to Edward CAVANOUGH.

p. 13: Victor MOREAU is entitled to hold estate in Morrisville although he is an alien.

p. 13: Lewis DORLEANS has his name changed to Lewis EMERY.

p. 18: Anthony BEELEN, Alexander M'LAUGHLIN, Zachariah A. TANNEHILL, exrs. of William PORTER, are auth. to execute a deed to George WALLACE for 1/4 of a lot in Pittsburg. Trust estate to cease & fee-simple vest in the children of William PORTER when they arrive at the age of 21.

p. 35: John M'DOWEL is to receive $40 & $40/year is payable to Alexander M'CLEAN for the use of M'DOWEL.

p. 35: A road is to be laid out from Strasburgh road near John G. PARKE's house, Chester co., to M'CALL's ferry on the Susquehanna R.

p. 39: Jonathan GROUT has erected a line of telegraphs from Phila. to Port Penn, Delaware. The use of Reedy Island at the head of Delaware Bay is granted to him for a telegraph station.

p. 39: A loan of $3000 is granted to William M'DERMETT from Pa.

p. 45: John BOYLS, sergeant in the Rev. War, is granted $40 & $40/yr.

p. 46: Samuel M'NEILL is granted $40 & $40/yr.

p. 48: John HUTON, a soldier in the Rev. War, is granted $40 & $40/yr.

p. 49: Moses WILLSON, Israel MERRICK are auth. to sell land in Tioga Co. for the benefit of Henry STRATER, a lunatic.

p. 50: Escheated lands are vested in Hannah HART, Hannah Morris HART & John Jaffry HART. John J. HART is auth. to sell Hannah Morris HART's share as she is non compos mentis.

p. 50: Managers for relief & employment of the poor, Germantown, Phila. Co.: Samuel MECHLIN, Jacob SUMMERS for the lower district; John JOHNSTON & Anthony JOHNSTON for the middle district; Jacob HOLGATE & Joseph MILLER for the upper district.

p. 56: William LANE & Thomas DAVIS are auth. to build a bridge across the Juniata R. near the mouth of Yellow Ck.

p. 58: John CRAIG is granted $40. Samuel KINKEAD is granted $40/yr. for the use of John CRAIG. John STEWART is granted $40 for the use of Robert VARNOR & $40/yr.

p. 60: Samuel BRADY is granted $40 & $40/yr. It will be paid to James MCCOMB for his use.

p. 61: Robert E. JONES is to be paid $40 for the use of Michael LYNCH, a Rev. soldier, & $40/yr.

p. 61: Samuel RAY, Jr., is auth. to erect a toll bridge over French Ck. opposite Buck St., Franklin Co.

p. 61: William LEEK, Joseph EDGAR, Thomas HENRY are auth. to lay out a road from Beaver-town toward New Lisbon, OH.

p. 63: Straban Twp., Adams Co., near George LASHELL's will vote at the courthouse, Gettysburg. Beaver Co. near John KELSO's mill & Alexander WRIGHT's will vote at David PATTON's. Hopewell Twp., Bedford Co., will vote at William LANE's on the south side of the Juniata, near the mouth of Yellow Ck. Tulpehocken Twp., Berks Co., will vote at Henry HORSH's. Springfield & Durham Twp., Bucks Co., will vote at William BURSON's, Springfield Twp. Falls Twp., Morrisville Borough, Bucks Co., will vote at Hugh MORTON's. Conemaugh Twp., Cambria Co., will vote at John GROSENICKEL's. Wayne, Fairfield & part of Fallowfield Twp., Crawford Co., near Uriah PETERSON's, will vote at James HERRINGTON's. McKean Twp., Erie Co., will vote at Thomas DUNN's. Conneotte Twp., Erie Co., will vote at John B. CULBERTSON's. Harbour Ck. Twp., Erie Co., will vote at Andrew ELLIOTT's. Beaver Dam Twp., Erie Co., will vote at William HUSTON's. Richhill Twp., Greene Co., will vote at Thomas CRAIG's. Morris Twp., Greene Co., will vote at Nathaniel PETTIT's. Dublin & Springfield Twps., Huntingdon Co., will vote at William WATER's, Dublin. Franklin, Tyrone, Warrior-mark Twp., Huntingdon Co., will vote at Bernard SWENEY's, Birmingham. Center Twp., Indiana Co., will vote at James DIXON's. The 4th district, Lycoming Co., will vote at George QUIGGLE's, now occupied by Sebastian SHADE. The Lower Tioga election district, Lycoming Co., will vote at Wright LOOMIS'. Washington Twp., south of Bald Eagle or Nittany Mt., Lycoming Co., will vote at George DORLAND's. The Kingston district, Luzerne Co., will vote at James WHEELER's. Greenwood Twp., Mifflin Co., will vote at Joseph SELLERS'. Milford Twp., Mifflin Co., will vote at Nicholas OKESON's. Franconia Twp., Montgomery Co., will vote at Lawrence JACOBY's, Summany Town, Marlborough Twp. W. Buffaloe near Adam LAUGHLIN's & William FORSTER's, Northumberland Co., will vote at Benjamin GOODWIN's, Hartleton. The 3rd election district, Northumberland Co., will vote at Eve METZGAR's, Lewisburg. The 11th election district, Northumberland Co., will vote at Stephen BREARLY's, Washington Twp. Southampton Twp., Somerset Co., will vote at Adam LEPLEY's, Esq. Brothers Valley & Stony Ck. Twp., Somerset Co., will vote at John KIMMEL's, Esq., Berlin. Conemaugh Twp., Somerset Co., will vote at Nicholas KIME's. Irwin & Scrubgrass Twp., Venango Co., will vote at Robert DONALDSON's. The 10th election district, Washington Co., will vote at Samuel SAYERS', Amity. Delaware Twp., Wayne Co., will vote at Alexander VANGORDON's. Middle-smithfield Twp., Wayne Co., will vote at John COOLBAUGH's.

p. 70: Thomas BODLEY will receive $40/yr. for the use of Hugh QUAY.

p. 70: John COLEMERY will receive $40 for the use of George BLAKELY. Thomas FORGY will receive $40/yr. for the use of George BLAKELY.

p. 74: Enrolled militia south of Loyalsock Ck., Lycoming Co., composed of the 2nd battalion of 1st Regiment & 10th Division is now commanded by Maj. Arthur M'KISSON. Williamsport is the usual place of the regimental meeting.

p. 77, 1810: Charles BILES is auth. to sell 35 acres in Bucks Co. for the benefit of his 4 minor children, which is the estate of his wife, the late Sarah WAMSLEY, decd.

p. 77: The small personal estate of Peter FRANKLIN (alias Peter HYWAY, an illegitimate son of Patty HYWAY), who died intestate & without issue, has escheated to the state. Patty HYWAY is aged, infirm & poor.

p. 77: John Lachausee BUJAC, a native of France, now a citizen of the U.S. & a resident of Pa., had 2 children: Patrick & Matthew, by Celiste ROBIN, a native of St. Domingo, before his marriage with Celiste, now his wife. The children are declared equal to children born in wedlock.

p. 79: Charles V. BONNHORST, an alien, is enabled to hold certain real estate, having declared his intention to become a citizen.

p. 80: Joseph WILLIAMS, the committee of Clement BROWN, a lunatic, is auth. to sell his estate.

p. 83: Michael MULLEN is granted $40 & $40/yr. Fullerton WOODS is to make an annual return to Orphan's Court.

p. 83: The right of John SCARLET to 2 tracts of land in Little Britain Twp., Lancaster, purchased at a sheriff's sale by a trustee, is confirmed.

p. 84: French Ck., Erie Co., from it's junction with Le Boeuff Ck. to a saw mill now or formerly owned by Leverick BISSELL, is declared a public highway.

p. Lewis RUSH, Phila., is auth. to convey ground granted to his minor children by George MARSHALL, decd., for a bridge over the Schuylkill River.

p. 84: Augustine Demetrius GALLITZEN, having assumed the name of SMITH & was by that name naturalized, is auth. to reassume his former name.

p. 85: Ulrich KISSINGER, Berks Co., is auth. to erect a bridge over the Schuylkill River at his mill.

p. 87: Robert HARRIS, George HOYER, George ZEIGLER are commissioners to establish a seat of the Pa. government at Harrisburgh, Dauphin Co.

p. 91: Green Ck., Northumberland Co., from it's mouth to a saw mill owned by John LEMON on the north branch to a saw mill owned by Samuel WATT on the north west branch is declared a public highway.

p. 100: The interest of the commonwealth in land is vested in the legal representatives of John TAYLOR, decd.

p. 101: Hugh CONNER is auth. to sell the land of Elizabeth WIGTON.

p. 103: The guardians of Mary & Elizabeth WOODWARD, heirs of Edward WOODWARD, decd., are auth. to sell land.

p. 104: Peter PENCE is granted $40 & $40/yr. is payable to John FORSTER, Lycoming Co., for the benefit of PENCE.

p. 107: The marriage of David & Mary CARMACK is annulled.

p. 108: James GIBSON is auth. to purchase land in the names of John GEORGE & Hains COUSLAND.

p. 110: The marriage of Isaac & Susannah PECK is dissolved.

p. 111: A bridge will be erected over the Delaware R. at Adam ROMIG's.

p. 113: Taxes due on the lands late the property of John NICHOLSON, decd., are to be paid.

p. 114: William WALLACE is exonerated from obligation of settlement on certain lands.

p. 115: The adminis. of William IRWIN, decd., are enabled to sell to John IRWIN, a part of a lot of ground.

p. 116: An artificial road from the west end of Lancaster, Elizabeth-town & Middletown Rd. to William MACLAY's will be built.

p. 117: Martin HYLEMAN is to be paid $40 & $40/yr.

p. 118: #101.10 is to be paid to Frederick ERRINGER, Samuel RICHARDS, William WEIR, for ammunition for the regiment of artillery in Phila.

p. 123: Philip JONES is to receive $40 & $40/yr will be paid to Michael M'CLEES for JONES' use.

p. 148: Charles SWIFT, Jr., is changing his name to Charles RICHE.

p. 154: Robert KENNEDY is to receive $.50 from each person navigating through his lock.

p. 158: The title of lot #97, Beaver, is vested in Matthew Taylor STEEN.

p. 179: Lots are granted to John WOODS.

p. 180: Election districts: Colerain Twp., Lancaster Co., will vote at William BARCLAY's, innkeeper. Oxford Twp., Phila. Co., will vote at Mahlon DUNGAN's. Hill's district, Washington Co., will vote at John BERRY's at the intersection of Washington & Pittsburg roads. Brothers-valley & Stoney Ck. Twp., Somerset Co., will vote at Peter GLASSNER's, Berlin. Burlington Twp., Lycoming Co., will vote at Mary GODDARD's. Delmar Twp., Tioga Co., will vote at Israel BUCKLEY's. Cliftsburg election district, Lycoming Co., will vote at William FURMAN's. Canton Twp., Luzerne Co., will vote at Joseph WALLACE's. Plum-Creek Twp., Armstrong Co., will vote at John THOMAS'. Allegheny Twp., Armstrong Co., will vote at William WATSON's. Redbank Twp., Armstrong Co., will vote at John SLOW's. N. Beaver Twp., Beaver Co., will vote at John DUNNING's. Parts of Big Beaver & Little Beaver Twp., Beaver Co., near Christopher WORMAN's will vote at Noble KOYL's. The 8th district, Erie Co., will vote at Henry BURGHART's. Sandy Lake Twp., Mercer Co., will vote at William PERRINE's. Wolf Ck. Twp., Mercer Co., will vote at Robert GLENN's. The 4th district, Chester Co., will vote at John BLACK's, W. Fallowfield Twp., commonly known as Gumtree Tavern, now occupied by William GILLILAND. W. Bradford, Newlin Twp., Chester Co., will vote at James CHAMBERLAIN's, Marshalton. Oil Ck. Twp., Crawford Co., will vote at John KERR's. Sadsburg Twp., Crawford Co, will vote at James BIRTCH's. Augusta Twp., Northumberland Co., will vote at Jacob REAKER's. Moore Twp., Northampton Co., will vote at George GREBER's. Wayne Twp., Crawford Co., will vote at Abraham KIGHTLINGER's. Warwick, Warminster, Warrington Twp., Bucks Co., will vote at William HART's. Warwick Twp., Lower Makefield Twp., Bucks Co., will vote at Jacob CHAPMAN's. Haycock Twp., Bucks Co., will vote at Mary STRAUN's. Deer Twp., Allegheny Co., will vote at Felix NEGLEY's, late in the tenure of John FRAZER. Newport Twp., Luzerne Co., will vote at Christian STOUT's. Mahoning Twp., Mercer Co., will vote at Henry ROBESON's.

p. 183: Commissioners will lay out a road from Washington to the Va. state line near William SLATOR's.

p. 185, 1811: John Harris PUGSLEY has his name changed to John Levet HARRIS.

p. 186: James CHAMBERS is a trustee of the Methodist Episcopal Congregation, Washington. They are auth. to sell a lot to John HOGE.

p. 188: William KERNICHON is to receive $40. $40/yr. will be paid to John HOUGH for his use.

p. 188: Isaac IVANS & others are managers of the Governor's Creek Meadow co.
p. 188: Jacob DODRIDGE is to receive $40 & $40/yr. will be paid to Daniel UDREE for his use.

p. 189: The marriage of Philip J.G. DE FRANQUEEN & his wife, Elizabeth, is dissolved. Their son is legitimatized.

p. 189: Amos JOURDAN is to be paid $40/yr. John HUTTON, a Rev. War soldier, is to receive the use of the $40. Michael MULLEN is to receive an annuity.

p. 190: A patent is made in the names of John SHEPARD & Benjamin DORRANCE for the greater part of Clavernack Twp.

p. 191: A writ of petition is sued out by Thomas SHIPLEY against John SHIPLEY, Phila.

p. 191: John EDIE, et al., are appted. commissioners to make the road from Michael GEISELMAN's mill to Abbotstown, York Co.

p. 194: $3000 is loaned to William EICHBAUM so he can manufacture wire.

p. 195: Armantine & Arman MONGES are declared legitimate.

p. 195: Lewis OVERDEER is auth. to sell land as executor of Philip BOTTENFIELD.

P. 196: Seneca LUKENS is auth. to sell land.

p. 198: John UMSTEAD is auth. to erect a mill-dam in the Schuylkill River.

p. 198: Samuel GARRETSON & James WICKERSHAM are auth. to sell land in Newbury Twp., York Co.

p. 198: John KERR & Andrew KAUFFMAN are to take care of John KAUFFMAN, a lunatic.

p. 200: Rev. Soldiers: William GLENDY, Atcheson MELLON, John FAUST, Abraham BODLE are to be paid $40 & $40/yr. Ernst GREESE & Duncan M'VICKAR are to receive $40.

p. 204: Matthew THOMPSON & Adam BOYD are executors of the will of William BOYD, late of Cumberland Co.

p. 205: James STEWART, Luzerne Co., formerly owned land there.

p. 206: Thomas HILL is granted $40 & $40/yr. is to be paid to Thomas CAMPBELL for his use.

p. 211: Joseph KIRKBRIDE is auth. to build a toll bridge over Frankford Ck.

p. 212: John KELSO's property in Erie is to be a public landing.

p. 216: John BARCLAY is appted. to erect a bridge over the Delaware River.

p. 217: The official acts of Abraham MULFORD & Abisha WOODWARD, late high sheriffs of Wayne Co., are declared valid.

p. 218: Ichabod BUCK & William BUCK are auth. to erect a wingdam on the north branch of the Susquehanna River, Luzerne Co.

p. 218: The title of Christopher FAATZ, Jacob HEINTZ, Christian HEINTZ, Christopher HEINTZ, Adam GREINER, Nicholas GREINER, aliens, to land in Wayne Co., is allowed.

p. 219: Elizabeth BOISE is given an escheated estate.

p. 221: Abraham SHERIDAN has a floating bridge in Phila. Co.

p. 228: John Philip DEGRUCHY & George KREMER are commissioners to erect a bridge over the north east branch of the Susquehanna River,

Northumberland Co., from the plantation of Thomas GRANT to Shamokin Island.

p. 241: A road is to be made from Phila. & Wilmington post road near John M'ILVAIN's to intersect the Phila., Brandywine, & New London road on the land of George DAVIS, Delaware Co.

p. 242: Rebecca MILES, Phila., widow, is auth. to sell lots.

p. 246: John WATSON is to be paid $40 & $40/yr. is to be paid to Isaac LEWIS for his use.

p. 246: Jacob BAKER is to be paid $40 & $40/yr. paid to William BINDER for his use.

p. 253: Henry BEARDT is to be paid $40 & $40/yr.

p. 253: Ross Twp., Allegheny Co., will vote at Samuel ALLEN's. Pine Twp., Allegheny Co., will vote at William COCHRANE's. The 8th election district of Tioga Co. voted in the past at Joshua EMLIN's, Wellsborough & now will vote at Alpheus CHENY's, Wellsborough. Bridgewater Twp., Susquehanna Co., will vote at Isaac POST's. Mohontongo Twp., Northumberland Co., will vote at Henry SHADLE's, miller. Toamensing, E. Penn Twp., Northampton Co., will vote at John KLUTZ's, Lehighton, E. Penn Twp. Beaver Co. near Christopher WORMAN's will vote at Armstrong DRENNON's, S. Beaver Twp. Brecknock Twp., Lancaster Co., near Henry GOOD, Peter BEAM, John BEAM, Baltzer SHEDER, John GOOD, will vote at John HUSTON, Esq.'s, now occupied by Isaac GOSHEN, Church town. Warren Twp., Franklin Co., will vote at the school house on Michael COOK's land. Morris Twp., Washington Co., will vote at Ebenezar GOBLE's, Esq. Hamilton Twp., Adams Co., will vote at Jacob KOCK's, Berlin. W. Penn, Rush Twp., Schuylkill Co., will vote at George SIMON's, W. Penn Twp. Mahoning Twp., Indiana Co., will vote at Isaac M'HENRY's. Hereford Twp., Berks Co., will vote at George HOOFF's. Nescopeck Twp., Luzerne Co., will vote at John BRIGGS'. Menallin Twp., Adams Co., will vote at Frederick HOPKEE's. Streban Twp., Adams Co., will vote at David FREEMAN's, Hunterstown. Washington Twp., York Co., will vote at Michael BOWEN's. Bedford & St. Clair Twp., Bedford Co., near John SILLS, Widow TODD, John ROWSER will vote at George ROCK's.

p. 259: Robert CLARK is the adminis. of the estate of James LAND, late of Brownsville, Fayette Co.

p. 261: Huntingdon Ck. from it's mouth to Amos BUCKLEW's saw mill is a public highway.

p. 262: John MORRIS is to receive $40 & $40/yr. The title to donation land is to be released to him.

p. 264: Daniel DOBBINS, James WESTON, James POLLOCK are commissioners to lay off a piece of land east of Erie on the bank of the lake to erect a lighthouse.

p. 265: The claim of Pa. to certain land is released in favour of Elizabeth SHAEFFER.

p. 267: John GILL & George WALLACE are empowered to sell land which is real estate of Michael HELMAN, a lunatic.

p. 268: John STAPLER is appted. treasurer of the Bucks Co.

contributionship for insuring house & other buildings from loss by fire.

p. 268: Christiana BEAR, widow & adminis. of Isaac BEAR, decd., is to sell land in Muncy-Ck. Twp., Lycoming Co.

p. 268: Joseph WREN is to receive $40 & $40/yr.

p. 270: Nathan BEACH, Phila.; Robert HARRIS, John SCHOCK, Harrisburg; William M'CANDLESS, Adamson TANNEHILL, Pittsburg; are commissioners to make a road from Harrisburg to Pittsburg.

p. 273: John FLETCHER & Samuel WRIGHT, Somerset Co., are commissioners to open a road between Connelsville, Fayette Co. & Berlin, Somerset Co. John STATLER, George GRAHAM, John DENNISON are commissioners to improve roads in Somerset & Cambria co.

p. 274: James MILLIGAN, John M'DOWELL, John GILLESPIE, Mifflin Co.; Isaac CAMPBELL, Robert LEONARD, John CRUMB, Huntingdon Co., are commissioners to lay out a road from John CAMPBELL's bridge, Huntingdon Co., to a public road leading up from the Kishicoquillas Valley.

p. 275: A bridge is to be erected over Wallanpaupack Ck. between William CHAPMAN's & Silas PURDEY's, Wayne Co. A road is to be opened from Blooming Grove to Ephraim KIMBLE's at the falls of the Lackawaxen, Wayne Co. A road is to be improved from GREEN's mill over Peter's Mt. to MOOREHEAD's ferry, Dauphin Co. A road is to be improved from Fishing Ck. at M'ALISTER's mill to CLARKE's ferry, Dauphin Co. Tioga Co. is to improve WILLIAMSON's road between Aaron BLOSS' & the south line between Ezra SPALDING's & the state line road from Muncy to Towandee in Ontario Co. The road is to be improved from David REYNOLD's up Lycoming Ck. to Ontario Co. John LITLE & James WESTON are to improve roads in Erie Co.

p. 276: Navigation of Conewango Ck. is to be improved by Martin REESE & Ralph MARLIN. In Venango Co., a road is to be improved where it passes through Venango Co. & crosses the Allegheny River at Eli HOLEMAN's ferry. In Allegheny Co., a bridge is to be built over Turtle Ck., where the road crosses it near Myers POWELL's tavern. In Greene Co., the road from Waynesburgh to Richard SARGEANT's near the confluence of Hunter's Fork, Wheeling Ck., will be improved.

p. 279, 1812: The title to a house & lot in Corporation St., Newville, Cumberland Co., lately held by William FERGUSON, is vested in his widow, Elizabeth FERGUSON.

p. 279: John SMITH, Matthew M'CALL, & James PEDAN, guardians of the minor children of Robert M'CALL & Elizabeth PEDAN are auth. to sell real estate to a company erecting a bridge over the Susquehanna River at M'CALL's ferry.

p. 283: John GAMBLE, late an alien, is granted a piece of land in Luzerne Co.

p. 284: Voltaire Goldsmith JONES' name is changed to Thomas Watkin JONES.

p. 284: Richard JOHNSTON, an old ranger of the Rev., is granted $40/yr.

p. 286: Andrew MILLER is Justice of the Peace, Crawford & Venango Cos.

p. 287: George GANTZ, Henry KUNKLE, et al. are elders, church wardens, & trustees of the Lutheran congregation of Codorus, Shrewsbury, Hopewell Twp., York Co.

p. 287: John WOODS is granted lots.

p. 288: A tract of donation land is granted to the heirs of James GORDON, late of Westmoreland Co., upon their releasing one in N.Y.

p. 288: A bridge will be erected over the North East branch of the Susquehanna River, Northumberland Co., from the highway opposite Thomas GRANT's plantation to Shamokin Island.

p. 288: A bridge is to be erected over the Susquehanna River at Great Bend where the ferry is now kept opposite the houses of Abraham DUBOIS & Sylvanus HATCH, Willingborough, Susquehanna Co.

p. 289: The marriage of Eleanor & Abraham HOULTZ is annulled.

p. 289: Joseph BRUTON, decd., received a wound in the Rev. war. His widow, Bridget, is to be paid $40 & $20/yr. which will be paid to Joseph CLUNN, a trustee.

p. 290: John M'GUIRE, a disabled Rev. soldier, is to be paid $40 & $40/yr. is to be paid to William MITCHEL, his trustee.

p. 291: Jacob PLUMB, a wounded militia man, is to be paid $40 & $40/yr. is to be paid to Adam LEPLEY as trustee, Somerset Co.

p. 291: Trustee of the Loller Academy, Hatborough, Montgomery Co., is Nathaniel B. BOILEAU, by the will of Robert LOLLER, decd.

p. 292: William SCOTT & Archibald [John] GALLOWAY, adminis. of the estate of Archibald SCOTT, are auth. to sell land.

p. 299: The commissioners of Indiana Co. are auth. to buy land from Conrad RICE (conveyance executed 11 Oct., 1806) for the use of Indiana inhabitants to build a church.

p. 301: Henry PENSINGER, an old soldier who lost a leg in the Rev., is to receive $40 & $60/yr.

p. 302: James WILSON, a wounded soldier of the Rev., is to receive $40 & $40/yr.

p. 304: Elections in Lehigh Co. will be at George SAVETZ's, Northampton Borough.

p. 307: A state road in Bedford beginning at the run near William TODD's & westward to John EWALT's to branch off Glade Road at John EWALT's is altered.

p. 308: A committee of Abraham COOK, a lunatic, York Co., is to sell real estate.

p. 311: The estate of Frederick ANTES is exonerated from the effects of a certain judgment.
p. 311: Jacob ROUSE, a wounded soldier, is to receive $40/yr.

p. 312: John HOSKINS, old soldier, will receive $45 & an annuity to be paid to Thomas BAIRD for his use. Daniel DOUGHERTY, old soldier, will receive $40 & an annuity to be paid to James SCOTT for his use.

p. 313: John BINNS is to print 750 copies of English statutes.

p. 314: The resolution directing Charles Wilson PEALE to take care of the State House year is repealed.

p. 314: James SCOTT is to receive $40. An annuity of $40 will be paid to Joseph JOHNSON in trust for SCOTT. A tract of donation land is granted to JOHNSON.

p. 315: The guardians to David MACLAY & Robert MACLAY, minor children of Samuel MACLAY, Northumberland Co., decd., are to partition real estate.

p. 315: James ARMSTRONG is appted. in place of Thomas STUBBS, decd., to improve roads.

p. 318: David DAVIDSON, an old soldier, will receive $40 & $40/yr.

p. 331: Judges of the 2nd district will meet at Joshua EVANS', Trediffrin Twp., Chester Co. Judges of the 3rd district will meet at Michael COBLE's, Elizabeth-town, Lancaster co. Judges of the 5th district will meet at Patrick COCHRAN's, Shippensburgh. Judges of the 7th district will meet at Abraham BAILEY's, Hamburgh, Berks Co. Judges of the 9th district will meet at William M'ALEVY's, Huntingdon Co. Judges of the 10th district will meet at John JONES', Berwick, Northumberland Co. Judges of the 13th district will meet at Jeremiah DAVISON's, Luzerne Twp., Fayette Co. Judges of the 14th district will meet at Sarah CARNAHAN's, Allegheny Co.

p. 333: A road will be laid out from John G. PARKS', Chester Co., by M'CALL's ferry on the Susquehanna R. to the Md. line.

p. 334: Magdalena ENNES, widow of the late Lt. Benjamin ENNES, who was slain in battle by Indians during the Rev. war, will receive $40 & $40/yr.

p. 335: Ferdinand RITTER is auth. to sell land in Northampton Co. belonging to the German Calvinist Congregation of Bethel Church, Albany Twp., Berks Co., & the Calvinist congregation of Jacob's Church & the Calvinist congregation of Ebethnezer Church, Lynn Twp., Northampton Co.

p. 335: $40 & $40/yr. is to be paid to Philip HORNBECKER, Michael M'NULTY. John M'MULLIN & James PURDY, old soldiers & William CURRAN will get a gratuity.

p. 336: George FEIDT is auth. to sell land in Dauphin Co. & to execute a title to Michael SHADEL for the land as directed by the Lutheran Congregation in Upper Paxton Twp. Thomas WILSON, John BOYD, John LYTLE, Erie Co. commissioners, are to take charge of certain lands in Erie.

p. 338: Part of Northumberland Co. in Beaver-dam Twp., near John RITTER's tavern, is annexed to Mifflin Co.

p. 339: The marriage of Benjamin HARRISSON & wife, Margaret, is annulled.

p. 339: Jesse HOMER changes his name to Jesse Henderson JONES.

p. 341: The elections of Moyamensing Twp., Phila. Co., will be at William DAILY's.

p. 352: Isaac & Elizabeth WOOD, minors, children of Benjamin WOOD, Phila., decd., are to receive $1320.73 due to their eviction from a messuage & lot, sold by Pa. as confiscated property.

p. 353: Claims of John SHEPHERD & Benjamin DORRANCE to the Mammoth Farm are valid.

p. 352: Annuities of $40 are granted to John LEHMAN, Matthew WILSON & George BUYERS, old soldiers.

p. 356: $40 is granted to David EDGAR & annuities of $40 are granted to Levi GREFFITH & George FUNK, old soldiers.

p. 357: $60 is granted to Henry M'EUEN, a wounded soldier & $40/yr. of $40 to Mary GORDON, widow of Thomas GORDON, decd., a soldier.

p. 357: Simon MEREDITH & David HILLIS are auth. to sell lands & pay 5% annually to Ann BALDWIN.

p. 357: $40 is paid to George WISEMAN & $40/yr. to Samuel SMILEY & Henry SHADE. $40/yr. is granted to William JOHNSON. James M'CALMONT is a trustee.

p. 358: Edward DE LA MONTANYE is auth. to sell the interest of Ann MONTANYE, decd., in certain real estate, Phila. Co.

p. 359: $40 is paid to Edward QUIGLEY, a wounded soldier of the Rev. $40/yr. is paid to John G. LOWREY for QUIGLEY's use.

p. 359: The bridge over Conestogoe River built by Abraham WITMER, Lancaster Co., is to be purchased & made free.

p. 360: Peter M'BRIDE, an old wounded soldier, will receive $40. $40/yr. is paid to Jacob BLOCHER for M'BRIDE's use.

p. 361: A gratuity & $40/yr. is paid to John KEASY.

p. 361: Nathaniel B. BOILEAU, Thomas B. MONTANYE & Gove MITCHELL are auth. to sell a school house on the land of Isaac PICKERING, Moorland Twp., Montgomery Co.

p. 362: Margaret BEECHLER & others are auth. to sell real estate of Henry BEECHLER, a lunatic.

p. 363: Fairfield & Fallowfield Twp., Crawford Co. will vote at Alexander DUNN's, Fairfield Twp. Nescopeck Twp., Luzerne Co., will vote at Christian ASH's, at the mouth of Wopehawley Ck. Bensalim Twp., Bucks Co., will vote at the Indian Queen Tavern now occupied by Daniel LURREW. Upper Smithfield Twp., Wayne Co., will vote at George BUCHANAN's, Milford. North Huntingdon Twp., Westmoreland Co., where Joseph BYERLEY formerly lived & now belonging to Andrew BYERLEY is where the election will be held. Bloom Twp., Northumberland Co., will vote at Casper CRISTMAN's, Bloomsburg. Hemlock Twp., Northumberland Co., will vote at William M'BRIDE's.

Plainfield Twp., Northampton Co., will vote at Frederick WOLLE's, innkeeper, Jacobsburg. Donegall Twp., Butler Co., will vote at Rudolph BARNHART's. Jenner Twp., Somerset Co., will vote at John DENNISON's. Conemaugh Twp., Somerset Co., will vote at James MITCHELL's. Stony Ck. & Quemahoning Twp., Somerset Co. at the mouth of JEMISON's Breastwork run, near Frederick CRAMER's, BROLIER's mill, will vote at Peter MILLER's. Northampton Twp., Bucks Co., will vote at Philip SAGER's. Berks Co. near Dicter SNYDER, John SEAMAN, John PATIERGER, Jr., George RIEGLE, John BACKENSTOS, Michael NUNNEMACHER, Michael's Church, will vote at George SHARTEL's, Bern Twp. Berks Co. near Jacob KOCH, George LONG, Frederick SPANG's forge will vote at Henry KEELY's. Ulalia Twp., Potter Co., will vote at Isaac LYMAN's. Pittsburg & Pitt Twp., Allegheny Co. near ROUP's mill, Henry FULTON's farmhouse & William KNOX's farmhouse, will vote at the courthouse. Long Swamp Twp., Berks Co. near Jacob CORLE, Theobald CORLE, Michael TREAS, Christian RITZ, John FREDERICK, John ONNAR will vote at George HOOF's, Hereford Twp. District Twp., Berks Co., near Adam BARDMAN, David JOHNSON, George WYEAND, will vote at George HOOF's. The 9th election dist., Erie Co., voted at Timothy TUTTLE's before & now at the schoolhouse, Greenfield. Bridgewater Twp., Susquehanna Co. near Zebulon DEAN's & Thomas CROCKER's will vote at Thomas PARKS'. New Sewickly Twp., Beaver Co., will vote at Stanton SHOALS'. The 3rd election dist., Wayne Co., will vote at George BUCHANAN's. Little Britain Twp., Lancaster Co., will vote at Robert CAMPBELL's. Black Lick Twp., Indiana Co., will vote at Amos LAWRENCE's. Hanover Twp., Northampton Co., will vote at George SAVITZ's. M'Kean, a provisional county, will vote at James HITTS', Ceres Twp. Miles Twp., Centre Co., will vote at Godfrey HARLOFF's, Resersburg. Lausanne Twp., Northampton Co., will vote at John KLUTZ's, Whighton, E. Penn Twp. Bethlehem Twp., Northampton Co., will vote at George BUTZ's, Bethlehem Twp.

p. 368: Henry MANIFOLD & Andrew CLARKSON, York Co., are to sell the real estate of Joseph MANIFOLD, a lunatic.

p. 371: Alexander BROWN is to receive $40 & $40/yr. Samuel WATT, Patrick MARTIN, old soldiers, will receive $40.

p. 374: Jacob PALMER, a lunatic, will have his real estate sold by John B. PALMER.

p. 376: A tract is released to Robert GREGG, Pikerun Twp., Washington Co., late the estate of William GREGG.

p. 376: The claims of Pa. released to Elizabeth FRANTZ were the estate of Henry MONEY, late of Westmoreland Co.

p. 378: A permanent bridge is to be erected over the Schuylkill R. near the floating bridge of Abraham SHERIDAN, "Upper Ferry," Phila. Co.

p. 381: Bethuel VINCENT, guardian of the minor daughters of Peter HOUSEL, decd., is auth. to sell a house & lot in Milton, Northumberland Co.

p. 382: There will be a review of a road from Butler to Franklin lying between James PHILIPS' lane, 6 miles from Butler, to the Venango Co. line. There will be a review of a road from Butler to Mercer, lying between the county line of Mercer & Butler & John M'MULLEN's farm, Mercer Co.

p. 382:   The marriage between Elsa & Levi MIDDOUGH is annulled.

p. 382:   The adminis. of the estate of John HANNAH, decd., is auth. to sell land, Orphan's Court of Allegheny Co.

p. 383:   The guardian of William O'HARRA, a minor, is auth. to sell real estate.

p. 384:   George SPANGLER & Elizabeth WILSON, a committee of York Co., are auth. to sell the real estate of Thomas WILSON, lunatic, to James PATTERSON.

p. 385:   The marriage between William & Isabella M'GLAUGLIN is annulled.

p. 386:   Frederick HAYMAKER is a Justice of the Peace for Allegheny & Crawford Co.

p. 386: $40 is paid to Catharine FISHER, widow of the late Garrat GRAFF, an officer in the Rev., & $20/yr.

p. 389:   The militia of W. Penn Twp., & Rush Twp., Schuylkill Co., are attached to a regiment commanded by Lt. Col. Bernard KEPNER, Schuylkill Co.

p. 390:   Jacob YOUNG, son of Christian & Lehna YOUNG, Passyunk Twp., Phila. Co., has the estate of John HANNIS, decd., also a son of Lehna, vested in him.

p. 391:   Samuel ANDERSON, guardian of Matthias Richard SAYRES & Edward Smith SAYRES.

p. 399:   C.W. PEALE is granted use of certain parts of the State House to display his museum.

THE LAWS OF PENNSYLVANIA
1812-13, 1813-14

p. 2:   Benjamin BURDS, George DANSDILL, John BURDS, Michael WALLET, Bedford Co., occupy land adj. to a state road being altered.

p. 5:   Jacob MIDDLEKAUFF owned lands on which a German church was situated in Petersburg.

p. 6:   Heirs of Matthew SHAW, decd., are given relief.

p. 8:   Michael FOX & Samuel FOX are adminis. with the will annexed of John FOX, decd., brickmaker, Phila.

p.8:   The title of Olof STROMBERG, an alien, to land in W. Chester, Chester Co., is confirmed.

p. 19:   Commissioners to make a road from the Spring House Tavern, Montgomery Co., to Bethlehem, Northampton co.: William TILGHMAN, Peter KNEPLAY, Phila.; John ROBERTS, Evan JONES, Silas HOUGH, John WEAVER, Montgomery Twp., Montgomery Co.; Samuel SELLERS, Andrew STICHLER, William GREEN, Bucks Co.; James GREENLEAF, Abraham RINKER, Jacob HARTZEL, Philip WINT, Lehigh Co.; George HUBER, Owen RISE, Northampton Co.

p. 30: Sarah HOPKINS, late MEWHORTER, was married 31 Mar., 1806 to Jesse HOPKINS, who has since deserted her & is imprisoned in the N.Y. State Prison for passing counterfeit in Washington Co. in June last. Sarah & Jesse, both late of Northampton Co., have marriage annulled.

p. 31: John M'GILL, an old & wounded soldier, receives $40 & $30/yr.

p. 31, 1813: Marsh Ck., Centre Co., which runs through Jacob BOONE's saw mill, is declared a public highway.

p. 32: Commissioners of Wayne Co. to make a road from the narrows at Big Eddey by Bethany to the intersection of the Milford & Owago Tpk. with the Clifford & Wilkesbarre Tpk., Luzerne Co.

p. 35: Commissioners to make a road from the Centre tpk. near the Bear Gap to the northeast branch of the Susquehanna at the end of the Blue Hill near Danville, Northumberland Co.: Lewis REESE, James MAY, Reading; Daniel MONTGOMERY, Jr., William MONTGOMERY, Jr., Danville; Jacob GEARHART, John JONES, Shamokin; Bethuel VINCENT, Seth IREDALE, Milton; John FUNSTON, John FRUIT, Derry; Jacob SHOEMAKER, George WEBB, Pennsborough; Joseph EVES, Richard DEMET, Fishing-Creek.

p. 39: Executors of the will of William BALL, decd., late of Phila.: Joseph BALL, John HEWSTON, Joseph L. INGLES.

p. 40: John MCGOWAN is to receive a tract of land. In 1776, he entered the flying camp. He served an active tour of duty, was a volunteer in several engagements with the British, in one of which he lost his servant. He settled on a tract of donation land by mistake, believing it was vacant. Patent is issued for the tract he now resides on, #3, 1st district, 250 acres.

p. 41: William SHARPLESS is auth. to sell a part of William SMITH's estate, a lunatic, Chester co.,

p. 45: William GILL, an old soldier of Mercer Co., is given $40 & $40/yr.

p. 45: Trustees of Venango Co: William MOORE, Alexander MCDOWELL, John MCDONALD, William CONNELLY, George POWER, Alexander MCCALMONT.

p. 48: Commissioners to make a road--The Marietta, Richland & Mountjoy Tpk. Rd.: Henry SHARE, Henry CASSEL, Jacob ROHRER, Christian LEIB, James MAHAFFEY, James PATTERSON, George SNYDER, Jacob GRAYBILL.

p. 51: Added to the surviving managers of Lancaster: James HUMES, William MONTGOMERY, Emanuel REIGART, John GUNDACKER, John HOFF, Samuel WHITE, Jonas METZGAR, John SWAR, Christian HOOVER, John BOMBERGER, Benjamin SHAUM, Abraham WITMER.

p. 53: William LAMB, Centre Co., purchased 100 acres of land in Bald Eagle Twp. from his step-son, John WATSON, decd. The land is part of a larger tract surveyed in pursuance of an application to Philip SMITH, 3 Apr., 1769. William MCEWEN & David WATSON are adminis. of John WATSON.

p. 56: Uriah MATSON & Thomas CULBERTSON were appted. to take care of William GUTHRIE's person & estate. GUTHRIE, decd., was a lunatic, Derry Twp., Westmoreland Co.

p. 57: Margaret ALLEN, who arrived in the U.S. since the Rev., is enabled to hold real estate in Holmesburg, Phila. Co.

p. 57: John CHRISTY was late a Justice of the Peace for Allegheny Co. He also performed his duties in Mercer Co. George FOWLER & Alexander M'DOWELL, Justices of the Peace for Crawford Co. also performed their duties in Venango Co.

p. 58: A state road from Butler to Mercer lies between the 15 mile tree in Butler Co. & William M'MELLIN's farm, Mercer Co.

p. 58: Charles CAPPLE & Francis STACKHOUSE, Bucks Co., Rev. War veterans, will receive $40 & $40/yr.

p. 59: Arthur ST. CLAIR, Maj. General in the Rev., is given $200 & $200/yr.

p. 60: On 24 Sept., 1779, John MCNAIR purchased 189 acres of confiscated estate of Andrew ALLEN, Allen Twp., Northampton Co. Since then, the land was vested in George NAGLE. In Oct., 1809, he was evicted by a title paramount in Margaret DELANEY of the Kingdom of Great Britain.

p. 62: John BIOREN was contracted to print SMITH's edition of the laws. He is to be paid $2.50 for 600 pages.

p. 62: John VOGAN is granted a tract of land #147 in the 1st district of donation lands on which he now resides. He is to pay $1/acre & interest.

p. 63: Cornelius VANHERN is a Pa. claimant of lot #20 in Sunbury Manor, Kingston Twp., Luzerne Co. It is now a Connecticut claim. He is to receive $2225.83.

p. 65: Wilson SMITH was a Quarter-master General of Pa. John KELSO was a Brigadier General.

p. 65: Charles BISSON, old soldier of Montgomery Co., is to receive $40 & $40/yr. Same for John COLMAN, Indiana Co.

p. 67: George WYMAN formerly occupied a sand-stone house in Lancaster Co. One SHROYER, decd., formerly occupied a house on the great road leading from Lebanon to Manheim. One HENRY has a house at the cross roads leading from Harrisburg to Reading.

p. 73: John RANKIN, Mercer Co., is granted a tract of donation land on which he now resides in the 4th donation district, lot #706 for $1/acre & interest.

p. 73: Members of the "Society of Artists of the United States" or "The Columbian Society of Artists": Thomas JEFFERSON, Paul HAMILTON, Gideon GRANGER, Joel BARLOW, Robert FULTON, Benjamin H. LATROBE, Benjamin TROTT, George MURRAY, Robert MILLS, John VALLANCE, William HAMILTON, Samuel F. BRADFORD, John CONRAD, William P. DEWEES, James PEALE, Benjamin TANNER, Samuel SEYMOUR, Samuel LEWIS,

William KNEASS, Jacob EICHOLTZ, Maurice FURST, Edward MILES, John James BARRALET, George MAGRAGH, Alexander RIDER, Henry S. TANNER, David KENNEDY, James GIBSON, N. LEFAVRE, Arnold VIGNIER, Thomas BIRCH, Charles O'HARRA, John DRAPER, Henry CONNELLY, John BOYD, Archibald BINNY, John MEER, Isaac FORSYTH, Dennis A. VOLOZAN, William WOOLLET, William R. JONES, John A. WOODSIDE, John CRAWLEY, John BINNEY, Alexander LAWSON, Benjamin Smith BARTON, James MCALPIN, Robert FIELDING, Abraham I. NUNES, William STRICKLAND, Christian GOBRECHT, George HYDE, George BRIDPORT, William CARR, Burgess ALLISON, Adam TRAQUAIR, Zaccheus COLLINS, John VAUGHN, Cornelius TIEBOUT, James PALMER, William HARRISON, Samuel HARRISON, Dr. N.S. ALLISON, Joseph H. SEYMOUR, Joseph SANSOM, George E. BLAKE, David EDWIN, John CONNELLY, William CHARLES, George HOLMES, John DORSEY, John REICHE, S. CHAUDRON, William ROGERS, William HOOD, James WORRELL, William THACKARA, Joseph H. HOPKINS, Cephas THOMPSON, John GILPIN, Charles MARQUEDANT, Thomas L. PLOWMAN, Edward GRAY, William S. LENEY, Alexander ANDERSON, Anthony FANNEN, Robert WELLFORD, Abel BREWATER, Feilding LUCUS, Samuel B. WILEY, Thomas WATERMAN, David H. MASON, William MASON, I.L. KRIMMELL, James COX, George ORD, John L. ROBBINS, James EARLE, John LOWE, Thomas AMIES, Cornelius STEVENSON, Joseph WORRELL, John W. JARVIS, Joshua GILPIN, Ebenezer HILLYARD, Robert Carey LONG, Francis GUY, Mathew CAREY, Maxmillion GODFROY, Thomas BISHOP, Caleb LOWNES, William POTTS, Alphonso C. IRELAND, Edward DAVIS, Thomas MITCHELL, Alexander WILSON, David MEREDITH, Samuel ALEXANDER, Edward HUDSON, Joseph ANDRIE, John FRANZONIA, George HATFIELD, Reubens PEALE, John I. HOLLAND, Hugh REINAGLE, John DIXEY.

p. 77: Hannah DYER, Northampton Twp., Bucks Co., decd., in her will, bequeathed a parcel of land to Andrew BOZORTH, Sarah Dyer BOZORTH & Dr. Phineas JENKS.

p. 83: John SMITH, old soldier, is granted $40 & $40/yr.

p. 83: Amos Austin HUGHES, late of Buckingham Twp., Bucks Co., willed the trustees of the Hughesian Free School a plantation in Buckingham Twp., for the school. Trustees are: John ELY, Nicholas AUSTIN, John WATSON, Jr., William ELY, Thomas BYE, John WILSON, M.D., Samuel JOHNSON, Joseph SHAW, Isaiah JONES, Joshua ANDERSON, Joseph WATSON & Stephen WILSON.

p. 86: Ralph EWART & Archibald EWART are aliens & are enabled to convey a certain tract of land named "Mountjoy" adj. George REYNOLDS, James SEATON, Thomas WRIGHT, Paul DOWLAN, Robert WHITEHILL, Cumberland Twp., Greene Co., to George REYNOLDS.

p. 87: Joshua WILLIAMS, late a Captain in the 4th Pa. Regiment, in 1776, entered the service in the flying camp. In 1779, he rendered essential service to Gen. WAYNE. He is given $100.

p. 88: Commissioners to build a road from the Lewistown courthouse to Alexander REED's in the Kishacoquillas Valley: William P. MACCLAY, Andrew KISER, John ALEXANDER, Robert MEANS, William BROWN, Jr., James MELLIGAN, John MCDOWELL, Richard HOPE, James POTTER.

p. 91: Thomas BOWEN, St. Clair Twp., Bedford Co., is decd. exrs. are Thomas BLACKBURN, Jonathan BOWEN. Owners of land bordering his are Thomas PENROSE, Thomas GRIFFITH, Andrew ALLISON, John GRIFFITH. Abraham MOORE purchased some of BOWEN's land in St. Clair Twp.

p. 92: Trustees of the Beaver Academy, Beaver Co.: James ALLISON,

Jr., Robert MOORE, Samuel LAWRENCE, Samuel POWER, James LYON, James DENNIS, Jonathan COULTER, Joseph HEMPHILL, James ALEXANDER, Guion GREER, John LAWRENCE.

p. 94: Moses WADHAMS, Plymouth Twp., Luzerne Co., decd., had minor heirs: Phebe & Lydia WADHAMS. Ellen WRIGHT & Noah WADHAMS are their guardians. Freeman THOMAS shall convey land in the n-w corner of lot #52, in the 1st tier & 4th division lots in Plymouth Twp. to the guardians & will receive land in the s-w corner.

p. 97: Philip GLEIM, Dauphin Co., was a sergeant during the Rev. War. He is to receive $48 & $48/yr. Francis MILLER, decd., was a sergeant in the Pa. Line. His heirs are granted a 250 acre tract of donation land.

p. 99: Commissioners to make a road between Manheim & Richland, Lancaster Co.: David CASSEL, John ROHRER, George MYERS, Christian LIPE, Jacob ERISMAN, Henry STRICKLER, Christian METZ, Samuel ENSMINGER, Christian METZ, Jr., of Abraham.

p. 102: Delaware Academy Commissioners: John COOLBUAGH, George W. NICE, Dan DIMMICK. Trustees: John NICE, Daniel JAYNE, John WESTBROOK, John LATTIMORE, Matthew RIDGWAY. Commissioners of Beach-woods Academy, Wayne Co.: Samuel STANTEN, Abisha WOODWARD, Seth GOODRICH. Trustees of Beach-woods Academy: Silas KELLOG, Isaac DIMMICK, Joseph WOODBRIDGE, Jason TORREY.

p. 104: The estate of Thomas GALLAGHER, Mifflin Co., decd., paid a sum of money to the state treasurer in 1793. Lydia GALLAGHER is adminis.

p. 105: Matthew KNOX, Montgomery Co., is granted 2 tracts of donation land. He was formerly a lieutenant in the Rev. War.

p. 106: Land owners along the boundaries of Orwigsburg, Schuylkill Co.: Jacob ORWIG, Daniel STROHECKER, Philip HEY, George KIMMEL, John KELLY, Peter FRAILEY, George HILLEGAS, Adam LANTZER, Wendell SEIP.

p. 112: Joseph HOLLAR is reimbursed for repairing a bridge over the Raystown branch of the Juniata River.

p. 113: Rebecca FLEMING (late Rebecca OGLESBY) & James FLEMING had a son, James FLEMING, the younger, before their marriage. The child is declared legitimate.

p. 114: Gen. Henry TAYLOR, Washington Co., is decd. His daughter, Elizabeth, minor, has Andrew SWEARINGEN as her guardian. James MORTON & James LINN own adj. lands to the TAYLOR's, Strabane Twp.

p. 115: James SHIELDS, Indiana Co., an old soldier, is granted relief of $40 & $40/yr.

p. 115: Abraham WALKER obtained a patent for land on 8 Mar., 1811 in Belfast Twp., Bedford Co. He was not a citizen of the U.S. Isaac GRAY & Henry DAVIS owned adj. land. WALKER's patent is made valid.

p. 115: Timothy CURRENS, decd., E. Nottingham Twp., Chester Co. died intestate without issue or kindred. His widow is Elizabeth.
p. 116: Catharine WALDHAUR is adjudged a lunatic. The committee to

take care of her estate, including real estate in Allegheny Co., is Casper WALDHAUR & James IRWIN. Catharine lives in Westmoreland Co.

p. 117: A brick dwelling house & lot in Phila. is conveyed on 10 Sept., 1810 by Benjamin POWELL & wife to John WILLIAMS, Phila., a man of colour.

p. 118: Jacob WARNER, a Rev. War soldier, is granted a tract of donation land.

p. 121: Henry YOUNG, Washington Co., Md., is granted a tract of donation land & the treasurer is to pay him $40.

p. 123: Alexander MACK, the elder, willed 1/5 of his real estate in Germantown Twp. & Springfield Twp., Phila. & Montgomery Co., to Agness MACK. Agness lately died intestate, leaving 9 children. From the records of the Orphans' Court, Adams & Bedford Co., Alexander MACK, the elder, was appted. guardian of the 3 minor children aforesaid.

p. 124: Thomas FORSTER is auth. to convey a tract of land located in Mifflin Twp., Lycoming Co., to James MCCLURE. The contract is made with Samuel FIELDS & his wife, Lovina, late FORSTER. Children of Samuel & Lovina FIELDS: Dorcas FIELDS, Forster FIELDS, Sarah FIELDS, Samuel FIELDS, John FIELDS, Daniel FIELDS, Lovia FIELDS, Rachel FIELDS, Stephen FIELDS, William FIELDS, Freeborn FIELDS.

p. 126: Enoch MORGAN, late pay-master during the Rev. War, receives $80.

p. 127: James PURDY is granted $60 which will be paid to William CURRIN, Sr., Mifflin Co., for clothes, diet & other necessaries.

p. 127: Casper WIGHT died intestate. He had purchased a tract of land called "Rich Land," 312 acres, in Antis Twp., Huntingdon Co. His partner in the purchase was John BARLET. Thomas WILSON & Jacob WIGHT are adminis. of WIGHT.

p. 128: Commissioners to make a road from John GUTHRIE's on the Downingstown, Ephrata & Harrisburg Tpk., past George LIGGET's mill to Nathaniel LIGHTNER's, Lancaster Co.: James HAMILTON, Jacob C. ELLMAKER, Joseph DICKESON, Nathaniel F. LIGHTNER, Barton HENDERSON, Samuel MARTIN, all of Lancaster Co. & Alexander MAITLAND, Benjamin VASTINE, Bernard VANLIER, John UMSTEAD, James GREENE, Isaac REESE, Chester Co.

p. 131: James HOPKINS, Lancaster, & George FISHER, Harrisburg, are additional commissioners to make the road from Middletown to Harrisburg.

p. 133: Commissioners to make a road from Manchester to intersect the York, Conewago & Canal Tpk., between the 5th & 7th mile stones: George SMALL, Andrew CRAMER, Frederick NAGLE, James MEHAFFEY, Matthias RANK, Lewis LEADER, Abraham ZUBLIN, Henry CASSEL, Lancaster Co.

p. 154: Joseph FREEMAN, decd., Chester Co., owned a tract of land in Willistown Twp., Chester Co. He was not a U.S. native & may not have been naturalized. Jesse MARIS, Joshua ASHBRIDGE, Daniel SINQUEST owned land bordering FREEMAN's. Tacy FREEMAN was Joseph's wife. The land was willed to her.

p. 155: Samuel LUCAS, Indiana Co., & Samuel BURNS, Montgomery Co., soldiers of the Rev. War, are to receive $40.

p. 155: Margaret DUNCAN, widow of Robert DUNCAN, decd., Phila., has the right of his estate released to her. Peter WILLIS, Philip ROUSCULP, & Mathias DEIBLER own adj. land in Upper Paxton Twp., Dauphin Co.

p. 155: George MARSHALL, decd., Montgomery Co., left a will dated 5 Nov., 1798. Lewis RUSH was willed a tract of land in Roxborough Twp., Phila. Co., in trust for RUSH's children.

p. 157: Trustees of Franklin School, Greene Co.: William CRAWFORD, William SEALS, Andrew BUCHANAN, William T. HAYS, Robert ADAMS, Jacob BALTZEL, Asa MCCLELLAND, Nathaniel JENNINGS, Barnet REINHART, Jr.

p. 162: Trustees of the Athens Academy, Bradford Co.: Clement PAINE, George WELLES, John FRANKLIN, Julius TOZOR, Stephen HOPKINS, David PAINE, John SALTMARSH, John SHEPARD, Abner MURRAY.

P. 164: Thomas LITTLE, Franklin Twp., Fayette Co., a soldier in the Rev. War, is granted a tract of donation land.

p. 167: A warrant for land in Conamaugh Twp., adj. Thomas SMITH, James SMITH, Nathan DOWTHAT, John HENERY, is given to John HENERY, James SMITH & David HUTCHESON, Indiana Co., in trust for a school to be built on the land.

p. 167: John CARLILE, late of Lewistown, Mifflin Co., decd. had adminis. John CARLILE & George BRATTON. John CARLILE sold a house & ½ lot of ground to William CRISWELL. John CARLILE died intestate, leaving some minor children.

p. 170: Elizabeth MARTIN, Bucks Co., a lunatic, is in the care of a committee of John BROWN & Joseph BROWN who are auth. to sell her real estate.

p. 175: Jacob HASSINGER, decd., late of Beaver, now Centre Twp., Northumberland Co. His exr., Daniel HASSINGER, is auth. to make conveyances to trustees of the United Lutheran & Calvinist Church, called "Christian Church."

p. 178: Thomas VAUGHN, an old soldier, is granted 200 acres of donation land.

p. 178: William CAMPBELL served as quarter master to a detachment of volunteer militia that marched to the frontier of Pa. on an alarm that the Indians & British had in large numbers landed at Cleveland, immediately after the surrender of Gen. HULL.

p. 179: William WASON & Jemima WILKINSON were married 14 Feb., 1811. Last Nov., she was convicted on 2 indictments for larceny & is confined to gaol. The marriage is annulled.

p. 181: Trustees of the New Providence Congregation are auth. to convey a tract of land to Timothy SMITH, which was bequeathed to the congregation by the will of William HALE. The land is in Cumberland Twp., Greene Co., & is bounded by Samuel WRIGHT, Rev. Moses ALLEN, James FLENNIKEN. Trustees are: Elias FLENNIKEN, James FLENNIKEN, Samuel HARPER, Samuel HUSTON, Robert MORRISON, Andrew MCCLELLAND,

Jr.

p. 181: James BARNES, Wilkesbarre, is granted exclusive right of navigating the east branch of the Susquehanna by aid of fire or steam.

p. 182: Caleb JOHNSON is granted a loan for a furnace in Harrisburg to cast hinges & weights.

p. 182: William NOBLE, decd., was a sergeant in the Rev. War. His widow & children are granted donation lands of 200 acres. Robert HAMILTON, an old soldier in the Rev., is granted 200 acres of donation lands.

p. 183; Adam GREIGHER, decd., late of Allen Twp., has as adminis. of his estate, William BOOR & Lewis ZERING. They are auth. to convey land to Philip PIZEL which lies in Monaghan Twp., York Co. GREIGHER was from Cumberland Co.

p. 185: Thomas MEANS is to receive 200 acres of donation land which lies in N.Y. in lieu of a tract granted to him for services in the Rev. War.

p. 186: Charles CAMPBELL owned a mill on Blacklick Ck., Indiana Co. Blacklick Ck. is declared a public highway.

p. 187: Andrew FINLEY, a lieutenant in the Rev. War, is granted donation land.

p. 189: Thomas MCCREARY, Mercer Co., decd., gives his minor children a conveyance of land which is released to Samuel MCCREARY (half of lot #1895, in the 2nd district of donation lands) on which he now lives in Mercer Co.

p. 190: John JACOBS, a.k.a. John YOUGHY, decd., Washington Twp., Franklin Co., died intestate. JACOBS had purchased 222 acres from Christopher DULL which was adj. land of Frederick HOWARD & Ulrich FREIDLY. The land had been purchased from John JACOBS & his brother, David JACOBS. George COOK was the guardian of the minor children of John JACOBS.

p. 191: Dennis DALEY & John HARRIS, old soldiers of Lancaster Co., are given $40. HARRIS is given $40/yr. as well. John MCMURDY, Washington Co., an old soldier, is given $40 & $40/yr.

p. 192: John HUHN, decd., late of Springhill Twp., Fayette Co., made a will dated 20 Oct., 1803. Michael CROW is adminis.

p. 193; Michael MILLER, Guildford Twp., Franklin Co., married Catharines ROCK on 8 Nov., 1803. They had 3 children & on 8 July, 1811, she eloped with a married man. The marriage is annulled.

p. 194: John BLAIN, Venango Co., an old soldier, is given $40 & $40/yr. David RITCHEY, Washington Co., an old soldier, is given $40

p. 194: Samuel MASON, Phila., is enabled to execute a deed to sell a lot of ground for Elizabeth GILL, a lunatic.

p. 196: William P. DEWEES & Hardman PHILIPS are required to furnish a statement to the auditors of Centre Co., of the manner in which certain sums of money have been expended.

p. 296: James BRINGHURST, Phila., decd., on 13 Apr., 1807, under the direction of John CONNELLY, one of the auctioneers of Phila., sold a frame messuage & lot in Passyunk Twp., Phila. Co., on the road from Phila. to GRAY's ferry, TO Augustine BOSQUET, merchant, Phila., for $2025. John C. EVANS & Joseph BRINGHURST, Wilmington, Del., are acting exrs. of his will. George MORTON owns land bordering BRINGHURST's.

p. 198: Henry ZERFAS, Armstrong Co., is granted $80.

p. 198: Trustees of the Orwigsburg Academy, Schuylkill Co.: Daniel GRAEFF, William GREEN, Jr., James MCFARLAND, Jacob KREBS, Barnet KEPNER, Jeremiah REED, Abraham REIFFSNYDER, Philip HEY.

p. 201: Samuel WRIGHT, Columbia, Lancaster Co., decd., has as adminis. James WRIGHT & James WRIGHT, Jr.

p. 202: James BONES occupies a house at Yellow Springs, Pikeland Twp., Chester Co.

p. 203: Samuel WINPENNY, an alien, purchased real estate formerly of John THOBURN, Blockley Twp. (Schuylkill Falls), Phila. Co.

p. 204: John MYERS, Lycoming Co., is given the right to establish a ferry across the west branch of the Susquehanna River.

p. 206: Jared INGERSOLL is compensated for his report on the penal code. John COCHRAN is secretary of the land office.

p. 208: The following owned land bordering Reading, Berks Co.: Adam WITMAN, decd., Philip SAYLOR, Jonathan POTTS, decd., Michael BRIGHT, Isaac LEVAN, Michael CROWSE.

p. 216: George SMITH, Bedford Co., & Bartholomew MELOY, Washington Co., old soldiers, are granted $40 & $40/yr.

p. 219: The Commonwealth sells land to Ebenezer SLOCUM & Benjamin SLOCUM in Luzerne Co., one lot in the name of George FULLERTON & one in the name of Andrew CALDWELL. They were the property of John NICHOLSON, decd.

p. 220: Commissioners to make a road from Millerstown by Daniel SPRENKLE's to the Franklin Co. line: Samuel WITHEROW, James WILSON, William MCMILLEN, James MCKESSON, William MONEY, Robert CROOKS.

p. 224: Centre Twp., Indiana Co., will vote at Michael MCANULTY's. Warwick Twp., Lancaster Co., will vote at Christian HALL's, Litiz near Martin GROSS', Abraham REIST, Sr.'s, Samuel HERSHEY's, Sebastian HOFFMAN, Jacob WOLF, David WISSLER, Christian HURSLY, BRICKER's tavern, Jacob BENDER's smith shop. Drumore Twp., Lancaster Co., will vote at Philip HOUSEKEEPER's. Montgomery & Guwyned Twp., Montgomery Co., will vote at George HEIST's, innkeeper, Guwyned Twp. Moorland Twp., Montgomery Co., will vote at Joseph KERR's, innkeeper. Dauphin Co.'s 13th election district is annexed to the 2nd district now in Lebanon Co. & will vote at Thomas HARPER's. The 14th district will vote at Peter ZATTERZAHM's. The 5th district will vote at George STINE's., Jonestown, Lebanon Co. Sadsbury Twp., Lancaster Co., will vote at Josiah Kennedy IRWIN's. French Ck. Twp., Mercer Co., will vote at William REED's. St. Tammany district, Damascus Twp., Wayne Co., will vote at William

TYLOR's. Salem Twp., Wayne Co., south of the road leading from John ANSLEY's to Wilkesbarre (election district to be called Newfoundland district) will vote at John CLEMENT's. Howard Twp., Centre Co., will vote at Frederick SHANK's. Walker Twp., Centre Co., will vote at Thomas WILSON's. Chinclecamoose Twp., Clearfield Co., near John CANNON's, James HUNTER's, George MEADE's surveys, will vote at Andrew OVERDORF's, at the forks of the Sinnemahoning. Rostravor Twp., Westmoreland Co., voted formerly at Samuel WILSON's & now at Richard STEEL's. Upper Makefield Twp., Bucks Co., will vote at William M'MASTER's. Decatur Twp., Mifflin Co., will vote at William STUMPS's. W. Bethlehem, Washington Co., will vote at John CONKLE's. Greenville Twp., Somerset Co., will vote at Peter DEAL's. Allen Twp., Cumberland Co., will vote at Maj. John SNYDER's. Moore Twp., Northampton Co., will vote at John MICHAIL's. Chestnut-hill Twp., Northampton Co., will vote at George WOODS'. Shanango Twp., Beaver Co., will vote at James KELLEY's. Green Twp., Beaver Co., will vote at James PRESTON's. Hempfield Manor, Rapho Twp., Lancaster Co., near ANDERSON's ferry, Christian RIGGLE's spring, Christian HERR's mill, John ESHELMAN's blacksmith shop & Philip SOWER's, will vote at the school house in Columbia. Connamaugh Twp., Cambria Co., will vote at George WEIMOR's, Johns town. Rush & Schuylkill Twp., Schuylkill Co., will vote at James BLEW's, Schuylkill Twp. The 3rd election district, Union Co., will vote at Andrew REEDY's, Buffalo Twp. Briar Ck., Columbia Co., will vote at William RITTENHOUSE's. The 5th election district, Huntingdon Co., will vote at William M'JIMSEY's, innkeeper, Williamsburgh. Providence Twp., Luzerne Co., will vote at Stephen TRIPP's. Nescopeck Twp., Luzerne Co., will vote at George KEEN's. Braintrim Twp., Luzerne Co., will vote at Joseph BURGESS'. Bridgewater & Russ Twp., Susquehanna Twp., will vote at Levi SMITH's. Middletown Twp., Bucks Co., will vote at David CARPENTER's tavern, Attleborough. Allegheny Twp., Armstrong Co., will vote at Eliab EAKMAN's. Washington & White Deer Twp., Union Co. near Matthew LAIRD's platation, William BOAL's, will vote at Dan CALDWELL's, White Deer Twp. Salem Twp., Luzerne Co., will vote at James CAMPBELL's. Hanover Twp., Luzerne Co., will vote at Frederick CRISMAN's, innkeeper. Milford Twp., Mifflin Co., will vote at Benjamin KEPNER's. The 2nd election district, Butler co., will vote at Guy HILLIARD's.

p. 231: The governor is auth. to purchase from William DUANE 2000 copies of the Hand Book for Infantry & 100 copies of the Hand Book for Riflemen for $2363.

p. 234: James CRAWFORD, Lycoming Co., a major of the late 12th Pa. Regiment, is given $60 & $40/yr.

p. 235: Tobias KRIDER & Martin MELLINGER, a committee of Henry MUSSER, Lancaster Co., who was found to be insane, are auth. to sell a messuage & lot held in common with John MILLER which is situated in Marietta Borough.

p. 237: Swatara Ck. from John WEIDMAN's forge dam, Dauphin Co., to Good Spring Ck., Schuylkill Co., is declared a public highway.

p. 237: Casper TARR, Westmoreland co., is to receive $40 for the use of George BAUMGARTNER, Westmoreland co., & $40 is given to John DOWNS, Huntingdon Co. Robert LYON, Northumberland Co., is given $40/yr. James SWEENY is to receive a tract of donation land (500 acres) in trust for the heirs of Isaac SWEENY, late a captain in the Rev. War.

p. 238: Louisa ROBB late Louisa ST. CLAIR, in 1796, married Samuel

ROBB, Westmoreland Co. Two years ago, ROBB abandoned her with 6 small children & left them destitute. The marriage is annulled.

p. 239: John HALDEMAN, Henry SHARE, Henry SLAYMAKER, Adam REIGART, Jr., Abraham WITMER, Jacob GROSH, John GREER, John SWAR, John PEDAN, James MAHAFFY, James WRIGHT, Sr., Samuel MILLER, James DUFFY, Samuel WHITE, Samuel CLENDENIN are commissioners to open a lock navigation & canal on the eastern side of the Susquehanna opposite Conewago Falls.

p. 245: Daniel WELKER, Franklin Co., an old soldier, is to receive $40 & $40/yr.

p. 246: Joseph WORRELL, George BARTRAM, Matthew WEAVER, Isaac HERBERT, Thomas T. STILES are commissioners to raise $8000 for the use of the African Episcopal Church of St. Thomas, Phila.

p. 247: A patent for donation land (200 acres) is given to the heirs of John KNAPSNYDER, decd., late a soldier in the Pa. line.

p. 248: Robert GILMORE, Mercer Co., attorney for the heirs of John SMITH, an old soldier, receives $65 for arrearages of pay.

p. 263: Charles READHEFER, Phila. Co., has invented a machine declared to have the power of self-motion. Henry VOIGHT, Robert PATTERSON, Nathan SELLERS, Oliver EVANS, Archibald BINNY, Lewis WERMWAG, Josiah WHITE, Phila. Co., Samuel D. INGHAM, Bucks Co., are requested to make a strict examination of the machine respecting it's alleged importance.

p. 264: Thanks is given to Commodore Stephen DECATUR of the frigate United States & Lt. James BIDDLE of the ship Wasp for gallantry & skill in their late engagements & a sword not to exceed $400.
1813-1814
p. 2: Arthur ST. CLAIR, late a major general in the U.S. Army, is placed on the pension book & given an annuity.

p. 4: Eliston PERROT, Paul BECK, William SANSOM, Jacob DOWNING, William DAVIDSON, James TAYLOR, Phila.; Edward BRIEN, John NEFF, Nathaniel W. SAMPLE, Rudolph KEGEY, Lancaster Co.; Gen. Charles RIDGELEY, Hampton; Benjamin ELLICOTT, James CARROLL, Luke TIERNAN, Henry PAYSAN, William WILSON, John M'KIM, Jr., Robert MILLER, James CAREY, Charles JESSOP, Baltimore, MD, are commissioners to make a road from the Phila. & Lancaster Co. Tpk. to the Susquehanna bridge at M'CALL's ferry & then to Baltimore.

p. 16: Samuel WETHERILL, Jr., Levi PAWLING, Isaac MARKLEY, John SHANNON, Norriton; Joseph CRAWFORD, John FRANCIS , Henry HIGHLY are commissioners to make a road from the intersection of Eqypt Rd. with Ridge Tpk. 2 miles above Norristown, Montgomery Co. & then to PAWLING's ford bridge over the Schuylkill River.

p. 21: John BROADHEAD, Matthew RIDGWAY, George BUCKANNEN, John CROSS, John B. QUECK, Jacob WESTBROOK, Mathias KEEN, Garrit VANAUKER, Francis A. L. SMITH are commissioners to make a road from Milford & Owego Tpk. to CARPENTER's ferry on the Delaware River.

p. 23: Robert DARRAH, David HAYS, Thomas HENRY, Jonathan MENDINHALL are commissioners to erect a toll bridge over Big Beaver Ck. near Wolf Lane, Beaver Co.
p. 25: John HALDEMAN, Jacob STRICKLER, Daniel MUSSER, Samuel

MILLER, Abraham REIMER, Henry CASSEL, Christian SHIRK, John GREINDER, merchant, are commissioners to make a road from Lancaster & Susquehanna road near the river shore in Columbia to Bridge St., Marietta.

p. 29: Caleb HOOPES' title to a messuage & tract in Thornbury Twp., Delaware Co., which was purchased in Jan., 1812 from Joseph MOORE, an alien, through his agent, James GIBBONS, is confirmed.

p. 33: Charles CAMPBELL has the exclusive right to use a salt spring he recently discovered in Conemaugh River, Black-lick Twp., Indiana Co.

p. 35: Isaac W. NORRIS, adminis. with the will annexed of Joseph SUMMERL, late of Phila., merchant, is auth. to sell his real estate.

p. 36: Henry CASSEL, James MEHAFFEY, George SNYDER, Mathias RANK, Thomas R. BUCHANNON, Christian KEESEY, John HOUTZ, Christian HERTZLER, Andrew BOGGS, John GUNDACKER, Samuel GROSH, David CASSEL, Jacob ROHRER, Henry SHARE, Lancaster Co.; John MILLER, George SPANGLER (surveyor), George UPP, York Co. are commissioners to erect a bridge over the Susquehanna River near Marietta, Lancaster Co.

p. 49: John WALTZ, late of Bucks Co., died intestate without issue or known kindred & owned real & personal estate. John & Magdalena EASTERLINE were children of the late wife of John WALTZ by a subsequent marriage. The right to a lot in Springfield Twp., Bucks Co., adj. Conrad HESS, Joseph HESS, Samuel TREIGLER is released to the EASTERLINES & the right of Pa. to personal estate of WALTZ in the hands of George RODROCK & Valentine OPP, adminis. of WALTZ, is released to the EASTERLINES.

p. 50: Henry WALKER, Schuylkill Co., an old soldier, is given $40 & $40/yr.

p. 51: Francis MILLER was late a sergeant in the Pa. Line. His heirs are issued a patent for 250 acres for lot #4 in Beaver Co., 1st donation district. MILLER left 2 female twin children: Isabella, wife of John ROGERS, & Nancy, wife of William LAWSON. The children were born a short time before the marriage of their parents & they are legally disqualified from succeeding to the land. Now, they are declared entitled to the estate.

p. 53: A road leading from Harrisburg to Pittsburg shall pass from John BLAIR's, east side of Allegheny Mt., to Martin REIGART's on the west side of Laurel Hill. George ANSHUITZ, C. COWEN, Thomas CROMWELL, Allegheny Co.; Daniel SMITH, Indiana Co., are commissioners to receive subscriptions to the stock of the road co.

p. 54: Christian BOWMAN, Jacob GORGAS, Abel WITMER, Samuel FAHNESTOCK, Jacob KIMMEL, Jr., Obed FAHNESTOCK, Jacob KOENIGMACHER are trustees of the German Religious Society of Seventh Day Baptists of Ephrata, Cocalico Twp., Lancaster Co.

p. 55: John A. KELP, Jonathan KELP, Catharine KELP, Christian LUTHER are now residing on the premises of the above society.

p. 59: Thomas SMITH, Dauphin Co., & Levi G. HOLLINGSWORTH, Lebanon Co., & Jacob HIBSHMAN, Lancaster Co., are commissioners to run the boundary lines between the 3 counties.

p. 64: John LOYER, late of Unity Twp., Westmoreland Co., decd., died intestate without heirs or known kindred. John left a widow, Anna Maria. A small tract was sold to LOYER on 17 Apr., 1809 by John BOSSERT & wife, Elizabeth, in Unity Twp., Westmoreland Co. containing 27½ acres. It is released to Anna Maria LOYER as well as any personal estate in the hands of Jacob POORMAN, adminis.

p. 67: Road from Susquehanna River through lands of Henry CASSEL & John CROW to Henry SHARE's new buildings at the intersection of Marietta, Richland & Mountjoy Tpk. William CHILD is to turn over all money received from lot owners in the east end of Marietta.

p. 70: William CLYMER, Jonathan HUDSON, David MORGAN, Berks Co.; Christian MAST, George JENKINS, John ZELL, Martin RINGWALD, Joseph WEAVER, Richard JACOBS, George WEAVER, Lancaster Co., are commissioners to make a road from the end of Little Conestoga Tpk. Rd., Berks Co. to the Blueball Tavern, Lancaster Co.

p. 83: Jabez BAILEY, late of Chester Co., died by casualty, intestate, unmarried, without issue, owning a messuage & land in E. Marlborough Twp. He was the reputed & acknowledged son of Isaac BAILEY, Newlin Twp., Chester Co., but was born before the parent's marriage. Jabez BAILEY is declared legitimate. Isaac released his claim to part of the estate of which his father died intestate & which had been bequeathed to Samuel BAILEY, his brother.

p. 84: Adam BRANDT, the elder, & Martin BRANDT, the younger, are adminis. of David BRANDT, late of Allen Twp., Cumberland Co., decd. James CORBET sold land in Allen Twp., Cumberland Co., to the decd. The land was adj. Michael EGE & Martin BRANDT.

p. 86: Robert HARRIS, Jacob BUCHER, Benjamin KURTZ, Dauphin Co.; John BOWMAN, John CAROTHERS, Matthew ERWIN, Andrew BODEN, George FAHNESTOCK, James WOODBERN, John SIMPSON, William KILGORE, George HAMMIL, Alexander STEWART, John WEAKLY, John WOODBERN, Cumberland Co.; William RIPPEY, John CULBERTSON, John STUMP, Jacob SNYDER, Jacob HEISSER, Franklin Co., for the Harrisburg, Carlisle & Chambersburg Tpk. Rd., Andrew DUNLOP, John HOLLIDAY, Jacob BRINDLE, Thomas M'DOWELL, Conrad STINGER, Franklin Co.; John ANDERSON, Jacob BONNET, Andrew WORK, Anthony SHOEMAKER, Bedford Co., for the Chambersburg & Bedford Tpk. Rd. Co., William PROCTOR, John SCHELL, Jr., George ROCK, Bedford Co.; John TANTLINGER, Alexander OGLE, Henry FISHER, Somerset Co.; Joseph HUSTON, Jacob BOWMAN, Isaac MEASON, Jr., Fayette Co.; Neil GILLESPIE, Jr., Zephaniah BEALL, Thomas ATCHESON, Washington Co. for the Bedford & Somerset Tpk. Rd. Co., Jacob ANKENNY, John DENNISON, John FLETCHER, Somerset Co.; William JACK, Sr., Arthur CARR, Peter GAY, John GROVE, Hugh MARTIN, John WHITE, James HURST, Alexander JOHNSTON, Westmoreland Co.; Samuel TREVOR, John LYON, Richard WEAVER, Fayette Co., for the Somerset & Greensburg Tpk. Rd. Co., Simon DRUM, Jr., William FRIEDT, Robert STEWART, Jeremiah MURRAY, Westmoreland Co.; William M'CANDLESS, Philip GILLAND, John DARRAH, James MORRISON, George STEWART, Allegheny Co.; David BRUCE, Robert BOULAND, Jr., Washington Co., for the Greensburg & Pittsburg Tpk. Rd. Co., are commissioners to make a road from Susquehanna River opposite Harrisburg to Pittsburg.

p. 91: Joshua DAVIS is late a Justice of the Peace in E. Penn Twp., Northampton Co.

p. 91: Joseph HORNER bought from Andrew ALLEN, 182 acres, 67 perches in Allen Twp., Northampton Co., in 1776. It was confiscated by the Commonwealth for it's use. HORNER was, in Oct., 1809, evicted from the premises by a title paramount in a certain Margaret DE LANCY of Great Britain. HORNER is paid $354.88 as compensation.

p. 92: On 1 May, 1776, John LATIMORE bought from Andrew ALLEN 159 acres, 60 perches in Allen Twp., Northampton Co., 96 3/4 acres of which has since been vested in John STENGOR, from which he was evicted by title paramount in Oct., 1809, in Margaret DE LANCY, Great Britain. STENGOR is paid $151.60 as compensation.

p. 93: On 1 May, 1776, John LATIMORE bought 159 acres, 60 perches from Andrew ALLEN in Allen Twp., Northampton Co., of which 66 acres, 2 perches has since been vested in John FOGLE, from which he was evicted by title paramount in Oct., 1809 in Margaret DE LANCY, Great Britain. FOGLE is compensated $113.45.

p. 94: Michael KAPP, Jr., Harrisburg, has been in the habit of ill treating his wife, Catharine, & has neglected to provide for her support & has given himself up to an irregular & immoral life. The marriage is annulled.

p. 94: A new loan certificate #14865 is issued to James ARMSTRONG for £11 19s 5p. It shall be paid to Robert JAMISON, surviving exr. of ARMSTRONG, for the use of his heirs.

p. 99: Samuel POWERS was appted. by the volunteers who marched in Aug., 1812, from Beavertown for the defence of the frontiers of Ohio.

p. 104: The interest of Pa. by escheat arising due to the death of Timothy REED, late of George's Twp., Fayette Co., to land adj. James DOWNARD, William VANCE, James FOUTZ, is released to Rebecca REED, widow.

p. 105: The interest of Pa. by escheat arising due to the death of John PATTON, late of Phila., to land on the west side of the Delaware 10th St., Phila., is released to Melshey PATTON, widow.

p. 108: William LEET, John WOLF, Sr., Beaver Co.; James DENNIS, Beaver borough, are auth. to lay out in lots of land at the mouth of Big Beaver Ck.

p. 110: Henry LUTZ, Michael LANGENBACK, & George GIEGHY, old soldiers, Northampton Co., are given $40.

p. 111: The following soldiers are given money: Thomas BUTTS, Cumberland Co., $40 & $40/yr; William RUSSEL, Beaver Co., $40; Henry BRENEMAN, Westmoreland Co., $100; John GILBERT, Westmoreland Co., $100.

p. 111: The road from John CAMPBELL's bridge, Huntingdon Co., by Sinkey's Gap, is to be reviewed.

p. 112: Martha ROSE, late Martha TAYLOR, married in 1797 to John ROSE. In Feb., 1812, ROSE, Somerset, Somerset Co., was convicted of horse stealing & sentenced to serve 5 years in the Penitentiary, Phila. The marriage is divorced.

p. 113; Simon GRATZ & Joseph REED, Phila., are commissioners for making a road from Waterford, Erie Co., to the Susquehanna River near the mouth of ANDERSON's Ck., Clearfield Co.

p. 114: James O'HARA, old soldier, now or late of Phila., is given $40 & $40/yr.

p. 114: Jonathan JONES, Benjamin BROOKS, John ELLIOTT, Upper Merion; Matthew ROBERTS, Jacob VOGDES, John HUGHES, Montgomery Co.; Isaac ANDERSON, Chester Co. are commissioners to make a road from Valley Forge, Montgomery Co. to John ELLIOTT's sign of the King of Prussia, to Thomas LOWRY's sign of the Bird in Hand to intersect the Phila. & Lancaster Tpk. Rd.

p. 117: Elizabeth HARKINS, Butler Co., widow of Robert HARKINS, decd., who lately died at Buffalo, whilst in the service of his country, will receive $100.

p. 121: Caleb KIRK, Isaac KIRK, Henry IRWIN, Jacob SPANGLER, Cornelius GARRETSON, John MYER, John MOSSER, Benjamin KURTZ, Jacob M. HALDEMAN, Jacob BOAS, John SHOCH, Andrew CREMER, Jesse WICKERSHAM, Peter A. KARTHOUSE, Robert BARRY, John FRICK, Joseph DONALDSON are commissioners to make a tpk. from Harrisburg bridge to the head of York & Conewago Canal Tpk.

p. 129: Trustees of the Allentown Academy, Northampton borough, Lehigh Co.: Peter RHOADS, John HORN, John MILLER, TAYLOR, James WILSON, George RECK, Adam REEP, Jacob MARTIN.

p. 132: John SHOCH, Harrisburg; David BRENIZER, Jacob MERKLE, Christian MOHLER, William HARKNESS, Jr., John BEELMAN, John MUSSELMAN, William BRYSON, Cumberland Co.; Frederick EICHELBERGER, John HURST, Abraham KINSLEY, Thomas WILSON, Thomas BLACK, Emanuel SMITH, York Co.; Jacob HARBAUGH, Valentine HOLLINGAR, Adams Co., are commissioners to make a road from Harrisburg to EICHELBURGER's tavern to Berlin, Adams Co. near Michael GEYSELMAN's mill.

p. 135: John SHOCH, John FORSTER, Robert HARRIS, Andrew DERSHEIMER, Michael DREHL, Daniel STINE, Henry BEADER, Jacob BOAS, Jacob BUCHER, Obed FAHNESTOCK, Abraham OVES, John BIGLER are commissioners to make a canal & lock navigation on the Susquehanna River near Harrisburg between John CARSON's & Archibald M'ALLISTER's.

p. 145: Henry M'EWEN, an old soldier, is to receive $40 & $40/yr. which will be paid to Francis M'EWEN, Centre Co., for his use. John ROSENSTELLE, an old soldier, Westmoreland Co., will be paid $50.

p. 146: Bellefonte & Smithfield, Centre Co., are erected near John M'KEE's field & Benjamin WILLIAMS' lots.

p. 151: John ROBISON, Fayette Co., an old soldier, will receive $134.81. Alexander M'CURDY, an old soldier, will receive $40.

p. 156: Commissioners of banks: Thomas PARKER, Joseph BURDEN, Ephraim CLARK, Robert MERCER, William THACKARA, Jr., Joseph MORRIS (C.) for the Mechanics' Bank of Phila. Andrew BAYARD, William NEWBOLD, Edward CARRELL, Charles PLEASANTS, Henry LENTZ for the Commercial Bank of Pa. Simon GRATZ, Richard BACHE, John HORNOR, Thomas M. SOUDER, Paul BECK, Jr. for the Schuylkill Bank, Phila. Daniel GROVES, John THOMPSON, (S.), Joseph GRICE, John NAGLEE, Michael BAKER, Joseph R. JENKS, Jesse SHELMIRE, John TAYLOR, George GORGAS, Frederick FOERING, Daniel BUSSIER for the Bank of Northern Liberties. Samuel HARVEY, William FISHER, John CONARD, Jacob HOLGATE, Joseph STARNE, Michael RITER for the Bank of Germantown.

Jonas PRESTON, Abraham SHARPLESS, Preston EYRE, Joseph GIBBONS, John WILCOX for the Bank of Delaware Co. Dr. William DARLINGTON, John W. CUNNINGHAM, Jesse JOHN, James KELTON, Joseph TAYLOR, Henry CHRISMAN, Matthew STANLEY, Esq., Joshua EVANS, Jr. for the Bank of Chester Co. John HAHN, John HEISTER, Daniel DEWEES, John WEBER, Stephen PORTER, John WENTZ, Samuel LEECH, Jr. for the Bank of Montgomery Co. Conrad SWARTZ, John SWAR, Banjamin SCHAUM, Samuel CARPENTER, John MICHAEL & John GUNDACKER for the Farmer's Bank of Lancaster. Robert COLEMAN, James WHITEHILL, James HUMES, Cyrus JACOBS, William KIRKPATRICK, Leonard EICHOLTZ, Christian HUBER, Christopher B. MAYER, John HUBLEY, Nathaniel WATSON, Samuel BETHEL, Charles SMITH, Jacob HIBSHMAN, Edward BRIEN, Christian CARPENTER, Isaac ELLMAKER, Adam REIGART of the Union Bank of Lancaster. Henry SHARE, Jacob ROHRER, George SNYDER, Jacob HOUTZ, Henry BEAR, Daniel CASSEL, John PEDAN, James PATTERSON, Jr., James MEHAFFY, Alexander BOGGS, Jacob GISH, Matthias RANK, Christian STEHMAN for the Marietta & Susquehanna Trading Co. John HALDEMAN, Christian BRENNEMAN, Samuel MILLER, Thomas BOUDE, John B. HALDEMAN, Jacob STRICKLER, Benjamin KAUFMAN for the Columbia Bank of Pa. Casper SHAFFNER, jr., Abraham WITMER, Henry REIGART, Jacob LONG, William HAMILTON, Joel LIGHTNER, Jr., Dr. Abraham CARPENTER, Jacob DUCHMAN, Isaac HINEY, Jacob KAUFMAN, Henry SLAYMAKER, Andrew BOGGS, Matthias TSCHUDY for the Lancaster Trading Co. John FORSTER, Jacob BOAS, William WALLACE, John DOWNEY, Thomas BROWN, John M'CLEERY, Daniel FERREE, Joseph CLOKEY, Isaac HERSHEY, Abraham BRANDT, John LANDIS, Spring Ck; John FOX, Jr. for the Harrisburg Bank. Thomas R. BUCHANAN, George BOWER, Isaac W. VANLEAR, Henry BERRY, George FISHER, John SHELLY, James WILSON, Jacob HERSHEY, James HAMILTON, Christian SPAYD, Elisha GREEN, Ephraim HELLER, William LOWMAN for the Bank of Swatara. Peter GLONINGER, Peter LEINAWEBER, John HAUTZ, Christian SELTZER, Jr., John WOLFERSBERGER, John SHERTZER, Samuel REX, John BADORF, Samuel LIGHT, John HARRISON, Edward GODWIN, Charles GLEIM for the Bank of Lebanon. John BARNITZ, Henry IRWIN, Jacob SPANGLER, Daniel HECKERT, David CASSAT, Jacob KLINE, Charles EMIG, Robert GEMMIL, Michael HELMAN, Isaac KIRK, Frederick EICHELBERGER, Jr., Matthew CLARK, Sr., Adam HENDRIX for the York Bank. James DUNCAN, Solomon GORGAS, Joseph KNOX, Joseph SHROM, James WOODBURN, Dr. John SIMPSON, William ANDERSON, Thomas DUNCAN, David WATTS for the Carlisle Bank. Richard O'BRIEN, Jacob HENDLE, Jacob ALTER, James STEWARD, James LAMBERTON, John GOOSEWEILER, David MORELAND, George M'GINNIS, David NEVIN, Robert PORTER, John HEAP, Charistian GEESE, Robert CLARK, George STROOP, John WALLACE, John EWALT for the Pa. Agriculture & Manufacturing Bank. Patrick CAMPBELL of Peters, George CHAMBERS, John COX, Andrew ROBINSON, John NEVIN, John HOLLIDAY, for the Chambersburg Bank. William ALLISON, Daniel MILLER, Archibald RANKIN, Joseph SNIVELY, Matthew LIND, John M'LENAHAN, Jr., William BLAKENEY, Samuel M'EWEN for the Farmers' & Mechanics' Bank of Greencastle. Alexander COBEAN, James GETTYS, Walter SMITH, Realph LASHELLS, Jacob EYSTER, Bernhart GILBERT, William MAXWELL, Esq., Michael NEWMAN, Robert HAYES, Esq., Dr. James H. MILLER, George SCHMISER for the Bank of Gettysburg. John HOUPT, William LONG of Durham, Abraham CHAPMAN, Lewis CORYELL, Enos MORRIS, Anthony TAYLOR, Josiah Y. SHAW, Abraham JACOBY, John KEETH, John FOX, Samuel SELLERS, Dr. Samuel MOOR, Hugh ELY, John HULME & George HARRISON for the Farmers' Bank of Bucks Co. Christian BIXLER, William LATTIMORE, Conrad KRIDER, Jr., James HOLLINGSHEAD, Matthias GRESS, James CLYDE, John DAVISON, Abraham LEVAN, Abraham HORN, Jr., George BEIDLEMAN of Easton; George BUTZ, Northampton Co.; John COOLBAUGH, John BRODHEAD, Daniel DIMMICK, Wayne Co. for the Easton Bank. Jacob MARTIN, John KEPER, George BREINIG, Peter RUCH, Joseph FRY, Jr., Peter DORNEY, saddler, Ferdinand FOLWEILER, John FOGLE, Jr., Peter RUMBLE, Joseph

SEAGER, for the Northampton Bank. John SPAYD, David KERPER, Peter NAGLE, Jr., Conrad STOUGH, Gabriel HEISTER, Jr., Frederick SMITH, Jacob K. BOYER, Samuel D. FRANKS, Abraham MENGLE, Samuel ELY, Peter KNAB, John MILLER, Jacob KREBS, James M'FARLAND, Jacob LEVAN for the Farmer's Bank of Reading. Thomas LOGAN, James AGNEW, David FORE, Joseph SHANNON, John RINE, John ANDERSON, William PROCTOR, Jr., Peter SCHELL, Alexander OGLE, James CARSON, Robert PHILSON, John FLETCHER, George GRAHAM, Isaac PROCTOR, James MELOY for the Allegheny Bank of Pa. Elias W. HALE, John M'DOWELL, Joseph KYLE, Jr., David REYNOLDS, John BROWN, Joseph B. ARD, William ARMSTRONG, John PATTERSON, Ezra DOTY, James KNOX, James BANKS, for the Juniata Bank of Pa. William ORBISON, Samuel STEEL, William R. SMITH, Thomas H. STEWART, Robert PROVINCE, Jacob ISATT, Abraham VANTRICE for the Huntingdon Bank. Andrew GREGG, James DUNCAN, Roland CURTIN, James HARRIS, John G. LOWREY, Samuel STEWART, John HAYS, John TURK, George WEBB for the Centre Bank of Pa. Daniel MONTGOMERY, John P. DE GRUCHY, James SANDERSON, John BOYD, Daniel LEBO, Jacob DENTLER, John DREISBACH, Matthew CALVIN, John COWDEN, Bethuel VINCENT of the Northumberland, Union & Columbia Bank. George DENNISON, George M. HALLENBACH, Abiel FELLOWS, Cyrus AVERY, Noah WADHAMS, Luzerne Co. for the Susquehanna Bank. Benjamin LATHROP, Daniel ROSS, Susquehanna Co.; Reuben HALE, George SCOTT, Bradford Co.; Samuel STAUNTON, Abisha WOODWARD, Wayne Co. for the Silver Lake Bank. Thomas BAIRD, Alexander MURDOCH, David CRAIG, John WATSON, Eleazer JENKINS, John CLEMENS, Isaac MAYES, James GORDON, Robert BOWLAND, Jr. for the Bank of Washington. John KENNEDY, Joseph HUSTON, Ellis BAILEY, Robert LONG, Jacob BEESON, Jr., Samuel TREVOR, Isaac MASON, Jr., Fayette Co.; Samuel HUSTON, Robert WHITEHILL, Greene Co. for the Union Bank of Pa. Jacob BOWMAN, Israel GREGG, Israel MILLER, John M'CADDEN, Samuel COOPE, Fayette Co., Rees HILL & Samuel HARPER, Greene Co. for the Monongahela Bank of Brownsville. John M. SNOWDEN, Daniel S. SCHULLY, John SPEAR, Thomas CROMWELL, George DAWSON, James MARTIN, Joseph WILSON, Robert HILANDS, Allegheny Co.; Guion GREER, Joseph HEMPHILL, Thomas HENRY, Beaver Co.; Samuel WILLIAMSON, John GILMORE, Jacob MECHLIN, Butler Co. for the Bank of Pittsburg. Jacob NEGLEY, John NEAL, George EVANS, John FERRIS, Thomas HAZLETON, George STEWARD, George ROBINSON, Allegheny Co.; Matthew B. LOWRIE, William CAMPBELL, Robert LEMAN, Butler Co.; for the Farmers' & Mechanics' Bank of Pittsburg. Jeremiah BARKER, James COCHRAN, John CHRISTMAN, Evan PUGH, Jarvis ALLISON, James LONG, Aaron MENDENHALL, Robert MOORE, William CLARK for the Bank of Beaver. Rufus S. REED, Amos JUDSON, Thomas FORSTER, Thomas KING, Erie Co.; Thomas ATKINSON, Henry HURST, John BROOKS, Samuel TORBETT, Crawford Co.; Ebenezer MAGOFFIN, William M'MILLAN, James CLARK, Jonathan SMITH, Mercer Co.; George M'CLELLAND, John M'DONALD, William MOORE, Venango Co.; John ANDREWS, Warren Co. for the North Western Bank of Pa. John B. ALEXANDER, John REID, Thomas M'GUIRE, John LOBINGUIER, Clements BURLEIGH, John GAMBLE, Joseph MARKLE, Thomas POLLOCK, James CLARK, Samuel M. REED, Nicholas DAY, Westmoreland Co.; James M'KNIGHT, John DENNISTON, James M. KELLY, Indiana-town; Thomas LUCAS, Jefferson Co.; Thomas HAMILTON, Robert BROWN, Robert ROBINSON, Sr., Kittanning for the Westmoreland Bank of Pa.

p. 176: Land in Redbank Twp., Armstrong Co., is bounded by land of John SLOAN, George LATIMORE, Joseph REID, John REID, Robert WILSON.

p. 177: John BAILY, John TEMPLIN, Samuel SHAFER, John MERIDITH, Samuel TOWNSEND, William SHULER, John REINHART, Enoch WALKER, John MORGAN, Henry CHRISTMAN, Jr., Lewis WARMWAG, David POTTS, Thomas BAIRD are commissioners to make a road from PAWLING's ford bridge to the Little Conestogoe road near Samuel JACOB's tavern, Berks Co.

p. 181: Robert WALLACE, John NAGLEE (lumber merchant, Northern Liberties), Thomas STEWARDSON, Joseph GRICE (shipbuilder, Northern Liberties), John GIBSON, for the city & county of Phila.; Asher MINER, Samuel SELLERS, Hugh ELY, Joseph SMITH, Anthony TAYLOR, Adam ROMIG, for Bucks Co.; John ROSS, William LATIMORE, Joseph RICE, John D. BOWMAN, Jacob STEM, Northampton Co.; James WILSON, Jacob NEWHART, Jacob BLUMER, Nicholas SAEGER for Lehigh Co.; Redman CUNNINGHAM, Ebenezer BOWMAN, Jacob CIST, Joseph PRUNER, Luzerne Co.; Andrew SHINER, Philip MERLIN, John CHAMBERLIN for Columbia Co. are commissioners to improve the navigaion of the Lehigh River.

p. 192: William P. MACLAY, Mifflin Co., will receive $40 for the use of Henry SHULER & $40/yr. Matthias ARMBRUSTER, Phila., will receive $40 & $40/yr.

p. 193: Martin REILY, Bedford, owns a lot #2 in the plan of the manor of Bedford. A state road is laid through it & relief granted.

p. 194: Trustees of Harts-Log Valley Presby. Church, Huntingdon Co.: John DEAN, John CRAWFORD, John CANAN, Sr., Conrad BUCHER, David CALDWELL, William STEWART.

p. 196: John MEANS built a bridge over Turtle Ck., Allegheny Co.

p. 197: John EWING, Isaac MOORE, Charles JOHNSTON are commissioners to review a road from Indiana to Pittsburg.

p. 199: Jacob ELDER, printer, Harrisburg, is to print the laws of the Commonwealth.

p. 200: Mahantango Ck., Schuylkill Co., from the mouth of Pine Ck. to Samuel KEIM's saw mill & Pine Ck. from Amos BUCKALEW's saw mill in Columbia Co. to the main forks above Jonathan WESTOVER's saw mill in Huntingdon Twp., Luzerne Co. & the western branch of Lackawaxen Ck. from Col. SEELY's mills to Silas KELLOGG's, Mt. Pleasant Twp., Wayne Co. & Little Swatara Ck., Schuylkill Co. from it's junction with big Swatara Ck. to John FIDLER's saw mill & Clearfield Ck. from Beaver Dam branch to Hugh GALLAHER's mill dam in Cambira Co. & Sugar Ck., Bradford Co. from it's mouth to RICH's mills, all are declared public highways.

p. 202: Commissioners of Potter Co. will hold their office at the house of Benjamin BURT. Samuel DALE & Alexander M'CALMONT are appted. to run the division line between M'Kean & Warren Co.

p. 204: Roswell WELLES & Sarah HODGE, exrs. of the will of Jeremiah COLEMAN, decd., are auth. to give, as soon as Amza B. BALDWIN & Summers BALDWIN pay the exrs. ¼ of the purchase money for patenting same, a deed for the ¼ part of lot #40 in the second tier, 5th division, Plymouth Twp., Luzerne Co.

p. 207: John K. WOODWARD is auth. to mark a division line between Wayne & Pike Co.

p. 210: Anthony TAYLOR, John HULME, Jonathan BUCKMAN, Joseph RICHARDSON, Jr. are commissioners of a company to open a lock navigation on Neshaminy Ck., Bucks Co.

p. 223: Jacob DENTLER, John P. DEGRUCHY, John BOYD, John COWDEN,

Northumberland Co.; John VAUGHN, Henry TOLAND, Simon GRATZ, Phila., John DREISBACH, Jacob BROBST, William HAYS, William M'QUEHA, James GEDDIS, Andrew REEDY, Union Co.; James DUNCAN, Lyons MUSSINA, Centre Co. are commissioners to erect a bridge over the west branch of the Susquehanna River from Lewisburg, Union Co., to the opposite shore.

p. 229: McConnellsburgh, Bedford Co., is bounded by the lands of George DARRAH, John COOK, Anthony SHOEMAKER, James AGNEW, George HOCK, Mary M'CONNELL.

p. 233: York Haven Company is to improve the Conewago Canal. Directors: Thomas Willing FRANCIS, William COLE, William WILSON, James WILSON, Thomas WILSON, William GWYNN (of John), Joseph TOWNSAND, Herman Henry HACKEMAN, Justus HOPPE, Isaac BURNESTON, Robert BARRY, Edward IRELAND, John HEATHCOTE, William M'MENCHEN, Frederick WAESHE, James LABES, James NELSON, John DAVIS, Joshua STEVENSON. President is William COLE. Other directors are Justice HOPPE & John DAVIS. All property owned by Thomas Willing FRANCIS, Phila., in Newberry Twp., York Co., which by indenture of 21 Nov., 1810, he sold to John WEATHERBURN, Joseph TOWNSEND & Thomas WILSON in trust for the benefit of themselves & other stockholders, is vested in the York Haven Co.

p. 237: Six warrants in the new purchase, #4070 to #4075, are owned by Charles HUSTON & Robert MORRIS.

p. 240: Martin BRECHALL, Northampton Co., a Rev. War soldier, is to receive $40. John BARR, Washington Co., will receive $40 & $40/yr. Joseph JOHNSON & Daniel DOUGHERTY, old soldiers of Butler Co., are to be paid the money that is due them. Charles TIPPER, Bedford Co., will receive $40.

p. 241: Walter CLARK, late of Londonderry Twp., Dauphin Co., decd., sold, by parole, to Samuel THOMPSON, 3 acres, being part of the land CLARK resided on at his decease. The full balance of purchase money is to be paid to James WILSON & William CATHCART, exrs. of the will of Clark.

p. 243: Jacob EARLY, William EARLY, adminis. of the estate of John EARLY, late of Londonderry Twp., Dauphin Co., now Lebanon Co., are auth. to deed to Daniel WONDERLICK, a lot in Palmyra, Lebanon Co., bounded by Adam DONINGER, Christopher MILLER, Jacob EARLY & Jacob KREMER. Daniel MILLER, one of the adminis. of the estate of Samuel MILLER, decd., is auth. to sell to Thomas MILLER, a lot in Mt. Pleasant. MARY hutcheson, Matthew BOWLAND, adminis. of the estate of Thomas HUTCHESON, late of Washington Co., decd., are auth. to sell land, part of a tract of Alexander HUSTON, late of said county, decd., which he possessed by virtue of a parole contract with Matthew RITCHIE, late of said county, decd., to the widow of Alexander HUSTON & children of Hugh HUSTON, late of said county, decd. Isabella RITCHIE, surviving exr. of Matthew RITCHIE, is auth. to sell 66 3/4 acres.

p. 244: George FOX, Joseph Parker NORRIS, Robert RALSTON, Jonathan SMITH, devisees of Samuel M. FOX, in trust for the purposes of his will; John ADLUM; Edward TILGHMAN, Jr., & wife Rebecca; Samuel Burge RAWLE & wife, Anne; Jesse WALN; Rebecca Waln WHARTON; Susan Lloyd WHARTON (heirs of Jesse WALN); minors by their guardians John HALLOWELL, Rebecca WALN & Moore WHARTON; Sarah BULKELEY (wife of Thomas BULKELEY & heir of Jesse WALN, decd.); Francis R. WHARTON, Thomas J. WHARTON, Hannah M. WHARTON, Joseph WHARTON, Jr., Rebecca

L. WHARTON, minors by their guardian, Margaret R. WHARTON (heirs of Isaac WHARTON, decd.); Patteson HARTSHORNE, John LARGE, James LARGE, Thomas MIFFLIN & wife, Sarah, devisees of Ebenezer LARGE; Robert WALN; David LEWIS, all petition that they hold sundry tracts of land in surveyors district #1, #5, #6, which they are desirous of dividing. Charles BIDDLE, Thomas STEWARDSON, James VAUX, Matthew M'CONNEL, Benjamin R. MORGAN, Phila., are empowered to partition the land.

p. 247: Benjamin BURD lives at Littleton, Bedford Co.

p. 248: Hardman PHILIPS, Centre Co., is auth. to receive from his father, John PHILIPS, & from his brothers, John Leigh PHILIPS & Francis PHILIPS, a deed for lands in PA.

p. 252: Joseph FLORA, formerly of Paxton Twp., Lancaster (now Dauphin) Co., by will dated 16 Sept., 1783, bequeathed to the 2 children of his son, Abraham, then decd., a certain part of his estate (£337 6s 6p). The legatees, with their mother, left Pa. ca 1778 & have never been heard of since. It is not known if they are living or dead but in the past 36 years, diligent inquiry has been made as to their whereabouts. Joseph FLORA left 6 other children whose descendents are numerous & many are poor. John WOLFLEY, one of the exrs. of Conrad WOLFLEY, who was one of the exrs. of Joseph FLORA & Christian SPAYD & John M'CAMMON, exrs. of Jacob WOLFLEY, an exr. of Conrad WOLFLEY, are auth. to distribute the £337 6s 6p plus interest.

p. 253: Robert NEILSON, Armstrong Co., is given $40 & $40/yr. The amount due on a certificate of funded debt, #13,326, is issued to Robert M'NITT for £10 10s. The amount due on a certificate of funded debt, #12845, is issued to William WILSON for £10 10s. The sum is to be paid to Thomas M'KINLEY, exr. of William WILSON, late of York Co., decd. Mary Anna SCOTT, Bedford, is to give a certificate of funded debt, #12611, in the name of Frederick WOER for 14s & a bill of credit #13,338 for 50s & another, #21,502 for 10s.

p. 254: Jared INGERSOLL is given $200 for expenses incurred in preparing 3 bills amending the penal law of Pa.

p. 254: Magdalena HAWK is executrix, & Martin RENNINGER, exr. of the will of John HAWK, late of E. Pennsborough Twp., Cumberland Co., decd. George GRAHAM conveyed a tract to John ORR. ORR sold the tract to George HAWK.

p. 255: William HENDRESON was appted. treasurer of Montgomery Co. for 1801, 1802, & 1803.

p. 256: John Carlisle STEWART, John SANKEY, Crawford WHITE, Mercer Co., are commissioners to alter part of a road from Blair's Gap to the western boundary of Pa., Mercer Co.

p. 257: John SWAR, Martin GREIDER, John HOUTZ, Daniel GREIDER, Jacob ROHRER, Abraham HARNLY, Jacob GISH, David RAHM, Christian HARTZLER, Lancaster Co.; James WILSON, James WALLACE, John HOFFER, Christian SHANK, Martin HOCKER, Samuel WILSON, David FERGUSON, James JOHNSTON, Dauphin Co., are commissioners to make a road from Lancaster, Elizabethtown, Middletown tpk. to Swatara Ck. ferry near the mill formerly owned by James WALLACE.

p. 260: Henry SHEARER, James MAHAFFY, Matthias RANK, Alexander BOGGS, John LONGNECKER, Henry HALDEMAN, Jacob BRUBACK, Lancaster Co.; George FISHER, James HAMILTON, Christian SPAYD, John SHELLY, John ELLIOT, Martin NEISLEY (miller), Dauphin Co.; Henry ERWIN, William BARBER, George SPANGLER, York Co., are commissioners to make a road from Marietta to Harrisburg.

p. 266: Michael LYNCH is a Justice of the Peace, Chester Co., & Thomas CANNON is a J.P. of Allegheny Co.

p. 271: Henry HOFFMAN, decd., Westmoreland Co., willed to his wife, Eleanor, the use of 49 acres. At her decease, a Dutch Lutheran Church is to be erected on the land. Exrs. are Charles MITCHELL & Andrew FINDLEY.

p. 271: Sir William PULTENEY, late of London, owned land in Wayne Co. He died intestate, leaving Henrietta Laura PULTENEY as his only child. She lately died in London, intestate & without issue. The land willed to her came by descent to Sir John Lowther JOHNSTON & to other collateral relations, some in England, Scotland, Europe, the East, the West Indies, some minors & some non compos mentis. Robert TROUP, a citizen of N.Y., acted as Sir William's agent.

p. 274: Elijah FUNK, Lewis MORGAN, Dr. Samuel NIXON, John EMERY, Matthias PENNYPACKER, Lawrence HIPPLE, Robert RALSTON, Chester Co.; John MARKLEY, Lewis SHRACK, George HAWKE, Montgomery Co., are commissioners to make a road from PAWLING's ford bridge over the Schuylkill River to intersect the Little Conestogoe tpk. near the western line of Herman PENNEPACKER's land, Chester Co.

p. 277: Kingsessing & Blockley Twps., Phila. Co., will vote at George C. LINTENER's, on West Chester Rd. Lower Salford & Franconia Twp., Montgomery Co., will vote at George SCHWENCK's, innkeeper, Lower Salford Twp. Hopewell Twp., Cumberland Co., will vote at James RODGERS', innkeeper. Braintrim, Rush Twp., Susquehanna co., will vote at Joab PICKET's, Rush Twp. Greenfield Twp., Bedford Co., will vote at Jacob GLASS'. Oley Twp., Berks Co., will vote at Jacob KEMP's. Manor election dist., Chester Co., will vote at Jacob HOWER's, innkeeper, Brandywine Twp. Salisbury Twp., Lancaster Co., will vote at Barton HENDERSON's. Donegal Twp., Lancaster Co., will vote at Jacob BARR's, innkeeper, Maytown. Chilisquaque Twp., Columbia Co., near William WILSON's, decd., & William MURRAY's, decd., will vote at Milton. Parts of Elizabeth, Cocalico & Warwick Twp., formerly in Lancaster Co., & now in Lebanon Co., will vote at Samuel REX's. Part of Rapho Twp., now in Lebanon Co., will vote at Abraham DOEBLER's. Part of Mt. Joy Twp., now in Lebanon Co., will vote at Casper DASHER's. Sadsbury Twp., Crawford Co., will vote at David BRACKENRIDGE's. Fayette Twp., Allegheny Co., will vote at Matthew M'COY's, Noblestown. Upper & Lower Nazareth Twp., Northampton Co., will vote at Henry JARRETT's, JARRETT's Villa, Lower Nazareth Twp. Towamensing, Northampton Co., will vote at Henry BOMAN's. Union Twp., Luzerne Co., will vote at John T. MILLER's. Clifford Twp., Susquehanna Co., will vote at James WELLS'. Pike Twp., Bradford Co., will vote at Jesse ROSS'. Stony Ck. Twp., Somerset Co., will vote at Andrew PORCUPINE's. Centre Twp., Indiana Co., near James M'CLENAHAN, Daniel M'KISSICK, David CUMMINS will vote at the courthouse, Indiana.

p. 283: Title to land in Toboyne Twp., Cumberland Co., adj. John FLEICHER, John ERNEST, containing 10 acres, is vested in Daniel BLOOM, John BARBER & John FLEICHER as trustees for the use of a school.

p. 284: Nathaniel WATSON, John GRAFF, William RAMSEY, James REA, William NOBLE, Lancaster Co.; John G. PARKS, Joseph CLOUD, William FLEMING, tanner, Chester Co., are app'ted commissioners to make a road from the Susquehanna River at M'CALL's ferry permanent bridge on the state road by Nathan THOMPSON, Jr., & William NOBLE's store to John G. PARKS in the Great Valley to the Phila. & Lancaster tpk.

p. 287: The title to land in Nether Providence Twp., & one lot in Upper Providence Twp., Delaware Co., is vested in George MILLER, Upper Providence Twp., Joseph PENNEL, Jr., James EMLIN, Middletown Twp.; Enos SHARPLESS, Eli D. PEIRCE, Nether Providence Twp.; Joseph RHOADS, Marple Twp., as Quakers of the Chester Monthly Meeting. Mathew LONGWELL, Walter SMITH, George SMYSER, Samuel SLOAN, Mathew DOBBIN, John F. M'FARLAND are the present president & directors.

p. 292: Trustees of the German Reformed Church of Heidleberg Twp., Lebanon Co. (formerly Dauphin Co.), are auth. to sell land adj. Abraham ANDREAS, John DEIFENBACH & Peter MUSSELMAN.

p. 292: Stroudsburg Academy trustees: Daniel STROUD, Samuel REES, Jacob POSTENS, Jacob BROWN, William VAN BUSKIRK, William D. WALTON, Asa HERRING, John ALLABACH, James HOLLINGSHEAD. They will hold their first meeting at George DROER's.

p. 295: Simon CORURIGHT, Daniel STEWART, John GUSTIN, Israel CAULFIELD, Sussex Co., N.J.; John BROADHEAD, John BRINK, Daniel DIMMICK, John CROSS, James WALLACE, Wayne Co., Pa., are commissioners to erect a bridge over the Delaware River near Milford, Wayne Co., Pa.

p. 302: William SMITH, Fayette, is declared lunatic. Andrew OLIPHANT is appted. guardian. SMITH inherited real estate in Fayette Co., late the property of his father, William Augustus SMITH (reserving to Sarah SMITH, widow of William Augustus SMITH, her right of dower). Esther GRIFFIN, sister of William SMITH (married to Samuel GRIFFIN), is to sell her interest in the real estate lying within Pa.

p. 304: Samuel GRAVES was appted. by the orphan's court, Bedford Co., guardian of the 5 minor children of John BREWER, decd.: Jonathan, Sarah, William, John & Abigail, Bethel Twp., Bedford Co. John BREWER died intestate, owning 1/10 of 250 acres. Henry BREWER owned the other part. The land is adj. Christian WALTZ, Bethuel COVALT & Jacob MANN.

p. 305: Henry BRUSTAR, late of Northern Liberties, Phila., decd., willed to his wife, Catharine, 1/3 of his real estate. He had 8 children: Mary STOY, Ann STOY (wife of Peter), Sarah BATTISS (wife of Elijah BATTISS), Elizabeth BENNETT (wife of Daniel BENNETT), James BRUSTAR, Susanna BRUSTAR, Merza BRUSTAR, Phoebe BRUSTAR & grandson Henry BRUSTAR, son of his decd. son, John BRUSTAR. John CLUNN, Phila. Co., is the adminis. of Henry BRUSTAR.

p. 310: Certificates are granted to John SHEPARD & Benjamin DORRANCE & their right to 12,328 acres in Claverack, Luzerne Co. (now Bradford Co.) are being investigated.

p. 311: William PURVIS, Robert PURVIS, Cumberland Co., aliens, are auth. to sell land in Southampton Twp.

p. 312: George RAWLS is to be paid $48.10 for provisions furnished to militia under Brig. Gen. CROOKS. Jacob BUCHER is one of the commissioners appted. to superintend the erection of a public bldg.

p. 313: Daniel BRODHEAD, decd., in 1795, procured a title under 17 warrants dated 1794 for 6240 acres, 121 perches in the twps. of Plymouth, Kingston & Exeter, Luzerne Co.

p. 313: It is not lawful to sell for taxes within 2 years any land late the property of John NICHOLSON which was purchased for the use of Pa. by the commissioners or the land of Peter BAYNTON on which the state has a lien.

p. 315: Timothy O'NEAL, Indiana Co., an old soldier, is to receive $40 & $40/yr. Thomas BRODNOX, John MURPHY, Bucks Co.; Philip KENNEDY, Centre Co., will receive $40. Peter SMITH, late a lieutenant in the Rev. War, is given $80 & $80/yr.

p. 316: Thomas COCHRAN, Caleb NORTH, William POWER, David WATTS, William RAMSAY, Cumberland Co.; John MAGORY, William BELL, David WALKER, John BROWN, William P. MACLAY, Elias W. HALE, Mifflin Co.; Robert T. STEWART, Joseph PATTON, Jr., Centre Co.; Robert ALLISON, William STEEL, Huntingdon Co., are commissioners to erect a toll bridge over the Juniata River near Millerstown, Cumberland Co.

p. 317: Henry SHARE, George SNYDER, James MEHAFFEY, Jacob GRAYBILL, Thomas R. BUCHANON, Lancaster Co.; John MILLER, John SULTZBAUGH, George UPP, George SPANGLER (surveyor), York Co., are add'l. commissioners of ANDERSON's ferry & the York Tpk. Rd.

p. 318: A tract in Penn Twp., Union Co., is granted by patent on 12 Aug., 1813, to Abraham BROUSE & Jacob HARMAN in trust for the United Congregation of the German Lutheran & Calvinists worshipping at Hessler's Church, adj. land of Simon ESPY, Michael HESSLER, Martin MICHAEL, John REEM.

p. 366: Eliston PERROT, Paul BECK, William SANSOM, Jacob DOWNING, William DAVIDSON, James TAYLOR, Phila.; Edward BRIEN, John NEFF, Nathaniel W. SAMPLE, Rudolph KEGEY, Lancaster Co.; Gen. Charles RIDGLEY, Hampton; Benjamin ELLICOTT, James CARROLL, Luke TIERNAN, Henry PAYSAN, William WILSON, John M'KIM, Jr., Robert MILLER, James CAREY, Charles JESSOP, Baltimore, Maryland, are commissioners to make a road from the Phila. & Lancaster tpk. road to the Susquehanna bridge at M'CALL's ferry & then to Baltimore.

p. 380: Thanks of the government is conveyed to Capt. Oliver Hazard PERRY for the brilliant action in which he succeeded in capturing his Britanic Majesty's fleet on Lake Erie. Thanks are conveyed to Master Commandant Jesse Duncan ELLIOTT, Lt. John J. YARNALL for their gallant & brave conduct.

THE LAWS OF PENNSYLVANIA
1814-15, 1815-16

p. 4: Overseers of the public school in Phila. are empowered to make competent releases of lots of land to Mary GARDINER, Elizabeth GARDINER, Mary GARDINER, the younger, Richard GARDINER, Mary RHOADS, Samuel RHOADS, Ann WILSON, Ann SKYRIN, William DRINKER, John GARDINER, Jr., in trust; Elizabeth WALLACE, Joseph WALLACE, Euphrosyne SONTAGG, Matilda WILLIAMS, Rachael TAYLOR, Hannah

WIDDIFIELD, wife of James WIDDIFIELD; Hannah WIDDIFIELD, daughter of James WIDDIFIELD; Noah SIMMONS, Elizabeth MOORE, Ann WILSON, Carolina COOK, devisees of Sarah JERVIS.

p. 4: Calvin HATHAWAY, late of Washington Co., decd., agreed to sell to Odel SQUIRE 102 acres of land. Jacob HATHAWAY & Luther DAY are adminis. of the estate of Calvin HATHAWAY, late of Morris Twp. The land is bounded by Jacob HATHAWAY, John PARCEL, Jonathan SHORES, Luther DAY & heirs of Calvin HATHAWAY.

p. 5: Joseph G. CHAMBERS is to supply 25 of his newly invented repeating swivels of 224 shots each with 5 carriages.

p. 6: Brownsville, Fayette Co., is bounded by land of Jonah CADWALADER's mill dam, William HOGG, Adam JACOB, BOWMAN's lot, FLETCHER's lot, M'CADDON's lot. Elections will be at Jacob COPLAN's.

p. 11: John DAVENPORT, Thomas DAVENPORT, Robert DAVENPORT, Jesse FELL are executors of the will of Thomas DAVENPORT, late of Plymouth Twp., Luzerne Co. Abraham VAN LOON & Stephen VAN LOON assigned a certificate to Thomas DAVENPORT for a lot which was to be patented by DAVENPORT. Matthias VAN LOON is decd.

p. 14: John SWAR, Henry BEAR, Henry KEFFER, Samuel WHITE, James HUSTON, William DICKSON, Christian HERR, Jr., Joseph OGELBY, Jr., John BOMBERGER, Benjamin OBER, James HUMES, Henry HUFFNAGLE, Christian STAUFFER, Jr., Henry CASSEL, Christian ROHRER are directors of the Manufacturing Co. of Lancaster.

p. 16: Edward TILGHMAN, Phila., is the legal owner of 83 warrants. Samuel MEREDITH & trustees names in the will of George CLYMER, Phila., decd., are legal owners of 108 warrants for lands formerly in Northampton & Luzerne Co. dated 3 Apr., 1792.

p. 19: Directors of the Manufacturing Co. of Waterford in Susquehanna Co.: Jacob TYLER, John SEYMOUR, Amasa PETERS, Cyril GIDDINGS, Joshua MILES, Jr.

p. 21: Canonsburg, Washington Co. is bounded by land of William HARTUPEE, Nathan ANDREW, James BELLENTINE's lot, William DONALDSON's lot.

p. 24: Charles BIDDLE, Thomas STEWARDSON, James VAUX, Matthew M'CONNEL, Benjamin R. MORGAN, Phila., are auth. to partition land in Armstrong, Indiana & Jefferson Cos. with respect to John ADLUM.

p. 25: The title of some land was conveyed to Sophia PHILLIPS of Phila., in trust for Hardman PHILIPS & before a deed could be executed by Francis PHILIPS, John Leigh PHILIPS & John PHILIPS.

p. 27: John WOODEND is granted the exclusive right to use a salt spring he discovered in Toby's Ck., Venango Co.

p. 29: Pottstown, Montgomery Co., is bounded by Jacob LESHER, land of the estate of Mary JONES, decd., Mary GRAHAM, David RUTTER, the estate of Clifford SMITH, decd., & Joanna POTTS, Peter RICHARD, Jacob HUBLEY.

p. 33: Daniel STROUD, Samuel BROOK, Peter HOLLINGSHEAD, Northampton Co., are commissioners of a manufacturing co. at Stroudsburg.

p. 39: The trustees of the Presby. Congregation of Three Ridges, Washington Co.: David FRAZIER, John BLEYNEY, Barnet BONER, John M'KOY, Samuel DICKEY, James ARMSTRONG, Samuel M'MURRAY, George SUTHERLAND, Jr., William M'DONALD, Jr.

p. 40: The marriage of Francis D. CUMMINS & Eliza L. CUMMINS is annulled.

p. 41: Hugh MOORE, James HERRINGTON, Samuel EVANS are to erect a toll bridge on French Ck., at "EVANS' Ferry," Mercer Co.

p. 43: Henry VOIGHTS, an alien, has title to a tract called "Babtist" on Big Whitely Ck., Greene Co., confirmed. He purchased it from Lewis & Rachel EVANS.

p. 44: Samuel WEBB, Jr., Columbia Co., & Alexander JAMESON & Abiel FELLOWS, Luzerne Co., are commissioners to mark the boundary line between Columbia & Luzerne Co.

p. 45: Thomas HALE owned land in Rye (now Juniata) Twp. He died intestate leaving two children: Matthew (father of Mary, Thomas, Elizabeth & Matthew) & Mary (married to William Hawkins WOOD). William & Mary WOOD died intestate, leaving one son, Thomas Hale WOOD who died intestate, unmarried & without issue. Elizabeth HALE, Phila., is guardian of Mary Wood HALE, Thomas, Elizabeth & Matthew HALE.

p. 47: Thomas ARMAT, Daniel STROUD, Jacob BROWN, James BURSON, John HOUSE, Evan THOMAS, Samuel STOKES, John BAKER, Peter KOCHER, John P. ARNDT, Stephen TUTTLE are commissioners of the Smithfield tpk. road. The road will begin near Pimple Hill, Northampton Co., to the house of Henry DILL, Upper Mt. Bethel Twp.

p. 50: Philip WEAVER, John ELLIOTT, Melchior HOFFER, Isaac TOD, William KITH, Andrew HIKES, Hugh REED, Rudolph CREICH, Jacob SQUIRE, trustees of the Methodist Episcopal Congregation, Carlisle, Cumberland Co., are auth. to sell land which William & Mary RAINEY, on 3 Mar., 1792, sold to William HUNTER, Thomas JONES, Henry BURCHSTEAD, trustees of the Methodist Episcopal Congregation.

p. 50: Kutztown, Berks Co., is bounded by John LEVAN, land late of John TEIPHER, Philip MOYERS, Jacob KUTZ. Elections will be held at Daniel LEVAN's.

p. 55: On 6 Apr., 1794, a patent was issued to Clement BIDDLE, Phila., for a lot #1283 in the 6th district of donation lands, in the right of Philip HICKCRICK, personating Philip RICHCRICK for services in the Revolution. Philip sold the patent & claim to the land to James HERRINGTON, Crawford Co.

p. 55: Martin UPDEGRAFF, Daniel UPDEGRAFF, Samuel UPDEGRAFF, Lycoming Twp., Lycoming Co., are auth. to repair the fishery opposite their lands on the west branch of the Susquehanna River by raising a gravel bar 3 feet.

p. 61: In 1813, Christian HIEST & Barbara REIGELSBAUGH, Lancaster Co., married. Barbara had a son 5 months later; the parties separated as a consequence of the birth, it being conceded by the parties that Christian wasn't the father. The marriage is annulled.

p. 62: George PARSON is to receive $100 for a waggon horse which died of a wound received by a bayonet while in the service of the state & attached to the volunteers & militia which marched from Harrisburg to Baltimore in Sept., 1814.

p. 62: Broadhead's Ck., from John PRICE's mill, Pike Co., to the mouth of the creek at the Delaware River, Northampton Co., is declared a public highway.

p. 63: Jacob NELL, who served as a volunteer in Capt. Michael H. SPANGLER's Co., was shot through the breast at the battle of North Point, near Baltimore. He is unable to labor & will receive $100.

p. 64: Andrew M'DOWEL, Greene Co., will receive $40 & $40/yr. Adam HILL, Mercer Co., will receive $40.

p. 65: Public highways: Big Cattawissa Ck., Luzerne Co., near Andrew GILBERT's saw-mill & the south branch of Swatara Ck., Schuylkilol Co., near Jacob CAPP's saw-mill & Beech Ck., Centre Co., & Kittle Ck., Lycoming Co.

p. 65: The borough of Hanover is erected with a tract of land of Richard M'ALISTER, decd. Elections will be held at Jacob EICHELBERGER,'s, Frederick St. Michael HELLMAN & Henry WELSH will superintend the election.

p. 69: Francis RHOADS & Jacob RHOADS are executors of Francis RHOADS, late of Selins-Grove, Union Co., decd. Francis owned lot #10 in Selins-Grove. The executors sold it to Jacob LECHNER.

p. 70: John SNYDER & Peter COOK, trustees of the German Presby. Cong., Guilford Twp., Franklin Co., are auth. to sell land adj. Daniel HELLMAN, Daniel BONEBREAK, & the land late of Ezekiel CHAMBERS.

p. 70: Henry FUNK, late of Bucks Co., decd., sold land to John FUNK. Executors of the estate of Henry FUNK, late of Springfield Twp., were Ralph FUNK & John W. BURSON. The land was bounded by Jacob REINSIMER, Jacob FUNK & Henry FUNK, Jr.

p. 71: Charles ELLET, Isaac PARSON, Samuel REYNOLD, John HUME, Robert CROZER, Samuel CROZER, Barclay IVINS, Hector THOMPSON, Isaac ROBBINS, Bucks Co.; John GEYER, Adolph ERINGHAUS, Phila., executors of John DE KARNS, decd., are to run Penns Manor Meadow Co.

p. 73: Samuel WETHERILL, Jr., Jonathan WILLIAMS, Samuel RICHARDS, Robert KENNEDY, Josiah WHITE, Phila.; Levi PAWLING, Matthias HOLSTINE, Philip HAHN, Jesse BEAN, Thomas LOWRY, Andrew TOD, Joseph POTTS, David RUTTER, Amos EVANS, Montgomery Co.; Lewis WERNWAG, Joshua MALIN, Enoch WALKER, John RHINEHART, John HEISTER, Jr., Chester Co.; Lewis REES, John S. HEISTER, John WILEY, James MAY, Jacob K. BOYER, John BREWER, Matthias BROOKE, Robert SCOTT, Abraham BAILEY, Abraham WOLF, Berks Co.; James M'FARLAND, John POTT, Daniel GRAEFF, George DREIBILBIS, John MULLOWNY, Schuylkill Co., are commissioners to make a lock navigation on the Schuylkill River.

p. 83: John BRODHEAD, Daniel W. DINGMAN, James WALLACE, Daniel DIMMICK, James BARTON, John CROSS, Edward MOTT, Jr., Thomas NEWMAN & George BOWHANNON are commissioners of a company for manufacturing hemp, flax, wool & cotton near Milford, Pike Co.

p. 87: William HENDERSON, late treasurer of Montgomery Co., has his account credited for money from exempt fines.

p. 88: William PROCTOR, John SCHELL, Jr., George ROCK, Bedford Co.; John TANTLINGER, Henry FISHER, George GRAHAM, Somerset Co. are commissioners to make a road from the bank of the Susquehanna River opposite Harrisburg to Pittsburg (the section from Bedford to Stoystown) & Jacob ANKENY, John DENISON, John LEHMER, Somerset Co.; William JACK, Sr., Alexander JOHNSTON, John RAMSEY, Abraham HORBAUGH, Westmoreland Co., for the part between Stoystown & Greensburg.

p. 89: On 21 Apr., 1794, John NICHOLSON applied for 202 & 400 acres & gave a check on the Bank of Pa. for the purchase money, which was presented & dishonored; upon which he tendered $27,261.33 on 14 June, which was refused. He transferred his right to the application to Joseph BOONE, who obtained the decree on the board of property for warrants to issue in his favor which was transferred by him to Philip NICHLIN & Robert E. GRIFFITH, merchants.

p. 90: Jacob BOWER, late a captain in the Pa. Line, is to receive an annuity equal to ¼ his pay.

p. 93: Return judges for the Senate are to meet:
Berks & Schuylkill Co.: at Abraham BAILEY's, Hamburg, Berks Co.
Dauphin & Lebanon Co.: at the public house of Jacob GREENAWALT, Hummelstown.
Northumberland, Columbia, Union, Luzerne, Susquehanna Co.: at John BROWN's, Berwick, Columbia Co.
Mifflin & Huntingdon Co.: at John READ's, Bellville, Mifflin Co.
Bedford, Somerset & Cambria Co.: at George GRAHAM's, Stoystown.
Westmoreland, Indiana, Jefferson Co.: at John KELLY's, Newport, Blacklick Twp., Indiana Co.
Washington, Greene Co.: at Henry CARTER's, Amity, Washington Co.
Allegheny, Armstrong, Beaver, Butler Co.: at James CARNAHAN's, Deer Twp., Allegheny Co.
House of Representatives return judges are to meet:
Armstrong, Indiana, Jefferson Co.: at Abaslom WOODWARD's, Arms. Co.
Luzerne, Susquehanna Co.: at Charles OTIS', Luzerne Co.
Bradford, Tioga Co.: at the house late of Moses TAYLOR, at the head of Sugar Creek, Bradford Co.
Allegheny, Butler Co.: at James CARNAHAN's, Deer Twp., Allegheny Co.
Somerset, Cambria Co.: at George GRAHAM's, Stoystown, Somerset Co.

p. 97: Trustees of Lewistown Academy, Mifflin Co.: Rev. James JOHNSTON, Rev. William KENNEDY, Rev. John HUTCHESON, Rev. Thomas SMITH, Rev. John COULTER, David REYNOLDS, James KNOX, Matthew TAYLOR, William LYON, Richard HOPE, James SHARARD, Robert M'CLELLAND, William P. MACLAY, John OLIVER, Andrew BANKS.

p. 99: Charles HALL, Andrew ALBRIGHT, Daniel LEBO, Jonas WEAVER, Sunbury; James DUNCAN, James POTTER, Centre Co.; Christopher SEABOLD, Frederick STEES, Robert BARBER, James HUMMEL, Adam LIGHT, John GRAYBILL, Joseph FEHRER, Union Co.; Simon GRATZ, Stephen GIRARD, Phila.; Jacob K. BOYER, Lewis REES, Berks Co.; James M'FARLAND, Daniel GRAEFF, Schuylkill Co., are commissioners to erect a bridge over the Susquehanna River opposite Sunbury, Northumberland Co.

p. 108: Robert RITCHIE, Peter MURKIN, John W. THOMPSON, John WORKMAN, John Y. BRYANT, Francis JOHNSTON, Peter SCRAVENDYKE, John C. STOCKER, John KAIGHN, James SLOAN, Joseph RIGERS, William E.

HOPKINS are trustees of the Pa. & N.J. Steamboat Co.

p. 111: Jacob GITT is imprisoned for debt. He is relieved as though he had resided in this state for 6 months immediately preceding his confinement in Adams Co.

p. 112: William HOGE is late of Washington Co. Samuel MILLER, decd., is late of Mt. Pleasant Twp., Washington Co.

p. 114: John RHINEHART, William SHULER, David POTTS, John HEISTER, Jr., John DITLOW, Thomas BAIRD, Rudolph STAUFFER, Chester Co.; David RUTTER, Jacob LESHER, George LEAFF, Thomas P. MAY, John HEISTER, Jesse IVES, Samuel BAIRD, Montgomery Co., are commissioners to erect a bridge over the Schuylkill River, opposite Pottstown, Montgomery Co.

p. 120: Commissioners to make a road from the west end of York borough to Gettysburg: David CASSAT, Jacob HAY, Penrose ROBISON, Godfrey LENHART, Frederick BAGHER, Jacob FAHNESTOCK, George HIMES, Samuel GRAYBLE, George LASHELLS, James GETTYS, Alexander COBEAN, Walter SMITH, Ralph LASHELLS, John MURPHEY.

p. 123: William HUNTER, son & devisee of William HUNTER, late of Muddy Ck. Twp., Butler Co., decd., is to sell to Matthew M'CULLOCH, 50 acres of land adj. John WOODS & Andrew M'GOWAN. HUNTER's will dated 29 Apr., 1811. He gave land to his 2 grandchildren: Mary & William MCCULLOCH, children of Matthew M'CULLOCH. William HUNTER, the son, is to sell to John M'CULLOCH, 50 acres adj. William DODDS & John NEGLEY in Butler Co. which William HUNTER, decd., left in his will to his grandchildren, John & William M'CULLOCH, minor children of John M'CULLOCH.

p. 124: Henry DOUGHERTY, Lycoming Co., old soldier, is to receive $40 & $40/yr. George MOSSER, Lehigh Co., Alexander MCCURDY, Beaver Co., & Thomas SMITH, Mifflin Co. are to receive $40 & $40/yr

p. 125: The Ridley Tpk. Co. is auth. to extend the road from John M'ILVAIN's along the Phila. & Wilmington Post Rd. to the Delaware & Pennsylvania state line near Naaman's Ck.

p. 128: Samuel KEARSLEY, a Capt. in the Rev. War, is to receive $50 & $50/yr.

p. 129: William COLEMAN, Henry MOYER, Samuel LIGHT, John WEIDMAN, Abraham RAGUEL, Tobias STEOVER, & Peter GLONINGER are commissioners to make a road from the South end of Market St., Lebanon borough, to Cornwall furnace.

p. 132: Heirs of Jacob REAM, late of Dauphin Co., decd.,: brothers Abraham, Isaac, Daniel & sisters Barbara (wife of Jacob PALMER), Esther (wife of John PARTHEMER), Elizabeth BERRINGER; three children of brother Samuel, decd. (Samuel, Esther, & Catharine who was married to John FELTY & died suddenly leaving a minor daughter, Catharine). They were tenants in common of a tract of land bounded by Jacob BERRINGER, heirs of William MACLAY & Henry HARE.

p. 134: Joseph CHARLES, Christian BINKLEY, John HABACKER, Barbara HARTMAN all owned lots on Market St., Charleston, Lancaster Co. Joseph CHARLES & Barbara HARTMAN died intestate. BINKLEY sold his lot to William MITCHENOR. The lot of Joseph CHARLES was vested in Daniel MUSSER, Isaac KAUFMAN, Abraham CHARLES, adminis. of Joseph

CHARLES, decd. The lot of BINKELY is to be vested in William MITCHENOR. Christian HABACKER is adminis. of Barbara HARTMAN.

p. 136: Martin BRECHAL, Northampton Co., a private in Capt. SEELY's Co., Rev. War, served until June, 1783, was honorably discharged. He is a native of Pa., old & infirm & is given $40 & $40/yr.

p. 137: A board of property has dismissed a caveat entered by Samuel BOWMAN & Mary BOWMAN v. John BIGLER in consequence of a land dispute over land which was formerly a part of the Conodoguinet Ck., Cumberland co., which was declared a public highway.

p. 137: In 1813, Col. Rees HILL, Greene Co., then commanding a regiment of Pa. militia, marched to Lower Sandusky & performed a tour of duty without being furnished by the government with sufficient pecuniary resources. $2400 is loaned to him.

p. 138: Matthew ROBERTS, Matthias HOLSTEIN, John ELLIOT, Levi PAWLING, George W. HOLSTEIN, Philip HAHN, Jr., Thomas HUMPHREY, David HENDERSON, Montgomery Co., are commissioners to erect a bridge over the Schuylkill River near Norristown, Montgomery Co.

p. 145: John L. FINNEY, recorder of deeds, Northumberland Co., is auth. to transcribe deed book A into a new book.

p. 146: A marriage between Joseph St. Leger DE HAPPART & wife, Elizabeth (formerly THOMPSON) is dissolved.

p. 146: Samuel AYRES, late of Bedford Twp., Luzerne Co., owned land in Bedford Twp., subject to a lien & another tract in Ohio. His widow & children (all minors) have moved to the land in Ohio. Amariah WATSON & James NISBITT are adminis. of Samuel AYRES.

p. 147: Thomas CHRONEMILLER, York borough, is changing his name to Thomas BAUMGARDNER.

p. 148: George BUCHANAN, Phila., physician, died intestate, owning a lot upon which there are 3 brick messuages. He left 7 minor children, now living. Latitia BUCHANAN is the guardian of the minor children. The lot is bounded by ground granted to Francis WAYNE by John H. BRINTON.

p. 154: Mordecai LEE, Samuel KENDAL, Jonas KERN, Henry LEVAN, Bucks co.; John HUGHES, John MULLOWNY, Daniel GRAEFF, Schuylkill Co.; Henry SCHAEFFER & Andrew ALBRIGHT, Northumberland Co., are commissioners of Mill Ck. Tpk. Road Co., leading from David PHILLIPS' to John MULLOWNY's saw mill & then to John HUGHES' saw mill to Orwigsburg.

p. 157: John TROYER, late of Somerset Co., decd., owned land in Stony Ck. Twp., Somerset Co., adj. land of Uly SOMERS, John YOTHER, Joseph YOTHER & warranted in the name of Nathaniel SMITH. He sold it to David LAHMAN. Yost MILLER is adminis. of the estate of John TROYER.

p. 159: Paul MORROW & Samuel GUTHRIE, Greensburg, Westmoreland Co., are guardians of Jane & George HAYS, minor children of George KAYS, Kittanning, Armstrong Co., decd. HAYS owned land in Kittanning.

p. 160: Rebecca GREER is widow & adminis. of Thomas GREER, late of North East Twp., Erie Co., decd. Daniel CALDWELL is another adminis. John M'CORD is guardian of the minor children of the decd. Thomas GREER exchanged 100 acres with Arnold CUSTARD. GREER sold the land to James GREER & John GREER.

p. 163: Lewis RUSH, James TRAQUAIR, Phila.; Joseph STARNE, Horatio Gates JONES, William ALEXANDER, Phila. Co.; Abijah STEVENS, Lloyd JONES, Conrad KRECKBAUM, Lewellin YOUNG, Montgomery Co., are commissioners to make a road beginning where the Flat Rock bridge road intersects the Ridge Tpk. Rd. near ROBINSON's mill & then to Bird-In-Hand Tavern, Montgomery Co.

p. 166: James KEAN, Westmoreland Co., will receive $40 and $40/yr. Mary TAYLOR, York Co., will receive $40. An annuity of $40 which was granted to Peter M'BRIDE is to be paid to Philip LANDIS, East-town Twp., Chester Co. & he will provide for JONES.

p. 167: Abraham WARFEL, Lancaster, shall have a right to improve an island called "Willow Island" in the Susquehanna River.

p. 167: Adam HOPE, Mt. Pleasant Twp., Westmoreland Co., died in 1813, owning land in the township. He left a widow, 2 sons, 5 daughter, one of whom married William SPEAR & died leaving 5 children, all minors. William SPEAR, Clements BURLEIGH, Westmoreland Co., are guardians of Mary, Jane, Nancy, Joseph & John SPEAR.

p. 168: Elections districts: Moore Twp., Beaver Co., will vote at Thomas MOORE's. Hopewell Twp., Beaver Co., will vote at Robert WALKER, decd.'s house. Hanover Twp., Beaver Co., will vote at John BOYD's. Greene Twp., Beaver Co., will vote at James PRESTON's, Hoakstown. Ohio Twp., Beaver Co., will vote at Samuel EWING's. South Beaver Twp., Beaver Co., will vote at William RAYL's. Big Beaver Twp., Beaver Co., will vote at Hugh MARSHALL's. Little Beaver Twp., Beaver Co., will vote at Robert MOORE's. North Beaver Twp., Beaver Co., will vote at John DUNNAN's. Shenango Twp., Beaver Co., will vote at James CLARNACK's. North Seweekly Twp., Beaver Co., will vote at John HAZEN's. New Seweekly Twp., Beaver Co., will vote at Stanton SHOLE's. Franklin Twp., Westmoreland Co., will vote at James HUTCHESON's. Somerset Twp., Washington Co., will vote at George M'ILVAIN's. Little Mahanoy Twp., Northumberland Co., will vote at Conrad REAKER's. Dunstable Twp., Lycoming Co., will vote at John QUIGLEY's, Youngwomanstown. Palmyra Twp., Wayne Co., will vote at William PURDY's. Ruscombmanor Twp., Berks Co., will vote at Jonathan PRICE's, inn-keeper. Franklin Twp., Huntingdon Co., will vote at Christian HUET's. Upper Paxton Twp., Dauphin Co., will vote at Jonathan COLLIER's, Millersburg. New Milford Twp., Susquehanna Co., will vote at Hezekiah LEECH's. Shenango Twp., Mercer Co., will vote at James SAMPLE's. Sandy Ck. Twp., Mercer Co., will vote at Jacob WILLIAMSON's. Richland Twp., Venango Co., will vote at William M'CALL's. South Huntingdon Twp., Westmoreland Co. & parts of the twps. of Mt. Pleasant & Hempfield will vote at Charles FOOLWOOD's, Mt. Pleasant. Waterford, Laboeuff & Beaver-dam Twps., Erie Co., will vote at Samuel GRAHAM's, Waterford. The 9th election district, Washington Co., will vote at David SIGHTS'. Franklin Twp., Adams Co., will vote at John MARKS'. Upper Mahantango Twp., Schuylkill Co., will vote at Peter YODER's. Huntingdon Twp., Luzerne Co., will vote at Stephen HARRISON's.

p. 174: Gideon DUNN, Delaware Co., left his family in Aug., 1799, while owning considerable property. Now, the property is vested in his wife & legal representatives.

p. 175: James BARTON, George BIDDIS, Milford, Pike Co., are to convey water from a spring or stream of water called Vankine Kill, into Milford.

p. 183: Accounts of Wilson SMITH, late quartermaster general, are to be adjusted. Accounts of Isaac LYNN for transporting baggage of a militia detachment from Fayette Co. to Erie & the accounts of George BOYD for supplies furnished to that detachment are to be adjusted. The accounts of Henry JARRETT, a capt. of a troop of cavalry, late in the service of this commonwealth, are to be adjusted.

p. 187: Daniel W. COX, Samuel WRIGHT, Jr., Peter T. SMITH are auth. to erect a wing dam in the Delaware River to connect Yard's Island with the mainland at Bloomsburg.

p. 188: Due to the Rev. services of Commodore BARNEY & the signal exertions & good conduct at Bladensburg in Aug. last in defence of the capital of the U.S., BARNEY is auth. to procure a sword with devices & emblems similar to the one presented to him by the legislature in 1782.

p. 191: A re-survey is to be made on the lands claimed by John SHEPARD & Benjamin DORRANCE, Claverack Twp., Luzerne Co. (now Bradford)

1815-16

p. 1: Catharine LEIDIG, late of Jonestown, Lebanon Co., died intestate owning real estate. It was thought she had no heirs but actually she left 2 children, Christopher HASSINGER & Elizabeth HESS (wife of Philip HESS). The land is bounded by lots of Ludwig SHADE & Frederick HERMAN.

p. 2: A warrant is issued for land in Somerset Twp., Washington Co., bounded by Benjamin LEYDA, David BILLMAN, John LEYDA, to Jacob KINTNER, John ONSTOTT, George MILLER for the use of the German Lutheran & Calvinist Congregation.

p. 4: The title that the commonwealth acquired by escheat from the want of heirs of Emmor VERNON, late of Delaware Co., decd., is vested in Sarah VERNON, mother of Emmor.

p. 4: Mary M'CREARY, one of the guardians of the minor children of Thomas M'CREARY, late of Mercer Co., decd., is auth. to release to Samuel M'CREARY, half of lot #1895 in the 2nd district of donation land on which Samuel improved & now lives.

p. 5: Elizabeth DEAL, Charles ALBRECHT are executors of Jacob DEAL, decd., & Peter DEAL & Daniel DEAL are brothers of the decd. Peter DEAL, their father, by his will of 9 Apr., 1798, devised his estate to be equally divided between his three children: Jacob, Peter & Daniel, & his granddaughter, Susanna. Jacob died leaving 7 children (of which 4 are minors).

p. 7: Part of Chillisquaque & Turbit Twp., Northumberland Co., near Montaur's Mountain, WILSON's mills, James MURRAY's, is annexed to Columbia Co. They will vote at William DALE's.

p. 8: Commissioners are to be appointed to review a part of a state road near the land of the heirs of Jacob TETWILOR, Newton Twp.,

Cumberland Co., through the land of David MICKEY to the land of Christopher AUS.

p. 13: James WILSON, Amos M'GINLEY, Yost HORBAUGH, Simon PECHER, William BLAKELY, Daniel ROYER, David FULLERTON, John M'LENAHAN (farmer), James BUCHANAN, Archibald RANKIN, Enoch SKINNER, James AGNEW are commissioners to make a road from the state line near Emmetsburg, MD to intersect the Chambersburg & Bedford Tpk. Rd. near the east end of M'Connelsburg.

p. 30: The "Orphan Society of Phila.": Managers: Sarah RALSTON, first directress; Julia RUSH, 2nd directress; Maria DORSEY, secretary; Mary YORKE, treasurer; Susanna LATIMER, Elizabeth M'LANE, Rebecca GRATZ, Abigail H. WARDER, Hannah PARKE, A. DENMAN, Sarah HENRY, Margaret LATIMER, Laetitia BUCHANAN, Elizabeth ABERCROMBIE, Debby H. MALCOM, Elizabeth HARKINS, Williamina E. SMITH, Sarah BACON, Eliza BRODHEAD, Ann L. EYRE, Rebecca RALSTON, J.H. PHILLIPS, Mary RICHARDS, Hannah JONES.

p. 31: Henry JARRETT, Northampton Co., is auth. to build a toll bridge across the Lehigh River near CURRIES' ferry.

p. 34: Isaac THOMPSON, an old soldier, formerly of Mifflin Co., but now of Ohio, is to receive $40 & $40/yr.

p. 35: Thomas CURTIS, late a sergeant in the 11th Pa. Regiment in the Rev. War, has left an unclaimed depreciation certificate in his name for £69 5s 8p. It is paid to him.

p. 42: George SPANGLER, William NESS, John BARNITZ, George SMALL, Charles F. FISHER, Abraham GARTMAN, Jacob SMYSER are commissioners of the York Water co.

p. 48: Lebanon Academy trustees: Rev. William HIESTER, Rev. William HENDEL, Rev. William G. ERNST, Rev. Philip GLONINGER, J. Andrew SHULZE, Peter SHINDEL, Samuel LIGHT, John HARRISON, Edward GODWIN, Dr. George REIDENAUR, Dr. Duncan KING, Philip GREENAWALT, Philip WOLFERSBURGER, Jr., Peter LINAWEVER, Abraham DOEBLER, John BATDORFF, Jacob WEIDMAN.

p. 51: Andrew BOZORTH is one of the executors of the will of Hannah DYER, decd.

p. 52: Michael WHEELAND, Milton, Northumberland Co., is to receive $40 & $40/yr.

p. 54: William MILLER, William BOOLS, Emanuel STOVER, John M'LAIN, Lazarus BROWN, Benjamin KYSER, Alexander M'COY, Jeremiah HAMILTON, James M'DOWELL, Thomas SCOTT are commissioners to make a road from the state line near Emmetsburg, MD to intersect the Chambersburg & Bedford Tpk. near Loudontown, Franklin Co.

p. 56: The adminis. of the estate of John BURNSIDE, an alien, petition to sell land in W. Caln Twp., Chester Co., bounded by Peter WAGONER, Dillman ZEIGLER.

p. 57: The estate of Thomas M'INTYRE, formerly of Phila., is vested in Isabella M'INTYRE, his widow.

p. 58: Thomas ALLIBONE, late of Phila., decd., before his death, contracted with John R. COATES, attorney of John PENN, Esq., of

Great Britain, for the purchase of a lot. ALLIBONE died 1 Aug., 1809. George W. JONES, William ALLIBONE, Jr., & Thomas ALLIBONE are adminis. of the estate. The lot was purchased by John LARGE. William LOWBER & wife, Francenia, George W. JONES & wife, Esther, Thomas ALLIBONE & wife, Mary E.B., William ALLIBONE, Jr. & wife Sarah, John HUMPHREYS & wife, Susan, Caleb NORTH, guardian of Sarah, Eliza, Mary & Rebecca ALLIBONE are auth. to sell the lot to John LARGE.

p. 59: Joseph CRAWFORD, William HAMILL are the executors of the will of William CLENNAL, an alien, late of Lower Province Twp., Montgomery Co. They are auth. to sell real estate.

p. 60: Peter NEWHARD, Charles H. MARTIN, Peter SNYDER, William BOAS, Solomon GANGEWERE are commissioners of the Northampton Water Co.

p. 65: Improvement of a road beginning where Coshecton & Great Bend Tpk. Rd. passes through Moosic Mt. to the west line of the state...to Susquehanna Co., $3000 is to be paid to Hosea TIFFANY, Jr., Jonah BREWSTER, Jabez HYDE, Jr...to Bradford Co., $300 is to be paid to George SCOTT, Samuel WOOD, Ebenezer KENDAL...to Tioga Co., $3000 is to be paid to Daniel KELSEY, Elijah PUTNAM, Richard ELLES...to Potter Co., $3000 is to be paid to Nathaniel PALMER, Isaac LYMAN & William AYRES...to M'Kean Co., $3000 is to be paid to Samuel STANTON, David BROWN & James ANDREWS...to Erie Co., $3000 is to be paid to Wilson SMITH, Thomas KING, John BOYD.

p. 67: Francis GIBSON, George STROOP, John MAXWELL, William POWER, Samuel ANDERSON, John CREIGH, Moses WATSON, Isaiah CARL, Robert ADAMS are commissioners to remove obstructions out of Sheerman's Ck.

p. 68: In the summer of 1815, $294 was stolen from John THOMPSON, West Chester. He charged Richard R. WILLIAMS with larceny & had him arrested. WILLIAMS fled. His bail of $300 was forfeited.

p. 69: James WILSON, Chanceford Twp., York Co., is auth. to sell claims of his sister, Mary WILSON, a lunatic, in land devised to Mary & others by the will of her father, John WILSON, late of Drumore Twp., Lancaster Co., decd.

p. 70: John MORE, present trustee of the Lutheran congregation, Upper Paxton Twp., Dauphin Co., is auth. to execute a deed for 10 acres adj. John NOLL & George FORNEY to George FORNEY.

p. 75: Mary HUTCHESON & Matthew BOWLAND, adminis. of the estate of Thomas HUTCHESON, late of Washington Co., are auth. to execute a deed to Robert HENRY, agreeably to a parol contract between Mathew RITCHIE, late of Washington Co., decd., & Robert HENRY. The land was part of a tract called "Mary's Bower" on Chartiers Ck. surveyed to Mathew RITCHIE on 24 Dec., 1794.

p. 77: Israel BRINGHURST, late of Montgomery Co., decd., died intestate. During his life, he agreed to sell to Cornelius TYSON, a tract of 13 acres in Montgomery Co. on the road from Trap to Wismersford. TYSON also died intestate. Mary BRINGHURST & Moses HOBSON are adminis. of the estate of Israel BRINGHURST.

p. 78: Militia fines on those who neglected or refused to march to the frontier under orders of Maj. Gen. MEADE & Gen. KELSO will be applied to road repairs.

p. 78: John KEATING, Thomas STEWARDSON, George VAUX, Phila.; John P. DE GRUCHY, John BOYD, Northumberland Co.; Hugh WHITE, James COLLINS, Thomas M'CLINTOCK, Samuel STEWARD, Robert M'CLURE, Andrew D. HEPBURN, Lycoming Co., are commissioners to make a road from Jersey Shore, Lycoming Co. to Coudersport, Potter Co.

p. 81: Daniel BUSSIER is paymaster of the Pa. Militia.

p. 83: A road from John BLAIR's, on the east side of the Allegheny Mt. to Huntingdon borough, & west from Martin REGART's on the west side of Laurel Hill to the Big Connemaugh River is to be extended. John DENNISTON, Indiana Co., & William JOHNSTON, Westmoreland Co., are commissioners to receive subscriptions to the road stock.

p. 84: Aaron BLOSS, Elijah PUTNAM, Asa MANN, Ambrose MILLARD, John GRAY, Tioga Co.; Henry HEWS, John HAYS, Esq., Samuel REED, John HERMAN, Lycoming Co.; George VAUX, Samuel MILLIGAN, John GIBSON, Phila., are commissioners to make a road from Henry HEWS', Lycoming Co. to Aaron BLOSS', Tioga Co.

p. 89: Mathew BROOK, William MOORE, Paul GEIGER, Curtis LEWIS, William HIGH, Abraham YOST, Abraham BROWER, Sr., Elijah GEIGER, Berks Co. are commissioners to erect a bridge over the Schuylkill River near LEWIS' ferry, Berks Co.

p. 90: Daniel LEIMBACH, Abraham KNABB, Oley Twp.; Daniel LEVAN, Benjamin SCHNEIDER, Exeter Twp.; John STROHECKER, Reading; Samuel BAIRD, Montgomery Co.; John MILLER, Sinking Spring, are commissioners to fix the site of a bridge.

p. 96: James ALEXANDER, Guion GREER, James LOGAN are empowered to sell, in Beaver borough, all the remaining lots which are the property of PA.

p. 100: Peter PEDERSON, minister from Denmark, has for many years past, resided in the U.S. & now wishes to purchase real estate to enable him to form a permanent residence. Owing to his public official station, he is unable to declare an intention to become a citizen of the U.S.

p. 101: In 1803, a fractional part of the reserved tract at the mouth of Big Beaver Ck., Beaver Co., was granted to James MOORE at $1.50/acre. MOORE has failed to pay the purchase money. He shall pay $250.

p. 101: Jean Victor Marie MOREAU, decd., by his will & codicil of 19 June, 1813, devised real estate in Bucks Co. to his wife, Eugenia MOREAU & his daughter, Isabella MOREAU, yet a minor. Eugenia & Isabella reside in France. John S. ROULET, executor of MOREAU, is auth. to sell the real estate.

p. 108: George EISENHUTH, George ORWIG, John ORWIG, Jacob ORWIG, Union Co., are auth. to dig a mill-race on the north side of Penn's Ck., near New Berlin, Union Co.

p. 112: David PORTER, Joseph ENGLE, William GRAHAM are commissioners to erect piers in the Delaware River, Chester borough, Delaware Co.

p. 113: Amos JUDSON is issued a patent for an in-lot in Waterford, Erie Co.

p. 116: Enoch SOUTH, Baltzer KRAMER, James VANCE, Lewis WRITEZ, Alexander VANCE are present managers of Greenesburg Mfg. Co., Greene Co.

p. 117: The borough of Strasburg, Lancaster Co., is bounded by Widow HERR, George LEFEVER, John HOWRY, John KINDIG, Widow LONGNECKER, Tobias HERR, Henry BRECHBILL, John BRECHBILL, Jacob FRITZ, John FUNK, Abraham GRAFF. They will vote at CRAWFORD's.

p. 123: Nicholas DAY, William DENNISTON, Zebulon DOTY, Joseph BARNES, James REED are commissioners to make a road from Harrisburg to Pittsburg. Commissioners to make a tpk. from New Alexandria, Westmoreland Co., to Pittsburg, Allegheny Co.: Nicholas DAY, Samuel DENNISTON, Jeremiah MURRAY, Hugh BIGHAM, Westmoreland Co.; Nathaniel IRISH, George SUTTON, Anthony BELLEN, Francis WILSON, Jr. & James HORNER, Allegheny Co.

p. 126: Land in Bethel Twp., Bedford co., is bounded by John GRAVES, Samuel GRAVES, Daniel SNIDER. It is sold to John STILLWELL, John VAN BUSKIRK, Nathaniel HART, Bethuel COVALT, Jacob MANN, Jacob HART, Jacob HESS for the use of the Baptist Congregation.

p. 128: Richard SMITH, John A. HENDERSON, William ORBISON, John H. LAMBERT, William SIMPSON, Patrict GWINN, William Wermiss SMITH, William R. SMITH are commissioners to erect a bridge over the Juniata River, Huntingdon borough.

p. 132: Edward DUFFIELD, Joseph K. SWIFT are executors of the will of John SWIFT, Moreland Twp., Phila. Co., decd.

p. 134: The treasurer must pay $600 to Edward BRIEN & Benjamin HART, Martick Twp., Lancaster co., for a road from Middle ferry to M'CALL's ferry.

p. 134: Cadwallader EVANS, Samuel WETHERILL, Jr., Phila.; Samuel BAIRD, Montgomery Co.; J.K. BOYER, Lewis REECE, Gabriel HEISTER, Jr., Berks Co.; James SINTON, Daniel SEAGER, Lehigh Co.; Daniel GRAFF, Dr. James M'FARLIN, Schuylkill Co.; Christian BROBST, Joseph PAXTON, Leonard RUPART, Philip MARLING, William BAIRD, Isaiah WILLETS, Richard DEMUTT, Columbia Co., are commissioners to erect a bridge over the north east branch of the Susquehanna River between Catawissa & the mouth of Fishing Ck.

p. 141: Samuel ROBERTS wrote a book on the British statutes in force in PA.

p. 142: It is lawful for Andrew FLEMMING to erect a toll bridge over Oil Ck., Venango Co. near FLEMMING's mills.

p. 145: Benjamin JENNINGS, an old soldier, is given $40 for losses sustained by him in the service of Pa. during the Rev.

p. 149: Samuel PRESTON, George M'HUBBELL, Samuel MOGRIDGE, Abraham DILLON, Buckingham Twp., Wayne Co.; Peter SPENCER, Benjamin KING, Levi GEER, Jirah MUMFORD, Jr., Mt. Pleasant Twp.; Lucas ELMENDORFF, Daniel BROADHEAD, Jr., Kingston Twp., Ulster Co., N.Y.; Levi DODGE, Samuel S. SEYMOUR, Newburg, N.Y.; Gilbert WALSWORTH, Ezra MAY, John KNIGHT, Charles LEONARD, Hancock, Delaware Co., N.Y. are commissioners to erect a bridge over the Delaware River at Stockport, Wayne Co.

p. 156: The amount due on a certificate of funded debt #13,451, issued to Peter OLINGER, late of York Co., decd., for £20 20s is to be paid to the executors of OLINGER. The amount due on a certificate of funded debt #15,672, issued to Col. James CUNNINGHAM, late of Lancaster Co., decd., for £2 is to be paid to Jane CUNNINGHAM, executor of the will of CUNNINGHAM.

p. 157: Joseph BUDD & Joshua BUDD are auth. to build a toll bridge across the Youghiogheny River, Westmoreland Co. Isaac MEASON & Zachariah CONNEL are auth. to erect a bridge across the Youghiogheny River at Connelsville, Fayette Co.

p. 171: Alexander MURDOCK, Joseph PENTECOAST, Thomas H. BAIRD, James MITCHELL, David HAMILTON, Esq., Alexander REED, John HILL, Jacob KINTNER, Andrew MENROW, Washington Co. for the Washington & Williamsport Tpk. Rd. Co.; William FLINN, James CONNER, Casper TARR, Henry FOX, James B. OLIVER, Dr. James BEATTY, Joseph MARKLE, John NICHOLAS, Joseph BEDSWORTH, Westmoreland Co., for the Robbstown & Mt. Pleasant Tpk. Rd. Co.; John LOBENGIER, James HURST, James JONES, Dr. James ESTEP, Westmoreland Co. & Abraham MORRISON, James CLARK, John HINDMAN, Abraham BROUGH, James HANNA, Somerset Co. for the Somerset & Mt. Pleasant Tpk. Rd. Co.; Jacob SNYDER, Henry ANKENY, Robert PHILSON, Jacob STONER, William C. DORSEY, Somerset Co. & James M. RUSSEL, David MANN, Jacob BONNETT & Samuel RIDDLE, Bedford Co. ofr the Somerset & Bedford Tpk Rd. Co. All are to make a road from Washington to Bedford.

p. 182: Loyalsock Ck., Lycoming Co., from the mouth to ROGER's factory; Crooked Ck., Armstrong Co., from the mouth to Jacob FRANTZ's mill; Tamaqua., commonly called Little Schuylkill from it's confluence with Big Schuylkill to David LONGAIRE's saw mill; Oil Ck., commonly called Mill Ck., Crawford Co. from it's mouth to the southern boundary of a tract belonging to Charles PLUMB, Crawford & Warren Co.; Tomhicken Ck.; a branch of Catawissa Ck., from the mouth to the line of a tract patented to Jeremiah WARDER, Jeremiah PARKER & Richard PARKER called Turn Hick; & Pemmapecha, commonly called Pennepack, Phila. Co., from the mouth to David LEWIS' saw-mill race are all declared public highways.

p. 183: Commissioners to erect a bridge over the Susquehanna River at Danville: John MILLS, William MONTGOMERY, Thomas WOODSIDE, Danville; Thomas MOOREHEAD, Mathew CALVIN, Derry; Dr. Thomas WOODS, Pennsborough; Alexander MOORE, Shamokin; Jacob K. BOYER & Lewis REESE, Reading.

p. 188: The U.S. recently purchased from William B. FORSTER, a tract on the Allegheny River, 2 miles above Pittsburg. The land is bounded by John EWART & will be the site of a military station.

p. 189: Walter CLARK, late of Londonderry Twp., Dauphin Co., decd., auth. Charles CLARK as his agent. On 24 Feb., 1812, he sold to Thomas DAVIS, a tract then the property of Walter CLARK partly in Derry & partly in Mahoning Twp., now Columbia Co. The executors of Walter CLARK are James WILSON & William CATHCART.

P. 190: A mortgage was executed by Thomas RYERSON on land in Greene Co. in 1806. RYERSON has since defaulted in payment. The land was eventually purchased by William T. HAYS, prothonotary of Greene Co. for $250 in trust for the use of Pa.

p. 192: Edward W. CARR, Phila., is to receive $221.63 for cleaning

& repairing public arms. Samuel POLAND, Franklin Co., is to receive $40 & $40/yr. Martin WILSON, Beaver Co., is to receive $50 for services in the medical dept. during the late war. Christopher Peter BENNER, late a soldier in the Rev. War, has an unclaimed final settlement certificate in his name for £5 4s dated 23 Apr., 1787. Jehu LEWIS, Bucks Co., is to receive $200 for a tract of donation land. William RUSH, Lycoming Co., is to receive $40 & $40/yr. Patrick MARTIN, Greene Co., is to receive $40 & $40/yr. Adam NITHREW, Lehigh Co., is to receive $50. Bernard VALLENTINE, Mifflin Co., is to receive $40 & $40/yr. is to be paid to David REYNOLDS for his use. Henry WOOLLERY, Northampton Co., is to receive $40. The claim of John HUGHES, Washington Co., will be adjusted. Jacob DEWITT, Pike Co., is to receive $50 for services rendered during the Rev. War. James KARR, Washington Co., is to receive $40 & $40/yr. Adam HILL, Mercer Co., a Rev. soldier, is to receive $40 & $40/yr. John M'MULLEN is to receive $150 for expenses incurred in consequence of being wounded whilst in the service under Gen. BROWN. James MITCHELL, Cumberland Co., is to receive $40 & $40/yr. Eleanor FOY, widow of John FOY, who died 28 Dec., 1814, whilst in the service of his country in Col. John THOMPSON's regiment, is to receive $50.

p. 195: Huntingdon Academy trustees: Rev. John JOHNSON, William STEEL, Richard SMITH, Patrick GIVIN, William R. SMITH, Samuel STEEL, William ORBISON, Thomas KERR, Robert ALISON, William KERR, John M'CONNEL, David NEWINGHAM, William SIMPSON, Martin GRAFFIUS.

p. 196: Trustees of the Susquehanna Academy: William THOMPSON, David DIMOCK, Isaac POST, Jabez HYDE, Jr., Daniel ROSS, Wright CHAMBERLAIN, Hosea TIFFANY, Jr., Robert H. ROSE, Jonah BREWSTER, David POST, Austin HOWEL, Charles FRAZIER, Isaac BROWNSON, Putnam CATLIN.

p. 200: Adam SMITH, Robert SIMONTON, Jacob DETRICH, Northampton Co., are commissioners to erect a bridge over the Delaware River at the Columbia Glass Manufactory. N.J. commissioners: Francis MAERHOFF, John JOHNSON, Michael ODENWELDER, Gershom BARTOW, Daniel SWAYZE, John LOCK, Jacob SHARP, N.J.; Joseph ARMAT, Phila.; David SMITH, Robert BUTTZ, James HOLLINGSHEAD, Peter HILLIARD, Evan THOMAS, Pa.

p. 208: James LINN is Secretary of State of N.J.

p. 208: Election districts: Fishing Ck., Columbia Co. will vote at Daniel PEALOR's. Sugar Loaf Twp., Columbia Co. will vote at Ezekiel COLE's. Greenwood Twp., Columbia Co. will vote at Jonathan HARTLY's. The 6th election district of Montgomery Co. will vote at Michael COLP's, Potstown. Part of Springfield & Wells Twp., Bradford Co., will vote at Noah MURRY's. Part of Wells & Columbia Twp., Bradford Co. will vote at Sarah MORGAN's. Allen Twp., Cumberland Co. will vote at Jacob GHEAR's. Rockland Twp., Berks Co., will vote at Andrew SHIFFERT's. Hilltown Twp., Bucks Co., will vote at John HOCKMAN's. Chippaway Twp., Beaver Co. will vote at Samuel CUNNINGHAM's. Fallowfield Twp., Crawford Co. will vote at Alexander CLARK's. Shenango Twp., Crawford Co. will vote at Hugh M'GILL's. Beaver & Cussawago Twp., Crawford Co., will vote at James FETTERMAN's, Cussawago. Londonderry Twp., Lebanon Co. will vote at John WOLFERSBERGER, Jr.'s, Campbellstown. Jackson Twp., Tioga Co. will vote at David NICHOLS'. Covington Twp., Tioga Co. will vote at Samuel HIGLEY's. Sullivan Twp., Tioga Co. will vote at John GRAY's. Penns & Mahantongo Twp., Union Co., near KREMER's saw mill run,

George GAMBYS', Henry RAMSTINE's, Christopher MOYER's, Henry GERMAN's will vote at Frederick MOYER's, Freeburg, Penns Twp. Greenwood Twp., Cumberland Co., will vote at Henry RAYMON's. Finley Twp., Washington Co., will vote at Edward CARROL's. Tunkhannock, Luzerne Co. will vote at Charles OTIS'. Gibson Twp., Susquehanna Co. will vote at James BENNET's. Indiana Twp., Allegheny Co. will vote at David STEWART's. Hempfield Twp., Westmoreland Co. from Jacob PAINTER's mill on Sewickly Ck. to the twp. line will vote at Greensburg. Brighton Twp., Beaver Co. will vote at Robert WILSON's. Turbutt Twp., Mifflin Co. will vote at John MORRISON's. Pike Twp., Berks Co. will vote at George OYSTER's. Venango & Parker Twp., Butler Co. will vote at James CONLY's, Parker Twp. Donegal Twp., Westmoreland Co. will vote at Robert CAMPBELL's, Mansville.

p. 214: Valentine KLOESS, Bethlehem Twp., Northampton Co., died owning two tracts in Northampton Co. & one in Northumberland Co. He willed them to his widow & 7 children. Maria Eva KLOESS is executrix & Jacob KLOESS, Abraham KLOESS & John SMITH are executors.

p. 215: Henry SHROEDER, Adams Co., an alien, has his title to a lot in Gettysburg confirmed. David SCOTT, Luzerne Co., has his title to a messuage in Wilkesbarre confirmed. John JONES, a former claimant, was an alien at the time of purchase. Hugh MULHOLLAND, Luzerne Co., formerly an alien, has his title in land confirmed.

p. 216: Charles TIPPER, Bedford Co., an old soldier, is to receive $40 & $40/yr.

p. 217: The volunteers & militia of Pa., who volunteered to cross lines into the province of Upper Canada in 1814, under the command of Maj. Gen. BROWN, distinguished themselves by their patriotism & bravery at Chippawa & Bridgewater & at the defence of Fort Erie.

p. 217: Everard PENROSE, Berks Co., wold land to Jacob FRY. It was sold to PENROSE by John NESTOR in trust for Margaret FORTMAN, who has since died. PENROSE is trustee of FORTMAN & is auth. to sell to Jacob FRY the land in Herefod Twp., Berks Co., adj. George HOFFMAN & Nicholas HUNTER.

p. 218: Edward CAVANOUGH is granted an annuity.

p. 219: William ELLIS, late of Lycoming Co., decd., died owning land in Lycoming & Tioga Co. Mercy ELLIS, Joseph WHITACRE, Samuel W. MORRIS are guardians of the minor children of William ELLIS.

p. 221: Militia commanders:
<u>1st Division, 1st Brigade</u>: #9--Edward TILGHMAN; #19--Thomas M'EUEN; #81--Peter A. BROWN; #72--Joshua SULLIVAN; #74--Isaac BOYER; #96--Anthony SIMMONS.
<u>1st Division, 2nd Brigade</u>: #3--Samuel CASTOR; #47--Robert WATKINS; #79--John SHINN; #4--John GOODWIN; #84--John GOODMAN; #93--John THOMPSON; #100--John ZANE.
<u>2nd Div., 1st Brig.</u>: #33--William LONG; #42--Lewis BACHE; #59--Jacob KITNOR.
<u>2nd Div., 2nd Brig.</u>: #56--Philip BOYER; #63--William M. WHITE; #92--Thomas HUMPHREY.
<u>3rd Div., 1st Brig.</u>: #38--John L. PEIRSON; #49--Gideon HUMPHREY; #57--William RALSTON.
<u>3rd Div., 2nd Brig.</u>: #41--Robert MORTON; #91--David DICKY; #95--Jacob HUMPHREY.
<u>4th Div., 1st Brig.</u>: #18--Samuel L. GEHR; #51--David SHIRK;

#69--Jeremiah MOSHER.
4th Div., 2nd Brig.: #35--John HAMILTON; #65--James ANKRIM; #75--William M'MULLEN; #101--John M'CLURE.
5th Div., 1st Brig.: #25--Henry STOVER; #64--Robert COLVIN; #94--Michael SPANGLER.
5th Div., 2nd Brig.: #80--Thomas C. MILLER; #39--George SHERMAN; #90--Frederick EICHELBERGER.
6th Div., 1st Brig.: #14--Adam RITSCHER; #16--William COCHRAN; #36--Frederick HUMMEL; #44--Abraham GULDIN; #98--Thomas WALKER.
6th Div., 2nd Brig.: #1--Daniel LEVAN; #11--John NEIKERCH; #30--Jacob HUNTZINGER; #53--John LUTZ; #77--Jonathan CLEAVER.
7th Div., 1st Brig.: #26--Henry WINTERS; #34--James SHAFFER; #97--Jacob SEIPLE.
7th Div., 2nd Brig.: #68--James JAMISON; #82--Jacob SHAFFER.
8th Div., 1st Brig.: #7--George WEYRICH; #43--Aaron CHAMBERLAIN; #48--John DARR; #45--John ROBINS; #71--James M'CLURE.
8th Div., 2nd Brig.: #2--Isaac BOWMAN; #70--Isaac DIMMICK; #76--Frederick BAILEY.
9th Div., 1st Brig.: #17--Jonathan SMITH; #54--John M'MEENS.
9th Div., 2nd Brig.: #15--Harry SPALDING; #21--Samuel M'KEAN.
10th Div., 1st Brig.: #12--William SMITH; #22--William TURNER; #73--Mathew ROGERS.
10th Div., 2nd Brig.: #29--Charles CADWALLADER; #32--Thomas M'PHERSON; #62--William R. SMITH.
11th Div., 1st Brig.: #23--John RIPPY; #39--John MAXWELL; #86--John WEISS.
11th Div., 2nd Brig.: #5--John SNYDER; #6--James WOOD; #50--Stephen WILSON.
12th Div., 1st Brig.: #55--John R. REID; #85--Moses GORDON.
12th Div., 2nd Brig.: #8--Isaac PROCTOR; #13--Michael DIEVELY.
13th Div., 1st Brig.: #60--Thomas M'QUAID; #67--James GUTHRIE; #88--James B. OLIVER.
13th Div., 2nd Brig.: #20--James A. M'CLELLAND; #52--Andrew MOORE.
14th Div., 1st Brig.: #10--Joshua DICKERSON; #37--House BENTLY; #66--Samuel SCOTT.
14th Div., 2nd Brig.: #40--Andrew SUTTON; #46--Andrew BUCHANAN.
15th Div., 1st Brig.: #28--George O. VALENDEGEM; #61--James LOGAN; #87--Magnus M. MURRAY.
15th Div., 2nd Brig.: #58--Robert ORR, Jr.; #99--John DOUGLASS.
16th Div., 1st Brig.: #24--Robert MARTIN; #83--Robert MOORE.
16th Div., 2nd Brig.: #31--David NELSON; #27--Andrew CHRISTIE; #78--George MOORE.

p. 230: Abraham BAILEY, Abraham WOLF, Robert SCOTT, John SCHOME, Henry LEWARS, William WITMAN, Jr., Frederick SMITH, Daniel LEVAN, Henry HEIST, George SHERTEL, Berks Co., are commissioners to erect a bridge over the Schuylkill River near Hamburg, Berks Co.

p. 236: John DICKSON may execute a deed to Jacob CASSAT, John KING, & James NEELY, trustees of the Presby. congregation of Great Connewago, Straban Twp., Adams Co., for a tract granted by patent to James DICKSON in trust for the use of the congregation.

p. 237: William HAMILTON, late a Lt. Col. of volunteer rifle & his troops marched to the defence of Baltimore. Lt. Col. John L. PEARSON, Delaware Co., is repaid for rations furnished the detachment of militia under his command in the service of the U.S. in the late war with Great Britain. John PHILIPS, late a pay master of the Pa. Militia, is reimbursed for monies expended by him.

p. 238: Commissioners to improve navigation of the Lehigh River:

John LARDNER, Thomas STEWARTSON, George VAUX. William PENROSE, John GIBSON, Phila. City & Co.; Asher MINOR, Joseph SMITH, Lewis S. CORYELL, James VANUXEM, Jr., Bucks Co.; Joseph RICE, Henry JARRET, Jacob STEN, George BUTTZ, Northampton Co.; George M. HOLLENBACH, Redmond CONYNGHAM, Joseph SENTON, David RICHARDS, Luzerne Co.; Jacob SEAGER, James WILSON, William ECKART, George YUNDT, Lehigh Co.; Jacob SHINER, Philip MARLIN, John CHAMBERLIN, John BROWN, Columbia Co.

p. 243: A deed of trust from Robert ANDERSON, James GILMORE to Hugh WILSON, Daniel MOORE, David SHIELDS, conveying a lot in Bell St., Washington, is confirmed to Hugh WILSON, Daniel MOORE & David SHIELDS in trust for the 1st Baptist Church of Washington.

p. 245: Capt. Charles STEWART, native of Pa., commanded a U.S. frigate Constitution, has highly distinguished himself by his valor & conduct in capturing the British ships of war Cyane & Levant. He is given a sword.

THE LAWS OF PENNSYLVANIA
1816-17, 1817-18

p. 2: John CONRAD, late of Phila., decd., willed land to the German Religious Society of Roman Catholics, of the Holy Trinity Church of Phila.

p. 2: The right of the commonwealth in an escheated estate of Francis DOERING, formerly of Phila., decd., is vested in the German Religious Society of Roman Catholics of the Holy Trinity Church.

p. 3: John OTTINGER, Springfield Twp., Montgomery Co., died owning land which he bequeathed to his wife until his youngest child reached 14 years. The child is now 1 year old. Esther OTTINGER, Jacob HOLGATE & Aaron KEYSER are executors.

p. 4: Richard HOPE, Mt. Pleasant Twp., Westmoreland Co., died in 1813 & owned 165 acres in Mt. Pleasant Twp. He left as his heirs 2 brothers & 5 sisters, one of whom married William SPEER & died leaving 5 minor children. Clements BURLEIGH was appointed guardian of the children but declined. John LOBINGIER was appointed in his room. William SPEER, Fayette Co., & John LOBINGIER, Westmoreland Co., were guardians of Mary, Jane, Nancy, Joseph & John SPEER.

p. 6: Jacob FUNK & Jacob TRICHLER, adminis. of John W. BURSON, late of Springfield Twp., Bucks Co., who died intestate, are auth. to sell to Nicholas KRAMER, Northampton Co., land near Jacob FULLMER's, William BURSON's, Joseph AFFLEBACH's, & Philip BARRON's.

p. 7: George Peter WOEBLER, late of Hempfield Twp., Westmoreland Co., died intestate & without kindred. He left a widow, Mary Magdalena. Under the articles of agreement with Daniel BUSH, 4 Dec., 1809, he bought land adj. Henry HIESLY, Thomas WILLIAMS.

p. 9: A tract in Moore Twp., Northampton Co., was granted by deed from William BECK, 30 Sept., 1782, to Philip DRUM, Casper ERB & Henry BARTHOLOMEW in trust for the use of Moore Twp's. German congregation. John HEINEY, John SILFIUS, John FULTON & William KLIPPENGER are trustees.

p. 10: James JEFFERIES, William DOWNING, Humphrey MARSHALL, William

WEBB, Jesse JOHN, Isaac TRIMBLE, Isaac BENNET, Caleb BRINTON, Jr., James JONES are commissioners of the Kennet & Dowingtown Tpk. Rd. Co.

p. 12: Patrick ARCHBOLD, late of Adams Col., died intestate, without kindred. He left a widow, Eleanor.

p. 15: John ALLEN, Phila., merchant, by indenture of 19 Aug., 1811, sold to Thomas William FRANCIS, Phila., merchant, real estate. Thomas W. FRANCIS died intestate, leaving several minor children. Dorothy William FRANCIS & Thomas Mayne WILLING are adminis.

p. 19: John CAVANOUGH is to be paid an annuity.

p. 19: Mary PAINTER, late Mary M'CREARY, one of the guardians of the minor children of Thomas M'CREARY, late of Mercer Co., decd., is auth. to sell to Samuel M'CREARY ½ of a lot #1892 in the 2nd donation land district, Mercer Co., which Samuel improved & on which he now lives.

p. 20: Hugh M'LAUGHLIN, late of Union Co., decd., by parole contract, sold to Uriah SILSBY, a piece of land in White Deer Twp. John BOAL & Thomas WILSON, adminis. of Hugh M'LAUGHLIN, are auth. to make a deed.

p. 21: The right of the commonwealth in the estate of William WILLIAMS, late of Radnor Twp., Delaware Co., is vested in Margaret WILLIAMS.

p. 22: William PAINE, late of Conestogo Twp., Lancaster Co., died intestate without heirs. He owned land adj. Abraham HARNISH & Henry HESS with a small, one story house thereon. PAINE left a widow, Susanna, since intermarried with John CRAWFORD.

p. 23: The right of the commonwealth in the estate of John TODD, late of East Whiteland, Chester Co., is vested in Margaret HOFFMAN.

p. 23: It is lawful for Catharine Augusta NEWBOLD, Herman LE ROY, Caleb NEWBOLD, Jr., Herman LE ROY, Jr., adminis. of the estate of Thomas NEWBOLD, late of Phila., merchant, to sell his real estate.

p. 24: Giles STEPHENS, Thomas STEPHENS purchased from Joseph BURLEY, 2 adj. tracts in Tyrone Twp., Huntingdon Co. Joseph BURLEY died intestate. The article of agreement was destroyed by the accidental burning of the house of James E. STEWART. John TEMPLETON & Joseph MEREDITH are adminis. of Joseph BURLEY's estate.

p. 25: Thomas CLUGAGE is to be paid $200 for services as a captain in the Rev. War.

p. 26: Joseph JOHNSTON, Beaver Co., is paid #375 for his claim for a tract of donation land in the 2nd district, Mercer Co., #1881, which was granted to JOHNSTON but had been previously granted to another.

p. 26: Daniel MONTGOMERY, Mathew S. COLVIN, Nathaniel SPENCE, Thomas MOORHEAD, Philip GOODMAN, Columbia Co.; John M'MEANS, Joseph WOOD, George WEBB, John BECHER, John BRINDLE, Jacob SHOEMAKER are commissioners to make a road from Danville, Columbia Co. to Pennsborough, Lycoming Co.

p. 29: Christopher SEEBOLD is to buy land in New Berlin, Union Co., from the commissioners of Union Co. SEEBOLD sold the land to the commissioners for a new jail yard.

p. 32: The officers of the Bethany & Canaan Tpk. Rd.: Moses THOMAS, Esq., Isaac DIMMICK, Jason TORREY, Mathias KEEN, George RIX, Wayne Co.

p. 35: Noah STEVENS, Stephen GRIFFIN, Isaac HART, John I. DING, John WATERS are commissioners to improve the navigation of the Lackawana Ck.

p. 39: David C. CULP is Justice of the Peace for the 4th district, Montgomery Co., & Assistant Assessor of the direct tax of the U.S.

p. 40: Peter S.V. HALMOT sustained losses in the purchase & sale of rations under the orders of Gen. MEADE.

p. 47: David MANN & James M. RUSSELL, Bedford, will superintend the elections. Bedford is bounded by land of Thomas RAY, Jacob BONNETT, Dr. John ANDERSON.

p. 49: Philip REED & Henry SNYDER can recover the surplus money which remains unexpended from the Sumanytown school-house lottery.

p. 50: Mary WALKER, Pike Co., the widow of John WALKER, is to be paid $40 & $40/yr.

p. 51: Gabriel BLAKENEY, Washington Co., an officer of the Rev. War, is to be paid $80 & $80/yr.

p. 52: David KROUSE, late of Upper Hanover Twp., Montgomery Co., decd., in his life, exchanged land with John GAREY which was bounded by Jacob SHULTZ, John GAREY, et al. Isaac SHULTZ & Daniel SHULTZ are guardians of the minor children of David KROUSE.

p. 54: Capt. Isaac SEELY's heirs are granted relief.

p. 56: A road is to be laid out in Washington Co. near Daniel DYE's, Canton Twp., to intersect the Va. state road near Alexander M'KETTRICKS' on the state line.

p. 57: Executors of John GEMMIL, Jr., decd., & adminis. of Zachariah GEMMIL, decd., are auth. to join with the surviving heirs of John GEMMIL, Sr., to sell land in Fermanagh Twp., Mifflin Co., adj. James BANKS, to Andrew & James BANKS.

p. 57: John SNYDER, late of York Co., Adam SPECHT, Union Co., old soldiers, will receive $40 & $40/yr. Daniel STOY, Somerset Co., is to receive $200 & $50/yr. for his meritorius services. Henry LEBO, Lycoming Co., is to receive $40.

p. 58: John EPLER, late of Bern Twp., Berks co., decd., by parole contract agreed to sell to John LERCH, a lot. EPLER died suddenly without making a deed. Jacob LINEBACH & Catharine (late Catharine EPLER) & Henry SHELL, surviving adminis. of John EPLER are to sell the land to John LERCH, bounded by John MOSER, et al.

p. 60: Newville, Cumberland co., is bounded by land of heirs of Gabriel GLENN, land formerly of Robert WALKER, land formerly of Andrew WALKER, land of the heirs of Jeremiah M'KIBBEN.

p. 69: Milton, Northumberland Co., is bounded by Daniel BICHLEY's farm, D. SCUDDER's farm, HILL's farm, William & Thomas POLLOCK's farm, David MARR's farm. Thomas COMLEY, Arthur M'GOWAN & the constable of Turbet Twp., are to superintend the elections.

p. 76: Samuel PRESTON, Sandford CLARK, George W. HUBBLE, Joseph TANNER, Peter SPENCER, Benjamin KING & Thomas MEREDITH are to make a road in Wayne Co.

p. 79: Thomas SMITH sold land in Clearfield Twp., Butler Co., to James SHARP in trust for the children of Thomas SMITH. SHARP died & SMITH sold the land to Abraham BRINKER.

p. 80: Abraham AURAND, adminis. of Jacob WOLF, late of Union Co., decd., is auth. to sell to Henry NULL, land in Buffaloe Twp., Union Co.

p. 81: Thomas MEREDITH, Ira MUMFORD, Jr., Sandford CLARK, Joseph TANNER, Benjamin LONG. Asa STANTON, Thomas SPANGENBERG, Walter LYON are commissioners to make a road from Bellmont, Wayne Co., to Oghquaga on the Susquehanna River.

p. 86: Michael BOLLINGER is adminis. of Wyand SMITH, late of Centre Co., who sold by parole contract, a house & lots in Millheim-town, Centre Co., to Martin TRESTER.

p. 87: John PHILLIPS, late a paymaster of militia, is to be credited with $286.52, being the amount paid by him to Maj. Gen. David MEAD & his aides for their services at Erie in the summer of 1813.

p. 88: Mary ZIMMERMAN, adminis. of Peter ZIMMERMAN, late of Union Co., is auth. to sell a lot in Hartleton, Union Co., to Elizabeth SMITH, wife of Melchior SMITH, Jr.

p. 88: William MEANS, George SCOTT, John HOLLENBACK, J.M. PIOLETTE, Jacob BOWMAN, Charles F. WELLES, Eliphalet MASON, Burr RIDGWAY, Jonathan STEVANS are commissioners to erect a bridge over the Susquehanna River at Meansville, Bradford Co.

p. 94: Elections in M'Connelsburg, Bedford Co., will be at Mary SCOTT's.

p. 99: John L. PEARSON, Delaware Co., is to be paid $150 for money refunded by George THOMAS for rations furnished a detachment of militia under his command late in the service of the U.S. Thomas HARSHE is paid $40 for services rendered at Erie during the campaign of 1814.

p. 100: Arthur ST. CLAIR is to be paid $200 & $350/yr.

p. 102: Ruth HATRICK, widow of William HATRICK, late of Berks Co., a soldier in the late war, is to receive $50.

p. 102: A suit is instituted by representative of George CROGHAN, decd., against persons holding titles to land in Beaver Co.

p. 102: Ann Dorothy GETTIG, Northumberland Co., widow of the late Lt. GETTIG, an officer in the Rev. army, will receive $40 & $40/yr.

p. 106: Jacob MIXSELL, Easton Borough, & Lewis S. CORYELL & Col.

John KINSEY, Bucks Co., are commissioners to improve the navigation of the Delaware River. William ERWIN, Bucks Co., & William BARNET, Northampton Co., shall view places where money has been expended.

p. 111: Jacob HERRINGTON, Crawford Co., is to receive $40 & $40/yr. He is an old soldier.

p. 112: Casper STONER, an old soldier, & Eve DOUGHERTY, Armstrong Co., widow of Patrick DOUGHERTY, soldier in the late war, will receive $40 & $40/yr. Elizabeth STICKLE, widow of John STICKLE, late a soldier, will receive $50.

p. 114: Jane VAN SCHUYVER, wife of Samuel VAN SCHUYVER, Bristol, Bucks Co., was born a short time before the marriage of her parents. She is declared legitimate.

p. 115: John BROOKS & William M'GRADY, Crawford Co., & William MILES, Erie Co., are commissioners to lay out a road from the northern line of Pa. to Meadville.

p. 131: Managers of the West Newton Bridge Co.: John NICOLLS, John ROWAN, Joseph MARKLE, Dr. James BEATTY, James B. OLIVER.

p. 135: John LACKEY, surviving adminis. of Charles CLARKE, late of N. Beaver Twp., Beaver Co., is auth. to sell land to William ADAIR, James FULLERTON, John NESBIT, in trust for the congregation of Westfield. John HUNTER & John CLARKE, executors of Walter CLARKE, late of N. Beaver Twp., Beaver Co., are auth. to sell to ADAIR, FULLERTON & NESBIT, land in trust for the congregation of Westfield. Executors of Thomas DAVENPORT, late of Plymouth Twp., Luzerne Co., are auth. to sell to Abraham VAN LOON, a part of lot #4 in the river tier of meadow lots, Plymouth Twp., adj. Joshua PUGH.

p. 144: Michael MURPHY, late of Cambria Co., sold to Samuel MOSS, a tract & in error, another tract was deeded instead. MOSS afterward sold it to John LANEY. MURPHY is since decd., leaving devisees named in his will, who are underage. Luke M'GUIRE is executor of MURPHY. Land is in Southampton Twp., Bedford Co., & is part of a large tract called "Armagh" which was granted to MURPHY by patent 1 Feb., 1799. MURPHY also sold land to Leonard NICHUM.

p. 146: George FISHER, William ALLISON, Enoch SKEER, John DETWILLER, John SWAR, John ELLIOT are commissioners to erect a bridge over Swatara from State St., Portsmouth, Dauphin Co.

p. 152: Henry ANTES, Jr. has the right to build a ferry on the west branch of the Susquehanna River at the mouth of Nippenose Ck., Lycoming Co.

p. 153: John STODDART, Ebenezer SLOCUM, Ebenezer DRAKE, John GARDNER, Eleazer CARY are commissioners of the Lackawana Tpk. Rd.

p. 156: Benjamin CHAMBERS & wife, Sarah, on 28 Sept., 1784, sold land to James MAXWELL as trustees for Franklin co. to erect a new jail.

p. 157: David MEAD, on 23 June, 1796, sold to Cornelius VANHORN, Henry REICHARD & Luke HILL, a lot in Meadville, #37, for a school. Cornelius VANHORN, Henry REICHARD, Samuel LORD, Samuel TORBETT, William FORSTER, Mead Twp., Crawford Co., are trustees of the school.

p. 158: Philip MORR, Jacob ROUSCH, trustees of the Evangelical German Lutheran Church of Zion's Church, Penns Twp., Union Co., are auth. to sell land.

p. 159: Frederick FOERING, Phila. Co., is appointed deputy quarter master general of the militia & paid $510.

p. 159: Henry BACH, late of Menallin Twp., Adams Co., died intestate. He left a widow, Elizabeth, who later married Peter CRUM. His estate adj. Thomas BALDWIN & George WILSON.

p. 160: Nicholas ANGST, Schuylkill Co., an old soldier, is to receive $40 & $40/yr.

p. 161: William BERRY, Huntingdon Co., Abraham KEAGY & Greenwood BELL, Clearfield Co., will receive $800 to improve the road from Logan's Narrows, Huntingdon, to the road to Presque Isle.

p. 163: Managers of the Pa. Botanic Garden: Jonas PRESTON, Pres.; Robert RALSTON, Simon GRATZ, Joseph CLOUD, Benjamin TUCKER, Robert VAUX, Reuben HAINS, Isaac C. JONES, Joshua LONGSTRETH, Edward CLARK, Adam ECHFELDT, Lewis CLAPIER, managers & directors.

p. 164: Commissioners of the Wind Gap, Nazareth & Hellerstown Tpk. Rd. Co.: William HENRY, Sr., Christian D. SENSEMAN, John HAMAN, Henry JARRET, George BUTZ, George HESS, Christian ROTH, Jacob GEISINGER, Jonas ROTHRICK, Northampton Co.; Abraham FERTZ, Joseph FRY, Sr., Lehigh Co.; William GREEN, Bucks Co.

p. 167: Commissioners to erect a bridge over French Ck., Franklin, Venango Co.: George M'CLELLAND, Alexander M'ALMONT, William CONNELY, Franklin; Henry HURST, John BROOKS, Meadville.

p. 173: Frederick SHRIVER, Lancaster Co., William HAMSON, Lebanon Co., are to receive $40 & $40/yr. Elizabeth M'CULLOUGH, widow of Robert M'CULLOUGH, Rev. soldier, is to receive $40. James COLLINS, Lycoming Co., will receive an annuity for the use of Atcheson MELLON.

P. 175: A warrant was granted to John KERR & John MONTEETH for land in trust for the congregation of the Pines, Straban Twp., Adams Co. Both are now decd. Said congregation is extinct. William GILLILAND, William KERR, Moses M'ILVAIN are auth. to sell the land adj. Abraham FICKES, William CASHMAN, reserving enough land for a burial ground.

p. 176: Jacob ARNDT, John HERSTER, Easton, Northampton Co., were tenants in common of a lot & messuage #88 & #89. They sold a stone messuage & lot to Philip H. MATTES. ARNDT has since died. Francis SWAINE & wife, Elizabeth, late Elizabeth ARNDT, Abraham ARNDT & John NICE are the executors.

p. 178: Atcheson LAUGHLIN, William KILGORE, John GETTIS, Richard WOODS, James PURDY, David STERRET, Alexander THOMPSON are trustees of the 1st Presby. Congregation of Big Spring, Newtown Twp., Cumberland Co.

p. 179: Cornelius COSYN sold an acre of land to Francis COSSART, David VANDINE, & David DEMORAST, in trust for the Low Dutch Congregation of Calvinists, Adams Co. Wilhelmus HOOGHTALEN, Jacob CASSAT, Garret BRINKERHOOF are auth. to sell land in Straban Twp.,

212

Adams Co.

p. 180: If the heirs of Christian CROLL require it, the board of property will examine his title to a tract in Salem Twp., Luzerne Co., surveyed on a warrant of 30 Jan., 1786, in the name of Jacob SMITHERS, for 250 acres. If it is found that the land was certified to Connecticut claimants & that CROLL was entitled to the land, CROLL's estate will get the money back that he paid & interest.

p. 181: John BORROWS, Abraham GRAFIUS, Jonathan SMITH, Benjamin WARNER, Lycoming Co., & John BROWN, David C. OWEN, Columbia Co., are commissioners to make a road from Berwick, Columbia Co. to Williamsport, Lycoming Co.

p. 185: Joseph STURGEON, late of West Hanover Twp., Dauphin Co., decd., by parole agreement, sold a tract to Joseph WILSON, bounded by Christian HERSHIE, Joseph WILSON, Joseph STRUGEON. STURGEON died intestate before making a deed. His heirs are minors. James DIXON, William CATHCART are adminis. of STURGEON & are auth. to complete the sale to WILSON.

p. 188: William PORTERFIELD, John M'CALMONT, Jr., John M'KINNEY, John MARTIN, Jr., Richard PATCH are agents to expend $1000 to improve the Allegheny River & Conowango Ck.

p. 189: Thomas Hartley CRAWFORD, Philip BERLIN, George BROWN, James WRIGHT, Jacob GROVE are commissioners of the Chambersburg Water Co.

p. 195: Peter FRICKER, an old soldier, is to receive $40 & $40/yr. will be paid to Frederick HELLER, Reading, for FRICKER's use.

p. 202: Joseph THORNHILL, late of Phila., carpenter, decd., granted on 2 Feb., 1788, to William YOUNG, Oxford Twp., Phila Co., cordwainer, & his wife, Rebecca, 3 acres of ground on the condition that they provide all the necessities of life to their son, Joseph YOUNG, who has been blind since infancy. William & Rebecca are now decd. & the estate is in ruinous condition. They left 6 children: Joseph, William, & David YOUNG, Keziah HUGHES, Susan CASNER, Ann YOUNG. Isaac WORRALL & Nathan HARPER, tanner, both of Frankford, are auth. to sell the real estate for Joseph's welfare.

p. 205: Henry BALDWIN, William ROBESON, Pittsburg; William CAMPBELL, Jacob MECKLIN, Butler; James MILLER, Bevan PEARSON, Mercer, for the Pittsburg, Butler & Mercer Tpk. Rd. Co.; John REYNOLDS, Thomas ATKINSON, Meadville; Joseph SMITH, Jacob HERRINGTON, Mercer, for the Mercer & Meadville Tpk. Rd. Co., are commissioners to make a road from Pittsburg to Meadville.

p. 217: Commissioners to be appointed to lay out a state road from Samuel HILLS', Franklin Twp., Greene Co. to Middle Island Ck., Va.

p. 219: Lower Chichester Ck., Delaware Co., from the mouth to David TRAINER's & Gideon JAQUES' mill, is declared a public highway.

p. 221: Jacob FOX, late of Bedminister Twp., Bucks Co., by will of 31 Mar., 1783, after certain bequests to his wife & grandchildren & a bequest of 1 shilling to each of his sons, he left the rest of his estate to the poor of Bedminister Twp. The estate is granted by the directors of the poor, Bucks Co., to the heirs of FOX in such a manner as if he had died intestate.

p. 222: The right of the commonwealth in the estate of Patrick CARROL, late of Londonderry Twp., Chester Co., is vested in Hanna CARROL.

p. 224: The title of John O'NEIL, Easton, Northampton Co., an alien, to land in Easton, on the general plan as lot #244 (part being sold to Jacob SHOUSE) is confirmed as if he was a citizen. Title of William ALEXANDER, an alien, to land in Hempfield Twp., Lancaster Co., containing 4 acres, purchased from Hugh KENEDY, is confirmed.

p. 226: Commissioners to erect a bridge over Big Beaver, near the ferry occupied by Charles MORROW: Joseph T. BOYD, Charles MORROW, William FORBES, William LOWRY, Stewart BOYD, David WHITE, James COCHRANE.

p. 228: President & managers of the Beaver & Greersburg Tpk. Rd.: Thomas HENRY, James LYON, Robert MOORE, John R. SHANON, Robert DARRAUGH, Samuel M'CLURE, John M'DONNAUGH, Beaver Borough; Stewart BOYD, John R. SCOGGS, James COCHRAN, John DUNLAP, John THOMAS, Greersburg.

p. 231: Easton Water Co. commissioners: Nathaniel NICHLER, John HERSTER, John GREEN, James HAYS, William BARNET, George WOLF, Peter H. MATTES.

p. 236: John WORMLEY & Abraham NEIDIG are to build a bridge over the Conedogwinit Ck.

p. 237: Trustees of Allegheny College, Mead Twp., Crawford Co.--for Crawford Co.: Roger ALDEN, William MACARTHUR, Jesse MOORE, John BROOKS, William CLARK, Henry HURST, Samuel LORD, Samuel TORBETT, Ralph MARLIN, Patrick FARRELLY, Thomas ATKINSON, John REYNOLDS, Daniel BEMUS, William FOSTER, Daniel PERKINS, Rev. Amos CHASE, Rev. Timothy ALDEN, Rev. Robert JOHNSTON; for Erie Co.: Judah COLT, Rufus S. REED, John C. WALLACE, John VINCENT, James WESTON, Rev. Johnson EATON, Rev. Robert REED; for Venango Co.: David IRVINE, William CONNELLY, Samuel HAYS; for Mercer co.: Alexander BROWN, Jacob HERRINGTON, Nathan PATTERSON; for Butler Co.: Walter LOWRY, Rev. John M'PHERRIN; for Beaver Co.: Robert MOORE; for Allegheny Co.: James ROSS, Henry BALDWIN, Rev. Joseph STOCKTON; for Westmoreland Co.: Alexander W. FOSTER; for Dauphin Co.: Rev. George LOCHMAN; for Phila. Co.: Callender IRVINE, John B. WALLACE, Rev. J.J. JANEWAY, D.D.; for New Jersey: William GRIFFITH; for Massachusetts: James WINTHROP, Rev. Joseph M'KEAN, L.L.D.; for Ohio: Simon PERKINS, Rev. Joseph BADGER.

p. 241: Commissioners to make a lock navigation system on the Monongahela River: George SUTTON, Anthony BEELEN, Thomas BAIRD, Pittsburg; John WILSON, John ROBINSON, Elizabethtown; William LAUGHEAD, James EVANS, M'Keesport, Allegheny Co.; Charles BOLLMAN, Joel BUTLER, James P. STEWART, Williamsport; Henry P. PEARSON, Joseph ALEXANDER, Fredericktown, Washington Co.; Andrew LINN, Esq., Hugh FORD, Freeport; James TOMLINSON, Elisha HUNT, George DAWSON, William HOGE, Jacob BOWMAN, Basil BRASHEAR, Joseph THORNTON, Israel MILLER, Brownsville, James W. NICHOLSON, Thomas WILLIAMS, Esq., New Geneva, Fayette Co.; George REPPART, Alexander VANCE, Greensburg, Greene Co.

p. 251: John MAY is auth. to erect a toll bridge over French Ck., Crawford Co.

p. 257: Robert WHARTON, Anthony GALE, Benjamin B. HOWELL, Thomas T. STILES, William FLINTHAM, Samuel W. HARRISON, Isaac BROWNING, James MATLACK, Robert L. ARMSTRONG are commissioners of the Gloucester & Greenwich Point Ferry Co.

p. 266: Road to be improved--Blockhouse road (otherwise known as WILLIAMSON's Road) along Lycoming Ck. across the head of Towanda near Ezra SPALDING's to the New York State Line. Money for improvements will be paid to John GRAHAM, Henry HEWS, John HARMAN, Noah WILSON, John WILBER & William FERMAN.

p. 268: Commissioners to erect wharves in Kittanning, Armstrong Co.: Robert BROWN, Henry JACK & Michael MACKLIN.

p. 269: Joseph ENGLE, William ANDERSON, William GRAHAM are commissioners to erect piers in Chester, Delaware Co.

p. 270: William TRAVIS, Joseph MARSHALL are commissioners to improve the navigation of Mahoning Ck. Levi GIBSON & Samuel C. ORR are commissioners to improve the navigation of Red Bank & Toby Ck.

p. 270: The Conemaugh River is to be improved from Conemaugh, Cambria Co. to Jacob LIEBENGOOD's. Commissioners to improve the Conemaugh River from Frankstown to Conemaugh are Isaac PROCTOR, Garret RHEAM, Cambria; & Fullerton WOODS, Indiana Co.

p. 271: A public road is to be laid out from Easton, Northampton Co., to Adam ROMIG's tavern. Commissioners are James HAYS, Christian BIXLER, Northampton; & Michael FACKENTHAL.

p. 272: Commissioners to improve state road from Blair's Gap to the western boundary of the state between GRIFFITH's mill, Indiana Co. & the Frankstown Rd., Cambria Co. & to erect a bridge over the west branch of Black Lick Ck.: David TODD, John GRAHAM, John DENNISTON.

p. 273: Commissioners to improve a road over White-deer Hole Mt., through Rattling Gap & into Nippinose Valley, Lycoming Co.: Henry ANTES, Jr., Abraham LAWSHA, James COLLINS.

p. 273: Part of the Huntingdon, Cambria & Indiana Tpk. Rd. exists between Blair's Gap & Martin REGER's.

p. 275: Commissioners to improve a state road from Indiana to Pittsburg: Nathaniel M'BRIER, James M'CULLOUGH, Jr., Washington Twp., Westmoreland Co.

p. 275: William MAJOR is to receive money to improve the road from Jonestown, Lebanon Co. to Wilkesbarre.

p. 275: David FIELDS & George DANSDILL, Dublin Twp., Bedford Co., are to receive money to improve the road from the Franklin Co. line to the forks of the road atop Sideling Hill, Bedford Co.

p. 276: John DEARDORF, Joseph COLE, James M'CURDY, Esq., Franklin Co.; David FIELDS, Bedford Co., are commissioners to improve a road from Carlisle, Cumberland Co. to Littleton, Bedford Co.

p. 276: George M'CLELLAND & Philip LAUFMAN, Franklin Co., are commissioners to improve a road from Strasburg to Letterkenny Twp. line.

p. 276: Henry ZIMMERMAN & John ALBRIGHT are to improve navigation of Big Swatara Ck., Schuylkill Co., between Barnhart MINICH's & Fox Valley.

p. 277: Charles RENO, William BUDD, Bevan PEARSON are to improve the road from Mercer Co. to Warren, Ohio.

p. 277: Alexander CRAIG, Nicholas DAY, Robert RAINEY are commissioners to erect a bridge over Loyalhanna Ck.

p. 280: A road will commence near Jacob BIGLER's, E. Pennsborough Twp., Cumberland Co., to intersect the Harrisburg & Pittsburg Tpk. Rd.

p. 281: John FISHER, Lancaster, Lancaster Co., is paid $115 for services rendered as a teamster at Baltimore in the fall of 1814.

p. 281: Election districts; Fawn Twp., York Co., will vote at John NICKEL's. Springfield Twp., Bradford Co., will vote at Gurdon GROVER's. White Deer Twp., Union co., will vote at Samuel MILLER's. Harford & Lenox districts, Susquehanna Co., will vote at Jacob BLAKE's. Maiden Ck. Twp., Berks Co., will vote at Catharine GIFT's. Long Swamp Twp., Berks Co., will vote at Peter TREXLER's, Mertztown. Baccaria Twp. & part of Bradford Twp., Clearfield Co., will vote at John CREE's, Baccaria Twp. Part of Rush Twp., Centre Co., will vote at George SMELL's, Bradford Twp. Earl Twp., Berks Co., will vote at Jacob PENNEPACKER's. Union Twp., Luzerne Co., will vote at Ichabod SHAW's. Part of Indiana Twp., Allegheny Co. near Alexander LOGAN's ferry will vote with the Deer Twp. election district. Springville Twp., Susquehanna Co., will vote at Leonard BALDWIN's. Allegheny Twp., & part of Brokenstraw Twp., Venango Co., formerly voted at Thomas GOTT's & now will vote at William NEILL's, Allegheny Twp. Fairfield Twp., Westmoreland Co., will vote at James LAWSON's. Conneaut Twp., Crawford Co., will vote at Thomas O. HALL's. W. Buffaloe Twp., Union Co., will vote at Jacob STITZER's. Shade Twp., Somerset Co., will vote at Jacob CABLE's. Sergeant Twp., M'Kean Co., will vote at Edmund NEWTON's, Instanter. Old Chinchaclamoose Twp., Clearfield Co., will vote at William BLOOM, Jr.'s. Neshanock Twp., Mercer Co., will vote at John HUNTER's. The 4th election district, Adams Co., will vote at Isaac SADLER's, Petersburg, Huntingdon Twp. Hartly Twp., Union Co., will vote at John WILSON's, Hartleton. Bridgewater Twp., Susquehanna Co., will vote at Chapman CARS'. Waterford Twp., Susquehanna Co., will vote at Cyril GIDEON's. Gibson & Jackson Twp., Susquehanna Co., will vote at James BENNET's, Gibson. Perry Twp., Jefferson Co., will vote at John BELL's. N. Beaver Twp., Beaver Co., will vote at William HENRY's. Lower Paxton Twp., Dauphin Co., will vote at Jacob PLANK's tavern, now occupied by John WALBORN. Greenfield Twp., Luzerne Co., will vote at Micha VAIL's. Nicholson Twp., Luzerne Co., will vote at Ebenezer STEPHENS'. Bristol Twp., Phila. Co., will vote at Jonathan CHILDS', Branchtown. The unincorporated part of Northern Liberties, Phila. Co., bounded by LOGAN's mill, will vote at Jacob VANDIKE's, at the sign of the White Horse on the Frankford Tpk. Rd. Part of Bradford Twp., Bradford Co., will vote at Benjamin I. WOODRUFF's, Windham Twp. Assylum Twp., Bradford Co., will vote at Jonathan TERRY's. Lawrence Twp., Tioga Co., will vote at Enos SLAWSON's. Deerfield Twp., Tioga Co., will vote at Daniel CUMMINGS'. Elkland Twp., Tioga Co., will vote at John RYAN's. Columbia Twp., Bradford Co., will vote at James MORGAN's. Connequenessing Twp., Butler co., will vote at WILSON's tavern, Harmony. Muddy Ck. Twp., Butler Co., will vote at Samuel RIDDLE's.

St. Clair Twp., Allegheny Co., near John BELL's, WILLET's on Streat's Run, will vote at James PATTERSON's, lock smith. Moon Twp., Allegheny Co., will vote at Philip HOOPER Sr.'s. Buckingham Twp., Bucks Co., will vote at Thomas HARRIS', New Britain Sq. Bedminister Twp., Bucks Co., will vote at Frederick GARIS'. Rockhill Twp., Bucks Co., will vote at John HOOT's. Springfield Twp., Bucks Co., will vote at Abraham RADABUSH's. Durham Twp., Bucks Co., will vote at Dennis RILEY's. Towamensing Twp., Northampton Co., will vote at John ANTHONY's. Ross Twp., Northampton Co., will vote at Jacob FRANTZ, Sr.'s. Parts of Manheim & Pinegrove Twp., Schuylkill Co., near Peter BERKHEISER, John A. BROWN's mill, Peter CONFER's saw mill, will vote at Daniel FENSTERMACHER, Friedensburg. Mt. Joy & part of Donegal Twp., Lancaster Co., will vote at George REDSECKER's. The 17th election district, Lancaster co., near Brice CLARK's road, Christian GRAYBILL, Francis EVANS, Thomas BAILEY, decd., will vote at the school house, Marietta. Plum Twp., Venango Co., will vote at John LAMBERTON's. Tell Twp., Huntingdon Co., will vote at Nesbit JEFFRIES'. Dublin Twp. & part of Springfield Twp., Huntingdon Co., will vote at Alexander BLAIR's, Dublin Twp. Part of Brunswig Twp., Schuylkill Co., near Michael HARTMAN's mill, Christian BOYER, John MATZ, Samuel STECHTER, Peter ALBRIGHT, John SCHOENER, Peter SHEIB will vote at John HEISSLER's, M'Keansburg. East Hanover Twp., Lebanon Co., will vote at John HARPER, Jr.'s. Cherrytree & part of Sugar Ck. Twp., Venango Co., formerly voted at Thomas GOTT's & now will vote at James HAMILTON's, Cherrytree Twp. E. Huntingdon & part of Hemfield & Mt. Pleasant Twp., Westmoreland Co., will vote at John LOYD's, innkeeper, Mt. Pleasant.

p. 289: Peter ALBERT, late of Mahanoy Twp., Northumberland Co. (now Upper Mahanoy Twp.), lately died leaving a widow & issue: Peter, Elizabeth (wife of Moses VAIL), Rachel (wife of John DARRECK), Phillipina (wife of John BUNDY), Eve (since decd., leaving one child, George DARRECK), Margaret. The widow is since decd. Margaret has been declared a lunatic, & her committee is Jacob ZARTMAN, Adam LINKER, Abraham M'KINNEY. Samuel BLOOM, Esq., Augusta Twp., is auth. to sell land adj. Henry LATCHA, Sr., Widow BOYER, Henry LATCHA, Jr., & Widow SMITH.

p. 291: Thomas BINGHAM, Mercer Co., is to receive $50 for losses sustained in the Rev. War.

p. 291: Isaac SEELY, a captain in the 5th regiment of the Pa. line, was entitled to a tract of donation land of 500 acres. On 8 May, 1803, a patent was issued to Elizabeth HUNT, late a widow, & the children of Isaac SEELY for 500 acres in district #10, Erie Co. for tract #193. $750 will be paid in lieu of the land.

p. 293: The road from Lewistown to intersect the great road from Mifflintown up the Tuscarora Valley near John ROSS', is to be improved.

p. 294: Commissioners to erect a bridge over the Lehigh River at Water Gap, Northampton Co.; David SNYDER, Peter RUMBLE, William FENSTERMAKER, Stephen BALLIET, Jr., Jacob SAEGAR, Lehigh Co.; Thomas CRAIG, John SNYDER, Nicholas SNYDER, Jacob STEM, Northampton Co.

p. 297: A road is to be made from Phila. & Wilmington Post Rd. near John M'ILVAIN's to intersect the Phila., Brandywine & New London Tpk. Rd. on the land of George DAVIS, Delaware Co.

p. 299: The Washington & Pittsburg Tpk. Rd. Co.: David ATCHESON, Alexander MURDOCK, David SHIELDS, Alexander REED, Parker CAMPBELL, John HOGE, Thomas H. BAIRD, Washington; Joseph CLOKEY, George MORGAN, Craig RITCHIE, Robert MAHON, Canonsburg; William M'CANDLESS, Henry BALDWIN, William WILKINS, Thomas CROMWELL, George EVANS, Pittsburg.

p. 302: Erie Academy trustees: Rev. Robert REID, Rufus S. REED, Robert BROWN, Thomas FORSTER, Thomas WILSON, John C. WALLACE, Judah COLT, Thomas H. SILL, Giles SANFORD.

p. 304: Trustees of Wellsborough Academy, Tioga Co.: Justus DART, James GRAY, Nathan ROWLAY, Jr., William D. BACON, Uriah SPENCER, Robert TUBBS, Eday HOWLAND, Samuel W. MORRIS, Isaac BAKER, Joseph M'CORMICK, John KNOS, Alpheus CHENEY, Assa MANN, Nathan NILES, Jr., John NORRIS, William BACHE, Daniel LAMB, Ambrose MILLARD.

p. 307: Daniel W. COX, Samuel WRIGHT, Jr., Peter T. SMITH are auth. by N.J. to erect a wing dam in the Delaware River. Lewis CONDICT, George HOLCOMB, John BEATTY are commissioners in behalf of N.J. for the wing dam. Cadwallader EVANS, Jr., Phila.; William ERWIN, Bucks Co.; Samuel SITGREAVES, Easton, Northampton Co. are commissioners in behalf of Pa.

p. 314: Walter LOWRIE is appointed commissioner to meet with the commissioners from Ohio, Va., Ky., & Indiana to examine obstructions in the Ohio River.

p. 314: Benjamin R. MORGAN, Phila.; Robert HARRIS, Dauphin Co.; John BOYD, Northumberland Co.; William WILSON, Lycoming Co.; John HOLLENBACK, Bradford Co. are commissioners to examine the Susquehanna River.

1817-1818

p. 2: Michael DEARMOND, Columbia Co., an old soldier, is to receive $40 & $40/yr.

p. 3: Elections of Greencastle, Franklin Co., will be held at John BESORE's.

p. 4: John READ, guardian for his children: John M. READ, Henry M. READ, Margaret M. READ. Their mother was Martha, daughter of Samuel MEREDITH, Wayne Co. She is decd.

p. 5: Isaac RAYMOND, an old soldier, Montgomery Co., will receive $40 & $40/yr.

p. 6: The title of John Jacob SMITH, Bethlehem Twp., Northampton Co., late an alien, to land in Hanover Twp., Lehigh Co., for 119 acres, sold to him by Nicholas KREAMER & wife on 30 Sept., 1816, & two smaller tracts, one of 6 acres in Forks Twp., & one of 2 acres in Altona, Bethlehem Twp., Northampton Co., is confirmed.

p. 6: The rector, church wardens & vestrymen of the United Swedish Lutheran Churches of Wicaco, Kingsessing & Upper Merion Twps., called Gloria Dei, St. James & Christ Church: Rev. Nicholas COLLIN, rector; Hugh DE HAVEN, Paul BECK, Jr., wardens. William JONES, George SHEED, Andrew KEER, Samuel RAMBO, Charles WHEELER, William COX, John M. JUSTIS, Sevan BOON, Matthias HOLSTEIN, vestrymen.

p. 7: The interest of the commonwealth to an estate of John COOK, formerly of E. Fallowfield Twp., Chester Co., is vested in Mary

COOK, widow.

p. 8: The interest of the commonwealth to an estate of Randolph M'DONALD, formerly of Phila., is vested in Ann GIBSON, M'DONALD's mother.

p. 9: The interest of the commonwealth to an estate of Samuel HERMAN, late of York, York Co., is vested in Catharine HERMAN, the widow.

p. 10: John SHREVE, Samuel COOPE, Jesse TOWNSEND, adminis. of the estate of Jonah CADWALADER, late of Bridgport, Fayette Co., decd., who died intestate, are auth. to sell to John MALCOMSON, a lot in Bridgport adj. Robert TOWNSEND.

p. 10: John LAMB, late of Cumberland Co., decd., sold to Michael HOOVER, a part of a tract in Allen Twp., Cumberland Co. The land was not patented.

p. 11: The right of the commonwealth in the estate of Dr. John C. BARGMAN, late of Huntingdon, Huntingdon Co., is vested in Sophia BARGMAN, widow.

p. 12: Andrew EMMINGER, executor, & Barbara SHELLY, executrix of Peter SHELLY, late of E. Pennsboro Twp., Cumberland Co., are auth. to sell to Peter PHILIPS, 5 acres in E. Pennsboro Twp.

p. 14: Almond H. READ, Bela JONES, Philander STEPHENS, Joseph WILLIAMS, Seth MITCHELL, Nicholas M'CARTY, David POST, John SNOW, Hezekiah LEECH, Jr., John BENNET, Susquehanna Co., are commissioners of the New Milford & Montrose Tpk. Rd.

p. 16: Henry DITMAN, by parol agreement, sold 2 acres in Hempfield Twp., Westmoreland Co., to Emick ROYER. ROYER afterwards died intestate. The land was sold to Jonas KIMMEL. Henry ALSHOUSE & James IRWEN were ROYER's adminis. DITMAN sold land to Adam BRINEY who became insolvent & left the county. That land was sold at a sheriff's sale. Christian CLINE & John DITMAN were adminis. of Henry DITMAN's estate.

p. 18: John EISENHARD, one of the adminis. of Andrew EISENHARD, late of Maccungie Twp., Lehigh Co., is auth. to convey to Jacob EISENHARD, 31 acres 43 perches & to George EISENHARD, 35 acres 7 perches of land in the same twp.

p. 19: Joseph WHARTON, Phila. Co., is adjudged a lunatic. Thomas J. WHARTON is the committee of his estate.

p. 21; Agnes CRAWFORD, Lycoming Co., widow of an old soldier, is granted $40 & $40/yr.

p. 21: James IRWIN, William PARKS are adminis. of the estate of John CHRISTY, decd., Versailes Twp., Allegheny Co. CHRISTY entered into an agreement with Robert AKINS on 9 June, 1789, to assign the title of 100 acres in North Huntingdon Twp., Westmoreland Co., held by warrant taken out for land partly in Westmoreland & partly in Allegheny Co. Both CHRISTY & AKINS are decd. William AKINS was willed the property by Robert AKINS.

p. 22; Jacob WOLMER, late of Montgomery Co., purchased from James HOOK, a tract in Washington Co. (now Greene). He died intestate, leaving a minor son, Henry WOLMER, who died shortly afterward, not yet of lawful age. Daniel THOMPSON was the adminis. of WOLMER.

p. 24: Susanna ALBRECHT, John ALBRECHT, & Jacob STEFFEN, executors of Dewalt ALBRECHT, formerly of Northampton Co., decd., are auth. to sell land in Williams Twp., Northampton co., which ALBRECHT bought from Stephen KRUMREIN, now also decd.

p. 24: Mary BENEZET, Montgomery Co., has real estate in Phila. held jointly with her brother, James ENGLE. Mary is the wife of Anthony BENEZET. They are auth. to rent the real estate.

p. 25: Appollonia HITNER, widow of Frederick HITNER, Phila., says her husband died intestate in 1784, owning a lot & small brick tenement in Phila. Appollonia is old, infirm & poor.

p. 27: John BROWN, John VENET, Samuel HEADLEY, Sherman CLARK are commissioners of the Berwick Water Co.

p. 35: Meetings of the Berwick, Columbia & Luzerne Co. town council will be at Samuel HEADLEY's.

p. 63: Caleb PEIRCE, late of E. Marlborough Twp., Chester Co., by a codicil to his will of 15 Aug., 1809, nominated John MARSHALL, Amos HARVEY, Isaac BENNET, James PYLE, Caleb PENNOCK trustees to equalise his estate among his children.

p. 64: John CADWALLADER, late of Huntingdon Co., decd., owed on a mortgage to the commonwealth $400. His wife & children are indigent. Payment is suspended for 5 years.

p. 74: Armstrong, Indiana & Cambria Tpk. Rd. commissioners: David STEWART, John BLAIR, Huntingdon Co.; George ROBERTS, Philip NOON, David TODD, Cambria Co.; John DENNISTON, Daniel STANARD, Thomas SHARP, Joseph MOORHEAD, William CUMMINGS, Indiana Co.; Thomas HAMILTON, David REYNOLDS, Philip TEMPLETON, Robert NELSON, Michael MACKLIN, Armstrong Co.; John NEGLEY, John PARKER, Walter LOWRIE, Butler Co.

p. 85: Thomas LOGAN's title to a tract in Air Twp., in the Big Cove, Bedford Co., for 153 acres 61 perches, is confirmed as if he had purchased it from a citizen & not from Samuel IRWIN, an alien.

p. 87: Joseph DARLINGTON bound himself by articles of agreement on 1 Oct., 1794, to sell land in Fayette Co. to Isaac M'DONALD, decd. Before the execution of the deed, DARLINGTON sold the rest of the tract to Rev. David SMITH, late of Westmoreland Co., decd. The land of M'DONALD was sold to Noble M'CORMICK. A deed will be made to Abner M'DONALD for the part of the tract in Fayette Co. sold by the heirs of Isaac M'DONALD to Noble M'CORMICK.

p. 88: William M'CLEAN claims compensation for 6 days service of the team he had in the service of the state & he is allowed compensation of pay equal to the pay of an ensign during his time as forage master in Col. Rees HILL's regiment of the Pa. Militia.

p. 89: The Presby. Congregation of Salem, Derry Twp., Westmoreland Co. trustees: Hugh CULBERTSON, Robert M'MILLAN, Thomas GALLAGHER, James GUTHRIE, William STERLING.

p. 92: A tract of land called "Devotion" was granted by patent 11

Dec., 1817, to Conrad KIRSHNER, Jacob PHILIPS, John STAUDT, Jacob SCHWENK, in trust for the Lutheran Congregation of St. Paul's Church, Manheim Twp., Schuylkill Co., for 205 acres 52 perches. The congregation is auth. to sell 81 acres to Christian LUCKENBILL, who transferred his rights to his son, Abraham LUCKENBILL.

p. 94: Chester, Delaware Co., is bounded by land of Jeremiah M'ILVAIN, Hugh ROBERTS, Joseph ENGLE, heirs of Joseph NEIDE, William GRAHAM, Richard FLOWER.

p. 99: John ERNST, successor of Christopher ERNST, & Samuel SHERER are auth. to erect a toll bridge over Swatara Ck., near ERNST's or SHERER's ferry, Dauphin Co.

p. 103: A lot in Beaver borough is granted to Thomas HENRY & John R. SHANON for the purpose of building a glass manufactory & ware house.

p. 106: William FORSTER, guardian of William KRATZER, son of John KRATZER, decd., is auth. to sell land in Mifflinsburg, Union Co.

p. 108: Marinda MERRILLS, late Marinda BENNET, Hanover Twp., Luzerne Co., in Nov., 1815, married John MERRILLS. At the court of quarter sessions, Wilkesbarre, Luzerne Co., the first Monday of Aug., 1816, John MERRILLS was convicted of larceny & horse stealing & sentenced to hard labor in the Phila. gaol. The marriage is annulled.

p. 109: James CARSON, late recorder of deeds in Phila., died owning Pa. tax on proceeds of his office. He left a widow & minor children. Payment is suspended for 5 years.

p. 115: The title of the estate of George BOWDERY, late of Northumberland co., decd., is vested in Lydia BOWDERY, widow.

p. 119: By the original charter from William PENN to Phila., 25 Oct., 1701, a piece of ground described as a swamp between BUDD's buildings & Society Hill, was granted to the city to be used a docks & harbors. The ground was previously covered by the survey of John MARSH.

p. 121; $5000 is appropriated to erect a bridge over Limestone Run & will be paid to Dr. James DOUGAL, Bethuel VINCENT, & John CHESTNUT, commissioners to superintend the building.

p. 131: Elections in the are of Columbia & Luzerne Co. which was annexed to Schuylkill Co., will be at John BIDLER's, Union Twp.

p. 132: Jacob ERNST, adminis. de bonis non with the will annexed of Richard CHESTER, late of York Co., is auth. to sell real estate.

p. 133: Joseph CLOUD, William BLACK, John SMITH are commissioners to lay out a road from John G. PARKE's, Sadsbury Twp., Chester Co., to M'CALL's ferry, Susquehanna River, beginning at John MOORE's limekiln, Sadsbury Twp.

p. 134: Peter YARNELL agreed to sell to Jacob KUNKEL, a tract in Norwegian Twp., Schuylkill Co. In Feb., 1792, there was a new agreement. On 17 Feb., 1812, Jacob KUNKEL assigned the agreement to Thomas REED. REED & YARNELL are both decd. & intestate. The land was sold by the adminis. of REED to Isaac REED. Mary REED & Jacob

REED are the adminis. of Thomas REED. Charles CLARKE sold to John HUNTER & John CLARKE, executors of Walter CLARK, decd., in trust for the 2 minor grandchildren, a tract in N. Beaver Twp., Beaver Co. Charles CLARKE died intestate. John LACKEY is surviving adminis. of Charles CLARKE.

p. 141: Trustees of the Pittsburg & Steubenville Tpk. Rd. Co.: Alexander MURRAY, John FIELD, Alexander WILSON, Jonathan W. CONDY, John PURDON, John STEELE, Phila.; James ROSS, Dennis S. SCULLY, Henry BALDWIN, Andrew SCOTT, Pittsburg; William BROWN, Samuel E. MARKS, Andrew M'CURDY, James BEATTY, Alexander M'FARLAND, Allegheny Co.; James CHRISTY, James BRICELAND, John DUNCAN, John BUCHANAN, James PROUDFOOT, Washington Co.

p. 145: The west branch of Oil Ck., Crawford Co., near M'CRAT's, now WINTEN's mill, James HAMILTON's mill, Bloomfield Twp., is declared a public highway.

p. 146: The executors of the estate of Mary ANDREWS, formerly of Phila., decd, are decd. Richard PETERS, Esq., is one of the trustees of the estate of William PETERS, decd. Mary's will was dated 10 June, 1757. Some of the executor's survivors live in England.

p. 147: Parker CAMPBELL & Daniel MOORE for themselves & on behalf of Thomas PATTERSON, Thomas H. BAIRD, David SHEILDS, Thomas M'GIFFIN, Thomas HOGE, Alexander MURDOCK, Washington Co., have entered into an agreement with the Phila. Bank for property to change the branch bank of Phila. at Washington into an original institution, The Franklin Bank of Washington Co.

p. 158: Trustees of the Presby. Congregation, Easton, Northampton Co.: John GREEN, William KENNEDY, Esech HOWELL, Robert INNES, Joseph BURKE, Absalom REEDER, Benjamin GREEN, Ralph TINDALL & Jesse M. HOWELL.

p. 161: John NEAL is auth. to build a toll bridge across the Monongahela River, Washington & Westmoreland Cos., at Columbia. It will be one the same footing as the bridge erected by Isaac MEASON & Zachariah CONNEL across the Youghiogheny River at Connelsville, Fayette Co.

p. 164: The commissioners of the Gettysburg & Hagerstown Tpk. Rd. Co.: Alexander COBEAN, John MURPHY, Ralph LASHELLS, Bernard GILBERT, James GILLILAND, Walter SMITH, William MILLER, Amos MAGINLEY, Andrew MARSHAL & John ROBINSON, Adams Co.; Daniel ROYER, Michael STONER, William BLAKELY, Franklin Co.

p. 168: On 12 Feb., 1740, John, Thomas & Richard PENN sold to Henry WORK, Alexander CRAIGHEAD, Robert MATHEWS, Hugh BARKLEY, in trust for the Presby. Congregation of Middle Octorara, Lancaster Co., 100 acres & 50 perches. Present trustees: James STEELE, James BAXTER, William HERD, William BROWN, Thomas MORGAN, John PATTERSON, Alexander MORRISON, Robert ANDERSON are auth. to sell some real estate.

p. 170: Enos MORRIS, Thomas G. KENNEDY, Jacob JANNEY, Dr. Phineas JENKS, Joseph WORSTALL, Jr., Thomas BUCKMAN are trustees of the Newtown Common, Bucks Co.

p. 172: Robert BROOKE, one of the commissioners appointed to explore the route of the intended canal from Tioga River to Seneca Lake, is to be paid $250 & to Charles TREZIYULNY, another commissioner, $264.

p. 174: Samuel W. FISHER, late of Phila., died 10 Feb., 1817, intestate, owning tracts of land in Luzerne, Lycoming, Tioga, Huntingdon, Cambria, Clearfield, Indiana & Bradford Cos., a total of 28,000 acres. Sarah W. FISHER, Coleman FISHER, S. Rhoads FISHER, adminis. of the estate of Samuel W. FISHER, are auth. to sell the lands.

p. 175: James ENGLISH, a sergeant in the Pa. Line during the Rev. War, in Capt. Jacob BOWER's Co., will receive $48 & $48/yr.

p. 176: Peter BROWN alias BRADY, Lower Paxton Twp., Dauphin Co., died intestate & without heirs. He left a widow, Elizabeth, who sold his land to George KNOLL for £125. He paid £40 before he died, leaving a widow, Catharine, & several children. Around 1797, Elizabeth BROWN died & left a will, devising the land to Francis SWEENY, Northumberland Co. Catharine KNOLL is willing to pay the balance to SWEENY for the land.

p. 177: The Roman Catholic Congregation of Christ's Church, Chambersburg, Franklin Co., purchased from Thomas HARTLY as per indenture made by HARTLY & wife, Catharine, on 3 Sept., 1792, to Rev. John CARROLL, D.D., Rev. Denis CAPAL, Laurence CLANEY, Jacob STILLINGER, Jeremiah MAHANY, & Barnabas DOYLE, in trust for the congregation, a lot. The congregation afterwards purchased a house & lot adj. the lot from George COOK as per indenture from COOK & wife, Liddy, on 12 Aug., 1809 & sold it to John CARROLL, D.D., John CHAMBERS, & Peter COOK as trustees for the congregation. The Rev. Nicholas ZOCCHY, Patrick CAMPBELL, Thomas MURRAY, John DIVINE, Patrick BROWN, Richard HEYDON, George GARLAND are the present trustees.

p. 185: Henry GUTHARDT, Northumberland Co.; John MURPHY, John M'KINNEY, Bucks Co.; Thomas ANDERSON, Westmoreland Co.; Christian HUBBARD, Phila. Co.; William MARKS, Berks Co.; William M'CONNELL, Armstrong Co.; Jacob VANGORDER & William RUSSELL, Beaver Co.; John SHOOK, Thomas M'MULLIN, Northampton Co.; Charles CHRISTMAN, Schuylkill Co.; John DOUGHERTY, Somerset Co.; Jesse GRINDING, Greene Co.; John HARDCHY, Phila. Co.; Benjamin LYON, Mifflin Co.; John KELER, Lehigh Co., old soldiers, will receive $40 & $40/yr. Thomas M'MILLEN, Allegheny Co., will receive $80 for his services & suffering during the Rev. War & afterwards as a volunteer in several expeditions against the Indians to the north western parts of Pa. Abraham HORN, Northampton Co., will receive $48 & $48/yr.

p. 192: David M'CORMICK, John MORAN, John WHITE, Samuel DONNEL, James CUMMINGS, Lycoming Co.; George BRESSLER, Francis M'EWEN, William SMITH, Roland CURTIN, John MAGEE, merchant, Centre Co.; Arthur BELL, Robert MAXWELL, Clearfield Co.; I.P. DE GRUCHY & Andrew ALBRIGHT, Northumberland co.; Simon GRATZ, Francis INGRAM, Phila., are commissioners to erect a bridge over the west branch of the Susquehanna River at Dunsburg, Lycoming Co.

p. 195: Sarah POLLOCK & Thomas POLLOCK, adminis. of the estate of William POLLOCK, late of Milton, Northumberland Co., are auth. to sell real estate in Upper Milford.

p. 197: Josiah WHITE, George F.A. HAUTO & Erskine HAZARD, Phila.

Co., are auth. to improve the navigation of the Lehigh River.

p. 219: William P. DEWEES, Reuben HAINS, Charles NORRIS, Phila.; Hardman PHILIPS, Joseph M. FOX, Centre Co.; George KREMER, William HAYS, Union Co.; John TAGGART, John B. HAINES, Northumberland Co., are commissioners to make a road from Waterford, Erie Co. to the Susquehanna River near the mouth of ANDERSON's Ck.

p. 220: Sarah SASSAMAN, Montgomery Co., is to be paid on a loan certificate drawn in favor of Joseph GROSS for £10 10s 6p, dated 1 Jan., 1787.

p. 223: William SCHLATTER, William GUIER, William W. HOWELL, John M. PRICE, Caleb CRESSON, Benjamin WARNER, Charles BRUGIERE, Condy RAGUET, Simon GRATZ are managers of the Phila. & Pittsburg Transporting Co.

p. 224: Robert SMITH, Archibald RANKIN, William M'KINSTRY, David HUMPHREYS, James BUCHANAN, Franklin Co.; Jacob HART, Andrew MANN, Bedford Co.; John JOHNSTON, Hancock, Maryland, are managers of the Mercersburg & Hancock Tpk. Rd. Co.

p. 228: Daniel Stewart BEIDEMAN, minor son of Daniel BEIDEMAN, decd., is entitled to an interest in real estate in Northampton, Northumberland, Columbia, Luzerne Co., is common with the children & heirs of Christian KUNCKLE, decd. George W. TRYON has been appointed guardian of the minor.

p. 231: Trustees of the Danville Academy, Columbia Co.: John B. PATTERSON, Assa DUNHAM, Daniel MONTGOMERY, William B. MONTGOMERY, Alexander MONTGOMERY, Thomas WOODSIDE, John MILLS, James LAUGHEAD, John MONTGOMERY, William MONTGOMERY, James DONALDSON, Robert CURRY.

p. 235: Thomas STOKELY is to be paid $2400 for services rendered during the Rev. War.

p. 238: Richard MARIS died intestate, leaving a widow, Rachael Ross MARIS & issue: Thomas Ross MARIS, Richard MARIS, George Guest MARIS, William MARIS..the eldest being around 12 years of age & the youngest not yet 4 years. MARIS owned land in Luzerne & Susquehanna Cos. Thomas ROSS & Caleb NEWBOLD, Jr. are the adminis. of the estate of MARIS & are auth. to sell the land.

p. 240: John Ewing PARKER's name is changed to John Ewing PORTER. Samuel TATE, a Justice of the Peace from Franklin Co., has his name changed to Samuel Tate SWANSY.

p. 242: William Tilghman CHEW is the grandson of William TILGHMAN, Phila., & the only child of Benjamin CHEW, Jr., Phila., & his late wife, Elizabeth Margaret CHEW, daughter & only child of William TILGHMAN. James ALLEN, decd. is former proprietor of all the land within the borough of Northampton. His widow, Elizabeth ALLEN, is also decd.

p. 245: George LONG, John WORK, James COCHRAN are commissioners to lay out a road from Meadville to the western line of Pa.

p. 249: Commissioners to make a tpk. rd. from Tunkhannock, Luzerne co., to Wysox, Bradford Co.: J.M. PIOLLET, Jonathan STEVENS, John HOLLENBACK, Salmon KEENEY, Daniel STERLING, Cyrus AVERY & John BUCKINGHAM.

p. 251: Auditors to settle the commissioners accounts for a lottery to build a church in Somerset: Peter KIMMEL, Abraham MORRISON, Jacob SCHNEIDER, Abraham MILLER, John KANTLINGER, James CLARK.

p. 253: Commissioners to make a bridge over the Susquehanna River in Dauphin & Cumberland Cos., at CLARK's ferry: Christian GLEIM, Archibaldn M'ALLISTER, Innis GREEN, Abraham GROSS, Dauphin Co.; Robert CLARK, John BODEN, Dr. Samuel MEALY, Cumberland; William BELL, Lewis EVANS, David HULING, Robert ROBINSON, Maj. John IRWIN, Mifflin; William STEEL, Patrict GWINN, Maxwell KINKEAD, Huntingdon; James POTTER, John RANKIN, John IRWIN, Penn's Valley, Centre Co. Commissioners to erect a bridge over the Susquehanna River near Marietta, Lancaster Co.: John Andrew SHULTZ, Esq., Lebanon Co.; James MEHAFFEY, Jacob GROSH, Henry CASSEL, Andrew NOBLE, James GRAHAM, Henry SHARE, Henry HAINES, Jr., Francis BOGGS, James WHITEHILL, John EAGAN, Samuel GROSH, William RICHENBACH, Thomas WENTZ, John ROBERTS, George COLEMAN, Brice CURRAN, James DUFFEY, James PATTERSON, Jr., Christian STAUFER, Jacob GAMBER, John HUBER, Daniel GROSH, William NOBLE, Lancaster Co.; Michael WELSH, John SULTZBACH, York Co.; Christian HERTZLER, Phila.

p. 256; Col. Rees HILL is loaned $2400.

p. 260: William FINDLAY, late treasurer of Pa., is paid $690 as an indemnification for the receipt of counterfeit bank notes.

p. 261: Managers of the Lewistown & Kishacoquillas Tpk. Rd. Co. are auth. to extend the road from Alexander REED's tavern to the division line between Huntingdon & Mifflin Cos.

p. 263: Part of Wayne Twp., Lycoming Co., including the east end of Sugar Valley to the headwaters of Sinking Fishing Ck., including Henry BARNERS' farm, is annexed to Miles Twp., Centre Co.

p. 265: Commissioners to make a road beginning between Brownsville & FROST's tavern, Fayette Co., to intersect the Washington & Bedford Tpk. Rd. near Somerset: Thomas M'KIBBEN, Valentine GIESY, James PAUL, John B. TREVOR, Daniel ROGERS, Hugh THOMPSON, Abraham BALDWIN, Fayette Co.; Godfrey STALL, Adam STARNER, Jacob LAUD, George CHORPPONING, Peter WILL, John KUSER, Sr., George GEBHART, Michael KING, Somerset Co.

p. 270: A road is to be laid out from the meeting house at Mr. JOHNSTON's, Kishacoquillas Valley, to intersect the state road from Bellefonte to Erie at GLEN's tavern on Bald Eagle Ck. A road is to be laid out beginning on the road from Carlisle to Fort Littleton between Fannettsburg & Tuscarora Mt., Franklin Co., to intersect the state road from Burnt Cabins to CLARK's ferry near the house of Thomas PURDAY, merchant, Tyrone Twp., Cumberland co.

p. 278: John DAILY, guardian of Margaret & Ann THOMPSON, minor children of Mathew THOMPSON, decd., is auth. to sell land in Elizabeth Twp., Allegheny Co., bounded by Mathew M'KENNIS, Joseph COOK.

p. 279: Election districts: Middletown Twp., Susquehanna Co., will vote at Philo BOSTWICK's. Salem Twp., Wayne Co., will vote at William WOODBRIDGE's. Canaan Twp., Wayne Co., will vote at John FOBES', Esq. The 5th district, Lycoming Co., will vote at Sarah HUCKELL's. Clearfield Twp., Butler Co., will vote at John M'COY's. Caernarvan Twp., Berks Co., will vote at Thomas L. JONES',

Morgantown. Connemaugh Twp., Somerset Co., will vote at Jacob BRUBAKER's. Ury's district, Washington Co., will vote at Daniel M'GOGIN's, West Middleton. Whiteley Twp., Greene Co., will vote at Nathaniel CAMPBELL's. Bald Eagle Twp., Centre Co., will vote at Hugh WHITE's. Lemarre Twp., Centre Co., will vote at James BROWN's. Moreland Twp., Lycoming Co., will vote at John SHIPMAN's. Auburn & Springfield Twp., Susquehanna Co., will vote at Salmon THOMAS'. Kingston Twp., Luzerne Co., will vote at Philip MYERS'. Blakely Twp., Luzerne Co., will vote at George HARBARGER's. Washington Twp., Indiana Co., near James THOMPSON's house, M'KEE's mill, William PATTERSON's house, Robert WALKER's house, will vote at Francis FAIRMAN's. Pike Twp., Bradford Co., will vote at Cornwall BRUSH's. Wyalusing Twp., Bradford Co., will vote at John STALFORD's. Covington Twp., Clearfield Co., will vote at Hugh BIDDLE's, Esq. East Nottingham Twp., Chester Co., will vote at Allen F. CUNNINGHAM's, New London Crossroads. Rockland Twp., Venango Co., will vote at James CRAWFORD's. Mt. Pleasant Twp., Wayne Co., will vote at Sanford CLARK's. Brokenstraw Twp., Warren Co., formerly voted at Arthur RANDLE's & now will vote at Amasa RANSOM's. Madison Twp., Columbia Co., will vote at William MARSHAL's. District Twp., Berks Co., will vote at John WELLAR's. Hellam Twp., York Co., will vote at Peter KLINE's. Tinicum Twp., Bucks Co., will vote at Peter BARNETS'. Nockamixon Twp., Bucks Co., will vote at John BUCK's. Ohio Twp., Beaver Co., will vote at Andrew CAROTHERS'. Pimatuning Twp., Mercer Co., will vote at Samuel CLARK's. Buffaloe Twp., Cumberland Co., will vote at Frederick DEAL's. Moore Twp., Northampton Co., will vote at John STEHLEY's. Part of Hamilton & Peters Twps., Franklin co., near Patrick M'DOWELL, CLAPSADLE's mill, CHRISTMAN & KRIDER's mill, William TEMPLETON's house, Widow ARMSTRONG, Thomas M'KINSTRY's will vote at Michael SELLERS', St. Thomas, Peter's Twp. Louisville Twp., Susquehanna Co., will vote at Allen UPSON's. Mahoning Twp., Indiana Co., will vote at Christian BARE's. The north part of Centre Co. will vote at Anthony KLECKNER's, Sugar Valley. Pocono & Stroud Twps., Northampton Co., will vote at Michael KEENER's, Stroudsburg. The 6th district, Chester Co., will vote at the public house of John EVERHART, Pughtown, Coventry Twp. Hatfield Twp., Montgomery Co., will vote at John BUCHAMMER's. Breighton Twp., Beaver Co., will vote at David EAKEN's. The 9th district, Huntingdon Co., will vote at Thomas JOHNSTON's, Antis Twp. Cousawago Twp., Crawford Co., will vote at Thomas POTTER's.

p. 296: Patton ROSS, Lancaster Co., is auth. to erect wharves in the Susquehanna River opposite Washington, Lancaster Co.

p. 299: Ellis PASSMORE's will of 6 Oct., 1817, was authenticated by the clerk of Loudon Co., Va. The Register of Wills in Chester Co. is to file it & issue letters testamentary to Samuel IRWIN & Josiah KIRK, executors.

p. 303: Roger DAVIS, late of Charlestown Twp., Chester Co., Esq., decd., willed to his sons, Isaac & Roger, all the real estate he owned in the county. His widow has been some time decd. It is the wish of all parties that a house, plantation & tract in Charlestown Twp., Chester co., bounded by Peter YOUNG, William LLEWELLYN, Isaac DAVIS should be sold. Thomas DAVIS, another son, & Roger are both minors. Jacob NEILOR is guardian of Roger DAVIS & is auth. to make the sale.

p. 307: Christian PEMBERTON, Phila.; Charles KEAN, Washington Co.; Adam ANDERSON, Westmoreland Co.; John CAREY, Northampton Co.;

William M'GREDY, Crawford Co.; John JEMISON, Butler Co. are given $40 & $40/yr. The heirs of Capt. John BRADY, late of Northumberland Co., decd., are to be given $750 in lieu of donation land #182 situated within the triangular tract of land on Lake Erie, formerly supposed to be in the 10th donation district (500 acres). The annuity granted to Thomas BAIRD, Allegheny Co., is repealed & it shall be paid hereafter to John HASKINS. Capt. John BRISBEN, Dauphin Co., is to receive $75 & $75/yr. William ROSS is to receive money for arrearages of pay & rations due him for his services in performing a tour of military duty during the late war.

THE LAWS OF PENNSYLVANIA
1817-1822

Revolutionary & Military Service Pensions: 1817--Michael DEARMOND; 1818--Isaac RAYMOND, Agnes CRAWFORD, James ENGLISH. Henry GUTHARDT, John MURPHY, John M'KINNEY, Thomas ANDERSON, Christian HUBBARD, William MARKS, William M'CONNELL, Jacob VANGORDER, William RUSSEL, John SHOOK, Thomas M'MULLEN, Charles CHRISTMAN, John DOUGLERTY, Jesse GRINDING, John HARDCHY, Benjamin LYON, John KELER, all are given $40 & $40/yr. Abraham HORN is given $48 & $48/yr. Christian PEMBERTON, Charles KEAN, Adam ANDERSON, John CAREY, William M'GREDY & John JEMISON are given $40 & $40/yr. John BRADY, decd., is given $750 in lieu of donation land. John HASKINS is to receive an annuity granted to Thomas BAIRD. John BRISBEN is given $75 & $75/yr. Rosina PRICE, widow of Thomas PRICE, is given $40 adn $30/yr. Charle BOWMAN, Jacob KREIDER will receive $40 & $40/yr. 1819--Elizabeth CARMINE, widow of William CARMINE, will receive $40 & $40 for five years. Joshua WILLIAMS will receive $80 & $80/yr. Alexander BURNES, Hugh CAMPBELL, Michael LONGENBACH, Elizabeth BROADHEAD (widow of Luke BROADHEAD), Henry WOLLERY (annuity will be paid to David HALLER for the use of Henry WOLLERY), Charles WILLOUGHBY, Joseph GEDDIS will receive $40 & $40/yr. John MARSHALL will receive $120 & $120/yr. Maria, widow of Matthias KELCHNER, will receive $40 & $30/yr. Isabella CAMPBELL, widow of Thomas CAMPBELL, will receive $60 & $60/yr. Joseph WREN will receive an annuity as will Atchison MELON. 1820--Jane, widow of William GODFREY, will receive $60 & $60/yr. in lieu of donation land. Peter GORDON, Jacob RUDOLPH, Daniel GRIDLEY, Jacob MUMMY, Jacob GEIGER, John ADAMS, Stephen CARTER, Henry WAGGONER, Henry LUTZ, David MARSH are all to receive $40 & $40/yr. John HUTON's auth. of payment of an annuity to Henry BULL is repealed & the annuity will be paid to John EWALT. John M'DOWELL will receive an annuity which will be paid to Reuben BAILEY for his use & so much as requires an annuity to be paid to Alexander M'CLEAN is repealed.
1821--Frederick WENDT, Joseph REED, William M'FADEN, Jacob BALMER, John MORRISON, Joseph KING, Christian YEGER, Samuel ROBB, Samuel PORTER, Conrad HITE, Peter SWARTZ, John VASEY, William MILLER, John BRANDON, Henry ZERFOSS, Thomas GAY, Hugh MOORE will be paid $40 & $40/yr. Henry WOOLERY is to receive an annuity which will be paid to David HALLER for his use. John DENNISSON is given the auth. which has been given to Fullerton WOODS. 1822--Daniel M'NEIL, Molly M'KOLLY, William HARBISON, Peter KIDD, Robert CRAWFORD, Michael YEISLY, Peter CRAWFORD, Frederick BIRD, John M'CLAIN, Sidney PENDERGRASS (widow of Lawrence PENDERGRASS), Debroah M'COY (widow of Daniel M'COY), Margaret CAPPEL (widow of Charles CAPPEL), John M'CALLISTER, John M'LEOD, Jeremiah BANNER, Solomon ADAMS, James BARRETT, Charles WALLACE, William GUTHRIE, Mary GUYER (widow of Peter GUYER), Samuel KELLY, Charles OLDWINE, Andrew STOLL, Robert THOMPSON, Joseph GOOD, Bridget BRUTON (widow of Joseph BRUTON), Ann

KANE (widow of Charles KANE), Eve LORENTZ (widow of Wendle LORENTZ), Elizabeth BOYLES (widow of John BOYLES), Andrew LUCKEY, William BRADLEY, Peter CONNER, James ANDERSON, George SIDLE, John NEIL, Andrew SOX, Hezekiah DAVIES, Samuel BLAIR will receive $40 & $40/yr. Peter FRICKER had an annuity which was to have been given to Jacob GOODMAN for his use & that is repealed. Barnard VALENTINE is to receive an annuity which will be paid to Daniel CHRISTY & is to be expended to provide clothing & diet for VALENTINE, Mifflin Co. David REYNOLDS is the person to whom the annuity was formerly payable. Hartman LEITLHEISER will receive $78/yr. Catharine PINKERTON & William JOHNSON will receive $40/yr.

p. xviii: In 1817, the admin. of the estate of Jacob WOLF, late of Union Co., were auth. to sell land. William SPEER & Clements BURLEIGH are auth. to sell land in 1815. Eleanor MOTT, late Eleanor ALEXANDER, is vested with the estate of Charles ALEXANDER, Phila. Co., decd., in 1820.

p. 1, 1817: The electors of Greencastle, Franklin Co., are to meet at John BESORE's.

p. 2: The New Milford & Montrose Tpk. Rd. will begin at Nicholas M'CARTY's, New Milford.

p. 28: An act to suspend the collection of debt due to Pa. by John CADWALLADER, Huntingdon Co., decd.

p. 41: Conrad KIRSHNER, Jacob PHILIPS, John STAUDT, Jacob SCHWENK are members of the Lutheran Congregation of St. Paul's Church, Manheim Twp., Schuylkill Co.

p. 42: John ERNST & Samuel SHERER are to erect a toll bridge over Swatara Ck. near "ERNST's" or "SHERER's" ferry, Dauphin Co.

p. 65: James STEELE is auth. to sell land granted on 12 Feb., 1740 to Henry WORK after setting aside 10 acres for a house of worship, school house & burying place for the Presby. Church, Middle Octorara, Lancaster Co.

p. 142, 1819: Real estate for the use of the German Lutheran Church & Calvinist Congregation, Hempfield Twp., Westmoreland Co., is vested in John SHRUM & Adam BAUGHMAN.

p. 164: Samuel WEBB, Columbia Co.; Isaac A. CHAPMAN, Luzerne Co.; John W. ROSEBERRY, Schuylkill Co., are commissioners to lay out a road from the bridge over the Susquehanna River at Nescopeck Falls, Luzerne Co., to Orwigsburg, Schuylkill Co.

p. 165: The commonwealth has claims against Peter PAYNTON, formerly state treasurer & against the estate of John NICHOLSON, decd.

p. 166: Daniel MONTGOMERY & John GEARHART own a ferry over the north branch of the Susquehanna River & the landing opposite Danville, Columbia Co.

p. 166: David MARCHAND, Daniel SCHAEFFER, Jacob KUHNS, Westmoreland Co., are auth. to dig for salt in the Conemaugh Riverbed adj. their land in Derry Twp.

p. 171: All of that part of Decatur Twp., Mifflin Co., near John EBERHART's stillhouse is annexed to Union Co.

p. 205: Matthias SHIRK & Co. is auth. to sell 40 acres in Cocalico Twp., conveyed by John BALMER to Adam GRILL for several congregations of Presby. or Reformed Churches in Cocalico, Earle, Warwick Twp., Lancaster Co.

p. 207: Election districts: Bradford Co., Wyalusing Twp., will vote at Joseph BLACK's. Warren Twp., Bradford Co., will vote at Abner BOWINGS'. Ridgeberry Twp., Bradford Co., will vote at Griswold OWENS'. Athens & Ulster Twp., Bradford Co., east of the Susquehanna River, will vote at Samuel BARTLETT's. Albany Twp., Berks Co., will vote at Jacob FOOSSELMAN's. Berks Co., that part of Colebrookdale Twp., included in Henry KEELY's election district, is re-annexed to John MUTHARD's. St. Clair Twp., Bedford Co., will vote at John BERKHIMER's. Muddy Ck. Twp., Butler Co., will vote at Andrew M'GOWAN's. Mt. Pleasant Twp., Columbia Co., will vote at Frederick MILLER's. Alleppo Twp., Greene Co., will vote at David KINNEY's. Springfield Twp., Huntingdon Co., will vote at William HUDSON's. Leacock Twp., Lancaster Co., will vote at Marks GROVE's, innkeeper. Brecknock Twp., Lancaster Co., will vote at Jacob MASONER's. Sadsbury Twp., Lancaster Co. will vote at Stephen HALL's, innkeeper. Dallas Twp., Luzerne Co., will vote at Abel WHEELER's. Covington Twp., Luzerne Co., will vote at George BUCK's. Mahoning Twp., Mercer co., will vote at Alexander THOMPSON's. Hanover Twp., Northampton Co., formerly voted at George BUTZ's & now will vote at Christian MENSCH's, Allen Twp. Moore Twp., Northampton Co., will vote at George GREBER's. Turbut Twp., Northumberland Co., will vote at William MORITZ's. Milton Twp., Northumberland Co., will vote at Daniel ECHERT's. Quemahoning Twp., Stony Ck. Twp., Somerset Co., will vote at John KENNEDY's. Stoystown. Sterling Twp., Wayne Co., will vote at Phineas HOW's. Pikerun Twp., Washington Co., will vote at John GREER's. Richland Twp., Venango Co., will vote at Henry BEST's (mill). Codorus Twp., York Co., will vote at Jacob B. WENTZ's, Jefferson. Windsor Twp., York Co., will vote at George OBERDORF, Jr's. Lancaster Co. near Henry STRICKLER's spring (near Chiquesalungo Ck., Rapho Twp.) to Abraham BRUBAKER's school house to John SLOREY's tenant house to Adam FIRST's, to Christian BRUBAKER's mill, past Widow STAUFER's, Jacob HERSHEY, Sr.'s, John BRENNEMAN's, Martin NISSLEY's including Andrew HEISTAND's, will vote at the school house, Mount Joy. Upper Paxton Twp., Dauphin Co., will vote at George BUFFINGTON's. Lykens Twp., Dauphin Co., will vote at Conrad FRY's, Gratz. The 2nd district, Delaware Co., will vote at Joseph HANNUM's, Concord Twp. Norwegian Twp., Schuylkill Co., including Abraham YODER's & John SLONECKER's, will vote at Michael BOLIG's, innkeeper.

p. 224: On 26 Apr., 1783, a compact was made between Abraham CLARK, Joseph COOPER, Thomas HENDERSON, N.J. commissioners, & George BRYAN, George GRAY, & William BINGHAM, Pa. commissioners, to clear the Delaware River.

p. 226: John KELKER lived in Swatara Twp., Dauphin Co.

p. 248, 1820: Michael NEWMAN & Peter WINEBRENNER are trustees of the German Reformed Congregation of Hanover, York Co.

p. 249: An act to record a deed from William ELLIOTT & his wife for land on 27 July, 1795 is acknowledged before John JOHNSTON in Allegheny.

p. 251: John NISSLY lived in Dauphin Co.

p. 255: Stony Ck. from it's mouth up to Peter BERKEY's mills, Somerset Co., is declared a public highway.

p. 260: Northern Liberties, Phila. Co., near land late of --- GIBSON, land late of Isaac NORRIS, decd., & now of J.P. NORRIS, is called the Kensington District.

p. 288: George BROWN, Berlin, is a Justice of the Peace in Adams Co.

p. 297: William P. BEATTY is treasurer of a lottery to raise money to improve navigation of the Susquehanna River.

p. 298: James BARTON is to convey water into Milford, Pike Co.

p. 303: James HOPKINS, Lancaster, recently erected an illegal dam in the Susquehanna River at Conewago Falls.

p. 305: James HOPKINS is auth. to create a slack water navigation in the Connestoga River.

p. 315: Election districts: St. Clair Twp., Allegheny Co., which formerly voted at James PATTERSON's, now will vote at Dominic O'CORNER's, Birmingham. Deer Twp., Allegheny Co., will vote at John M'COOL's. Greenfield District, Luzerne Co., will vote at Samuel VAIL's. Mifflin Twp., Dauphin Co., will vote at George BUFFINGTON's. Upper Paxton Twp., Dauphin Co., will vote at Jonathan COLLIER's. German Twp., Fayette Co., will vote at Frederick STRUBLE's, McClellandtown. Springhill Twp., Fayette Co., will vote at Absalom MORRIS'. The 12th election district, Huntingdon Co., will vote at Jacob GOOSEHORN's house (now James ORR's, Tell Twp.). Union Co. near Robert BADGER's, West Buffalo Twp., to James MATHERS' lane, near John KLAPP's saw-mill, to George MITCHELL's upper mill, to John BISHOP's, to George OTT's, to Henry MOYER's, will vote at Joseph LECHNER's, Centreville. Addison Twp., Somerset Co., will vote at Henry STULLER's, Petersburg. Mahoning Twp., Mercer Co., will vote at Henry ROBINSON's. French Ck. Twp., Venango Co., will vote at George KAPP's. Robinson Twp., Washington Co., will vote at Joseph CRAFFORD's. Hanover Twp., Washington Co., will vote at David TUCKER's. Penn Twp., Chester Co., will vote at Dr. Allen CUNNINGHAM's, New London crossroads. E. Caln, W. Whiteland Twp., Chester Co., will vote at Jesse EVANS' public house, Dowingtown, E. Caln Twp. Sugar Ck. Twp., Venango Co., will vote at Alexander BOWMAN's. Plumb district, Venango Co., will vote at Daniel HERRING's. Bloomfield Twp., Crawford Co., will vote at Gilbert A. GEROWS'. E. Bethlehem Twp., Washington Co., will vote at Jacob SPENCER's, Fredericktown. Hanover Twp., Northampton Co., will vote at Simon BUTZ's, Bethlehem Twp. George's Twp., Fayette Co., will vote at David MILLER's. Germantown Twp., Phila. Co., will vote at Andrew TROLLINGER's. Clearfield Twp., Butler Co., will vote at Peter HENRY's. Southampton Twp., Franklin Co., will vote at Daniel WONDERLICKS'. Norwegian & Schuylkill Twp., Schuylkill Co., will vote at Jacob SHELLY's, Pottsville, Norwegian Twp. Rush Twp., Northampton Co., will vote at John KOLKIT's. Shamokin Twp., Northumberland Co., will vote at Daniel STAMBACH's. Wheatfield & Washington Twp., Indiana Co., near Gen. CAMPBELL's mill, Isaac GREFETH's mill, will vote at David FULTON's, Washington Twp. Springfield & Troy Twp., Bradford Co. will vote at Samuel CONANT's, Troy Twp. Montour Twp., Allegheny Co., will vote at Aaron ATON's, Montour Twp. Sugar Ck. & Toby Twp., Armstrong Co., near John

MARTIN's mill, will vote at Samuel KELLY's on the east side of the Allegheny River. Bensalem Twp., Bucks Co., will vote at Benjamin FLEMMING's until the former house is rebuilt. Northmoreland Twp., Luzerne Co., will vote at Orange FULLER's. Washington & Perry Twp., Union Co. near Simon SNYDER's paper mill, John GERMAN, Sr.'s, John LONG's. Grub Church in Perry Twp., Wiandt NEWMAN's at Mohontongo Ck. will vote at Philip HAROLD's. Decatur Twp., Mifflin Co., will vote at Stephen HINDS'. Burlington Twp., Bradford Co., will vote at James LONG's. New Sewickly, Beaver Co., will vote at Philip GRIMM, Sr.'s. West Bethlehem Twp., Washington Co., will vote at Stephen HILL's, Hillsborough. Versailles Twp., Allegheny Co., will vote at Thomas NEEL's. Patton Twp., Centre Co., will vote at Isaac HICKS'. Gibson & Jackson Twp., Susquehanna Co., will vote at Joseph WASHBURN, Esq.'s, Gibson Twp. Venango Twp., Crawford Co., will vote at James SKELTON's. Pocono Twp., Northampton Co., will vote at Christian SINGER's. Potter Twp., Centre Co., will vote at Walter LONGVILLE, Earlysburg. Halfmoon Twp., Centre Co., will vote at Joseph B. SHUGERT's. Hamilton Twp., Northampton Co., will vote at James SHAFER's.

p. 321: Peter BAYNTON has lands in Huntingdon, Centre & Venango Co.

p. 331: Jacob KREIDER, Centre Co.,; James DALE, Union Co.; John HANNA, Lycoming Co., are commissioners to run the line between Union & Centre Co.

p. 332: Isaac A. CHAPMAN, Luzerne Co.; Jacob ANTES, Lycoming Co. are commissioners to run the line between Luzerne & Lycoming Co.

p. 334: Sandy Lick Ck. is declared a public highway from it's mouth to Henry NULFF, Jr.'s saw mill, Jefferson Co.

p. 339: Alexander M'CALMONT & others are commissioners to review state roads, Warren town. Arnold HUNTER & others are commissioners to review state roads, Bradford Co. Benjamin STOKELY & others are commissioners to review state roads, Franklin, Venango Co.

p. 352: William KELLY is to establish a ferry on the north branch of the Susquehanna River, Bradford, Bradford Co.

p. 352, 1821: A warrant is issued for 30 acres in Upper Mahonoy Twp., Northumberland Co. adj. John KARES, to John HAAS, Martin ZARTMAN & Jacob TRESTLER, trustees of the Presby. & Lutheran Congregations.

p. 357: Samuel MEREDITH, George CLYMER on 13 May, 1807, purchased land from Cadwallader EVANS, Jr. & Joseph HIESTER, Esq. (2 Pa. commissioners appointed to settle debts due from the estate of the late John NICHOLSON). MEREDITH & CLYMER are since decd. The Governor issues process to Henry CLYMER, George CLYMER, John READ, James GIBSON or their survivors (who survived Dr. Casper WISTAR), devisees in trust of the estate of George CLYMER, late of Phila.; & Samuel DICKINSON, John READ, Thomas CADWALLADER, James GIBSON, adminis. of Samuel MEREDITH, decd.

p. 366: The heirs of James MOORE, decd., are to receive $943.69. The heirs of William M'CORD & Alexander HUNTER sued to recover money paid to them by mistake.

p. 381: Two tracts of land in the will of Rev. Theodore BOWERS are vested in Dennis CONNOR, et cet, trustees of the Roman Catholic

Church, Westmoreland Co.

p. 389: Commissioners to erect a state penitentiary in Phila: Thomas WISTAR, Dr. Samuel P. GRIFFITTS, Peter MIERCKEN, George N. BAKER, Thomas BRADFORD, Jr., John BACON, Caleb CARMALT, Samuel R. WOOD, Thomas SPARKS, James THACKARA, Daniel H. MILLER.

p. 396: William COURTNEY, Allegheny Co.; James ADAMS, Pittsburg; Thomas FOSTER, Georgetown, Beaver Co., are appointed to make contracts to spend money to improve navigation of the Ohio River.

p. 397: Agents to improve the Susquehanna River & branches: Henry HALDEMAN, Elisha GREEN, Abbot GREEN, Derrstown; Erastus HILL, Daniel STERLING, George BENNET, Matthew OGDEN, Clearfield; Samuel EDMISTON, Henry MILLER, Huntingdon; Henry BARNHART, John AULT, George TOMB, William MAHAFFEY, Johnston BUCKLEY, Peter DIMM.

p. 398: George MULHOLLAND, Jr., Peter WALLACE, Andrew BOGGS, John HILL & Jacob DRUM are commissioners to spend money to improve the navigation of the Connemaugh & Kiskiminitas Rivers. Commissioners to improve navigation of the Delaware River: Benjamin METTLER, Easton; Lewis S. CORYELL, John KIRKBRIDE, Bucks Co.; Luke BROADHEAD, Northampton; Jacob QUICK, Pike; George BUSH, Wayne. Joseph BURKE, Easton, & Richard MITCHELL, Bucks, are to view the river. John COLLBAUGH, Abisha WOODWARD are to view the river.

p. 399: Jonathan BRINK, Benjamin KIMBLE, Wayne Co., are commissioners to improve the Lackawaxen.

p. 401: James ALLISON, John PUGH, Edward WRIGHT, Beaver Co.; Auther CHENWITH, Samuel CLARK, Mercer Co., are commissioners to improve navigation of the Beaver River.

p. 401: James HANAGAN, Joseph MARSHALL, Armstrong Co.; James M'COMB, William TRAVIS, Indiana Co.; Charles C. GASKILL, Carpenter WINSTOW, Jefferson Co.; David FORGESON, Moses BOGGS, Clearfield Co., are commissioners to improve a state road from the mouth of Anderson's Ck., Clearfield Co. to Kittanning.

p. 402: David LAWSON, James COCHRAN, John SLOAN, Jr., Armstrong Co.; John MATTSON, John LUCAS, Jefferson Co.; Brewster FREEMAN, Joseph OTTO, McKean Co., are commissioners to superintend the improvement of a road from Kittanning to Hamilton, N.Y. Jarret SHADUCK, John BROOKS, Crawford; James IRVINE, Warren, are commissioners to complete a road from Warren to Meadville.

p. 403: Daniel D.B. KEIM, John ADAMS, et al., are former managers of the Centre Tpk.

p. 404: John GEBHART, Sr., John BRUBAKER, Esq., Peter HEFFLEY, Somerset; Thomas BOYD, Daniel ROGERS, Joseph TORRENCE, Fayette, are commissioners to improve a road through Greene Co., to the flats of Grave Ck. A road between RICHARDSON's old tavern & the Milford & Owego Tpk. is to be completed. Aaron BLOSS, Richard HAYS, John SHAFER are to improve a road between John HARMAN's, Lycoming Co., & Aaron BLOSS', Tioga Co. Asa MANN, William WILLIARD, Jr., Robert TUBBS are to improve the road between Widow SLAWSON's & Ayres TUTTLE's, Tioga Co. William L. MILLER, Samuel RANKIN, Alexander PLUMER are commissioners to improve navigation of the Youghiogheny River from Connelsville to it's mouth.

p. 405: George KECK, Philip WIND are to improve the road from KECK's to GANGWER's tavern, Lehigh Co. John HOOT & Thomas V. BUSKERCH are to improve the road from LANDES' hill & the rocks between John ROBERTS' & the late Samuel SELLER's taverns in Bucks Co. Lord BUTLER & John GARDNER are to improve the road in Luzerne Co. from the Lackawanna River to KELLER's ferry. Peter STEM, Charles CRAIG, John HAGENBACH are to improve the road between the Lehigh Gap.

p. 406: William MEANS, Harry SPALDING, Edmund LOCKWOOD are to improve a road between Sugar Ck., Towanda Twp., & the house of Thomas OVERTON, Ulster Twp., Bradford Co. John HARMAN, Ezra LONG, Reuben WILBER are to improve the road from John HARMAN's, Lycoming Co. & Ezra SPALDING's, Bradford Co.

p. 407: Edward HERRINGTON, William CARROL, Jr., Samuel HAYS & Arthur ROBINSON, Jr. are to improve the road from Franklin to Mercer.

p. 407: James ADAMS, Sr. & Charles WHITNEY are to complete a road from CLARK's ferry to Burnt Cabins. The road is to be improved from John PIATT's through Loyalsock Gap to George PORTER's, Lycoming Co. The road is to be improved from Henry ANTIS' to the head of Whitedeer Valley.

p. 408: Hugh DONALY, David READ are to improve the post road from Union Co. to Whitedeer Hole Ck. Frederick DERING, John FISHER are to repair a bridge across Black Ck. & the road between Middle Ck. & Samuel WHITMOR's. The road between Meadville & the Ohio state line near Andrew BETT's mill is to be repaired by James HERRINGTON, Hugh ANDREWS & Thomas ATKINSON.

p. 409: William MITCHELL & Joseph SMITH are to improve a road from New Hope to Durham Ck. John RICHARDS & John CAREY, Jr. are to improve a road from Easton to Durham Ck. John M'ALLEN, Alexander WALKER, George DANSDILL are to improve a road from Strasburgh to Sideling Hill.

p. 410: James CREE & James M'CURDY are to improve a road from Roxbury to the north side of Tuscarora Mt., Huntingdon.

p. 410: Robert BARBER, Jr., Peter RICHTER are to improve navigation of Penn's Ck., Union Co. Caspar HARTMAN, John YOTERS, John RITTER, Columbia, are to improve a road from the foot of the north side of Little Mt. to Mahonoy Gap, Columbia & Schuylkill Co.

p. 411: James ALLEN, Benjamin RICE are to improve a road across North Mt. at M'CLURE's Gap between Landisburg & Newville. George SWART & Robert BRITTIN, Northampton Co., are to improve the river road from Easton to MARTIN's Ck. bridge.

p. 424: James LOCKHART has a tract of land in Salem Twp., Luzerne Co. It was surveyed on a warrant 4 Jan., 1786 to Frederick KUHNS & Nicholas KERNS, Jr. The land may be claimed by Connecticut.

p. 439: A road is to be laid out from John BLAIR's, through Munster & Ebensburg to Martin RAIGART's.

p. 443: Thomas WOODSIDE, Joseph PRUTZMAN, Samuel WEBB, Columbia Co., are commissioners to lay out a road from Mahony Bridge, Schuylkill River to Cattawissa, Columbia Co.

p. 444: Zephon FLOWERS, Bradford Co.; William D. BACON, Ambrose MILLARD, Tioga Co., are commissioners to lay out a road from the west side of the Tioga River to John LANARD's to Widow Rachel BERRY's to Wellsborough.

p. 454: William P. BEATTY is treasurer of the Susquehanna Lottery.

p. 457: John KOONS is granted compensation for tracts of land certified to Connecticut. The claims are in 17 townships of Luzerne Co. The land was surveyed to Samuel MORRIS, Jacob CRAMER, David or Daniel SHOEMAKER.

p. 460: The religious society of Friends of Phila. has land adj. Elizabeth POWEL.

p. 467: Levi PAWLING is auth. to sell in Montgomery & Chester co., the corporate rights of Pawlingsford Bridge over the Schuylkill River.

p. 470: William HARVEY, Greene Co.; Walter CRAIG, Washington Co.; David SCOTT, Beaver Co., are commissioners to lay out a road from Waynesburg, Greene Co., to Beaver, Beaver Co.

p. 476: Robert BOYD, John BUTE, Freeman LEWIS are to review a road from White Horse, Somerset Co., to the Va. line near George OLDSHOE's tavern. Joshua DICKERSON, Richard CROOKS, Henry HEATON are commissioners to re-locate a road through Waynesburg to the flats of Grave Ck., between Waynesburg & David BRADBERRY's & part lying between Low Gap near HODGE's improvement.

p. 478: Ephriam ESTEP, James WIER, Washington Co.; Charles FULWOOD, Westmoreland Co., are to lay out a road from Mt. Pleasant, Westmoreland Co. to intersect the National Road not further east of Washington than the house of Peter DAGER.

p. 481: Election districts: Middletown, Upper Providence, Ashton, Thornbury Twp., Delaware Co. near Jacob PARKS' will vote at the Black Horse Tavern occupied by George ERWIN, Middletown Twp. Silver Lake Twp., Susquehanna Co., will vote at Ansel HILL's. Clifford Twp., Susquehanna Co., will vote at Warren DIMOCK's, Dundarff. Allegheny Twp., Westmoreland Co., will vote at James M'COLLOUGH's. Eaton Twp., Luzerne Co., will vote at Jesse LEE's. Beaver Twp., Union Co. will vote at Henry MICK's. Abington Twp., Luzerne Co., will vote at Russel CAHOON's. Penn Twp., Union Co. formerly voted at Joseph FREEHRER's, Esq. & will now vote at Jacob RHOADS', Selin's Grove. Patton Twp., Centre Co., will vote at William DAVIS'. Shippen Twp., M'Kean Co., will vote at David CROW's. Sergeant Twp., M'Kean Co., will vote at Nathaniel C. GALLUP's. Warren Co. will vote at Samuel OLDHAM's. Heidleberg Twp., Lebanon Co., will vote at Frederick OBERLEY's, Shaefferstown. Londonderry Twp., Bedford Co., will vote at Jacob CARPENTER's. Union Twp., Huntingdon Co. will vote at John PORT's. Centre Twp., Butler Co., will vote at Sylvanus AGERS'. Muddy Ck. Twp., Butler Co., will vote at Cadwalader BAKER's. Windham Twp., Bradford Co., will vote at Joseph WEBSTER's, Esq. Franklin Twp., Bradford Co., will vote at Amos KNAPP's. Centre Twp., Greene Co., will vote at Ephraim MORRIS', Clinton. Honeybrook Twp., Chester co., will vote at Samuel BEAR's. Lower Chanceford Twp., York Co., will vote at the house occupied by John DOUGHERTY, the property of Henry SHENK. Hopewell Twp., York Co., will vote at Abraham MILLER's, innkeeper. Upper Nazareth Twp., Northampton Co., will vote at John T. HAMAN's, Nazareth. Palmyra

Twp., Pike Co., will vote at Jacob KIMBLE's. Lackawaxen Twp., Pike Co., will vote at Mordecai ROBERTS'. Ohio Twp., Beaver Co., will vote at John DIXON's, on the Georgetown Rd. Windsor Twp., York Co., will vote at Jacob KAUFFELT's, innkeeper. Northern Liberties Twp., Phila. Co., will vote at John WICKERMAN's, New Front St. Rd., known as Rose Hill tavern. Tulpehocken Twp., Berks Co., will vote at Christian LONG's. Perry Twp., Berks Co., will vote at John BINKLEY's. Middlesmithfield Twp., Pike Co., will vote at Solomon WESTBROOK, Jr.'s. Sterling Twp., Wayne Co., will vote at John BORTREE's. Maiden Ck. Twp., Berks Co., will vote at Samuel BEARD's.

p. 499, 1822: Abraham TAYLOR, Lycoming Co.; Daniel MONTGOMERY & Matthew COLVIN, Columbia Co. are commissioners to lay out a road from Pennsborough, Lycoming Co. to Danville, Columbia Co.

p. 502: The land of the Holland Land Co. was warranteed to Richard, Samuel & Peter GILL. The land is near Daniel M'COMB's land, Moses LONG's, & the Crawford & Warren Co. line.

p. 503: John M'ALLEN, Alexander WALKER, George DANSDILL are auth. to review the road from Strasburg, Franklin Co., to the top of Sideling Hill, Bedford Co., near C. REAMER's.

p. 505: A report was made by Ephraim ESTEP & James WIER on the road from Mt. Pleasant, Westmoreland Co., to the National Road, east of Washington, Washington Co.

p. 506: Moses RANKIN, York Co.; James HINDMAN, Chester Co.; Peter FRAILEY, Schuylkill Co.; David FULLERTON, Franklin Co.; James AGNEW, Bedford Co. are commissioners to view possible seats of justice for Perry Co.

p. 511: Richard ALLEN, Luzerne Co.; James HAYS, Jacob SHOUSE, Northampton Co., are commissioners to view roads from Lehigh Bridge to Water Gap.

p. 515: Return judges for senators will meet:
Berks & Schuylkill Co.: at John BAILY's, Hamburg.
Dauphin & Lebanon Co.: at the public house of John WOLFERSBERGER, Campbellstown.
Northumberland & Union Co.: at Randal WILCOX's, Lewisburg, Union Co.
Luzerne & Columbia Co.: at Samuel HEADLEY's, Berwick, Columbia Co.
Lycoming, Centre, Clearfield, M'Kean, Potter Co.: at Asker HUNT's, Bald Eagle Bridge, Centre Co.
York & Adams Co.: at Henry BEAR's, Hanover, York Co.
Huntingdon & Mifflin Co.: at John REED's, Belleville, Mifflin Co.
Washington & Greene Co.: at Henry CARTER's, Amity, Washington Co.
Allegheny, Beaver, Butler Co.: at Martin BYRNES', Pine Twp., Allegheny Co.
Somerset & Bedford Co.: at John STATLER's, Allegheny Mt.
Venango, Warren, Armstrong, Indiana, Jefferson, Cambria Co.: at Philip CLOVER's, Armstrong Co.
Return judges for the House of Representatives will meet:
Lehigh, Northumberland, Union, Columbia, Washington, Westmoreland, Armstrong, Indiana & Jefferson Co.: at Robert WOODWARD's, Armstrong Co.
Fayette, Bedford, Franklin, Montgomery, Dauphin, Lebanon, Luzerne, Susquehanna Co.: at John BRICKINGHAM's, Tunkhannock Twp., Luzerne Co.
Mifflin, Delaware, Somerset, Cambria Co.: at George GRAHAM's,

Stoystown, Somerset Co.
Erie, Warren Co.: at William MILES', Union Twp., Erie Co.
Crawford, Venango Co.: at Col. James COCHRAN's, Wayne Twp., Crawford Co.

p. 519: Samuel BELL, Berks Co., is auth. to erect a toll bridge over the Schuylkill River opposite LARDNER's Lane.

p. 521: Thomas BARR, Armstrong Co.; Thomas ENOCHS, William M'CANDLESS, Allegheny Co., are to lay out a road from Kittanning to Pittsburg.

p. 525: White Deer Ck. is declared a public highway from STITZEL's forge to Samuel FORESMAN's milldam (Northumberland Co.), now Lycoming Co.

p. 529: An opinion was signed by E. THURLOW (afterwards Lord THURLOW), Al. WEDDERBURN (afterwards Lord LOUGHBOROUGH), R. JACKSON & J. DUNNING (afterwards Lord ASHBURTON). An eminent lawyer, Sir Charles PRATT (then attorney-general) (afterwards Lord CAMDEN) also made an opinion. Both opinions concerned Connecticut's title to land in Pa.

p. 545: Auchwick Ck., Huntingdon & Bedford Co., from it's mouth to John WILDE's mill, is declared a public highway. Bald Eagle Ck., Centre Co., from Joseph WILLIAMS' saw mill to the mouth of Laurel Run, is a public highway. Little Juniata River, Antes Twp., Huntingdon Co. to the saw mill dam of Alexander & Daniel ALE is declared a public highway. Stoney Ck., Somerset Co., from the mill dam of Peter BERKY, Esq., to the mill dam of George KIMMEL, Esq., is a public highway.

p. 552: Solomon KRIPPS & Joseph ENOCHS, Fayette Co.; William LECKEY, Pittsburg, are commissioners to improve the navigation of the Monongahela River. Henry HEATON, Fayette Co.; John BROWNLEE, Washington Co.; John WALKER, Allegheny Co., shall view the river.

p. 555: Lycoming Co. auth. a bridge over Pine Ck. near Widow HAYS'.

p. 556: Heirs of Michael ROSS may establish a ferry on the west branch of the Susquehanna River adj. Williamsport, Lycoming Co.

p. 557: James MOORE, Beaver Co., owes Pa. money on account of a part of a reserved tract at the mouth of Big Beaver Ck., Beaver Co.

p. 557: Mathew CHAPMAN owned lot #165 in York Co. He died without heirs. The west half of the lot is vested in Lewis ROSENMILLER & James SHALL. The rest is vested in Catharine HOOVER.

p. 561: A section of the land office is to issue a patent for land surveyed in 1796 (400 acres on the southwest side of BATE's fork of 10 Mile Ck., adj. land of John HOGE, Henry PURVIANCE) in trust to Jeremiah COLE, Mary COLE & Michael RUPE.

p. 568: John ERNST, Samuel SHERER are to erect a toll bridge over Swatara Ck., Dauphin Co. Daniel ADAMS, John BEER, John CLARK are add'l commissioners.

p. 569: Luzerne & Wayne Co. tpk. is to end at the east bank of Wallenpaupack Ck. near Ira KELLUM's, Pike Co.

p. 574: Thomas R. PETERS is auth. to erect a dam across Toby's Ck. (Clarion River).

p. 576: John HAMIL, John PEW, John FINDLEY, Mercer Co., are to review a road from Mercer to Warren, OH near the west end of John WRIGHT's land.

p. 580: Election districts: Washington Co., Fallowfield Twp., will vote at James GALLAGHER's. Moon Twp., Allegheny Co., will vote at Adrian ATON's. Findlay Twp., Allegheny Co., will vote at John CHARLES'. Wilkins Twp., Allegheny Co., will vote at Francis WILSON's. Salem Twp., Westmoreland Co., will vote at Jacob LINSIBIGLER's, innkeeper. Washington Twp., Westmoreland Co., will vote at Widow KIRKWOOD's. East Huntingdon, Mt. Pleasant, Hempfield Twps., Westmoreland Co., will vote at Frederick BAUDER's, innkeeper, Mt. Pleasant. Wharton Twp., Fayette Co., will vote at George INKS'. Dunkard Twp., Greene Co., will vote at John SOUTH's mill. Ohio Twp., Beaver Co., will vote at Andrew CAROTHERS'. Toby Twp., Armstrong Co., voted at Thomas M'KIBBEN's & now will vote at James M'CELVEY's. Greene Twp., Indiana Co., will vote at David FULTON's. Mercer Twp., Butler Co., will vote at Samuel M'MURRAY's. Elk Ck. Twp., Erie Co., will vote at Fowler CRANE's. Beaverdam Twp., Erie Co., will vote at James GRAHAM's. The third election district, Erie Co., will vote at John HAY's, Ridge Road, Fairview Twp. The second election district, Erie Co., will vote at Warren STAFFORD's, M'Kean Twp. Northwest & Spring Ck. Twps., Warren Co., will vote at James CULBERTSON's, Spring Ck. Sugar Grove Twp., Warren Co., will vote at John J. WILLIAMSON's. Deerfield Twp., Warren Co., will vote at John THOMPSON's. Pine Grove Twp., Warren Co., will vote at Robert MILES'. Stoeny Ck. Twp., Somerset Co., will vote at Jacob SHANK's. Greenville Twp., Somerset Co., will vote at Peter KEEFER's. E. Pennsborough Twp., Cumberland Co., near Leonard SPONG's on Blue Mt., across Conodoguinet Ck. at Joseph STAYMAN's ford & then in a straight line to intersect the line of Allen Twp., at Baltzer TITLER's will vote at Matthias SWILER's, Hogestown. Conawago Twp., Adams Co., will vote at Adam OYSTER's. Newberry Twp., York Co., will vote at David KISTER's, Newberry. Franklin Twp., York Co., will vote at Frederick HOKE's. Fairview Twp., York Co., will vote at Henry TYSON's. Wisenburg Twp., Lehigh Co., will vote at Peter ZELNER's. Lynn Twp., Lehigh Co., will vote at John SEIBERLING's, Lynnville. Plumstead Twp., Bucks Co., will vote at Josiah BROWN's, which is now occupied by Jesse CALLENDER. Warwick Twp., Bucks Co., will vote at John JAMESON's. Warrington Twp., Bucks Co., will vote at Francis G. LUKENS'. Warminster Twp., Bucks Co., will vote at Thomas BEANS'. Vincent Twp., Pikeland Twp., Chester Co., will vote at Frederick SHEADER's, innkeeper. E. Fallowfield Twp., Chester Co., will vote at Robert YOUNG's, innkeeper. W. Nantmeal Twp., Chester Co., will vote at John SMITH's. Westcaln Twp., Chester Co., will vote at John MARCH's. Cocalico Twp., Lancaster Co., will vote at Jacob STEHLEY's, Reamstown. Martick Twp., Lancaster Co., will vote at Julius HUBERT's. East Hempfield & Manheim Twps., Lancaster Co., near Jacob KAUFFMAN's mill & John STEMAN's, will vote at Frederick SMITH's, Petersburg. Swatara Twp., Lebanon Co., will vote at Jacob HEILMAN's, Jonestown. Anville Twp., Lebanon Co., near Isaac SNEVELY's, Nicholas BOAR's, will also vote at HEILMAN's. Upper Bern Twp., Berks Co., will vote at Benjamin HAAS'. Union Twp., Berks Co., will vote at Peter MARTIN's. Douglass Twp., Berks Co., will vote at Henry KEELY's. Amity Twp., Berks Co., will vote at John POTT, Jr.'s. Rush & Schuylkill Twps., Schuylkill Co., will vote at John BITLER's, Union Twp. M'Keansburg district near Michael HARTMAN's & John MARTZ's, excluding the house of Christian BOYER, will vote at the courthouse, Orwigsburg. Tulpehocken Twp., Berks Co., will vote at John LEISE's tavern. Washington Twp., Fayette Co., will vote at Thomas PATTERSON's. Northumberland Co., Chilisquaque Twp., will vote at Lott CORSON's. Harmony Twp., Susquehanna Co., will vote at Martin LANE's. Clifford Twp., Susquehanna Co., will vote at James WELLS', late the property of PHINNEY & PHELPS. Choconut Twp., Susquehanna Co., will vote at the house formerly occupied by Colvin STANLEY on the farm of Samuel MILLEGAN. Ulster election district (now called Sheshequin election district), Bradford Co., formerly voted at Samuel BARTLETT's & now will vote at Thomas MARSHALL's, Sheshequin Twp. Wysox district, Bradford Co., will vote at Thomas MARSHALL's. Orwell election district, Bradford Co., will vote at Artemas JOHNSON's. Ridgebury Twp., Bradford Co., will vote at James BURNHAM's. Canton Twp., Bradford Co., will vote at Zephaniah RODGERS'. Springfield Twp., Bradford Co., will vote at William BRIGDEN's. Monroe Twp., Bradford Co., will vote at Abner C. ROCKWELL's. Tyrone Twp., Adams Co., will vote at Michael BOWERS', Hidlersburg. Fox Twp. & Gibson Twp., Clearfield Co., will vote at James GREEN, Sr.'s, Fox Twp. Howard Twp., Centre Co., will vote at Enos MILES'. Rush Twp., Centre Co., will vote at Jacob TEST's, Phillipsburg instead of at George SHMEAL's. Middle Smithfield Twp., Pike Co., will vote at John BRICE's. Lewisburg Borough, Union Co., will vote at William HAYES' house, now occupied by Randall WILCOX. Scott Twp., Wayne Co., will vote at John STARBIRD, Jr.'s. Liberty Twp., Columbia Co., will vote at Charles MOORE's, Mooresburg. Shenango Twp., Mercer Co., will vote at Moses CANNON's.

p. 592: CORNPLANTER's lands which were granted to him by Pa., are exempted from taxes.

p. 659: John SHREVE, James TODD, Fayette Co.; Joseph RITNER, Washington Co., are commissioners to review a road in Greene Co. between Waynesburg & David BRADBERRY's.

p. 668: Judges of election will meet: 6th district at John WOLFERSBERGER's, Campbellstown, Lebanon Co. 7th district at George FRESTER's, Kutztown, Berks Co. 9th district at John P. SCHUYLER's, Pennsborough, Lycoming Co. 11th district at Patrick COCHRAN's, Shippensburg. 12th district at Alexander ENNIS', Ennisville, Huntingdon Co. 13th district at John STOTLER's, Allegheny Mt., Somerset Co. 14th district at Jeremiah DAVISON's, Luzerne Twp., Fayette Co. 17th district at Robert ELDER's, Blacklick Twp., Indiana Co.

p. 678: Thomas FORSTER, Giles SANFORD, George MOORE are commissioners to chart Presque Isle harbour, Erie Co.

p. 678: Charles REDHEFFER invented machinery 17 Dec., 1812. A sword was presented to Capt. Stephen DECATUR & Lt. James BIDDLE on 15 Feb., 1816.

p. 679: A gold medal was presented to Capt. Oliver Hazard PERRY for capturing a British fleet commanded by Capt. BARCLAY. The same was given to Jese Duncan ELLIOT & John J. YARNALL on 6 Jan., 1814. Commodore BARNEY is auth. to procure a sword similar to one presented to him by the legislature in 1782. This was auth. on 4 Mar., 1815. On 5 Mar., 1816, a sword was presented to Capt. Charles STEWART of the U.S. Frigate Constitution for valor in the capture of the British ships of war Cyane & Levant. On 11 Mar., 1816, a copy of SMITH's laws was presented to Thomas SPANGENBERGER, Justice of the Peace of Wayne Co.

p. 680: Walter LOWRIE is appointed commissioner to examine obstructions to navigation of the Ohio River. Benjamin R. MORGAN is appointed commissioner to view the Susquehanna.

p. 695: Murder case: Commonwealth vs. Richard SMITH. On 20 Jan., 1816, Richard SMITH shot John CARSON through the head. CARSON died 4 Feb., 1816. On 17 Jan., SMITH & CARSON dined together at CARSON's house on the corner of 2nd & Dock St. They had a fight. On 20 Jan., Capt. CARSON came to his house between 7:00 & 8:00, when Mrs. CARSON & SMITH both left. CARSON sent for Thomas & Jane BAKER, Mrs. Ann CARSON's parents. They found CARSON in the china store. Between 10:00 & 11:00 that evening, Thomasw ABBOT went home & when told the BAKERS who lived under his roof had gone to Mrs. CARSON's, he followed them there. He saw Mrs. CARSON near the house & went with her to the office of Jonathan B. SMITH. They went to the CARSON house where SMITH shot CARSON in the mouth. Capt. BAKER pursued SMITH, heard him tumble among the china & overtook him.

THE LAWS OF PENNSYLVANIA
1818-1819, 1819-1820

p. 1: The estate of Esther ELY, late of Delaware Co., decd., who died without heirs or known kin, is vested in her illegitimate son, George ELY, 21 Dec., 1818.

p. 2: Ephriam KEYS, Fayette Co., died intestate without kin. Violet KEYS, widow, & George PALMER, nephew of Violet, reared in the family of Ephraim KEYS, petitioned to be vested with the estate. KEYS had land in Manallin Twp., Fayette Co., adj. William DIXON.

p. 3: On 14 Apr., 1818, David WELLS, Fayette Co., married Mary DELANY, Harrison Co, OH. Mary was found to have had criminal connections before the marriage. On 30 July, 1818, she had a child that she said was not David's. The marriage is dissolved.

p. 4: Elections in Waynesburg, Franklin Co., will be at John COCHRAN'S.

p. 9: Rosina PRICE, Union Co., widow of Thomas PRICE, a Rev. War veteran, will receive $40 & $30/yr.

p. 10: Charles BOWMAN, Phila. Co., soldier of the Rev., will receive $100 & $40/yr.

p. 12: James & Charles CAMPBELL, two sons of William CAMPBELL, Franklin Co., decd., owned land willed by their father & conveyed by William CAMPBELL, the younger. Charles sold his share to John WILSON. James is now decd. James & McFarland CAMPBELL are executors of the will of James CAMPBELL, decd.

p. 15: Shippensburg, Cumberland Co., was bounded by lands of Patrick COCHRAN, James CHESTER, Dr. SIMPSON, David MANON's heirs, William BARR, Isaac MILLER, William BEARD, Benjamin REYNOLDS, John RAHN.

p. 20: A patent was issued to David MARCHAND on 14 Nov., 1792 for 347 ½ acres in Hempfield Twp., Westmoreland Co. 182 acres was held in trust for the German, Lutheran & Calvinist Reformed congregations. The conveyance to the trustees was executed 20 July, 1797. MARCHAND has since died. The land adj. Henry DITTMAN. It is now vested in John SHRUM & Adam BAUGHMAN for these congregations.

p. 21: John LORAIN, late of Phila., merchant, & wife, Lydia, purchased a house in Phila. & a house in Germantown with Lydia's share of the sale of her father, Stephen SHEWELL's, real estate. John MORREL, the elder, & John A. M'CUTCHEON can sell the house in Phila., & James WILMER & John A. MCCUTCHEON can sell the house in Germantown.

p. 23: In 1794, George MCCARTNEY, the elder, of Westmoreland Co., died, leaving 7 children: Andrew, George, Samuel, Jane, Martha, Elizabeth, Mary (since married to Mathew DILL, Jr.). Jane later married James COULTER, Indiana Co., & had 2 children--Mary B. COULTER & Elizabeth W. COULTER, both minors, & Jane is lately decd.

p. 24: Jacob KREIDER, Northampton Co., Rev. soldier, will receive $40 & $40/yr.

p. 27: William RIPPY, John CREMER, Samuel BROTHERTON, George M'CLELAND, John M'ALLEN, John CAMPBELL, John WALKER, John PATTERSON, John SKINNER, Franklin Co.; William PYMN, John WILDS, Michael WILLET, George D. RITTENHOUSE, John KERR, Bedford Co., are commissioners for Strasburg & Fannetsburg Tpk. Rd.

p. 37: Elizabeth CARMINE, Bucks Co., widow of William CARMINE, a volunteer soldier in the late war, is to receive $40 & $40/yr.

p. 45: David TOWNSEND, Evan PUGH, John DICKEY, Frederick HAYMAKER, Robert DARRAGH, Thomas HENRY, Milo ADAMS, Charles S. RENO, James ALLISON, Joseph M'FERRON, Beaver Co.; Arthur SHENOWITH, Jacob HERRINGTON, Bevan PEARSON, Mercer Co.; Mathias EVANS, Hugh DAVIS, Allegheny Co., are commissioners for the Beaver Canal Co.

p. 57: William NICHOLS, decd., had a lien on his estate at the suit of Henry MILLER on 8 Feb., 1819.

p. 59: Benjamin SHAW, an alien, has title to real estate confirmed.

p. 60: In 1813, James KITE, then of Phila., & Eliza DONNELLY, Phila., married & lived together until 1815. James KITE abandoned his wife. They are divorced.

p. 61: The marriage between Vachel STEPHENS & Rachel PEAIRS, Fayette Co., is dissolved.

p. 62: Trustees of Western University of Pa.: James ROSS, George STEVENSON, Francis HERRON, Joseph STOCKTON, Robert BRUCE, John BLACK, John SCULL, John M. SNOWDEN, William WILKINS, George EVANS, Morgan NEVILLE, Henry BALDWIN, George POE, Jr., Walter FORWARD, John DARRAH, Samuel ROBERTS, Ebenezer DENNY, Peter MOWRY, Pittsburg; William ROBERTSON, Jr., Allegheny; John M'PHERRIN, John GILMORE, Butler Co.; John YOUNG, James POSTLEWAITH, John REED, Westmoreland Co.; Robert MOORE, James ALLISON, Beaver Co.

p. 65: Robert HUTCHISON sold 102 acres to James TODD, Centre Twp., Indiana Co., adj. James KELLY, James M'LAIN. William HUTCHISON, who died intestate, leaving several minor children, owned ½ of said land.

p. 66: Matthias ARMBRUSTER, Phia., is given $300 in full claim of a tract of donation land to which he was entitled for service as a soldier in the Pa. Line during the Rev.

p. 67: James LANG, late of Brownsville, Fayette Co., died intestate without issue. Before his death, he said his heir would be Cynthia BENNET & her brother, Richard DENNY, children of the wife of James LANG by a former husband. The wife is also decd. James LANG got most of his estate from her. Richard left Pa. several years ago & no one knows if he is living or dead.

p. 69: James CARSON, late recorder of deeds for Phila., died in debt to the Commonwealth for $1250. He left a widow & minor children.

p. 70: The Manufacturing Co. of Lancaster is vested in: John SWAR, William DICKSON, John HERR, James HUMES, Jacob MILLER, Henry BEAR, Joseph OGILBY, James HUSTON, Christian HERR (Pequea), Christian ROHRER.

p. 71: Lt. John PAINTER, Lt. Richard MARTIN, Thomas MARTIN, & William HOFFMAN, Northumberland Co.; performed considerable military service during the Rev. War in aiding to protect frontier settlements. Col. Thomas HARTLEY was commandant of that district of country. The men were not paid.

p. 72: Isaac REES sold 2 tracts of land in Brandywine Twp., Chester Co., adj. William MOORE, Job WINDEL, William JACKSON, George PIERCE, Jr. REES' wife is non compos mentis.

p. 75: Elizabeth BOYES, Maytown, Donegal Twp., Lancaster Co., died owning a lot in the village. Her will was dated 2 Dec., 1815. Joseph VANCE & John CLARK are executors.

p. 76: Joshua WILLIAMS, Centre Co., an officer of the Rev., is to receive $80 & $80/yr.

p. 77: Henry BALDWIN, William ROBINSON, Robert CAMPBELL, Hugh DAVIS, Allegheny Co.; Dunning M'NAIR, John DAVID, William CAMPBELL, John GILMORE, Butler co., are commissioners for the Pittsburg & Butler Tpk. Co. Jacob MECHLING, John BREDIN, David M'JUNKIN, John BROWN, Butler Co.; James MILLAR, Bevan PEARSON, John FINDLAY, Mercer Co., are commissioners of the Butler & Mercer Tpk. Co.

p. 80: Andrew BAYARE, Samuel ARCHER, Richard BACHE, Charles N. BANCKER, Clement C. BIDDLE, Samuel BRECK, Turner CAMAC, Reuben HAINES, Thomas HALE, Adam KOENIGMACHER, Ludwig KRUMBHAAR, John M'CREA, Samuel B. MORRIS, Isaac W. NORRIS, Richard PETERS, Jr., Condy RAGUET, Joseph ROTCH, William SCHLATTER, Samuel SPACKMAN, John C. STOCKER, John STRAWBRIDGE, Roberts VAUX, John VAUGHN, Daniel B. SMITH, Matthew C. RALSTON are the corporate body of the Phila. Saving Fund Soc.

p. 84: Alexander BURNS, Washington Co., a Rev. War soldier, will receive $40 & $40/yr.

p. 85: Abraham ARMSTRONG and wife, Maria, late Maria ABERCROMBIE, both late of Phila., have their marriage annulled.

p. 92: John ARNDT, late of Easton, Northampton Co., Esq., is decd. His will was dated 20 Mar., 1813 & a codicil was dated 14 Apr.,

1814. George Washington ARNDT & Charles LOMBAERT are trustees. John ARNDT's daughter, Elizabeth, married William INNIS & had children.

p. 94: Margaret CONNELL & John B. TREVOR are the adminis. of the estate of Zachariah CONNELL, late of Fayette Co., decd.

p. 96: Jacob FOLTZ, Union Co., married Polly SWINEFORD, Union Co. They cohabitated several years & had several children. Jacob deserted his wife & children & has since been convicted of a felony in Adams Co., was sentenced to hard labor in the penitentary but was pardoned by the Governor & has since been convicted of burglary in Cumberland Co. & sentenced to hard labor in the pentientary.

p. 97: Samuel WEBB, Columbia Co., Isaac A. CHAPMAN, Luzerne Co., & John W. ROSEBERRY, Schuylkill Co., are commissioners to lay out a state road.

p. 98: Peter BAYNTON was formerly state treasurer. John NICHOLSON, decd., was formerly comptroller general.

p. 100: Daniel MONTGOMERY & John GERHART are owners of a ferry over the north branch of the Susquehanna, opposite Danville, Columbia Co.

p. 101: David MARCHAND, Daniel SCHAEFFER & Jacob KUHNS, Westmoreland Co., are auth. to dig for salt water in the Conemaugh River bed adj. their land in Donegal Twp.

p. 105: Thomas LAUGHLIN, decd., Franklin Co., has his estate vested in John & Agnes BOYLES.

p. 105: Benjamin R. MOORE, Condy RAGUET, John READ, Thomas STEWARDSON, Thomas P. COPE, Robert VAUX, John STODDARD, Phila.; Isaac RYNEERSON, Ithamer MOTT, William WARD, Thomas MEREDITH, Benjamin T. CASE, Susquehanna Co.; Henry W. DRINKER, William CLARK, Luzerne Co., are commissioners of the Phila. & Great Bend Tpk. road.

p. 108: George BAIRD, John MARSHELL, James CLERK, Thomas M'CALL, David CRAIG, Daniel HUSTON, Robert HERVEY & David T. ARCHER are commissioners for a road from Washington, Washington Co., to the Va. state line near the farm of Francis M'GUIRE.

p. 116: John Marshall, Washington Co., a captain in the Rev. War, is to receive $120 & $120/yr.

p. 116: Patrick M'GOWAN, late of Fayette Co., decd., has his estate vested in Patrick MILLER, late of Huntingdon Co., now Butler Co.

p. 117: John SPAYD, Frederick HELLER, John ADDAMS, George D.B. KEIM, John BERKENBINE are commissioners of the Reading Water Co.

p. 127: Hugh CAMPBELL, Rev. War soldier of Chester Co., will receive $40 & $40/yr.

p. 129: George LEITNER & George SKELTON were the executors of the will of Ignatius LEITNER, late of York Borough, decd. He had a lot bounded by Benjamin WEISER, Daniel WEAVER. Ignatius had a dau., Elizabeth SHAEFFER.

p. 148: George HOFFMAN, decd., owned land in Chester Co., Uchland Twp. John RIDDLE & David LAIRD, Allegheny Co., were guardians of

George HOFFMAN's minor children.

p. 149: Jacob BUCK, Jr., decd., left a widow & 2 children. He had land in Buffalo Twp., Cumberland Co., adj. John M'GINNIS, Philip RODEPOUCH, Philip DECKERT, Benjamin STROW, Richard BEARD. Jacob BUCK, father of the decd., died intestate before his son.

p. 154: John ROSS, Indiana Co., is to sell land in Centre Twp., Indiana Co., adj. Alexander ROSS, for the minor child of John ROSS, John Dean ROSS, who holds lands with James & Jane SAMPLE, & William & Mary WILKINS, heirs of William DEAN, decd.

p. 156: William RAMSAY, Andrew HIKES, James WOODBURN, Robert PEEBLES, David STERRETT, James ROGERS, Cumberland Co.; Samuel Tate SWANSY, James M'CURDY, William ALEXANDER, William MACLAY, Roxbury, Franklin Co.; Isaac THOMPSON, Abraham LONG, Samuel FINDLAY, John BLAIR, Huntingdon Co.; James JAMESON, John WILS, George DANSDILE, George RITTENHOUSE, John KARR, John WILLIS, George BURD, Bedford Co., are commissioners of the Newville & Roxbury Tpk. Road.

p. 160: Conrad CODERMAN, decd., Rev. War soldier, also called Conrad CATTERMAN, is to receive $300 for donation land.

p. 168: William WILKINS, George STEWART, Philip GILLAND, George SUTTON, Pittsburg; Thomas DUNCAN, Birmingham; James BRICK & George A. BAYARD, Elizabethtown; Joseph BARNETZ, Perryopolis; John WITHEROW, John LYON, Thomas IRWIN, Henry W. BEASON, Uniontown, are commissioners for the Pittsburg & Uniontown Tpk. Rd.

p. 172: Daniel M'CONNELL, late of M'Connelsburg, Bedford Co., gave a lot to the trustees of an English school in M'Connelsburg. Trustees were: George W. DARRAH, George DENIG, Thomas LOGAN, Andrew WORK, John FLETCHER, James AGNEW, Andrew LINDSAY.

P. 175: David STEWART, John BLAIR, Huntingdon Co.; George ROBERTS, Philip NOON, David TODD, Cambria Co.; John DENISTON, Daniel STANARD, Thomas SHARP, Joseph MOORHEAD, John M. STEWART, James M. KELLY, John DOUGLASS, Robert NIXON, Indiana Co., are commissioners of the Indiana & Ebensburg Tpk. Rd. Thomas HAMILTON, David REYNOLDS, James MONTIETH, Philip TEMPLETON, Robert WOODWARD, Michael MACKLIN, Armstrong Co.; John NEGLEE, John PARKER, Walter LOWRIE, Butler Co.; William CUMMINS, Thomas LUCAS, John TAYLOR, Thomas SUTTON, Indiana Co., are commissioners of the Armstrong-Indiana Tpk. Road.

p. 177: Charles FULWOOD, William HINDMAN, James IRWIN, Robert STEWART, Andrew BYERLY, Christian BREENEMAN, James M'GUIRE, Peter POOLE are commissioners of the Mt. Pleasant Tpk. Rd., Westmoreland Co.

p. 180: Trustees of the Ebensburg Academy, Cambria Co.: Demetrius Augustin GALLITZEN, George ROBERTS, Abraham HILDEBRAN, James C. MAGUIRE, John MURRAY, Moses CANNAN, James MELOY, Charles B. SEELY, John AGNEW, William O'KEEFE, Cornelius M'DONALD, Richard M'GUIRE, Samuel M'ANULTY.

P. 183: Enoch MARVIN & Guion GREER are appointed additional commissioners for the Beaver & Greersburg Tpk. Rd.

p. 186: Thomas SILVERWOOD, Mifflinburg, Union Co., an alien, had title to two islands: "Cherry Island" & "Round Island" in the Susquehanna River opposite land surveyed to James SILVERWOOD,

Augusta Twp., Northumberland Co. William MILNE, an alien, had land in Bedminster Twp., Bucks Co.

p. 189: Thomas ALLIBONE, William ALLIBONE, Phila.; Charles L. HUTTER, Stephen BALLIOT, Jr., Lehigh Co.; John HAGENBUCH & Jacob WEISS, Northampton Co.; William ROSS & David RICHARDS, Luzerne Co., are commissioners of the Northampton & Wilkesbarre Tpk. Road.

p. 193: John BALMER, Cocalico Twp., Lancaster Co., & wife, Rachel, sold land 11 Sept., 1779, to Adam KRILL, Peter FANGHAUSER, John MILLER, et al., elders & trustees of 4 congregations of Presby. or Reformed Churches in Cocalico, Earle & Warwick Twp. Matthias SHIRK, Adam GRILL, Christian WOLF, Jacob ROCK are auth. to sell the land.

p. 195: Heirs of Capt. John BRADY, late of Northumberland Co., decd., a soldier, are to receive $750 for their claim on a tract of donation land. Michael LONGENBACH, Northampton Co.; Elizabeth BROADHEAD, widow of Luke BROADHEAD, late of Northampton Co., a Capt. in the Rev. War; Henry WOLLERY, Northampton Co.; Charles WILLOUGHBY, Beaver Co.; are to receive $40 & $40/yr. Maria KELCHNER, widow of Matthias KELCHNER, late of Berks Co., will receive $40 & $30/yr. Isabella CAMPBELL, widow of Thomas CAMPBELL, late of York Co., formerly a Capt. in the Rev. War, will receive $60 & $60/yr. James Smith POLLOCK, Columbia Co., will receive $80. Atchison MELON's annuity is to be paid to James COLLINS (24 Mar., 1817). That act is repealed & the annuity will now be paid to MELON. John BEISEL's heirs will be paid $300 for donation land given for service during the Rev. War. Joseph GEDDIS, Huntingdon Co., will receive $40 & $40/yr. Joseph DUNLAP will receive $300 in lieu of donation land. Joseph WREN's annuity is repealed.

p. 202: Election districts: Wyalusing Twp., Bradford Co., will vote at Joseph BLACK's. Warren Twp., Bradford Co., will vote at Abner BOWING's. Ridgeberry Twp., Bradford Co., will vote at Griswold OWENS'. Ulster Twp., Athens Twp., Bradford Co., will vote at Samuel BARTLETT's. Albany Twp., Berks Co., will vote at Jacob FOOSSELMAN's. Colebrookdale Twp. (the part included in Henry KEELY's election district), Berks Co., is re-annexed to John MUTHARD's district. St. Clair Twp., Bedford Co., will vote at John BERKHIMER's. Muddy Ck. Twp., Butler Co., will vote at Andrew M'GOWAN's. Mt. Pleasant Twp., Columbia Co., will vote at Frederick MILLER's. Aleppo Twp., Greene Co., will vote at David KINNEY's. Springfield Twp., Huntingdon Co., will vote at William HUDSON's. Leacock Twp., Lancaster Co., will vote at Mark GROVE's, innkeeper. Breaknock Twp., Lancaster Co., will vote at Jacob MASONER's. Sadsubry Twp., Lancaster Co., will vote at Stephen HALL's, innkeeper. Dallas Twp., Luzerne Co., will vote at Abel WHEELER's. Covington Twp., Luzerne Co., will vote at George BUCK's. Mahoning Twp., Mercer co., will vote at Alexander THOMPSON's. Hanover Twp., Northampton Co., formerly voted at George BUTZ's & now will vote at Christian MENSCH's, Allen Twp. Moore Twp., Northampton Co., will vote at George GREBER's. Turbut Twp., Northumberland Co., will vote at William MORITZ's. Milton borough, Northumberland Co., will vote at Daniel ECKERT's. Quemahoning & part of Stoney Ck. Twp., Somerset Co., will vote at John KENNEDY's, Stoystown. Sterling Twp., Wayne Co., will vote at Phineas HOW's. Pikerun Twp., Washington Co., will vote at John GREER's. Richland Twp., Venango Co., will vote at Henry BEST's, (mill). Codorus Twp., York Co., will vote at Jacob B. WENTZ's, Jefferson. Windsor Twp., York Co., will vote at George OVERDORF, Jr.'s. Part of Lancaster Co. near Henry STRICKLER's spring, Abraham BRUBAKER's school house, John FLOREY's tenant house,

Adam FIRST's house, Christian BRUBAKER's mill & house, Widow STAUFER's, Jacob HERSHEY, Sr.'s, John BRENNEMAN & Martin NISSLEY's, Andrew HEISTAND's, will vote at the public school house, Mountjoy. Upper Paxton Twp., Dauphin Co., vill vote at George BUFFINGTON's. Lykens Twp., Dauphin Co., will vote at Conrad FRY's, Gratz. Second election district, Delaware Co., will vote at Joseph HANNUM's, Concord Twp. Norwegian Twp., Schuylkill Co., including John SLONECKER's & Abraham YODER's, will vote at Michael BOLIG's, innkeeper.

p. 207: John CHESNUT & Dr. James S. DOUGAL are auth. to sell a lot in Milton, Northumberland Co., which was conveyed on 3 Mar., 1808 by the executors of Andrew STRAUB to John CHESNUT for the use of the Presby. Church of Milton.

p. 209: Stoystown, Somerset Co., is bounded by lands of George HARTZEL's tan-yard, John LEHMER's, George KIMMEL's, Peter KIMMEL's. John KENNEDY will hold elections at his house.

p. 214: Samuel HODGDON, Benjamin TILGHMAN & Richard PETERS, Jr., Phila.; George CALHOON, Benjamin DORRANCE, Joseph BURGESS, Luzerne Co.; William MEANS, Reuben HALE & Jacob BOWMAN, Bradford Co., are commissioners to make a road from Meansville, Bradford Co., to Wilkesbarre, Luzerne Co.

p. 218: Abraham WISMER & John MICHENER, adminis. of John FUNK, late of Hilltown Twp., Bucks Co., decd., are auth. to convey to Jacob LANDIS, Henry ANGLEMOYER & Andrew WILSON, a lot for use of a school.

p. 220: Electors in Elizabethtown, Lancaster Co. will vote at Michael COBLE's.

p. 221: The Lutheran Cong. of Springfield Twp., Bucks Co., by virtue of an indenture by Elias BIDDLEMAN & Anna Maria, his wife, dated 1 Aug., 1768, became seized of a lot. Paul APPLE & Michael BARNET, trustees of the Lutheran Cong. are auth. to sell the lot which is bounded by Elias BIDDLEMAN, Casper HEITER.

p. 228: Thomas CROMWELL, David EVANS, William ROBINSON, Jr., John WAY, William COURTNEY, Hugh DAVIS, Robert CAMPBELL, Allegheny Co.; David SHIELDS, Washington Co.; Abner LACOCK, Joseph HEMPHILL, Robert DARRAGH, Beaver Co., are commissioners of the Pittsburg & Beaver Tpk Rd. Co.

p. 233: Samuel WETHERILL, Jr., John K. HELMUTH, Abraham BARKER, Jacob HOLGATE, James ASH, George W. MORGAN, Charles GRAFF, Phila.; George D. B. KEIM, Jacob K. BOYER, Curtis LEWIS, William WITMAN, John M'KNIGHT, George BOON, Berks Co.; Charles SNOWDEN, Daniel GRAEFF, Philip FRAILEY, George RAUSCH & Abraham REIFSCHNEIDER, Schuylkill Co., are commissioners to make a lock navigation on the west branch of the Schuylkill.

p. 245: Daniel BUSSIER, late a paymaster of the Pa. militia, has his accounts settled.

p. 246 David RUTTER, Ruth Anna LINDLEY, John Clement STOCKER & wife, Mary Catharine, died owning as tenants in common, various lots in Berks, Chester, Montgomery, & Wayne Cos. John Clement STOCKER & wife, Mary Catharine, Ruth Anna LINDLEY, died owning as tenants in common, lots in Pottsgrove, Montgomery Co.

p. 248: Octararo Navigation Co. Commissioners: Jesse MOORE, Joshua WEBSTER, David DICKEY, Phineas ASH, David THOMAS, John ANDREWS, Arthur ANDREWS, James ANDREWS, James STEELE, William NOBLE, Simeon POWNELL, Timothy KIRK, Pa.; William STANSBURY, Charles CARROL, Eli BALDERSTON, Thomas TENANT, Baltimore; James JENNY, Samuel ROWLAND, Rev. James M'GRAW, Samuel CLENDENNIN, Thomas RICHARDS, Jonas PRESTON, Cecil Co., Md. Books will be opened at ANDREW's tavern, Lancaster, Strasburg borough; John HILL's tavern in Lancaster, George PHILLIP's tavern, David THOMAS's tavern in Chester Co.; Nathaniel EWING's tavern at Baldfryer ferry, Md.

p. 258: By indenture of 10 Dec., 1796 between Moses LEVY, Esq., Phila., counsellor at law, & his wife, Mary; Thomas RYERSON, Phila., merchant, & his wife, Mary; Rev. Joseph TURNER, Southwark district, Phila. Co., a lot was granted to LEVY & TURNER in trust for the use of Thomas & Mary RYERSON. Thomas & Mary RYERSON are still alive & have 6 children: George Ormesby RYERSON, Marriell & Thomas, all of full age; Ann Catharine, Esther Turner & Joseph Turner RYERSON, minors.

p. 261: Adminis. of Samuel SELLERS, late of Bucks Co., decd., are auth. to sell a tract in E. Penn Twp., Northampton Co., on Mahoning Ck., adj. Philip SENDEL.

p. 261: A compact was entered into on 26 Apr., 1783 by Abraham CLARK, Joseph COOPER, Thomas HENDERSON, commissioners of N.J.; & George BRYAN, George GRAY, William BINGHAM, commissioners of Pa. to prevent obstructions to the navigation of the Delaware River.

p. 265: A road through the land of John KELKER, Swatara Twp., Dauphin Co., is vacated.

p. 267: Union Canal Co. commissioners: Cadwallader EVANS, Jr., Thomas CADWALLADER, Thomas BIDDLE, Samuel MIFFLIN, Jacob RIDGEWAY, Samuel RICHARD, Turner CAMAC for Phila.; John SPAYD, Lewis REESE, Samuel BELL for Reading; Peter GLONINGER, Peter SHINGLE, John Andrew SHULTZ for Lebanon; Obed Fahnestock, Christian SPAYD, Jacob HUMMEL for Harrisburg.

p. 277: Reuben HAINES, Phila., John ADAMS, Berks Co.; John P. DE GRUCHY, Jacob DENTLER, Northumberland Co.; George KREAMER, Jacob MUSSER, Hugh WILSON, (ridge) Union Co., are appointed commissioners for a section of road lying between Northumberland & Youngmanstown. George LATIMER, Phila.; William WHITMAN, Berks Co.; John DRIESBOUGH, John WILSON, (Hartleton), & Henry ROUSH, Union Co.; & James DUNCAN, Centre Co., are commissioners for a section of road between Youngmanstown & Aaronsburg. Richard WISTAR, Phila.; Jacob K. BOYER, Berks Co.; Michael BOLLINGER, John KEEN, William IRWIN, John FURY & John MITCHEL, Centre Co., are commissioners of a section of road between Aaronsburg & Bellefonte. Simon GRATZ, Phila.; Thomas BURNSIDE, Joseph M. FOX, Joseph MILES, Roland CURTIN, John RANKIN, James FORSTER, Centre Co., are commissioners for a section of road between Bellefonte & Philipsburg. William RAWLE, Phila., Hardman PHILIPS, John LORAINE, William BLOOM, Job ENGLAND, Clearfield Co., are commissioners for a section of road between Philipsburg & the Susquehanna River near the mouth of Anderson's Ck.

p.282: Isaac A. CHAPMAN, Luzerne Co.; Jason TORRY, Wayne Co.; John BRODHEAD, Pike Co., are commissioners to explore a route to open a direct communication from Millford, Pike Co. to Wilkesbarre, Luzerne Co.

1819-1820

p. 5: The right of the Commonwealth in the personal estate of William WALLACE is released to Jane SHAW.

p. 5: Rudolph HARLEY & Adam FISHER, guardians of the minor children of Henry CROUSE, late of W. Nantmill Twp., Chester Co., decd., are auth. to sell a ¼ part of a forge called Springton & a parcel of land.

p. 7: Commissioners of Cambria Co. are auth. to pay Thomas CROYLE, Cambria Co., part of his expenses in erecting a bridge over a branch of the Connemaugh River.

p. 11: Thomas SMILEY, being a good citizen, strongly attached to his country, was on 24 June, 1801, employed by Col. Abraham HORN, an agent of government, to receive relinquishments from certain settlers on Towanda Ck., Luzerne Co. While on duty, he was attacked by a company of insurgents from other parts of the county & was abused & compelled to leave the country for a considerable length of time. He is paid $250.

p. 13: Andrew BAYARD, Mathew CAREY, Samuel MIFFLIN, Clement C. BIDDLE, Andrew PETITT, Adam ECKFELT, Andrew M. PREVOST are commissioners to superintend the distribution of property in a lottery for promoting the sciences & useful arts. George MURRAY, Gideon FAIRMAN, John DRAPER, Robert BALD, Thomas UNDERWOOD, co-partners of the firm of MURRAY, FAIRMAN & Co., engravers of Phila., will be paid for their expenses.

p. 17: Andrew MANN, Moses GORDON, Abraham MARTIN, James GRAHAM, Uria AKERS, James PARSONS, George ENSLOW, George MORGAN & James M. RUSSEL, Bedford Co., are commissioners of the Warfordsburg & Juniata Tpk. Rd.

p. 23: Jane GODFREY, Cumberland Co., widow of William E. GODFREY, a capt. of artillery in the Rev. War, will receive $60 & $60/yr., in lieu of donation land due her husband.

p. 26: Michael NEWMAN, Peter WINEBRENNER, trustees of the German Reformed Congregation of Hanover, York Co., are auth. to sell land in York St., Hanover.

p. 28: A deed of conveyance executed by William ELLIOTT & wife, Barbara, for a tract of land in Westmoreland Co., to John HINDMAN, dated 27 July, 1795 & acknowledged before John JOHNSTON, a Justice of the Peace, Allegheny Co., is put on the record.

p. 29: Trustees of Salem Congregation are Hugh CULBERTSON, Uriah MATSON, John GALLAGHER, James GUTHRIE & William STERLING.

p. 30: Isaac A. CHAPMAN & John BROADHEAD surveyed a road from Milford, Pike Co. to Wilkesbarre, Luzerne Co.

p. 30: John AGNEW, James AGNEW, Samuel AGNEW, Robert MARSHELL & Robert ANDERSON, the parents & natural guardians of their children, Samuel C. AGNEW, Samuel A. MARSHELL, Samuel AGNEW, Samuel M. AGNEW & Samuel A. ANDERSON, are auth. to sell land in Washington Co., devised to them by their grandfather, Samuel AGNEW.

p. 31: Benjamin SLOCUM, Philip SWARTZ, Comer PHILIPS & John COBB, Luzerne Co.; Seth GOODRICH, Amos POLLY, Reuben PURDY, William

WOODBRIDGE, Peter PURDY & Simeon ANSLEY, Wayne Co., are commissioners of the Luzerne & Wayne Co. Tpk. Rd.

p. 34: Peter GORDON, Southwark district, Phila. Co., is to receive $40 & $40/yr.

p. 36: Marriage between John CULBERTSON, now a lieutenant in the U.S. Army, & his wife, Polly, is annulled.

p. 44: A petition of John PYLER, Christian DITWEILER, Sarah LANTZ, widow of Christian LANTZ, decd., Christian KING, & Abraham KURTZ, executors of Jacob LANTZ, late of Henderson Twp., Huntingdon Co., decd., David LANTZ, Anna LANTZ, Christian DITWEILER, as guardian of Henry LANTZ & Lydia LANTZ, minor children of Henry LANTZ, decd., Solomon KING, as guardian of Maria LANTZ & Magdalena LANTZ, minor children of John LANTZ, decd., John BLACK, intermarried with Fanny LANTZ, says Jacob LANTZ died owning land in Huntingdon Co. & willed it to his sons, Jacob, David & Christian. Land is to be divided by 6 Ammisch men. Christian LANTZ died a minor, leaving a widow & a number of brothers & sisters, nephews & nieces, his heirs. Jacob LANTZ is a lunatic.

p. 47: Marriage of Samuel MOORHEAD, Westmoreland co., & wife Sarah, late Sarah SWAN, is annulled

p. 48: Stoney Ck., from it's mouth to Peter BERKEY's mills, Somerset Co., is declared a public highway.

p. 49: The annuity which was to be paid to Henry BULL is repealed. The annuity will be paid to Col. John EWALT, Cumberland Co.

p. 54: Kensington district of the Northern Liberties, Phila. Co., is bounded by land of ----- GIBSON, land late of Isaac NORRIS, decd., & now of J.P. NORRIS. Election of commissioners will be at Jacob VANDIKE's tavern, sign of the White Horse.

p. 67: Pierce BUTLER, Robert WALN, William MEREDITH, Andrew BAYARD, Charles PENROSE, Edward PENNINGTON, Edward SHARP, Caleb NEWBOLD, Isaac MICKLE, Samuel L. HOWELL, Samuel HARRIS, Henry CHEW are commissioners of the Pa. & N.J. communication company.

p. 82: A division line run by Peter HAGENBERG between Union & Mifflin Co. will continue.

p. 88: George BRYAN, Esq., late of Phila., decd., died owning 5 tracts in Northumberland (now Armstrong & M'Kean Cos.), & in consequence of the derangement in mind of one of the daughters & the death in a state of insolvency of one of the sons of BRYAN, a partition cannot be made. George BRYAN, Harrisburg, one of the sons of George BRYAN, Esq., cares for his sister. Jacob SPANGLER & Thomas SMITH, Harrisburg, Dauphin Co., & Robert ORR, Jr., Armstrong Co., are auth. to partition the land. Sarah BRYAN is the daughter of BRYAN who is deranged.

p. 90: The interest of Peter BARNCORD, late of Franklin Co., decd., in a house & lot in Greencastle, Franklin Co., is vested in his son, Jacob BARNCORD.

p. 91: William SCOTT, Mercer Co., guardian of the minor children of Benjamin LODGE, decd., is auth. to execute a deed for tracts of land in Mercer Co. (on the waters of Shenango), surveyed in the following names: Aaron LEVI, John KAPP, Daniel WILLIAMS, John LEACOCK, Nathan FALKNER, Daniel REAS, all patented to James HAMILTON, since decd.

p. 97: Hugh MEANS, Mercer Co., is auth. to sell the right of the heirs of Thomas WOODS, late of Bedford Co., decd., to land on the waters of Chartier's run, Westmoreland Co., granted by patent of 13 Apr., 1785.

p. 107: All acts of George BROWN, Berlin, a Justice of the Peace for the 3rd district, Adams Co., done from 22 Mar., 1815 to 30 Mar., 1818, are declared legal. He was acting as an assistant assessor of the direct tax of the U.S. during this period.

p. 108: Cornelius VANHORN, adminis. of the estate of Thomas VANHORN, is to be paid $1773.68, for the use of the heirs of the decd., which is due from a suit in which the heirs were plaintiffs & the Commonwealth was the defendant. He must post bond of $3000 in Crawford Co. first.

p. 109: Trustees of the Fire Assoc. of Phila.: Frederick HOECKLY, Benjamin THAW, Michael FOX, William WAGNER, Mordecai Y. BRYANT, Daniel H. MILLER, Jeremiah BOONE, James HARPER, Jr., Townsend SHARPLESS, John D. SMITH, Benjamin MARTIN, William ABBOTT, Caleb CARMALT.

p. 117: Commissioners of the Wilsonsville Tpk. Rd.: Jason TORRY, Daniel KIMBLE, Jonathan BRINK, Jesse REYNOLDS, Joseph AITKINSON, Wayne Co.; Leonard LABARR, Amasa DANIELS, Pike Co.

p. 126: Thomas S. RIDGWAY & Jonathan FELL, Phila., are add'l commissioners of the Northampton & Wilkesbarre Tpk. Rd.

p. 130: Ezekiel SANKY, an old soldier, will be paid $300 in lieu of a tract of donation land.

p. 131: James BARTON, Milford, Pike Co., has petitioned that the town has an insufficient water supply. He is the proprietor of a spring & streams of water in the rear of the town, sufficiently elevated to addommodate most of the inhabitants. He is auth. to convey the water to Milford.

p. 136: Commissioners of the Lock Navigation of the waters of Brandywine Ck.: John PIMM, Abraham BAILEY, Thomas A. PARKE, Charles LUKENS, Caleb BRINTON, Jr., Chester Co.; Thomas LEA, James CANBY, Edward GILPIN, Victor DUPONT, New Castle Co., Delaware.

p. 137: Commissioners of the Connemaugh Bridge Co.: George MULHOLLAN, Jr., Moses MURPHY, Nathaniel DOTY, Samuel BARD, Edward HOWARD.

p. 139: In 1808, an act was passed naming as commissioners of a lottery to raise $10,000 for the Society of Universalists, Phila.: Israel ISRAEL, Elisha GORDON, Thomas AMIES, Jacob THOMAS, Thomas TOMPKINS, John MURRAY, Thomas KINGSTON, Thomas F. GORDON. John MURRY is since decd. Elisha GORDON has moved out of the state.

p. 142: Elizabeth HENDERSON, adminis. of the estate of William HENDERSON, late of Montgomery Co., decd., is auth. to sell land.

p. 143: An annuity granted to John M'DOWEL in 1809, will be paid half yearly to Reuben BAILEY, Fayette Co., for the use of M'DOWEL.

The annuity granted to Alexander M'CLEAN is repealed.

p. 144: James HOPKINS made an illegal dam at the head of the Conewago falls, on the east side of the Susquehanna River.

p. 145: Archibald S. JORDAN, inspector of the first brigade of the 5th division of Pa. militia, is to be compensated for extra services rendered under the Governor's order of 16 Mar., 1815.

p. 146: The right of the Commonwealth due to escheat in the estate of Charles ALEXANDER, Phila., decd., who died without heirs, is vested in Gershom MOTT & William MOTT, the sons & only heirs of Eleanor MOTT, late Eleanor ALEXANDER, widow of Charles ALEXANDER.

p. 148: Directors of the York Co. Manufacturing Co.: John DEMUTH, Philip SMYSER, Martin EBERT, Peter BUTT, Jacob EICHELBERGER.

p. 150: James HOPKINS may create a slack water navigation near the Conestoga River, Lancaster Co.

p. 162: Election districts: The part of St. Clair Twp., Allegheny Co., who voted at James PATTERSON's will now vote at Dominic O'CONNER's, Birmingham. Voters of Deer Twp., Allegheny Co., will vote at John M'COOL's. Voters of Greenfield district, Luzerne Co., will vote at Samuel VAIL's. Mifflin Twp., Dauphin Co., will vote at George BUFFINGTON's. Upper Paxton Twp., Dauphin Co., will vote at Jonathan COLIER's, Millersburg. German Twp., Fayette Co. will vote at Frederick STRUBLE's, McClellandtown. Springhill Twp., Fayette Co., will vote at Absalom MORRIS'. The 12th election district, Huntingdon Co., will vote at Jacob GOOSEHORN's house, now occupied by James ORR, Tell Twp. Part of Union Co. from Robert BADGER's, W. Buffaloe Twp., to James MATHERS' lane, to near John KLAPP's saw-mill, George MITCHELL's upper mill at Penn's Ck., to John BISHOP's, to George OTT's, on the Long Ridge, then to Henry MOYER's, will vote at Joseph LECHNER's, Centreville. Addison Twp., Somerset Co., will vote at Henry STULLER's, Petersburg. Mahoning Twp., Mercer Co., will vote at Henry ROBINSON's. Part of French Ck. Twp., Venango Co., will vote at George KAPP's. Robinson Twp., Washington Co., will vote at Joseph CRAFFORD's. Hanover Twp., Washington Co., will vote at David TUCKER's. Penn Twp., Chester Co., will vote at Dr. Allen CUNNINGHAM's, New London crossroads. E. Caln & W. Whiteland Twps., Chester Co., will vote at Jesse EVANS' public house, Downingtown. Sugar Ck. Twp., Venango Co., will vote at Alexander BOWMAN's. Plumb district, Venango Co., will vote at Daniel HERRING's. Bloomfield Twp., Crawford Co., will vote at Gilbert A. GEROWS'. E. Bethlehem Twp., Washington Co., will vote at Jacob SPENCER's, Fredericktown. Hanover Twp., Northampton Co., will vote at Simon BUTZ's, Bethlehem Twp. George's Twp., Fayette Co., will vote at David MILLER's. Germantown Twp., Phila. Co., will vote at Andrew TROLLINGER's. Clearfield Twp., Butler co., will vote at Peter HENRY's. Southampton Twp., Franklin Co., will vote at Daniel WONDERLICKS'. Part of Norwegian & Schuylkill Twps., Schuylkill Co., will vote at Jacob SHELLY's, Pottsville, Norwegian Twp. Rush Twp., Northumberland Co., will vote at John KOLKIT's. Shamokin Twp., Northumberland Co., will vote at Daniel STAMBACH's. Part of Pine-Ck. Twp., west of Hugh WHITE's, Lycoming Co., will be annexed to the 4th election district. Part of the electors of Wheatfield & Washington Twps., Indiana Co., near General CAMPBELL's mill, Isaac GREFETH's mill, will vote at David FULTON's, Washington Twp. Springfield & Troy Twp., Bradford Co., will vote at Samuel CONANT's, Troy Twp. Montour Twp., Allegheny Co., will vote at Aaron ATON's.

Parts of Sugar Ck. & Toby Twps., Armstrong Co., near John MARTIN's, will vote at Samuel KELLY's, on the east side of the Allegheny River. If the house at which the electors of Bensalem Twp., Bucks Co., were to vote, is not rebuilt by 1 Oct., next, the electors will vote at Benjamin FLEMMING's. Northmoreland Twp., Luzerne Co., will vote at Orange FULLER's. Part of Washington & Perry Twps., Union Co., near Simon SNYDER's paper mill, John GERMAN, Sr.'s road, John LONG's house, Wiandt NEWMAN's house at Mohontongo Ck., will vote at Philip HAROLD's, Washington Twp. Decatur Twp., Mifflin Co., will vote at Stephen HINDS'. Burlington Twp., Bradford Co., will vote at James LONG's. New Sewickly Twp., Beaver Co., will vote at Philip GRIMM, Sr's. W. Bethlehem Twp., Washington Co., will vote at Stephen HILL's, Hillsborough. Versailles Twp., Allegheny Co., will vote at Thomas NEEL's. Patton Twp., Centre Co., will vote at Isaac HICKS'. Gibson & Jackson Twps., Susquehanna Co., will vote at Joseph WASHBURN's, Esq. Venango Twp., Crawford Co., will vote at James SKELTON's. Pocono Twp., Northampton Co., will vote at Christian SINGER's. Potter Twp., Centre Co., will vote at Walter LONGVILLE's, Earlysburg. Half Moon Twp., Centre Co., will vote at Joseph B. SHUGERT's. Hamilton Twp., Northampton Co., will vote at James SHAFER's.

p. 176: Jacob KREIDER, Centre Co., James DALE, Union Co., & John HANNA, Lycoming Co., are commissioners to employ 2 surveyors to run the line between Union & Centre Cos.

p. 177: Joseph TREGO, Joshua WEAVER, exrs. of the will of William TREGO, are auth. to sell land in Honeybrook Twp., Chester Co.

p. 177: The trust estate vested in Samuel EVANS by Evan Rice EVANS, adminis. of Jane EVANS, decd., for land in London-Britain Twp., Chester Co., in trust for the use of Elizabeth E. WILKIN, then a minor, is declared executed to the cestui que trust of Elizabeth E. WILKIN.

p. 177: The adminis. of George STROOP, decd., Jacob STROOP, & John SHUMAN, are auth. to sell 4 lots in Landisburg, Perry Co. to the adminis. of John HIPPLE.

p. 178: Elijah DIX, late guardian of the minor children of Benjamin DIX, decd., is auth. to sell land in Mt. Pleasant Twp., Wayne Co., adj. Ichabud STARK, Thomas MEREDITH, et al.

p. 178: William REYNOLDS, Franklin Co., guardian of Catharine REYNOLDS, is auth. to make a deed to Samuel WEAVER for land in Southampton Twp., Franklin Co. Samuel WEAVER, previous to making the deed, shall grant to Peter HENDRICKS, the right of way through the land.

p. 179: George YOUNGMAN & John DREISBACH, adminis. of the estate of Elias YOUNGMAN, late of Mifflinsburg, Union Co., are auth. to sell land in Mifflinsburg.

p. 179: Mary HANNA, adminis. of John A. HANNA, decd., & Andrew S. DEARMOND, adminis. of James DEARMOND, who was adminis. of Richard DEARMOND, decd., are auth. to sell land on Lake Erie, at the mouth of Walnut Ck., Erie Co.

p. 179: Rhinehart BAUSMAN, Allegheny Co., is auth. to sell, with the consent of his guardian, land in St. Clair Twp., Allegheny Co., purchased by him from Peter H. PATTERSON & Elizabeth, his wife.

p. 179: Daniel BACON, William D. BACON, guardians of the minor children of Alvan BACON, late of Jackson Twp., Tioga Co., decd., are auth. to sell land in Jackson Twp.

p. 179: Title of George DAWS to a tract of land in Mt. Pleasant Twp., Wayne Co., bounded by John DOUGLAS, is confirmed. Henry BEAR & his wife were aliens when they conveyed the land to DAWS.

p. 181: Daniel GRIDLEY, Luzerne Co.; Jacob RUDOLPH, Butler Co.; Jacob MUMMY, Northampton Co.; Jacob GEIGER, Lebanon Co.; John ADAMS, Stephen CARTER, Northumberland Co.; Henry WAGGONER, Cumberland Co.; Henry LUTZ, David MARSH, Northampton Co., are paid $40 & $40/yr. Samuel JOHNSTON, Cumberland Co., & John BRANNON, Westmoreland Co., are to be paid $300 in lieu of donation land to which he is entitled for Rev. War services. Margaret CAPPLE, Bucks Co., widow of Charles CAPPLE, Rev. soldier; Nancy FELTY, Phila. Co., widow of Henry FELTY, Rev. soldier; Margaret REIM, Union Co., widow of Nicholas REIM, Rev. soldier; Ann KANE, Washington Co., widow of Charles KANE, Rev. soldier; Mary MONTZ, Northumberland Co., widow of Nicholas MONTZ, Rev. soldier, are to receive $40.

p. 182: Isaac A. CHAPMAN, Luzerne Co., Jacob ANTES, Lycoming Co., are commissioners to run a line between Luzerne & Lycoming Co.

p. 185: Greersburg, Beaver Co., is bounded by Thomas SPROTT, Calvin AUSTIN, George DONNEHUE. David TOWNSEND, Evan PUGH, Benjamin TOWNSEND, John PUGH, Abel W. TOWNSEND, James TAYLOR, Mathias EVANS & John WALKER are the body politic of the Beaver Co. Water Co.

p. 188: Sandy Lick Ck., from mouth to Henry NULFF, Jr.'s saw mill, Jefferson Co., is declared a public highway.

P. 192: John M'CLUNEY, Washington Co., employed a guard to assist him in conveying Nathaniel PEEK to the penitentiary.

p. 193: Alexander M'CALMONT, Venango Co., James STEWART, Hugh WILSON, Warren Co., are commissioners to view certain state roads.

p. 194: Benjamin STOKELEY, William CARROLL, Mercer Co.; James MARTIN (son of John), Venango Co., are commissioners to lay out a state road.

p. 196: Arnold HUNTER, Timothy S. COATS, Charles BLANCHARD are commissioners to lay out a state road from Newtown, N.Y. to King's settlement, McKean Co.

p. 197: A road between Robert STURGEON & Richard GREHAM, Armstrong Co., is to be reviewed.

BIBLIOGRAPHY

CHARTER TO WILLIAM PENN, AND LAWS OF THE PROVINCE OF PENNSYLVANIA BETWEEN THE YEARS 1682 AND 1700, PRECEDED BY DUKE OF YORK'S LAWS IN FORCE FROM THE YEAR 1676 TO THE YEAR 1682 WITH AN APPENDIX (1879).

THE STATUTES AT LARGE OF PENNSYLVANIA FROM 1682 TO 1801, VOLUME 2 - 1700-1712 (CLARENCE M. BUSCH, STATE PRINTER OF PA., 1896).

THE STATUTES AT LARGE OF PENNSYLVANIA FROM 1682 TO 1801, VOLUME 3 - 1712-1724 (CLARENCE M. BUSCH, STATE PRINTER OF PA., 1896).

THE STATUTES AT LARGE OF PENNSYLVANIA FROM 1682 TO 1801 VOLUME 4 - 1724-1744 (CLARENCE M. BUSCH, STATE PRINTER OF PA., 1897).

THE STATUTES AT LARGE OF PENNSYLVANIA FROM 1682 TO 1801 VOLUME 5 - 1744-1759 (WM. STANLEY RAY, STATE PRINTER OF PA., 1898).

THE STATUTES AT LARGE OF PENNSYLVANIA FROM 1682 TO 1801 VOLUME 6 - 1759-1765 (WM. STANLEY RAY, STATE PRINTER OF PA., 1898).

THE STATUTES AT LARGE OF PENNSYLVANIA FROM 1682 TO 1801 VOLUME 7 - 1765-1770 (WM. STANLEY RAY, STATE PRINTER OF PA., 1903).

THE STATUTES AT LARGE OF PENNSYLVANIA FROM 1682 TO 1801 VOLUME 8 - 1770-1776 (WM. STANLEY RAY, STATE PRINTER OF PA., 1904).

THE STATUTES AT LARGE OF PENNSYLVANIA FROM 1682 TO 1801 VOLUME 9 - 1776-1779 (HARRISBURG, PA., 1906).

THE STATUTES AT LARGE OF PENNSYLVANIA FROM 1682 TO 1801 VOL. 10 - 1779-1781 (HARRISBURG, PA., 1906).

THE STATUTES AT LARGE OF PENNSYLVANIA FROM 1682 TO 1801 VOLUME 11 - 1782 (HARRISBURG, PA., 1909).

THE LAWS OF PENNSYLVANIA FROM 14 OCT., 1790 TO 20 MAR,
1810   VOLUME 2 - 1781-1790 (PHILADELPHIA, 1910).

THE STATUTES AT LARGE OF PENNSYLVANIA FROM 1682 TO 1801
VOLUME 12 - 1785-1787 (HARRISBURG, PA., 1911).

THE STATUTES AT LARGE OF PENNSYLVANIA FROM 1682 TO 1801
VOLUME 13 - 1787-1790 (HARRISBURG, PA., 1911).

THE STATUTES AT LARGE OF PENNSYLVANIA FROM 1682 TO 1801
VOLUME 14 - 1791-1793 (HARRISBURG, PA., 1911).

THE STATUTES AT LARGE OF PENNSYLVANIA FROM 1682 TO 1801
VOLUME 15 - 1794-1797 (HARRISBURG, PA.).

THE STATUTES AT LARGE OF PENNSYLVANIA FROM 1682 TO 1801
VOLUME 16 - 1798-1801 (HARRISBURG, PA., 1915)

ACTS OF THE GENERAL ASSEMBLY OF THE COMMONWEALTH OF
PENNSYLVANIA (LAWS OF PENNSYLVANIA) - 1801 (etc.)
LANCASTER (etc.), ROBERT BAILEY (etc.)

INDEX

ABBOT Thomas 239
ABBOTT William 249
ABERCROMBIE Elizabeth 199
ABERNATHY W. 155
ABRAHAM 53
ACHESON Thomas 118
ACHISON Lt. Col. 142
ACKER Casper 12
  Jacob 12
ADAIR William 211
ADAM Jacob 133
ADAMS Alexander 60, 67
  Daniel 236
  James 232, 233
  John 227, 232, 246, 252
  Jonathan 62, 68
  Milo 240
  Nathaniel 92
  Robert 47, 55, 174, 200
  Samuel 47, 129, 153
  Solomon 227
ADCOCK William 103
ADDAMS John 242
ADDISON Alexander 74, 116
ADDLEMAN 57
ADERSON Joshua 27
ADKINSON Rebecca 124
  Thomas 124
ADLUM John 186, 191
  Joseph 73, 74
AFFLEBACH Joseph 207
AGERS Sylvanus 234
AGNEW James 184, 186, 199, 235, 243, 247
  John 29, 33, 35, 36, 38, 70, 115, 243, 247
  Lt. Col. 112, 142
  Samuel 137, 247
  Samuel C. 247
  Samuel M. 247
AISTER Jacob 14
AITKIN Robert 36, 70
AITKINSON Joseph 249
AKERS Uria 247
AKINS Robert 219
  William 219
ALBERGER Adam 71
ALBERT Elizabeth 217
  Eve 217
  Margaret 217
  Michael 14
  Peter 217
  Phillipina 217
  Rachel 217
  William 14

ALBERTS Dirck 2
ALBERTUS Lewis 153
  Zilla 153
ALBERTY Philip 34
ALBRECHT Charles 198
  Dewalt 220
  John 220
  Susanna 220
ALBRIGHT Andrew 110, 194, 196, 223
  John 144, 216
  Peter 217
  Philip 124
ALDAN Roger 128
ALDEN Roger 105, 110, 117, 138, 142, 214
  Timothy 214
ALDRICH Peter 4
ALE Alexander 236
  Daniel 236
ALEXANDER --- 100
  Alexander John 100
  Benjamin 115
  Charles 60, 67, 228, 250
  Eleanor 228, 250
  Hugh 38, 39
  James 113, 172, 201
  John 49, 86, 171
  John B. 184
  Joseph 214
  Lt. Col. 101, 111, 141
  Margaret 49
  Mariamne 100
  Robert 100
  Samuel 171
  William 100, 113, 197, 214, 243
ALIBONE William 41
ALISON Robert 204
ALLABACH John 189
ALLEN --- 39
  Ananias 112, 142
  Andrew 31, 35, 60, 61, 62, 67, 68, 102, 170, 180, 181
  Ann Penn 102
  David 33
  Elizabeth 44, 102, 224
  Isaac 60, 67
  James 26, 44, 102, 145, 224, 233
  John 25, 35, 140, 208

  Joseph 28
  Margaret 170
  Margaret Elizabeth 102
  Moses 174
  Nathaniel 48, 133
  Peter 30, 31
  Richard 235
  Samuel 35, 36, 129, 162
  William 15, 20, 31, 35, 48, 58, 65, 85, 102, 118, 143
ALLENTON John 56
ALLER Ulrich 13
ALLESON Archibald 137
  Gawin 137
  Hugh 137
  James 137
  Jane 137
  John 137
  Thomas 137
ALLIBONE --- 200
  Mary 200
  Mary E. B. 200
  Rebecca 200
  Sarah 200
  Thomas 109, 113, 128, 141, 199, 200, 244
  William 43, 89, 200, 244
ALLICE James 70
ALLISON Andrew 171
  Burgess 171
  George 143
  James 74, 107, 171, 232, 240
  Jarvis 184
  John 25, 33, 38
  Matthew 122
  N. S. 171
  Patrick 99
  Robert 132, 154, 190
  Samuel 80
  William 183, 211
ALLMAN Hannah 100
  Lawrence 100
ALLOWAY William 6
ALLSHOUSE Henry 21
ALLUMMAPIS 52
ALRICHS Jacob 2
  Peter 4, 5, 7
ALRICKS Jacob 1
  Peter 2
ALSHOUSE Henry 219
ALTEMUS John 65

INDEX

ALTER Jacob 183
  Nathaniel 126
ALTMAN Anthony 105
ALTMORE Caleb 79
AMBERSON James 104
AMBROSE John 126
AMBROSURE Mathias 150
AMIEL John 43
AMIES Thomas 145, 171, 249
ANDAGGY-JUNKQUAGH 52
ANDERSON --- 177, 181, 190, 224
  Adam 226, 227
  Alexander 80, 171
  Isaac 182
  Jacob 98
  James 31, 37, 38, 40, 70, 228
  John 69, 75, 100, 128, 138, 146, 180, 184, 209
  Joshua 32, 37, 45, 171
  Lt. Col. 101
  Patrick 42
  Robert 207, 222, 247
  Samuel 68, 168, 200
  Samuel A. 247
  Stephen 61, 68
  Thomas 119, 223, 227
  William 55, 70, 112, 183, 215
ANDREAS Abraham 189
ANDREW 52, 246
  Daniel 30
  Hugh 84
  Nathan 191
  Nicholas 105
  Wendall 30
ANDREWS Arthur 246
  Hugh 95, 106, 233
  James 200, 246
  John 35, 98, 104, 132, 143, 184, 246
  Joseph 138
  Mary 222
  Robert 50, 55
ANDRIE Joseph 171
ANDRIESEN Lars 2
ANDROSSE Edmund 2
  Gov. 2
ANGLEMOYER Henry 245
ANGST Nicholas 212
ANGUS John 89
ANKENNY Jacob 180

ANKENY Henry 203
  Jacob 194
  Peter 147
  Rosina 147
ANKRIM James 206
ANNESLY Thomas 79
ANSHUITZ George 179
ANSLEY John 177
  Simeon 248
ANSLY Thomas 109
ANSPACH Lt. Col. 111
ANTES Frederick 164
  Henry 211, 215
  Jacob 231, 252
ANTHONY John 217
  Joseph 79, 89
  Peter 34, 39, 58, 66
ANTIS Frederick 32, 34, 37, 38, 39
  Henry 12, 233
  William 34
ANUCHNAXQUA 53
APP Christian 71
  Michael 71
APPLE Paul 245
  Peter 119
APPOWEN Hannah 48
  Samuel 48
ARBO John 26
ARCHBOLD Eleanor 208
  Patrick 208
ARCHER Adam 19
  David T. 242
  Jacob 19
  Samuel 241
ARD Joseph B. 184
ARMAT Joseph 204
  Thomas 79, 80, 192
ARMBRUSTER Matthias 185, 241
ARMOR James 50
  Robert 27
ARMSTRONG --- 64
  Abraham 241
  Andrew 98
  Col. 155
  James 65, 96, 116, 165, 181, 192
  John 25, 33, 42, 45, 70, 76, 116
  Lt. Col. 111, 141
  Quintain 73
  Robert L. 215
  Thomas 15, 20, 21, 33, 109
  Widow 226

  William 66, 76, 184
ARNDT Abraham 33, 212
  Elizabeth 212, 242
  George Washington 242
  Jacob 39, 40, 71, 212
  John 36, 37, 45, 91, 241, 242
  John P. 137, 192
ARNOLT Peter 109
ARRETS Lenartt 8
ARRETT Christian 156
ARRISON Jephta 102
ARSKEN Edward 54
ART James 79
ARTHURS John 92
ARTZ Michael 107
ASH Christian 166
  James 89, 129, 245
  Phineas 246
ASHBAUGH Martin 152
ASHBRIDGE Joseph 27, 97, 173
  William 60, 67
ASHBURTON Lord 236
ASHBY William 79
ASHCOM Charles 154
ASHDON Robert 6
ASHLEMAN Daniel 11
ASHMAN George 64
ASHMEAD John 23
  Samuel 32, 50
  William 50
ASHTON George 80
  Isaac 19
  Jacob 72
  Joseph 72
  Samuel 147
  Thomas 72
ASPDEN Matthias 42, 62, 68
ASSARODUNQUA 53
ATCHESON David 218
  Thomas 180
ATCHISON Lt. Col. 112
ATKINS William 103
ATKINSON Joseph 15
  Thomas 184, 213, 214, 233
  Wilton 36
ATLEE Col. 118
  Samuel 69
  William 38, 69
ATON Aaron 230, 250
  Adrian 237
ATTIN 63

INDEX

ATTLEE William P. 142
ATTMORE Thomas 109
AUFRERE George 19
AULT John 232
AURAND Abraham 210
AURANT John 83
AUSTIN Calvin 252
  Isaac 50, 51
  Nicholas 171
  William 50, 51, 62
AVERY Cyrus 184, 224
AWARTZ Peter 95
AWL Jacob 50, 51, 57, 86
AX John Frederick 12
AYAMACKAN 52
AYBE John 12
  Peter 12
AYRES David 102
  John 91
  Samuel 196

BABB Matthias 73
BABLE Thomas 61, 68
BACH Elizabeth 212
  Henry 212
BACHE Benjamin Franklin 89
  Lewis 205
  Richard 42, 153, 182, 241
  William 218
BACHENSTOFE Andrew 70
BACHMAN George 12
  Lt. Col. 101
BACHSINOSA 53
BACKENSTOS John 167
BACKHOUSE John 154
  Mary 151
  Richard 151
  William 132, 144
BACON Alvan 252
  Daniel 252
  Job 30
  John 232
  Joseph 79
  Sarah 199
  William D. 218, 234, 252
BADER Henry 128
BADGER Joseph 214
  Robert 230, 250
BADOLET John 118
BADORF John 183

BAER Jacob 140
  John 140
BAGG James 92
BAGHER Frederick 195
BAILEY Abraham 133, 144, 165, 193, 194, 206, 249
  Asa 126
  Ellis 184
  Francis 79, 112, 139
  Frederick 206
  Isaac 180
  Jabez 180
  John 73
  Jonathan 6, 7
  Reuben 227, 249
  Samuel 180
  Thomas 86, 217
  William 33, 36, 61, 68, 74, 144
BAILIE James 70
  John 70, 184, 235
BAILY Robert 75
BAIRD Absalom 88
  Alexander 74
  Archibald 70, 113
  David 55
  George 128, 242
  Hugh 153
  James 98
  John 41, 153
  Lt. Col. 142
  Samuel 49, 94, 195, 201, 202
  Thomas 165, 184, 195, 214, 227
  Thomas H. 203, 218, 222
  William 202
BAKER Adam 74
  Capt. 239
  George 152
  George Adam 51
  George N. 232
  Henry 4, 5, 6, 7
  Henry Cleland 77
  Hilary 79
  Isaac 218
  Jacob 80, 109, 162
  Jane 239
  Johan 12
  John 65, 192
  Ludwick 138
  Michael 112, 182
  Richard 32

  Samuel 79
  Thomas 239
BALD Robert 247
BALDERSTON Eli 246
BALDRIGE Joseph 128
BALDWIN Abraham 225
  Amza B. 185
  Ann 166
  Henry 213, 214, 218, 222, 240, 241
  John 9, 10, 26
  Josiah 109
  Leonard 216
  Lt. Col. 142
  Summers 185
  Thomas 212
BALDY Lt. Col. 111, 141
BALFOUR Elizabeth 56
  George 56
BALICHWANONACH-SHY 53
BALIO Peter 12
BALL Blackall William 88
  Joseph 88, 169
  William 18, 23, 24, 32, 49, 169
BALLIET Stephen 217
BALLIOT Stephen 74, 130, 146, 244
BALMER Jacob 227
  John 229, 244
  Rachel 244
BALTZEL Jacob 174
BAMBERGER Arnold 11
BANCKER Charles N. 241
BANFORD Thomas 29
BANKS Andrew 194, 209
  James 110, 184, 209
  Lt. Col. 111, 141
BANKSON Andrew 1, 4, 7, 18, 19, 23, 43, 50
BANNER Jeremiah 227
BANTLEON George 145
BARBER John 148, 188
  Nathaniel 132
  Robert 33, 138, 194, 233
  William 140, 188
BARCLAY Capt. 238
  David 19, 80
  Gilbert 22
  Hugh 118
  John 19, 72, 86, 114, 161
  Thomas 96
  William 160

INDEX

BARCLAY & MITCHELL 96
BARD George 99, 120, 138
  Samuel 249
BARDMAN Adam 167
BARE Christian 226
  Henry 11
  Jacob 12, 14
  John Henry 12
BARGE Jacob 38, 42
BARGMAN John C. 219
  Sophia 219
BARKER Abraham 245
  Jeremiah 97, 184
  John 118
  Jonathan 150
  Lt. Col. 111
  Thomas 3, 10
BARKLEY Hugh 222
BARLET John 173
BARLEY Jonathan 7
BARLOW Joel 170
  John 146
BARNCORD Jacob 248
  Peter 248
BARNDOLLAR Michael 142
BARNES Barnaby 28, 155
  Christopher (Xtoper) 3
  Cornelius 31
  Henry 225
  James 175
  John 4, 5, 6, 79
  Joseph 202
  William 99
BARNESLY John 63, 70
BARNET Henry 32, 33, 78
  John 97
  Joseph 133
  Michael 245
  William 211, 214
BARNETS Peter 226
BARNETT Joseph 132
  S. 80
BARNETZ Joseph 243
BARNEY Commodore 198, 238
  Joshua 93
BARNHART Henry 232
  Rudolph 167
BARNITZ George 113
  Jacob 99
  John 183, 199
BARNS Cornelius 32
BARR Jacob 188
  James 36, 39, 104
  John 94, 186
  Samuel 71, 74

Thomas 236
  William 239
BARRALET John James 171
BARRET William 89
BARRETT James 227
BARRON Michael 134
  Philip 207
BARRY Robert 182, 186
BARTELLS Henry 8
  Senwes 8
BARTHOLD Frederick 78
BARTHOLOMEW Benjamin
  31, 32, 39
  Edward 38, 39
  Henry 207
BARTLETT Samuel 229,
  238, 244
BARTLING Christieb 145
BARTOLETT Jean 12
BARTON Benjamin 87
  Benjamin S. 133
  Benjamin Smith 171
  Daniel 55
  David R. 142
  James 134, 193, 198,
    230, 249
  Matthias 100
  Thomas 155
BARTOW Gershom 204
  Thomas 79
BARTRAM Alexander 93
  George 178
  John 5
  Moses 32
BASSELER Henry 14
  Johan Henry 14
BATDORF John 148
BATDORFF John 199
BATE --- 236
BATES John 46
BATHO Charles 22
BATON John 36
BATTISS Elijah 189
  Sarah 189
BAUCHMAN Lt. Col. 101
BAUDER Frederick 237
BAUGHMAN Adam 228, 240
BAULDIN Henry 117
BAUM --- 56
  Lt. Col. 111, 141
BAUMAN Charles 76
  Johan Ditterig 14
  John 128
BAUMGARDNER Thomas 196
BAUMGARTNER George 177

BAUNA Lt. Col. 101
BAUSMAN Andrew 70
  Jacob 59, 66
  Nicholas 86
  Rhinehart 251
  William 32, 129
BAXTER James 222
BAY Thomas 80
BAYARD Andrew 99, 182,
  247, 248
  George A. 243
  James 51
  John 21, 23, 32, 34,
    38, 47
  Samuel 95
  Stephen 71, 74
BAYARE Andrew 241
BAYLOR Henry 86
BAYNTON John 16, 17, 20,
  41, 42, 156
  Peter 5, 73, 151, 190,
    231, 242
BAYNTOR Peter 51
BEACH Nathan 64, 77, 131,
  163
BEACK George 105
BEADER Henry 182
BEAKES William 4
BEAKS Stephen 7, 28
BEAL David 65
BEALE David 64, 78, 104
  Lt. Col. 111, 141
BEALL Zephaniah 180
BEAM John 162
  Peter 162
BEAN James 94
  Jesse 193
  John 76
BEANER Henry 140
BEANS Thomas 36, 237
BEAR Christian 103
  Christiana 163
  Henry 183, 191, 235,
    241, 252
  Isaac 163
  Jacob 109
  Samuel 234
BEARD James 34
  John 38
  John George 13
  Richard 243
  Samuel 235
  Thomas 128, 138
  William 239
BEARDSLEY Alexander 7

INDEX

BEARDT Henry 162
BEASON Henry W. 243
BEASORE Peter 97
BEATON John 37
BEATTY James 203, 211, 222
  John 98, 218
  Lt. Col. 141
  Robert 77
  William 92
  William P. 123, 132, 230, 234
BEATY Alexander 112
  Hugh 112
  James 112
BEAUMENT William 90
BEAVER John 64, 78, 208
BECHTLEY George 12
  Hans Jacob 12
BECK --- 86
  Henry 65
  Lt. Col. 111, 141
  Paul 73, 89, 117, 125, 178, 182, 190, 218
  William 207
BECKER Jacob 14
  Michael 14
BEDFORD Gunning 23, 41, 64
  Nathaniel 71, 97, 130
BEDSWORTH Joseph 203
BEDWELL Bobert 1
  Robert 4
  Thomas 7
BEECH Nathan 120
BEECHLER Henry 166
  Margaret 166
BEEKMAN William 1, 2
BEELEN Anthony 156, 214
BEELER Anthony 136
  George 116
BEELMAN John 182
BEER John 129, 236
BEERBROWER Mary 149
BEERE Mary 84, 121
BEESON Jacob 118, 184
BEESTON Francis 75
BEIDEMAN Daniel 224
  Daniel Stewart 224
BEIDLEMAN George 183
BEIER Peter 70
BEIL Henry 133
BEISEL John 244
  Peter 33
BEKER Cadwalader 234

BELITZ Lorence 12
BELL Arthur 223
  Greenwood 212
  Henry 30
  Isaiah 60, 67
  James 125
  John 22, 86, 216, 217
  Peter 37
  Samuel 100, 236, 246
  Thomas 89
  William 55, 190, 225
  Zephania 118
BELLEN Anthony 202
BELLENTINE James 191
BELLIS Matthew 48
BELSTERLING Peter 110
BEMUS Daniel 214
BENDER Adam 96
  Jacob 176
  Johannes 14
  Leonhart 14
BENEZET Anthony 13, 220
  Daniel 16
  James 16, 17, 32, 33
  John 31
  Mary 220
  Philip 79
  Samuel 77
BENFELL Engle 124
  George S. 124
BENLEY Shasbazer 63
BENNER Christopher
  Peter 204
  George 59, 61, 67, 68
  Jacob 61, 68
  John 106, 150
  Lt. Col. 141
BENNET Aaron 78
  Cynthia 241
  Edmond 4
  Edmund 5
  Edward 5
  George 232
  Isaac 208, 210
  Jacob 30
  James 205, 216
  John 125
  Marinda 221
  William 44
BENNETT Daniel 189
  Edmund 6
  Elizabeth 189
  William 27, 30, 37
BENNEZETT Samuel 148
BENNINGHOVE Jacob 145

BENSEL Charles 14, 32
BENSELL Conrad 13
BENSON Peter 140
BENTLEY 102
  Joseph 34
BENTLY House 206
BENTZEL Johannes George 12
BENZEIN Christian 74
BERGER Michael 13
BERKENBINE John 242
BERKEY Peter 230, 248
BERKHEISER Peter 217
BERKHIMER John 229, 244
BERKY Peter 236
BERLAIN Abraham 32
BERLIN --- 40
  Abraham 39
  Philip 213
BERLITS Elias 150
BERNHART Henry 14
BERRELL John 107
BERRINGER Elizabeth 195
  Jacob 195
BERRY Daniel 98
  Henry 124, 127, 183
  John 160
  Rachel 234
  Thomas 122
  William 4, 5, 212
BERRYHILL Alexander 92, 94
BERWICK Edward 69
BESHORE John 126
BESK John Admundson 1
BESORE John 218, 228
BESSONET Charles 58, 65, 97
BEST Henry 229
  William 99
BETHEL Robert 133
  Samuel 28, 123, 132, 137, 183
BETHELL Robert 60, 67
BETT Andrew 233
BETTERTON Benjamin 31, 34
BETTON Samuel 98, 105
BETTS John 5, 6, 7
BEVAN John 5, 7, 8
BEYER Abraham 14
BEZAR Edward 5
BEZER John 1, 4, 97
BHEME Jacob 11
BHREIN Jacob 76
BICHLEY Daniel 210

INDEX

BICKER Maria 139
BICKHAM George 74, 90, 128
BICKLER Catharine Salome 129
BICKLEY Abraham 9, 84, 134
  Daniel 145
BIDDIS George 198
  John 111, 119, 127, 134
BIDDLE --- 57, 140
  Charles 78, 98, 187, 191
  Clement 26, 27, 79, 86, 118, 153, 192
  Clement C. 241, 247
  Ed. 31
  Hugh 226
  James 32, 75, 178, 238
  John 24, 35, 51, 99, 113
  Owen 31, 32, 39, 42
  Sophia 113
  Stacy 80
  Thomas 128, 246
BIDDLEMAN Anna Maria 245
  Elias 245
BIDGOOD William 28
BIDLER John 221
BIERE Jacob 11
BIGHAM Hugh 202
BIGLER Jacob 216
  John 182, 196
BIGONY Francis 97
BIKKER Gerrit 1
BILES Charles 158
  Sarah 158
  William 3, 5, 6, 7, 13, 15, 41, 145
BILGER George 139
BILLINGTON Thomas 109
BILLMAN David 198
BILLMEYER Andrew 64, 76
  Jacob 43
  Mary 43
  Michael 83, 89, 91
BILLOP Christopher 2
BINCKSON Andros 4
  John 3
BINDER William 162
BINGHAM James 48
  John 140
  Maria M. 102
  Thomas 217

  William 21, 43, 45, 46, 72, 86, 102, 229, 246
BINKELY 196
BINKLEY Christian 106, 195
  John 235
BINNEY Barnabas 109
  John 171
BINNS John 165
BINNY Archibald 171, 178
BIOREN John 112, 170
BIRCH Thomas 171
BIRCHFIELD James 127
BIRD --- 63
  Benjamin 33
  Frederick 227
  James 32
  John 20
  Mark 29, 33, 38, 42
  Robert 130, 139
  Silvanus 145
  William 15, 18
BIRKBY James 74
BIRTCH James 160
BISBING Bernard 65
  George 144
BISHIP John 49
BISHOP Benoni 1, 4, 5
  Jacob 37, 104
  John 75, 230, 250
  Thomas 171
BISSELL Leverick 158
BISSON Charles 170
BITLER John 237
BITTENBENDER Jacob 120
BIXLER Christian 183, 215
BLACK Fanny 248
  James 58, 66, 106
  John 45, 99, 107, 160, 240, 248
  Joseph 229, 244
  Lt. Col. 111, 141
  Robert 69
  Samuel 153
  Thomas 182
  William 221
BLACKBURN Thomas 171
BLACKFORD John 60, 67
BLACKISTON Presley 64, 69
BLACKWELL John 3, 5
  Robert 73

BLADEN Mart. 10
BLADENEY William 183
BLAIN John 175
BLAINE Ephraim 43, 55
BLAIR Alexander 217
  Charles 108
  John 132, 179, 201, 220, 233, 243
  Randle 75
  Samuel 228
  William 35
  William Lawrence 42
BLAKE Edward 5, 6
  George E. 171
  Jacob 216
  John 89
BLAKELY George 158
  William 199, 222
BLAKENEY Gabriel 209
  William 153
BLANCHARD Charles 252
BLAND Elias 19
BLANDT 53
BLAZER George 64
BLEAKLEY John 79
BLEIKERS Johannes 8
BLEUER Joseph 80
BLEW James 177
BLEWER Joseph 32, 36, 38, 39, 41, 44, 73
BLEYNEY John 192
BLIGHT Peter 88, 89
BLOCHER Jacob 166
BLOCK Hans 2
BLODGET Samuel 88
BLOEMMAERT Samuel 1
BLOOM Daniel 188
  Samuel 217
  William 216, 246
BLOSS Aaron 163, 201, 232
BLOTTENBERGER John 71
BLUM John 14
BLUMER Abraham 72
  Jacob 185
BLUMSTON John 1, 3, 4, 5, 6, 7, 8, 10
  Michael 5
BLUNSTON Samuel 54, 155
BLYTH Benjamin 38
  David 115
  William 24
BLYTHE David 70
  Samuel 127
BOAHLER Francis 74

INDEX

BOAL David 97
  John 105, 208
  Lt. Col. 111, 141
  Robert 97
  William 177
BOAR Nicholas 237
BOAS Jacob 182, 183
  William 200
BOATICAR Alexander 117
  Lucy 117
BOB Nicholas 140
BOBBITT Jacob 133
BOCHIUS Peter 60, 67
BODEN Andrew 180
  John 225
BODLE Abraham 161
BODLEY Thomas 158
BOEHLER Lewis 74
BOEHM Philip 32, 36, 42
BOELHAM William 3
BOELSEN Jan 3
BOGGS Alexander 100, 130,
    143, 183, 188
  Andrew 179, 183, 232
  Francis 225
  James 103
  John 51, 80, 103
  Robert 103, 122, 123,
    135
  William 144
BOHLEN Bohl 89, 119
BOHM Anthony 13
  John Philip 12
BOHMAN John 11
BOILEAU Nathaniel B. 134,
    164, 166
BOISE Elizabeth 161
BOISLE Joseph 140
BOKENSTOSE John 33
BOLE David 64, 78
BOLIG Michael 229, 245
BOLLINGER Emanuel 154
  Michael 210, 246
BOLLMAN Charles 214
  Lewis 117
BOLTON Everard 9
  Samuel 23
BOMBERGER John 169, 191
BOND John 80
  Joseph 106
  Lewis 55
  Samuel 32
  Thomas 23, 59, 65, 67
BONEBREAK Daniel 193
BONER Barnet 192

BONES James 176
BONHAM Ephraim 35, 37
BONNER Rudolph 14
BONNET Jacob 180
  Lt. Col. 101, 112,
    142
BONNETT Jacob 128, 203,
    209
  John 128
BONNHORST Charles V.
    158
BONSALL Isaac 79, 84
  James B. 92
  Vincent 76
BOOLS William 199
BOON --- 19
  Andrew 73
  George 245
  Hezekiah 136
  Peter 30
  Sevan 218
BOONE --- 75
  Jacob 169
  Jeremiah 249
  Joseph 194
  Samuel 105
BOOR William 175
BOOS William 75
BOOTH Joseph 7
BORDNER John 132
BORROWS John 213
BORTREE John 235
BOSQUET Augustine 176
BOSSERT Elizabeth 180
  John 180
BOSTLER Henry 28
BOSTWICK Philo 225
BOTTENFIELD Philip 161
BOTTIMORE Jacob 139
BOUDE Samuel 20
  Thomas 90, 97, 100,
    123, 137, 143, 183
BOUDENOT Elias 109
BOUDINOT Elias 99
BOULAND Robert 180
BOUQUET Col. 53
BOURNE Thomas 16, 41
BOUSQUET Augustine 119
BOVARD Lt. Col. 111,
    141
BOWCOMB Peter 3
BOWDERY George 221
  Lydia 221
BOWEL David 65

BOWEN David 127
  Jonathan 171
  Michael 162
  Thomas 47, 171
  Thomas B. 148
BOWER George 183
  Jacob 86, 98, 194, 223
  Samuel 127, 144
BOWERS Michael 238
  Theodore 231
BOWES Hugh 24
BOWHANNON George 193
BOWING Abner 244
BOWINGS Abner 229
BOWLAND Matthew 186, 200
  Robert 184
BOWMAN --- 191
  Alexander 230, 250
  Charle 227
  Charles 239
  Christian 12, 179
  Ebenezer 137, 146, 185
  Henry 1, 4, 5, 188
  Isaac 206
  Jacob 13, 118, 180,
    184, 210, 214, 245
  John 12, 138, 180
  John D. 185
  Joseph 102
  Lt. Col. 141
  Mary 196
  Samuel 137, 196
  Thomas 131
BOWNE Samuel 120
BOWSMAN William 32, 38
BOYD Adam 97, 128, 161
  Alexander 47, 84, 129
  Andrew 37, 73, 106, 125
  David 71
  George 198
  James 45, 94, 122, 139
  John 32, 69, 130, 138,
    139, 151, 165, 171,
    184, 185, 197, 200,
    201, 218
  Joseph T. 214
  Lt. Col. 101, 111, 141
  Robert 234
  Stewart 214
  Thomas 232
  William 148, 161
BOYDEN James 1, 4, 48
BOYER Christian 217, 237
  Frederick 97
  Isaac 205
  J. K. 202

INDEX

Jacob 37
Jacob K. 184, 193, 194, 203, 245, 246
Philip 94, 205
Valentine 136
Widow 217
BOYES Elizabeth 241
BOYLE Charles 140
BOYLES Agnes 242
  Elizabeth 228
  John 228, 242, 156
BOYLS Lt. Col. 112, 142
BOYS Nathan 79
BOZORTH Andrew 171, 199
  Sarah Dyer 171
BRACKEN Thomas 88
  William 88
BRACKENRIDGE David 188
BRACY Bobert 4
  Thomas 4
BRADBERRY David 234, 238
BRADDOCK --- 108
BRADFORD David 71, 74, 128, 149
  Samuel F. 109, 170
  Thomas 83, 232
BRADLEY Dominick 154
  William 228
BRADON Thomas 129
BRADSHAW John 4, 7
BRADY James 113
  John 120, 227, 244
  Peter 223
  Samuel 103, 157
BRAKIN Jesse 85
BRAND Adam 12
  David 105
BRANDON John 152, 227
BRANDT Abraham 183
  Adam 97, 180
  David 180
  Jacob 76
  Martin 180
BRANNAN Benjamin 65
BRANNIFF John 142
BRANNON John 35, 252
BRANSCON Thomas 6
BRANT Jacob 64
BRASEY Thomas 10
BRASHEAR Basil 214
  Lt. Col. 142
BRASHIERS Lt. Col. 112
BRASSIE Robert 1
  Thomas 1
BRASSY Thomas 3

BRATTON George 174
  John 110, 123, 136
  Lt. Col. 111, 141
BREADING Nathaniel 118
BREADY James 143
BREARLY Stephen 157
BRECHAL Martin 196
BRECHALL Martin 186
BRECHBILL Henry 202
  John 202
BRECHT John 13
BRECK Samuel 241
BREDEN Nathaniel 55
BREDIN John 241
BREED Ebenezer 80
BREENEMAN Christian 243
BREIDENBACH Philip 148
BREINIG George 39, 183
BRENEMAN Henry 181
  Jacob 130
BRENIZER David 182
BRENNEMAN Christian 123, 132, 183
  John 229, 245
BRENNON Benjamin 33
BRESSLER George 223
BRETTER Anthony 14
BREUTIGAM Daniel 145
BREWATER Abel 171
BREWER Abigail 189
  Henry 189
  John 189, 193
  Jonathan 189
  Sarah 189
  William 189
BREWSTER Jonah 200, 204
  Samuel 38
BRICE James 58, 70, 74
  John 238
BRICELAND James 222
BRICK James 243
BRICKER 176
BRICKINGHAM John 235
BRIDGES John 4
  Robert 66
BRIDPORT George 171
BRIEN Edward 137, 142, 178, 183, 190, 202
BRIGDEN William 238
BRIGGS John 3, 4, 162
BRIGHT Jacob 26, 32, 33, 42
  John 65
  Lt. Col. 111, 141
  Michael 32, 46, 176

BRILLINGER John 138
BRINCKLOE John 4
BRINDLE Jacob 180
  John 208
BRINEY Adam 219
BRINGHURST George 50
  Israel 200
  James 83, 109, 176
  John 21, 50, 62, 69
  Joseph 176
  Mary 200
  Samuel 50
BRINK John 100, 111, 119, 134, 189
  Jonathan 232, 249
BRINKER Abraham 210
BRINKERHOOF Garret 212
BRINKLOE John 1, 4, 5, 6, 7
BRINTON Caleb 65, 208, 249
  John H. 196
  Moses 28
BRINZER George 97
BRISBAND William 80
BRISBEN John 227
BRISON James 97
BRISTOW John 5, 6
BRITAIN John 37
BRITTAIN Nathaniel 30
BRITTIN Robert 233
BRITTON Abraham 33
  John 45
BRITTON & MASSEY 89
BROADHEAD --- 84
  Daniel 75, 202
  Elizabeth 227, 244
  John 178, 189, 247
  Luke 46, 227, 232, 244
BROADLEY Daniel 49
BROBST Christian 136, 202
  Jacob 186
  Valentine 145
BROCKDEN Charles 9
BROCKHOLLS Anthony 2, 3
BRODHEAD Daniel 54, 129, 190
  Eliza 199
  John 119, 134, 183, 193, 246
BRODNOX Thomas 190
BROEN Thomas 2
BROLIER 167
BROOK Mathew 201
  Samuel 191

INDEX

Thomas 97
BROOKE John 146
  Matthew 134, 146
  Matthias 193
  Robert 222
BROOKES Edward 10
BROOKS Benjamin 182
  Edward 59, 62, 66, 69, 79
  John 37, 49, 127, 138, 142, 184, 211, 212, 214, 232
  Matthew 38
BROTHERTON Samuel 240
BROUDE Thomas 132
BROUGH Abraham 203
BROUSE Abraham 190
BROWDEN Joseph 7
BROWER Abraham 201
BROWN Alexander 20, 131, 167, 214
  Andrew 83, 89
  Anna Margaret 23
  Basil 152
  Bazil 54
  Benjamin 131
  Charles 71, 137
  Clement 158
  Daniel 1, 4, 5, 6, 7
  David 200
  Elizabeth 223
  Gen. 204
  George 213, 230, 249
  Godfrey 23
  Hannah Fisher 131
  Henry 88, 121
  Jacob 63, 69, 189, 192
  James 8, 39, 226
  John 20, 31, 33, 34, 44, 58, 92, 113, 120, 136, 141, 143, 153, 154, 174, 184, 190, 194, 207, 213, 220, 241
  John A. 217
  Joseph 174
  Josiah 237
  Lazarus 199
  Lt. Col. 141
  Maj. Gen. 205
  Mary Frances 131
  Matthew 39
  Moses 80
  Nathaniel 69, 86
  Patrick 223
  Peter 45, 122, 223

Peter A. 205
Richard 33
Robert 136, 184, 215, 218
Samuel 16
Thomas 183
William 19, 33, 36, 37, 38, 41, 46, 47, 51, 57, 64, 65, 78, 86, 94, 137, 154, 171, 222
William M. 113
BROWNBACK Garratt 13
BROWNE George 2
  John 3
  Peter 107, 109
BROWNING Isaac 215
BROWNLEE John 236
BROWNSON Isaac 134, 204
BRUBACK Jacob 188
BRUBAKER Abraham 229, 244
  Christian 229, 245
  Jacob 226
  John 11, 232
BRUCE David 180
  George 133
  Robert 240
BRUGIERE Charles 224
BRUMECK Michael 26
BRUSH Cornwall 226
BRUSTAR Ann 189
  Catharine 189
  Elizabeth 189
  Henry 189
  James 189
  John 189
  Mary 189
  Merza 189
  Phoebe 189
  Sarah 189
  Susanna 189
BRUTON Bridget 164, 227
  Joseph 164, 227
BRYAN George 16, 17, 20, 32, 46, 50, 112, 156, 229, 246, 248
  Samuel 24, 133
  Sarah 156, 248
BRYANT John Y. 194
  Mordecai Y. 249
BRYSON James 71
  Samuel 99
  William 182
BUCH Elizabeth 149
  John 149

BUCHAMER -- 59, 67
BUCHAMMER John 226
BUCHANAN Andrew 174, 206
  Arthur 58, 64, 66, 78, 98
  George 98, 166, 167, 196
  James 100, 199, 224
  John 222
  Laetitia 199
  Latitia 196
  Thomas 56
  Thomas R. 183
  William 129
BUCHANNAN -- 57
BUCHANNON Thomas R. 179
BUCHANON Thomas R. 190
BUCHER Conrad 185
  Jacob 97, 180, 182, 190
BUCHOLTZ Henry 8
BUCK George 229, 244
  Ichabod 161
  Jacob 243
  John 226
  Joseph 87
  William 161
BUCKALEW Amos 185
  John 98
BUCKANNEN George 178
BUCKBEE Isaac 80
BUCKENMEYER Erasmus 14
BUCKHOLDER Peter 39
BUCKINGHAM John 224
BUCKIUS Philip 71
BUCKLEW Amos 162
BUCKLEY Daniel 100
  Israel 160
  John 7
  Johnston 232
  Phineas 106
  Thomas 120
  William 119
BUCKMAN Jonathan 185
  Thomas 222
BUCKWALTER Johannes 12
  Joseph 11
  Turst 14
BUDD --- 221
  John 29
  Joseph 79, 109, 203
  Joshua 138, 203
  Levi 34, 42, 74
  Levy 65
  Rebecca 29
  William 216

INDEX

BUDDEN Francis 77
  James 42, 59, 66, 67, 77, 142
BUFFINGTON George 114, 229, 230, 245, 250
  Thomas 61, 68
  William 68
BUGH Peter 87
BUHLER George 117
BUJAC Celiste 158
  John Lachausee 158
  Matthew 158
  Patrick 158
BULKELEY Sarah 139, 186
  Thomas 139, 186
BULL Henry 227, 248
  John 29, 32, 38, 39
  John G. 138
  Thomas 38, 41, 49, 51, 69, 71, 75
BULLA Thomas 45
BULLMAN Thomas 91
BULLOCK Joseph 42, 46
BULLY Robert 17
BUMGARNER Peter 11
BUNDY John 217
  Phillipina 217
BUNEL Joseph Robert Eustache 129
BUNNER Jacob 60, 67
  John 67
  Rudolph 62, 68
BUNT --- 53
BUNTING John 100
  Philip S. 109
  Samuel 92
BURBERRY Samuel 7
BURBURY Samuel 5
BURCH William Y. 137
BURCHFIELD James 138
BURCHSTEAD Henry 192
BURCKHART Andrew 43
BURD Benjamin 37, 187
  George 243
  John 34, 39, 49
  Thomas 124
BURDEN Benjamin 30
  Joseph 182
BURDS Benjamin 168
  John 168
BURG John 71, 138
BURGE Samuel 15, 16
BURGESS Joseph 177, 245
BURGESSER George 153
BURGET George 85

BURGHART Henry 160
BURK Cornelius 117
  Edward 72
  Elizabeth 117
  John 118
BURKE John 60, 67
  Joseph 222, 232
BURKHALTER Peter 33
BURKHAM Charles 54
BURKHOLDER Abraham 11
  John 11
BURLEIGH Clements 140, 184, 197, 207, 228
BURLEY John 45, 100
  Joseph 208
BURNES Alexander 227
BURNESTON Isaac 186
BURNHAM James 238
BURNS
  Alexander 241
  George 45
  Peter 104
  Samuel 33, 174
BURNSIDE John 199
  Thomas 246
BURR Hudson 62, 68
BURRAS Susanna 154
BURROWS Isaac 140
  John 30
BURSON James 192
  John W. 193, 207
  William 157, 207
BURT Benjamin 185
BURTON Benjamin 77
  John 5
BUSAIN Mathys 2
BUSH Daniel 207
  George 232
  Michael 73
  Philip 21
BUSHING John 14
BUSKERCH Thomas V. 233
BUSSIER Daniel 182, 201, 245
BUSTIE Paul 117
BUTCHER John 59, 66, 67
BUTE John 234
BUTLER Anthony 89
  Joel 214
  Lord 97, 113, 137, 141, 146, 233
  Pierce 248
  Richard 74, 134, 135, 148
  Simon 13

  Thomas 88, 121
  William 1, 47, 71, 115, 147
  Zebulon 63, 70, 71
BUTT Peter 250
BUTTERBACK 57
BUTTS George 131
  Thomas 181
  William 64
BUTTZ George 207
  Robert 204
BUTZ George 167, 183, 212, 229, 244
  Peter 146
  Simon 230, 250
BUYERS George 166
BYE Thomas 171
BYERLEY Andrew 166
  Joseph 166
BYERLY Andrew 243
  Jacob 13
  Michael 13
BYERS James 55
  John 20, 29, 33, 126
  Robert 50
  Robert A. 153
  Samuel 119
BYRNE James 75
  Redmond 150
BYRNES Martin 235

CABLE Abraham 33, 36
  Jacob 216
CACHNAORA-KATACK-KE 53
CADWALADER John 31
  Jonah 191, 219
  Lambert 31
  Thomas 17, 20
CADWALLADER Charles 206
  John 32, 220, 228
  Lambert 89
  Rees 80
  Thomas 231, 246
CAHOON George 53
  Russel 234
CALDWELL Andrew 24, 43, 50, 77, 92, 176
  Dan 177
  Daniel 196
  David 185
  James 54, 61, 68
  Joseph 33
  Samuel 42, 50, 51, 61, 68

INDEX

Sarah 77, 84, 109, 115, 121
William 40
CALHOON George 245
James 155
CALHOUN James 110
John 113, 147
William 109
CALLENDER Jesse 237
Robert 26
William 18, 20
CALLOWHILL Thomas 13, 54
CALVIN Mathew 203
Matthew 184
CAMAC Turner 241, 246
CAMDEN Lord 236
CAMPBEL Charles 125
William 63
CAMPBELL Adam 140
Charles 49, 71, 88, 136, 175, 179, 239
Francis 20
Gen. 230, 250
Hugh 227, 242
Isaac 163
Isabella 227, 244
James 150, 177, 239
John 24, 46, 73, 93, 99, 138, 163, 181, 240
John R. 138
Joseph 126
Lt. Col. 101, 112, 142
McFarland 239
Nathaniel 226
Parker 218, 222
Patrick 53, 183, 223
Peter 61, 67
Robert 38, 167, 205, 241, 245
Terence 146
Thomas 16, 138, 151, 152, 153, 161, 227, 244
William 97, 174, 184, 213, 239, 241
CANAN John 98, 135, 185
CANASATAGO 53
CANASSATEGO 52, 53
CANBY James 249
Thomas 89
CANDLE Nicholas 14
CANECHWADEERON 53
CANN John 4, 5, 6
CANNAN Moses 243
CANNON James 32, 34, 39
John 80, 136, 177

Moses 238
Thomas 188
CANTLER David 74
CANTWELL Edmund 2, 3, 4
CAPAL Denis 223
CAPP Christopher 95
Jacob 193
CAPPEL Charles 227
Margaret 227
CAPPLE Charles 170, 252
Margaret 252
CARAHAN 40
CARE Philip 89
CAREY James 178, 190
John 226, 227, 233
Mathew 112, 171, 247
Matthew 142
CARGIL David 87
CARL Isaiah 200
CARLILE Abraham 84
John 121, 174
CARLISLE Abraham 60, 67
John 137
CARMACK David 159
Mary 159
CARMALE Caleb 72
CARMALT Caleb 79, 232, 249
CARMICHAEL James 134
John 39
Margaret Eskridge 134
William S. 134
CARMICK Stephen 16, 28
CARMINE Elizabeth 227, 240
William 227, 240
CARMONY Anthony 127
Joseph 146
CARNAGHAN Elizabeth 50
CARNAHAN Hannah 109
James 109, 152, 194
Sarah 165
CAROL Charles 70
CAROLUS John 118
CAROTHERS Andrew 226, 237
James 56, 58
John 58, 128, 138, 180
Lt. Col. 142
William 58
CARPENTER --- 178
Abraham 94, 183
Christian 183
Conrad 147

David 177
Emanuel 12, 17, 20, 32
Gabriel 12
Hannah 9
Henry 12
Jacob 87, 113, 155, 234
John 155
Joshua 41
Samuel 3, 5, 6, 7, 8, 9, 10, 12, 13, 83, 154, 183,
Thomas 16, 17, 19
CARR Arthur 180
Edward W. 203
John 44, 71
William 171
CARRE Robert 2
CARRELL Edward 89, 104, 182
John 110, 150
CARROL Edward 205
Hanna 214
John 75
Patrick 214
Richard 55
William 233
CARROLL Charles 246
Edward 100
James 178, 190
John 223
William 252
CARRY Robert 66
CARS Chapman 216
CARSON --- 122
Andrew 79
Ann 239
Christian Febiger 147
James 184, 221, 241
John 33, 75, 77, 153, 182, 239
Joseph 60, 67
Richard 43
William 150
CARTER Henry 194, 235
Robert 7, 8
Samuel 97
Stephen 55, 227, 252
Thomas 126
William 4, 8
CARTWRIGHT George 2
CARUCHIANACHAQUI 53
CARY Eleazer 211
CASE Benjamin T. 242
CASHMAN William 212
CASNER Susan 213

INDEX

CASSAT David 183, 195
  Jacob 206, 212
CASSEL Christian 105
  Daniel 183
  David 172, 179
  Henry 169, 173, 179,
    180, 191, 225
  Jacob 113
CASSELL Nicholas 47
CASTOR Frederick 74
  George 74
  Jacob 74
  Samuel 205
CATHCART William 186,
  203, 213
CATHER Lt. Col. 112, 142
  Robert 42
CATHRALL Isaac 83
CATLIN Putnam 204
CATTERMAN Conrad 243
CAULFIELD Israel 189
CAVAL James 33
CAVANOUGH Edward 151,
  156, 205
  John 208
CAVAT James 34
CAVEAT John 29
CAVENOUGH John 152
CAVET John 49, 50
CAVODE Garrett 74
CAYANOCKEA 53
CAYUGAS 53
CECIL William 153
CESSNA Charles 33
  John 39
CHADS Elizabeth 65
CHALFANT James 61, 68
  Thomas 115
CHALMERS James 22
CHALONER John 51
CHAMBERLAIN Aaron 206
  Jacob 47
  James 160
  Wright 204
CHAMBERLEN Hugh 3
CHAMBERLIN John 185, 207
CHAMBERS --- 63
  Benajmin 9, 15, 20, 51,
    113, 114, 211
  Col. 119, 131
  Ezekiel 193
  George 183
  James 160
  John 36, 46, 223
  Joseph 114

Joseph G. 191
  Sarah 211
  Stephen 69, 72
CHANCELLER William 109
CHANCELLOR William 11,
  79
CHANDLER John 125
  Thomas 14, 15
CHAPMAN Abraham 11, 15,
  28, 41, 183
  Isaac A. 228, 231,
    242, 246, 247, 252
  Jacob 160
  James 130
  John 80
  Joseph 13
  Mathew 236
  Nicholas 136
  Seth 121
  William 88, 163
CHARLES --- 52
  Abraham 195
  John 237
  Joseph 195, 196
  William 171
CHARLTON --- 53
CHASE Amos 214
CHAUDRON S. 171
CHENEY Alpheus 218
  Thomas 35, 37
CHENUGHIATA 53
CHENWITH Auther 232
CHENY Alpheus 162
CHESTER James 239
  Richard 221
CHESTNUT John 221, 245
CHEVALIER John 23, 24
  Peter 16, 17, 18, 20
CHEW Benjamin 57, 71,
  98, 105, 139, 224
  Elizabeth 71
  Elizabeth Margaret
    224
  Henry 248
  Joseph 2
  William Tilghman 224
CHILCOT Joshua 104
CHILD James 16, 17, 18,
  20
  William 180
CHILDS Jonathan 216
CHISSELDEN --- 140
  CharlesEdward 139
CHORPPONING George 225
CHRIEST Henry 33

CHRISMAN Henry 183
CHRIST Henry 34, 42
CHRISTIAN Peter 133
CHRISTIE Andrew 206
  Capt. 134
  John 61, 68, 77
CHRISTLER Leonhart 14
CHRISTMAN --- 226
  Charles 223, 227
  Frederick 101
  George 79
  Henry 184
  John 184
CHRISTMEN Henry 79
CHRISTOPHER Charles 11
CHRISTY Daniel 228
  James 222
  John 151, 170, 219
CHRONEMILLER Thomas 196
CHRYSTLER Jacob 142
CHURCHMAN George 154
  Mordicai 79
CHURTS Jacob 12
CIRKEL Ludowick 14
CISNA Charles 32
CISS Henry 59, 67
CISSNA Charles 34
  John 34
CIST Jacob 185
CLAMENS Christian 123
CLANEY Laurence 223
CLAPHAMSON Samuel 80
CLAPIER Lewis 212
CLAPSADLE --- 226
  Daniel 105
CLARE Thomas 110, 127
CLARK --- 225, 233
  Abraham 46, 229, 246
  Alexander 204
  Benjamin 125, 126
  Brice 130, 217
  Bryce 70
  Charles 203
  Edward 212
  Ephraim 122, 182
  George 55, 63, 113, 153
  James 123, 184, 203,
    225
  John 9, 28, 32, 70, 74,
    99, 123, 125, 136,
    236, 241
  Jonas 143
  Joseph 79, 99, 109, 136
  Joshua 58
  Lt. Col. 142

INDEX

Mary 134
Matthew 183
Rebecca 11
Robert 38, 72, 162, 183, 225
Samuel 226, 232
Sandford 210
Sanford 226
Sherman 220
Thomas 33
Walker 34
Walter 39, 40, 96, 186, 203, 222
William 1, 3, 4, 5, 6, 7, 11, 37, 38, 128, 136, 184, 214, 242
CLARKE --- 163
 Charles 211, 222
 David 115
 John 211, 222
 Lt. Col. 112
 Rebecca 10
 Walter 211
 William 3, 7, 9, 10, 39
CLARKSON Andrew 167
 Gerardus 73, 77
 Joseph 100
 Mathew 49
 Matthew 16, 17, 31, 32, 69, 80, 90, 116
 William 77
CLARNACK James 197
CLARSON Thomas 80
CLAXTON James 27
CLAY Curtis 89
 George 89
 Slaitor 76
 Slator 121
CLAYDER Jacob 131
CLAYPOLE John 79
CLAYPOOL James 37
CLAYPOOLE David C. 98
 George 149
 James 4, 5, 10, 35
 John 5
 Norton 5
 Septimus 98
CLAYTON William 1, 3, 4
CLEAVER Jonathan 206
CLECKNER Frederick 49
CLEMENS John 184
 Thomas 80
CLEMENT John 177
CLEMENTS Gerhard 12
 Jacob 126

CLEMMINS William 56
CLEMSON James 32, 69, 100
 John 20
CLENDANIN Robert 69
CLENDENEN John 92
CLENDENIN Samuel 178
CLENDENNIN Samuel 246
CLENNAL William 200
CLERK James 242
CLEVER Jesse 109
 Peter 8
CLEVINGER Aaron 150
CLEYN Elmerhuysen 1
CLIFFORD Thomas 15, 16, 17, 21, 27, 129
CLIFFTON William 31
CLIFTON Robert 4, 6, 7
 Thomas 6
 William 44
CLINE Christian 219
 Jacob 63
CLINGAN William 41, 49, 51, 71, 75
CLINGEN William 32
CLINTON James 65, 78
CLOKEY Joseph 183, 218
CLOPPER Nicholas 114
CLOUD Joseph 189, 212, 221
CLOVER Philip 235
CLOWES John 1, 4
CLOYD David 33, 71, 77
CLUGAGE Thomas 208
CLUGGAGE George 49, 58, 64, 66
CLUNI James 64, 76
CLUNN John 189
 Joseph 114, 164
 Lt. Col. 141
CLURE William M. 34
CLYDE James 183
CLYMER Daniel 60, 67, 69, 75
 George 21, 39, 71, 72, 125, 128, 131, 191, 231
 Henry 121, 231
 William 180
COATES Isaac 45
 John R. 199
 Jonathan 18
 Lindsay 30, 73
 Maj. 41
 Moses 87

Samuel 27, 30, 79, 83, 89
William 32, 38, 39, 66, 92
COATS George 48
 John R. 124
 Lindsey 49
 Lt. Col. 101, 111
 Timothy S. 252
 William 59
COBB John 247
COBEAN Alexander 129, 140, 183, 195, 222
 Samuel 106
COBLE Michael 165, 245
COBOURN Thomas 119
COCHRAN James 70, 98, 184, 214, 224, 232, 236
 John 58, 176, 239
 Lt. Col. 111, 141
 Patrick 165, 238, 239
 Robert 138, 139
 Samuel 50, 54
 Thomas 136, 190
 William 206
COCHRANE James 214
 William 162
COCK Lacey 3
 Lansa 2
 Lasse 3, 4, 5
 Lawrence 4, 6
 Moens 3
 Otto Earnest 2
 Otto Ernest 2
 Otto Ernst 3
 Peter 2
 Pieter 2
COCKER Peter 155
COCKS Widow 75
CODERMAN Conrad 243
COE Robert 109
COFFMAN Andrew 11
 John 11
COFFY Robert 140
COFMAN Isaac 11
COLDEN Cadwallader 78
COLE Ezekiel 204
 Harmonis 104
 Jeremiah 236
 Joseph 215
 Mary 43, 236
 William 43, 186
COLEBROOKE George 17
COLEMAN George 225
 Henry 3

267

INDEX

Jacob 34
Jeremiah 185
Joseph 10
Robert 86, 128, 153, 183
William 195
COLEMERY John 158
COLFRODE Jacob 104
COLHOON John 38
Samuel 113
COLIER Jonathan 250
COLLARD John 127, 144
COLLBAUGH John 232
COLLEEN Nicholas 73
COLLIER John 2
Jonathan 197, 230
COLLIN Nicholas 79, 218
COLLINS Edward 23
James 51, 201, 212, 215, 244
Jane 85
John 25
Lewis 134
Lt. Col. 111, 142
Ralph 85
Stephen 26
Zaccheus 80, 171
COLLOM John 51
COLMAN John 170
COLP Michael 204
COLT Arnold 137, 146
Jabiz 117
Judah 104, 117, 214, 218
COLVIN Mathew S. 208
Matthew 235
Robert 206
COMELY Isaac 37
COMFORT Jacob 148
COMLEY Jonathan 59, 66
Joseph 66
Thomas 210
COMLY Joshua 118
COMRON Abraham 47
John 47
Mary 47
Rebecca 47
CON Robert 154
CONANT Samuel 230, 250
CONARD John 182
CONCHY James 36
CONDICT Lewis 218
CONDIT David 108
CONDY Jonathan W. 222
CONFER Peter 217

CONKLE John 177
CONKLIN John 121
CONLY James 205
CONNARD Edward 45
Henry 45
CONNEL Zachariah 203, 222
CONNELL Margaret 242
Zachariah 104, 242
CONNELLY Henry 171
John 142, 171, 176
William 102, 169, 214, 212
CONNER Hugh 159
James 203
Peter 228
CONNIGSMARK 3
CONNOR John 153
CONOR Patrick 155
CONOWAY Barbara 130
CONRAD Frederick 94
Henry 23
John 170, 207
CONYNGHAM David H. 89
David Hayfield 135
Redmond 16, 22, 207
COOB Joseph 14
COOK Abraham 164
Arthur 4, 5, 6
Carolina 191
Edward 32, 35, 36, 38, 39, 47, 71
Francis 7
George 175, 223
John 6, 186, 218
Joseph 225
Liddy 223
Mary 84, 219
Michael 162
Nathan 41
Peter 193, 223
Richard 26
Ziba 133
COOKE Alexander 107
Arthur 3, 6
Cha. 10
John 109
William 39, 120
COOKER John Peter 14
COOKS Zeba 148
COOKSON Thomas 15, 24
COOLBAUGH John 158, 172, 183
Lt. Col. 102

COOMB Ed. 33
Edward 34
COOMBE Thomas 19, 27
COOPE Samuel 184, 219
COOPER --- 131
Calvin 16
Daniel 11, 130
David 80
Jacob 16, 18, 20, 23, 47, 69, 72, 149
Jeremiah 45
John 49
Joseph 46, 229, 246
Marmaduke 44, 47
Mary 44
Robert 45
Samuel 30
William 11, 131
COPE Caleb 85
Thomas P. 242
COPELAND Caleb 12
Isaac 61, 68
COPLAN Jacob 191
COPPACK Barth. 5
COPPERTHWAITE Joseph 32
COPPICK Barth. 6
COPPOCK Bart. 6
Barth. 5, 7
CORBET James 180
CORBETT Roger 6, 7
CORBIT William 98
CORBLY John 74
CORBYN George 80
CORE Casper 27
COREY John 152
Levy 152
CORLE Jacob 167
Theobald 167
CORNELIUS 24
CORNELL Gilliam 30, 44
Wilhelmus 36
CORNPLANTER 96, 238
CORNWALLIS 134, 135
CORRYS Lt. Col. 101
CORSON Lott 238
CORTWRIGHT William Ennis 93
CORURIGHT Simon 189
CORYELL Lewis 183
Lewis S. 207, 210, 232
COSSART Francis 212
COSTILLOE James 150
COSYN Cornelius 212
COTTMAN Benjamin 72
Joseph 72

INDEX

COTTRINGER John 75
COUCHRIN John 117
COULTAS James 18, 22
COULTER Eli 76
  Elizabeth W. 240
  James 240
  Jane 240
  John 194
  Jonathan 104, 172
  Mary B. 240
  Nathaniel 145
  Thomas 26, 33, 36, 39
COURTER Harnam 71
COURTNEY William 232, 245
COURTRIGHT Cornelius 146
COUSIE John B. 72
COUSLAND Hains 159
COVALT Bethuel 189, 202
COVELL Matthew 137, 146
COWAN Catharine 119
  David 119
  John 69
COWDAN James 51, 57, 86
COWDEN John 125, 184, 185
COWEN C. 179
COWPERTHWAIT Joseph 109
COWPLAND Ann 44
  Caleb 14, 20, 44
  David 32, 91
  Grace 44
  Jonathan 44
  Mary 44
  Sarah 44
COX 155
  Charles 155
  Daniel W. 198, 218
  Gabriel 80
  George 92
  Hannah 48
  Isaac 27
  Issac 26
  James 89, 171
  John 38, 183
  Michael 108
  Paul 37, 137
  Thomas 15, 145
  William 154, 218
COXE Andrew 73
  John 62, 68
  John D. 80
  John R. 131
  Tench 79, 134
  William 22
CRABB William 94, 118, 128

CRAFFORD Joseph 230, 250
CRAFT Lawrence 55
CRAIG Alexander 125, 216
  Charles 233
  David 184, 242
  Isaac 74, 97
  James 23, 41, 89
  John 61, 68, 72, 88, 96, 104, 119, 157
  Lt. Col. 101, 111
  Robert 36, 37
  Thomas 15, 20, 120, 149, 157, 217
  Walter 234
  William 48, 69
CRAIGE Daniel 15
CRAIGHEAD Alexander 222
  Thomas 70
CRAIN George 49
CRAMER Andrew 173
  Frederick 167
  Jacob 234
CRAMMOND William 117
CRANE Fowler 237
  George 123
  Lt. Col. 102
CRATHO John 10
CRATO John 2
CRAUSE Mchael 35
CRAVEN Giles 37
  Gills 44
  Isaac 136
  Thomas 37
CRAWFORD --- 202
  Agnes 219, 227
  Alexander 121
  Andrew 37
  Charles 79
  Christopher 22, 70, 72
  Col. 99
  Edward 51, 114, 147
  George 55
  James 39, 63, 103, 177, 226
  John 103, 185, 208
  Joseph 95, 178, 200
  Josiah 50, 51, 57, 113
  Peter 227
  Robert 227
  Sampson 137
  Susanna 208

  Thomas Hartley 213
  William 43, 46, 174
CRAWLEY John 171
CRAYTON William 72
CREAIN Ambrose 49
CREAT Elizabeth 121
  John 121
CREE James 233
  John 216
CREESMAN George 14
CREICH Rudolph 192
CREIGH John 34, 35, 38, 200
CREMER Andrew 182
  John 240
CREPS Henry 100
CRESMAN John Nicholas 48
CRESS Andrew 106, 122
CRESSON Caleb 224
  Joshua 83
CRIDER George 95
CRISMAN Frederick 177
CRISPIN William 31
CRISTMAN Casper 166
CRISWELL William 174
CROAL Michael 23
CROCKER Thomas 167
CROGHAN George 16, 53, 54, 210
CROHAN George 156
CROLL Christian 213
  Michael 37, 66, 101
CROMELL Lt. Col. 101
CROMLEY Joseph 59
CROMWELL Lt. Col. 111, 142
  Thomas 179, 184, 218, 245
CROOKS Brig. Gen. 190
  Richard 234
  Robert 176
  Thomas 74
CROPT Casper 43
CROSBY John 10, 32
  Thomas 15, 16
CROSS John 22, 178, 189, 193
CROUCH James 124
CROUSE Henry 247
CROUSILLET Lowis 89
CROUT John 144
CROW --- 57
  David 234
  John 180
  Michael 175

INDEX

CROWLEY Miles 153
CROWSE Michael 176
CROWSER Michael 46
CROYDER John 12
CROYLE Thomas 54, 247
CROZART Francis 39
CROZER John 103
   Robert 193
   Samuel 193
CRUCKSHANK Joseph 79
CRUKSHANK Joseph 44
CRUM Elizabeth 212
   Isaac 95
   Peter 212
CRUMB John 163
CRUTHERS Anthony 76
CRYDER Michael 58
CULBERTSON Andrew 36
   Hugh 220, 247
   James 237
   John 58, 70, 148, 180, 248
   John B. 157
   Polly 248
   Robert 35, 110
   Samuel 35
   Thomas 169
CULIN George 18
   Samuel 18
   Swan 18, 103
CULLIN Daniel 18
CULNAN Charles 112
CULP David C. 209
CUMINGS Lt. Col. 111, 141
CUMMINGS Daniel 216
   James 223
   John 150
   Lt. Col. 102
   Thomas 15
   William 220
CUMMINS David 188
   Eliza L. 192
   Francis D. 192
   John 131
   William 243
CUMPSTON Thomas 109, 117
CUNNARD Henry 50, 57
CUNNINGHAM Allen 230, 250
   Allen F. 226
   David H. 42
   James 25, 38, 77, 203
   Jane 203
   John 114, 118
   John W. 183
   Lt. Col. 112, 142

   Margaret 58
   Patrick 140
   Redman 151, 185
   Robert 58, 83
   Samuel 39, 70, 114, 153, 204
   Widow 133
CUNRADS Cunrad 8
   John 8
   Mathias 8
CUREVEN George 119
CURFAS Margaret 25
CURFMAN Philip 104
CURRAN Brice 225
   Richard 58
   William 165
CURREE William 109
CURRENS Elizabeth 172
   Timothy 172
CURRIE Mary 50
   William 77
CURRIES 199
CURRIN William 173
CURRY Robert 49, 224
CURTIN Roland 122, 184, 223, 246
   Rowland 143
CURTIS John 1, 4, 5, 6, 7
   Rebecca 10
   Richard 6
   Thomas 199
CURVEN Joseph 117
CUSSEWAGO 56
CUSTARD Arnold 197
CUSTER Samuel 137
CUTHBERT John 45
   Thomas 32, 36, 38
CUTTS Nicholas 14

D'ARTOIS Peter Bonaventure 110
D'HAAS Jonathan 5
D'HAES J. 6
   Johannes 5
   John 3
D'HINNOYOSSA Alexander 2
D'HINOYOSSA Alex. 1
DAGER Jacob 118
   Peter 234
DAGGER Martin 63
DAILY John 225
   William 166

DALE James 231, 251
   Lt. Col. 142
   Samuel 56, 110, 138, 151, 185
   William 119, 143, 198
DALECKER Frederick 72
DALEY Dennis 175
   John 138
DALLAS Alexander James 86, 98
DANIELS Amasa 249
DANNEHOWER Christian 147
DANNELFELSER Jacob 79
DANSDELL George 142
DANSDILE George 243
DANSDILL George 168, 215, 233, 235
DARBIE John 1
DARBY John 4, 5, 6
DARK Samuel 7, 8
   William 4
DARKE Samuel 1, 4
DARLINGTON Amos 99
   Edward 97
   John 64, 75, 99
   Joseph 220
   Thomas 64, 75
   William 69, 183
DARR John 206
DARRAGH Robert 240, 245
DARRAH George 186
   George W. 243
   John 136, 180, 240
   Robert 178
DARRAUGH Robert 214
DARRECK Eve 217
   George 217
   John 217
   Rachel 217
DART Justus 218
DARVALL William 4, 5
DASHER Casper 188
DATWEILLER Hans 12
DAUFTON Edm: 3
DAUGHERTY Bernard 26
DAVENPORT John 191
   Robert 191
   Thomas 191, 211
DAVEY Hugh 65
DAVID Caleb 34
   John 113, 241
   Margaret 127
   Owen 127
   Zaccheus 32

INDEX

DAVIDSON David 136, 165
  George 70
  James 34
  John 36, 70
  Patrick 116
  Robert 70
  Samuel 33, 37, 38, 146
  William 178, 190
DAVIE Richard 3
DAVIES Gabriel 69
  Hezekiah 228
  John 29
  Walter 21
DAVIS --- 57
  Benjamin 24, 33, 49,
    59, 66, 71, 76, 143
  Caleb 33, 38, 103
  Daniel 110
  David 18
  Edward 123, 171
  Gab. 38
  George 80, 137, 162,
    217
  Henry 172
  Hugh 33, 240, 241, 245
  Isaac 226
  James 43, 77
  Jerman 100
  John 25, 33, 56, 77,
    96, 97, 109, 128, 138,
    186
  Joseph 41, 49, 51, 71,
    75
  Joshua 114, 180
  Llewellin 121
  Lt. Col. 111, 141,
  Patrick 153
  Roger 226
  Samuel 79, 137
  Thomas 16, 17, 59, 67,
    76, 157, 203, 226
  William 9, 234
DAVISON Jeremiah 165, 238
  John 58, 183
DAWES Abijah 87, 89, 94
  Rumford 87, 89, 117
DAWS George 252
DAWSON --- 57
  Abraham 140
  Benoni 55
  Daniel 109
  George 184, 214
  John 13
  Michael 63, 69
  Nicholas 55

Thomas 69
William 61, 68
DAY Luke 72
  Luther 191
  Nicholas 136, 184,
    202, 216
  Thomas 80
De BENEVILLE Daniel 114
De FRANQUEEN Elizabeth
    160
  Philip J. G. 160
De GRUCHY I. P. 223
  John P. 184, 201, 246
  John Philip 130, 139
De HAAS John Philip 26
De HAES Johanes 2
  Johannes 5
De HAPPART Elizabeth
    196
  Joseph St. Leger 196
De HAVEN Hugh 218
De KARNS John 193
De La MONTANYE Edward
    166
De LANCY Margaret 181
De NORMANDIE Abraham 16
  John Abraham 35
De TILLY Alexander 102
  Maria M. 102
De VRIES David
    Pietersen 1
DEAL Daniel 198
  Elizabeth 198
  Frederick 226
  Jacob 198
  Peter 177, 198
  Susanna 198
DEAB Alexander 80
  Benjamin 155
  Jacob 85
DEAN John 80, 128, 185
  Joseph 27, 36, 38,
    42, 51, 96, 128
  Mary 128
  Robert 95
  William 128, 243
  Zebulon 167
DEAN & PURVIANCE 96
DEANE Joseph 59, 60, 67
  William 61, 68
DEARDORF John 215
DEARMAN Joseph 74
DEARMOND Andrew S. 251
  James 251
  Michael 218, 227

Richard 251
DEARY Mark 152
DEBOAES John 4
DeCAMP Gideon 48
DECATUR Stephen 89, 139,
    147, 178, 238
DECKERT Capt. 138
  Philip 243
DEERINGER Henry 14
DEGRUCHY John P. 185
  John Philip 161
DEHART Cornelius 30
DeHAVEN Hugh 73
  Peter 31
  Peter 87
DeHUFF Capt. 118
  H. 38
  Henry 22, 129
DEIBER Michael 146
DEIBLER Mathias 174
  Matthias 90
DEIFENBACH John 189
DEIMER James 86
DEINIG Henry 14
DELANEY Margaret 170
  Sharp 32, 38, 79
DELANY Mary 239
  Sharp 31, 78
DELAPLAINE Nehemiah 94
DELAVALL John 6
DEMET Richard 169
DEMORAST David 212
DEMUTH John 250
DEMUTT Richard 202
DENCKE Jeremiah 74
DENEY William 32
DENIG George 243
DENISON John 194
DENISTON John 243
DENLOP James 122
DENMAN A. 199
DENNIS James 172, 181
  John 125
DENNISON George 184
  John 163, 167, 180
DENNISON Nathan 46
DENNISSON John 227
DENNISTON John 184, 201,
    215, 220
  Lt. Col. 141
  Samuel 202
  William 202
DENNY, David 37, 70, 119
  Ebenezer 240
  Richard 241

271

INDEX

DENTLER Jacob 184, 185, 246
DEPUE Benjamin 38
  Nicholas 38
DEPUI Nicholas 26, 58, 63, 66
  Samuel 26
DEREBACHER Jacob 119
DERIE George 79
DERING Frederick 233
DERMOND Richard 49
DERR Lewis 96
DERRINGER Henry 33
DERSHEIMER Andrew 182
DESHLER Adam 85
  David 14, 35, 37, 38, 39, 40, 50, 71
DESHLOR David 23
DESTLER Lt. Col. 141
DETRICH Jacob 204
DETTENBURN Ludowick 14
DETTERMER Hartman 14
DETWILLER John 211
DEVOIR Jacobus 43
  John 43
DEVOSS John 134
  Joseph 134
DEWEES Daniel 183
  David 107
  Mary 121
  Thomas 122
  William 29, 35, 37, 76
  William P. 170, 175, 224
DEWET Morgan 3
DEWIT Paul 155
DEWITT Jacob 204
  Simeon 65, 78
DIARYHOGON Christian 53
DIBLER John 104
DICK Alexander 113
  Catharine 113
  Nicholas 127
DICKENSON Philemon 89
DICKERSON Joshua 206, 234
DICKERT Jacob 118
DICKESON Joseph 173
DICKEY David 58, 246
  John 240
  Robert 128
  Samuel 192
  Thomas 58
  William 58
DICKINS John 80

DICKINSON Edward 71
  John 31, 32, 45
  Jonathan 7
  Samuel 231
DICKSON James 38, 206
  John 206
  Robert 112
  Samuel 58, 66
  William 112, 148, 191, 241
DICKY David 205
DIEHL Lt. Col. 101
DIEMER James 75, 94
  John 13
DIEVELY Michael 206
DIFFEDERFER Michael 27
DIFFENDEFFER Philip 104
DIFFENDERFER Philip 95, 123, 132
DIHL Alexander 13
DILBECK Isaac 8
  Jacobus 8
DILL Caleb 146
  Elizabeth 146
  Henry 192
  James 33, 35, 37, 146
  John 146
  Mary 240
  Mathew 240
  Matthew 33
  Priscilla 146
  Thomas 146
DILLON Abraham 202
DILLWYN George 21
DILWORTH Charles 78, 87
  George 129
  James 4
DILWYN William 80
DIMM Peter 232
DIMMICK Dan 172
  Daniel 183, 189, 193
  Isaac 172, 206, 209
DIMOCK David 204
  Warren 234
DIMSEY Richard 108
DING John I. 209
DINGMAN Daniel W. 183
  Lt. Col. 111, 141
DITMAN Henry 219
  John 219
DITTMAN Henry 240
DITWEILER Christian 248
DIVINE John 223

DIX Benjamin 251
  Elijah 95, 251
DIXEY John 171
DIXON --- 143
  James 136, 145, 157, 213
  John 235
  William 239
DOANE Aaron 45
  Abraham 45
  Joseph 45
  Levi 45
  Mahlon 45
DOBBIN Alexander 104, 129
  Mathew 189
DOBBINS Alexander 45
  Daniel 162
DOBSON Thomas 89, 91, 109, 125
  William 92, 143
DOCKEY Anthony 140
DOCMINIQUE P. 10
DODD Thaddeus 55, 74
DODDS William 195
DODGE Levi 202
DODRIDGE Jacob 160
DOEBLER Abraham 131, 188, 199
DOEDEN John 8
DOERING Francis 207
DONALD Moses 65
DONALDSON Arthur 31
  James 224
  John 6, 7, 8, 50, 51, 72, 86, 89
  Joseph 39, 182
  Lt. Col. 142
  Robert 158
  William 191
  William T. 146
DONALY Hugh 233
DONATT George 13
DONEDER Michael 11
DONGAN Thomas 52
DONINGER Adam 186
DONNALDSON Hugh 22
  William T. 109
DONNEHUE George 252
DONNEL Henry 138, 151
  Samuel 223
DONNELL John 26
DONNELLY Eliza 240
DOOGALL James 125
DORLAND George 157

INDEX

DORLEANS Lewis 156
DORLEY John 37
DORNEY Peter 183
DORRACH Henry 45
DORRANCE Benjamin 160, 166, 189, 198, 245
DORSEY Benedict 29
  John 131, 137, 151, 171
  Maria 199
  Nathan 77
  William C. 203
DOTTERER Bernhard 14
  Conrath 14
  George Philip 14
  Michael 14
DOTTS Henry 60
  Henry 67
DOTY Ezra 110, 136, 184
  Nathaniel 249
  Zebulon 202
DOUGAL --- 57
  James 221
  James S. 245
DOUGHERTY Barnard 36
  Bernard 31, 33, 40, 45
  Daniel 165, 186
  Eve 211
  Henry 41, 55, 132, 195
  James 47
  John 223, 234
  Patrick 211
DOUGHTY James 46, 80
DOUGLAS George 31, 33
  John 252
DOUGLASS Ephraim 118
  George 31, 42, 98, 136
  John 69, 206, 243
  Thomas 69
DOUGLERTY John 227
DOVER Andrew 46
DOWDLE Michael 74
DOWERS John 79
DOWLAN Paul 171
DOWMAN John 65
DOWNARD James 181
DOWNEY John 183
DOWNING Jacob 89, 178, 190
  William 207
DOWNS John 177
DOWNY John 146
DOWTHAT Nathan 174
DOYLE Barnabas 223
  John 149
DOZ Andrew 46, 73

DRAFTGATE Richard 10
DRAIS Daniel 50
DRAKE Ebenezer 211
DRAPER Alexander 4
  John 171
  John 247
DRASON Matthew 48
DREHL Michael 182
DREIBILBIS George 193
DREISBACH John 184, 186, 251
  Simon 39
DRENNON Armstrong 162
DRESHBACH Siman 39
DRESHER Philip 139
DRIESBOUGH John 246
DRIESTLE John 12
DRINKER Henry 21, 24, 26, 28, 44, 55, 57, 83, 84, 85, 92, 113, 120
  Henry W. 242
  John 62, 69, 83, 92
  Joseph D. 119
  William 190
DRIVER Gaspar 137
DROER George 189
DRUM Jacob 232
  Lt. Col. 111, 141
  Philip 207
  Simon 180
DRURY Michael 151
Du BOIS Abraham 77
DUANE Lt. Col. 141
  William 177
DUBOIS Abraham 28, 37, 41, 164
  Daniel 28
  Isaac 28
  Menna 121
  Philip 28
  Solomon 28
DUBRE Jacob 13
DUCHE Andrew 61, 68
  Anthony 60, 67
  Esther 107
  Jacob 16, 35, 60, 67, 107
  Sophia 107
DUCHEE Jacob 21
DUCHMAN Jacob 183
DUCKET Thomas 4
DUCKETT Thomas 5, 6
DUFFEY James 225
DUFFIELD Benjamin 77
  Ed. 16

  Edward 21, 27, 50, 97, 202
  George 137
  Jacob 19, 72, 124
  John 51
  Samuel 77
  William 39, 140
DUFFIN George 87
DUFFY James 178
DUGUID John 46
DULL Christian 118, 126
  Christopher 175
DUN --- 63
DUNANT Edward 89
DUNCAN David 74
  James 122, 128, 132, 138, 183, 184, 186, 194, 246
  John 140, 222
  Margaret 174
  Robert 174
  Stephen 32, 45, 76
  Thomas 183, 243
  William 114, 118
DUNDAS Thomas 33, 86, 94
DUNDASS Thomas 75
DUNGAN Benjamin 73
  Mahlon 160
  Thomas 36, 37, 52
DUNHAM Assa 224
DUNLAP Andrew 123, 128, 138
  James 33, 100, 107
  John 59, 66, 67, 89, 124, 139, 142, 147, 214
  Joseph 244
  Robina 124
  William 20
DUNLOP Andrew 147, 180
  James 103, 131
  John 122, 131, 143
DUNN Alexander 166
  Gideon 197
  Henry 47
  Thomas 157
  William 61, 68
DUNNAN John 197
DUNNING J. 236
  John 160
  Mary 28
  Robert 29
DUNTON William 93
DUNWOODY James 70
DUPLESSIS Peter Le Barbier 152

INDEX

DUPNI Ncholas 33
DUPONT Francis Clery 80
  Victor 249
DUPUE Nicholas 39
DUPUI Benjamin 33
  Nicholas 40
DUPUY Nicholas 34
DURBUROW John 10
DURVALL William 5
DUTHILL & WACHSMUTH 89
DUTILH Stephen 119
DUTTON Jonathan 119
DYE Daniel 209
DYER Hannah 171, 199
  Thomas 35, 36, 137
  William 5, 8
DYLANDER Joannes 14
DYMOCK Tobias 8

EAGAN John 225
EAGEN James 125
  David 226
EAKERD Valentine 38
EAKMAN Eliab 177
EALER Peter 95
EARLE James 171
EARLY --- 143
  Jacob 186
  John 186
  William 186
EARNEST Christopher 64, 76
EASTBURN -- 61, 68
  Benjamin 154
EASTBURNE Benjamin 54
  Joseph 41
EASTERLINE John 179
  Magdalena 179
EASTERLY George 153
EASTON James 32, 39
  Jonathan 80
EATON Johnson 214
EBERHART John 228
  Joseph 13
  Michael 13
EBERLE Henry 50
EBERLIEN John 149
EBERT Martin 250
ECARD George 104
ECHERT Daniel 229
ECHFELDT Adam 212
ECK Joseph 75
ECKARD Peter 146
ECKART George 58, 66
  Jacob 38

  Nicholas 123
  Valentine 35, 37, 39
  William 207
ECKERT Daniel 244
  John 75
ECKFELT Adam 145, 247
ECKHART Valentine 93
ECKLESWICH Thomas 8
ECKLEY John 5
ECKMAN Henry 95
ECKSTEIN Johannes 12
ECKSTINE Leonard 49
  Mary 49
EDDY Daniel 55
  George 79, 89, 95
  James 19
  Thomas 79
EDGAR David 166
  James 38, 39, 42, 74, 107
  John 58, 65, 138, 140
  Joseph 157
EDGE Jacob 20
EDIE John 99, 161
  Lt. Col. 101
  Samuel 33
EDINGTON Widow 90, 91
EDMISTON Samuel 135, 232
EDMOND Robert 7
EDMONDS Aaron 79
  Deborah 28
  Roger 28
  William 31
EDMONSTONE Charles 55
EDWARDS Alexander 32
  Enoch 38, 50, 73
  Ezekiel 30
  Thomas 20, 35, 37, 69
EDWIN David 171
EGE George 75, 123, 124
  Michael 180
EGERSDORF John 65
EHLER Daniel 85
EHRHART Thomas 108
EHRMAN Casper 85
EICHBAUM William 161
EICHELBERGER --- 182
  Frederick 182, 183, 206
  Jacob 121, 140, 147, 193, 250
  Leonard 108
  Martin 33

EICHHOLTZ Leonard 123, 138
EICHOLTZ George 118
  Jacob 171
  Leonard 132, 183
EIGHELBERGER Frederick 14
EIGSTER John 14
EISENHARD Andrew 219
  George 219
  Jacob 219
  John 219
EISENHUTH George 201
ELALAPIS 52
ELBERSCHIDT Frederick 13
ELDER Abraham 107
  David 36
  Jacob 185
  John 50, 72, 114, 146
  Joshua 27, 50, 51, 57, 86, 155
  Lt. Col. 111
  Robert 36, 238
  Samuel 97
  Widow 148
ELFRETH Jeremiah 18, 19
ELFRITH --- 48
ELGAR Joseph 88
ELICK George 97
ELIENST Daniel 135
ELIOT John 94
ELLES Richard 200
ELLET Charles 193
ELLICK John 62, 68
ELLICOT Andrew 65, 78, 112
ELLICOTT Benjamin 178, 190
ELLIOT Andrew 62, 68
  Benjamin 33, 36, 64, 80, 91
  Daniel 38, 49
  Jese Duncan 238
  John 107, 188, 196, 211
  Robert 32
  Widow 58, 63
  William 33, 38, 93
ELLIOTT Andrew 157
  Barbara 247
  Benjamin 34, 39
  Christopher 75
  Jesse Duncan 190
  John 182, 192
  Lt. Col. 101
  Nathaniel 37
  Robert 40, 54

INDEX

Samuel 69
Widow 66
William 33, 34, 104, 113, 229, 247
ELLIS Cadwalader 28
  Mercy 205
  Rowland 8, 9
  William 120, 130, 144, 145, 205
ELLISTON Thomas 89
ELLMAKER Isaac 183
  Jacob C. 173
  Leonhart 14
  Peter 97
ELMAKER Leonard 100
ELMENDORFF Lucas 202
ELMERHUYSEN Herr 2
ELROD Lt. Col. 142
ELVES Henry 19
ELWES Henry 23
ELY Esther 239
  George 239
  Hugh 183, 185
  Isaac 135
  John 80, 171
  Samuel 184
  William 171
EMBREE Effingham 120
EMERSON William 45
EMERY John 188
  Lewis 156
EMIG Charles 183
EMLEN George 16, 28
  Joshua 143
EMLIN George 89
  James 189
  Joshua 162
EMMETT William 4
EMMINGER Andrew 219
EMPSON Cornelius 4, 6, 7
EMRICH Baltes 145
  George 79
EMRICK Andrew 107
  Michael 143
END Johannes Dewalt 12
ENDREAS Peter 12
ENGELL Jacob 8
  Paul 8
ENGHERT Philip 14
ENGLAND Job 246
  Joseph 6, 7
  Thomas 48
ENGLE Henry 91
  Jacob 124
  James 220

Joseph 201, 215, 221
Levi 124
Mary 220
Paul 50, 124
ENGLISH David 63
  James 223, 227
  Rebecca 47
ENNES Benjamin 165
  Magdalena 165
ENNIS Alexander 238
ENOCH David 63
ENOCHS Joseph 236
  Thomas 236
ENSLOW George 247
ENSMINGER Lt. Col. 101, 111, 141
  Samuel 137, 172
ENTRICKEN James 123
  Lt. Col. 111, 142
ENTZMINGER Peter 13
EOMUS 52
EPLER Catharine 209
  John 209
  Lt. Col. 111, 141
ERB Casper 207
  Jacob 38
  John 114
ERINGHAUS Adolph 193
ERISHMAN Melcor 11
ERISMAN Jacob 172
ERNEST John 188
ERNST --- 228
  Christopher 93, 221
  Jacob 221
  John 113, 146, 221, 228, 236
  William G. 199
ERRINGER Catharine 107
  Frederick 107, 159
  Jacob 107
ERWIN Archibald 36
  George 234
  Henry 188
  Lt. Col. 101
  Matthew 180
  Morris 35
  Robert 119, 123
  Samuel 32, 33, 51
  William 211, 218
ESHELMAN John 177
ESKES Peter 110
ESLING Nicholas 110
  Paul 75

ESPY Daniel 32
  David 36, 37, 38, 39, 45
  Simon 190
  William 144
ESSEPENAICK 52
ESSEPENAIKE 52
ESSEXAMARTHAKE 52
ESTEP Ephraim 235
  Ephriam 234
  James 203
ETSHBERGER Jacob 14
ETTWEIN John 74
EUAN David 132
EVAN Evan 121
  Jesse 132
EVANS 57, 192
  Abel 30, 31
  Amos 69, 193
  Baner 133
  Benjamin 61, 68
  Cadwalader 133
  Cadwallader 85, 118, 121, 202, 218, 231, 246
  Daniel 134
  David 245
  Edward 118
  Elisha 94
  Evan 32, 38, 103
  Evan Rice 251
  Francis 217
  George 184, 218, 240
  Griffith 119
  James 69, 146, 214
  Jane 251
  Jenkin 37, 47
  Jesse 132, 230, 250
  Joel 26, 27, 59, 62, 67, 68
  John 47, 48, 69, 79, 109, 118, 123, 132
  John C. 176
  John J. 126, 136
  Jonathan 15, 16, 21, 23
  Joshua 165, 183
  Lewis 192, 225
  Margaret 44
  Mary 44
  Mathias 240, 252
  Nathan 69, 110
  Oliver 73, 178
  Owen 146
  Peter 32, 35, 47
  Rachel 192
  Robert 79

275

INDEX

Rowland 32
Samuel 192, 251
Sarah 135
Thomas 33, 47
William 34, 38, 61, 68
EVE John 60, 67, 102
　Oswald 19
　Oswell 22, 26, 60, 62, 67, 68
EVERHART John 226
EVERLY Anna Maria 135
EVERSOLL Peter 103
EVES Joseph 169
　Joseph Benet 122
EVIG John 114
EVY George 106
EWALT John 164, 183, 227, 248
　Lt. Col. 111, 141
　Samuel 55, 117, 128
EWART Archibald 171
　John 203
　Ralph 171
EWING James 45
　Jasper 94
　John 50, 55, 155, 185
　Nathaniel 246
　Samuel 197
　Thomas 89
EYCHELBERGER Martin 32
EYERLY Jacob 93, 135
EYRE Ann L. 199
　Manuel 136
　Preston 183
EYRES Emanuel 37
EYSTER Jacob 183

FAATZ Christopher 161
FACKENTHAL Michael 215
FAGAN Lawrence 62, 68
FAHNESTOCK George 180
　Jacob 195
　Obed 136, 179, 182, 246
　Samuel 179
FAIL Philip 118
FAIRLAMB John 21
　Nicholas 31
　Samuel 38
FAIRLAMBE Nicholas 32
FAIRMAN Francis 226
　Gideon 247
　Thomas 3
FALCONAR Lester 19
FALCONER Nathaniel 39, 41, 42, 50, 51, 91

FALKNER Nathan 249
FANDERALL Adam 148
FANGHAUSER Peter 244
FANNEN Anthony 171
FARIES Owen 60, 67
　William 27
FARMER Edward 9
　Lewis 43, 72
　Robert A. 96
FARRELLY Patrick 214
FARRINBORROUGH Thomas 3
FAULKNER Lt. Col. 101, 111
　William 41
FAUST John 161
FAY Thomas 15
FEAGAN Lawrence 40
FEAGLY Abraham 57
FEARON John 122
FEATHER Peter 93
FEBIGER Christian 120, 147
　Christian Carson 147
　Elizabeth 120
FEE Lt. Col. 101, 111
FEHRER Joseph 194
FEIDT George 165
FEIGLE John 80
FELFE John 24
FELL Jesse 137, 191
　Jonathan 249
FELLOWS Abel 131
　Abiel 184, 192
FELT Adam 106
FELTY Catharine 195
　Henry 252
　John 195
　Nancy 252
FENSTERMACHER Daniel 217
　William 217
FERGUSON David 187
　Ebenezer 109, 137
　Elizabeth 42, 163
　Henry Hugh 42
　Hugh 156
　James 57
　Lt. Col. 141
　Thomas 122
　William 163
FERIE John 11
FERMAN William 215
FERN Joshua 6
FERNE Joshua 4

FERREE Daniel 183
　Isaac 126, 131
　Joseph 50
　Richard 38
　Thomas 111
　William 123, 132
FERRIE John 32
FERRIS John 184
FERTICH John 79
FERTZ Abraham 212
FETTER Casper 59, 66
FETTERMAN James 204
FEW Ann 23
FICKES Abraham 212
　John 105
FIDLER John 185
FIELD John 28, 79, 83, 89, 222
　Nathan 79, 89
　Nehemiah 7, 8
　Robert 19
FIELDING Robert 171
FIELDS Daniel 173
　David 215
　Dorcas 173
　Forster 173
　Freeborn 173
　John 173
　Lovia 173
　Lovina 173
　Rachel 173
　Samuel 173
　Sarah 173
　Stephen 173
　William 173
FIERE Philip 12
FILBERT Peter 62, 68, 99, 105, 136
FILERAPPOMOND 52
FILSON John 114
FINCHER Francis 4, 61, 68
FINDLAY James 145
　John 241
　Lt. Col. 111
　Samuel 243
　William 225
FINDLEY Andrew 188
　John 114, 119, 150, 237
　Lt. Col. 141
　William 107, 136
FINK Sebastian 14
FINLAY Samuel 57
FINLEY Andrew 175
　David 84
　James 71

INDEX

Joseph 64
Samuel 75
FINNEY John L. 196
  Robert 73
  Samuel 8
FIRST Adam 229, 245
FISH Abraham 144
  Jabez 141
FISHBOURN Ralph 8
  William 9, 10, 12, 13
FISHBURN Peter 146
FISHER -- 14
  Adam 247
  Catharine 168
  Charles F. 199
  Coleman 223
  George 94, 173, 183,
    188, 211
  Henry 78, 140, 180, 194
  Herman 14
  James C. 89, 98, 105,
    114, 120
  John 14, 140, 216, 233
  Joseph 5
  Joshua 40
  Mary 14
  Miers 80, 89, 107
  Peter 138
  S. Rhoads 223
  Samuel 28, 89, 91
  Samuel W. 120, 130, 223
  Sarah W. 223
  Thomas 7, 27, 80, 83
  William 8, 16, 17, 19,
    21, 26, 28, 48, 182
FISSELL Michael 105
FITCH John 72
FITZGERALD Thomas 79, 100
FITZGERRALD Robert 80
FITZPATRICK Daniel 148
FITZRANDOLPH Robert 55
FITZSIMMONS Thomas 43,
  71, 75
FITZSIMONS Thomas 88, 89,
  119, 139
FITZWATER Georege 10
  Thomas 1, 4, 5, 6
FIZIMMONS Thomas 130
FLACHER John 116
FLAM Matthias 99
FLANAGAN James 74
FLAUGHERTY 84
FLEESON Plunket 16, 36,
  46, 60, 67
FLEICHER John 188

FLEMING Elizabeth 154
  James 155, 172
  John 87, 130, 145
  Rebecca 172
  Richard 154
  William 189
FLEMMING -- 202
  Andrew 202
  Benjamin 231, 251
  John 39
  William 57
FLENNIKEN Elias 174
  James 174
FLETCHER --- 191
  Benjamin 3, 6
  Elizabeth 36
  Jacob 146
  John 128, 163, 180,
    184, 243
FLINN William 203
FLINTHAM John 130
  William 130, 215
FLORA Abraham 187
  Joseph 187
FLOREY John 244
FLOWER Enoch 16, 18,
    19, 43
  Richard 221
FLOWERS Zephon 234
FOBES John 225
FOERING Frederick 182,
    212
FOGLE John 181, 183
FOLKNER George 80
FOLTZ Jacob 242
  Polly 242
FOLWEILER Ferdinand 183
FOOKS Paul 41
FOOLWOOD Charles 197
FOOSSELMAN Jacob 229,
    244
FORBES James 39
  William 214
FORD Hugh 214
  Philip 10, 52
  Simon 132
  Standish 88
FORDNEY Caspar 70
FORE David 184
  Henry 55
  Jacob 150
FOREE Richard 37
FOREMAN Charles 35, 36,
    109
FOREPAUCH Lt. Col. 111

FOREPAUGH George 45
FORESMAN Samuel 236
FOREST Walter 7
FORGEMAN Robert 33
FORGESON David 232
FORGY Thomas 158
FORMAN George 6
FORNEY George 200
FORREST Thomas 79, 145
  William 89
FORREY John 126
FORRY John 140
FORSTER James 246
  John 8, 159, 182, 183
  Lovina 173
  Lt. Col. 101, 112, 142
  Thomas 117, 173, 184,
    218, 238
  William 157, 211, 221
  William B. 203
FORSYTH Isaac 171
FORTMAN Margaret 205
FORWARD Walter 240
FOSTER Alexander 89
  Alexander W. 214
  Benjamin 80
  James 98
  John 50, 138, 151
  Strickland 97, 114
  Thomas 232
  William 214
FOULKE Andrew 30
  Charles 30
  John 77, 79
  Theophilus 32, 37
  William 20
FOULKS James 154
  Judah 155
FOUR Jacob 108, 110
FOUST Henry 155
  Philip 155
FOUTS Christian 35
  Jacob 37
FOUTZ --- 34, 58
  James 181
  Lt. Col. 101
FOWLER Alexander 71, 74
  David 105, 119
  George 104, 132, 170
  Robert 154
FOX Edward 51, 86
  George 79, 186
  Henry 203
  Henry Justus 118
  Jacob 213

277

INDEX

James 5, 6, 7
John 60, 67, 83, 168, 183
Joseph 15, 17, 18, 20, 23, 25, 26, 41, 62, 68
Joseph M. 224, 246
Justus 50
Michael 145, 168, 249
Philip 23
Regina 118
Samuel 168
Samuel M. 79, 89, 131, 186
Samuel Mickle 87
William 118
FOY Eleanor 204
John 204
FRAILEY Lt. Col. 101, 111
Peter 124, 172, 235
Philip 245
FRAMPTON William 4, 5
FRANCIS Col. 154
Dorothy William 208
Fench 86
John 69, 178
Tench 42, 86
Thomas W. 208
Thomas William 208
Thomas Willing 186
FRANCIS & RELFE 19, 22
FRANCISCUS Christopher 12
FRANKLIN Benjamin 17, 31, 32, 37, 39, 79, 80, 85
John 71, 131, 174
Lt. Col. 101
Peter 158
Temple 78
Thomas 69
William 65
William T. 79
FRANKS David 16, 22, 54
Isaac 98
Lt. Col. 101
Samuel D. 184
FRANTZ Elizabeth 167
Jacob 203, 217
FRANZONIA John 171
FRASER Persifier 36
FRASHER Ludwig 105
FRAZER John 160
Paul 94
Persifor 47
FRAZIER --- 155
Charles 204
David 192

John 89
Nalbro 89
Persifer 37
FREAME Margaret 13
Thomas 13, 154
FREDERICK John 11, 94, 126, 167
Philip 138
FREE Lt. Col. 142
FREEH Jacob 14
FREEHRER Joseph 234
FREELAND William 5, 6
FREEMAN Brewster 232
David 162
John 122
Joseph 173
Maurice 145
Richard 109, 135
Tacy 173
William 6
FREEMEN Randolph 133
FREES Jacob 88
FREIDLY Ulrich 175
FRELICH Jacob 50
FRENCH James 153
Robert 8
FRESTER George 238
FRETE John 95
FREY George 64, 78
Jacob 14
John 65
FRICK John 182
FRICKER Peter 213, 228
FRIE Jacob 90
FRIED Johannes 12
Paul 12
FRIEDLEY Peter 59, 66
FRIEDMAN Adam 155
FRIEDT William 180
FRITCHER William 4
FRITCHMAN Barbara 152
John 152
FRITZ Jacob 202
John 43
FROMBERGER John 98, 105, 142, 144
FROST --- 225
FRUIT John 169
FRY Conrad 229, 245
Daniel 116
George 84, 118
Jacob 205
John 50, 87, 88, 89, 94

Joseph 75, 83, 89, 183, 212
FUCKESS Christopher 155
FULLER Benjamin 36, 49, 89
Edward 150
Orange 231, 251
FULLERTON Alexander 130, 139
David 199, 235
George 176
James 211
FULLMER Jacob 207
FULTON Alexander 73
David 230, 237, 250
Henry 167
James 70
John 207
Robert 170
FULTZ Frederick 125
FULWOOD Charles 234, 243
FUNK Adam 110, 133
Christopher 12
Elijah 188
George 166
Henry 11, 58, 193
Jacob 11, 193, 207
John 11, 94, 97, 129, 193, 202, 245
Ralph 193
FUNSTON --- 57
Jesse 55
John 169
FURMAN Moore 23, 27, 63
William 160
FURRY Jacob 57
FURST Maurice 171
FURY John 246
FUSS Valentine 79
FUTCHER William 1

GABLE Henry 126
Philip 133
GABRIEL George 24
GADDIS Samuel 38
GAIN Thomas 80
GALAR Adam 13
GALBRAITH Andrew 71
Bartram 38, 143
George 143
Robert 34, 71, 83
GALBREATH --- 142
Bartram 39, 55
James 20, 21
John 24

INDEX

Robert 74
GALBUCK Frederick 125
GALE Anthony 215
GALLAGHER James 237
  John 247
  Lydia 172
  Thomas 172, 220
  William 95
GALLAHER Hugh 185
  James 155
  Thomas 153
GALLAUDET Peter W. 134
GALLESPIE John 143
GALLETTE Jacob 14
GALLITZEN Augustine
  Demetrius 158
GALLITZEN Demetrius
  Augusin 243
GALLOWAY --- 53
  Archibald 164
  John 55, 121, 140
  Joseph 16, 17, 20, 23,
    24, 26, 35, 36, 41,
    60, 61, 67, 68, 69,
    84, 103, 151
GALLUP Nathaniel C. 234
GALT Nathaniel 79
GAMBER Jacob 225
GAMBLE John 163, 184
GAMBYS George 205
GANGEWERE Solomon 200
GANGWER --- 233
GANTZ --- 133
  George 164
GARANGER Lewis 108
GARBER --- 38
GARDINER Elizabeth 190
  George 49
  John 190
  Joseph 38
  Mary 190
  Richard 48, 190
  Sarah 48
GARDNER Hugh 45
  John 211, 233
  Joseph 33, 34
  Philip 37
  William 92
GAREY John 209
GARIS Frederick 217
GARLAND George 223
GARRET Jonathan 28
  Lawrence 18
GARRETSON Cornelius 108,
  182

John 108
  Samuel 108, 161
GARRIGUES Abraham M.
  109
  Edward 109
  Jacob 39
  Samuel 62, 68, 109
  William 109
GARRISON Charles 36
GARTMAN Abraham 199
GARTNER Martin 99
GARVER John 114
GARWOOD Joseph 116
GASKILL Charles C. 232
GASSELL Hubbard 12
GAST Nicholas 122
GATE Henry 105
GATEAU Nicholas 10
GATTIS Samuel 34
GAUBLE Philip 134
GAUFF Diter 13
GAULT Willliam 126
GAUSTARAX 53
GAUT Mathew 144
GAW Catharine 121
  Chambers 121
  Gilbert 109
  Mary 121
GAY Peter 180
  Thomas 227
GAYLORD Charles E. 104
  Justus 108
GAZARD --- 56
GAZZAM William 117
GEAR Balzar 33
GEARHART Jacob 169
  John 228
GEBHART George 225
  John 232
GEDDIS James 186
  Joseph 227, 244
  William 41
GEE Joshua 54
GEER Levi 202
GEESE Charistian 183
GEHR Joseph 148
  Lt. Col. 101
  Philip 64
  Samuel L. 205
GEIGER Elijah 201
  Jacob 59, 66, 147,
    227, 252
  Paul 201
GEISBERTS Andreas 14
GEISELMAN Michael 161

GEISINGER Jacob 212
GELBAUGH Frederick 122
GELDBACH Johannes 14
GEMELIN Mathias 12
GEMMIL John 121, 209
  Robert 183
  Zachariah 209
GEORGE -- 59
  John 159
  Thomas 154
GEPHART John 112
GERARD Stephen 128
GERHART John 39, 97, 242
GERICH Hans Martin 12
GERMAN Henry 205
  John 231
  John 251
GERNON Richard 114, 119,
  135, 137
GEROWS Gilbert A. 230
  Gilbert A. 250
GETTIG Ann Dorothy 210
  Lt. 210
GETTIS John 212
  Samuel 58, 66
GETTY Lt. Col. 111
GETTYS James 140, 183,
  195
GETZ John 70
GEYER Andrew 79
  Casper 55
  John 193
GEYSELMAN Michael 182
GHEAR Jacob 204
GHEER Balser 42
GHETTYPENEEMAN 52
GIBBONS Jacob 94
  James 27, 76, 179
  James M. 97
  John H. 77
  Joseph 79, 183
  William 80, 92
GIBBS Edward 7
  Josiah W. 89
  W. 89
GIBSON -- 230, 248
  Ann 219
  David 18, 19, 23, 149
  Francis 200
  James 104, 110, 117,
    125, 136, 138, 159,
    171, 231
  John 21, 23, 27, 28,
    60, 67, 71, 74, 118,
    130, 185, 201, 207

INDEX

Levi 215
Nathan 50
GIDDINGS Cyril 191
GIDEON Cyril 216
GIEGHY George 181
GIESY Valentine 225
GIGGEN John 40
GIFFIN Lt. Col. 111, 141
GIFFS Edward 7
GIFT Catharine 216
GILBAUGH Frederick 130
GILBERT Andrew 193
  Bernard 222
  Bernhart 183
  Henry 100, 103
  John 181
  Margaret 96
  Thomas 21
  William 96
GILCHRIST John 118
GILCRIST John 50
GILL Elizabeth 175
  John 37, 131, 162
  Peter 235
  Richard 235
  Samuel 235
  William 169
GILLAND Lt. Col. 101
  Philip 180, 243
GILLESPIE John 123, 163
  Neal 118
  Neil 180
GILLIARD John 27
GILLILAND James 222
  Lt. Col. 112, 142
  William 106, 160, 212
GILLINGHAM Elizabeth 90
  Joseph 90
GILMAN Adolph 63, 69
GILMORE James 207
  John 128, 184, 240, 241
  Moses 114, 128
  Robert 178
GILPIN Edward 249
  Henry 124
  John 171
  John B. 97
  John Bernard 72, 107
  Joshua 80, 89, 117, 171
GILVEX Frederick 121
GIRARD Stephen 89, 118, 194
GIRTY -- 55
GISH Jacob 183, 187
GITHEN Thomas 80

GITLING David 98
GITT Jacob 195
GIVIN Patrick 204
GLANCEY Jesse 56
GLASKOW Ann 144
  Jennet 144
  Margaret 144
  Mary 144
  Rachel 144
  Samuel 144
GLASS Jacob 188
GLASSGOWE 133
GLASSNER Peter 160
GLEIM Charles 183
  Christian 225
  Philip 172
GLEN --- 225
  James 48
  John 98
GLENDY William 161
GLENN Gabriel 209
  Robert 160
GLENTWORTH George 46, 77
  James 65
  Plunket F. 147
GLONINGER Peter 183, 195, 246
  Philip 199
GLOVER John 4
GLUNN Lt. Col. 111
GOBLE Ebenezar 162
GOBLIN Charles 62, 68
GOBRECH Christian 171
GODDARD Mary 160
  William 30
GODFREY Jane 227, 247
  William 227
  William E. 247
GODFROY Maxmillion 171
GODWIN Edward 183, 199
GODYN Samuel 1
GOHMAN Michael 11
GOLTSHALK Peter 98
GONDY Christian 14
GONTER Peter 118
GOOD George 14
  Henry 162
  John 162
  Joseph 227
  Michael 14
GOODMAN Daniel 41
  Jacob 228
  John 145, 205
  Philip 208

GOODRICH Seth 172, 247
GOODSON Job 10
  John 3, 4, 7
GOODSONN John 3
GOODWIN --- 63
  Benjamin 157
  George 38, 46, 65
  John 133, 205
  Thomas 28
GOOLDIN Samuel 14
GOOSEHORN Jacob 230, 250
GOOSEWEILER John 183
GOOT Hans 12
  Jacob 11
GORDON --- 40
  Elisha 114, 145, 249
  Harry 44, 135
  James 164, 184
  John 93
  Mary 65, 166
  Moses 206, 247
  Peter 98, 227, 248
  Robert 119
  Thomas 16, 17, 20, 21, 65, 75, 84, 166
  Thomas F. 145, 249
GORGAES John 8
GORGAS George 182
  Jacob 179
  Solomon 183
GORING Jacob 99
GORMLEY Benj. 7
GORNER Philip 125
GORNET Gilliam 33
GORTNER Jacob 145
GOSHEN Isaac 162
GOSLAR Philip 99
GOSLER Philip 132
GOSLINE John 45
GOSLING John 45
GOTSHALL Frederick 14
GOTT Thomas 122, 216, 217
GOTTSHALL Philip 56
GOTTSHICK George 8
GOULD Samuel 87
GOULDIN Christian 12
  Samuel 12
GOULDNEY Henry 54
GRAAF Andrew 38
  Hans 11
  Martyn 12
GRAEFF Daniel 176, 193, 194, 196, 245
  George 137
GRAEFLY John George 65

INDEX

GRAEME Elizabeth 42
  Patrick 135
  Thomas 135
GRAESAL Lawrence 75
GRAFF Abraham 202
  Charles 245
  Daniel 94, 202
  Garrat 168
  Hans 14
  Jacob 36, 95
  John 145, 189
  Joseph 13
GRAFFIUS Martin 204
GRAFIUS Abraham 213
GRAFT Andrew 154
GRAFTS Isaac 102
GRAHAM George 140, 148, 163, 184, 187, 194, 235
  Henry Hale 27, 30, 65, 80
  James 55, 225, 237, 247
  John 104, 215
  Mary 191
  Robert 114
  Samuel 197
  Thomas 137
  William 46, 79, 201, 215, 221
GRAM Frederick 143
GRANGER Gideon 170
GRANT Josiah 143
  Thomas 55, 57, 132, 162, 164
  William 4, 6, 15, 16
GRANTHAM John 94
GRANTUM Charles 19
GRASSOLD Christian 14
GRATZ Bernard 53
  Rebecca 199
  Simon 136, 181, 182, 186, 194, 212, 223, 224, 246
GRAVES John 202
  Samuel 189, 202
GRAY 176
  Alexander 104
  Ann 129
  Daniel 126
  David 63, 132
  Edward 171
  George 19, 22, 23, 30, 31, 32, 39, 42, 46, 129, 229, 246
  George W. 129
  Henry 25
  Isaac 172
  James 218
  John 156, 201, 204
  Martha 129
  Mary B. 129
  Neigal 38, 39, 69
  Neigel 39
  Neigle 40
  Richard 142
  Samuel 4, 5, 6
  William 34, 35, 51, 96, 129, 154
GRAYBILL Christian 217
  Jacob 169, 190
  John 194
GRAYBLE Samuel 195
GRAYDON William 97
GREAFF Daniel 123
GREBER George 160, 229, 244
GREEN --- 58, 111, 163
  Abbot 232
  Ashbel 99, 109
  Benjamin 222
  Edward 108
  Elijah 118
  Elisha 183, 232
  Innis 225
  James 24, 238
  John 214, 222
  Joseph 38
  Timothy 33, 35
  William 130, 168, 176, 212
GREENAWALT Jacob 124, 143, 194
  Matthias 152
  Philip 38, 103, 124, 199
GREENE Edward 4
  Gen. 115
  James 173
  Joel 106
GREENLEAF Isaac 15
  James 130, 131, 168
GREENLEAFE Isaac 19, 21
GREENWALT Philip 33
GREENWAY Robert 48
GREER David 74
  Guion 172, 184, 201, 243
  James 197
  Jane 90
  John 130, 178, 197, 229, 244
  Joseph 35, 90
  Lt. Col. 141
  Rebecca 196
  Thomas 138, 196, 197
GREESE Ernst 161
GREFETH Isaac 230, 250
GREFFITH Levi 166
GREGG Amos 80
  Andrew 64, 65, 78, 103, 117, 122, 184
  Israel 184
  John 56, 129
  Robert 167
  William 56, 57, 167
GREGORY Asahel 143
  Asuhel 121
  James 38
GREHAM Richard 252
GREIDER Daniel 187
  Martin 187
GREIFF Stephen 14
GREIGHER Adam 175
GREINDER John 179
GREINER Adam 161
  John 145
  Nicholas 161
GREISS Eve Dorthea 129
GRENLEE William 113
GRESS Matthias 183
GRICE Joseph 182, 185
GRIDLEY Daniel 227, 252
GRIER Guion 113
  John 39, 86, 120, 128
  Lt. Col. 111
GRIESWOLD Joseph 66, 67
GRIFFETH Enoch 127
GRIFFIN Esther 189
  Samuel 189
  Selwood 59, 67
  Stephen 209
GRIFFITH --- 215
  Christopher 100
  Daniel 72
  David 20
  Even 109
  John 20, 77, 171
  Levi 72
  Robert E. 117, 139, 194
  Thomas 171
  William 72, 146, 214
GRIFFITHS Abraham 135
  Henry 103
  John R. 125
  Samuel P. 79
  Samuel Powell 109

INDEX

GRIFFITS Nathaniel 11
  Samuel P. 91
  Samuel Powel 77
GRIFFITTS Abigail 19
  Nathaniel 10
  Samuel P. 232
  William 16, 19
GRILL Adam 229, 244
GRIM George 119
  Lt. Col. 101
GRIMES Michael 27
GRIMM Philip 231, 251
GRINDING Jesse 223, 227
GRIPE Daniel 55
GRISPIN William 30
GRISWOLD Joseph 59, 142
GROCE Henry 100
GROENWALDT Philip 72
GROFF George 14
GROFFCOOP Paul 35
GRONINGDYCK Peter 5
GRONINGDYKE Peter 4
GRONO Lewis 38
GROOM William 30
GROSENICKEL John 150, 157
GROSH Daniel 225
  Jacob 178, 225
  Samuel 179, 225
GROSS Abraham 225
  Henry 119
  Joseph 224
  Martin 176
  Michael 143
GROSSCUP Paul 75
GROTH Andreas Henry 20
GROTZ Jacob 91
GROUT Jonathan 156
GROVE Jacob 213
  John 180
  Mark 244
  Marks 229
  Sylvanus 54
  Thomas Cotterell 23
GROVER Gurdon 216
GROVES Daniel 182
  Michael 92
GROWDEN Joseph 4, 5, 6, 7
GROWDON Joseph 3, 5, 8
  Lawrence 52
GRUBB Adam 30, 37, 42
  Ann 23
  Curtis 23, 34, 129
  George C. 129
  John 6, 7
  Martha G. 129

  Mary 129
  Michael 70
  Nathaniel 16, 17
  Peter 23
GRUBE Bernhard Adam 74
GRUM John 103
GRYMER John 142
GUEST Henry 41
  William 1, 4, 8
GUIER William 224
GUIN Patrick 136
GULDIN Abraham 206
GULICK Samuel 100
GUNCKEL Jacob 96
GUNDACKER John 138,
  169, 179, 183
  Michael 132, 137,
  138, 139
GUNDAKER John 118
  Michael 123
GUNN James 116
GURNEY Francis 32, 38,
  43, 50, 51, 64, 89,
  93
  Henry 48
  Lt. Col. 101
GUSTIN John 189
GUSTON John 119
GUTHARDT Henry 223, 227
GUTHRIE James 99, 128,
  145, 206, 220, 247
  John 173
  Samuel 196
  William 170, 227
GUY Francis 171
  Jonathan 151
GUYER Lt. Col. 101
  Mary 227
  Peter 227
  William 128
GWINN Patrict 202, 225
GWYNE Joseph 146
GWYNN John 186
  William 186
GYERHART John 150

HAAN Philip 14
HAAS Benjamin 237
  Conrad 70, 145
  Jacob 122
  John 79, 231
  Peter 33
HABACKER Christian 196
  John 195
HACKEMAN Herman Henry
  186

HACKER George 65
HACKETHORN George 58
HACKNEY Joseph 117, 138
  Lt. Col. 142
HADDEN Thomas 145
HADLEY Simon 91
HAFERTY Lt. Col. 101
HAFFOLD Thomas 4
HAGA Godfrey 91, 97, 109,
  12, 128
HAGEMAN Ulrich 11
HAGENBACH John 233
HAGENBERG Peter 248
HAGENBUCH John 244
HAGENBUCK Andrew 40
HAGEY Jacob 110
HAGGERTY Hugh 129
HAGHN John 79
HAGNER Frederick 37
HAGUE John 76
HAHN Henry 73, 75
  Jacob 140
  John 183
  Michael 45, 72
  Philip 133, 193, 196
HAIG William 1
HAIGE William 3, 4
HAINES -- 61, 68
  Caspar W. 79, 98
  George 138, 151
  Henry 225
  John 61, 68
  John B. 224
  Reuben 26, 55, 241, 246
  Rudolph 28
HAINS Casper W. 105
  Reuben 212, 224
HAKE Frederick 153
HALDEMAN Henry 188, 232
  Jacob 38
  Jacob M. 182
  John 123, 130, 136,
  178, 183
  John B. 183
HALDIMAN John 106, 143
HALE Elias W. 184, 190
  Elizabeth 192
  Mary 192
  Mary Wood 192
  Matthew 80, 192
  Reuben 131, 184, 245
  Thomas 192, 241
  William 174
HALIWELL Richard 6

INDEX

HALL Charles 125, 194
  Christian 176
  Clement 80
  Jacob 37, 48, 114
  John 60, 67, 122
  Joseph 28, 29
  Robert 1, 4, 5
  Solomon 18
  Stephen 229, 244
  Thomas O. 216
HALLENBACH George M. 184
HALLER David 227
  Henry 38, 42, 49
HALLING Michael Jansen 14
HALLIWELL Richard 6, 7, 8
HALLMAN Michael 79
  William 144
HALLOWELL Israel 79
  John 186
HALLWELL Richard 6
HALMOT Peter S. V. 209
HAM Isaiah 80
HAMAKER Adam 86, 103
  Frederick 104
HAMAN John 212
  John T. 234
HAMBLETON John 127
HAMBRIGHT John 47
  Lt. Col. 101
HAMERSLY Robert 138
HAMIL John 237
HAMILL Robet 121
  William 200
HAMILTON Alexander 126
  Andrew 10, 13, 20, 28
  David 203
  Gavin 152
  James 17, 28, 118, 143,
    154, 173, 183, 188,
    217, 222, 249
  Jeremiah 199
  John 107, 113, 206
  Lt. Col. 102
  Paul 170
  Robert 87, 175
  Thomas 100, 184, 220,
    243
  William 38, 72, 104,
    133, 142, 170, 183,
    206
HAMITT Francis 21
HAMM Mary 149
  Samuel 149
HAMMER John 98
HAMMERSLEY Robert 74
HAMMIL George 180

HAMPHER John 12
HAMPTON Joseph 20
HAMSON William 212
HANAGAN James 232
HANBURY John 17
HANCOCK Isaac 84
HAND Col. 131
  Edward 69, 85, 86,
    90, 95, 97, 151
HANDELL A. M. 45
  William 45, 72
HANDIE --- 63
HANISON George K. 141
HANKE Anna Maria 135
  Matthew 135
HANNA Edward 119
  James 203
  John 231, 251
  John A. 94, 251
  Lt. Col. 101
  Mary 251
  Robert 29, 32, 33,
    34, 49
HANNAH John 168
HANNIS John 19, 168
HANNUM Alice 148
  John 16, 20, 49, 71,
    87, 148
  Joseph 229, 245
HANSE Conrad 79
  Jacob 22
HANSON Matthys 2
HAPPLE John 150
HARB Joseph 44
HARBARGER George 226
HARBAUGH Jacob 182
HARBESON Benjamin 32,
  33, 41, 60, 67
HARBISON William 227
HARDCHY John 223, 227
HARDEN John 54
  Martin 54
HARDING John 1, 4, 126
  Philip 154
  Richard 153
HARDY John 155
  William 40
HARE Abraham 11
  Henry 195
  John Powel 145
  Lt. Col. 112
  Robert 84, 109, 145
HARKINS Elizabeth 182,
  199
  Robert 182

HARKNESS William 58, 182
HARLAND George 7
HARLEY Rudolph 247
HARLOFF Godfrey 167
HARMAN Casparus 1
  Elizabeth 62, 69
  Jacob 28, 190
  John 215, 232, 233
  William 21
HARMAR John 71
HARMER Ruth 28
  William 28
HARNISH Abraham 208
HARNIST Martin 11
HARNLY Abraham 187
HAROLD Philip 231, 251
HARPER James 249
  John 143, 217
  Josiah 18
  Nathan 114, 213
  Robert 60, 67
  Samuel 174, 184
  Thomas 176
HARRIS --- 86
  James 131, 184
  James B. 146
  John 27, 37, 38, 39,
    50, 51, 57, 86, 109,
    175
  John Levet 160
  Lt. Col. 101, 111
  Robert 77, 86, 97, 106,
    119, 124, 128, 159,
    163, 180, 182, 218
  Samuel 248
  Simpson 153
  Theophilais 124
  Thomas 77, 217
  William 42, 93, 96, 99
HARRISON Francis 4
  George 89, 183
  Henry 16, 17, 20, 21,
    22
  James 3, 4, 34, 98
  John 69, 96, 183, 199
  Mary 84
  Samuel 171
  Samuel W. 215
  Stephen 197
  Thomas 71, 79, 120, 152
  William 171
HARRISSON Benjamin 165
  Margaret 165
HARRY David 9
HARSHE Thomas 210
HARSHORN Pattison 79

INDEX

HART Benjamin 202
  Hannah 157
  Hannah Morris 157
  Isaac 209
  Jacob 202, 224
  John 1, 4, 39, 48, 109, 114, 134, 144
  John J. 157
  John Jaffry 157
  Joseph 32, 34, 37, 38, 39, 47, 48, 128
  Josiah 37
  Lt. Col. 101, 111
  Nathaniel 202
  Robert 2
  Seymour 79
  Silas 48
  Thomas 74
  William 42, 87, 160
HARTLEY Col. 85, 121
  James 28
  Martin 145
  Thomas 45, 73, 99, 241
HARTLINE Leonhart 14
HARTLY Catharine 223
  Jonathan 204
  Thomas 132, 223
HARTMAN Barbara 195, 196
  Caspar 233
  Jacob 14
  John 75
  Michael 217, 237
HARTSHORNE Hugh 28
  Patteson 187
HARTSHORNE, LARGE & Co. 89
HARTUPEE William 191
HARTZEL George 245
  Jacob 168
  Jonas 63
HARTZELL Jonas 39, 77, 91, 96
HARTZLER Christian 123, 187
HARVEY --- 63
  Amos 149, 220
  Catharine 90
  Elizabeth 90
  John 90
  Jonathan 87
  Joseph 14, 41
  Robert 9
  Samuel 90, 109, 137, 182
  Thomas 90

  William 55, 90, 234
HASENCLEVER Francis
  Caspar 29, 32
HASKINS John 4, 227
  William 60, 67
HASLET James 50
HASSART Arent 11
HASSINGER Abraham 127
  Christopher 198
  Daniel 174
  Jacob 174
HASSOLD Thomas 1
HASTINGS David 154
  Henry 3
  Jno. 1
  Joshua 4
HATCH Sylvanus 164
HATFIELD George 171
HATHAWAY Calvin 191
  Jacob 191
HATRICK Ruth 210
  William 210
HATZ John 70
HAUGHENBAUGH Henry 95
HAUKE William 14
HAUSMAN George Jacob 30
  Paul 73
HAUTO George F. A. 223
HAUTZ John 183
HAVELL Sgt. 37
HAVERSTOCK Conrad 55
HAWGER John 92
HAWK George 187
  John 187
  Magdalena 187
HAWKE George 188
HAWKINS George 26
  Henry 139
  Phoebe 48
  William 48
HAY -- 18
  Charles 65
  David 72, 121
  George 107, 120, 140
  Jacob 99, 128, 195
  John 27, 37, 38, 39, 50, 74, 145, 237
  John D. 104
HAYES Christopher 54
  David 115
  Henry 42
  John 87
  Johnathan 7
  Jonathan 5, 8, 10
  Richard 13

  Robert 183
  Samuel 61
  William 48, 238
HAYMAKER --- 57
  Frederick 56, 168, 240
HAYN Michael 38
HAYS --- 196
  David 178
  George 196
  James 214, 215, 235
  Jane 196
  John 184, 201
  Richard 232
  Samuel 68, 128, 214, 233
  Widow 236
  William 186, 224
  William T. 174, 203
HAZARD Ebenezer 99
  Erskine 223
  Samuel 15
HAZELTON Thomas 184
HAZELWOOD John 41, 50, 51
HAZEN Col. 94
  John 197
HAZLEHURST Isaac 89
HAZLET James 37
HAZLEWOOD John 107, 128
HEADLEY Samuel 220, 235
HEADY Thomas 132
HEALD Nathan 102
HEAP John 43, 48, 183
HEARLY Samuel 149
HEARN Anthony 148, 149
  William 10
HEARNLY Abraham 143
HEATHCOTE John 186
HEATLY Charles 78
HEATON Henry 234, 236
  John 118
  Joseph 7
  Lt. Col. 112
HECHLING Jacob 241
HECK Ludwig 71
HECKERT Daniel 183
HEESTER Joseph 37
HEFFLEY Peter 232
HEGAN James 130
HEGER Stophel 71
HEILMAN Jacob 237
  Stephen 79
HEINEY John 207
HEINITSH Charles 71
HEINS John 106

284

INDEX

HEINTZ Christian 161
  Christopher 161
  Jacob 161
HEINTZELMAN John 100
HEISER Jacob 128, 138, 180
HEISSLER John 217
HEIST George 176
  Henry 206
  Peter 46
HEISTAND Andre 245
  Andrew 229
HEISTER Daniel 72, 75, 133
  Gabriel 39, 184, 202
  John 42, 183, 193, 195
  John S. 193
  Joseph 72, 75, 86, 94, 98, 124, 125, 143
  Lt. Col. 101
HEISZ Frederick 103
HEITER Casper 245
HEIZER Andrew 28
HELFENSTEIN Albert 50
  Albertus 72
HELLER Ephraim 183
  Frederick 213, 242
  Jacob 94
  Simon 102
HELLMAN Daniel 193
  Michael 193
HELMAN Eva 128
  Michael 162, 183
HELMBOLD George 116
HELME Israel 2
HELMUTH John Henry Christian 72
  John K. 245
HEMBELL William 28
HEMOR Moses 140
HEMPHILL Joseph 104, 172, 184, 245
HENDEL Jacob 146
  William 70, 199
HENDERSON Andrew 65, 80, 106, 135, 136
  Archibald 100
  Barton 173, 188
  Daniel 100
  David 196
  Elizabeth 249
  James 100
  John 59, 67
  John A. 202
  Lt. Col. 111, 141, 142

  Mathew 71
  Matthew 33, 74, 100, 126
  Thomas 46, 58, 63, 66, 229, 246
  William 103, 149, 187, 193, 249
HENDLE Jacob 183
HENDRICKS Hendrick 8
  Lawrence 8
  Lt. Col. 111
  Peter 251
  William 8
HENDRICKSON Isaac 76
  Israel 18
HENDRIKS Jan 3
HENDRIX Adam 138, 183
HENERY John 174
HENING Matthias 63
HENLY John 8
HENNING Daniel 127
HENNINGTON 133
  James 133
HENRY --- 170
  Ann 148
  Conrad 79
  George 58, 146
  Hugh 137
  Jane 153
  Job 87
  John 107
  Peter 230, 250
  Robert 200
  Samuel 118
  Sarah 199
  Sophia 107
  Thomas 157, 178, 184, 214, 221, 240
  William 32, 33, 34, 36, 37, 91, 141, 212, 216
HEPBURN Andrew D. 201
  James 55, 129
  Stacy 51
  William 125
HERBEIN Jonathan 12
HERBERGS John 22
HERBERT Isaac 178
  Lawrence 109
HERBST John 72, 74
HERD William 222
HERGELRAT Valentine 14
HERGER George 63, 69
  Gottlieb 13
  Michael 14

HERLEMAN Conrad 79
HERMAN Catharine 219
  Christian 11
  Daniel 12
  Frederick 198
  Gasparus 4
  Jacob 12
  John 201
  Samuel 219
HERMANS Ephriam 2
HEROLD Simon 123
HERON James G. 132
HERR Benjamin 99
  Christian 177, 191, 241
  John 241
  Tobias 202
  Widow 202
HERRING Asa 189
  Daniel 230, 250
HERRINGTON Edward 233
  Jacob 211, 213, 214, 240
  James 116, 127, 138, 157, 192, 233
HERRISON Isaac 97
HERRON Francis 240
HERSH John 86
HERSHEY Andrew 31
  Isaac 183
  Jacob 183, 229, 245
  John 154
  Samuel 176
HERSHIE Christian 213
HERSHNER Conrad 33
HERSTER John 91, 113, 212, 214
HERTZEL George 133
  Jonas 37
HERTZLER Christian 179, 225
HERVEY Robert 242
HESLER --- 98
HESLET William 32
HESLIP Thomas 35, 37
HESS Conrad 179
  David 153
  Elizabeth 198
  George 143, 212
  Henry 208
  Jacob 202
  John 11
  Joseph 179
  Philip 198
HESSLER Michael 190
HESTING Enoch 64

INDEX

HETTLESTEIN Jacob 12
HEVERLAN Jacob 34
HEVERSTRITE Elizabeth 149
   Jonas 149
HEWES Isaac 42
   Josiah 31, 89
HEWIT Thomas 38
HEWITT Thomas 34
HEWS Henry 201, 215
HEWSON John 77
   William 97
HEWSTON John 169
HEY Philip 172, 176
HEYDON Richard 223
HEYER Leonhart 14
HEYSHAM William 24
HIBBARD Daniel 59, 67
HIBSHMAN Jacob 179, 183
HICKCRICK Philip 192
HICKMAN James 153
HICKNER Hans George 14
HICKOQUEON King 52
HICKS Charles 27
   Edward 28
   Gilbert 35
   Giles 42
   Isaac 231, 251
   Samuel 80
   William 72
HICKSON Woolman 80
HIDDLESTON --- 53
HIESLY Henry 207
HIEST Christian 192
HIESTER Daniel 32
   Joseph 38, 84, 231
   William 199
HIGBY Joseph 154
HIGGINS Andrew 78
HIGH William 201
HIGHLANDS Martha 55
HIGHLY Henry 178
HIGLEY Samuel 204
HIKES Andrew 192, 243
HILANDS Robert 184
HILBORN John 100
   Joseph 16
HILBOURN Amos 21
HILDEBRAN Abraham 243
HILDEBRAND Christian 27
HILGER Henry 148
HILL --- 210
   Adam 126, 193, 204
   Alexander 136
   Ansel 234
   Cato 71

   Daniel 134
   Deborah 17
   Erastus 232
   Esther 107
   Hannah 17
   Harriet 17
   Henry 17, 32, 38, 39,
      42, 43, 45, 50
   Jacob 13
   John 1, 4, 5, 6, 7,
      203, 232, 246
   Luke 211
   Margaret 17
   Mary 17
   Milcah 17
   Peter 103
   Rachel 17
   Rees 184, 196, 220,
      225
   Richard 9, 17, 48,
      154
   Sarah 17
   Stephen 231, 251
   Thomas 161
   William 107
HILLBORN Joseph 17
HILLEGAS George 172
   Michael 18, 23, 26,
      30, 31, 41, 49, 76
   Peter 13
HILLEGASS Adam 48
HILLENGAS Frederick 14
HILLER Henry 37
HILLGART William 11
HILLIARD Guy 177
   Isaac 102
   John 1, 3, 4, 7
   Peter 204

HILLIS David 166
HILLS Samuel 213
HILLYARD Ebenezer 171
   John 2
HILMAN Antonius 12
HIMES George 195
   Lt. Col. 141
HINCKEL Lt. Col. 111
HINDMAN James 235
   John 203, 247
   William 243
HINDS Stephen 231, 251
HINES Lt. Col. 101
HINEY Isaac 183
HINKEL Anthony 14
HINKS Matthew 3

HINNIGE Ludowick 14
HIPPLE Frederick 144
   John 251
   Lawrence 188
HIRLEMAN Catharine Salome
   129
   Eve Dorthea 129
   John 129
   John Henry 129
   John Jacob 129
   John Michael 129
   John Philip 129
   John Stephen 129
HIRSH Henry 123
HIRST John 118
HITCHCOCK Enos 80
HITE Conrad 227
HITNER Appollonia 220
   Frederick 72, 220
   George 21
HITTS James 167
HOAG Michael 110
HOBART Enoch 24
HOBBY Jonathan 26
HOBENSACK John 108
HOBSON Moses 94, 200
HOCH Hans 12
   Jacob 12
   Melchor 12
   Samuel 12
HOCK George 186
   Johan 14
HOCKER John 115
   Martin 115, 187
HOCKLEY James 29, 49
   Thomas 38
HOCKMAN John 204
HODGDON Samuel 120, 245
HODGE --- 234
   Andrew 21, 34, 41
   Henry 14
   Hugh 41
   Sarah 185
   William 23
HODGSON Thomas 109
HOECKLY Frederick 249
HOEKLY Henry 148
HOFF John 138, 169
HOFFER John 187
   Melchior 192
HOFFMAN Eleanor 188
   George 205, 242, 243
   Henry 188
   Jacob 62
   Margaret 208

INDEX

Peter 51, 57, 59, 66
Sebastian 176
William 241
HOGE David 42, 71
  John 55, 74, 114, 160, 218, 236
  Jonathan 33, 39
  Thomas 222
  William 195, 214
HOGELAND Daniel 44
HOGERMOED Mathias Adams 12
HOGG George 7
  William 191
HOGGE Samuel 121
  Sarah 121
HOKE Frederick 237
  Henry 104, 140
HOLCOMB George 218
HOLDEMAN John 125
HOLDING Joseph 5
HOLEMAN Eli 163
HOLGATE Jacob 157, 182, 207, 245
HOLLADY John 147
HOLLAND Benjamin 89
  John I. 171
  Samuel 65, 78
HOLLANDARE Peter 1
HOLLANDER --- 18, 19, 23
HOLLAR Joseph 172
HOLLENBACH George M. 207
HOLLENBACK John 210, 218, 224
  Mathias 146
  Matthias 97
HOLLENBAIK George 12
HOLLERBACK Matthias 137
HOLLICK William 80
HOLLIDAY --- 57
  Adam 135
  John 119, 180, 183
  Lt. Col. 101, 111
  William 33, 55, 57
HOLLINGAR Valentine 182
HOLLINGER George 125
HOLLINGSHEAD James 149, 183, 189, 204
  Peter 148, 149, 191
  William 33
HOLLINGSWORTH Henry 10
  Jehu 88, 89
  Levi 29, 89, 91, 105, 109, 120, 131, 147
  Levi G. 146, 179

Paschal 117
Samuel 87
Val. 5
Valentine 1, 4, 5
Zebulon 80
HOLLINGWORTH Henry 7
  Valentine 7
HOLLINSHEAD William 41
HOLLIS James 95
HOLMAN Elias 132
  Martin 37
HOLME John 97
  Jonatha 43
  Thomas 1, 97
HOLMES George 171
  John 22, 25, 33, 50, 55, 73, 114
  Thomas 3, 4
  William 43
HOLMES & RAINEY 89
HOLMS Jonathan 29
HOLSTEIN George W. 196
  Matthias 196, 218
  Samuel 73
HOLSTERMAN Peter 34
HOLSTINE Matthias 193
HOLSTON Peter 37
HOLT Lt. Col. 101
  Thomas 26
HOMER Jesse 166
  William 30
HOMES John 32
HOOD John 80
  Samuel 95
  William 171
HOODT Caspar 8
HOOF George 167
HOOFF George 162
HOOFNAGLE Peter 34, 70, 72
HOOGHTALEN Wilhelmus 212
HOOGLAND Daniel 36
HOOK James 219
HOOKY Anthony 76
HOOPER Philip 217
  Robert Lettis 22
HOOPES Caleb 179
  Joshua 7
HOOPS Abner 99
  Adam 16, 26, 27
  George 28
  Joshua 5, 6
  Thomas 64, 75, 91
HOOT John 217, 233

HOOTON Thomas 5
HOOVER Catharine 236
  Christian 169
  Michael 219
HOPE Adam 197
  Richard 171, 194, 207
HOPKEE Frederick 162
HOPKINS James 86, 133, 137, 173, 230, 250
  Jesse 169
  John 100, 153
  Joseph H. 171
  Robert 18
  Samuel 80, 83
  Sarah 169
  Stephen 174
  William 16, 17
  William E. 195
HOPKINSON Francis 23, 26, 36, 73, 78
  Joseph 131
HOPPE Justice 186
  Justus 186
HOPPER Isaac T. 109
HOPSON John 22, 32
HORBAUGH Abraham 194
  Yost 199
HORN Abraham 183, 223, 227, 247
  John 136, 182
  Lt. Col. 111, 141
HORNBECKER Philip 165
HORNE Edward 11
  Henry 76
HORNER Benjamin 79
  Hugh 153
  Jacob 109, 153, 202
  Jaocb 36
  John 108, 126, 150
  Joseph 180, 181
  Lt. Col. 141
  Robert 153
  William 153
HORNOR John 182
HORSEFIELD Joseph 94, 97
HORSH Henry 157
HORST George Ludowick 14
HOSAC John 73
HOSKIN William 103
HOSKINS John 10, 165
  Joseph 27
HOSSETT Giles 1
HOSTERMAN Jacob 122
HOSTETTER Abraham 129

INDEX

HOUGH Jacob 91, 134
  John 73, 123, 160
  Richard 4, 5, 6, 7, 8
  Silas 168
HOULTZ Abraham 164
  Eleanor 164
HOUPT John 183
HOURZ John 148
HOUSE John 192
HOUSECKER Nicholas 61, 68
HOUSEKEEPER Philip 176
HOUSEL Peter 167
HOUSER Hans 155
  Jacob 55
  Ulrich 108
  Woolrick 12
HOUSMAN Frederick 146
HOUSTON Anthony 10
  James 137
  John 78
  William 8, 9
HOUTZ Jacob 183
  John 179, 187
HOUVER John Woolrick 12
HOW Phineas 229, 244
HOWARD Edward 249
  Fredrick 175
  Richard 78
HOWEL Austin 204
HOWELL Abraham 24
  Arthur 109
  Asron 98
  Benjamin B. 215
  David 45
  Ebenezer 80
  Esech 222
  Isaac 30, 31, 34, 36, 42, 69, 86
  Jacob S. 42, 50, 51
  Jesse M. 222
  Joshua 16, 19, 23, 26
  Reading 54
  Samuel 16, 27, 32, 39, 86, 89
  Samuel L. 248
  William 1
  William W. 224
HOWER Jacob 188
HOWLAND Eday 218
HOWRY John 202
HOWSER John 11
HOYER George 124, 136, 159
HOYT Andrew 137

HUBBARD Christian 223, 227
HUBBLE George W. 210
HUBER Abraham 140
  Christian 183
  George 135, 138, 168
  John 95, 225
HUBERT Julius 237
HUBLEY Adam 27, 31, 72
  Bernard 27, 57, 71, 138
  Frederick 103
  Jacob 191
  John 32, 39, 57, 71, 72, 85, 90, 95, 136, 137, 183
  Lt. Col. 149
  Michael 27, 71
HUBNER Andrew 74
  George 14
HUCKELL Sarah 225
HUDDE Andries 1
HUDDELL Joseph 109
HUDDLESON Isaac 121
HUDSON Edward 171
  George 98
  Harry 44
  John 69
  Jonathan 180
  Martha 44
  Mary 44
  Robert 44
  Samuel 21, 27, 44, 47
  Sarah 44
  William 44, 125, 229, 244
HUET Christian 197
HUFFNAGLE Arnold 12
  Henry 191
HUFFORD Melcor 11
HUFNAGLE Michael 33
HUGHES Amos Austin 171
  Edward 23
  Ellis 26
  Hezekiah 80
  Isaac 33
  James 55
  John 16, 17, 18, 20, 21, 55, 124, 133, 136, 182, 196, 204
  Keziah 213
  Thomas 55
  Thomas E. 129
  William 107

HUGHS John 15
  Michael 147
HUHL Marcus 12
HUHN John 175
HULING David 225
HULINGS Marcis 125
  Marcus 50, 57, 111, 121
  Michael 22, 26
HULL Francis 57
  Gen. 174
HULME John 183, 185
HUME Dennison 71
  John 193
HUMES James 169, 183, 191, 241
  Samuel 118, 128, 136, 137
HUMMEL Frederick 206
  Jacob 246
  James 194
  Valentine 86
HUMPHREY Gideon 205
  Jacob 205
  Thomas 196, 205
HUMPHREYS Benjamin 59, 66
  Charles 17, 25, 27, 31, 41
  Daniel 83
  David 224
  James 17
  Jane 130
  John 130, 200
  Joshua 27
  Richard 23, 30, 79
  Susan 200
  Whitehead 34
HUMPHRIES Daniel 94
HUMPHRYS James 16
  Jane 139
  John 139
HUMPTON Col. 137
  Richard 129
HUNN John 89, 105
HUNSUCKER Valantine 12
HUNT Asker 235
  Elisha 214
  Elizabeth 217
  Jesse 148
  John 77, 79, 92, 94
  Wilson 89
HUNTCHINSON John 79
HUNTER Alexander 231
  Andrew 99
  Arnold 231, 252
  Daniel 32, 38, 39

INDEX

David 150
James 41, 177
John 17, 211, 216, 222
John W. 136
Lt. Col. 101, 112, 142
Nicholas 205
Robert 70, 77, 150
Samuel 26, 27, 31, 32, 57, 110
William 192, 195
HUNTZINGER Jacob 206
HURLING James 105
HURSLY Christian 176
HURST Henry 127, 136, 138, 142, 184, 212, 214
James 180, 203
John 143, 182
HUSBANDS Harman 34
HUSK John 54
HUSSEY John 7
Nathan 15
HUSTON Alexander 23, 186
Anthony 11
Charles 186
Daniel 242
Hugh 186
James 108, 154, 191, 241
John 69, 97, 118, 143, 152, 162
Jonathan 11
Joseph 180, 184
Lt. Col. 142
Matthew 105
Rachael 154
Samuel 174, 184
William 9, 10, 157
HUTCHESON David 174
James 197
John 102, 194
Mary 186, 200
Thomas 186, 200
HUTCHINS Joseph 72
Thomas 46
HUTCHINSON --- 129
James 60, 61, 67, 68, 77, 79
William 55
HUTCHISON Robert 240
William 240
HUTON John 156, 227
HUTTER Charles L. 244
Christian J. 112
HUTTON John 160
Joseph 108

HUY John 124
HUYSTON Thomas 115
HYDE Ezekiel 104
George 171
Jabez 200, 204
Lt. Col. 111
Nathan 27
Samuel 54
HYLEMAN Martin 159
HYNDSHAW James 91
HYSHAM William 41
HYWAY Patty 158
Peter 158

I'ALBO Andries 2
IACHNECHDORUS 53
IANNOTTOWE 52
ICQUOQUSHAN 52
IDEN John 13
IDQUOQUEYWAN 52
IDQUOQUEYWON 52
IMHOFF Evert 8
Gerhard 8
Henry 150
Herman 8
Peter 8
IMMEL Henry Michael 14
INCORN -- 18
INGELO Richard 4
William 1
INGERSOLL Jared 41, 176, 187
Jaret 71, 99
INGHAM Jonathan 85
Samuel D. 178
INGLE Samuel 33
INGLES James 133
Joseph L. 169
INGLIS John 22
Samuel 43
INGOLD William 72, 75
INGRAM Francis 223
Matthew 72
INKS George 237
INMAN Lt. Col. 141
INNES Robert 222
INNIS Elizabeth 242
William 242
INSKEEP John 79, 109, 114, 117, 122, 142
IREDALE Seth 169
IREDEL Charles 155
Robert 155
IRELAND Alphonso C. 171
Edward 186

IRELEY Abraham 104
IRICK Michael 121
IRISH Nathaniel 97, 128, 138, 202
IRONCUTTER John 24, 25
IRONS Simon 1, 4, 6, 7
IRVIN Archibald 113
James 70
John 128
Thomas 51
IRVINE Callender 117, 214
David 214
Deborah 66
James 29, 66, 232
William 46
IRWEN James 219
IRWIN Francis 154
George 35, 154
Henry 182, 183
James 55, 152, 173, 219, 243
John 49, 55, 133, 136, 138, 159, 225
Joseph 29, 49, 58
Josiah Kennedy 176
Martha 51
Matthew 146
Moses 21, 33
Nathan 99
Nathaniel 51
Richard 154
Samuel 220, 226
Thomas 243
William 43, 76, 159, 246
IRWINE William 99, 100
ISATT Jacob 184
ISH Peter 155
ISQUAHON 52
ISRAEL Israel 90, 145, 249
Samuel 152
IVANS Isaac 160
IVES Jesse 195
IVINS Barclay 193

JACK Henry 215
James 37
William 93, 99, 101, 115, 125, 128, 138, 180, 194
JACKS James 45
JACKSON Daniel 150
David 99, 109, 121
George 61, 68

289

INDEX

Holliday 91
John 61, 62, 68
Jonathan 61, 68
Josiah 72
R. 236
Samuel 80, 89, 118, 139
Stephen 10
Susanna 139
Thomas 91
William 37, 48, 79, 241
JACKSON & EVANS 89
JACOB Adam 191
John 39
Samuel 185
JACOBS --- 40
Albertus 5, 6
Benjamin 26, 34, 76
Cyrus 114, 153, 183
David 175
John 45, 49, 71, 79, 175
Joseph 21
Richard 99, 180
JACOBSON Marcus 3
JACOBY Abraham 183
Lawrence 133, 157
Lt. Col. 141
JACQUET John Paul 1
JACQUETT John Paul 2
JAGER Andreas 14
George 12
Nicholas 14
JAMES Abel 16, 21, 22, 78
Able 44
Bael 26
Isaac 47
Joseph 79
Thomas C. 120, 131
JAMES & DRINKER 19
JAMESON Alexander 192
James 243
John 237
William 58, 66
JAMISON James 206
Robert 181
JANEWAY J. J. 214
JANNEY Jacob 222
Thomas 4, 6
JANSEN Claus 8
Conrad 8
Dirk 8
John 8
Peter 8
William 8

JANUARY Peter 36
William 104
JAQUES Gideon 213
JARGER Hans George 14
JARGERT Peter 14
JARMAN Jeremiah 72
JARRET --- 92
Henry 207, 212
Jonathan 96
JARRETT Henry 188, 198, 199
JARVIS John W. 171
JAVISON John 90
JAWERT John 8
JAY John 80
JAYNE Daniel 172
JEANS Ebenezer 100
JEFFERIES Emmor 152
James 207
Joseph 38
JEFFERSON Thomas 170
JEFFRIES Nesbit 217
JEKYL John 44
JEMISON 167
John 227
JENKINS Aaron 54
David 33, 38, 51, 123
Eleazer 184
George 180
Joseph 69
Lewis 148
Lt. Col. 102, 112, 142
Philip 37
Robert 128
William 6, 7
JENKS Joseph R. 182
Phineas 171, 222
Thomas 77
William 121
JENNEY Thomas 46
JENNINGS Benjamin 202
Hannah 109
Henry 127
Jacob 109
John 41, 155
Nathaniel 174
JENNY James 246
JERVIS Charles 28, 30, 79
Sarah 191
JESS James 80
Zacariah 79
JESSOP Charles 178, 190
JEWELL William 143

JOB Nicholas 70
JOBSON Samuel 3
JOCKIE Christian 155
JOCKUM Peter 3
JODER Joest 12
John 12, 13
JOE 52
JOFFMAN Jacob 68
JOHE Adam 20
JOHN Benjamin 127
Daniel 127
David 127
Jacob 127
Jesse 183, 208
Joseph 127
Margaret 127
Reece 79
Samuel 127
JOHNS Matthew 18
JOHNSON Artemas 238
Caleb 175
David 167
Francis 61
Gershom 58, 65
Isaac 122, 127, 144
Jacob 130
John 50, 204
Joseph 18, 19, 24, 43, 62, 69, 139, 165, 186
Robert 97
Samuel 145, 171
William 53, 166, 228
JOHNSTON --- 225
Alexander 32, 180, 194
Andrew 80
Anthony 157
Benjamin 72, 119
Caleb 80
Charles 185
David 119
Edward 83
Francis 30, 31, 35, 68, 79, 90, 102, 134, 194
James 49, 73, 97, 187, 194
John 57, 75, 144, 150, 157, 224, 229, 247
John Lowther 188
Joseph 208
Lt. Col. 101
Martha 155
Richard 163
Robert 56, 112, 113, 115, 214

290

INDEX

Samuel 32, 98, 112, 113, 119, 133, 252
Thomas 155, 226
William 33, 56, 74, 136, 154, 201
JONES --- 24, 144, 197
  Amos 116
  Arthur 48
  Bela 219
  Charles 15, 16, 17
  Daniel 4, 5, 6
  David 33, 60, 67, 96
  Edward 65
  Elizabeth 83
  Esther 200
  Evan 168
  George W. 200
  Griffith 3, 4, 5, 6, 7, 48, 84
  Hannah 199
  Henry 2
  Holton 60, 67
  Horatio Gates 197
  Isaac 15, 23, 69
  Isaac C. 212
  Isaiah 171
  Israel 37
  James 203, 208
  Jesse 39
  Jesse Henderson 166
  John 15, 20, 21, 32, 49, 69, 77, 78, 102, 121, 126, 165, 169, 205
  Jonathan 79, 90, 182
  Joshua 70, 73, 124, 128
  Lloyd 197
  Lt. Col. 142
  Margaret 59, 66
  Mary 191
  Matthew 24, 73, 92
  Nathan 42
  Nicholas 34
  Norris 79
  Owen 15, 19, 28, 59, 66, 72, 85
  Philip 152, 159
  Richard 79
  Robert 50, 74
  Robert E. 157
  Robert Strettell 26
  Samuel 73, 105
  Thomas 39, 54, 70, 99, 105, 128, 132, 138, 144, 192
  Thomas L. 225

Thomas W. 136
Thomas Watkin 163
Voltaire Goldsmith 163
William 19, 24, 27, 28, 73, 218
William R. 171
JORDAN Archibald S. 250
  John 152
  Michael 30
JOSHIA James 115
JOURDAN Amos 131, 160
  John 131
  Sophia 131
JUDD William 30
JUDSON Amos 184, 201
  Joseph 45, 46
JUNG Mattheas 14
JUSTICE Charles 18, 73
  Lawrence 73
JUSTIS John M. 218

KACHLEAN Col. 41
KACHLEIN Peter 78
KACHNEGHDACKON 53
KACHNOARAASEHA 53
KAERNS Godfrey 150
KAGHRADODON 53
KAHICHDODON 53
KAIGHN John 194
KAISS John 123
KAMMERER Henry 43, 65
KAMMERSLY Robert 80
KANADAKAYON Johannes 53
KANALSHYIACAYON 53
KANATSANY-AGASHTASS 53
KANE Ann 228, 252
  Charles 228, 252
KANGWEER Jacob 13
KANTLINGER John 225
KAPP Catharine 181
  George 230, 250
  John 249
  Michael 181
KARAGHIAGDATIE Nichai 53
KARCHER Ludwig 55
KARES John 231
KARPER Julius 117
KARR James 204
  John 243
  Matthew 54
KARTHOUSE Peter A. 182
KASDROP Jacob 12
KASE William 145

KASNER George 50
KATZ Henry 106, 144
KAUFFELT Jacob 235
KAUFFMAN Andrew 132, 161
  Jacob 237
  John 161
KAUFMAN Benjamin 183
  Isaac 195
  Jacob 183
  John 99
KAUSMAN --- 74
KAY Thomas 55
KAYS George 196
KEAGY Abraham 212
KEAN Charles 226, 227
  James 197
  John 86, 124, 146
KEARNEY Edmond 16
  Edmund 21, 22
  Philip 22
KEARNEY & GILBERT 19
KEARSLEY John 74
  Samuel 195
KEASY John 166
KEATING John 135, 137, 201
KEBLE John 46, 147
KECHLEIN Abraham 66
KECHLER Anthony 59
KECHLINE Peter 26
KECK --- 233
  George 136, 233
KEEFER Peter 237
  Valentine 14
KEEHMLE Elizabeth 28
  George 28
KEELEY Jacob 146
KEELY Henry 167, 229, 237, 244
  Mathias 89
KEEN George 177
  Jacob 127, 144
  John 97, 125, 246
  Mathias 178, 209
  Reynold 28, 35, 36, 51, 73
KEENER Michael 226
KEENEY Salmon 224
KEEPER John 131
KEER Andrew 218
  Conrad 13
KEESEY Christian 179
KEETH John 183
KEEVER Christian 128
KEFFER Henry 191

291

INDEX

KEGEY Rudolph 178, 190
KEHNOLE Conrad 26
KEICHLEIN Abraham 58
KEIFT William 1
KEILWEIN Philip 12
KEIM Daniel D. B 232
  George D. B. 127, 242, 245
  John 94, 124
  Samuel 185
KEINER Godfrey 101
KEIPER John 131
  Lt. Col. 141
KEISINGER Philip 12
KEITH Margaret 120
  Timothy 120
KEKELAPPAN 52
KEKETAPPAN 52
KELCHNER George 34
  Maria 227, 244
  Matthias 227, 244
KELER John 223, 227, 229, 246
KELLER --- 233
  Jacob 114, 116
  John 12, 39
  Joseph 77
KELLEY James 177
  Lt. Col. 101
KELLINGER Andrew 124
KELLOG Silas 172
KELLOGG Silas 185
KELLUM Ira 236
KELLUP Lt. Col. 142
KELLY James 136, 240
  James M. 184, 243
  John 39, 145, 172, 194
  Jonas 142
  Lt. Col. 101, 111, 141
  Samuel 227, 231, 251
  William 231
KELP Catharine 179
  John A. 179
  Jonathan 179
KELSEY Daniel 200
KELSO Gen. 200
  John 157, 161, 170
KELTON James 149, 183
KELTZ George 110
KEMBLE Peter 89
KEMP Jacob 13, 188
KENDAL Ebenezer 200
  Samuel 196
KENDALL Benjamin 19, 27
KENDING Henry 99

KENEDY Hugh 214
KENEHAN Richard 121
KENGETH Jacob 62, 68
KENLY William 31
KENNEDY David 113, 171
  George 36
  John 145, 148, 184, 229, 244, 245
  Philip 190
  Robert 94, 140, 143, 147, 159, 193
  Thomas G. 222
  Thomas R. 77, 110, 117, 128, 138, 142
  William 194, 222
KENNER John 139
  Mary 139
KENNY Charles 149
  Patrick 149
KENSETT 139
KENT Thomas 48
KEPER John 183
KEPLER Andreas 14
  Bernard 28
KEPLINGER Peter 120
KEPNER Barnet 176
  Benjamin 177
  Bernard 168
KEPPELE Henry 28, 39, 43
  Michael 117, 136
KEPPLE Henry 32
KERCHER Martin 123
KERL George 148
KERN Jacob 29
  Jonas 196
  Lt. Col. 101
  Nicholas 96, 97
  Peter 146
KERNEGHEY William 126
KERNEY William 63
KERNICHON William 160
KERNS Nicholas 233
KERPER David 184
KERR Alexander 149
  James 90, 104, 107, 118, 140
  John 114, 140, 160, 161, 212, 240
  Joseph 65, 176
  Lt. Col. 141
  Ruth 149
  Thomas 204
  William 50, 204, 212
KERSBERGER Jacob 13

KERSTITLER Leonard 154
KESSLEBERRY Henry 8
KESSLER Charles 127, 153
  John 149
  Lt. Col. 141
KESTAR John 76
KESTER John 26
KESTLER George 145
  Lt. Col. 111
KEYS Ephriam 239
  Richard 86
  Violet 239
KEYSER Aaron 207
  Dirk 8
  Henry 144
  Michael 144
  Nicholas 13
  Peter 8, 109
KICKLIN Andrew 35
KID Mary 121
KIDD Alexander 49
  Edith 49
  John 21, 27, 32, 38, 92, 96
  Peter 64, 76, 78, 227
KIEN Jonas 3
KIESY Philip 65
KIGHTLINGER Abraham 160

KILBUCK William Henry 153
KILE John 39
KILGORE Capt. 125
  William 180, 212
KILLWEATHER Margaret 26
KIMBER Emmor 109
KIMBLE Benjamin 232
  Daniel 249
  Ephraim 163
  Jacob 235
KIME George D. B. 136
  Nicholas 158
KIMMEL George 128, 172, 236, 245
  Jacob 152, 179
  John 138, 158
  Jonas 219
  Lt. Col. 102, 112, 142
  Peter 123, 128, 138, 225, 245
KINCAID Michael 73
KINCHLEY Catharine 49
KINDICK George 11
KINDIG John 202
KING Benjamin 202, 210
  Christian 248

INDEX

Duncan 199
Francis 138, 151
Frederick 110
John 45, 79, 108, 153, 154, 206
Joseph 15, 16, 227
Lawrence 79, 88
Lt. Col. 101, 111
Michael 225
Samuel 93
Simeon 12
Solomon 248
Thomas 36, 53, 184, 200
Walter 4
William 92
KINGSLEY Samuel 79
KINGSTON Thomas 145, 249
KINKEAD James 29, 34
John 36, 37, 41, 49, 51, 71, 75
Maxwell 225
Samuel 157
KINKING Abraham 12
KINKNER John George 13
KINLEY William 34
KINNEY David 229, 244
KINSER George 126
KINSEY John 13, 14, 15, 20, 154, 211
Philip 30
KINSLEY Abraham 182
Frazer 36, 70
KINSOLE Benjamin 54
KINTNER Jacob 198, 203
KINTZEL Rudolph 131
KIP Hendrick 2
KIPSHAVEN John 1, 3, 4
KIRBRIDE Joseph 41
KIRK Caleb 80, 138, 182
Ezekiel 108
Isaac 138, 182, 183
Josiah 226
Roger 41, 49, 51, 71, 75
Timothy 246
KIRKBRIDE Col. 40
John 232
Joseph 7, 8, 9, 13, 14, 15, 20, 32, 39, 161
Mahlon 15, 19, 21
KIRKPATRICK Francis 89
William 118, 137, 183
KIRKWOOD Widow 237
KIRSHNER Conrad 221, 228

KISER Andrew 171
KISSINGER Ulrich 158
KISTER David 237
KITCHAM Philip 95
KITE Benjamin 109
Eliza 240
James 240
KITH William 192
KITHCART Robert 99
KITLOW John 195
KITNOR Jacob 205
KITTERE John 80
KITZLY Godlieb 148
KITZMILLER George 54
Martin 54
KLAMTER Adam 13
KLAPP John 230, 250
KLECKNER Anthony 226
KLEIM Johan 14
KLEIN John 47
John Isaac 12
Michael 14
KLEINE --- 63
KLEINHOOF Caspar 8
KLEMMER Jacob 12
Christian 13
KLINE George 14
Jacob 148, 183
John 93
Lt. Col. 111, 141
Nicholas 118, 139
Peter 226
Philip 144
KLINGSOHR John August 74
KLINUPGES Paul 8
KLIPPENGER William 207
KLOESS Abraham 205
Jacob 205
Maria Eva 205
Valentine 205
KLUTZ John 162, 167
KNAB Peter 184
KNABB Abraham 201
KNAPP Amos 234
KNAPPENBERGER Michael 14
KNAPPER George 59, 66
KNAPSNYDER John 178
KNAUS Ludowick 14
KNAUSS John 152
Paul 152
KNEASS William 171
KNEPLAY Peter 168
KNERR Henry 79

KNIGHT -- 61, 67
Isaac 62, 68
John 62, 69, 202
Joseph 62, 68
Joshua 60, 61, 62, 67, 68
Peter 23, 26, 32, 44, 131
KNOLL Catharine 223
George 223
KNOS John 218
KNOUFF Adam 153
KNOWLES James 129
John 18, 21, 30, 48
KNOWS Lewis 77
KNOX Andrew 33, 34
David 36
George 71
James 99, 136, 184, 194
John 42
Joseph 183
Mathew 40
Matthew 172
Robert 23, 32, 42, 44, 80
William 167
KOCH Adam 130
Jacob 167
KOCHER Peter 192
KOCK Jacob 162
KOCKEN Johannes 12
KOEHLER Daniel 74
KOELER Jacob 70
KOENIGMACHER Adam 241
Jacob 179
KOLB Conrath 14
Dielman 12
Jacob 12
Leonard 106, 144
Martin 12
KOLER Peter 33
KOLKIT John 230, 25
KONAPOT John 95
KONIGMACHER Abraham 152
KONKAPOT John 102
KOOCKOOYAEI Samuel 145
KOOKEN Henry 26, 33
KOON Peter 119
KOONS John 234
KOPLIN Matthias 14
KOPP Michael 86
KOPPENHAFER Henry 148
KOPPENHEFFER Michael 14
Thomas 14
KORN Michael 118

INDEX

KOSTER John 62, 68
KOUFFMAN David 12
KOYL Noble 160
KRAEMER Matthias 62
KRAFT Peter 43
KRAMER Baltzer 202
  Nicholas 207
KRATZER John 221
  William 221
KRAUS Michael 14
KRAUSE David 103, 124
  Michael 73
KRAVER Andreas 13
KREAMER George 246
  Matthias 68
  Nicholas 218
KREBBS George 109
KREBS Jacob 176, 184
KRECKBAUM Conrad 197
KREESTMAN Daniel 14
KREHL Michael 57
KREIDER Jacob 227, 231, 240, 251
KREINER John Dieterich 12
KREMER --- 204
  George 161, 224
  Jacob 186
KREPS Henry 143
  Michael 66
  Peter 105
KREPSE Michael 59
KRESS Charles 50
KRESSMAN Johann Nicholas 12
KREWSON Derrick 59, 67
  Detrick 60, 67
  Henry 30
  John 30
KREY John 8
  William 8
KRIDER --- 226
  Conrad 183
  John 122
  Tobias 177
KRIERS David 108
KRILL Adam 244
KRIMMELL I. L. 171
KRIPNER Paulus 13
KRIPPS Solomon 236
KRIPS Lt. Col. 141
KRITZER Nicholas 112
KROESEN Henry 44
KROUP Andrew 78
KROUSE David 209
KRUG Jacob 71, 129, 137

KRUGH Jacob 95
KRUMBHAAR Ludwig 241
KRUMREIN Stephen 220
KUCHER Christopher 72
  Peter 20
KUCHLEIN Andrew 34
KUHL Frederick 20, 28, 32, 38, 39
KUHN Adam 77, 89
  Adam Simon 28
  Casper 38
  Jacob 154
  Lt. Col. 101, 111
  Peter 89
KUHNS Frederick 233
  Jacob 228, 242
  John 136
KUNCKLE Christian 94, 128, 131, 224
KUNDERS Dennis 8
KUNIUS Bathsheba 110
  John 110
KUNKEL Jacob 221
KUNKLE Baltzer 107
  Christian 97
  Henry 164
KURTZ Abraham 248
  Benjamin 180, 182
  Christopher 138
  Nicholas 72
KUSER John 225
KUSTER Hermanus 12
KUSTOR Conrad 13
KUTZ Jacob 192
KYLE John 37
  Joseph 184
KYSER Benjamin 199

La FAYETTE La Marquis de 80
La TERRIERRE Charton de 80
LABAR Daniel 47
  Peter 155
  Philip 14, 47
LABARR Leonard 249
LABES James 186
LACKEY John 211, 222
LACOCK Abner 245
LACY Michael 110
LAFFERTY Samuel 98
  William 55
LAGAUZ Peter 86
LAHMAN David 196
LAHR Nicholas 79

LAIB Christopher 99
LAIRD David 242
  Hugh 71
  John 89
  Matthew 95, 177
  Robert 46
  Samuel 29, 43, 70
  William 72
LAMB Daniel 218
  John 219
  William 169
LAMBE Hugh 3
LAMBERT John H. 202
LAMBERTON James 183
  John 217
LANARD John 234
LAND James 45, 51, 162
LANDAS Felix 11
LANDAVER Johannes 20
LANDEN Nathaniel 63
LANDES --- 233
LANDIS Abraham 112
  Jacob 245
  John 183
  Philip 197
LANE Edward 76
  Isaac 24
  Martin 238
  Presley Car 145
  Presly Carr 113
  Susanna 125
  William 157
LANEY John 211
LANG James 241
  Thomas 36
LANGEBACK Michael 181
LANGENECKER Daniel 12
  Johannes 12
LANGHORN Thomas 5
LANGHORNE Jeremiah 7, 9, 12, 13, 15, 41
LANTZ --- 133
  Anna 248
  Christian 248
  David 248
  Fanny 248
  Henry 248
  Jacob 248
  John 248
  Lydia 248
  Magdalena 248
  Maria 248
  Sarah 248
LANTZER Adam 172
LAPPAWINZOE 52

INDEX

LARDNER --- 236
 John 207
 Lynford 17, 20
 William 97
LAREW Daniel 70
LARGE Ebenezer 187
 James 187
 John 187, 200
LASHEL George 105
LASHELL George 157
LASHELLS George 153, 195
 Ralph 195, 222
 Realph 183
LATCHA Henry 217
LATHROP Benjamin 184
LATIMER George 79, 84,
 89, 94, 246
 Henry 94
 Margaret 199
 Susanna 199
 William G. 118
LATIMORE George 33, 184
 John 181
 William 185
LATROBE Benjamin H. 112,
 170
LATTA Thomas 33
 William 33, 90
LATTIMER George 51
 James 119
LATTIMORE Arthur 40
 John 172
 William 183
LAUB Conrad 120
LAUBE Conrad 99
LAUD Jacob 225
LAUER Christian 35
LAUFMAN Philip 215
LAUGHEAD James 65, 224
 William 214
LAUGHLIN --- 57
 Adam 157
 Atcheson 212
 Thomas 106, 242
 William 55
LAUGHLY --- 63
LAUMAN Christopher 74
 Ludwig 32, 71
LAUNT Gabriel 136
LAURAMORE Joseph 104
LAURENCE Thomas 142
LAURENS Lt. Col. 142
LAVENGUTH Lt. Col. 141
LAVERTY Jesse 126
LAVINGAIR Christopher 39

LAW Richard 4
LAWALD Henry 33
LAWLER Mathew 89
LAWMOT Francis 146
LAWRENCE Amos 167
 Effingham 120
 Henry 112
 John 113, 124, 134,
 172
 Samuel 172
 Thomas 48, 59, 66,
 67, 79
LAWSHA Abraham 215
LAWSON Alexander 171
 David 232
 James 216
 Lt. Col. 141
 Nancy 179
 William 179
LAYCOCK Abner 116
LAZARUS Lt. Col. 101
Le FEVRE Samuel 16
Le GAUX Peter 73
Le GUEN Lewis 121
Le ROY Herman 208
LEA Thomas 249
LEACOCK John 249
LEADER Lewis 173
LEADLY George 154
LEAFF George 195
LEAMAN Samuel 110
LEAMEN Peter 11
LEAMY John 88, 100
LEANORD George 20
LEARCH Anthony 37
LEARD Samuel 33
LEAS William 32
LEASURE Abraham 53
LEBO Daniel 184, 194
 Henry 209
LECHLER Henry 85
LECHLET George Ernest
 76
LECHNER Jacob 193
 Joseph 230, 250
LECKEY William 236
LEDEN Benjamin 35
LEDLEY William 26
LEDLIE Andrew 40
LEE Anthony 15
 Francis 59, 66
 Jesse 234
 Mordecai 196
LEECH Hezekiah 197,219
 Jacob 19

 John 105
 Richard T. 114
 Samuel 51, 183
 Thomas 14, 15, 17, 19,
 20, 29, 31
 Toby 9, 18
LEEDOM Richard 118, 128
LEEK William 157
LEEMAN Christian 14
LEES James 45
 William 33
LEET Daniel 86, 93
 Jonathan 55
 William 181
LEFAVRE N. 171
LEFEVER George 202
 Isaac 23
LEFFERTS Aart 44
LEFFLER George Lewis 74,
 93
LEHMAN John 166
 Samuel 145
 William 43
LEHMER John 140, 194, 245
LEIB Christian 169
 George 45, 65
 Michael 77
LEIBERGERD John 14
LEIDIG Catharine 198
 Charles 61, 68
LEIDIGH Michael 97
LEIGHTE John 12
LEIGHTHOUSER Henry 43
LEIMBACH Daniel 201
LEINAWEBER Peter 183
LEIPER Charles 75
 James 38
 Thomas 109, 115, 121,
 125, 129, 139, 147
LEISE John 238
LEISHER Nicholas 13
LEITHEUSER Jacob 73
LEITHHEISER Hartman 228
LEITNER Elizabeth 242
 George 242
 Ignatius 242
LEMAN Jacob 13
 Robert 184
LEMES Christopher 25
LEMMON Thomas 155
LEMON John 159
 Thomas 23, 27
LENEY William S. 171
LENHART Godfrey 113, 195
LENKER Adam 140

295

INDEX

LENOX Hugh 41
LENSON John 8
LENTZ Henry 182
LEONARD Charles 202
  George 27
  John 110
  Robert 163
LEPLEY Adam 158, 164
LERCH John 152, 209
LEROW Jonas 12
LESCHER Nicholas 12
LESEBER Johannes 12
LESHER Jacob 191, 195
  John 35, 39, 145
  William 143
LESLIE Robert 77
LETCHWORTH John 79, 90
LETTSOM John Okely 80
LEVAM Daniel 75
LEVAN Abraham 183
  Bastian 33
  Daniel 46, 123, 192, 201, 206
  Henry 196
  Isaac 18, 20, 46, 176
  Jacob 184
  John 192
LEVAND Abraham 12
  Isaac 12
LEVERING Abraham 126
  Anthony 29, 49
  Nathan 37, 42
  Septimus 30
LEVERS Robert 35, 37, 38, 39, 55
LEVI Aaron 249
LEVINGSTON Henry Walter 102
LEVIS Lt. Col. 101
  Samuel 6, 7, 10
  Thomas 38
  William 147, 149
LEVY Aaron 83
  Benjamin 22
  Mary 246
  Moses 131, 246
  Paul 136
  Peter 135
LEVY & Co. 16
LEWARS Henry 206
LEWES Jacob 16
LEWIS --- 201
  Benjamin 40
  Curtis 201, 245

  David 109, 117, 130, 139, 187, 203
  Eli 80, 105
  Evan 9
  Freeman 234
  Henry 1
  Isaac 162
  Jacob 18, 20, 21, 28
  James 79
  Jehu 204
  John 18, 19, 129
  Josiah 65
  Mordecai 28, 89
  Nathaniel 89, 94
  Robert 19, 38
  Samuel 5, 6, 170
  William 59, 66, 80, 116
LEY Christopher 14
LEYDA Benjamin 198
  John 198
LIBOUGH John 14
LICQUERS --- 55
LIDDON Abraham 79
LIEBENGOOD Jacob 215
LIGGET George 173
LIGGINS Mary 153
  William 153
LIGHT Adam 194
  Jacob 49
  John 99
  John Jacob 12
  Matthew 44
  Samuel 183, 195, 199
LIGHTFOOT Benjamin 15, 18, 24
  Michael 91
LIGHTNER Joel 183
  John 97
  Nathaniel 115, 173
  Nathaniel F. 173
LIHMAN Jacob 105
LILLY Joseph 136
  Thomas 38, 54
LIMBER John 127, 138
LINAWEVER Peter 199
LINCOLN Abraham 49, 98
  Mordecai 33
LIND Mathew 183
LINDEMUTH Michael 37
LINDENBERGER George
  Adam 71
LINDLEY Jacob 94
  Ruth Anna 245
LINDSAY Andrew 243

LINDSEY Richard 69
  William 90
LINDSLEY Caleb 133
  Demas 133
LINE John 12
LINEBACH Catharine 209
  Jacob 209
LINEHAN Patrick 110
LINGAHONE 52
LINK --- 55
LINKER Adam 217
LINN Andrew 214
  James 172, 204
  John 45
  William 45
LINNARD William 109, 137
LINSIBIGLER Jacob 237
LINTENER George C. 188
LINTON David 76
  William 77
LINUGES John 8
LIPE Christian 172
LIPPENCOTT Jacob 62, 68
  William 79
LISLE Henry 24
LITCHWORTH John 109
LITE Daniel 42
LITLE John 163
LITTLE Archibald 119
  Francis 10
  John 35, 112
  Joseph 70
  Thomas 174
LIVENGUTH Jacob 149
LEVEZLEY Thomas 21
LLEWELLYN William 226
LLOYD David 3, 6, 7, 9
  Henry 33
  Hugh 32, 38, 77, 92, 94
  James 131
  John 126
  Martha 44
  Peter Zachary 83
  Rees 44, 126
  Robert 44
  Samuel 44
  Sarah 44
  Stephen 126
  Thomas 3, 4, 5, 6, 44
  William 21
LOBENGIER John 138, 203, 207
LOBINQUIER John 184
LOCHMAN George 214
LOCK John 204

INDEX

LOCKART Reuben 143
LOCKHART James 233
  Robert 70
LOCKRAY William 33, 40
LOCKRY Jeremiah 70
LOCKWOOD Edmund 233
LOCUM Ebenezer 146
LODGE Benjamin 76, 134, 248
LOFT Capel 80
LOGAN --- 216
  Alexander 216
  George 98
  Hannah 85
  James 10, 52, 85, 154, 156, 201, 206
  John 85
  Thomas 184, 220, 243
  William 15, 24, 85, 105
LOLLAR Maj. 41
  Robert 38, 114
LOLLER Robert 34, 38, 39, 164
LOMBAERT Charles 242

LONEY John 116
LONG --- 95
  Abraham 243
  Andrew 37
  Christian 14, 235
  Ezra 233
  Francis 100
  George 138, 152, 167, 224
  Jacob 125, 183
  James 184, 231, 251
  John 50, 231, 251
  Lt. Col. 111, 141
  Moses 235
  Robert 109, 184
  Robert Carey 171
  Thomas 32, 72, 93
  William 44, 183, 205
LONGACRE Andrew 73
LONGAIRE David 203
LONGANICKAR David 12
LONGBOROUGH John 67
LONGEBACH Michael 244
LONGENBACH Michael 227
LONGENECKER Henry 146
  John 153
LONGNECKER Jacob 105
  John 188
  Widow 202

LONGSTRETH Bartholomew 48
  Daniel 48
  David 47
  Joshua 212
  Mahlon 121
LONGVILLE Walter 231, 251
LONGWELL Mathew 189
LOOFBOURROW David 47
LOOMIS Wright 157
LOOSLEY Robert 62, 68
LORAIN John 240
  Lydia 240
LORAINE John 246
LORD Samuel 211, 214
  Thomas 4
LORENTZ Eve 228
  Wendle 228
LOTMAN George 138
LOUDGE Jonathan 34
LOUDON John 26, 27
LOUGHBOROUGH John 59
  Lord 236
LOUGHLIN Randel 125
LOUGHMAN Caspar 12
LOUGHREY Jeremiah 136
LOUGHRY John 155
LOUKS Jacob 138
LOUSH George 60, 67
LOVE Robery 153
  Samuel 61, 68
LOVELACE Francis 2
LOVETT Daniel 137
LOWBER Francenia 200
  William 200
LOWDEN Archibald 92
LOWE John 171
LOWER Christian 14, 33, 37, 124
  Christopher 75
  George 131
  Jacob 14
  Lt. Col. 101
LOWMAN Christopher 33, 113
  Lodowick 38
  William 38, 183
LOWNES --- 63
  Caleb 79, 90, 149, 171
  David 79
  John 30
  Joseph 23, 79, 91, 149

LOWNS Curtis 137
  Joseph 109
LOWREY --- 56
  Alexander 26, 38, 39
  Col. 40
  David 63, 64
  James 147
  John G. 166, 184
  Lazarus 63
LOWRIE Matthew B. 184
  Walter 218, 220, 239, 243
LOWROW John 25
LOWRY Andrew 112, 143
  John G. 135
  Lazarus 136
  Thomas 182, 193
  Walter 214
  William 214
LOWTHER William 52
LOXLEY Benjamin 38
LOYD John 217
LOYDICK John 53
LOYER Anna Maria 180
  John 179, 180
LUCAS John 232
  Robert 1, 4, 5
  Samuel 174
  Thomas 184, 243
LUCKEN John 8
LUCKENBILL Abraham 221
  Christian 221
LUCKEY Andrew 228
LUCUS Feilding 171
LUDWICK Christopher 36, 43
LUDWIG Christopher 38
  Daniel 98
  Jacob 79
LUITHAUSER Henry 34
LUKENS Abraham 83
  Charles 38, 57, 249
  Elizabeth 83
  Francis G. 237
  Jesse 27, 155
  Jessee 57
  John 54
  Robert 83
  Seneca 73, 161
LUKINS Charles 80
  David 119
LUPTON Joseph 13
LURREW Daniel 166
LUSBY Josiah 80
LUSH Lt. Col. 101

INDEX

LUTGE Anthony Ulrich 105
LUTHER Christian 179
  John 80
LUTLE Roger 69
LUTZ Henry 181, 227, 252
  John 206
  Nicholas 38, 75

LYCON --- 53
LYLE Aaron 107
LYMAN Isaac 167
LYNCH Michael 157, 188
LYNN Isaac 198
  John 16
  Joseph 18
  Lt. Col. 102
LYON Benjamin 223, 227
  James 33, 172, 214
  John 133, 146, 180, 243
  Robert 153, 177
  Samuel 33, 58
  Walter 210
  William 25, 32, 39, 58, 76, 80, 120, 121, 194
LYONS Samuel 36, 112
  William 70
LYTEL Janet 31
  John 31
  Nathaniel 31
LYTLE James 100
  John 126, 165

M'ADAMS William 57
M'ALEVY William 165
M'ALISTER --- 163
  Richard 193
M'ALLEN John 233, 235, 240
M'ALLISTER Archibald 182, 225
M'ALMONT Alexander 212
M'ANULTY Samuel 243
M'BEATH Lt. Col. 141
M'BRIDE Alexander 133
  John 113
  Peter 166, 197
  William 166
M'BRIER Nathaniel 215
M'CADDEN John 184
M'CADDON 191
M'CAHRIN James 119
M'CALL --- 156, 165, 178, 189, 190, 202, 221
  Matthew 163
  Robert 163

Thomas 242
William 197
M'CALLEN Robert 105
  Thomas 105
M'CALLISTER John 227
M'CALMONT Alexander 185, 231, 252
  James 57, 113, 126, 166
  John 213
M'CAMMON Christiana 103
  John 187
M'CANDLESS George 133, 140
  William 163, 180, 218, 236
M'CANLESS Elizabeth 64
M'CARTNEY Laughlin 40
M'CARTY Nicholas 219,228
M'CELLAND George 143
M'CELVEY James 237
M'CLAIN John 227
M'CLANAHAN James 122
  Robert 122
M'CLARION James 104
M'CLAY 154
  William 40, 155
M'CLEAN --- 155
  Alexander 156, 227, 250
  John 118
  Lazarus Brown 143
  Moses 115
  William 115, 220
M'CLEERY John 183
M'CLEES Everet 110
  Michael 159
M'CLELAND George 240
  Lt. Col. 112
M'CLELLAN Capt. 130
  James 140
  John 39, 105
  Joseph 99
  William 38, 104
M'CLELLAND George 110, 132, 136, 184, 212, 215
  James A. 206
  Robert 194
M'CLELLEN John 152
  Margaret 152
M'CLENAHAN James 188
M'CLINTOCK Thomas 201
M'CLOSKEY Edward 148
M'CLUNEY John 252

M'CLURE --- 233
  Andrew 100
  Francis 137
  James 206
  John 206
  Robert 137, 201
  Samuel 147, 214
  William 58
M'COLLOUGH David 150
  James 234
M'COMB Daniel 235
  James 128, 232
  Lt. Col. 142
  William 40
M'COMBS Lt. Col. 112
M'CONAHEY John 151
M'CONNEL Daniel 65
  Henry 65
  James 114
  John 204
  Matthew 97, 187, 191
  Samuel 109
M'CONNELL Arthur 155
  Daniel 243
  Mary 186
  Matthew 56
  William 223, 227
M'COOL John 230, 250
M'CORD John 133, 197
  William 231
M'CORMICK Benjamin 55, 58
  David 223
  George 63, 64
  Joseph 218
  Noble 220
  Seth 154
  William 146
M'COY Alexander 199
  Col. 150
  Daniel 227
  Debroah 227
  John 225
  Joseph 104
  Matthew 188
  Robert 110
M'CRAT 222
M'CREA John 241
M'CREARY Mary 198, 208
  Samuel 198, 208
  Thomas 198, 208
M'CULLEY Thomas 126
M'CULLOCH John 195
  Matthew 195
  William 195

INDEX

M'CULLOUGH Elizabeth 212
  James 215
  Robert 212
M'CUNE Archibald S. 147
M'CURDY Alexander 182
  Andrew 222
  James 147, 215, 233, 243
  Mary 153
M'CUTCHEON John A. 240
M'DERMETT William 156
M'DONALD Abner 220
  Alexander 150
  Ann 219
  Cornelius 243
  Isaac 220
  John 184
  Malcolm 109
  Randolph 219
  William 192
M'DONNAUGH John 214
M'DOWEL Andrew 193
  John 154, 156, 249
  Lt. Col. 141
M'DOWELL Alexander 74, 104, 106, 170
  Charles 146
  James 199
  John 94, 106, 107, 113, 130, 163, 184, 227
  Lt. Col. 111, 112, 142
  Patrick 138, 226
  Thomas 180
M'ELNAY John 124
M'ELROY John 114
M'ELVEY William 64
M'ELWRATH Thomas 105
M'ENTIRE William 147
M'EUEN Henry 166
  Thomas 205
M'EWEN Francis 182, 223
  Henry 182
  Samuel 183
M'FADEN William 227
M'FALL Archibald 138
M'FARLAND Alexander 222
  Daniel 55
  James 184, 193, 194
  John F. 189
  Lt. Col. 112
  William 136
M'FARLANE James 127
M'FARLIN James 202
  Patrick 108

M'FARREN Ann 115
  John 129
M'FERREN Lt. Col. 111
M'FERRON Joseph 240
M'GARRY Michael 131
M'GAW Col. 148, 151
M'GEARY Clement 39
M'GEE Patrick 143, 152
M'GEHAN Brice 56
M'GIFFIN Thomas 222
M'GILL Hugh 204
  John 169
  Patrick 110
M'GINLEY Amos 199
  John 105, 115
M'GINNIS George 183
  James 143
  John 243
M'GLAUGHLIN Neal 55
M'GLAUGLIN Isabella 168
  William 168
M'GOGIN Daniel 226
M'GOWAN Andrew 195, 229, 244
  Arthur 210
  Patrick 242
M'GRADY William 211
M'GRAW James 246
M'GREADY Alexander 140
  Patrick 140
M'GREDY William 227
M'GUIRE Francis 242
  James 243
  John 164
  Luke 211
  Richard 243
  Thomas 184
M'GUNNIGLE John 100
M'GURK Peter 148
M'HAFFEY Margaret 120
M'HENRY Isaac 162
M'HUBBELL George 202
M'ILHENNEY --- 63
  William 41
M'ILVAIN George 197
  Jeremiah 221
  John 195, 217
  Moses 212
M'ILVANIN John 162
M'INTYRE Isabella 199
  Thomas 199
M'JIMSEY William 177
M'JUNKIN David 241
M'KAY John 38

M'KEAN Joseph 214
  Joseph B. 131
  Judge 155
  Samuel 206
  Thomas 60
M'KEE 226
  John 128, 133, 138, 182
  Robert 64
M'KEEHAN John 75
M'KEEN Lt. Col. 111, 141
  Thomas 126, 153
M'KENNIS Mathew 225
M'KENNY Abraham 111, 123
  John 111
  Lt. Col. 141
M'KETTRICKS Alexander 209
M'KIBBEN Jeremiah 209
  Thomas 225, 237
  William 152
M'KIM John 178, 190
M'KINLEY David 126
  Thomas 187
M'KINNEY Abraham 55, 217
  Isac 123
  John 213, 223, 227
  Walter 131
M'KINSTRY Thomas 226
  William 224
M'KINZIE --- 57
M'KISSICK Daniel 188
  David 110
  Margaret 110
M'KISSON Arthur 158
M'KNIGHT --- 155
  David 147
  Dennis 134
  James 184
  John 140, 245
M'KOLLY Molly 227
M'KOY John 192
M'LAIN James 240
  John 199
M'LANE Elizabeth 199
  Lt. Col. 111
M'LAUGHLIN Alexander 136, 156
  Hugh 208
  John 149
M'LEAN John 140
  William 99
M'LENAHAN John 183, 199
M'LEOD John 227
M'LURE Adiel 104
  Denny 104

INDEX

M'MAHON --- 57
  John 55
M'MANIMY William 55
M'MASTER William 177
M'MEANS John 208
M'MECHEN William 186
M'MEENS John 206
M'MELLIN William 170
M'MILLAN John 107
  Robert 220
  Thomas 115
  William 184
M'MILLEN James 107, 108
  Thomas 223
M'MILLIAN William 104
M'MULLEN John 38, 167, 204
  Lt. Col. 111, 141
  Robert 122
  Thomas 227
  William 114, 206
M'MULLIN George 104
  John 109, 165
  Robert 137
  Thomas 223
M'MURRAY Samuel 192, 237
  William 55
M'NAIR Archibald 153
  Dunning 241
M'NEIL Daniel 227
M'NEILL Hiram 148
  Samuel 156
M'NITT Robert 187
M'NULTY Michael 165
M'PHARRIN John 107
M'PHERRIN John 214, 240
M'PHERSON Col. 40
  Thomas 206
M'QUAID Thomas 206
M'QUEHA William 186
M'SHERRY James 140
M'VICKAR Duncan 161
M'WHORTER Alexander 99
MacARTHUR William 214
MacCLAY William P. 171
MacHALOHA 52
MACHLIN Samuel 65
MACK Agness 173
  Alexander 173
  Henry 150
MACKAY James 30
MACKEY David 73
  John 39
MACKINET Blasius Daniel 12

MACKLIN Michael 215, 220, 243
MACKNED Daniel 14
MACLAY David 165
  Robert 165
  Samuel 165
  William 27, 159, 195, 243
  William P. 185, 190, 194
MADDISON James 50
MADDOCK Henry 4
MADERIA D. 114
MAERHOFF Francis 204
MAGAU Robert 45
  Samuel 73
MAGAW David 15
  Robert 76
MAGEE John 223
  Thomas 53
MAGINLEY Amos 222
  John 70
MAGOFFIN --- 56
  Ebenezer 184
  Joseph 89
MAGORY John 190
MAGRAGH George 171
MAGRATH John 154
MAGUIRE James C. 243
MAHAFFEY James 169
  William 232
MAHAFFY James 178, 188
MAHANY Jeremiah 223
MAHON David 140
  Robert 107, 218
MAITHLAND John 149
MAITLAND Alexander 173
MAJOR William 215
MALCOM Debby H. 199
MALCOMSON John 219
MALEBORE 52
MALFESON Bernard J. 114
MALIBORE 52
MALIN Joshua 193
MALONE John 140
MALONEY John 151
MALTBY William 125
MANGHOUGSIN 52
MANIFOLD Henry 167
  Joseph 167
MANKIN Rich. 5
MANLOE George 6
  William 5, 6
MANLY Henry 80

MANN Abraham 4
  Abram 4
  Andrew 224, 247
  Asa 201, 232
  Assa 218
  David 203, 209
  Jacob 189, 202
  John 51, 92
MANOCKYKICHON 52
MANON David 239
MANUSMITH Christian 14
MAPLE Richard 59, 67
MARCH John 237
MARCHAND --- 240
  David 228, 239, 242
MARCHINTON Philip 61, 68
MARCKLEY Isaac 146
MARE Capt. 147
MARIS Elizabeth 147
  George 5, 6, 7
  George Guest 224
  James 137
  Jesse 45, 173
  John 9
  Rachael Ross 224
  Richard 224
  Thomas Ross 224
  William 224
MARKHAM William 1, 3, 4, 5, 6, 7
MARKL George 12
MARKLE Joseph 184, 203, 211
MARKLEY Benjamin 94
  George 104
  Isaac 178
  John 94, 121, 188
  Lt. Col. 101
  Solomon 115
MARKOE Abraham 73
MARKS John 197
  Joseph 22
  Samuel E. 222
  William 122, 223, 227
MARLIN Philip 207
  Ralph 163, 214
MARLING Philip 202
MARQUART Philip 96
MARQUAS Thomas 104
MARQUEDANT Charles 103, 171
MARQUIS Thomas 107
MARR David 210
MARRIOT Joseph 17
MARRIOTT Joseph 16, 17

INDEX

MARSH David 227, 252
  John 52, 221
  Joseph 65
MARSHAL Andrew 222
  William 226
MARSHALL --- 63
  Andrew 146
  Benjamin 28
  Charles 109
  Chris. 32
  Christopher 34, 35, 36, 38, 69, 86, 109
  David 127
  Frederick 22
  George 158, 174
  Hugh 197
  Humphrey 28, 207
  James 74, 136
  James Isaac Thomas 139
  John 20, 88, 104, 143, 146, 220, 227, 242
  Joseph 146, 215, 232
  Lt. Col. 101, 112
  Martha 139
  Moses 97
  Samuel 146
  Thomas 238
  William 36, 70, 146
MARSHELL John 242
  Robert 247
  Samuel A. 247
MARSTALLER Frederick 14
MARSTELLER Philip 39, 61, 68
MARTAIN Manning 152
MARTEN Charles 117
MARTER Henry 147
MARTIN --- 233
  Abraham 247
  Alexander 33
  Benjamin 138, 249
  Charles 154
  Charles H. 200
  Daniel 135
  Elizabeth 37, 174
  George 6
  Hugh 59, 66, 71, 128, 136, 138, 180
  Jacob 182, 183
  James 15, 20, 21, 23, 37, 83, 89, 136, 184, 252
  John 29, 213, 231, 251, 252
  Lewis 29
  Llewelyn 29
  Lt. Col. 111, 112, 141
  Manning 149
  Martha 29
  Patrick 167, 204
  Peter 237
  Richard 96, 241
  Robert 39, 46, 206
  Robert C. 152
  Samuel 173
  Thomas 29, 241
  William 29
MARTSTELLER Philip 23
MARTZ John 237
MARVIN Enoch 243
  Lt. Col. 142
MARY Christian 12, 88
MASON --- 63
  David H. 171
  Eliphalet 210
  Isaac 184
  Samuel 175
  William 171
MASONER Jacob 229, 244
MASSEY Isaac 79
  John 97
  Samuel 38
MAST Christian 180
MASTERS Thomas 9, 48
  William 17, 25
MATHER James 27
  Joseph 38
MATHERS James 230, 250
MATHEWS Robert 222
MATHIOTT John 148
MATLACK George 75, 99
  Isaiah 75
  James 215
  Jesse 99
  Jonathan 99
  Josiah 87
  Timothy 32, 38, 39, 43, 86
MATLOCK George 64
  Isiah 64
  Jonathan 64
  Jonothan 75
MATSON Uriah 169, 247
MATTER Jacob 146
MATTES Peter H. 214
  Philip H. 212
MATTHEW Benjamin 70
  Edward 70
MATTHEWS George 35
  James 116
  John 147
MATTHIAS Thomas 126
MATTSON John 232
MATZ John 217
MAUGRIDGE William 15
MAULSBY Samuel 94
MAUNTZ Janitze 2
  William 2
MAUS Philip 55
MAUSE Frederick 63, 69
MAVERICK Samuel 2
MAWHORTER Thomas 95
MAXFIELD Stephen 79
MAXWELL Isabella 123
  James 33, 38, 50, 57, 211
  John 77, 123, 200, 206
  Margaret 123
  Martha 123
  Mary 123
  Patrick 33
  Robert 223
  Sarah 123
  William 183
MAY Daniel 80
  Ezra 202
  James 46, 86, 94, 125, 169, 193
  John 214
  Lt. Col. 101
  Thomas 76
  Thomas P. 195
MAYBURY Thomas 21
MAYEMOE 52
MAYER Catharine 151
  Christopher B. 183
  George 105
  Henry 126, 131
  Jacob 29, 151
  Johannes 12
  John 124
  Ulrich 12
MAYERLE Frederick 34
MAYES Edward 8
  Isaac 184
MAYKEERICKKISHO 52
MAYLOR James 117
MAYNE Benjamin 12, 13
MAZURIE James 89
McALLISTER Archibald 97
  Richard 36
McALPIN James 171
McALVEY William 87

INDEX

McANULTY Michael 176
McARTHUR Thomas 50
McCALISTER Richard 33
McCALL Archibald 22, 89
   George 13, 89
   Samuel 22
McCALLA William 96
McCALLEM Thomas 72
McCALMON Thomas 122
McCALMONT Alexander 169
   Isaac 50
   James 50
McCAMANT J's. 38
McCAMMON Samuel 103
McCANDLISH George 38
McCANLESS Elizabeth 76
McCARTNEY Andrew 240
   Elizabeth 240
   George 240
   Jane 240
   Laughlin 32
   Martha 240
   Mary 240
   Samuel 240
McCASHLAN James 36
McCASKEY William 33
McCAULEY Cornelius 35
McCLAY John 33, 38
   William 24, 26, 45
McCLEAN Alexander 45, 118
   Archibald 33, 34, 42
   James 34, 39
   Joseph 51
   Moses 70
   Samuel 41
   William 33, 36, 70, 45
McCLELLAN David 73
   William 73
McCLELLAND Andrew 174
   Asa 174
   Joseph 93
   Samuel 75
McCLENACHAN Blair 46, 89
   John 97
   Robert 96
McCLOSKEY Samuel 45
   Samuel A. 70
McCLURE Alexander 50
   Charles 43
   David 36
   James 70, 173
   John 29
   Samuel 70
   William 37, 66
McCOMB James 157

McCONAUGHY David 15,
   20, 33
McCONNEL Daniel 95
McCONNELL Robert 39
   Thomas 108
McCORD William 55
McCORMICK Alexander 104
   George 83
   Hugh 38
   James 98
   John 15
McCOUSLAND Thomas 88
McCOWAN Fallix 27
McCOY John 122
   Robert 15
McCRACKING John 72
McCREA James 51
   Robert 26
McCREARY Samuel 175
   Thomas 175
McCREE John 79
McCREIGHT James 49
McCULLOCH Mary 195
   William 195
McCULLOUGH George 27
   Robert 119
McCUNE Samuel 36
   William 95
McCURDY Alexander 195
McDANIEL Hester 42
   John 26
McDONALD --- 43
   John 98, 169
   Lt. Col. 101
McDOWELL 100
   Alexander 91, 96, 169
   James 20
   John 20, 45, 73, 74,
     171
   Lt. Col. 101
   Robert 37
McELVAINE Joseph 42
McELWAINE George 72
McENTIRE James 15
   William 147
McEWEN John 49
   William 122, 169
McFADDEN John 50
McFADEN William 119
McFARLAND James 176
   John 46
   Lt. Col. 101
   Thomas 53
McFARLANE Lt. Col. 101
   Thomas 118

McFARLIN Andrew 33
McFARQUHAR Collin 70
McFARREN Ann 70
   Lt. Col. 101
   Samuel 70
McGAW Robert 22, 29
McGINLEY Amos 70
   Ann 70
   Hance 70
   James 70
   Samuel 70
   Sarah 70
   Temperance 70
McGLATHARTY Michael 66
McGLENACHEN Elijah 73
McGOWAN John 169
McGREW Archibald 88
   James 88
McHAFFEY Charles 120
McILHENNY William 47, 79
McILROY George 33
McILVAINE David 16
   Ferguson 89
   William 16
McINTIRE Alexander 122
McKAY Aeneas 47
   Elizabeth 47
   May 47
   Samuel 47
McKEAN Thomas 38, 67, 72
McKEE 108
   James 55
   John 48
   Lt. Col. 101
   Robert 76, 94
McKENNY David 37
   Lt. Col. 101
McKESSON James 176
McKIBBIN Thomas 142
McKINNEY Mordecai 35, 94
McKINSTRY Nathan 44
McKNIGHT John 45
McLANE James 38
   Lt. Col. 191
McLAUGHLIN Owen 94
   William 68
McLEAN Alexander 33
   Archibald 35
   William 37
McLEAVY William 33
McLELEN Hugh 83
McMANAS James 75
McMASTERS John 117
McMICHAEL Thomas 116
McMILLAN John 71, 74

INDEX

McMILLEN William 176
McMULLEN James 32
   Robert 117
McMURDIE John 120
McMURDY John 175
McMURTRIE David 22
   William 88
McNAIR James 45
   John 170
   Lt. Col. 101
   William 35, 36, 37
McNEAL Ann 23
   Archibald 23
McNEAR Samuel 51
McPHERSON Alexander 119
   Daniel 27
   Robert 33, 39, 45
   William 73
McTEER William 71
MEAD David 46, 117, 210, 211
MEADE David 56, 66, 104, 110, 126, 128, 138
   Gen. 209
   George 75, 78, 86, 89, 177
   Henry 56
   Maj. Gen. 200
MEALY Samuel 225
MEANS Hugh 249
   John 185
   Robert 171
   Thomas 175
   William 210, 233, 245
MEAR John 42
MEARS John 49
   William 153
MEARSE John 115
MEAS James 31
   John 31
MEASE James 23
   John 19, 21, 27, 36, 42
MEASES Jacob 101
MEASON Isaac 104, 180, 203, 222
   Issac 118
   Thomas 145
MECHLIN Jacob 184
   Samuel 50, 157
MECKLEY George 116
   Henry 116
MECKLIN Jacob 213
   Samuel 91
MEDAR John 74
MEDER John 74

MEEK Joshua 63
MEEKER Samuel 119, 128, 136
MEEKS Joshua 76
MEENES William 102
MEER John 171
MEETASHECHAY 52
MEHAFFEY James 173, 179, 190, 225
MEHAFFY James 183
MEILY Martin 131
MELCHER Adam 88
MELLIGAN James 171
MELLINGER Martin 177
MELLON Atcheson 161, 212
MELLOTT John 33
MELON Atchison 227, 244
MELOY Bartholomew 176
   James 153, 184, 243
MELVIN James 20
MENDENHALL Aaron 184
   Robert 32
MENDING Michael 25
MENDINHALL Jonathan 178
MENG Melchoir 60
MENGLE Abraham 184
MENGT Melchior 67
MENOUGH John 103, 149, 150
MENROW Andrew 203
MENSCH Christian 229, 244
MENSH Abraham 133, 143
MENTGES F. 140
   Francis 65, 76
MENTLY Benjamin 107
MERCER James 72
   John 107
   Robert 182
MEREDITH Charles 16, 28, 63, 69, 123
   David 171
   Hugh 123
   John 88, 123, 133
   Joseph 208
   Martha 218
   Samuel 42, 43, 86, 191, 218, 231
   Simon 166
   Thomas 210, 242, 251
   William 131, 248
MERIDITH John 184
MERIS George 4
MERKEL Christian 73

MERKENKOWON 52
MERKLE Bernard 93
   Jacob 182
MERLIN Philip 185
MERRICK Israel 156
MERRILLS John 221
   Marinda 221
MESHECONGA 52
MESSERSMITH George 138
   John R. 127
MESSIMER Cassimer 97
   Henry 97
   Jacob 97
MESSINGER George 78
METAWEQUAN 52
METOR Jacob 139
METOXEN John 92
METTAMICONT Richard 52
METTLER Benjamin 232
METTS Jacob 12
METZ Abraham 172
   Christian 172
   Peter 77
METZGAR Eve 157
   Jonas 138, 169
METZGER Jacob 146, 147
METZLER Ann 137
   Elizabeth 137
   Jacob 137
   John 137
MEWHORTER Sarah 169
MEY Cornelis Jacobsz 1
MEYER Adam 56
   Henry 108, 124
   John 144
   Lawrence 77, 141
   Solomon 112
MEYERS Jacob 74
MEYMAN John 116
MICHAEL George 98
   John 183
   Martin 190
MICHAIL John 177
MICHEL Joseph 59
MICHENER John 245
MICK Henry 234
MICKEY David 199
MICKLE Isaac 248
   John 33
   Samuel 44, 47
MIDDAGH Peter 102
MIDDLEKAUFF Jacob 168
MIDDLESWARTS Abraham 33
MIDDOUGH Elsa 168
   Levi 168

INDEX

MIERCKEN Peter 232
  Peter 27
MIFFLIN Emily 135
  Frances (Fanny) 135
  Francis 136
  John 17, 21, 24, 27
  John T. 109
  Jonathan 42, 44, 120, 135, 136
  Joseph 28
  Samuel 24, 26, 32, 39, 41, 42, 65, 131, 141, 246, 247
  Sarah 187
  Thomas 26, 27, 71, 72, 75, 103, 108, 187
  Warner 80
MILBERGER Michael 117
MILE Col. 126
MILES Catharine 114
  Charles 114
  Col. 39
  Edward 171
  Enos 238
  James 114
  Joseph 73, 122, 246
  Joshua 191
  Martha 139
  Rebecca 114, 162
  Richard 92, 122
  Robert 237
  Samuel 23, 28, 58, 84, 86, 87, 114, 124
  Thomas 104
  William 100, 104, 114, 211, 236
MILEY John 86
MILLAR James 241
MILLARD Ambrose 201, 218, 234
  Joseph 15, 18
MILLEGAN John 109
  Samuel 238
MILLER --- 63, 64, 110, 115
  Abraham 39, 119, 123, 141, 147, 225, 234
  Adam 104, 138
  Andrew 164
  Catharines 175
  Charles 23, 43
  Christian 58, 95
  Christopher 186
  Daniel 92, 183, 186
  Daniel H. 232, 249

David 119, 136, 230, 250
Elizabeth 28
Felix 14
Francis 172, 179
Frederick 229, 244
Gaven 9
George 14, 49, 144, 189, 198
Henry 9, 74, 86, 92, 156, 232, 240
Isaac 239
Isabella 179
Israel 184, 214
Jacob 11, 12, 49, 241
James 90, 91, 213
James H. 183
Johan 14
John 22, 27, 42, 65, 86, 89, 94, 95, 125, 130, 139, 177, 179, 182, 184, 190, 201, 244
John T. 188
Joseph 7, 157
Joseph I. 98
Lt. Col. 101, 141
Magnus 88
Martin 12
Michael 114, 175
Mordecai 49
Nancy 179
Nicholas 14, 34
Patrick 242
Peter 118, 167
Philip 79
Robert 22, 25, 29, 32, 33, 38, 43, 70, 76, 97, 178, 190
Samuel 102, 123, 150, 178, 179, 183, 186, 195, 216
Sebastian 94
Thomas 186
Thomas C. 206
Valentine 103
Wichard 65
Wiggard 117
William 26, 29, 199, 222, 227
William L. 232
Yost 196
MILLIGAN James 33, 38, 163
  Samuel 201
MILLIRON John 29

MILLISON Jacob 54
  John 54
  Philip 54
MILLS John 48, 203, 224
  Lt. Col. 101
  Robert 170
  Thomas 130
MILNE Edmund 62, 68, 97, 107, 128, 154
  William 244
MILNER Edward 59, 66
MILNOR Isaac 26
  James 109
  Mahlon 121, 137
MILTZEIMER Frederick
  Valentine 72
MINCH Abraham 126
MINER Asher 185
  Charles 137
MINICH Barnhart 216
MINICK Conrad 73
MINK Christopher 13
MINNICK Christian 28
MINOR Asher 207
  John 118
MINSHAL Thomas 20
MINSHALL Thomas 26
MINUET Peter 1
MIRE Abraham 12
  Jacob 11
  John 12
  Michael 11
  Roody 11
MIRES John 7
MIRRIL Jacob 106
MIRRY Sebastian 14
MITCHEL George 136
  James 135
  John 246
  Joseph 66
  William 154, 164
MITCHELL Charles 188
  George 230, 250
  Gove 166
  Hugh 37
  James 12, 31, 118, 167, 203, 204
  John 29, 33, 116
  Lt. Col. 101, 142
  Richard 13, 232
  Ross 43
  Seth 219
  Thomas 171
  William 38, 137, 233

INDEX

MITCHENOR William 195, 196
MIX Amos 150
MIXSELL Jacob 210
MOBLEY Denton 58
  Ezekiel 58
  Margaret 58
  Samuel 58
  Susanna 58
  William 58
MOENS Hans 3
MOGRIDGE Samuel 202
MOHLER Christian 182
MOLAND Hannah 153
  William 153
MOLESTINE Henry 5
MOLESTON Alexander 4
  Henry 7, 8
MOLESWORTH J. 10
MOLL John 1, 2, 3
MOLLISTON Alexander 1
MOLYNEAUAUX Robert 75
MOLYNEUX William 150
MONCRIEFF William 70
MONDERF Peter 80
MONEY Henry 167
  William 176
MONGES Arman 161
  Armantine 161
MONK Charles 19
MONOCKYKICHAN 52
MONTANYE Ann 166
  Thomas B. 166
MONTEETH John 212
MONTGOMERY --- 84
  Alexander 224
  Daniel 118, 123, 125, 169, 184, 208, 224, 228, 235, 242
  Hugh 71
  John 29, 31, 43, 45, 70, 76, 89, 224
  Lt. Col. 101, 111, 141
  Thomas 62, 68
  William 38, 45, 74, 84, 89, 94, 105, 118, 128, 169, 203, 224
  William B. 224
MONTIETH James 243
MONTOUR --- 46
  Andrew 53
MONTZ Mary 252
  Nicholas 252
MOOD Philip 46

MOODY Robert 27, 72
  Samuel 53
MOON John 4
MOOR Hans 14
  James 51
  John 21, 39
  Samuel 183
  William 29
MOORE Abraham 171
  Alexander 119, 145, 203
  Andrew 55, 129, 206
  Benjamin 77
  Benjamin R. 242
  Charles 22, 31, 238
  Daniel 207, 222
  David 104
  Elizabeth 191
  George 48, 56, 129, 206, 238
  Hannah 48
  Hugh 192, 227
  Isaac 185
  James 113, 139, 201, 231, 236
  Jesse 106, 138, 214, 246
  John 21, 32, 34, 35, 36, 39, 58, 126, 135, 221
  John Joseph 3
  Joseph 64, 75, 79, 99, 179
  Lt. Col. 101, 111, 112, 141, 142
  Mordecai 18
  Nicholas 10, 52
  Patrick 89
  Philip 60, 67
  Robert 26, 172, 184, 197, 206, 214, 240
  Samuel 145
  Samuel Preston 17, 21, 28, 48
  Thomas 16, 17, 19, 31, 37, 197
  Thomas Lloyd 78, 88
  William 18, 36, 49, 58, 66, 70, 71, 78, 127, 136, 154, 169, 184, 201, 241
  Zachariah 97
MOORE & KINSEY 19
MOOREHEAD Thomas 203

MOORHEAD 163
  Joseph 220, 243
  Samuel 34, 248
  Sarah 248
  Thomas 208
MOORY Jacob 33
MORAN John 223
MORE John 71, 200
  Nicholas 3, 4
MOREAU Eugenia 201
  Isabella 201
  Jean Victor Marie 201
  Victor 156
MORELAND David 183
MORETON William 7
MOREY Jacob 36
  William 13
MORGAN Andrew 134
  Benjamin 10, 21, 28, 44, 47, 48, 89
  Benjamin R. 105, 113, 131, 187, 191, 218, 239
  Catharine 48
  David 69, 102, 180
  Enoch 173
  Evan 15, 16, 17, 33, 48
  Francis 69
  George 218, 247
  George W. 245
  Isaac 137
  Jacob 33, 37, 38, 39, 69
  James 216
  Jane 44
  John 62, 68, 69, 77, 184
  Jonathan 137
  Lewis 188
  Sarah 137, 204
  Thomas 69, 89, 222
  William 69
MORGAN & PRICE 89
MORGARET Peter 123
MORITZ William 229, 244
MORR Philip 212
MORREL John 240
  William 24, 27
MORRELL William 21
MORREY Humphrey 5, 6
MORRIS Absalom 230, 250
  Andrew 20
  Anthony 7, 27, 48, 131, 141
  Benjamin W. 79, 130

INDEX

Cadwalader 21, 27, 42, 75
Cadwallader 43
  Charles 153
  Enos 183, 222
  Ephraim 234
  Gov. 71
  Henry 153
  James 14, 15, 41, 62, 69, 145
  John 32, 34, 39, 41, 45, 77, 79, 147, 162
  Joseph 15, 16, 17, 21, 26, 182
  Lewis 149
  Luke 16, 17, 20, 21, 23, 26, 27, 44 70
  Richard H. 80
  Robert 22, 26, 27, 31, 55, 71, 72, 73 79, 86, 186
  Robert Hunter 154
  S. 80
  Samuel 16, 17, 21, 22, 31, 32, 34, 39, 125, 234
  Samuel B. 241
  Samuel C. 38
  Samuel Cadwalader 31
  Samuel W. 145, 205, 218
  William 16, 17
MORRISON Abraham 118, 123, 128, 203, 225
  Alexander 73, 75, 222
  Archibald 46
  George 24
  James 97, 180
  John 79, 205, 227
  Robert 174
MORROW Abraham 105
  Abram 78
  Alexander 33, 38
  Charles 214
  James 38, 154
  Paul 196
MORSTOLLER Frederick 144
MORTIMORE William 114
MORTON Aaron 103
  Erasmus 119
  George 129, 176
  Hugh 157
  James 172
  John 18, 20, 24, 27, 31
  Lt. Col. 141 18

Robert 205
  Samuel 27
  Sketchley 31, 38
  Thomas 113, 143
  William 7
MOSER Adam 14
  John 209
MOSHER Jeremiah 129, 206
  Lt. Col. 101
MOSS Samuel 211
MOSSER George 97, 195
  John 182
MOTT Edward 193
  Eleanor 228, 150
  Gershom 250
  Ithamer 242
  John 137
  William 250
MOULDER Benjamin 128
  Joseph 32, 33, 38
MOUNT James 143
  William 53
MOUNTS Lt. Col. 142
  Providence 33
MOUREY Michael 140
MOWER Rudolph 74
MOWRY Peter 240
MOYER Christopher 205
  Frederick 205
  Henry 195, 230, 250
  John 65
MOYERS Lt. Col. 101
  Philip 192
MOYLAN Stephen 148

MUBLY Michael 33
MUCKS Jacob 30
MUHLENBERG Henry 45, 71, 72
  Henry Melchior 145
  Peter 72, 94
MUHLENBERT Henry 106
MUHLENBURGH Peter 112
MUIRHEAD James 70
MULFORD Abraham 161
MULHALLON Lt. Col. 101
MULHOLLAND George 232, 249
  Hugh 205
MULLAN Thomas 23
MULLEN Michael 158, 160
MULLOWNY John 193, 196
MUMFORD Ira 210
  Jirah 202

MUMMY Jacob 227, 252
  Samuel 117
MUNDORF Peter 74
MUNDORFF George 56
  John 56
MUNSTER Paul 74
MUNTS Benedictus 14
MURDOCH Alexander 184
  Samuel 51
MURDOCK Alexander 203, 218, 222
  William 122
MURKIN Peter 194
MURPHEY John 195
MURPHY Hugh 46
  John 190, 222, 223, 227
  Michael 211
  Moses 249
MURRAY Abner 174
  Alexander 89, 222
  Francis 27, 46, 77, 128
  George 170, 247
  James 33, 136, 198
  Jeremiah 136, 180, 202
  John 120, 145, 153, 243, 249
  Magnus M. 206
  R. 3
  Thomas 223
  William 123, 188
MURRAY, FAIRMAN & Co. 247
MURRY James 137
  Noah 204
MUSSELMAN Henry 12
  John 182
  Peter 189
MUSSER Daniel 178, 195
  George 71, 95
  Henry 177
  Jacob 246
  John 72
  Michael 71
MUSSGRAVE Aaron 109
MUSSINA Lyons 186
MUTHARD John 229, 244
  Joseph 88
MYER Abraham 22
  Adam 140
  Christopher 118
  Jacob 117
  John 182
  Michael 127
MYERS George 172
  Jacob 112
  John 149, 176

INDEX

Lawrence 64, 92, 113
Lt. Col. 111, 141
Michael 133
Philip 226
MYLES Samuel 1
MYLIN John 11
Martyn 11

NAGLE Col. 130
Frederick 133
Fredrick 173
George 170
Henry 59
Jacob 93
Peter 46, 62, 68, 75, 184
NAGLEE John 182, 185
NAHOOSEY 52
NANNAMSY 52
NANNESHESSHAD 52
NARGONG 57
NATHANS Moses 128
NAWGEL Anthony 146
NAYLOR James 38
Jeremiah 124
John 124
NEACE Mickael 14
NEAFF Henry 14, 93
NEAL John 184, 222
William 84
NEALE William 19
NEARLY Matthew 77
NEAVE Samuel 16, 21
NEBINGER Ann 87
George 87
NEEDHAM Ez. 6
Robert 2
NEEDLES John 80
NEEL John 144
Thomas 231, 251
NEELY James 206
NEES Jacob 65
NEFF Frederick 138
Jacob 74
John 178, 190
Rudolph 74, 103
NEGLEE John 243
NEGLEY Feliz 160
Jacob 184
John 12, 195, 220
NEGUS Shadlock 133
NEIDE Joseph 221
NEIDIG Abraham 214

NEIFF Francis 11
Henry 11
John Henry 11
NEIGH John 97
NEIGHLY John 122
NEIGHMAN William 55
NEIKERCH John 206
NEIL John 228
NEILL Hugh 19
William 216
NEILLY Hugh 55, 58
NEILOR Jacob 226
NEILSON Robert 187
NEIS Adam 148
NEISLEY Christopher 129
Martin 188
NELL Jacob 193
NELSON David 206
George 46
James 186
John 19, 99
Lt. Col. 101
Robert 116, 220
William 94
NENESHICKAN 52
NESBETT John Maxwell 26
NESBIT --- 57
Arnold 17
John 33, 38, 211
John Maxwell 22, 88
NESBITT John Maxwell 36, 43
NESHANOCKE 52
NESS William 140, 199
NESTOR John 205
NEUS Cornelius 8
Hans 8
John 8
Matthias 8
NEVIL Pressly 55
Priestly 71
NEVIL & RITCHIE 57
NEVILL Nicholas 55
Pressly 139
Prestly 97
Thomas 41
NEVILLE Morgan 240
NEVIN David 183
John 183
NEWBERRY Henry 76
NEWBOLD Caleb 208, 224, 248
Catharine Augusta 208
Thomas 208
William 182

NEWCOMAT Peter 12
NEWCOMB Baptist 5, 6
NEWCOMER --- 129
NEWHARD Peter 200
NEWHART Jacob 185
NEWINGHAM David 204
NEWLIN Cyrus 94, 137
Nath. 7
Nathaniel 9, 12
Nicholas 4, 5
NEWMAN Michael 183, 229, 247
Thomas 193
Wiandt 231, 251
NEWMIRE Henry 25
NEWTON Edmund 216
NICE George W. 172
John 172, 212
NICHLER Nathaniel 214
NICHLIN Philip 194
NICHLOW John 95
NICHOLAS --- 52, 57, 130
Anthony 44
Edward 57
Jane 44
John 44, 47, 93, 203
Martha 44
Mary 44
Michael 63, 70
Samuel 44, 47
Sarah 44
NICHOLASON John 43
NICHOLLS John 55
NICHOLS David 204
Francis 94
Lt. Col. 101
Thomas 140
William 40, 156, 240
NICHOLSON --- 38, 100
David 150
James W. 118, 145, 214
John 78, 86, 91, 107, 127, 129, 132, 133, 143, 151, 159, 176, 190, 194, 228, 231, 242
Samuel 127
NICHUM Leonard 211
NICKEL John 216
NICKLIN Juliana 139
Philip 89, 139
NICOLLS John 211
Richard 2
NILES Nathan 218
William 62, 69
NISBITT James 196

INDEX

NISLEY Jacob 11
NISSLEY Martin 229, 245
NISSLY John 229
  Martin 94
NITHREW Adam 204
NIXON John 19, 22, 26,
  36, 53, 89
  Robert 243
  Samuel 188
NOBELL Richard 129
NOBLE Andrew 225
  Henry 92
  Lt. Col. 112
  Richard 5
  William 175, 189, 225, 246
NOECKER John 64
NOHAKER Johan 14
NOLFLY Conrad 64, 76
NOLL John 200
NONES Benjamin 128
NOON Philip 220, 243
NOOTAMIS 52
NORCROSS William 155
NORRIS --- 25
  Charles 17, 19, 29, 62, 68, 224
  Isaac 8, 13, 17, 20, 59, 67, 154, 230, 248
  Isaac W. 179, 241
  J. P. 230, 248
  John 94, 136, 218
  Joseph P. 105
  Joseph Parker 79, 87, 89, 109, 186
  Mary 27
NORTH Caleb 190, 200
  Richard 147
  William 136
NORTHROP John 124
NORTON John 79
  Thomas 79
NOTTNAGLE, MONTMOLIN & Co. 89
NOWLIN Michael 153
NULFF Henry 231, 252
NULL Henry 210
NUNES Abraham I. 171
NUNNEMACHER Michael 167
NUTIMUS 52, 53
NYCE William 77

O'BRIEN Richard 183
O'CONNER Dominic 250
  Dominic 230

O'HARA James 138, 182
  John 110
O'HARRA Charles 171
  James 128
  William 89, 168
O'KEEFE William 243
O'NEAL Timothy 190
O'NEIL John 214
O'QUIN Toran 104, 114
OADE Thomas 54
OBER Benjamin 191
OBERDORF George 229
OBERLEY Frederick 234
OCKER Christian 58
ODENWELDER Michael 204
  Philip 91
ODERMAN George 99
ODEWELDER Philip 77
OELLERS James 76
OFFICER James 83
OGDEN Benaniel 64, 75, 99
  John 147
  Matthew 232
  Nathan 26
OGELBY Joseph 191
OGILBY Joseph 241
OGLE Alexander 126, 128, 134, 138, 149, 180, 184
OGLESBY Rebecca 172
OGLIVIA James 134
OHL Andrew 47
  Henry 87
  Lt. Col. 111
OHOPAMEN 52
OKELY John 63
OKESON Nicholas 157
OKETTARICKON 52
OKILL George 16
OKONICHON 52
OLD James 69
OLDEN James 79
  John 79
OLDHAM Samuel 234
OLDMAN Samuel 18
  Thomas 7
OLDSHOE George 234
OLDWINE Charles 227
OLINGER Peter 203
OLIPHANT Andrew 189
  Lt. Col. 111, 142
  William 66, 108

OLIVER James 33, 36
  James B. 203, 206, 211
  John 64, 65, 78, 194
OLMSTEAD Gideon 115
ONIONS John 30
ONNAR John 167
ONONDAGO 53
ONSTOTT John 198
ONTACHSAX Peter 53
OPASISKUNK 52
OPEKASSET 52
OPP Jacob 33
  Valentine 179
ORBISON William 184, 202, 204
ORD George 37, 41, 46, 50, 51, 73, 171
  John 16, 17, 21, 23, 36
OREEKTON 52
ORIAN William 3
ORLEDY Henry 126
ORLEIP Israel 97
ORMES Samuel 19
ORMSBY John 49, 130
ORNDT Jacob 26
  James 34
  John 34, 35
ORNER Valentine 79
ORONTAKAYON 53
ORR James 230, 150
  John 187
  Robert 206, 248
  Samuel C. 142, 215
ORTH Gotlieb 114
  Henry 137
ORWIG George 201
  Jacob 172, 201
  John 201
OSEREREON 52
OSGOOD Samuel 43
OSTERHOUT Gideon 64, 77
OSWALD Eleazer 83
OTIS Charles 194, 205
OTSINUGHYADA 53
OTSTOT Adam 148
OTT George 230, 250
  Michael 132
OTTER John 4, 5, 6
OTTINGER Christopher 14
  Esther 207
  John 207
OTTO Bodo 38
  Gerritt 2
  John 94
  Joseph 232

INDEX

M. Gerritt 2
OTTON John 75
OURAN John 35
OUTHOUT Foppo 2
OVERDEER Lewis 161
OVERDORF George 244
OVERDORG Andrew 177
OVERDUR Ludwig 147
OVERHOLSER Martin 126
OVERHOLTZ Jacob 61
  John 68
OVERTON Thomas 233
OVES Abraham 182
OWEN David C. 213
  Edward 4
  Evan 10, 83, 93
  Griffith 4, 5, 6, 16, 154
  Owen 48
  Robert 7
OWENS Francis 30
  Griswold 229, 244
OWINGS Robert 55
OYSTER Adam 237
  George 205
OZEAS Peter 43

PACK Edward 2
PACKENAH 52
PACKER William 35
PAHSCHAL John 19
PAINE Clement 174
  David 174
  Susanna 208
  Thomas 51
  William 208
PAINTER George 109
  Jacob 91, 103, 118, 205
  John 241
  Mary 208
PALMER Barbara 195
  George 239
  Jacob 103, 167, 195
  James 171
  John 98
  John B. 103, 167
  Nathan 146
  Nathaniel 200
  Thomas 80
  William 18, 42
PANCAKE Lt. Col. 111, 141
PANCOAST Samuel 79, 147
  Seth 147
PAPPEGOYA Amigart 1
  Jeffro Armagart 3

John 1
PARCEL John 191
PARE --- 52
PARIS Peter 60, 66, 67
  Sarah 124
PARISH Isaac 109
PARK James 54
PARKE Hannah 199
  Jacob 79
  John G. 156, 221
  Joseph 61, 68
  Thomas 71, 77, 134
  Thomas A. 249
PARKER Edward 37
  Hugh 43
  James 75
  Jeremiah 79, 89, 203
  John 220, 243
  John Ewing 224
  Jonathan 155
  Joseph 30, 31, 32
  Lt. Col. 101
  Philo 143
  Richard 62, 69, 79, 203
  Samuel 120
  Thomas 71, 79, 104, 182
  William 18, 33, 34, 50
PARKHURST Samuel 55
PARKINSON Joseph 43
  Sarah 44
  Thomas 102
PARKS Jacob 234
  John G. 165, 189
  Joseph 72
  Thomas 167
  William 219
PARR James 60, 61, 67, 68, 115, 125
  William 23, 48
PARRIN Francis 18
PARRIS Peter 59
PARRISH Isaac 79
PARROCK -- 18
  James 115
  John 59, 60, 61, 62, 63, 66, 67, 68, 115
PARRY James 153
  John 11
PARSON George 192
  Isaac 193
  James 142

PARSONS Eli 72
  James 247
  John 7
  William 54
PARTHEMER Esther 195
PARVIN Francis 15, 20
PASCHAL Benjamin 32
  Isaac 16
  John 14
  Jonathan 14, 32
  Mary 14
PASCHALL Elizabeth 44
  Jonathan 19
  Stephen 19, 24, 154
  Thomas 4, 5, 9, 59, 67
PASSAGE Hans George 14
PASSMORE Ellis 226
PASTORIUS Abraham 62, 69
  Daniel 5
  Francis Daniel 8
PATCH Richard 213
PATIERGER John 167
PATTERSON --- 56
  Adam 105
  Alexander 46, 117, 136
  Andrew 135
  Elizabeth 251
  James 95, 168, 169, 183, 217, 225, 230, 250
  John 61, 68, 127, 138, 184, 222, 240
  John B. 224
  Joseph 107
  Lt. Col. 101, 102
  Nathan 214
  Peter H. 251
  Robert 32, 75, 178
  Thomas 222, 238
  William 26, 155, 226
PATTON Benjamin 126
  David 157
  James 29
  John 33, 42, 43, 64, 75, 99, 125, 130, 181
  Joseph 190
  Matthew 33, 34
  Melshey 181
  Robert 46
  Thomas 51
  William 39, 80
PATTRIDGE --- 52
PAUL Caleb 45
  James 225
  Jeremiah 79, 109
  John 5, 45

INDEX

Joseph 49
Lt. Col. 102
Thomas 91, 118
William 103
PAULE Philip 74
PAWLING 184, 188
  Henry 18, 50, 57, 76
  John 28, 29, 76
  Joseph 28, 76
  Levi 121, 178, 193, 196, 234
  Nathan 76
PAXON Henry 4
  William 6, 8
PAXSON William 8, 9
PAXTON --- 63
  Henry 7
  John 75
  Joseph 62, 68, 202
  Thomas 35
  William 7, 13, 62, 68, 99
PAYNTON Peter 228
PAYSAN Henry 178, 190
PEAIRS Rachel 240
PEALE C. W. 168
  Charles Wilson 85, 112, 131, 165
  James 170
  Reubens 171
PEALOR Daniel 204
PEARCE Mary 117
  Matthew 117
PEARL Thomas 60, 67
PEARNE Richard 17, 19, 20
PEARSON Bevah 240
  Bevan 213, 216, 241
  Henry P. 214
  Isaac 18, 19, 23, 25, 30, 31, 50, 95, 109
  James 21, 106
  John 77
  John L. 206, 210
  Lt. Col. 141
  William 25
PEASON Isaac 79
PECHER Simon 199
PECK Isaac 159
  Susannah 159
PEDAN Benjamin 37
  Elizabeth 163
  James 163
  John 178, 183
PEDEN Hugh 58, 66
  John 118

PEDERSON Peter 201
PEDON Hugh 37
PEEBLES Robert 36, 243
PEEK Nathaniel 252
PEEL Oswald 41
PEELE Oswald 14
PEELMAN Christian 11
PEGG Daniel 11
PEIRCE Caleb 220
  Eli D. 189
  Henry 9
PEIRSON John L. 205
PELTZ Philip 149
PEMBERTON --- 19
  Christian 226, 227
  Israel 10, 85
  James 15, 44, 79, 80
  Joseph 27, 28
  Phineas 4, 5, 6, 7
  Phinehas 3
  Thomas 5, 6, 7
PEMMISON John 33
PENCE Peter 159
PENDANOUGHHAH 52
PENDERGRASS Lawrence 227
  Sidney 227
PENFINGER Henry 94
PENINGTON Ed. 16
  Edward 13, 15, 17
PENN George 67
  Hannah 13, 28
  John 13, 59, 67, 71, 78, 83, 130, 199, 222
  Margaret 13
  Richard 13, 76, 83, 154, 222
  Thomas 13, 76, 83, 154, 222
  William 1, 3, 10, 13, 52, 154, 221
PENNEBAKER Matthias 49
PENNEBECKER Henry 12
PENNEL Jesse 145
  Joseph 189
PENNELL Dell 129
  Robert 27
  William 128
PENNEPACKER Herman 188
  Jacob 216
PENNINGTON Edward 20, 41, 54, 61, 68, 91, 248
  Isaac 90
  Lt. Col. 141
  Sarah 90

PENNOCK Caleb 220
  Joseph 20
  Nathaniel 16
PENNYPACKER Matthias 188
PENROSE Ann 148
  Charles 248
  Clement 44
  Everard 205
  Isaac 44, 80
  James 44
  Johnathan 80
  Jonathan 79, 148
  Joseph 23, 26
  Samuel 42, 46, 89
  Thomas 22, 26, 44, 79, 89, 171
  William 103, 109, 207
PENSINGER Henry 164
PENTECOAST Joseph 203
PENTICOST Joseph 118
PEOPLES Widow 68
PEPAWMAMAM 52
PEPLER Frederick 23
PERES Peter 92
PERIT Maria 134
  Rebecca Hunt 134
PERKINS Daniel 214
  Joseph 78
  Simon 214
  Thomas 126
PEROT Elliston 85, 90
  John 89, 97, 109
PERRINE William 160
PERROT Eliston 178, 190
PERRY Benjamin 137
  James 38, 39, 86
  Oliver Hazard 190, 238
  William 109
PERSONS Mahlon 125
PESKOY 52
PESQUETOMEN 52
PESS 98
PETER --- 63
  Frederick 74
  Philip 83
  Richard 97
PETERKILL James 7
PETERS Abraham 53
  Amasa 191
  Gerhard 12
  Henry 53
  John 59, 66
  Richard 53, 73, 80, 85, 116, 222, 241, 245
  Thomas R. 237

INDEX

Widow 59, 67
William 222
PETERSON Adam 7, 8
 Derick 114
 Uriah 157
PETERY Christopher 85
PETIT Andrew 117
PETITT Andrew 247
PETRIKIN William 122
PETTIGREW James 77
PETTIT Andrew 51, 87
 Charles 21, 88
 Nathaniel 157
PEW John 237
PFAUT John 115
PFEIFFER Jacob 103
PFLEIGER George 100
PHILE Frederic 29
 Frederick 78
PHILIPS Charles 55
 Comer 247
 Francis 187, 191
 Hardman 175, 187, 191, 224, 246
 Jacob 221, 228
 James 80, 167
 John 63, 103, 187, 191, 206
 John Leigh 187, 191
 Jonas 60, 67
 Miles 97
 Peter 219
 Thomas 136
 William 58
PHILIPS, CRAMOND & Co. 89
PHILLIP George 246
PHILLIPS Catherine 90
 David 196
 Elijah 90
 Falkner 123
 J. H. 199
 John 69, 91, 210
 Nathaniel 123
 Sophia 191
 Theophilus 47
 William 33, 34, 134
PHILSON Robert 85, 184, 203
PHINNEY & PHELPS 238
PHIPPES Joseph 4
PHIPPS Joseph 1, 28
 Samuel 28, 45
PHYSICK Philip S. 109
PIATT John 233
PICKEL Rucolph 88

PICKERING Charles 6
 Isaac 166
 Timothy 71, 74, 76, 86
PICKET Joab 188
PICKLE Tobias 14
PIDGEON Joseph 10, 48
PIDON Benjamin 33
PIERCE Andrew 87
 Cromel 69
 Edward 10
 George 241
 Henry 9, 10
 John 61, 68
 Joseph 114, 128
 Lt. Col. 141
PIERSOL Mordecai 69
 Richard 69
PIGOU Frederick 55, 78
PILE Nicholas 9
 Robert 5, 6, 7, 8
PILES William 6, 8
PILMORE Joseph 72
PILSON Adam 122
PIMM John 249
 Thomas 20
 William 30
PINE Mary 78
 Robert Edge 78
PINGEMAN Hans 13
PINKERTON Catharine 228
 David 89
PINKLEY Joannes 14
PINNEL Jeffery 54
PIOLETTE J. M. 210
PIOLLET J. M. 224
PIPER John 33, 38
 Lt. Col. 111, 141
PITQUASSIT 52
PITT William 80
PITTING Lodwick 13
 Martin 13
PITTINGER Nicholas 129
PIZEL Philip 175
PLANK Jacob 216
PLAYFORD William 147
PLEASANTS Charles 182
 Israel 79
 Samuel 27
PLEIN John 60, 67
PLOWMAN Thomas L. 171
PLUMB Charles 203
 Jacob 164
PLUMER Alexander 232

PLUMMER Samuel 132
 William 102
PLUMSTEAD George 89
 William 65, 89
PLUMSTEAD & McCALL 89
PLUMSTED Clement 10, 30
 William 19
PLUNKET Dr. 155
 William 154
POALK Daniel 155
POE George 240
POKEHAIS 52
POLAND Samuel 204
POLLARD William 73
POLLING Henry 33
POLLOCK James 29, 33, 34, 43, 49, 162
 James Smith 244
 Joseph 129
 Oliver 93
 Sarah 223
 Thomas 184, 210, 223
 William 210, 223
POLLY Amos 247
POMEROY John 66, 71
POMROY John 59, 115, 125, 136
POOLE Joseph 123, 132
 Peter 243
 William 87
POORMAN Jacob 180
PORCUPINE Andrew 188
PORT John 234
PORTE Charles 145
PORTER Andrew 54, 121
 Charles 118
 David 201
 George 233
 James 34, 38, 58, 63, 66, 70
 John Ewing 224
 Nathaniel 70
 Robert 57, 66, 140, 183
 Samuel 227
 Stephen 183
 Thomas 39
 Washington 122
 William 72, 143, 144, 156
PORTERFIELD William 213
PORTEUS James 84
POST David 204, 291
 Isaac 162, 204
POSTENS Jacob 189
POSTLETHWAITE Samuel 43

INDEX

POSTLEWAITH James 240
POTT John 193, 237
POTTAR James 122
POTTER Charles William 133
  Col. 40, 132
  David 124, 129, 134
  James 25, 27, 39, 51, 117, 171, 194, 225
  John 16
  Thomas 226
POTTS David 184, 195
  Isaac 49
  James 38
  John 18, 35
  Joanna 191
  Jonathan 46, 176
  Joseph 119, 154, 193
  Martha 119
  Samuel 32
  Thomas 20, 29, 33, 39, 42
  William 171
  Zebulon 119
POULSON Zachariah 79, 91
POULTNEY John 79
  Thomas 79
POUPARD James 109
POWEL Elizabeth 234
  John Hare 145
  Samuel 86
  William 3
POWELL Benjamin 173
  Joseph 39
  Lawrence 46
  Myers 163
  Samuel 60, 67
POWER --- 100
  Alexander 121
  George 132, 169
  John 56
  Samuel 172
  William 190, 200
POWERS Alexander 60, 67
  J. 56
  James 71, 107
  Lt. Col. 101
  Samuel 181
  William 60, 67
POWL John 116
POWNELL Simeon 246
POYNTELL William 79, 109, 117, 121, 122, 131, 142
POYNTER Henry 6
PRAEZEL Godfrey 74

PRALL --- 63
PRATT Charles 236
  Henry 89, 128
PREMIR Adam 76
PRENIMAN Adam 11
  Christian 11
  Christopher 11
PRESTON James 177, 197
  Jonas 20, 183, 212, 246
  Samuel 6, 9, 150, 202, 210
PRETZLER George 132
PREVOST Andrew W. 247
PRICE Benjamin 109
  Elisha 31, 38
  John 119, 193
  John M. 109, 224
  Jonathan 197
  Joseph 109, 134
  Lt. Col. 101
  Philip 19, 77, 79
  Richard 79, 80, 104, 109
  Rosina 227, 239
  Samuel 119
  Thomas 5, 89, 126, 227, 239
PRICHARD Joseph 15
PRIESTLY John 17, 22
  Joseph 117, 125
PRINTZ Amigart 1
  Gov. 3
  John 1
PRIOR Thomas 22, 31, 51
PROBST John 109
  Mathias 36
PROCKTER William 26
PROCTOR --- 40
  Isaac 184, 206, 215
  John 37
  Joseph 54
  Thomas 80, 93, 96
  William 33, 146, 180, 184, 194
PROCTORS William 36
PROTSMAN John 78
PROUDFOOT James 222
PROUL John 70
PROVENCE Thomas 54
PROVINCE Robert 123, 184
  Thomas 136
PRUDYARD Thomas 3
PRUNER Joseph 185

PRUTZMAN Joseph 233
PRYER Thomas 50
PRYOR Thomas 42
PUCKLE Nathaniel 27, 28
PUE John 114
PUGH Elizabeth 149
  Evan 184, 240, 252
  John 114, 149, 232, 252
  Jonathan 79
  Joshua 211
  Lt. Col. 101
PUGSLEY John Harris 160
PULLIN Samuel 154
PULTENEY Dan. 10
  Henrietta Laura 188
  William 188
PUNKEY --- 63
PURDAY Thomas 225
PURDEY Silas 163
PURDON John 36, 70, 222
PURDY James 34, 42, 165, 173, 212
  Peter 248
  Reuben 247
  William 197
PURVIANCE Henry 236
  John 31, 42
  Samuel 155
PURVIS Robert 189
  William 189
PUSEY Caleb 5, 6, 7, 8, 9
  Ellis 139
  Joshua 94
PUTNAM Elijah 200, 201
PUTTS William 8
PYLE James 220
  Nicholas 9
  Robert 10
PYLER John 248
PYLES 48
PYMN William 240
PYSERHAY 52

QUALPAGHACH 53
QUAY Hugh 158
QUECK John B. 178
QUEE Leth 32
  Seth 36
QUENAMOCKQUID 52
QUICK Jacob 232
QUIGGLE George 157
QUIGLE Lt. Col. 141
QUIGLEY Christopher 128
  Edward 166
  John 197

INDEX

QUIN Bryan 109

RADABUSH Abraham 217
RADEMAN Anthony 2
RADER Henry 77
RAGUEL Abraham 195
  Abram 124
RAGUET Condy 224, 241, 242
RAHM David 187
  Jacob 147
RAHN John 239
RAIGART Martin 233
RAIGUEL Abraham 127
RAINEY Mary 192
  Robert 216
  William 192
RALFE James 24
RALSON Robert 99
RALSTON Andrew 87
  James 109, 136
  John 39, 69
  Lt. Col. 111, 141
  Matthew C. 241
  Rebecca 199
  Robert 88, 91, 109, 136, 186, 188, 212
  Samuel 107
  Sarah 199
  William 205
RAMBO Abraham 144
  Ann 144
  Ezekiel 73
  Gunner 4
  Peter 2, 73
  Pieter 2
  Samuel 218
RAMSAY Alexander 122
  William 126, 190, 243
RAMSEY Alexander 91, 98
  James 113
  John 194
  Robert 33, 143, 154
  Thomas 95
  William 95, 189
RAMSTINE Henry 205
RANDEL Joshua 143
RANDLE Arthur 226
RANK Mathias 179
  Matthias 173, 183, 188
RANKIN Abraham 87
  Archibald 183, 199, 224
  David 125
  Elizabeth 103
  James 35, 43, 87, 103

  Jesse 99
  John 43, 103, 170, 225, 246
  Moses 235
  Samuel 232
  William 33, 39, 99, 138
RANKING William 38
RANSOM Amasa 226
  Lt. Col. 101, 111
RASER William 32
RATTEN Aaron 69
RATTEU Aaron 69
RAUM Jacob 128, 138
RAUP William 78
RAUSCH George 245
RAWLE Anne 186
  Francis 10, 16, 48
  Martha 48
  Samuel Burge 186
  William 72, 79, 80, 89, 109, 131, 246
RAWLS George 190
RAY Richard 30
  Samuel 35, 157
  Thomas 209
RAYL William 197
RAYMON Henry 205
RAYMOND Isaac 218, 227
RAYNAL LeAbbe 80
REA James 189
READ Almond H. 219
  Ann 117
  Charles 10, 12, 13
  Collinson 75
  David 233
  Henry M. 218
  James 32, 33, 79
  John 194, 218, 231, 242
  John M. 218
  Lt. Col. 101
  Margaret M. 218
  Martha 218
  William 117
READHEFER Charles 178
READING George 36
REAKER Conrad 197
  Jacob 160
REAM Abraham 195
  Barbara 195
  Catharine 195
  Daniel 195
  Elizabeth 195
  Esther 195

  Everard 12
  Henry 104
  Isaac 195
  Jacob 195
  Lt. Col. 101, 141
  Michael 128
  Samuel 195
REAMER C. 235
  Frederick 114
REAS Daniel 249
REBENSTOCK Johannes 8
REBLE Conrad 13
RECK George 182
REDDICK David 55
REDFEKER George 118
REDHEFFER Andrew 72,135
  Charles 238
REDICK David 74
REDMAN John 41, 42, 77
  Joseph 9, 16, 31, 51
  Thomas 47, 80
REDSECKER George 217
REDWOOD Samuel 80
REEB-CAMP Charles 14
  Justis 14
REECE Lewis 202
REED Adam 14
  Alexander 171, 203, 218, 225
  Andrew 37
  Caspar 14
  Charles 119
  Hugh 192
  Isaac 221
  Jacob 37, 104, 222
  James 202
  Jeremiah 176
  John 61, 68, 86, 106, 235, 240
  Joseph 41, 144, 181, 227
  Lt. Col. 112, 142
  Mary 221
  Moses 35
  Philip 47, 209
  Rebecca 181
  Robert 214
  Rufus S. 184, 214, 218
  Samuel 201
  Samuel M. 184
  Thomas 221, 222
  Timothy 181
  William 95, 176
REED & PETIT 19
REED & PETITT 22

INDEX

REEDER Absalom 222
REEDY Andrew 177, 186
REEM John 190
  Nicholas 121
REEMER Philip 119
REEP Adam 182
REES David 45
  George 145
  Isaac 241
  Jeremiah 91
  John 69
  Lewis 193, 194
  Samuel 189
  Thomas 103, 104, 106
REESE Isaac 173
  Lewis 130, 169, 203, 246
  Martin 163
  Mary 154
REESER Baltzazar 14
REEVE Peter 16, 17, 20, 21, 22, 23, 24, 26, 27
REGART Martin 201
REGER Martin 215
REIBLE William 29
REICHARD Henry 127, 211
REICHE John 171
REICHEL Charles Gotthold 74
REID John 184
  John R. 206
  Joseph 184
  Robert 218
REIDENAUR George 199
REIF Conrad 12
  Jacob 12
  Joh. Geo. 12
  John George 12
  Peter 12
REIFFSNYDER Abraham 176
REIFSCHNEIDER Abraham 245
REIGART Adam 72, 86, 90, 94, 95, 118, 123, 128, 132, 137, 178, 183
  Emanuel 132, 169
  Gotliep 55
  Henry 183
  Martin 179
  Michael 136
REIGELSBAUGH Barbara 192
REILEY Philip 120
  Richard 38, 65
REILLY Thomas 22
REILY Martin 146, 185
  Richard 31

REIM Margaret 252
  Nicholas 252
REIMER Abraham 179
  Peter 28
REINAGLE Hugh 171
REINECKE Abraham 74
REINHART Barnet 174
  John 184
REINSIMER Jacob 193
REIS Zachariah 79
REISINGER Lt. Col. 111, 141
  Philip 146
REIST Abraham 176
REITMEYER Henry 33
REITZ Leonard 143
REITZALL John 85
REMSBERGER Paul 14
RENGEWALT Jacob 104
RENISON John 106
RENNINGER Martin 187
RENO Charles 216
  Charles S. 240
  Susanna 139
RENSHAW Richard 46
REPPART George 214
RERIGH William 14
RESSOR Bernard 12
REUGLE Henry 142
REVE Peter 17
REX George 20, 114
  Samuel 183, 188
REYMER Frederick 13
REYNELL John 15, 17, 19, 21, 47
  Johy 44
REYNOLD David 163
  Samuel 193
REYNOLDS Benjamin 239
  Catharine 251
  David 184, 194, 204, 220, 228, 243
  George 171
  Jesse 249
  John 27, 33, 213, 214
  Lt. Col. 142
  Richard 5
  William 146, 251
RHEA John 16, 23, 51
  Lt. Col. 101, 111
RHEAM Garret 215
  Nicholas 121
RHEEM Michael 138
RHEMOR Frederick 147
RHINEHART John 193, 195

RHOADS Francis 193
  George 93, 136
  Henry 33, 39
  Jacob 193, 234
  Joseph 147, 189
  Mary 190
  Peter 32, 39, 182
  Samuel 18, 19, 20, 21, 41, 43, 190
RHODDEN William 60, 67
RHODES Peter 120
  Samuel 15, 26
RICE Benjamin 233
  Conrad 164
  Henry 61, 68
  James 115
  Joseph 185, 207
RICH --- 185
RICHARD Henry 138
  Peter 191
  Samuel 246
RICHARDS Casper 108
  David 207, 244
  Frederick 95
  Isaac 61, 67, 91
  Jacob 119
  John 36, 37, 94, 233
  Jonathan 59, 66
  Lt. Col. 111, 141
  Mary 199
  Matthias 127
  Peter 143
  Samuel 79, 155, 159, 193
  Thomas 246
  William 21, 24, 27, 36, 84, 117, 122
RICHARDSON --- 232
  Arnold 102
  Awbray 84
  Edward 45, 84
  Elizabeth 84
  John 3, 5, 7, 80
  Joseph 16, 17, 19, 21, 84, 185
  Joshua 62, 68
  Rebecca 11
  Richard 84
  Samuel 5, 6, 7, 8, 84
  William 26
  Zachariah 11
RICHART Elizabeth 102
  Robert 102
  William 102

INDEX

RICHE Charles 159
  Thomas 22, 62, 68
RICHENBACH William 225
RICHIE George 79
RICHISON Richard 69
RICHTER Peter 233
RICKENBACH Ann 152
  Peter 152
RICKET Thomas 133
RICKIN Elizabeth 25
RIDDLE James 46
  John 69, 242
  Samuel 203, 216
RIDER Alexander 171
  George Michael 47
RIDGELEY Charles 178
RIDGEWAY Jacob 246
RIDGLEY Charles 190
RIDGWAY Burr 210
  Dillaplain 146
  Matthew 172, 178
  Thomas S. 249
RIEBER Sebastian 65
RIEGART Adam 94
RIEGLE George 167
RIFFERT Philip 96
RIFFET Paul 24
RIFFLE Nicholas 80
RIGERS Joseph 194
RIGGLE Christian 177
RIGHTER John 59, 66
  Peter 14
RIGHTMEYER Christopher 73
RILEY Dennis 217
  Richard 80
RINCHART John 97
RINE George 23, 96
  John 184
  Michael 132
RINGWALD Martin 180
RINKER Abraham 168
  Henry 13
  John 21
  Lt. Col. 101, 111
RIPPEY William 33, 180
RIPPY John 206
  William 240
RISE Owen 168
RISK Charles 51
RITCHEY David 175
  Gideon 33
RITCHIE Craig 107, 218
  Isabella 186
  Mathew 200
  Matthew 55, 186

  Robert 194
  William 29, 71
RITENHUYSEN Claus 8
RITIZ Christian 103
RITNER Joseph 238
RITSCHER Adam 206
RITTENHOUSE Abraham 50
  Benjamin 76
  David 29, 31, 32, 34,
    36, 39, 42, 49, 50,
    65, 78, 86, 93, 106,
    112, 116
  George 243
  George D. 240
  Rebecca 124
  William 177
RITTER Ferdinand 165
  John 127, 153, 165,
    233
  Michael 182
RITZ Christian 167
RIX George 209
  Samuel 92
RIXECKER Jacob 108
  John 108
ROAB Christopher 14
ROACH Isaac 79
ROADES John 3, 4
ROADS George 131
  John 3, 4
  Peter 95
ROAN Flavel 115
  Lt. Col. 111
ROBB Louisa 177
  Samuel 178, 227
ROBBINS Brintnel 93
  Isaac 193
  John L. 171
  Vincent 108
ROBERDEAU Daniel 16,
    26, 31, 36, 47, 65
ROBERT Robert 41
ROBERTS Aubrey 44
  Edward 30
  George 21, 79, 220,
    243
  Hough 43
  Hugh 6, 15, 18, 19,
    20, 47, 87, 221
  Israel 147
  James 72
  Jane 44, 84
  John 9, 20, 29, 59,
    62, 66, 69, 80, 84,

    118, 126, 143, 168,
    225, 233
  Jonathan 50, 57
  Lt. Col. 111
  Martha 44
  Matthew 182, 196
  Mordecai 235
  Owen 9, 27
  Patrick 88
  Robert 79
  Samuel 202, 240
  Sarah 44
  William 33, 36, 59, 67
ROBERTSON Robert 72
  William 240
ROBESON Andrew 6
  George 138
  Henry 160
  Israel 20
  James 41, 149
  Jonathan 13
  Joseph Richard 77
  Robert 80, 149
  William 89, 94, 213
ROBEY Thomas 16
ROBIN Celiste 158
ROBINS John 206
ROBINSON 197
  Andrew 46, 113, 183
  Arthur 233
  George 33, 84, 184
  Grizel 89
  Henry 230, 250
  Humphry 22
  James 45
  John 34, 49, 59, 62,
    66, 68, 73, 97, 146,
    214, 222
  Patrick 6, 7, 61, 68
  Richard 69, 95
  Robert 37, 89, 184, 225
  Thomas 80
  William 33, 38, 97,
    241, 245
ROBISON David 65
  George 136
  James 154
  John 182
  Penrose 195
ROBOTHAM George 19
ROCHEY Henry 23
ROCHFORD Dennis 1, 4
ROCK Catharine 175
  George 162, 180, 194
  Jacob 244

315

INDEX

ROCKWELL Abner C. 238
RODENEY William 7
RODEPOUCH Philip 243
RODGERS James 72, 188
  John 72
  John B. 100
  Robert 84
  Thomas 47, 79
  William 152
  Zephaniah 238
RODMAN James 99
  William 24, 25, 31
RODNEY William 5, 7
RODROCK George 179
RODTE Woolrick 11
ROEHRER Godfrey 65
ROGER --- 203
ROGERS Daniel 225, 232
  Isabella 179
  James 243
  John 38, 99, 179
  Jonah 63
  Mathew 206
  Philip 33
  Thomas 61, 68
  William 79, 103, 171
ROHRBACH Christian 105
ROHRER Christian 191, 241
  George 74
  Jacob 144, 169, 179,
    183, 187
  John 74, 172
  Mary 144
ROLAND John 6
ROMAN Jacob 30
  Philip 6, 7, 8
ROMANS Philip 8
ROMIG Adam 159, 185, 215
ROMISH Adam 13
ROMLER Leonhart 14
ROSA Elias 71
ROSE Daniel 98
  David 45
  John 181
  Martha 181
  Robert H. 204
  Samuel 154
  Sarah 154
ROSEBERRY John W. 228,
  242
ROSENMILLER Lewis 236
ROSENSTELLE John 182
ROSS --- 116
  Alexander 55, 243
  Andrew 77

Col. 40
Daniel 184, 204
George 26, 31, 39,
  86, 106, 115, 144
Hugh 119
James 71, 74, 133,
  214, 222, 240
Jesse 188
John 24, 25, 31, 48,
  49, 73, 86, 88, 185,
  217, 243
John Dean 243
Joseph 54
Mary 51
Michael 129, 236
Patton 226
Robert 78
Thomas 80, 224
William 55, 62, 68,
  76, 78, 99, 107,
  137, 146, 227, 244
ROSSETER John 110
ROSTAIN Tournier 119
ROTCH Joseph 241
ROTH Christian 212
  George 46, 47
  Johan Jacob 14
  Johannes 12
  John 47, 136
ROTHRICK Jonas 212
ROTHROCK John 113
ROUGH Michael 59, 66,
  71
ROULET John S. 135,
  137, 201
ROUP --- 167
ROUSCH Jacob 212
ROUSCULP Philip 174
ROUSE Jacob 164
ROUSH Geroge 102
  Henry 246
ROVER Henry 103
ROWAN James 60, 67, 80
  John 211
ROWLAND James 109
  John 5, 9, 33, 69
  Joseph 69
  Samuel 246
ROWLAY Nathan 218
ROWSE George 12
ROWSER John 162
ROYER Bastian 12
  Daniel 199, 222
  Emick 219
  Samuel 36

  Sebastian 127
RUBEL Ulrich 13
RUBEY Charles 46
  Jane 46
RUCH Peter 183
RUCKMAN John 150
RUDEBAGH Christopher 53
RUDEMAN Andrew 30
RUDICIL Jacob 99
RUDISELL Jacob 148
RUDOLPH Jacob 55, 227,
  252
  John 110
RUE Lewis 31
  Rachel 31
RUGAN John 145
RUGH Michael 105
RUIDISILL Melchior 71
RUMBLE Peter 183, 217
RUMSDALE Aquila 115
RUMSEY James 51, 78
RUNDLE Daniel 16, 17, 18,
  19, 20, 22, 42
RUNDLE & MURGATROYD 89
RUNK Jost 105
RUP Hans 12
RUPART Leonard 202
RUPE Michael 236
RUPERT Lt. Col. 111, 141
RUPLEY Lt. Col 141
RUPLY Lt. Col. 111
RUSH Benjamin 38, 45, 72,
  77, 79, 80, 109
  Julia 199
  Lewis 158, 174, 197
  Mary 124
  William 19, 23, 36, 60,
    67, 131, 204
RUSSEL Ann 92
  Edward 17, 22, 89
  James M. 203, 247
  Joseph 89
  Thomas 56
  William 181, 227
RUSSELL Alexander 93, 106
  Edward 29
  James 94
  James M. 209
  Joseph 79
  Joshua 46, 73
  William 223
RUST Jacob 50
RUTT Peter 14

INDEX

RUTTER David 191, 193, 195, 245
  George 79
RUTY Jacob 150
RYAN Charles 64, 75
  James 110
  John 131, 216
  Timothy 136
RYERSON Ann Catharine 246
  Esther Turner 246
  George Ormesby 246
  Joseph Turner 246
  Marriell 246
  Mary 246
  Thomas 132, 203, 246
RYNEERSON Isaac 242
RYSINGE John Claude 1

SACKET Joseph 45
SADLER Isaac 216
SAEGAR Jacob 217
SAEGER Nicholas 185
SAGAL Benjamin 33
SAGAR John 101
SAGEHSADON 53
SAGER Philip 167
SAGOCHSIDODAGON 53
SAGOGUCHIATHON 53
SAHLER Abraham 28
SAHOPPE 52
SALKELD John 91
SALMON Joseph 136
  Lt. Col. 101
  Samuel 100
SALSBURY William 63, 69
SALTER Thomas 23
SALTMARSH John 174
SALWAY William 5, 6
SAMPLE David 101
  James 197, 243
  Jane 243
  Nathaniel 140
  Nathaniel W. 178, 190
  Robert 94
  William 3
SAMUEL Christiana 55
SANDALL Andrew 30
SANDERS Joseph 21
  William 30
SANDERSON George 24
  James 184
SANDILAND James 5
SANDILANDS James 3
SANDS Joseph 75
SANFORD Giles 218, 238

SANKEY John 187
SANKY Ezekiel 249
SANSOM Joseph 91, 171
  Samuel 15, 83
  William 89, 178, 190
SAQUHSONYONT 53
SARGEANT Richard 163
SARGENT John 19
SARISTAGNOAH 53
SASSAMAN Sarah 224
SASSOONAH 52
SASSOONAN 52
SASTAGHREDOHY Abraham 53
SATAGANACHLY --- 53
SATFYHOWANO Johannes 53
SAULINER John Charles 21
SAUNDERS Isaac 27
  John 80
  Joseph 15, 16, 17
  Paul 6
SAUNDERSON Alexander 29
  George 29
SAVAGE James 38
SAVERY Thomas 79, 109
  William 109
SAVETZ George 164
SAVITZ George 131, 141, 167
SAVOY Isacq 3
SAWNWICH John 74
SAY Benjamin 69, 77, 79, 86, 92, 109, 120, 141
  Thomas 16, 17, 24
SAYERS Samuel 158
SAYHOPPY 52
SAYLOR Philip 46, 176
SAYR Jedediah 119
SAYRE John 16
SAYRES Edward Smith 128, 168
  Matthias Richard 168
  Matthias Richards 128
SCAIFE Jonathan 6
SCANLIN -- 25
SCANURATY 53
SCARLET -- 61, 67
  John 158
SCATTERGOOD Thomas 83
SCHAEFFER Daniel 228, 242
  Henry 196

SCHAFFER Charles 145
  Jacob 47
  John 59
SCHAFFNER Casper 72
SCHANK John H. 134
SCHAUM Banjamin 183
SCHAUT Henry 12
SCHEAFF William 89
SCHEID John 107
SCHEIMER Jacob 12
SCHELL John 180, 194
  Peter 184
SCHENKEL Martin 12
SCHITZ Conrad 59, 66
SCHLATTER William 224, 241
SCHLEGLE Henry 45
SCHLOSSER George 38, 39, 71
SCHMIDT John Frederick 65
SCHMISER George 183
SCHNEIDER Benjamin 201
  Caspar 148
  Christian 65
  David 37
  George 148
  Henry 13
  Jacob 225
  Nicholas 79
  Peter 13
  Sebastian Reiff 13
SCHNEYDER Henry 95
  Herman 40
  Jacob 95
SCHNIDER Catharine 96
  Jacob 123
  Nicholas 144
SCHNYDER Lt. Col. 141
SCHOCK John 163
SCHOENER John 217
SCHOLFIELD Jonathan 124
SCHOLL Johannes 8
SCHOLTZ George 13
SCHOLTZE David 13
SCHOME John 206
SCHONER Daniel 13
SCHRACK John Jacob 12
  John Joseph 12
  Philip 12
SCHRADER Lt. Col. 141
SCHREADER Lt. Col. 111
SCHREINER Jacob 32
SCHRIBER John 154
  Sebilla 154
SCHRINER Jacob 38

INDEX

SCHRIOCK --- 116
SCHRIVER --- 105
SCHRUNK Lt. Col. 102
SCHRYNER Jacob 32
SCHUBART Michael 33
SCHULER Gabriel 8
SCHULL Edward 24
  John 128
SCHULLY Daniel S. 184
SCHULTZ Peter 37
SCHULTZBACH Henry 99
SCHUTE Swens 2
SCHUYLER John P. 238
SCHWAARTZ Abraham 12
SCHWENCK George 188
SCHWENK Jacob 221, 228
SCOFIELD Nathan 87
SCOGGS John R. 214
SCOTT Andrew 222
  Archibald 164
  David 205, 234
  George 184, 200, 210
  George M. 129
  Hugh 42
  James 55, 129, 153, 165
  John 102, 120, 156
  Joseph 64
  Josias 33
  Lt. Col. 101, 111, 141
  Martha 48
  Mary 210
  Mary Anna 187
  Moses 136, 138
  Patrick 33, 38
  Philip 35
  Robert 36, 144, 193, 206
  Samuel 206
  Thomas 33, 74, 199
  William 33, 35, 42, 44, 99, 129, 143, 164, 248
SCOTT & McMICHAEL 22
SCRAVENDYKE Peter 194
SCUDDER D. 210
SCULL Edward 15, 155
  Jasper 154
  John 97, 240
  Joseph 154
  Nicholas 48, 53, 54
  William 24, 27, 46, 55, 154
SCULLY Dennis S. 222
SEABOLD --- 104
  Christopher 104, 114, 194

SEAGER Daniel 202
  Jacob 207
  Joseph 184
SEAGRIST Jacob 154
SEALS James 152
  William 174
SEAMAN John 167
SEATON Francis 134
  James 171
SEBOLD Lt. Col. 111
SECANE --- 52
SECHLER Michael 153
SEEBOLD Christopher 138, 209
SEEBOLT Lt. Col. 141
SEELY Barbara 25
  Capt. 196
  Charles B. 243
  Col. 185
  Isaac 209, 217
  John 46
  Jonas 20, 21
SEESHOLTZ David 14
SEGAR Frederick 104
SEGER Frederick 97
SEGLE Benjamin 38
SEIBERLING John 237
SEIDLE Philip 144
SEIJL Jacob 13
SEIP Wendell 172
SEIPLE Jacob 206
SELIN Anthony 86
SELL Eva 128
  Jacob 128
  Ludwig 64
SELLARS John 32, 78
SELLER John 27, 32
  Samuel 131, 185, 233
SELLERS David 79
  John 41, 49, 51, 71, 75
  Joseph 157
  Michael 226
  Nathan 79, 178
  Samuel 130, 168, 183, 246
SELLIN Henry 8
SELLINGER William 11
SELTZER Christian 183
  Jacob 12, 90
SEMPLE Caldwell 129
  David 32
  Nathaniel 72
  Nathaniel W. 75
SENDEL Philip 246

SENSEMAN Christian D. 212
SENSINIGH John 44
SENTON Joseph 207
SENUGHSIS 53
SEQUARISERA 53
SERGEANT Elizabeth 116
  Jonathan 34
SERRILL Isaac 77
SERVER Benjamin 133
SEVITZ George 120, 133
SEWELL Richard 48
SEYMOUR John 191
  Joseph H. 171
  Samuel 170
  Samuel S. 202
SHADE Henry 166
  Ludwig 198
SHADEL Michael 165
SHADLE Henry 162
SHADUCK Jarret 232
SHAEFFER Catharine 152
  Elizabeth 162, 242
  John 152
SHAFER James 231, 251
  John 232
  Samuel 184
SHAFFER Adam 14
  David 42
  Frederick D. 144
  Jacob 14, 206
  James 206
  Johannes 12
  John 66, 150
SHAFFNER Caspar 33, 95
  Casper 24, 86, 129, 152, 183
  Peter 90
SHAINLINE Jacob 144
SHAKHOPPOH 52
SHALL James 236
SHALLCROSS John 76
SHALLUS Francis 89
  Jacob 83
SHANK Christian 187
  Frederick 177
  Jacob 237
  John 11
  Michael 12
SHANNON David 84
  James 76
  John 178
  Joseph 184
  Robert 50, 57, 76
SHANON John R. 214, 221
SHANTZ Isaac 97

INDEX

SHARARD James 194
SHARDER Ottho 123
SHARDLE John 144
SHARE Henry 130, 169,
  178, 179, 180, 183,
  190, 225
SHARER Henry 144
SHARLOE William 10
SHARP Alexander 128, 138
  Daniel 72, 130
  Edward 248
  Eva 106
  Jacob 204
  James 210
  John 77, 107, 152
  Joseph 91, 127
  Peter 77, 91
  Philip 106
  Thomas 8, 220, 243
  William 37
SHARPE Conrad 55
  Granvolle 80
SHARPLESS Abraham 79, 183
  David 153
  Enos 189
  Joseph 79
  Townsend 249
  William 64, 75, 169
SHARSWOOD James 90
SHARTEL George 167
SHAUFLER Lt. Col. 101
SHAUGHAN Daniel 63
SHAUM Benjamin 138, 169
SHAURWASIGHON 52
SHAVER Bartholomew 14
  John 33
SHAW --- 149
  Benjamin 240
  Ichabod 216
  Jane 247
  Joseph 171
  Josiah Y. 123, 183
  Mathew 139
  Matthew 147, 168
  William 36, 38, 150
SHAWANAUGH 63
SHEADER Frederick 237
SHEAF Whilliam 72
SHEAFF Henry 29
  William 29, 97
SHEARER Andrew 106
  Bernard 50
  Henry 188
  Jacob 114
  James 143

John 50
SHEARMAN --- 53, 57
  Lt. Col. 101
SHEDER Baltzer 162
SHEE John 36, 134
SHEED George 218
  William 39
SHEERMAN 50
SHEFFER Henry 103
SHEIB Peter 217
SHEIDE Christian 134
SHEIFLEY Jacob 154
SHEINER Adam 55
SHELBY Evan 33
SHELL Henry 209
  Peter 14
SHELLEY Jacob 102
SHELLY Barbara 219
  Jacob 230, 250
  John 183, 188
  Peter 219
SHELMIRE Jesse 182
SHENK Henry 234
SHENOWITH Arthur 240
SHEPARD John 160, 174,
  189, 198
SHEPHERD John 166
  William 119
SHEPPARD Henry 6
  Henry Lennox 152
  Hercules 4
SHERER --- 228
  David 53
  John 108
  Samuel 93, 221, 228,
  236
  William 73
SHERIDAN Abraham 161,
  167
SHERMAN --- 25
  Conrad 146
  George 206
SHERRARD William 136
SHERRER Joseph 39
SHERRIFF William 114
SHERTEL George 206
SHERTZER John 127, 183
SHERWOOD William 4
SHETTLE George 149
SHEWARD Rosanna 75
SHEWART Caleb 22
SHEWELL Joseph 40
  Lydia 240
  Nathaniel 123
  Stephen 40, 240

SHEWMAN John 136
SHIBE Catharine 152
SHIEFFELIN Jacob 120
SHIDLES --- 57
  David 207, 218, 222,
  245
  James 172
  John 34, 59, 66, 71
  Thomas 64, 79
SHIFFERT Andrew 204
SHINDEL Peter 199
SHINDLE Peter 100, 103,
  124, 138
SHINER Andrew 185
  Chrisophel 116
  Christian 116
  Elizabeth 116
  Jacob 207
  Melchior 116
SHINGLE Peter 246
SHINKLE Frederick 62
SHINN John 205
SHIPLER Mary 49
SHIPLEY John 161
  Thomas 161
SHIPMAN John 226
SHIPPEN Edward 3, 7, 8,
  32, 65, 71, 73, 83,
  102, 154
  Joseph 10, 25, 69
  William 16, 23, 77
SHIRAS George 97
SHIRK Christian 179
  David 205
  Matthias 229, 244
SHISLER Henry 36
SHITMOR Samuel 233
SHMEAL George 238
SHOALS Stanton 167
SHOCH John 136, 182
SHOCHELEAR Albertus 48
SHOCK Joseph 154
SHOCKEY Christian 149
SHOCKLIER Henry 14
SHOEMAKER --- 63
  Anthony 180, 186
  Benjamin 16, 28, 79
  Charles 38, 39, 49, 75
  Daniel 234
  David 234
  George 8
  Henry 46, 95
  Isaac 8

319

INDEX

Jacob 8, 19, 21, 23, 26, 28, 35, 79, 109, 119, 169, 208
John 73, 114
Jonathan 22, 73
Lt. Col. 141
Peter 8
Samuel 16, 23, 35, 59, 60, 62, 67, 69, 108
Solomon 142
Thomas 30, 79, 149
William 61, 68
SHOENER Adam 143
SHOFF John 86
SHOLE Stanton 197
SHOMO Anthony 64
SHOOK John 223, 227
SHORES Jonathan 191
SHORP John 140
SHORT James 87
John 84
SHORTALL Thomas 104, 110
SHORTY Christopher 76
SHOTWELL Joseph 80
SHOUB Henry 14, 123
SHOUFFLER Valentine 131
SHOUP Lt. Col. 111
SHOUSE Jacob 214, 235
SHOUSLER Valentine 97
SHOWERS Adam 61, 68
SHRACK John 20
Lewis 188
SHRADER George 154
SHREINER Hans Adam 14
SHREVE John 150, 219, 238
SHRIVER --- 105
Andrew 37
Frederick 212
SHROEDER Henry 205
SHROM Joseph 146, 183
SHROPP John 85
SHROYER --- 170
SHRUM John 228, 240
SHRUPP Lt. Col. 101
SHRYOCK John 114
SHUBART Michael 42, 43, 66
SHUBERT Michael 56
SHUGERT Joseph B. 231, 251
SHULER Henry 185
William 184, 195
SHULL John 138
SHULTS Andrew 11

SHULTZ Christopher Emanuel 45, 72
Daniel 209
Frederick 121, 147
Isaac 209
Jacob 209
John 23
John Andrew 225, 246
SHULZE J. Andrew 199
Peter 148
SHUMAN John 251
SHUTE -- 44
Attwood 16
Sarah 44
SHWOPE John 12
SHYMER Edward 88
SIBLEY Jacob 74
SICHAIS 52
SIDLE George 228
SIGFRIED Hans 12
SIGHTS David 197
SILFIUS John 207
SILL Thomas H. 218
SILLS John 162
SILSBY Uriah 208
SILVER Francis 71
SILVERWOOD James 243
Thomas 243
SIMCOCK John 1, 8, 10
SIMCOCKS John 3
SIMENS Walter 8
SIMMERMAN Henry 114
SIMMONS Anthony 133, 205
Joseph 109
Leeson 41
Noah 191
SIMON George 162
SIMONDS Lt. Col. 141
SIMONTON Alexander 119
Robert 204
SIMPSON Dr. 239
John 26, 34, 92, 123, 138, 140, 147, 180, 183
Matthew 65
Michael 60, 67
Nathaniel 131, 153
Samuel 58
William 202, 204
SIMS Buckridge 16, 21
Joseph 19, 21, 27, 69, 89
SIMSMORE William 1
SINCLAIR George 68
SINCLAIRE George 76

SINGER Caspar 14
Christian 231, 251
John 139, 145, 147
SINQUEST Daniel 173
SINTON James 202
SIORTS Cornelius 8
SITGREAVES John 89
Samuel 78, 113, 141, 218
SKEER Enoch 211
SKELTON George 242
James 231, 251
SKILLING John 94
SKINNER Enoch 199
James 60, 67
John 240
Reuben 113
SKYRIN Ann 190
SLACK --- 63
SLAGLE Henry 33, 37, 38, 39, 121, 147
SLAREMAKER Mathias 12
SLATER Ann 139
Elizabeth 139
James 139
John 139
Mary 139
Prudence 139
Sibby 139
Thomas 95, 139
SLATOR William 160
SLAWSON Enos 216
Widow 232
SLAYMAKER Amos 50
Henry 39, 72, 129, 139, 178, 183
John 72
SLEMONS Thomas 50
SLINGLOFF Henry 13
SLOAN James 104, 116, 136, 194
John 126, 184, 232
Joseph 80
Lt. Col. 112
Samuel 29, 49, 189
SLOANE Samuel 33, 40
Thomas N. 136
SLOCUM Benjamin 176, 247
Ebenezer 176, 211
Joseph 137
SLONECKER John 229, 245
SLOREY John 229
SLOUGH George 142
Leonard 87
Matthias 71, 85, 95

INDEX

SLOW John 160
SMALL George 173, 199
   Peter 113
SMALLWOOD Richard 115
SMELL George 216
SMIDT Deryck 1
SMILEY John 38
   Samuel 166
   Thomas 247
SMILIE John 80
SMITH --- 63, 88, 158, 170, 238
   Abraham 117
   Adam 153, 204
   Alexander 62, 68
   Armstrong 11
   Bastian 12
   Charles 113, 136, 183
   Clifford 191
   Daniel 89, 94, 122, 133, 147, 179
   Daniel B. 241
   David 204, 220
   Deveraux/Debereux 49, 58, 66, 130
   Dr. 155
   Elizabeth 115, 210
   Emanuel 182
   Esther 189
   Ezekiel 29
   Francis A. L. 178
   Frederick 50, 71, 127, 184, 206, 237
   George 47, 50, 57, 88, 154, 176
   Hannah 85
   Henry 4, 5, 6, 14
   Jacob 103
   James 29, 34, 39, 40, 74, 79, 80, 99, 109, 137, 143, 174
   Jane 46
   Johannes 14
   John 8, 15, 18, 19, 22, 27, 40, 43, 60, 67, 80, 103, 108, 153, 154, 163, 171, 178, 205, 221, 237
   John D. 249
   John Jacob 218
   Jonathan 184, 186, 206, 213
   Jonathan B. 32, 34, 36, 38, 39, 41, 99, 239
   Jonathan Bayard 23, 57, 105, 126, 152

   Joseph 71, 74, 95, 104, 185, 207, 213, 233
   Leonhart 14
   Levi 177
   Lt. Col. 101, 111, 141
   Margaret 71
   Marthan 119
   Mary 153
   Mathew 151
   Melchior 210
   Michael 140
   Nathan Allen 79
   Nathaniel 196
   Newberry 109
   Peter 12, 55, 190
   Peter T. 198, 218
   Philip 169
   Richard 65, 133, 202, 204, 239
   Robert 39, 43, 51, 70, 84, 88, 89, 95, 99, 103, 112, 224
   Rowland 14
   Samuel 16, 32, 34, 39, 90, 104, 109, 137
   Samuel Stanhope 99
   Sarah 189
   Thomas 16, 18, 33, 39, 40, 45, 103, 108, 109, 111, 154, 174, 179, 194, 195, 210, 248
   Thomas Duncan 64
   Timothy 174
   Walter 183, 189, 195, 222
   Widow 217
   William 31, 33, 36, 41, 51, 69, 86, 89, 94, 169, 189, 206, 223
   William Augustus 189
   William Hooker 91
   William R. 184, 202, 204, 206
   William W. 77
   William Wermiss 202
   Williamina E. 199
   Wilson 117, 170, 198, 200
   Wyand 210
SMITH & RIDGEWAY 89

SMITHERS Jacob 213
SMITHS Michael 11
SMOUT Edward 69
SMYSER George 189
   Jacob 199
   Philip 250
SNEIDER Jacob 23
SNENER Adam 95
SNEVELY Casper 33
   Isaac 237
   Jacob 12
   John 11
   John Jacob 11
SNIDER Christian 50
   Daniel 202
   Jacob 147
   Lt. Col. 141
SNIVELY Joseph 183
SNODGRASS Benjmain 44
   William 72
SNOW John 219
SNOWDEN Charles 245
   Isaac 23, 33, 34, 41
   Jedediah 42
   John M. 138, 184, 240
   Joseph 117
   Thomas 148, 156
SNOWDEN & NORTH 89
SNYDER Daniel 146
   David 217
   Dicter 167
   George 132, 169, 179, 183, 190
   Henry 14, 209
   Jacob 138, 150, 180, 203
   John 12, 79, 177, 193, 206, 209, 217
   Joseph 110
   Lt. Col. 141
   Michael 99
   Nicholas 217
   Peter 200
   Philip 148
   Simon 86, 231, 251
SOLMS Count 106
SOLOSSER George 51
SOMERS Uly 196
SOMMER Jacob 128
SOMMERLAT William 65
SOMMERS Jacob 118
   John 37
SONGHURST John 4
SONGS John 1
SONTAGG Euphrosyne 190
SOTCHER John 9

INDEX

SOUBER George 13
  John 13
  Peter 13
SOUDER Jacob 12
  Thomas M. 182
SOUR Christopher 60, 67
SOUTH Enoch 202
  Humphry 3
  John 237
SOUTHERLAND 98
SOUTHERSBY William 4, 5
SOUTHRIN Edward 3, 4
SOUTHWORTHE John 1
SOWER Christopher 85, 93
  David 85
  Hannah 93
  Philip 177
SOWERS Christopher 11
SOX Andrew 228
SPACKMAN Samuel 241
SPALDING Ezra 163, 215, 233
  Harry 206, 233
  Lt. Col. 111, 141
  Simon 64, 77
SPANG Frederick 167
  Lt. Col. 101
SPANGENBERG Thomas 210
SPANGENBERGER Thomas 238
SPANGLER Baltzer 74
  Daniel 113
  George 120, 168, 179, 188, 190, 199
  Jacob 182, 183, 248
  Lt. Col. 111
  Michael 206
  Michael H. 193
  Peter 148
  Rudolph 132
  Samuel 120, 140
SPARK --- 39
SPARKS Thomas 232
SPAWLDING Simon 63
SPAYD Christian 183, 187, 188, 246
  John 136, 184, 242, 246
SPEAR Jane 197
  John 184, 197
  Joseph 197
  Mary 197
  Nancy 197
  William 197
SPEARS Robert 70
SPECHT Adam 209
SPEEDY William 26

SPEER Jane 207
  John 207
  Joseph 207
  Mary 207
  Nancy 207
  William 29, 207, 228
SPEIDER Jacob 153
SPENCE Nathaniel 208
  Thomas 118
SPENCER Jacob 230, 250
  Lt. Col. 101
  Peter 202, 210
  Thomas 143
  Uriah 218
  William 48
SPENGLER Henry 73
SPERING Elizabeth 44
  Henry 44
  Jane 44
  John 44
SPERRY Jacob 119, 128
SPIEGLE Mary 139
  Michael 139
SPIKE --- 19
SPIKER Benjamin 20
  Henry 123
  John 93
  Peter 35
SPONG Leonard 237
SPOON John 46
SPRAGUE William Peter 92
SPRENKLE Daniel 176
SPRING Marahal 56
SPRINGER Lt. Col. 102
SPRINGET Harbert 3
  Harbet 3
SPROAT Lt. Col. 112, 142
SPROGEL Ann 122
  Elizabeth 122
  John 122
  Ludwick 122
SPROTT Thomas 252
SPROUT Lt. Col. 101
SPYCHER Henry 37
SPYKER Benjamin 26, 39, 46
  Peter 33, 45, 97
SQUIRE Jacob 192
  Odel 191
ST. CLAIR Arthur 26, 36, 127, 170, 178, 210
  Louisa 177
STACKHOUSE Francis 170

STACKPOLE James 65
STAFFORD Warren 237
STAHL Jacob 138
STAHLEY George 23
  Jacob 110, 115
STAKE George 72
STELEY Jacob 60, 67
STALFORD John 226
STALL Godfrey 225
  Lt. Col. 102
  Michael 85
STALLS Caspar 8
STAM Warner 34
STAMBACH Daniel 230, 250
  Philip 145
STAMPER Joseph 21, 27
STANARD Daniel 220, 243
STANBURG Nathan 9
STANDFORD Abraham 122
STANER Christian 12
STANFIELD Francis 4
STANGERT Lewis 72
STANLEY Colvin 238
  Matthew 183
STANLY Matthew 114
STANSBURG William 246
STANTEN Samuel 172
STANTON Asa 134, 210
  Isaac 200
  Lt. Col. 111
  Samuel 121
STAPLER John 80, 162
STAR James 29
STARBIRD John 149, 238
  Lt. Col. 101
STARK Ichabud 251
STARNE Joseph 182, 197
STARNER Adam 225
STARR James 79, 80, 91
  John 79
STARTIN John 27
STATLER John 163, 235
  Lt. Col. 111
STAUCH Conrad 96
STAUDT John 221, 228
STAUFER Christian 225
  Widow 229, 245
STAUFFER Christian 115, 191
  Rudolph 195
STAUGH Conrad 124
STAUNTON Samuel 184
STAY Frederick 12
STAYER Christian 74
STAYMAN Joseph 237

INDEX

STEADMAN Charles 16
STECHTER Samuel 217
STEDMAN Charles 21
  James 95
STEEL --- 56
  Alexander 109
  James 47
  John 22, 25, 65, 144
  Lt. Col. 101
  Martha 47
  Peter 70
  Richard 177
  Robert 45
  Samuel 27, 184, 204
  William 136, 190, 204, 225
STEELE David 122
  James 222, 228, 246
  John 109, 114, 119, 133, 222
STEEN James 84
  Matthew Taylor 159
STEENE James 121
STEER Christian 42
STEES Frederick 126, 194
STEFFEN Jacob 220
STEHELY Jacob 61, 68, 237
STEHLEY John 226
STEHMAN Christian 183
STEIN Abraham 103
  Catharine 103
  Henry 97
  John 103
STEINER Melchior 43, 83
STEINMETZ Daniel 14
  John 28, 42, 86, 89
STEITZ George 14
STELL Charles 79
STEM Jacob 185, 217
  Peter 233
STEMAN John 237
STEN Jacob 207
STENGOR John 181
STEOVER Tobias 195
STEPHEN James 29
STEPHENS Ebenezer 216
  Giles 208
  Henry 79
  Luke 56
  Philander 219
  Thomas 208
  Vachel 240
STEPHENSON James 70, 115
  Lt. Col. 142

STERLING Daniel 224, 232
  James 97
  William 220, 247
STERRET David 75, 212
  Robert 110
  William 110
STERRETT David 243
  John 90
  Lt. Col. 101
STETLER Johan 14
STEUART Charles 19
STEUBEN Baron 51, 57
STEVANS Jonathan 210
STEVENS --- 56
  Abijah 197
  Ebenezer 133
  John 87
  Jonathan 224
  Noah 209
  Richard 27
STEVENSON Cornelius 171
  George 76, 97, 117, 240
  James 149
  Joshua 186
  Lt. Col. 112
  Robert 34, 36, 38, 58, 66, 104
  Thomas 9
STEWARD Catharine 49
  Daniel 119
  George 184
  James 183
  Robert 49
  Samuel 201
STEWARDSON Thomas 136, 185, 187, 191, 201, 242
STEWART Alexander 31, 147, 180
  Andrew 51, 57, 86
  Charles 26, 207, 238
  Daniel 189
  David 93, 135, 205, 220, 243
  George 180, 243
  James 26, 161, 252
  James E. 208
  James P. 214
  John 64, 65, 78, 97, 120, 140, 157
  John Carlisle 187
  John M. 243
  Lazarus 26

  Robert 37, 71, 73, 180, 243
  Robert T. 190
  Samuel 96, 184
  Thomas 123
  Thomas H. 184
  Walter 56, 78, 86, 87, 88, 151
  William 26, 97, 122, 185
STEWART & BARR 89
STEWARTSON Thomas 207
STICHLER Andrew 168
STICKLE Elizabeth 211
  John 211
STIEGELL Henry William 30
STILES Edward 60, 61, 67, 68
  Joseph 24, 47, 69, 86
  Thomas T. 178, 215
STILLE John 73, 89
  Oloffe 2
STILLINGER Jacob 223
STILLWELL John 202
STILTFORD Thomas 59, 60, 67
STINE Daniel 182
  George 176
STINGER Conrad 180
STITZEL--- 236
STITZER Jacob 216
STOCHER John 9
STOCK --- 114
STOCKDALE William 5, 6
STOCKDON Robert 138
STOCKELY Lt. Col. 101
STOCKER John C. 117, 122, 194, 241
  John Clement 69, 89, 109, 245
  Mary Catharine 245
STOCKER & FULLER 22
STOCKLEY John 7
STOCKTON Joseph 110, 214, 240
  Lt. Col. 142
STODDARD John 242
STODDART John 211
STOEVER Frederick 123
STOKELEY Benjamin 252
STOKELY --- 56
  Benjamin 104, 107, 231
  Lt. Col. 142
  Nehemiah 154
  Susanna 154

INDEX

Thomas 57, 224
STOKES James 109
  John 126
  Samuel 192
  Thomas 80
STOLL Andrew 227
STONE Frederick 104
  Ludowick 28
  Robert 150
STONEBURNER Ann 124
  Hester 124
  Leonard 124
  Mary 124
  Sarah 124
STONEMAN Christian 11
  Joseph 11
STONER Casper 211
  Christian 120, 132
  David 50, 57
  Jacob 203
  Michael 222
STOREY Thomas 154
STORM Peter 146
STORY Enoch 17, 18, 20, 21
  John 80
STOTLER John 238
STOUCH Conrad 123
STOUGH Conrad 184
STOUT Abraham 64
  Christian 160
  Joseph 24
STOVER Emanuel 199
  Henry 206
  John Casper 13
STOY Ann 189
  Daniel 209
  Mary 189
  Peter 189
STRATER Henry 156
STRAUB Andrew 245
STRAUCK Frederick 79
STRAUN Mary 160
STRAW Philip 126
STRAWBRIDGE John 241
  Joseph 73
  Thomas 39
STREEERS John 8
STREPERS William 8
STRETCH Isaac 21
  Joseph 17, 21
STRETCHER Henry 4, 5
STRETTELL Amos 16, 28
STRETTLE Amos 17
STRICKER William 77

STRICKLAND William 171
STRICKLER Henry 172, 229, 244
  Jacob 123, 132, 178, 183
  Lt. Col. 101, 141
STRICLER Jacob 100
STRIEPERS Peter Hendrick 22
STRIKEHOUSER Henry 105
STRING Jacob 155
STROHECKER Daniel 172
  John 73, 75, 201
STROMAN John 120
STROMBERG Olof 168
STROMES Henry 150
STRONG Horatio 89
  Martin 117
STROOP George 183, 200, 251
  Jacob 251
STROUD Daniel 189, 191, 192
  Jacob 26, 39, 148
  John 149
STROW Benjamin 243
  Michael 97
STRUBLE Frederick 28, 230, 250
STUART --- 43
  Jane 31
  John 31
  Josiah 150
STUBBS Thomas 94, 123, 131, 143, 165
STULLER Henry 230, 250
STUMP Caspar 14
  Frederick 24, 25
  John 180
  William 177
STUMPFF William 40
STURGEON Joseph 213
  Robert 252
  Thomas 55
  William 105, 143
SULLIVAN Gen. 115
  Joshua 205
  Lt. Col. 141
SULTZBACH John 225
SULTZBAUGH John 190
SUMMERL Joseph 179
SUMMERS Catharine 46
  Jacob 157
  Peter 46
SUMRALL John 49

SUNTRUGHWACKON 53
SURKETT John 8
SUTHERLAND George 192
SUTOR John 153
SUTTEN Peter 143
SUTTERFIELD James 129
SUTTON Amariah 34, 58, 66
  Andrew 206
  George 202, 214, 243
  James 45
  John 152
  Luke 25
  Thomas 243
  Woolman 89
SWAIN Woolle 2
SWAINE Elizabeth 212
  Francis 94, 121, 212
SWAMPES King 52
SWAN Hannah 116
  Lt. Col. 102
  Samuel 116
  Sarah 248
  William 37
SWANK Jacob 144
SWANPISSE 52
SWANSON Swan 4
SWANSY Samuel Tate 224, 243
SWANWICK John 86, 87, 88, 89
  Richard 61, 68
SWANZEY William 103
SWAR John 94, 118, 169, 178, 183, 187, 191, 211, 241
SWART George 233
SWARTSWOOD 63
SWARTZ Conrad 138, 183
  Peter 227
  Philip 247
SWAYNE Caleb 115
  Samuel 115
SWAYZE Daniel 204
SWEARINGEN Andrew 172
SWEARINGHAM Van 42
SWEENY Francis 223
  Isaac 177
  James 177
SWEET Samuel 29
SWENEY Bernard 157
SWENGLE Nicholas 26
SWENK John 86
SWENSON Jacob 2
SWENTZEL Henry 138

INDEX

SWERINGEN Andrew 80
  Daniel 55
SWIFT Charles 109, 159
  Edward 114
  John 5, 6, 7, 8, 16,
    22, 65, 202
  Joseph 22, 27, 44, 73,
    89
  Joseph K. 202
  Samuel 19, 37, 114
SWILER Matthias 237
SWINEFORD Albright 64,
  76, 114
  John 114
  Polly 242
SWOOPE George 15
  Michael 31, 32, 39, 42
SWOPE Michael 21
  Nicholas 134
SYLLIMAN Thomas 155
SYMCOCK John 3, 4, 5, 6,
  7
SYMONS John 5
SYMS Charles 99
SYNG Philip 18, 20, 21,
  23, 62, 69

TAGAAIA 53
TAGESHATA 53
TAGGARD John 104
TAGGART David 115
  John 224
  Robert 79
TAKACHQUONTAS 53
TAKEGHSATI 53
TALAWSIS 52
TAMANEN 52
TAMINENT King 52
TAMINY Sachem 52
TANGORAS 52
TANGORUS King 52
TANNAGHDORUS 53
TANNEHILL Adamson 128,
  138, 163
  Zachariah A. 156
TANNER Benjamin 170
  Henry S. 171
  Joseph 210
  Lt. Col. 141
  Michael 15
TANNYHILL Adamson 74
TANTLINGER John 123, 180,
  194
TARAGHORUS Aneeghnaxqua
  53

TAREEKHAN 52
TARR Casper 177, 203
  Christian 145
TATE Magnus 132
  Samuel 146, 224
TATNAL Joseph 94
TATNALL Thomas 14
TATNEL Thomas 41
TAUGHHAUGHSEY 52
TAWIS Tawis 53
TAYLOR --- 48, 182
  Abraham 235
  Anthony 183, 185
  Benjamin 13, 79
  Christopher 1, 3, 4
  Elizabeth 172
  Henry 42, 172
  Isaac 9, 10, 62, 69,
    71, 154
  Jacob 54, 122
  James 37, 38, 109,
    178, 190, 252
  Joe 52
  John 11, 16, 30, 43,
    49, 51, 69, 143,
    159, 182, 243
  John M. 97
  Joseph 183
  Lt. Col. 111
  Martha 181
  Mary 197
  Matthew 194
  Moses 194
  Nathaniel 69
  Philip 12
  Rachael 190
  Richard 30
  Thomas 48
TEA Richard 33, 54, 57
TEGAL George 80
TEIPHER John 192
TEMPLE William 2
TEMPLETON John 77, 208
  Philip 220, 243
  Samuel 138
  William 226
TEMPLIN John 184
TENANT Thomas 246
  William 154
  William M. 99
TENBROOK Jane 90
  John 90
  Mary 90
  Peter 90
  Samuel 90

  Vanransiller 90
  Willilam 90
TENNENT William 121
  William M. 51
TEPAKOASET 52
TERRANCE Joseph 108
TERRY Jonathan 216
TESHACOMIN 52
TESHAKOMEN 52
TEST Jacob 238
  John 3
TETWILOR Jacob 198
TEYER Andrew 70
THACKARA James 232
  William 171, 182
THARPE William 71
THAW Benjamin 249
  John 108
THOBURN John 176
THOM John 36
THOMAS Benjamin 69
  David 29, 42, 49, 72,
    126, 246
  Esther 125
  Evan 61, 68, 192, 204
  Evan W. 129
  Freeman 172
  Georg 90
  George 100, 154, 210
  Hazael 72
  Jacob 145, 249
  John 17, 79, 160, 214
  John Chew 92
  Joseph 37, 80, 119
  Leonard 47
  Levy 61, 68
  Lt. Col. 111, 141
  Martin 105
  Mordecai 73
  Moses 209
  Richard 33, 38, 45, 90,
    114
  Salmon 226
  Samuel 72
  William 61, 68
THOMB John 37
THOME John 33
THOMPSON --- 34
  Alexander 212, 229, 244
  Ann 225
  Cephas 171
  Charles 17, 142
  Daniel 220
  Elizabeth 196
  Esther 137

INDEX

George 71
Hector 193
Hugh 140, 225
Isaac 199, 243
James 226
John 37, 45, 72, 84,
  114, 121, 137, 182,
  200, 204, 205, 237
John W. 194
Joseph 109
Margaret 225
Mathew 225
Matthew 161
Nathan 150, 189
Peter 31, 69
Robert 33, 227
Samuel 29, 33, 79, 186
Shem 46
Thomas M'Kean 152
William 31, 91, 123,
  136, 204
THOMPSON & McLENACHAN 96
THOMSON Charles 16, 17
  Hannah 57
  James 48
  Peter 31, 86
  William 123
THORN Joseph 35
  William 34
THORNE William 42
THORNHILL Joseph 72, 213
THORNTON Joseph 214
THURLOW E. 236
  Lord 236
TICE Michael 119
TIEBOUT Cornelius 171
TIEFENDURFER Michael 23
TIENPOIONT Adriaen
  Jorissz 1
TIERNAN Luke 178, 190
TIETSWORTH Lt. Col. 101
TIFFANY Hosea 200, 204
TIFFENY Hosea 150
TILBURY Thomas 17, 24, 30
TILGHMAN Benjamin 245
  Edward 120, 125, 139,
  149, 186, 191, 205
  Elizabeth Margaret 102,
  224
  Lt. Col. 51
  Maj. Gen. Lt. Col. 57
  Margaret Elizabeth 102
  Rebecca 139, 186

William 95, 97, 102,
  120, 125, 130, 131,
  168, 224
TILLER William 67
TILLIER William 59
TILLYER Philip 30
TILTON William 51
TIMINGS Thomas 127, 144
TIMMONS John 40
TINDALL Ralph 222
TINGEY Thomas 88, 89
TIPPER Charles 186, 205
TISE Mathew 14
TISHEKUNK 52
TISTOAGHTON 53
TITLER Baltzer 237
TITTERY Joshua 48
TITTLE George 88
TITUS 57
TIYONENKOKARAW 53
TOD Andrew 193
  Isaac 192
TODD Alexander 28
  Andrew 134
  David 215, 220, 243
  James 238, 240
  John 79, 208
  Robert 77
  Widow 162
  William 32, 33, 34,
  38, 71, 164
TOEY Catharine 128
  Simon 128
TOHAGHDAGHGUYSERRV 53
TOHASOWANGARUS 53
TOKAAIYON 53
TOKAHOYON 53
TOLAND Henry 186
TOLLY John 61, 68
TOM William 2
TOMACKHICKON 52
TOMAS Janitze 2
TOMB George 232
TOMBAUGH Frederick 22
TOMKINS Thomas 145
TOMLINSON James 214
  John 17
  Joseph 58, 65
TOMPKINS Thomas 249
TOMPSON --- 98
TONGAN Thomas 52
TONKIN Israel 97
TOOT Lt. Col. 111
TOPPELL Jacob 125

TORBETT Samuel 184, 211,
  214
TORBUTT Thomas 110
TORRENCE Joseph 118, 232
  William 54
TORREY Jacob 172, 209
TORRY Jason 121, 246, 249
TOWERS Robert 72, 79
TOWIS 52
TOWNE Benjamin 46
TOWNSAND Joseph 186
TOWNSEND Abel W. 252
  Benjamin 252
  David 240, 252
  Jesse 219
  John 109
  Joseph 109, 186
  Noah 50
  Robert 219
  Samuel 184
TOZOR Julius 174
TRACY Peleg 137
TRAIL Robert 32, 33, 93
TRAINER David 119, 213
  Sarah 119
TRAPP Andrew 100
TRAQUAIR Adam 125, 171
  James 109, 125, 197
TRASEL Jacob 79
TRAVERS John 89
TRAVIS Elizabeth 124
  John 123
  William 215, 232
TRAXLER Peter 33
TREACHEL Elias Lewis 42
TREAS Michael 167
TREAT Christian 147
  Jacob 87
TREGO Joseph 251
  William 251
TREICHEL Ewis 26
TREIGLER Samuel 179
TREMBLE William 92
TRENCHARD James 79
TRENT William 16
TRESS Thomas 11
TRESTER Martin 210
TRESTLER Jacob 231
TREVOR John B. 225, 242
  Samuel 118, 180, 184
TREXLER Jeremiah 131
  Peter 12, 216
TREZIYULNY Charles 223
TRICHLER Jacob 207

INDEX

TRIEWIG --- 131
  Andreas 130
TRIMBLE Abraham 125
  Isaac 208
  James 79
  William 149
TRIMNUL Cornelius 127, 144
TRIPP Stephen 177
TROLDENIER George 72
TROLLINGER Andrew 230, 250
TROMBOUER Andreas 14
  Jacob 14
TROTH Bathsheba 110
TROTT Benjamin 170
TROTTER Daniel 79
  Joseph 14, 41
TROUP Robert 188
TROWERS Robert 74
TROY Michael 40
TROYER John 196
TRUBEY Christopher 40
TRUBY Christopher 34, 99
TRUMBOUR Henry 117
TRUMBOWER Andrew 47
TRYON George W. 224
TSCHUDY Matthias 183
TUBBEN Henry 8
TUBBS Robert 218, 232
TUCKER Benjamin 212
  David 230, 250
  Thomas 78
TUCKNISS Robert 30
TUNES Abraham 8
TUNIS Abraham 117
TURK John 184
TURNBULL William 43, 51, 106, 112, 120, 131
TURNER --- 48, 58, 59
  Joseph 19, 44, 46, 71, 246
  Michael 126
  Robert 4, 5, 6
  William 206
TUTLE Timothy 100
TUTROW George 123
TUTTLE Ayres 232
  Stephen 131, 192
  Timonty 167
TUYNEN Hermann 8
TWEED Robert 38
TWELLS Godfrey 31
TYANHASARE 53
TYBOUT Andrew 31, 51

TYCE Michael 26
TYLER Jacob 191
  John 121
TYLEROX 53
TYLLIER William 60
TYLOR William 177
TYSEN Matthias 8
TYSON Abraham 61, 68
  Cornelius 200
  Daniel 89
  Henry 237
  Isaac 108
  John 107
  Joseph 134
  Joshua 114
  Reinier 8
  Rynear 68
  Ryner 62
  Thomas 60, 67, 108

UDRE Daniel 75
UDREE Daniel 98, 160
UHLER Christopher 99, 103
ULRICH Caspar 13
  Peter 129
UMSTAT Jacob 26, 76
UMSTEAD John 161, 173
UNDERWOOD Elihu 99
  Thomas 247
UNGERMAN Elizabeth 115
  Nicholas 115
UNROOK George 14
UPDEGRAFF Ambrose 80
  Daniel 192
  Martin 149, 192
  Samuel 80, 192
UPDEGRAVE Abraham 5
UPDEGROVE Abraham 6
UPP George 179, 190
  Jacob 120
UPSON Allen 226
URIE Lt. Col. 111, 141
  Thomas 26
URIES Samuel 88
URMSTEAD Gideon 115
USHER Abraham 28
  Thomas 3, 4
USSELINCX William 1
UTREE Daniel 37

VAIL Elizabeth 217
  Micha 216
  Moses 217
  Samuel 230, 250

VALANCE John 147
VALENDEGEM George O. 206
VALENDIGHAM George 80
VALENTINE Barnard 228
  Bernard 204
VALLANCE John 170
VALLIANT James 110
Van AKEN Henry 13
Van BEBBER Matthias 8
Van BUSKIRK John 202
  William 189
Van CAMP John 33
Van Der GAEGH Cornelius 8
Van Der HEGGEN Gaetshalck 8
  Jacob Gaetshalck 8
Van Der SLUYS Adrian 8
  Reinier 8
Van Der WERF John Roeloffs 8
  Richard 8
Van DYCK Gregorius 2
Van DYDE Gregorius 1
Van GEZEL Cor. 2
Van HEER Capt. 145, 147
Van HORN Cornelius 249
  Gabriel 31
  Thomas 249
Van HORNE Isaac 105
Van LOON Abraham 191, 211
  Matthias 191
  Stephen 191
Van MIDLESWARTS Abraham 39
Van RYNEVELT Abraham 2
Van SCHUYBER Jane 211
Van SCHUYVER Samuel 211
Van SWERINGEN Gerritt 2
Van TWILLER Wouter 1
Van VLECK Jacob 74
Van ZANT Capt. 151
VANAUKER Garrit 178
VANBUSKIRK Jacob 72
VANCAMPEN --- 63
  Isaac 63
VANCE Alexander 202, 214
  David 109
  George 131
  James 202
  Joseph 107, 241
  Patrick 51
  William 181
VANCOURT Moses 36
VANDEEREN John 107
VANDEGRIFT Joshua 58

INDEX

VANDEREN John 50, 72
VANDERGRIFT Abraham 30
  Jacob 70
  John 70
  Joshua 65
VANDERIN John 128
VANDERSPEIGEL William 16
VANDIKE Jacob 216, 248
VANDINE David 212

VANGARDER Jacobus 39
VANGORDER Jacob 223, 227
VANGORDON Alexander 158
VANHERN Cornelius 170,
  211
VANHORN Isaac 93
  William 39
VANHORNE Cornelius 55
VANLASHETS Christian 60
VANLASKETS Christian 67
VANLEAR Isaac W. 183
  John 152
  Samuel 69
VANLEER Bernard 11
VANLIER Bernard 173
VANNOST John 83
VANNUXEM James 133
VANOKEN --- 63
VANSAND Elizabeth 31
  John 31
  Olshe 31
  Rachel 31
  Sina 31
  Soffel 31
VANSANT Garret 62, 68
  James 48, 60, 67
  Lt. Col. 111,141
  Nathaniel 37
VANSAVT Herman 70
VANSCIVER Esther 125
  George 125
  Jacob 125
  Susanna 125
VANSICKEL Richard 56
VANSINTERN Isaac 12
VANTRICE Abraham 184
VANUXEM James 89, 207
VARNOR Robert 157
VASEY John 227
VASSE Ambrose 89
VASTINE Amos 61, 68
  Benjamin 173
VAUGH Samuel 71

VAUGHN John 78, 88,
  130, 171, 186, 241
  Thomas 174
VAUN Azariah 23
VAUX George 201, 207
  James 187, 191
  Richard 30
  Robert 212, 242
  Roberts 241
VENET John 220
VERBOOF Cornelius 4
VERBYNEN Peter 8
VEREE Robert 80
VERHOOFFE Cornelius 1
VERNON --- 133
  Emmor 198
  Frederick 152
  Gideon 45
  John 36
  Joshua 90
  Nathaniel 35, 36
  Randel 5
  Sarah 198
  Thomas 36
VICKROY Thomas 150
VICORY Thomas 93
VIGNIER Arnold 171
VINCENT Bethuel 123,
  167, 169, 184, 221
  Cornelius 87
  John 214
VINES John 3, 5
VINING Benjamin 9
VINSON Samuel 80
VOGAN John 170
VOGDES Elizabeth 129
  Jacob 129, 182
VOGELS Gerard 80
VOIGHT Henry 178
VOIGHTS Henry 192
VOIGT Ludwig 79
VOLOZAN Dennis A. 171
Von MARSHALL Frederick
  William 74
Von SCHWEINITZ Hans
  Christian 74

WADDY Henry 5, 6
WADE Francis 51
  Robert 1, 3, 4, 10
WADHAMS Lydia 153, 172
  Moses 153, 172
  Noah 172, 184
  Phebe 153, 172
WAESHE Frederick 186

WAGENER Christopher 33
  Daniel 113
  John 135
WAGER Philip 69, 98
WAGGONER Daniel 99, 141
  Henry 227, 252
WAGLE Lt. Col. 112, 142
WAGNER John 109
  John Nicholas 92
  Philip 72
  William 249
WAGONER Christian 150
  Christopher 20
  Peter 199
WAIN Jacob 136
WALBORN John 216
WALBURN Herman 14
WALDHAUR Casper 173
  Catharine 172, 173
WALKER Abraham 172
  Alexander 116, 233, 235
  Andrew 209
  Charles 59, 66
  David 190
  Enoch 184, 193
  Henry 179
  John 4, 5, 6, 7, 20,
    57, 69, 71, 86, 91,
    147, 209, 236, 240,
    252
  Mary 209
  Richard 32, 44
  Robert 197, 209, 226
  Thomas 206
  William 44
  Zadoc 145
WALL --- 63
  George 63, 73, 89, 151
WALLACE Burton 79, 80,
  107
  Charles 227
  Elizabeth 190
  Ephraim 58, 66, 71, 74,
    93, 156, 162
  George 71, 74, 93, 156,
    162
  James 16, 32, 33, 38,
    88, 119, 187, 189, 193
  John 65, 140, 183
  John B. 141, 214
  John C. 214, 218
  Joseph 160, 190
  Peter 136, 232
  Robert 185
  Samuel 71
  Thomas 22

INDEX

William 90, 159, 183, 247
WALLER --- 88
  Nathan 146
WALLET Michael 168
WALLIS James 121
  Joseph 27, 57
  Samuel 21
WALN Ann 139
  Jesse 89, 91, 120, 130, 139, 186
  John 89
  Joseph 89
  Nicholas 9, 83
  Rebecca 139, 186
  Richard 80, 89
  Robert 79, 89, 94, 109, 120, 130, 139, 187, 248,
  Sarah 139
  William 130, 139
WALNE Nich. 5
  Nicholas 1, 4, 5, 6, 7
WALSWORTH Gilbert 202
WALTER Barnett 78
  Bernard 155
  Daniel 25
  Henry 27
  Jacob 120
  John 79
  Michael 61, 68, 120
WALTHOUR Barbara 152
  Casper 152
  Catharine 152
  Christopher 152
  Dolly 152
  Joseph 152
  Michael 152
WALTON Albertson 35, 60, 67
  Albinson 35
  George 102
  Henry 37
  James 153
  Jonathan 37
  William 37
  William D. 189
WALTZ Christian 188
  John 179
WAMPOLE Isaac 145
WAMSLEY Sarah 158
WANN Michael 153
WARBURTON Matthew 23
WARD Henry 2
  Lt. Col. 102
  William 242

WARDER Abigail H. 199
  Jeremiah 16, 26, 27, 89, 203
  John 30
WARE Charles 6
WARFEL Abraham 197
WARLIN Michael 98
WARMWAG Lewis 184
WARNER Benjamin 213, 224
  Dr. 62, 69
  Edmund 1
  Edward 18, 44, 47
  George 137
  Jacob 173
  John 79
  Joseph 60, 67, 69, 87
  William 3, 4, 137
WARVILLE I. P. Brissot de 80
WASHBURN Joseph 231, 251
WASON Jemima 174
  William 174
WATER William 157
WATERMAN Humphrey 97
  Jesse 79
  Thomas 171
WATERS Esther 116
  James 148
  John 209
  William 30
WATERSON James 99
WATKINS Joseph 42
  Robert 205
WATSHATUHON 53
WATSON Amariah 196
  David 35, 36, 169
  Isaac 93
  John 14, 15, 17, 99, 137, 162, 169, 171, 184
  Joseph 171
  Luke 1, 3, 4, 5, 6, 7
  Mark 15
  Moses 200
  Nathan 12, 13
  Nathaniel 183, 189
  Thomas 9, 15, 41, 52
  William 154, 160
WATT Col. 110
  Frederick 33
  Samuel 159, 167
  Stephen 73

WATTS David 99, 183, 190
  Samuel 23
  Stephen 36
WATTSON David 37
WAUGH Alexander 55
  Samuel 45
  William 70, 115
WAY --- 57
  John 245
WAYNE Anthony 31
  Col. 137
  Francis 196
  Gen. 55, 171
  Lt. Col. 141
WEABER Christian 96
WEAKLY John 180
WEATHERBURN John 186
WEATHERELL Samuel 23
WEAVER Adam 86, 95
  Albright 151
  Christian 126
  Daniel 242
  George 118, 130, 180
  Henry 12, 129
  Isaac 79, 113
  Jacob 12, 23, 37, 70, 85, 92, 146
  John 12, 92, 168
  Jonas 194
  Joseph 180
  Joshua 251
  Matthew 178
  Nicholas 20
  Philip 152, 192
  Richard 180
  Samuel 251
WEBB George 169, 184, 208
  James 16, 27, 41
  Samuel 90, 192, 228, 233, 242
  William 80, 99, 208
WEBER Adam 118
  Christian 13
  John 151, 183
WEBSTER Joseph 234
  Joshua 246
  Noah 80
  Pelatiah 134
  Peter 8
  Thomas 73
WEDDERBURN Al. 236
WEEBER Johan Hnery 14
WEED Elijah 37, 43
WEEDMAN Henry 155
WEEKLEY Samuel 138

INDEX

WEGERLY Adam 60, 67
WEGMAN Christopher 33
WEHEQUEEKHON 52
WEHR George Simon 107
WEIBER Michael 13
WEIBURG Caspar 72
WEIDLEY Michael 13
WEIDMAN Jacob 199
  John 60, 61, 67, 68, 103, 177, 195
WEIFFER John 123
WEIGELL Stoffel 154
WEIGERT Hans George 13
WEILE Josh 142
WEIMOR George 177
WEINMAN George 128
WEIR William 159
WEIRICH Jacob 103
  Lt. Col. 111
WEIRICK Valentine 154
WEISER Barbara 118
  Benjamin 118, 242
  Conrad 52, 53, 118
  Peter 53
  Samuel 53
WEISS Jacob 85, 244
  John 206
  Lewis 20, 43
WEISTER Frederick 26
WEITZEL John 32, 33, 34, 38, 39
WEITZELL John 39
WELCH John 116, 129
  William 4, 6
WELDON Isaac 5
WELDY Maria 149
  Philip 149
WELKER Daniel 130, 178
WELL --- 104
WELLAR John 226
WELLES Charles F. 210
  George 174
  Rosewell 97, 137, 146
  Roswell 185
WELLFORD Robert 171
WELLS Benjamin 55
  David 239
  James 4, 188, 238
  John 10
  Mary 239
  Richard 21, 26, 44, 64, 79
  William H. 145
  William Hill 130
WELLS & MORRIS 89

WELPER Jacob C. 153
WELSH George 74
  Henry 146, 193
  James 114
  John 119
  Michael 225
  Thomas 38
  William 80
WELTZHOOVER Jacob 99
WENDT Frederick 227
WENNER George 136
WENRICK Baltzer 61, 68
  Matthias 61, 68
WENTWORTH --- 56
  John 56
WENTZ Abraham 37
  Frederick 146
  Jacob 34
  Jacob B. 229, 244
  John 183
  Lt. Col. 101, 111, 141
  Peter 12, 23
  Philip 23
  Thomas 225
WERMWAG Lewis 178
  Lewis 193
WERTZ Christian 27, 59, 66
  Henry 128, 138, 146
  William 65
WESCOTT George 89
WESKEKITT 52
WESLEY Henry 154
  James 154
WESSAPOAK 52
WEST Benjamin 80
  Charles 19, 24, 88, 121
  Edward 102
  Francis 88
  Thomas 137
  William 16, 17, 24, 79, 139
WESTBROOK Jacob 178
  John 172
  Solomon 235
WESTFALL Abel 54
  John 54
WESTLEY John 147
WESTON James 162, 163, 214
  William 62, 68
WESTOVER Jonathan 185

WETHERILL Samuel 178, 193, 202, 245
WETZEL John 85
  Lt. Col. 111, 141
WEY Andrew 144
WEYBRECHT Martin 14
WEYGAND Jacob 78
WEYLAND Frederick 72
WEYMAN Robert 19
WEYMER Martin 133
WEYRICH George 206
WEYRICK George 14, 138
  William 104
WHALEY Lt. Col. 102, 112, 142
WHALIN Israel 32
WHARTON Charles 30, 89
  Francis R. 186
  Hannah M. 186
  Isaac 28, 89, 117, 120, 130, 139, 187
  James 16, 17, 27, 30, 36
  John 51, 69, 89
  Joseph 15, 16, 17, 19, 42, 186, 219
  Kearney 79
  Margaret R. 187
  Mary 139
  Moore 128, 139, 186
  Rebecca 139
  Rebecca L. 187
  Rebecca Wain 186
  Robert 89, 109, 215
  Samuel 16, 17, 156
  Susan 139
  Susan Lloyd 186
  Thomas 16, 20, 21, 31, 32, 39, 48
  Thomas J. 186, 219
WHARTON & GREEVES 89
WHATSON Luke 3
WHEELAND Michael 199
WHEELEN & MILLER 89
WHEELER Abel 229, 244
  Adam 72
  Charles 218
  Enoch 109
  Gilbert 4
  James 104, 153, 157
  Joseph 52
  Samuel 73, 117
WHELEN Isaac 100
  Israel 79, 85, 86, 87, 90

INDEX

Lt. Col. 101
WHELER Samuel 109
WHITACRE Joseph 205
WHITAKER Thomas 93
WHITE --- 48, 64
  Amos 45
  Artimus 115
  Crawford 187
  David 214
  Francis 78
  Hugh 123, 137, 201, 226, 250
  Isaac 127
  John 4, 5, 6, 180, 223
  Josiah 178, 193, 223
  Matthew 133
  Robert 24, 26, 31, 58
  Samuel 136, 137, 152, 169, 178, 191
  William 39, 53, 73, 84, 107, 109
  William M. 205
WHITEALL James 79
WHITEBY Philip 136
WHITEHALL Robert 27
  David 122
  George 97
  James 137, 140, 183, 225
  John 33, 36, 37
  Lt. Col. 111
  Robert 34, 39, 171, 184
WHITER Isaac 144
WHITESIDE Thomas 32, 75
WHITESIDES Thomas 36, 37
WHITEWELL Francis 3, 4
WHITMAN Adam 37
  Jacob 92
  John 98
  Michael 38
  Nathan 72
  William 246
WHITMIRE David 150
WHITNEY Charles 233
WHITPAIN Sarah 7
WHITPANE John 22
WHITTON Richard 73, 124
WHITWELL Francis 1, 2
WICK William 129
WICKERMAN John 235
WICKERSHAM Amos 79, 104
  James 108, 161
  Jesse 182
WICKERT George 32
WICKOFF Peter 105

WIDAGH 52
WIDDIFIELD Hannah 191
  James 191
WIER James 234, 235
WIERMAN Henry 153
  John 153
WIGGINS John 50
WIGHT Jacob 173
WIGTON Elizabeth 159
  Thomas 40
WIKOFF John 22
  Peter 19, 57, 126
WILBER John 215
  Reuben 233
WILCOCKS Alexander 89
  Andrew 73
  John 43, 73, 89
  Lt. Col. 101
WILCOX Barnaby 4
  John 88, 183
  Mark 38, 75, 148, 149
  Randal 235
  Randall 238
WILD William 40
WILDBOHN Frederick 75
WILDE John 236
WILDS John 240
WILEY Isaac 110
  John 193
  Samuel B. 171
  Thomas 135
WILHELM Johannes 14
WILKIN Elizabeth E. 251
WILKINS James 31, 33, 49, 155
  Janet 31
  John 33, 39, 56, 117, 144
  Mary 243
  William 31, 218, 240, 243
WILKINSON Anthony 41
  Jemima 174
  John 32, 39
  Joseph 80, 125
WILL Peter 225
  William 33, 34
WILLBANK Cornelius 7
WILLCOX Joseph 9
  Mark 149
WILLET --- 217
  Anthony 116
  Michael 240
WILLETS Isaac 26
  Isaiah 202

WILLETT Augustine 128
  Isaiah 98
WILLIAM Catherine 25
  Heinrich 4
WILLIAMS Amos 45
  Benjamin 1, 182
  Charles 79
  Daniel 15, 17, 26, 154, 249
  David 155
  Dunk 3
  Edward 154
  Elizabeth 154
  George 109, 112
  Hendrick 4
  Henry 6
  James 4
  John 7, 33, 39, 173
  Jonathan 96, 100, 193
  Joseph 158, 219, 236
  Joshua 171, 227, 241
  Margaret 208
  Mariamne 100
  Mary 155
  Matilda 190
  Mordecai 92
  Peter 107
  Richard R. 200
  Robert 99
  Thomas 134, 207, 214
  William 9, 133, 208
WILLIAMS, MOORE & Co. 96
WILLIAMSON --- 163, 215
  Dr. 155
  Gideon 64, 75
  Hugh 23
  Jacob 197
  Jam. 2
  John 104, 107, 108
  John J. 237
  Lt. Col. 101, 102
  Samuel 137, 184
  Thomas 64, 75
WILLIARD William 232
WILLING Richard 28
  Thomas 17, 20, 31, 43, 73, 89, 109
  Thomas M. 89
  Thomas Mayne 208
WILLING, MORRIS & Co. 22
WILLIS Henry 51
  Isaiah 136
  John 243
  Johnathan 79
  Lt. Col. 111

331

INDEX

Mary 51
Peter 174
William 54
WILLIAMMS John 80
WILLOT Augustine 118
WILLOUGHBY Charles 227, 244
WILLSON John 125
  Moses 156
WILMER Francis 69
  James 240
  Lambert 46
WILS John 243
WILSON --- 56, 99, 198, 216
  Alexander 171, 222
  Andrew 245
  Ann 190, 191
  David 13, 77
  Elizabeth 168
  Fleming 87
  Francis 202, 237
  George 29, 39, 49, 79, 212
  Henry R. 122
  Hugh 15, 20, 109, 114, 132, 207, 246, 252
  James 27, 29, 33, 41, 43, 45, 48, 71, 72, 76, 164, 176, 182, 183, 185, 186, 187, 199, 200, 203, 207
  John 32, 41, 49, 50, 51, 70, 71, 75, 98, 100, 153, 171, 200, 214, 216, 239
  Jonathan 37
  Joseph 184, 213
  Lt. Col. 101
  Martin 204
  Mary 200
  Matthew 51, 166
  Noah 215
  Peter 108
  Richard 4, 5, 6, 7
  Robert 184, 205
  Samuel 65, 84, 109, 124, 134, 177, 187
  Sarah 109, 121
  Stephen 171, 206
  Tempest 143
  Thomas 29, 37, 42, 43, 58, 65, 66, 69, 126, 151, 165, 168, 173, 177, 182, 186, 208, 218

William 51, 96, 178, 186, 187, 188, 190, 218
WILT Adam 138
  John 45, 149
  Maria 149
  Paul 149
WILTON Richard 36
WIND Philip 233
WINDEL Job 241
WINEBRENNER Peter 229, 247
WINEY Jacob 27, 28, 75
WINGEBONE 52
WINN Thomas 4
WINNE Thomas 5
WINNOTT Jacob 153
WINPENNY Samuel 176
WINROTT Jacob 105
WINSMORE William 4
WINT Philip 168
WINTEN --- 222
WINTEROTT Jacob 140
WINTERS Henry 206
WINTHROP James 214
WIREMAN Martin 59, 67
  William 146
WIRICH Jacob 100
WIRTZ Christian 33, 60, 67
WISEMAN George 166
WIESNER Isaac 153
WISER Martin 107
WISHAQUONTAGUSH 53
WISHART William 28, 30
WISINBURG Jacob 148
WISMER Abrahm 245
WISSAPOWEY 52
WISSLER David 176
WISTAR Bartholomew 79
  Caspar 10, 77, 79, 80, 135
  Casper 44, 109, 231
  John 80, 109, 114, 136
  Richard 16, 246
  Thomas 79, 232
  William 28
WISTER Daniel 42
  William 114
WISTOR John 12
WITHER Michael 94
WITHEROW John 243
  Samuel 176

WITHERS George 140
  John 74
  Michael 140
  Ralph 3
  Thomas 6
WITHINGTON Peter 40
WITHROW John 70
WITHY Mary 63, 70
WITMAN Adam 46, 176
  Christopher 14, 33, 93
  John 93
  William 65, 127, 147, 206, 245
WITMER Abel 179
  Abraham 64, 85, 86, 94, 95, 98, 118, 128, 132, 137, 166, 169, 178, 183
  Adam 14
  Benjamin 14
WOEBLER George Peter 207
  Mary Magdalena 207
WOELFLEY John 144
WOER Frederick 187
WOGLOM Peter 79
WOLBERT Frederick 118
WOLF Abraham 193, 206
  Catharine 113
  Christian 244
  Frederick 33
  George 214
  Henry 155
  Jacob 176, 210, 228
  John 181
  Peter 33
  Valentine 154
WOLFE Frederick 38
WOLFERSBERGER John 183, 235, 238
  Lt. Col. 141
WOLFERSBURGER John 204
  Philip 199
WOLFEY John 100
WOLFF Barnard 70
  Christian 147
WOLFLEY Conrad 187
  Jacob 187
  John 187
WOLLE Frederick 167
WOLLERY Henry 227, 244
WOLMER Henry 220
  Jacob 219
WONDERLICH Daniel 146
WONDERLICK Daniel 186
WONDERLICKS Daniel 230, 250

INDEX

WOOD Benjamin 166
  Elizabeth 166
  George 4, 33
  Isaac 166
  James 206
  John 1, 4, 9, 10, 46
  Joseph 8, 22, 208
  Mary 192
  Robert 79
  Samuel 200
  Samuel R. 232
  Thomas Hale 192
  William 4
  William Hawkins 192
WOODBERN James 180
  John 180
WOODBRIDGE Joseph 172
  William 225, 248
WOODBURN James 183, 243
WOODEND John 191
WOODMANSON William 3
WOODROW Hester 124
WOODRUFF Benjamin I. 216
WOODS Fullerton 158, 215, 227
  George 26, 36, 177
  James 135
  John 41, 52, 54, 138, 159, 164, 195
  Lt. Col. 101
  Matthew 49
  Richard 212
  Samuel 70
  Thomas 203, 249
  William 4, 108
WOODSIDE John A. 171
  Thomas 203, 224, 233
WOODWARD Abisha 161, 172, 184, 232
  Absalom 136, 148, 194
  Edward 159
  Elizabeth 159
  John K. 185
  Mary 159
  Robert 235, 243
WOOLERY Henry 227
WOOLEY Stephen 16, 17
WOOLGAST Otto 3
WOOLLERY Henry 204
WOOLLET William 171
WOOLSLEGLE John 11
WOOLSTON John 20
WOOLVERTON Lt. Col. 102

WORK Andrew 75, 180, 243
  Edward 136
  Henry 222, 228
  James 33
  John 224
  Samuel 152
WORKMAN John 194
WORLEY Francis 20
WORMAN Christopher 160, 162
WORMLEY John 214
WORRALL Isac 213
WORREL Elisha 147
  Lt. Col. 111
WORRELL Demos 72
  Isaac 114, 118, 128
  James 171
  Joseph 171, 178
  Lt. Col. 101
WORRILAW John 8
WORSTALL Joseph 222
WORTH Samuel 68
  Thomas 7
WORTHINGTON John 30
WRANGEL Charles Magnus 20
WREN Joseph 163, 227, 244
WRIGHT --- 74, 87, 90, 110
  Aaron 28, 138
  Abijah 59, 60, 67
  Alexander 55, 56, 74, 129, 157
  Anthony 89
  Benjamin 80
  Casper 173
  Edward 232
  Ellen 172
  Enoch 124
  James 15, 19, 26, 50, 176, 178, 213
  Jeremiah 54
  John 12, 14, 15, 50, 60, 67, 153, 237
  Jonathan 59, 67
  Lt. Col. 111, 141
  Samuel 163, 174, 176, 198, 218
  Thomas 26, 113, 146, 171
  William 113
  Zadock 54
WRITEZ Lewis 202

WROMLEY John 138
WUIBERT Anthony Felix 80
WUNDER George 149
WYEAND George 167
WYERELAND Frederick 100
WYKART George 35
WYMAN George 170
WYNCOOP Garrett 30
  Henry 38, 44
WYNKOOP Benjamin 27, 69
  Garret 51
  Gerardus 35
  Henry 27, 31, 32, 36, 38, 77, 118
  Jonathan 128
WYNKOP Henry 39
WYNN Isaac 71
WYNNE Thomas 1, 3

YAQUEEKHON 52
YARD James 89
YARDLEY Thomas 10, 26
  William 3, 4, 5, 6, 90
YARDLIE William 1
YARDLY Enoch 8
YARNAL Francis 15
YARNALL Ellis 79, 109
  Francis 19
  John J. 190, 238
YARNELL Peter 221
YEACKLE John 47
YEAGLEY Jacob 140
YEATES Jasper 7, 8, 9, 10, 69, 72
  Joseph 16
  Judge 155
YEDER Melchior 60, 67
YEGER Christian 227
YEGLESS John 60, 67
YEISLY Michael 227
YELDALL Anthony 108
YERKES Titus 133
YERKHAS Anthony 12
  Herman 12
YODER Abraham 229, 245
  John 57
  Peter 197
YORDEA Peter 11
YORK Thomas 124
YORKE Mary 199
  Thomas 17, 18, 20
YOST Abraham 201
  John 97, 150
YOTERS John 233

INDEX

YOTHER John 196
  Joseph 196
YOUGHY John 175
YOUNDT George 136, 153
YOUNG Ann 213
  Christian 168
  David 213
  Henry 173
  Jacob 87, 142, 168
  James 29, 32, 36, 37, 43
  John 34, 46, 107, 240
  Joseph 213
  Keziah 213
  Lehna 168
  Lewellin 197
  Mathias 92
  Matthias 85
  Peter 226
  Rebecca 213
  Robert 237
  Susan 213
  William 26, 109, 148, 213
YOUNGE Groote 53
YOUNGMAN Elias 251
  George 251
YUNDT George 207

ZAATZMENTZHOUSSEN Joest Hendrick 12
ZACHARIAS Johannes 14
ZADOUSKI Anthony 13
ZANCK Jacob 113
ZANE John 205
  William 79
ZANTZINGER Paul 71, 72, 85, 90, 94, 95
ZARTMAN Jacob 217
  Martin 231
ZATTERZAHM Peter 176
ZEFF Philip 133
ZEGLER Jacob 136
ZEIGLER David 61, 68
  Dillman 199
  George 159
ZEIMER John 147
ZEISBERGER David 74
ZEIWIZT George 13
ZELL John 180
ZELLER Michael 138
ZELNER Peter 237
ZERFAS Henry 176
ZERFOSS Henry 227
ZERING Lewis 175

ZETH Ulrich 126
ZIEGLER George 136
  Michael 12
  Wilhelm 13
ZIGLER Adam 108
ZIMMERMAN --- 101
  Abraham 13
  Chris. 12
  Christopher 85
  Henry 216
  Jacob 127
  Mary 210
  Michael 140
  Peter 210
  Sebastian 20
ZINN Eve 154
  Jacob 154
ZIRWER Johannes 13
ZOCCHY Nicholas 223
ZOLL Jacob 73
ZOOTZS Morris 45
ZUBLIN Abraham 173

INDEX TO PLACES [For personal names see preceding index.]

Aaronsburg 132, 246
Abbotstown 110, 161
Abington Twp. 36, 51, 60, 61, 62, 67, 68, 96, 107, 149, 150, 234
Adams County 104, 105, 106, 110, 111, 128, 129, 141, 157, 162, 173, 182, 195, 197, 205, 206, 208, 212, 213, 216, 222, 230, 235, 237, 238, 242, 249
Addison Twp. 116, 230, 250
Air Twp. 42, 58, 65, 95, 220
Albany Twp. 40, 64, 101, 145, 165, 229, 244
Alexandria 136
Allegheny 55, 56, 57, 229, 240
Allegheny County 54, 64, 65, 76, 78, 82, 84, 86, 87, 93, 95, 98, 99, 100, 101, 105, 108, 110, 112, 122, 124, 126, 128, 136, 139, 142, 148, 150, 160, 162, 165, 167, 168, 170, 173, 179, 180, 185, 188, 194, 202, 205, 214, 216, 217, 219, 222, 223, 225, 227, 230, 231, 232, 235, 236, 237, 241, 242, 245, 247, 250, 251
Allegheny Mountain 25, 179, 201, 235, 238
Allegheny River 47, 55, 81, 99, 106, 132, 163, 203, 213, 231, 251
Allegheny Twp. 90, 91, 109, 142, 150, 160, 177, 216, 234
Allen Twp. 58, 69, 92, 95, 109, 112, 133, 143, 170, 175, 180, 181, 204, 219, 229, 237, 244
Allen's town 39
Alleppo Twp. 229, 244
Alloa 70
Alsace 64
Alsace, Lower Rhine, France 129
Altona 218
Amboy 40, 41
Amity 133, 148, 158, 235
Amity Twp. 30, 65, 237
Amwell Twp. 133
Anderson's Creek 123, 181, 224, 232, 246
Anderson's Ferry 177, 190
Andrew's Tavern 246
Ansit Twp. 173
Antis Twp. 226, 236
Antrim Twp. 63, 126
Antwerp, Belgium 1
Anvil Twp. 105
Anville 127

Anville Twp. 237
Armagh 108
Armagh Twp. 58, 98, 133
Armstrong 's mill 64
Armstrong County 56, 104, 109, 110, 111, 112, 113, 116, 124, 136, 142, 148, 160, 176, 177, 184, 187, 191, 194, 196, 203, 211, 215, 220, 223, 230, 232, 235, 236, 237, 243, 248, 251, 252
Armstrong Twp. 84, 122, 128, 143
Armstrong's mill 64
Ash Swamp, New Jersey, battle of 130
Ashton Twp. 90, 234
Assylum Twp. 216
Athens Twp. 229, 244
Attin's two islands 63
Attleborough 177
Auburn Twp. 226
Auchwick Creek 236
Augusta Twp. 160, 244

Baccaria Twp. 150, 216
Bagg's Fork 92
Bald Eagle 157
Bald Eagle Bridge 235
Bald Eagle Creek 123, 143, 225, 236
Bald Eagle River 26
Bald Eagle Twp. 58, 92, 95, 106, 108, 122, 126, 169, 226
Bald Eagle's Nest 132
Baldfryer Ferry, Maryland 246
Baltimore, Maryland 178, 190, 193, 206, 216, 246
Bangor 110
Barbados 10, 29
Barnett's Mill 132
Barree Twp. 118
Barren Hill 106, 144
Bart 95
Bart Twp. 75, 150
Bath 11
Bear Gap 169
Beaver 98, 124, 234
Beaver Borough 181, 201, 214, 221
Beaver County 104, 110, 112, 113, 116, 126, 129, 133, 134, 142, 148, 157, 160, 162, 171, 177, 178, 179, 181, 194, 195, 197, 201, 204, 205, 208, 210, 211, 214, 216, 222, 223, 226, 231, 232, 234, 235, 236, 237, 240, 244, 245, 251, 252
Beaver Creek 56, 86
Beaver Dam Branch 185

INDEX TO PLACES [For personal names see preceding index.]

Beaver Dam Twp. 143, 157, 165, 197, 237
Beaver River 232
Beaver Run 112
Beaver Twp. 64, 76, 100, 116, 119, 174, 204, 234
Beaver-town 133, 134, 157, 181
Beavertown District 112
Beck's Run 86
Bedford 25, 26, 36, 43, 45, 123, 146, 164, 185, 187, 194, 203, 209
Bedford County 26, 32, 33, 34, 35, 36, 37, 38, 39, 40, 42, 44, 45, 46, 49, 58, 63, 65, 66, 72, 85, 86, 87, 90, 91, 93, 95, 102, 106, 109, 110, 112, 122, 126, 127, 128, 133, 142, 146, 148, 150, 157, 162, 168, 171, 172, 173, 176, 180, 186, 187, 188, 189, 194, 202, 203, 205, 210, 211, 215, 220, 224, 229, 234, 235, 236, 240, 243, 244, 247, 249
Bedford town 46
Bedford Twp. 162, 196
Bedminster Twp. 88, 89, 117, 213, 217, 244
Beech Creek 193
Beil's Mill 133
Belfast Twp. 85, 95, 150, 172
Bellefonte 126, 131, 225, 246
Belleville 235
Bellmont 210
Bellville 106, 194
Benley's Mill 63
Bensalem 70
Bensalem Twp. 150, 166, 231, 251
Bentley 81
Bentley's Mill 102
Bently's District 82
Berkey's Mills 230, 248
Berkley County, VA 78
Berks County 15, 20, 21, 30, 32, 33, 34, 35, 37, 38, 39, 40, 45, 46, 60, 61, 62, 64, 67, 68, 69, 73, 75, 82, 84, 88, 90, 93, 96, 98, 99, 100, 101, 107, 110, 111, 114, 116, 122, 123, 124, 127, 130, 133, 135, 136, 141, 144, 145, 147, 152, 154, 157, 158, 162, 165, 167, 176, 180, 185, 188, 192, 193, 194, 197, 201, 202, 204, 205, 206, 209, 210, 216, 223, 225, 226, 229, 235, 236, 237, 238, 244, 245, 246
Berlin 85, 116, 158, 160, 162, 163, 182, 230
Bern Twp. 64, 167, 209

Berry's Mountain 150
Berwick 131, 153, 165, 194, 213, 235
Berwick County 220
Berwick Twp. 105
Best's Mill Twp. 229, 244
Bethany 169
Bethel Twp. 42, 58, 59, 63, 65, 66, 90, 95, 96, 114, 142, 150, 189, 202
Bethlehem 85, 95, 110, 135, 168
Bethlehem Twp. 77, 88, 95, 135, 167, 205, 218, 230, 250
Bett's Mill 233
Biddle's Mill 140
Big Beaver Creek 112, 113, 178, 181, 201, 236
Big Beaver River 214
Big Beaver Twp. 160, 197
Big Cattawissa Creek 193
Big Connemaugh River 201
Big Cove 220
Big Creek 85
Big Eddey 169
Big Schuylkill River 203
Big Spring 212
Big Swatara Creek 97, 216
Big White Lick Creek 54
Big Whitely Creek 192
Biles Island 145
Bird's Island 63
Bird-in-Hand Tavern 197
Birmingham 157, 230, 243, 250
Birmingham Twp. 90
Black Creek 233
Black Horse Tavern 234
Black Lick Creek 175, 215
Blacklick Twp. 143, 148, 167, 179, 194, 238
Bladensburg, battle 198
Blair's Gap 187, 215
Blakely Twp. 226
Blockley Twp. 21, 59, 67, 96, 105, 131, 176, 188
Bloom Twp. 104, 119, 148, 150, 166
Bloomfield Twp. 222, 230, 250
Blooming Grove 163
Bloomsburg 166, 198
Blue Hill 169
Blue Mountain 237
Blue Rock 87
Blueball Tavern 180
Boon's Island 19, 75, 150

336

INDEX TO PLACES [For personal names see preceding index.]

Boston, Massachusetts 131
Boundbrook, New Jersey 125, 150
Braddock's Upper Fording 108
Bradford 231
Bradford County 174, 185, 188, 189,
  194, 198, 200, 204, 210, 216, 218,
  223, 224, 226, 229, 230, 231, 233,
  234, 238, 244, 245, 250, 251
Bradford Twp. 30, 150, 216
Braintrim 188
Braintrim Twp. 177
Branchtown 216
Brandywine Creek 87, 249
Brandywine Twp. 188, 241
Brandywine, battle of 130, 151, 152
Brantum Twp. 104
Breakneck Mountain 102
Brecknock 64
Brecknock Twp. 58, 63, 110, 162, 229, 244
Breighton Twp. 226
Briar Creek 177
Bricker's Tavern 176
Bridgewater, battle of 205
Bridgewater Twp. 150, 162, 167, 177, 216
Bridgeport 219
Brier Creek Twp. 105
Brighton Twp. 205
Bristleton 101
Bristol 8, 9, 10, 65, 114, 211
Bristol Borough 28, 58, 97, 106
Bristol Twp. 28, 97, 129, 216
Britain 27, 35
Broadhead's Creek 193
Broadhead's Road 84
Brokenstraw Twp. 143, 150, 216, 226
Brothers Valley 58, 158, 160
Brothers Valley District 85
Brothers Valley Twp. 85
Brown's Mill 217
Brownsville 152, 214, 225, 241
Brubaker's Mill 229
Brunswick 64
Brunswick Twp. 62, 68, 98
Brunswick, battle of 151
Brunswig Twp. 217
Buckingham 15
Buckingham Twp. 88, 145, 150, 171, 202, 217
Bucks 4, 5, 6, 7, 8, 9, 232
Bucks County 3, 10, 12, 13, 14, 15,
  16, 17, 20, 21, 22, 25, 28, 29,
  30, 31, 32, 33, 34, 35, 36, 37,
  39, 41, 42, 44, 45, 47, 51, 58,
  61, 62, 65, 66, 68, 70, 71, 72,
  73, 77, 81, 82, 84, 85, 87, 88,
  89, 90, 93, 96, 97, 101, 108, 110,
  111, 117, 121, 123, 126, 129, 131,
  132, 137, 141, 145, 150, 151, 157,
  158, 160, 162, 166, 167, 168, 170,
  171, 174, 177, 178, 179, 185, 190,
  193, 196, 201, 204, 207, 211, 212,
  213, 217, 218, 222, 223, 226, 231,
  232, 237, 240, 244, 245, 246, 251,
  252
Buffalo 34, 182
Buffalo(e) Twp. 56, 58, 64, 76, 96,
  108, 113, 121, 122, 123, 133, 142,
  177, 210, 216, 226, 243
Bullskin Twp. 80
Burbut Twp. 244
Burlington 133
Burlington District 126
Burlington Twp. 150, 160, 231, 251
Burlington, N.J. 9
Burnt Cabins 90, 225, 233
Bustletown 63, 70
Butler 213
Butler County 110, 111, 112, 113,
  114, 122, 129, 133, 142, 148, 167,
  170, 177, 182, 186, 194, 195, 205,
  210, 214, 216, 220, 225, 227, 229,
  230, 234, 235, 237, 240, 241, 242,
  243, 250, 252
Byberry Twp. 30, 35

Cadwalader's Mill Dam 191
Caernarvon 84
Caernarvon Twp. 58, 123, 126, 225
Calcoon Hook 19
Cambell's Bridge 163
Cambria 215
Cambria County 126, 136, 142, 148,
  150, 157, 163, 177, 185, 194, 211,
  215, 220, 223, 235, 243, 247
Campbell's Mill 230, 250
Campbellstown 204, 235, 238
Canaan Twp. 150, 225
Canonsburg 98, 107, 191, 218
Canton Twp. 160, 209, 238
Cape Henlopen 21
Cape Hinlopen 1
Carcus-Hook Marsh 19, 75
Carlisle 21, 22, 24, 25, 29, 37, 38,
  40, 43, 45, 57, 76, 147, 192, 215,
  225
Carlisle Borough 70
Carnarvon 64
Carnarvon Twp. 63, 69, 110

INDEX TO PLACES [For personal names see preceding index.]

Carolina 91
Carpenter's Ferry 178
Carpenter's Tavern 177
Catawissa 136, 202, 233
Catawissa Creek 203
Catawissa Town 98, 123
Catawissa Twp. 98
Catfishes Camp 42
Cecil County, Maryland 246
Center Twp. 157
Centre County 103, 106, 107, 108,
　110, 111, 117, 122, 126, 131, 132,
　135, 141, 143, 148, 150, 167, 169,
　175, 177, 182, 186, 187, 190, 193,
　194, 210, 216, 223, 224, 225, 226,
　231, 234, 235, 236, 238, 241, 246,
　251
Centre Twp. 122, 127, 143, 174, 176,
　188, 234, 240, 243
Centreville 230, 250
Ceres Twp. 167
Chambers' Island 63
Chambersburg(h) 38, 113, 114, 147,
　199, 223
Chanceford Twp. 34, 58, 200
Chansford Twp. 133
Charles Justice's Creek 18
Charleston 115, 195
Charleston Twp. 88
Charlestown 121
Charlestown Twp. 29, 95, 137, 226
Chartier's Run 249
Chartiers Creek 128, 200
Chatham 38
Cheat River 25
Cheltenham Twp. 23, 96, 144
Cherry Island 243
Cherry-run 109
Cherrytree Twp. 217
Chesapeake Bay 106
Chesnut Ridge 58
Chester 3, 4, 5, 6, 7, 8, 9, 21, 23,
　31, 38, 91, 215, 221
Chester Borough 27, 201
Chester County 10, 12, 13, 15, 16,
　17, 19, 20, 21, 22, 24, 25, 27,
　28, 29, 30, 32, 33, 34, 35, 36,
　37, 38, 39, 41, 42, 44, 45, 47,
　49, 51, 58, 61, 63, 64, 67, 68,
　69, 70, 71, 72, 73, 75, 77, 79,
　82, 84, 88, 90, 91, 92, 94, 95,
　97, 100, 101, 103, 106, 110, 111,
　114, 115, 119, 121, 125, 126, 127,
　134, 135, 137, 138, 139, 141, 148,
　149, 150, 153, 156, 160, 165, 168,
　169, 172, 173, 176, 180, 182, 188,
　189, 193, 197, 199, 208, 214, 218,
　220, 221, 226, 230, 234, 235, 237,
　242, 245, 246, 247, 249, 250, 251
Chester Twp. 63, 119
Chestnut Hill 105, 117
Chestnut Hill Twp. 58, 102, 177
Chestnut Ridge 84
Chestnut Street 20
Chichester 21
Childeisquaque Creek 95
Chillisquaque Creek 154
Chillisquaque Twp. 119, 188, 198, 238
Chinclecamoose Twp. 177
Chippawa, battle of 205
Chippaway Twp. 204
Chiquesalungo Creek 229
Chiquis Falls 113
Choconut Twp. 238
Church Town 69, 126, 162
Clair Twp. 139
Clapsadle's Mill 226
Clarion River 237
Clark(e)'s Ferry 163, 225
Claverack 117, 189
Claverack Twp. 198
Clavernack Twp. 160
Clearfield 232
Clearfield County 123, 126, 141, 148,
　150, 177, 181, 212, 216, 223, 226,
　232, 235, 238
Clearfield Creek 185
Clearfield Twp. 210, 225, 230, 250
Cleveland 174
Clifford Twp. 188, 234, 238
Cliftsburgh District 150, 160
Clinton 234
Clonmell 47
Coates Street 92
Cocalico Twp. 92, 110, 115, 148, 179,
　188, 229, 237, 244
Cocolamus Creek 87
Cocolico Twp. 58
Codorus River 107
Codorus Twp. 105, 164, 244
Colebrookdale 20, 88
Colebrookdale Twp. 65, 88, 116, 229,
　244
Colerain Twp. 109, 110

INDEX TO PLACES [For personal names see preceding index.]

Columbia 143, 148, 222
Columbia County 177, 185, 188, 192, 194, 198, 202, 203, 204, 207, 208, 213, 281, 220, 221, 224, 226, 228, 229, 233, 235, 238, 242, 244
Columbia Twp. 216
Colver Creek 58
Conamaugh Twp. 174
Conawago Twp. 237
Concord 21
Concord Twp. 90, 229, 245
Coneaut Creek 56
Coneaut Lake 56
Conecocheague Creek 113
Conedogwinet Creek 86, 91, 93, 214
Conemaugh 83
Conemaugh River 179, 215
Conemaugh River Bed 228, 242
Conemaugh Twp. 126, 157, 158, 167
Conemough District 150
Conenugayya 82
Conequenessing Twp. 133
Conequinessing Creek 113
Conestoga Creek 98
Conestoga River 94, 106, 129, 250
Conestogo 25
Conestogo Twp. 208
Conestogoe 54
Conestogoe Creek 64
Conestogoe River 26, 166
Conewago Falls 178, 230, 250
Conewago River 107
Conewango Creek 163
Conewango Island 81
Conewango River 81
Conewango Twp. 150
Coniatue Twp. 143
Connamaugh Twp. 177
Conneaut Twp. 116, 216
Connecticut 96, 134, 170, 213, 233, 234, 236
Connedaguinet River 26
Connellsville 104, 163, 203, 222, 232
Connemach 58
Connemach River 58
Connemaugh River 232, 247
Connemaugh Twp. 108, 226
Conneotte Twp. 157
Connequenessing Twp. 216
Connestoga River 230
Connewago Falls 86
Conniat Twp. 143
Conodoguinet Creek 196, 237
Conostogoe Creek 86
Conowango Creek 213

Coolspring Twp. 108
Cooper's Tavern 131
Cornwall Furnace 115, 195
Coudersport 137, 138, 201
Cousawago Twp. 226
Coventry Twp. 226
Covington Twp. 204, 226, 229, 244
Crawford 232
Crawford County 104, 106, 110, 112, 113, 116, 122, 126, 127, 128, 133, 136, 138, 142, 143, 157, 160, 164, 166, 168, 170, 188, 192, 203, 204, 211, 214, 216, 222, 227, 230, 231, 235, 236, 249, 250, 251
Creesham 117
Creutz Creek 99
Crooked Billet 37, 110
Crooked Creek 122, 124, 203
Cross Road 63
Croyle's Valley 54
Crum Creek 18
Cumberland 225
Cumberland County 15, 16, 20, 21, 22, 25, 26, 29, 32, 33, 34, 35, 36, 37, 38, 39, 42, 43, 45, 50, 57, 58, 63, 66, 70, 71, 75, 76, 77, 80, 82, 83, 84, 86, 90, 91, 92, 93, 94, 100, 101, 104, 108, 110, 111, 112, 114, 120, 121, 123, 128, 131, 136 141, 147, 155, 161, 163, 175, 177, 180, 181, 182, 187, 188, 189, 190, 192, 196, 199, 204, 205, 209, 212, 215, 216, 219, 225, 226, 237, 239, 242, 243, 247, 248, 252
Cumberland Twp. 34, 46, 70, 95, 171, 174
Cumberland Valley Twp. 87, 122
Cumru 64
Cumru Twp. 99
Cunningham's Mill 114
Curries' Ferry 199
Cussewago Twp. 116, 204

Dallas Twp. 229, 244
Damascus Twp. 176
Danville 114, 125, 169, 203, 208, 228, 235, 242
Darby Creek 18, 19, 103
Darby Twp. 19, 90
Dauphin County 51, 57, 59, 63, 64, 66, 72, 76, 77, 78, 82, 86, 88, 90, 91, 92, 94, 95, 96, 97, 101, 103, 105, 110, 111, 112, 114, 115, 122, 124, 126, 127, 128, 129, 131, 136, 138, 141, 142, 143, 146, 148,

339

INDEX TO PLACES [For personal names see preceding index.]

150, 153, 159, 163, 165, 172, 174, 176, 177, 179, 180, 186, 187, 188, 189, 194, 195, 197, 200, 203, 211, 213, 214, 216, 218, 221, 223, 225, 228, 229, 230, 235, 236, 245, 246, 248, 250
Decatur Twp. 177, 228, 231, 251
Deer Twp. 98, 108, 160, 194, 216, 230, 250
Deerfield Twp. 216, 237
Deerstown 232
Delaware 24, 73, 80, 94, 139 (State line), 156, 249
Delaware Bay 2, 20, 21, 27, 43
Delaware County 65, 78, 90, 91, 92, 94, 101, 111, 119, 125, 128, 129, 137, 141, 147, 149, 162, 179, 189, 197, 198, 201, 206, 208, 210, 213, 215, 217, 221, 234, 235, 239, 245
Delaware County, New York 202
Delaware River 2, 10, 14, 18, 20, 26, 43, 46, 52, 61, 81, 91, 93, 98, 103, 106, 108, 114, 119, 135, 145, 159, 161, 178, 189, 193, 198, 201, 204, 211, 218, 229, 232, 246
Delaware Twp. 58, 82, 158
Delmar Twp. 143, 145, 160
Denmark 20, 201
Derby Twp. 94
Derham Twp. 132
Derry 64, 169, 203
Derry Twp. 58, 59, 65, 66, 76, 84, 98, 170, 220, 228
Deshler's mill dam 85
District Twp. 226
Dixon's Fording 143
Donegal 55
Donegal Twp 58, 63, 70, 100, 122, 126, 143, 167, 188, 205, 217,
Donegal Twp. 241, 242
Douglass Twp. 58, 65, 96, 100, 143, 237
Dover Twp. 108, 149
Dovertown 108
Dowington 230
Dowingtown 250
Downingstown 115
Doylestown 123
Drumore Twp. 34, 58, 63, 66, 70, 84, 109, 154, 176, 200
Dublin Twp. 49, 58, 65, 98, 142, 150, 157, 215, 217
Duke's Ward 22
Dun's Island 63
Dundarff 234

Dunkard Twp. 237
Dunnsburg 95, 149
Dunsburg 106, 223
Dunstable Twp. 197
Durham Creek 233
Durham Twp. 87, 157, 217
Dutchy of Deuxponts, Germany 20
Dutchy of Wirtemberg 20

Earl Twp. 23, 58, 63, 65, 66, 102, 216
Earle District 88
Earle Twp. 229, 244
Early's Mill 143
Earlysburg 231, 251
East Bethlehem Twp. 230, 250
East Caln Twp. 61, 68, 75, 230, 250
East Fallowfield Twp. 95, 218, 237
East Hanover Twp. 59, 94, 95, 143, 217
East Hempfield Twp. 237
East Huntingdon Twp. 134, 217, 237
East Marlborough Twp. 61, 68, 114, 180, 220
East Nantmel Twp. 72
East Nottingham Twp. 95, 172, 226
East Penn Twp. 162, 167, 180, 246
East Pennsborough [Pennsboro] Twp. 92, 112, 187, 216, 219, 237
East Whiteland 208
East Whiteland Twp. 82, 95
East-town Twp. 197
Eastern Moiety 18
Easton 20, 39, 40, 43, 44, 77, 91, 117, 153, 212, 214, 215, 218, 222, 232, 233, 241
Easton Borough 78, 113, 210
Easton Island 63
Easttown Twp. 95
Eaton Twp. 234
Ebensburg 126
Eckart's Tavern 58, 66
Edgemont Twp. 90
Elder's District 98
Elizabeth Twp. 58, 82, 92, 95, 188, 225
Elizabethtown 38, 82, 94, 144, 165, 187, 214, 243, 245
Elk Creek Twp. 143, 237
Elk Lands Twp. 150
Elk-lick 116
Elkland Twp. 216
Elklick Twp. 85, 133
Emmetsburg, MD 199

340

INDEX TO PLACES [For personal names see preceding index.]

England 12, 188, 222
English's Mill 63
Ennisville 238
Enoch's Mill 63
Ephrata 92, 179
Erie 100, 161, 162, 198, 210, 225
Erie County 104, 110, 112, 116, 126, 142, 143, 150, 157, 158, 160, 163, 165, 181, 196, 200, 201, 211, 214, 217, 224, 236, 237, 238, 251
Erie Twp. 98, 100
Euan's Mill 132
Eve's Mill 102
Evens' Ferry 192
Evy's Mill 106
Ewing's Tavern 246
Exeter 64
Exeter Twp. 91, 190, 201

Fairfield Twp. 108, 116, 126, 166, 216
Fairview Twp. 150, 237
Falling Spring 113
Falling Springs 51
Fallowfield Twp. 154, 157, 166, 204, 237
Falls of the Delaware 9
Falls Twp. 90, 137, 145, 157
Falls-hill 108
Fan Twp. 132
Fannet Twp. 58, 63, 66, 93, 119
Fannetsburg 147, 225
Farmanagh Twp. 34, 42
Fawn Twp. 34, 143, 216
Fayette County 47, 54, 58, 72, 80, 82, 90, 93, 100, 102, 108, 110, 111, 118, 122, 124, 127, 132, 133, 142, 143, 144, 150, 152, 162, 163, 165, 174, 175, 180, 181, 182, 189, 198, 203, 207, 214, 219, 220, 222, 225, 230, 235, 236, 237, 238, 239, 240, 241, 242, 249, 250
Fayette Twp. 188
Ferguson Twp. 106, 122
Fermanagh Twp. 58, 122, 209
Ferree's Mill dam 126
Findlay Twp. 237
Finley Twp. 205
Finly Twp. 149
Fish-creek 136
Fisher's Island 14
Fishing Creek 93, 102, 154, 163, 169, 202
Fishing Creek Twp. 104

Flat Rock Bridge 197
Flaugherty's Run 84
Flemming's Mills 202
Followfield Twp. 116
Foresman's milldam 236
Forguson Twp. 133
Forks Twp. 218
Fort Augusta 26
Fort Casimer 1, 2
Fort Erie, battle 205
Fort Franklin 56
Fort Lee 135
Fort Littleton 34, 225
Fort Mifflin 93
Fort Nassau 1
Fort Pitt 25, 49, 58
Fort Pitt Twp. 58
Fort Washington 137
Foul Rift Island 63
Fourth Street 25
Foutz's Mill 58
Fox Twp. 238
Fox Valley 216
France 10, 80, 106, 112, 129, 158, 201
Franconia Twp. 96, 107, 133, 157, 188
Frankford 74, 114, 213
Frankford Borough 103
Frankford Creek 18, 161
Franklin 57, 98, 132, 212, 233
Franklin County 50, 51, 57, 58, 63, 64, 66, 87, 90, 92, 95, 97, 101, 110, 111, 114, 119, 125, 126, 127, 128, 130, 141, 143, 146, 147, 157, 162, 175, 176, 178, 180, 193, 199, 204, 211, 212, 215, 218, 222, 223, 224, 225, 226, 228, 230, 231, 235, 239, 242, 243, 248, 250, 251
Franklin Town 143
Franklin Twp. 84, 95, 108, 122, 157, 174, 191, 197, 213, 237
Frankstown 63, 83, 90, 95, 123, 215
Frankstown Branch 98
Frankstown Twp. 91
Franstown Branch 113
Frantz's Mill 203
Frederick County, Maryland 70
Frederick Twp. 27, 96, 100
Fredericktown 214, 230, 250
Freeburg 205
Freeport 98, 214
French Creek 55, 56, 57, 105, 111, 122, 125, 135, 157, 158, 192, 212, 214
French Creek Twp. 176, 230, 250

INDEX TO PLACES [For personal names see preceding index.]

Frost's tavern 225
Ft. Pitt 66
Ft. Washington, battle of 151

Gallaher's Mill 185
Gangwer's tavern 233
Gantz's Mill 133
Gap Tavern 94, 139
Garber's mill 38
Gelnhausen, Germany 28
Geneva, (Switzerland) 35
George's Creek 132
George's Germantown Twp. 230
George's Twp. 80, 132, 181, 250
Georgetown District 112, 126
Georgia 116
German Twp. 80, 127, 230, 250
Germantown 26, 34, 41, 50, 59, 62, 67, 97, 110, 157, 240
Germantown Twp. 65, 117, 173, 250
Germantown, battle 130
Germany 10, 11, 12, 13, 14, 22, 106
Germany Twp. 105, 108
Gettysburg 104, 129, 140, 153, 157, 195, 205
Geyselman's Mill 182
Gibson 216
Gibson Twp. 205, 216, 231, 238, 251
Girty's Run 55
Glassgow'es Farm 133
Glen's tavern 225
Gloucester 47
Gloucester Point, N.J. 1
Gloucester, N.J. 11
Good Spring Creek 177
Goodwin's two islands 63
Goshen Twp. 28, 149
Grace Church 11
Graeme Park 42
Grape Island 133
Gratz 229, 245
Grave Creek 132, 232, 234
Gray's Ferry 129, 176
Great Bend 164
Great Bend Ferry 150
Great Britain 10, 22, 28, 29, 80, 117, 124, 125, 170, 181, 200
Great Connewago 206
Great Valley 69, 189
Green Castle 97
Green County 125, 148, 174, 234
Green Creek 159
Green Twp. 92, 177
Green's Mill 58, 111, 163

Greencastle 63, 120, 125, 126, 218, 228, 248
Greene County 95, 100, 101, 110, 112, 118, 126, 127, 133, 134, 142, 146, 157, 163, 171, 174, 192, 193, 194, 196, 202, 203, 204, 213, 214, 219, 223, 226, 229, 232, 234, 235, 237, 238, 244
Greene District 100
Greene Twp. 197, 237
Greenfield 167
Greenfield District 230, 250
Greenfield Twp. 112, 126, 188, 216
Greensburg 99, 101, 194, 196, 205, 214
Greenville Allen Twp. 177
Greenville Twp. 237
Greenwich 101
Greenwich Island 18, 23
Greenwich Twp. 77, 91
Greenwood Twp. 58, 63, 65, 90, 104, 108, 131, 157, 204, 205
Greersburg 214, 252
Grefeth's Mill 230, 250
Griersburgh 129
Griffith's Mill 215
Guildford Twp. 175
Guilford Twp. 193
Gumtree Tavern 160
Gunner's Creek 18, 24
Gunner's Creek County 24
Gwyned(d) Twp. 96, 176

Hagey's Tavern 110
Hahoning Twp. 162
Haines Twp. 122
Half-moon Twp. 107, 122, 150, 231, 251
Halifax 114
Hamberg 144
Hamburg 65, 194, 206, 235
Hamburg, Germany 27
Hamburgh 125, 133, 165
Hamilton Twp. 58, 82, 95, 102, 146, 162, 226, 231, 251
Hamilton's Ban(n) Twp. 70, 105
Hamilton's Mill 222
Hamilton, New York 232
Hampton 178
Hancock 202
Hancock, Maryland 224
Handie's Island 63
Hannah's town 39, 43

342

INDEX TO PLACES [For personal names see preceding index.]

Hanover 38, 105, 121, 146, 147, 229, 235, 247
Hanover Borough 193
Hanover Twp. 49, 143, 167, 177, 197, 218, 221, 229, 230, 244, 250
Harbor Creek 99
Harbour Creek Twp. 143, 157
Harford District 216
Harford Twp. 150
Harmony 216
Harmony Twp. 238
Harris' Ferry 37, 86
Harrisburg(h) 86, 93, 94, 97, 115, 118, 128, 136, 138, 159, 163, 170, 173, 175, 179, 180, 181, 182, 185, 188, 193, 194, 202, 246, 248
Harrisburg Borough 106
Harrison County, Ohio 239
Hartleton 216, 246
Hartly Twp. 216
Hartman's Mill 217
Harvey's Lower Island 63
Harvey's Upper island 63
Hatboro(ugh) 73, 164
Hatfield Twp. 59, 60, 67, 96, 226
Haverford Twp. 90
Hay Creek 18
Hay Island 19
Haycock Twp. 88, 160
Haydensburg 132
Heidelberg 67, 103
Heidelberg Twp. 59, 60, 61, 62, 68, 92, 96, 105
Heidelburg(h) 87, 121
Heidleberg 64
Heidleberg Twp. 25, 189, 234
Heidleburg Twp. 101
Hellain Twp. 113
Hellam Twp. 99, 226
Heller's Tavern 94
Hemfield Twp. 217
Hemlock Twp. 114, 166
Hempfield Manor 177
Hempfield Twp. 58, 105, 156, 197, 205, 207, 214, 219, 228, 237, 239, 248
Heningston's District 133
Hereford Twp. 88, 162, 167, 205
Herr's Mill 177
Hesler's old mill 98
Hesse-Cassel 28
Hickory Tavern 98
Hidlersburg 238
Hill's District 160
Hill's Tavern 246

Hillsborough 231, 251
Hilltown Twp. 61, 68, 88, 117, 204, 245
Hispaniola 91
Hoag's Mill 110
Hoakstown 197
Hog Island 61, 68
Hogestown 237
Holeman's Ferry 163
Hollander('s) Creek 18, 19, 23
Hollidaysburg 101
Holmesburg 170
Honeybrook Twp. 234, 251
Hopewell Twp. 34, 91, 95, 132, 157, 164, 188, 197, 234
Horsham Twp. 42, 83, 96
Horthampton County 251
Hostetter's Mill 129
Howard Twp. 177, 238
Howell's Falls 81
Hummel's town 59
Hummelstown 66, 88, 93, 103, 143, 194
Hunter's Fork 163
Hunterstown 162
Huntingdon 57, 58, 132, 212, 215, 219, 225, 232, 233
Huntingdon Borough 106, 201, 202
Huntingdon County 64, 65, 80, 81, 82, 90, 91, 93, 95, 98, 101, 103, 104, 106, 110, 111, 118, 123, 132, 133, 135, 136, 141, 148, 157, 163, 165, 173, 177, 181, 185, 190, 194, 197, 208, 212, 217, 219, 220, 223, 225, 228, 229, 230, 231, 234, 235, 236, 238, 242, 243, 244, 248, 250
Huntingdon Town 64, 93
Huntingdon Twp. 21, 58, 64, 80, 104, 105, 108, 150, 185, 197, 216

Incorn's Kill 18
Indian County 215, 232
Indian Creek 143
Indian Queen Tavern 166
Indian Twp. 150
Indiana 185, 215, 218
Indiana County 115, 122, 125, 136, 142, 143, 148, 150, 157, 164, 170, 172, 174, 175, 176, 179, 188, 190, 191, 194, 201, 215, 220, 223, 226, 235, 237, 238, 240, 243, 250
Indiana Twp. 205, 216
Instanter 216
Ireland 31, 120, 149

INDEX TO PLACES [For personal names see preceding index.]

Ireland (Limerick) 52
Ireland (Londonderry) 83
Irwin Twp. 98
Isaac Vancampen's Island 63

Jackson Twp. 204, 216, 231, 251, 252
Jacob's Tavern 185
Jacobsburg 167
Jamaica 11
Jaques' Mill 213
Jarret's Fort 92
Jefferson County 141, 148, 191, 194, 216, 231, 232, 235, 252
Jefferson Town 100
Jefferson Twp. 100
Jemison's Breastwork Run 167
Jenner Twp. 167
Jenuch Shadega 82
Jersey Shore 201
Jersey Shore Village 143
Jersey 40
Johns Town 177
Jones Creek 149
Jones' Mill 144
Jonestown 88, 94, 97, 176, 198, 215, 237
Juniata 25, 99, 109, 123, 192
Juniata River 26, 45, 54, 90, 91, 92, 93, 95, 98, 113, 123, 143, 154, 157, 172, 190, 202
Juniata Twp. 108
Juniata, Big 53

Kauffman's Mill 237
Keller's Ferry 233
Kelly's District 244
Kelso's Mill 157
Kennett Twp. 114
Kensington 25, 49
Kensington District 230
Kent 3, 4, 5, 6, 7, 8
Kentucky 117, 218
Kercherstown 125
King's Ward 22
Kingessing 73
Kings Creek 64
Kingsess 19
Kingsess Twp. 18
Kingsessing Twp. 19, 22, 50, 75, 92, 105, 188, 218
Kingston 77
Kingston District 157
Kingston Twp. 170, 190, 202, 226
Kingstown District 64
Kishacoquillas Valley 163, 171, 225

Kishecoquillis 143
Kiskiminitas River 26, 232
Kiskiminitas Twp. 58
Kittanning 196, 215, 232, 236
Kittle Creek 193
Kreps' Tavern 66
Krepse's Tavern 59
Krider's Mill 226
Kutztown 192, 238

Laboeuff Twp. 197
Lack Twp. 65, 106
Lackawana Creek 209
Lackawanna River 233
Lackawanna Twp. 91
Lackawaxen 163, 232
Lackawaxen Creek 185
Lackawaxen Twp. 113, 235
Laird's Plantation 95
Lake Erie 227, 251
Lancaster 12, 22, 23, 25, 27, 28, 29, 31, 34, 72, 85, 86, 90, 94, 100, 128, 142, 151, 153, 159, 173, 187, 191, 197, 216, 230, 241, 246
Lancaster Borough 24, 38, 71, 90, 95, 106, 113, 118, 138
Lancaster County 11, 13, 14, 15, 16, 20, 21, 22, 23, 24, 25, 27, 28, 29, 31, 32, 33, 35, 36, 37, 38, 39, 44, 45, 47, 49, 50, 55, 58, 61, 63, 64, 66, 68, 69, 70, 72, 73, 75, 76, 77, 82, 84, 86, 87, 90, 92, 94, 97, 98, 99, 100, 101, 102, 104, 107, 108, 109, 110, 111, 114, 115, 122, 123, 125, 126, 128, 129, 130, 132, 136, 137, 139, 140, 141, 143, 144, 147, 148, 149, 150, 151, 152, 154, 155, 158, 160, 162, 165, 166, 170, 172, 173, 175, 176, 177, 178, 179, 180, 187, 188, 189, 190, 192, 195, 200, 202, 203, 208, 212, 214, 216, 217, 222, 225, 226, 228, 229, 237, 241, 244, 245, 250
Landes' Hill 233
Landisburg 233, 251
Lantz's Mill 133
Laughly's Island 63
Laurel Hill 58, 132, 179, 201
Laurel Run 236
Lausanne Twp. 150, 167
Lawrence Twp. 216
Le Boeuff Creek 158

INDEX TO PLACES [For personal names see preceding index.]

Leacock Twp. 58, 63, 72, 151, 229, 244
Lebanon 38, 61, 68, 99, 103, 170, 246
Lebanon Borough 195
Lebanon County 176, 186, 188, 194, 198, 204, 212, 215, 217, 225, 234, 235, 237, 238, 252
Lebanon Twp. 59, 77, 88
LeBoeuff Twp. 143
Leek Twp. 58
Lehigh Bridge 235
Lehigh County 164, 168, 182, 185, 195, 202, 204, 207, 212, 217, 218, 219, 223, 233, 235, 237, 244
Lehigh Gap 233
Lehigh River 26, 83, 85, 88, 95, 97, 131, 185, 199, 206, 217, 224
Lehigh Twp. 34, 58, 66
Lehighton 162
Leise's Tavern 238
Lemarre Twp. 226
Lenox District 216
Letterkenny Twp. 87, 215
Lewis' Ferry 201
Lewisburg 96, 105, 110, 157, 186, 235
Lewisburg Borough 238
Lewistown 132, 171, 174, 217
Lexington 100, 143
Liberties of Philadelphia 37
Liberty Twp. 105, 238
Ligget's Mill 173
Ligonia Valley 110
Limerick Twp. 58, 96, 100, 107, 146
Limestone Run 221
Lindsley's Mill 133
Linn Twp. 145
Lisburn 43
Little Beaver Twp. 160, 197
Little Britain Twp. 158, 167
Little Hay Creek 23
Little Hollander's Creek 23
Little Island 19
Little Juniata River 106, 236
Little Mahonoy Twp. 197
Little Mountain 233
Little Schuylkill River 102, 143, 203
Little Swatara Creek 185
Littleton 187, 215
Logan's Ferry 216
Logan's Mill 216
Logan's Narrows 212
London 11, 19, 24, 78, 120, 188
London-Britain Twp. 150, 251
Londonderry 72

Londonderry Twp. 59, 65, 105, 106, 122, 146, 186, 203, 204, 214, 234
Londonderry, Ireland 83
Long Island, 40 Battle of 118, 124, 126, 135
Long Ridge 250
Long Swamp Twp. 167, 216
Long's Tavern 95
Loor's Island 63
Loudontown 199
Louisville Twp. 226
Low Gap 234
Lower Bethel Twp. 102
Lower Chanceford Twp. 234
Lower Chichester Creek 213
Lower Chichester Twp. 119, 128
Lower Dublin 97
Lower Dublin Twp. 63, 70, 72, 73
Lower Makefield Twp. 160
Lower Merion Twp. 59, 66, 88, 133
Lower Mt. Bethel Twp. 100
Lower Nazareth Twp. 188
Lower Oxford Twp. 95
Lower Paxtang Twp. 64
Lower Paxton Twp. 51, 57, 76, 216, 223
Lower Province Twp. 200
Lower Salford Twp. 96, 188
Lower Sandusky 196
Lower Saucon Twp. 110
Lower Smithfield Twp. 34, 58, 66, 82, 108, 149
Lower Wopehawley 131
Lowhill Twp. 87
Lownes's Island 63
Loyalhanna Creek 216
Loyalsock Creek 150, 158, 203
Loyalsock Gap 233
Lurgan Twp. 64
Luzerne County 63, 64, 70, 71, 76, 77, 82, 84, 89, 90, 91, 92, 93, 94, 97, 98, 100, 101, 102, 104, 108, 110, 111, 113, 117, 121, 123, 126, 130, 131, 133, 134, 136, 141, 143, 148, 150, 153, 157, 160, 161, 162, 163, 166, 169, 170, 172, 176, 177, 185, 188, 189, 190, 191, 192, 193, 194, 196, 197, 198, 205, 207, 211, 213, 216, 220, 221, 223, 224, 226, 228, 229, 230, 231, 233, 234, 235, 242, 244, 245, 246, 247, 248, 250, 251, 252
Luzerne Twp. 165, 238
Lycoming 120, 232

INDEX TO PLACES [For personal names see preceding index.]

Lycoming County 95, 102, 106, 110, 111, 122, 125, 126, 129, 130, 131, 132, 133, 137, 139, 141, 143, 148, 149, 150, 157-160, 163, 173, 176, 177, 192, 193, 195, 197, 201, 203, 204, 205, 208, 209, 211, 212, 213, 215, 218, 219, 223, 225, 226, 231, 233, 235, 236, 238, 250, 251, 252
Lycoming Creek 163, 215
Lycoming Twp. 192
Lykens Twp. 229, 245
Lynn Twp. 87, 119, 165, 237
Lynnville 237

M'Alister's Mill 163
M'Bride's Mill 133
M'Call's Ferry 163, 165, 178, 190, 202, 221
M'Calmont's Mill 126
M'Clure's Gap 233
M'Connelsburg 199, 210, 243
M'Connelstown 150
M'Ilhenney's Island 63
M'Kean County 141, 148, 167, 185, 200, 234, 235, 248, 252
M'Kean Twp. 126, 143, 237
M'Keansburg 217
M'Keansburg District 237
M'Kee's Mill 226
M'Keesport 214
Maccungie Twp. 87, 219
Maccungy Twp. 82
Machanoy River 26
Madison Twp. 226
Mahanoy Twp. 92
Mahantango Creek 185
Mahantango Mountain 150
Mahantango Twp. 107, 126
Mahantongo Twp. 204
Mahoning 114
Mahoning Creek 215
Mahoning Twp. 114, 143, 203, 226, 229, 230, 244, 250
Mahonoy Gap 233
Mahonoy Twp. 140, 217
Mahony Bridge 233
Mahony Twp. 140
Maiden Creek 64
Maiden Creek Twp. 216, 235
Makefield 10
Manahan Twp. 64, 108
Manallen Twp. 88
Manallin Twp. 239
Manchester 173
Manchester Twp. 50

Manheim 76, 137, 170, 172
Manheim Three Rivers, battle 137
Manheim Twp. 90, 98, 100, 105, 148, 217, 221, 228, 237
Manor of Moreland 67
Manor Twp. 73
Mansville 205
Marietta 179, 180, 188, 217, 225
Marietta Borough 177
Marlborough 100
Marlborough Twp 46, 59, 96, 107, 157
Marple Twp. 90, 147, 189
Marsh Creek 73, 169
Marshall's Island 63
Marshalton 160
Martic Twp. 95
Martick Forge Road 86
Martick Twp. 202, 237
Martin's Creek Bridge 233
Martin's Mill 231
Martock Twp. 143
Maryland 24, 58, 70, 80, 113, 178, 190, 199, 224, 246
Mason's Island 63
Massachusetts 107, 131, 214
Massachusetts Bay 72
Maxatawney Twp. 64
Mayerstown 148
Maytown 122, 125, 130, 188, 241
McClellandtown 230, 250
McConnellsburgh 108, 186
McCormick's Mill 104
McDowell's District 100
McKean County 135, 232
McKean Twp. 157
McKee's Port 108
Mead Twp. 211, 214
Meadville 105, 110, 133, 136, 142, 211, 212, 213, 224, 232, 233
Meansville 210, 245
Menallen Twp. 162
Menallin Twp. 212
Mercer 213, 233, 237
Mercer County 104, 107, 108, 110, 111, 112, 114, 115, 119, 126, 142, 143, 146, 150, 160, 167, 169, 170, 175, 176, 178, 187, 192, 193, 197, 198, 204, 208, 214, 216, 217, 226, 229, 230, 232, 237, 238, 240, 241, 244, 248, 249, 250, 252

Mercer Twp. 237
Mercersburg 63, 120
Mertztown 216

346

INDEX TO PLACES [For personal names see preceding index.]

Metal Twp. 147
Methben 70
Middle Creek 24, 98, 233
Middle Ferry 202
Middle Island Creek, Virginia 213
Middle Octorara 75, 222, 228
Middle Paxton 91
Middle Paxton Twp. 114, 153
Middle Smithfield Twp. 158, 235, 238
Middleburgh 114
Middlesex Twp. 122, 133
Middleton Twp. 29
Middletown 64, 78, 90, 94, 120, 143, 173
Middletown Twp. 31, 62, 68, 96, 177, 189, 225, 234
Mifflin 57
Mifflin County 64, 65, 78, 81, 82, 83, 90, 92, 96, 97, 98, 99, 101, 104, 106, 110, 111, 122, 124, 131, 132, 133, 136, 141, 143, 148, 157, 163, 165, 172, 173, 174, 177, 185, 190, 194, 195, 199, 204, 205, 209, 223, 225, 228, 231, 235, 248, 251
Mifflin Twp. 86, 98, 173, 230, 250
Mifflinburg 243
Mifflinsburg 98, 221, 251
Mifflintown 99, 110, 122, 217
Miles Square, New York 131
Miles Twp. 122, 167, 225
Milesborough 92
Milesburgh 123
Milford 97, 111, 119, 166, 189, 193, 198, 230, 247, 249
Milford Twp. 58, 66, 85, 86, 88, 95, 112, 122, 177
Mill Creek 55, 203
Millar's town 108
Miller's Run 63, 64, 92
Miller's Tavern 110, 115
Millersburg 197, 250
Millerstown 105, 176, 190
Millerstown Twp. 87
Millford 246
Millford Twp. 42
Millheim-town 210
Milton 95, 125, 167, 169, 188, 210, 245
Milton Borough 244
Milton Twp. 229
Mingo Creek 57
Mohontongo Creek 231, 251
Mohontongo Twp. 98, 162
Molattin, Berks Co. 21

Monaghan Twp. 105, 175
Monahan Twp. 105, 146
Monmouth, New Jersey, battle 148
Monongahela 25
Monongahela River 43, 47, 48, 49, 54, 57, 59, 65, 66, 87, 108, 214, 222, 236
Monroe Twp. 238
Montaur's Mountain 198
Montgomery County 50, 51, 57, 58, 59, 66, 72, 73, 76, 82, 83, 88, 90, 92, 94, 96, 97, 100, 101, 103, 105, 106, 107, 110, 111, 116, 119, 121, 126, 130, 133, 134, 141, 142, 143, 144, 146, 148, 149, 157, 164, 166, 168, 170, 172, 173, 174, 176, 178, 182, 187, 188, 191, 193, 195, 196, 197, 200, 201, 202, 204, 207, 209, 218, 219, 220, 224, 234, 235, 245, 249
Montgomery Twp. 47, 63, 96, 127, 168, 176
Montgomery's mill 84
Montour Troy Twp. 250
Montour Twp. 230
Montour's Island 46, 99
Montour's Run 54, 64, 92
Moon Twp. 122, 126, 217, 237
Moore Twp. 58, 133, 160, 177, 197, 207, 226, 229, 244
Moorehead's Ferry 163
Mooresburg 238
Moorland Manor 30
Moorland Twp. 166, 176
Moosic Mountain 138, 200
Moreland Manor 37, 73
Moreland Twp. 96, 202, 226
Morgan Twp. 100
Morgan's Town 110
Morgantown 226
Morris County, New Jersey 140
Morris Twp. 91, 95, 98, 133, 143, 157, 162, 191
Morrison's Cove Twp. 63
Morrisville 114, 121, 156
Morrisville Borough 157
Mountjoy 245
Moyamensing Twp. 18, 19, 60, 67, 149, 166
Moyerstown 101
Mt. Joy Twp. 58, 70, 100, 105, 108, 126, 143, 188, 217, 229
Mt. Pleasant 186, 234, 235, 237

347

INDEX TO PLACES [For personal names see preceding index.]

Mt. Pleasant Twp. 105, 140, 150, 185, 195, 197, 202, 217, 226, 229, 237, 244, 251, 252
Muddy Creek 63
Muddy Creek Twp. 133, 195, 216, 229, 234, 244
Muncy 163
Muncy Creek Twp. 106, 163
Muncy Twp. 34, 66, 95, 106, 120
Munsey 58
Munsey Twp. 58
Muthard's District 244
Myer's mill dam 117

Naaman's Creek 195
Nanticoke Creek 123
Nazareth 135, 234
Nazareth Twp. 91
Nescopeck Falls 228
Nescopeck Road 83
Nescopeck Twp. 162, 166, 177
Neshaminy Creek 9, 10, 185
Neshanock Twp. 108, 143, 216
Nether Providence Twp. 125, 189
New Alexandria 202
New Berlin 104, 113, 201, 209
New Berlin District 114
New Bristol 9
New Britain Square 217
New Britain Twp. 45, 70, 88
New Brunswick, N.J. 41
New Castle 2, 3, 4, 5, 6, 7, 8, 9
New Castle County, Delaware 23, 73, 94, 249
New Garden Twp. 61, 67, 91
New Geneva 214
New Hanover 66, 143
New Hanover Twp. 58, 96, 97, 100, 116, 143
New Holland 38, 58, 63, 66, 104
New Hope 233
New Jersey 24, 46, 47, 63, 80, 91, 98, 110, 119, 125, 132, 140, 189, 204, 214, 218, 229, 246, 248
New Jersey (Sussex) 77
New Lisbon, Ohio 157
New London 73
New London Crossroads 226, 230, 250
New London Twp. 150, 153
New Milford 228
New Milford Twp. 197
New Netherlands 1
New Providence Twp. 76
New Seweekly Twp. 197
New Sewickly 231

New Sewickly Twp. 167, 251
New Stone Bridge 105
New Sweden 1
New York 2, 3, 24, 65, 78, 80, 94, 105, 120, 131, 142, 164, 169, 175, 188, 202, 215, 232, 252
Newberry 237
Newberry Twp. 64, 186, 237
Newburg, New York 202
Newbury Twp. 103, 105, 108, 161
Newcopeck 141
Newfoundland District 177
Newlin Twp. 114, 160, 180
Newport 194
Newport Twp. 160
Newport, Delaware 94
Newton Road 37
Newton Twp. 90, 198
Newtown 15, 38, 47, 77, 131
Newtown Twp. 75, 212
Newtown, New York 252
Newville 163, 209, 233
Nicholas Depui's Island 63
Nicholas' Tavern 130
Nicholson's District 100, 133
Nicholson's mill 38
Nippenose Creek 211
Nippenose Twp. 95
Nippinose Valley 215
Nittany Mount 157
Noblesburg 92
Noblesburgh District 112
Noblestown 188
Nockamixon Twp. 87, 132, 226
Noecker's mill 64
Norristown 178, 196
Norriton 178
Norriton Twp. 57
North Beaver Twp. 160, 197, 216, 222
North East Twp. 196
North Huntingdon Twp. 166, 219
North Liberties 23
North Mountain 233
North Point, battle of 193
North Quemahoning Twp. 97
North Seweekly Twp. 197
Northampton 44, 82, 85, 95, 215, 224, 232
Northampton Borough 164, 182
Northampton County 15, 20, 21, 25, 26, 32, 33, 34, 35, 36, 37, 38, 39, 40, 44, 45, 58, 66, 69, 71, 72, 77, 78, 82, 85, 87, 88, 90,

INDEX TO PLACES [For personal names see preceding index.]

91, 93, 94, 95, 97, 100, 101, 102, 107, 108, 109, 110, 111, 113, 117, 119, 125, 126, 131, 133, 135, 136, 141, 143, 145, 146, 148, 149, 150, 152, 153, 154, 162, 165, 167, 168, 169, 170, 177, 180, 181, 185, 186, 188, 191, 192, 193, 196, 199, 204, 205, 207, 211, 212, 214, 215, 217, 218, 220, 222, 223, 224, 226, 229, 230, 231, 233, 234, 235, 240, 241, 244, 246, 250, 251, 252
Northampton Twp. 30, 44, 167, 171
Northampton-town 131
Northern Liberties 45, 48, 59, 62, 66, 67, 74, 77, 78, 92, 102, 110, 114, 125, 127, 185, 189, 216, 230, 248
Northern Liberties Twp. 18, 24, 59, 61, 68, 82, 100, 107, 122, 140, 235
Northmoreland Twp. 231, 251
Northumberland 57, 246
Northumberland County 27, 30, 32, 34, 35, 36, 37, 39, 40, 45, 46, 55, 58, 63, 64, 66, 72, 73, 76, 81, 83, 84, 86, 87, 90, 92, 93, 95, 96, 98, 100, 101, 102, 104, 106, 110, 111, 112, 113, 114, 115, 116, 117, 118, 119, 120, 121, 125, 126, 127, 130, 131, 132, 136, 138, 140, 141, 143, 145, 148, 150, 151, 154, 155, 157, 159, 160, 162, 164, 165, 166, 167, 169, 174, 177, 186, 194, 196, 197, 198, 199, 201, 205, 210, 217, 218, 221, 223, 224, 227, 229, 230, 231, 235, 236, 238, 241, 244, 245, 246, 248, 250, 252
Northumberland town 123, 132
Northwest Twp. 237
Norwegian Twp. 221, 229, 230, 245, 250
Nova Scotia 16, 126
Number Nine (island) 135

Oghquaga 210
Ohio 157, 181, 196, 199, 214, 216, 218, 233, 237, 239
Ohio River 16, 49, 55, 99, 106, 133, 218, 232, 239
Ohio Twp. 126, 197, 226, 235, 237
Oil Creek 82, 116, 122, 202, 203, 222
Oil Creek Twp. 160
Old Chinchaclamoose Twp. 216
Oldshoe's Tavern 234
Oley 64
Oley Twp. 188, 201

Ontario County 163
Orewell District 238
Orwell Twp. 143
Orwigsburg(h) 98, 172, 196, 228, 238
Otter Creek 114
Oxford 19, 105
Oxford Twp. 18, 48, 60, 67, 72, 74, 75, 160, 213

Painter's Mill 91, 205
Paisley 70
Palmer's Fort 126
Palmyra 146, 186
Palmyra Twp. 197, 234
Parker Twp. 205
Parkinson's Old Mill 102
Passyunk Twp. 18, 19, 134, 168, 176
Path Valley 93
Patton Twp. 107, 122, 231, 234, 251
Pawling's Ford Bridge 178, 184, 188, 234
Paxton 51
Paxton Twp. 115, 187
Paxton's Island 63
Pemmapecha 203
Penn Twp. 58, 64, 76, 87, 98, 107, 190, 230, 234, 250
Penn's Creek 26, 86, 92, 98, 201, 233, 250
Penn's Twp. 118
Penn's Valley 225
Pennepack 203
Penns Twp. 24, 114, 204, 205, 212
Penns Valley 63
Pennsboro Twp. 91
Pennsborough 169, 203, 208, 235, 238
Pennsburg 106
Pennsbury 9
Pennsbury Twp. 114
Pensacola 46
Pequea 50, 69
Perkiomen 76
Perkiomen Creek 94, 105
Perkiomen Twp. 28, 96, 107
Perkioming Copper Mine 28
Perry County 235, 251
Perry Twp. 216, 231, 235, 251
Perry's ferry 86
Perryopolis 243
Perth Amboy, N.J. 27
Pess' Mill 98
Peter's Creek 63
Peter's Mountain 57, 163
Peters Twp. 63, 226

349

INDEX TO PLACES [For personal names see preceding index.]

Petersburg(h) 105, 140, 168, 216, 230, 237, 250
Pfaut's Mill 115
Philadelphia 1, 3-13, 15-32, 34, 36, 37, 39-52, 65, 66, 68, 70-78, 80-86, 90-95, 98, 100-105, 107, 109, 110, 111, 114, 115, 117-123, 125, 128-131, 134, 139, 141, 142, 144-152, 156, 158, 159, 161, 162, 163, 166, 168, 169, 173-176, 178, 179, 181, 182, 185, 186, 187, 190-194, 196, 197, 199, 201, 202, 203, 207, 208, 218-224, 226, 231, 232, 234, 240, 241, 242, 244, 245, 246, 248, 249
Philadelphia City 13, 14, 15, 30, 32, 33, 34, 35, 38, 39, 41, 42, 90
Philadelphia County 12, 13, 14, 15, 18, 19, 20, 21, 22, 23, 24, 26, 27, 28, 30, 32, 33, 35-39, 41, 42, 46, 47-50, 59, 60, 61, 63, 65, 66, 67, 68, 70, 72, 74, 78, 84, 85, 89, 92, 96, 97, 99, 101, 105, 106, 107, 110, 111, 114, 116, 117, 129, 131, 134, 135, 139, 140, 141, 144, 147, 150, 152, 157, 160, 161, 166-168, 170, 173, 174, 176, 178, 185, 188, 189, 197, 202, 203, 207, 212, 213, 214, 216, 219, 223, 228, 230, 235, 239, 246, 248, 250
Philipsburg 238, 246
Phillip's Tavern 246
Pidgeon Creek 43, 63
Pigeon Swamp 28
Pike 232
Pike County 185, 193, 198, 204, 209, 230, 235, 236, 238, 246, 247, 249
Pike Twp. 188, 205, 226
Pikeland Twp. 79, 176, 237
Pikerun Twp. 229, 244
Pimatuning Twp. 226
Pimple Hill 192
Pine Creek 82, 95, 120, 185, 236
Pine Creek Twp. 84, 95
Pine Grove Twp. 65, 96, 217, 237, 250
Pine Twp. 148, 162, 235
Pines 212
Piscataway, New Jersey, battle of 132
Pitt Twp. 49, 126, 167
Pittsburg 46, 47, 49, 66, 74, 111, 130, 133, 136, 138, 144, 152, 156, 163, 167, 179, 180, 185, 194, 202, 203, 213, 214, 215, 218, 222, 232, 236, 240, 243
Pittstown District 126
Plainfield Twp. 77, 91, 167

Plank's Tavern 216
Plum Twp. 217
Plum-Creek Twp. 160
Plumb District 230, 250
Plumb Twp. 65, 112
Plumstead Twp. 88, 237
Plymouth Twp. 119, 134, 172, 185, 190, 191, 211
Pocono Twp. 226, 231, 251
Pocopoco 85
Pohatcung Island 63
Point No Return Meadows 18
Ponteaudemer, Normandy, France 129
Poplar Lane 92
Port Penn, Delaware 156
Portsmouth 211
Pottar's Twp. 122
Potter County 137, 138, 141, 148, 167, 185, 200, 201, 235
Potter Twp. 58, 63, 83, 92, 106, 150, 231, 251
Pottsgrove 94, 245
Pottstown 100, 191, 195, 204
Pottsville 230, 250
Powell's Tavern 163
Power's District 100
Prall's two islands 63
Presque Isle 212, 238
Price's Mill 193
Prince's Ward 22
Providence Island 14
Providence Twp. 84, 91, 107, 110, 142, 177
Province Island 43
Prussia 20, 22
Pughtown 226
Punkey's Island 63
Pymatuning Twp. 108, 150

Quakertown Meetinghouse 131
Quebec 21, 24; battle of 151
Queen's Ward 22
Quemahoning District 85, 116
Quemahoning Twp. 58, 66, 87, 167, 229, 244

Raccoon Creek 55, 64
Race Street 25
Radnor Twp. 90, 208
Rapho Twp. 58, 66, 70, 100, 177, 188, 229
Rastrover Twp. 58, 66
Rattling Gap 215

INDEX TO PLACES [For personal names see preceding index.]

Raystown Branch 45, 54, 90, 95, 109, 123, 172
Reading 21, 26, 38, 46, 73, 86, 93, 94, 98, 125, 127, 135, 136, 169, 170, 176, 201, 203, 213, 246
Reading Borough 64, 75
Reading Twp. 64, 105, 108
Reamstown 110, 115, 237
Red Bank 215
Red Lion 34
Red Lion Tavern 114
Red Stone Creek 25
Redbank Twp. 142, 160, 182, 184
Reed's Tavern 225
Resersburg 167
Resolution Island 63
Restraver Twp. 65
Rhode Island 80
Rich's Mills 185
Richardson's Old Tavern 232
Richland 172
Richland Twp. 88, 90, 150, 197, 229, 244
Richmond 18, 24
Ridgeberry Twp. 229, 244
Ridgebury Twp. 238
Ridley Twp. 18, 19, 103, 137, 147
Riggle's Spring 177
Rising Sun Tavern 114
Ritter's Tavern 165
Robert's ferry 41
Robeson Twp. 84, 96
Robinson 64
Robinson Twp. 147, 230, 250
Robinson's Mill 197
Rockdale Twp. 113
Rockhill 34
Rockhill Twp. 88, 117, 217
Rockland Twp. 204, 226
Rocky Island 92
Romig's Tavern 215
Rosborough Twp. 174
Rose Hill Tavern 235
Ross Twp. 162, 217
Rosstown 108
Rostraver Twp. 49, 177
Round Island 243
Roup's Mill 167
Roxborough Twp. 60, 67
Roxbury 233, 243
Rummerfield Creek 102
Ruscomb Manor 64
Ruscombmanor Twp. 197

Rush Twp. 150, 162, 168, 188, 216, 230, 237, 238, 250
Russ Twp. 177
Rye Twp. 58, 63, 192
Sadsbury 95
Sadsbury Twp. 95, 107, 116, 119, 126, 133, 143, 160, 176, 188, 221, 229, 244
Salem 77, 220
Salem County, N.J. 13
Salem district 64
Salem Twp. 107, 177, 213, 225, 233, 237
Salisbury Twp. 50, 58, 63, 69, 107, 126, 188
Salsbury 133
Salsbury Twp. 63, 126
Salt Lick Twp. 100, 143
Sandy Creek 56
Sandy Creek Twp. 108, 197
Sandy Lake Twp. 126, 160
Sandy Lick 133
Sandy Lick Creek 132, 231, 252
Saw-Mill Run 49
Saxony 22
Schuylkill 52
Schuylkill County 162, 168, 172, 176, 177, 179, 185, 193, 194, 196, 197, 202, 212, 216, 217, 221, 223, 228, 229, 230, 233, 235, 237, 242, 245, 250
Schuylkill Falls 176
Schuylkill Point Meadow 44
Schuylkill Point Meadow Land 19
Schuylkill River 9, 14, 18, 26, 29, 41, 42, 49, 73, 84, 94, 97, 98, 103, 129, 130, 134, 140, 143, 147, 158, 161, 167, 178, 188, 193, 195, 196, 201, 206, 233, 234, 236
Schuylkill Twp. 177, 230, 237, 250
Scotland 119, 188
Scott Twp. 238
Scrubgrass Twp. 158
Seabold's Mill 104, 114
Seely's Mills 185
Selin's Grove Twp. 234
Selins Grove 98, 118, 193
Seller's Tavern 131, 233
Seneca Lake 223
Sergeant Twp. 216, 234
Sewickley Creek 91, 205
Shade Twp. 216
Shaefferstown 234

INDEX TO PLACES [For personal names see preceding index.]

Shafferstown 92
Shamokin 169, 203
Shamokin District 104
Shamokin Island 162, 164
Shamokin Twp. 145, 230, 250
Shanango Twp. 177
Shauchan's District 82
Shaver's Creek 103
Shawanaugh's Island 63
Shearman's Creek 29, 53, 57, 94
Shearman's Valley 104
Sheep Island 92
Sheerman's Creek 50, 200
Shenango Twp. 116, 197, 204, 238
Shenango, waters of 248
Sherer's Ferry 221
Sherman's Valley 25
Sheshequin District 238
Sheshequin Twp. 238
Shickasolungo Creek 31
Shippen Twp. 234
Shippensburg(h) 140, 147, 165, 238, 239
Shippensburg Twp. 77
Shirley Twp. 49, 58, 64, 66
Shirleysburg 98, 103
Shoemaker's Island 63
Shoemakerstown 114
Shrewsbury Twp. 108, 150, 164
Shriver's mill 105
Sideling Hill 215, 233, 235
Silver Lake Twp. 234
Silver Spring 71, 92
Sinkey's Gap 181
Sinking Fishing Creek 225
Sinking Spring 201
Sinnemahoning 177
Skepsholm 1
Skippack Creek 26, 76
Skippack Twp. 28, 96, 107
Slack's Three Islands 63
Slippery Rock Twp. 126, 142
Smeth's Port 135
Smith's Island 63
Smithfield 37
Snake Spring Creek 54
Snyder's Paper Mill 231
Solebury 10
Solebury Twp. 85, 108, 150
Somerset 132, 181, 225
Somerset County 95, 97, 102, 107, 108, 110, 112, 116, 118, 126, 128, 132, 133, 141, 142, 144, 147, 148, 149, 151, 157, 158, 160, 163, 164, 167, 177, 180, 181, 188, 194, 196, 203, 209, 223, 225, 226, 229, 230, 234, 235, 236, 237, 238, 244, 245, 248, 250
Somerset Twp. 95, 144, 197, 198
South Beaver Twp. 162, 197
South Huntingdon 91
South Huntingdon Twp. 90, 197
South Irwin Twp. 116
South's Mill 237
Southampton Twp. 36, 44, 64, 107, 118, 133, 143, 149, 157, 189, 211, 230, 250, 251
Southerland's Mill 98
Southwark 44, 61, 64, 68, 80, 85
Southwark District 246
Spark's fort 39
Spike's Creek 19
Spring Creek 237
Spring Creek Twp. 237
Spring House Tavern 168
Spring Twp. 122
Springfield Twp. 88, 90, 96, 98, 139, 157, 173, 179, 193, 204, 207, 216, 217, 226, 229, 230, 238, 244, 245, 250
Springhill Twp. 80, 175, 230, 250
Springville Twp. 216
St. Clair Twp. 86, 126, 150, 162, 171, 217, 229, 230, 244, 250, 251
St. Domingo 158
St. Jones County 2
St. Tammany District 176
St. Thomas Twp. 226
Standing Stone 89
Standing Stone Creek 87
State Island 43, 87
Stauffer's Mill 115
Stayman's Ford 237
Stenton 85
Sterling Twp. 229, 235, 244
Stitzel's Forge 236
Stockbridge 92, 95
Stockholm 1
Stockport 202
Stone Creek 18
Stoney Creek 236, 248
Stoney Creek Twp. 116, 160, 237, 244
Stony Creek 230
Stony Creek Twp. 87, 158, 167, 188, 196, 229
Stony Point, battle 154

INDEX TO PLACES [For personal names see preceding index.]

Stoystown 116, 141, 148, 194, 229, 236, 244, 245
Straban Twp. 157, 206, 212
Strabane Twp. 105, 172
Strasburg(h) 87, 95, 140, 202, 215, 233, 235
Strasburg Borough 246
Strasburgh Village 129
Streat's Run 217
Streban Twp. 162
Strickler's Spring 229, 244
Stroud Twp. 226
Stroudsburg 148, 191, 226
Stuart's Crossing 43
Stumpstown 150
Sugar Creek 185, 194, 233
Sugar Creek Twp. 142, 217, 230, 250, 251
Sugar Grove Twp. 237
Sugar Loaf Twp. 204
Sugar Valley 122
Sullivan Twp. 204
Sumanytown 209
Summany town 157
Summey Town 107
Summony-town 133
Sunbury 43, 93, 106, 125, 194
Sunbury Manor 170
Susquehanna 26
Susquehanna Bridge 190
Susquehanna County 162, 164, 167, 188, 191, 194, 197, 205, 216, 219, 224, 225, 226, 231, 234, 235, 238, 242, 251
Susquehanna River 26, 54, 56, 83, 84, 86, 87, 90, 93, 98, 99, 103, 112, 113, 123, 129, 131, 132, 134, 138, 141, 143, 149, 154-156, 161, 163, 164, 165, 169, 175, 176, 178-182, 186, 192, 194, 197, 202, 203, 210, 211, 218, 221, 223-226, 228-232, 236, 239, 242, 243, 246, 250
Susquehanna Twp. 177
Sussex 3-8
Sussex County, New Jersey 91, 119, 189
Sussex, New Jersey 77
Swartswood's Island 63
Swatara 211
Swatara Creek 82, 78, 86, 93, 94, 103, 112, 129, 143, 177, 193, 221, 228, 236
Swatara Creek Ferry 187
Swatara River 26, 123
Swatara Twp. 229, 237, 246

Sweden 20
Sweetara Creek 64

Tacony Creek 23
Tamaqua 203
Teboyne Twp. 58, 84, 114
Tell Twp. 217, 230, 250
Ten Mile Stone 105
Thomas's tavern 246
Thompsontown 123
Thornbury Twp. 47, 90, 179, 234
Three Ridges 192
Tiago County 201, 234
Tinicum Twp. 61, 72, 75, 77, 87, 90, 132, 226
Tioga 77, 120
Tioga County 77, 141, 145, 148, 150, 156, 160, 162, 163, 194, 200, 204, 205, 216, 218, 223, 232, 252
Tioga District 64, 104
Tioga River 223
Tioga River, New York 131
Tioga Twp. 122
Toamensing 162
Toboyne Twp. 188
Toby Creek 215
Toby Twp. 142, 230, 237, 251
Toby's Creek 191, 237
Tomhicken Creek 203
Tompson's Mill 98
Torbut Twp. 98
Towamensing 188
Towamensing Twp. 58, 96, 133, 217
Towanda 215
Towanda Creek 247
Towanda Twp. 233
Towandee 163
Trap 200
Trediffrin Twp. 165
Tredyfferin Twp. 69
Tredyffrin Twp. 77, 95, 135
Trenton, New Jersey 65, 98, 139
Triewig's Tavern 131
Troy Twp. 230
Tubmill Creek 84
Tulpehoccon Twp. 65
Tulpehocken 26
Tulpehocken Twp. 96, 157, 235, 238
Tunkhannock 77, 205, 224
Tunkhannock District 64, 133
Tunkhannock Twp. 235
Turbet Twp. 210
Turbit Twp. 198
Turbut Twp. 229

353

INDEX TO PLACES [For personal names see preceding index.]

Turbutt Twp. 84, 205
Turkey Foot Twp. 58, 85, 95, 151
Turn Hick 203
Turtle Creek 163, 185
Tuscarora 104
Tuscarora Mountain 225, 233
Tuscarora Valley 217
Tyrone Twp. 58, 63, 64, 66, 80, 84, 91, 105, 157, 208, Twp. 225, 238

Uchland Twp. 242
Ulalia Twp. 167
Ulster County, New York 202
Ulster District 238
Ulster Twp. 229, 244
Ulster, N.Y. 28
Unicorn 84
Union County 177, 186, 190, 193, 194, 201, 204, 208, 209, 210, 212, 216, 221, 224, 228, 231, 233, 234, 235, 238, 239, 242, 243, 246, 248, 250, 251, 252
Union Twp. 65, 83, 84, 95, 106, 116, 143, 150, 188, 216, 221, 234, 236, 237
Uniontown 47, 133, 243
Unity Twp. 179, 180
University of Pennsylvania 59
Upper Bern Twp. 237
Upper Bethel Twp. 102
Upper Canada 205
Upper Chichester Twp. 90
Upper Darby Twp. 90
Upper Dublin Tp. 96
Upper Ferry 167
Upper Hanover 100
Upper Hanover Twp. 59, 96, 107, 209
Upper Mahantango Twp. 197
Upper Mahonoy Twp. 143, 217, 231
Upper Makefield Twp. 177
Upper Merion 73, 182
Upper Merion Twp. 103, 144, 218
Upper Milford 223
Upper Milford Twp. 87
Upper Mt. Bethel Twp. 100, 192
Upper Nazareth Twp. 188, 234
Upper Oxford Twp. 95
Upper Paxton 229
Upper Paxton Twp. 51, 57, 66, 96, 114, 150, 165, 174, 197, 200, 230, 245, 250
Upper Pextang 59
Upper Providence Twp. 90, 189, 234
Upper Salford Twp. 59, 107
Upper Smithfield Twp. 58, 82, 166

Ury's District 226
Uwchlan Twp. 90

Valley Forge 182
Valley of the Swans 1
Vancampen's Island 63
Vandike's Tavern 248
Vankine Kill 198
Vanoken's Island 63
Venango 56, 164, 212, 231
Venango County 104, 105, 106, 110, 112, 116, 122, 132, 142, 143, 150, 158, 163, 167, 169, 170, 175, 191, 197, 202, 214, 216, 217, 226, 229, 230, 231, 235, 236, 244, 250, 252
Venango Twp. 126, 143, 150, 205, 231, 251
Vernon's Mill 133
Versailles Twp. 65, 112, 150, 219, 231, 251
Vincent Twp. 134, 237
Virginia 24, 50, 51, 78, 80, 99, 116, 124, 136, 209, 213, 218, 234, 242

Wahrton Twp. 100
Wakefield 124
Walker Twp. 177
Wall's Island 63
Wallanpaupack Creek 163, 236
Waller's Fort 88
Wallshire 2
Walnut Creek 251
Walnut Street 41
Warfordsburg 142
Warminster Twp. 36, 47, 96, 160, 237
Warren 138, 232
Warren County 104, 110, 112, 138, 142, 150, 185, 203, 226, 234, 235, 236, 237
Warren Town 231
Warren Twp. 162, 229, 244
Warren, Ohio 216, 237
Warrington 64
Warrington Twp. 34, 51, 64, 82, 88, 105, 108, 160, 237
Warrior-mark Twp. 157
Warwick 44
Warwick Twp. 69, 88, 100, 115, 160, 176, 188, 229, 237, 244
Washington 74, 98, 132, 160, 203, 207, 218, 226, 235, 242
Washington County 42, 45, 49, 54, 63, 64, 72, 74, 76, 78, 80, 81, 82, 88, 92, 93, 98, 101, 102, 104, 107, 112, 117, 133, 136, 137, 142,

INDEX TO PLACES [For personal names see preceding index.]

145, 148, 149, 150, 158, 160, 162, 169, 172, 175, 176, 177, 180, 186, 191, 192, 194, 195, 197, 198, 200, 203, 204, 205, 209, 214, 219, 222, 226, 229, 230, 231, 234, 235, 236, 237, 238, 241, 242, 244, 245, 247,, 250, 251, 252
Washington Twp. 63, 84, 95, 108, 143, 150, 157, 162, 175, 177, 215, 226, 230, 231, 237, 238, 250, 251
Water Gap 217, 235
Waterford 100, 106, 181, 191, 201, 224
Waterford Twp. 126, 197, 216
Waterford-town 143
Wayne 232
Wayne County 98, 100, 102, 110, 111, 113, 119, 121, 134, 141, 148, 150, 158, 161, 163, 166, 169, 176, 177, 185, 188, 189, 197, 202, 209, 210, 218, 225, 226, 229, 232, 238, 239, 244, 245, 246, 248, 249, 251, 252
Wayne Twp. 58, 83, 148, 157, 160, 225
Waynesburg(h) 95, 163, 234, 238, 239
Weidman's Forge Dam 177
Weisenberg Twp. 119
Weiserburg 118
Weiss' mill dam 85
Weissenburg Twp. 87
Well's Mill 104
Wells' Falls 81
Wells Twp. 204
Wellsborough 130, 145, 162, 234
West Bethlehem Twp. 133, 231, 251
West Bradford 61
West Bradford Twp. 68, 160
West Buffalo(e) Twp. 98, 230, 250
West Buffaloe 157
West Caln Twp. 61, 68, 95, 100, 126, 140, 199, 237
West Chester 75, 149, 168, 200
West Chester Borough 64, 99, 148
West Conecocheague Mountains 104
West Fallowfield Twp. 95, 160
West Hanover 111
West Hanover Twp. 51, 59, 88, 142, 213
West Middleton Twp. 226
West Nantmeal Twp. 237
West Nantmill Twp. 247
West Nottingham Twp. 95
West Penn Twp. 162, 168
West Penns Borough Twp. 29
West Whitefield Twp. 134
West Whiteland Twp. 45, 90, 230, 250

Westfield 211
Westmoreland 29
Westmoreland County 32-40, 43, 45, 49, 53, 54, 56, 58, 59, 65, 66, 71, 72, 74, 76, 82, 84, 88, 90, 91, 92, 93, 99, 101, 105, 108, 110, 112, 115, 124, 126, 128, 132, 134, 136, 140, 142, 144, 150, 152, 156, 164, 166, 167, 170, 173, 177-182, 188, 194, 196, 197, 201-203, 205, 207, 214-217, 219, 220, 222, 223, 226, 228, 232, 234, 235, 237, 239, 240, 242, 243, 247, 248, 249, 252
Westnantmel Twp. 70
Westnantmill Twp. 119
Wever's Mill 126
Weyalusing Twp. 108
Wharton Twp. 237
Wheatfield Twp. 84, 108, 230, 250
Wheeling Creek 149, 163
Whighton 167
White Deer Creek 236
White Deer Twp. 58, 95, 177, 208, 216
White Horse 38, 234
White Marsh Twp. 106
White's mill 64
White-deer Hole Mountain 215
White-hall Twp. 146
Whitedeer Hole Creek 233
Whitedeer Valley 233
Whiteland Twp. 47
Whiteley Twp. 226
Whitely Creek 54
Whitely District 133
Whitemarsh 19, 58, 66
Whitemarsh Twp. 72, 96
Whitpain Twp. 50, 57, 66, 68, 97
Whitpaine Twp. 61, 62
Whore Kill 3
Wicaco Meadows 19
Wicaco Twp. 218
Wicacoa 73
Wilde's Mill 236
Wilford Twp. 58
Wilkes-Barre district 64
Wilkesbarre 70, 94, 113, 130, 141, 146, 175, 177, 205, 215, 221, 245, 246, 247
Wilkins Twp. 237
Williams' landing 9
Williamsburg(h) 63, 95, 177
Williamsport 129, 158, 213, 214, 236
Willingborough 164
Willingborough District 104
Willingsborough District 150

355

INDEX TO PLACES [For personal names see preceding index.]

Willistown Twp. 95, 173
Willow Island 197
Wilmington, Delaware 94
Wilson's Island 99
Wilson's Mills 198
Wilson's Tavern 216
Wind Gap 212
Windham Twp. 216, 234
Windsor 64
Windsor Twp. 65, 229, 235, 244
Winten's Mill 222
Wisenburg Twp. 237
Wismersford 200
Wolf Creek Twp. 126, 160
Wolf Lane 178
Wolf-creek 108
Wolmesdorf 123
Woodbury 90
Woodbury Twp. 58, 87, 95
Woodrow's Alley 25
Wopehawley Creek 166
Worcester Twp. 23, 34
Wright's ferry 74, 87, 90
Wright's Tavern 110
Wyalusing District 104
Wyalusing Twp. 226, 229, 244
Wyconisco Creek 126
Wyoming 26, 66, 74, 121
Wyoming Twp. 46
Wyorocks Twp. 102
Wysock District 104
Wyson Twp. 150
Wysox 224
Wysox District 238

Yard's Island 198
Yellow Creek 157
York 21, 42, 43, 54, 219
York Borough 74, 113, 140, 195, 196, 242
York County 15, 20, 21, 27, 32, 33-37, 39, 43, 45, 46, 58, 64, 66, 70, 73, 82, 88, 89, 93, 99, 101, 103, 105, 108, 110, 111, 113, 116, 121, 128, 132, 133, 135, 138, 141, 146-149, 152, 161, 162, 164, 167, 168, 175, 179, 182, 186, 187, 188, 190, 197, 200, 203, 209, 216, 219, 221, 225, 226, 229, 234, 235, 236, 237, 244, 247, 250
Yorktown 34, 38, 73
Yorktown, battle of 134, 140, 149
Youghiogeny 25
Youghiogheny River 43, 48, 49, 65, 92, 93, 104, 203, 222, 232

Youghogheny County 54
Youngmanstown 246
Youngwomanstown 197

Zwanendal 1

www.ingramcontent.com/pod-product-compliance
Lightning Source LLC
Chambersburg PA
CBHW071953220426
43662CB00009B/1108